SP Pvt. Ltd.

Dedication

This book is dedicated to whole pharmaceutical world friends for their impact on the core of our being.

Pharmaceutical Industry
Quality Assurance

by

Manish Kumar
Shailendra Bhatt
Rishabh Srivastava

2019

Studium Press (India) Pvt. Ltd.

Pharmaceutical Industry
Quality Assurance

ISBN: 978-93-85046-44-5

Published by:

Studium Press (India) Pvt. Ltd.
4735/22, 2nd Floor, Prakash Deep Building
(Near Delhi Medical Association),
Ansari Road, Darya Ganj, New Delhi-110 002
Tel.: + 91-11-43240200-15 (15 lines); Fax: 91-11-43240215
E-mail: pubdir@studiumpress.in

Printed at India

About the Authors

Dr. Manish Kumar, completed M. Pharm (Pharmaceutics) from Rajiv Gandhi University of Health Sciences in 2005 and PhD (Pharmacy) from Karpagam University in 2014, is currently working as Professor and HOD, M. M. College of Pharmacy, Mullana, Ambala, with a total working experience of more than 13 years in this field. Along with this, I have also contributed in many research and review papers of international/national repute. I am also contributing to educate the future industrial pharmacist through short interactions and tutorials for the day to day challenges that we are facing in the industry.

Dr. Shailendra Bhatt, earned his M.Pharm from Rajasthan University of Health Sciences, Jaipur, Rajasthan and Ph.D. from K.S. Vishwa Vidyalaya, Gandhinagar, Gujarat. He has started his carrier in 2007 as a lecturer. Presently he is working as Associate Professor in Department of Pharmaceutics, MM College of Pharmacy, MM (Deemed to be University), Mullana, Ambala, Haryana. He has published various national and international research papers in reputed pharmaceutical journals. He has supervised more than 10 M.Pharm students and presently supervising 03 Ph.D candidates. He is also a member of numerous professional bodies like APTI, IPGA etc.

Mr. Rishabh Srivastava, completed M. Pharm (Pharmaceutics) from Gautam Buddha Technical University in 2011 and MBA (Operation Management) from Sikkim Manipal University in 2017, is currently working with Elys Chemical Industry Ltd, Nairobi, Kenya, as Officer Quality Assurance with a total working experience of more than 6 years in this field. Along with this, I have also contributed in many research and review papers of international/national repute. I am also contributing to educate the future industrial pharmacist through short interactions and tutorials for the day to day challenges that we are facing in the industry.

Acknowledgements

First and foremost, we are thankful to God Almighty for, without his help and blessings in completion of this work, it would not have been completed. Appreciation is extended to my superiors, colleagues, various companies and organisations we have been associated with, family, friends for their contribution towards this work.

We are indebted to Mr. Ashok Patel Managing Director, Elys Chemical Industries Ltd, Nairobi, Kenya for his support and guidance. We are thankful to Dr. Abhay Walvekar, Plant Manager, Elys Chemical Industries Ltd, Nairobi, Kenya and Dr. Sarah Vugigi, Manager QA, Elys Chemical Industries Ltd, Nairobi, Kenya for their insightful comments, scholarly advice and systemic involvement in all aspects of this book. We wish to acknowledge all industrial friends for their support, suggestions constructive criticism and consistent encouragement and their involvement in this work directly or indirectly.

We would like to give name of some friends and seniors from industry like Mr. Anil Saini, Mr. Neeraj Vishwakarma, Mr. Dharmendra Kumar, Mr. Ankur Tyagi and Mr. Shishpal to whom we owe much gratitude for their thoroughness in ensuring continuous learning, compilation in this manuscript. In addition to them authors would also like to thank various organisations they are and were associated with. We also thank various regulatory bodies to regularly updating the guidelines.

Last but not the least we would like to thanks our family and friends for their consistent encouragement and spiritual support while on this journey and their inspiration towards a mindset of scaling any wall and their selfless generosity which has contributed immensely to this realization.

Preface

This book has been written to meet requirement of students getting training in validation of quality assurance. A keen attempt has been felt for a book useful and interesting. Leaving aside all the unnecessary, only the essential facts have been discussed in this book. It has a directly link with practical work, that all the common and complicated troubles of validation and quality assurance have been explained very clearly.

It give us immense pleasure to present a book entitled "*Pharmaceutical Industry: Quality Assurance*". Need to write this book is ever increasing the study material on the subject matter of quality assurance. In the era of quality assurance, every industry need to be quality assured so that it can achieve its quality assurance laid by various Indian universities. Aim of this book is to provide primary and update knowledge of various quality assurance study material to master of pharmacy in the professional programme of their study. Special emphasis is given on validation and basic concept of quality assurance.

Table of Contents

1

Pharmaceutical Industry (Basic Concept)

ABSTRACT

With increase in the market need and supply requirements pharmaceutical sector has rapidly developed from just compounding and dispensing to a million dollar industry. During the developing phase, this industry has seen many ups and down. One by one pharmaceutical industry gained confidence and later developed various systems to assure product quality. Thereafter the terms like quality, safety and efficacy combined together to prove that product released for market is of desired quality to ensure safety to patient and to provide relief to patient. But also during this era various accidents took place which eventually helped the industry to improve and to lay down the guideline to ensure uniformity. In modern era industry follow these guidelines and get approval from various regulatory bodies to prove their system and to gain patient confidence. In this chapter we are going to learn about the pharmaceutical industry including basic GMP, history of industry, development and background, evolution of GMP, role of WHO and other authorities, current scenario and future prospects.

INTRODUCTION

A patient suffering from any ailment place their faith in the medical practitioner that the medicine they prescribed will eventually provide them a relief from the pain and suffering. Same way the patient also has faith in community pharmacist that he shall dispense the correct medicines. But these people like patient, medical practitioner or pharmacist on the retail store don't have the facility to analyse the medicine to detect if there is any defect in it or not. Thus the life of patient relies on the faith they have on medical practitioner and pharmacist. Similarly the medical practitioner and pharmacist in turn put their trust in the manufacturer who has a fundamental role in ensuring that the medicine is fit for its purpose and is safe to use [1]. Eventually manufacturer maintains that faith by ensuring that they are following the best of the GMP systems. Manufacturers have to face GMP inspections to certify that the manufacturer is suitable to manufacture any pharmaceutical finished product which in market is known as medicine.

This way following the GMP ensures that a quality system is in place into the organization and the product manufactured through the manufacturing process is of specified quality. But the activities involved in achieving quality, cover much more than the manufacturing operations like approved specifications for the raw materials, intermediate process bulk material, semi-finished product, finished product, packaging materials and other material used as the utility or support to manufacture that product, instructions and procedures covering processing, testing, handling, storage, receipt and dispatch, suitable premises, equipment and trained staff. [1]

With the advent of technology, system and procedure to develop new medicines also evolved. With the change in human lifestyle some older diseases or infections also developed resistances to the old medicines. Along with this some new diseases also developed. Due to increase in the population, now more people are taking pharmaceuticals. This raise in population also resulted in increased number of adverse events and some products also reflected their ability to cause adverse effects in some specific people. These all incidences make common factor to increase the number of market complaints. Same way the products which don't meet specifications but were released in the market for sale, have to be recalled due to quality concerns. However, the incidence of safety problems is quite low as a result of GMP systems, talented people and the use of advanced technologies [2].

Due to these reasons pharmaceutical industry needs to maintain high standards of Quality Management in the development, manufacture and control of medicinal products. An approved and established system at manufacturing site ensures that all medicinal products are assessed by a competent authority to ensure compliance with contemporary requirements of safety, quality and efficacy. Manufacturing authorisations are required by all pharmaceutical manufacturers.

WHAT IS GMP?

Good Manufacturing Practices or GMP is a part of quality management system to regulate pharmaceutical manufacturing ensuring products are consistently and continuously produced and controlled according to the quality standards appropriate to their intended use and as required by the marketing authorization, clinical trial authorization or product specification. GMP is concerned with both production and QC. GMP is aimed primarily at managing and minimizing the risks inherent in pharmaceutical manufacture to ensure the quality, safety and efficacy of products. Thus under GMP following subjects are covered:

1. All manufacturing processes are clearly defined, systematically reviewed for associated risks in the light of scientific knowledge and experience, and shown to be capable of consistently manufacturing pharmaceutical products of the required quality that comply with their specifications;
2. Qualification and validation are performed;
3. All necessary resources are provided, including:
   a. Sufficient and appropriately qualified and trained personnel,
   b. Adequate premises and space,
   c. Suitable equipment and services,
   d. Appropriate materials, containers and labels,
   e. Approved procedures and instructions,
   f. Suitable storage and transport,
   g. Adequate personnel, laboratories and equipment for in-process controls;
4. Instructions and procedures are written in clear and unambiguous language, specifically applicable to the facilities provided;
5. Procedures are carried out correctly and personnel are trained to do so;
6. Records are made (manually and/or by recording instruments) during manufacture to show that all the steps required by the defined procedures and instructions have in fact been taken and that the quantity and quality of the product are as expected. Any significant deviations are fully recorded and investigated with the objective of determining the root cause and appropriate corrective and preventive action is implemented;
7. Records covering manufacture and distribution, which enable the complete history of a batch to be traced, are retained in a comprehensible and accessible form;
8. The proper storage and distribution of the products minimizes any risk to their quality and takes account of good distribution practices (GDP);
9. A system is available to recall any batch of product from sale or supply;
10. Complaints about marketed products are examined, the causes of quality defects investigated and appropriate measures taken in respect of the defective products to prevent recurrence;
11. Trained personnel.

HISTORY OF PHARMACEUTICAL INDUSTRY

The modern pharmaceutical industry traces its roots to two sources *i.e.* local apothecaries and organic chemical synthesis. The local apothecaries system expanded from their traditional role distributing botanical or herbal drugs such as morphine and quinine to wholesale manufacture in the mid 1800s. Initial rational drug discovery from plants was done particularly with the isolation of morphine (named after Greek God of dreams, Morpheus), an analgesic and sleep-inducing agent from opium, by the German apothecary assistant Friedrich Sertürner. Multinational corporations including Merck, Hoffman-La Roche, Burroughs-Wellcome (now part of Glaxo Smith Kline), Abbott Laboratories, Eli Lilly and Upjohn (now part of Pfizer) began as local apothecary shops in the mid-1800s.

By the late 1880s, German dye manufacturers had perfected the purification of individual organic compounds from coal tar and other mineral sources and had also established rudimentary methods in organic chemical synthesis.[3]

With the development of synthetic chemical methods scientists get freedom to make systematic variations in the structure of chemical substances, and growth in the emerging science of pharmacology expanded their ability to evaluate the biological effects of these structural changes.

By the 1890s, scientist made remarkable discovery by identifying the effect of adrenal extracts on many different types of tissue. This discovery also led to understanding of the mechanism of drugs through chemical signalling and led to start efforts to exploit these observations for the development of new drugs. Adrenal extracts have effects like increasing the blood pressure and vasoconstriction, but these effects have attracted the interest surgeons as hemostatic agents and as treatment for shock, and a number of companies developed products based on adrenal extracts containing varying purities of the active substance. In 1897, John Abel of Johns Hopkins University identified the active principle as epinephrine, which he isolated in an impure state as the sulfate salt. Later Jokichi Takamine (an industrial chemist) developed a method to obtain epinephrine in a pure state, and licensed the technology to Parke-Davis which marketed it under the trade name Adrenalin. Injected epinephrine proved to be especially efficacious for the acute treatment of asthma attacks, and an inhaled version was sold in the United States until 2011 (Primatene Mist).[4, 5] By 1929 epinephrine had been formulated into an inhaler for use in the treatment of nasal congestion.

While highly effective, the requirement for injection limited the use of epinephrine and orally active derivatives were sought. A structurally similar compound, ephedrine, (actually more similar to norepinephrine) was identified by Japanese chemists in the Ma Huang plant and marketed by Eli Lilly as an oral treatment for asthma. Following the work of Henry Dale and George Barger at Burroughs-Wellcome, academic chemist Gordon Alles synthesized amphetamine and tested it in asthma patients in 1929. The drug proved to have only modest anti-asthma effects, but produced sensations of exhilaration and palpitations. Amphetamine was developed by Smith, Kline and French as a nasal decongestant under the trade name Benzedrine Inhaler. Amphetamine was eventually developed for the treatment of narcolepsy, post-encephalitic parkinsonism, and mood elevation in depression and other psychiatric indications. It received approval as a New and Nonofficial Remedy from the American Medical Association for these uses in 1937 and remained in common use for depression until the development of tricyclic antidepressants in the 1960s.[5]

In 1903, Hermann Emil Fischer and Joseph von Mering disclosed their discovery that diethylbarbituric acid, formed from the reaction of diethylmalonic acid, phosphorus oxychloride and urea, induces sleep in dogs. The discovery was patented and licensed to Bayer pharmaceuticals, which marketed the compound under the trade name Veronal as a sleep aid beginning in 1904. Systematic investigations of the effect of structural changes on potency and duration of action led to the discovery of phenobarbital at Bayer in 1911 and the discovery of its potent anti-epileptic activity in 1912. Phenobarbital was among the most widely used drugs for the treatment of epilepsy through the 1970s, and as of 2014, remains on the World Health Organizations list of essential medications. [6, 7]

The 1950s and 1960s saw increased awareness of the addictive properties and abuse potential of barbiturates and amphetamines and led to increasing restrictions on their use and growing government oversight of prescribers. Today, amphetamine is largely restricted to use in the treatment of attention deficit disorder and phenobarbital in the treatment of epilepsy. [8, 9]

A series of experiments performed from the late 1800s to the early 1900s revealed that diabetes is caused by the absence of a substance normally produced by the pancreas. In 1869, Oskar Minkowski and Joseph von Mering found that diabetes could be induced in dogs by surgical removal of the pancreas. In 1921, Canadian professor Frederick Banting and his student Charles Best repeated this study, and found that injections of pancreatic extract reversed the symptoms produced by pancreas removal. Soon, the extract was demonstrated to work in people, but development of insulin therapy as a routine medical procedure was delayed by difficulties in producing the material in sufficient quantity and with reproducible purity. The researchers sought assistance from industrial collaborators at Eli Lilly and Co. based on the company's experience with large scale purification of biological materials. Chemist George B. Walden of Eli Lilly and Company found that careful adjustment of the pH of the extract allowed a relatively pure grade of insulin to be produced. Under pressure from Toronto University and a potential patent challenge by academic scientists who had independently developed a similar purification method, an agreement was reached for non-exclusive production of insulin by multiple companies. Prior to the discovery and widespread availability of insulin therapy the life expectancy of diabetics was only a few months.[10]

The development of drugs for the treatment of infectious diseases was a major focus of early research and development efforts; in 1900 pneumonia, tuberculosis, and diarrhea were the three leading causes of death in the United States and mortality in the first year of life exceeded 10%.[11]

In 1911 arsphenamine, the first synthetic anti-infective drug, was developed by Paul Ehrlich and chemist Alfred Bertheim of the Institute of Experimental Therapy in Berlin. The drug was given the commercial name Salvarsan. [12] Ehrlich, noting both the general toxicity of arsenic and the selective absorption of certain dyes by bacteria, hypothesized that an arsenic-containing dye with similar selective absorption properties could be used to treat bacterial infections. Arsphenamine was prepared as part of a campaign to synthesize a series of such compounds, and found to exhibit partially selective toxicity. Arsphenamine proved to be the first effective treatment for syphilis, a disease which prior to that time was incurable and led inexorably to severe skin ulceration, neurological damage, and death. Ehrlich's approach of systematically varying the chemical structure of synthetic compounds and measuring the effects of these changes on biological activity was pursued broadly by industrial scientists, including Bayer scientists Josef Klarer, Fritz Mietzsch, and Gerhard Domagk. This work, also based in the testing of compounds available from the German dye industry, led to the development of Prontosil, the first representative of the sulfonamide class of antibiotics. Compared to arsphenamine, the sulfonamides had a broader spectrum of activity and were far less toxic, rendering them useful for infections caused by pathogens such as streptococci. [13] In 1939, Domagk received the Nobel Prize in Medicine for this discovery. [14,15] Nonetheless, the dramatic decrease in deaths from infectious diseases that occurred prior to World War II was primarily the result of improved public health measures such as clean water and less crowded housing, and the impact of anti-infective drugs and vaccines was significant mainly after World War II. [16, 17]

In 1928, Alexander Fleming discovered the antibacterial effects of penicillin, but its exploitation for the treatment of human disease awaited the development of methods for its large scale production and purification. These were developed by a U.S. and British government-led consortium of pharmaceutical companies during the Second World War.[18] Early progress toward the development of vaccines occurred throughout this period, primarily in the form of academic and government-funded basic research directed toward the identification of the pathogens responsible for common communicable diseases. In 1885 Louis Pasteur and Pierre Paul Émile Roux created the first rabies vaccine. The first diphtheria vaccines were produced in 1914 from a mixture of diphtheria toxin and antitoxin (produced from the serum of an inoculated animal), but the safety of the inoculation was marginal and it was not widely used [19]. The United States recorded 206,000 cases of diphtheria in 1921 resulting in 15,520 deaths. In 1923 parallel efforts by

Gaston Ramon at the Pasteur Institute and Alexander Glenny at the Wellcome Research Laboratories (later part of GlaxoSmithKline) led to the discovery that a safer vaccine could be produced by treating diphtheria toxin with formaldehyde.[20] In 1944, Maurice Hilleman of Squibb Pharmaceuticals developed the first vaccine against Japanese encephelitis.[20] Hilleman would later move to Merck where he would play a key role in the development of vaccines against measles, mumps, chickenpox, rubella, hepatitis A, hepatitis B, and meningitis.

BACKGROUND OF PHARMACEUTICAL INDUSTRY

Prior to the 20th century drugs were generally produced by small scale manufacturers with little regulatory control over manufacturing or claims of safety and efficacy. To the extent that such laws did exist, enforcement was lax. In the United States, increased regulation of vaccines and other biological drugs was spurred by tetanus outbreaks and deaths caused by the distribution of contaminated smallpox vaccine and diphtheria antitoxin.[2]

"Tragic events help us to wake up" this statement became true when several children died of tetanus in 1901 in USA. These children received antitoxin for diphtheria treatment. On investigation it was identified that the horse serum that used to prepare the antitoxin was contaminated with tetanus. This, accident is sufficient enough to demonstrate the importance of high-quality raw materials, along with the ability of animal-derived materials to pass diseases both known and unknown.

In 1902, "The Biologics Control Act" was passed to improve the assurance of safety and purity of sera, vaccines, and other biological products. Later in 1906, The Food and Drugs Act was first passed and put into law. In 1938 this act was revised as the Food, Drug and Cosmetic Act of 1938 [2].

In 1905, a book called The Jungle was published. His book acted as catalyst to make public opinion for change. This book was based on the Chicago Meat packing industry and was written by "Muckraker" and social reformer Upton Sinclair. This book explained the unsanitary conditions in which animals were slaughtered and processed and the practice of selling rotten or diseased meat to the public. Through this book, he also explained that the ground meat sometimes contained remains of poisoned rats and even unfortunate workers who fell into the machinery. The main interest of the author of the book was in bringing attention to the miserable working conditions and the plight of the impoverished factory workers, many of whom were immigrants. This book had a major impact on the American public and in 1906 Congress passed the Pure Food and Drug Act. It was for the first time in modern history became illegal to sell contaminated (adulterated) food or meat [2].

1906 was a major break point as this was same year when requirement of proper labelling on the drugs was also observed. It was also included in the act. It mentioned that selected dangerous ingredients like alcohol, opium, morphine which have the ability of addiction are required to be labelled. These were the common ingredients of the syrups and tonics. Inaccurate or false labeling was called misbranding, and that became illegal [21].

Shortcomings of the 1906 law was soon illustrated by a 1933 FDA exhibit of dangerous food, medicines, medical devices, and cosmetics. "America's Chamber of Horrors" included a womb supporter (also used as a contraceptive) that could puncture the uterus if inserted incorrectly; a weight-loss drug that caused death; a hair remover that caused baldness, even if not used on the head; lotions and creams that could cause mercury poisoning; hair dyes that could cause lead poisoning; and an eyelash dye that blinded women [22].

In 1937, sulphanilamide elixir formulation manufactured by S.E. Massengill Company of Tennessee and marketed for use in children caused another tragedy which killed 107 people most of them were children. On investigation it was found that this formulation contained a poisonous substance called diethylene glycol as solvent (the same chemical used in antifreeze nowadays). This tragedy leads Congress to pass the Federal Food, Drugs and Cosmetic (FD & C) Act of 1938. This act bound the companies for the first time to prove that their products were safe before marketing them[23].

Another tragedy took place in 1941, due to which nearly 300 people were killed or injured by one company's sulfathiazole tablets, a sulfa drug tainted with the sedative phenobarbital. That incident caused FDA to drastically revise manufacturing and quality control requirements, leading to what would later be called GMPs [24].

During the time period of World War II, batch certification by FDA became a requirement for certain drugs. Due to this companies were asked to submit samples from each lot to FDA for analysis. Agency would then give permission for their release only if the sample complied with the specified limits. In 1941 it was initially started for insulin but later included penicillin in 1945 later expanded to include all antibiotics[25].

In 1955, Jonas Salk discovered a way to vaccinate against polio. Many manufacturers began making his polio vaccine. One company failed to inactivate the virus completely in a single lot. Due to which about 60 individuals who were inoculated with vaccine developed polio. After this incident, FDA started to ensure safety of the vaccine [26].

Same way when regulatory agencies allowed thalidomide, a drug used as sleeping pills to treat morning sickness for sale in Europe, they were completely unaware of its side effects. Later on as it turned out to be teratogenic, this caused serious deformities in developing foetuses. Pregnant ladies for the first trimester who were taking this drug later gave birth to the child with severely deformed arms and legs. Approximately 10,000 cases of infant deformities in Europe were linked to thalidomide use. This thalidomide tragedy galvanized public opinion and legislators pushed more stringent legislation through Congress that required companies to test not only to ensure that the products were safe, but that they were efficacious for their intended uses through conducting clinical trials. Thus some amendments were required in the act so that drugs to be tested in animals before people. As per these amendments investigators were made responsible for supervising drugs under study. Along with this a drug manufacturer was expected to inform participants if a drug was being used for investigational purposes and to obtain their consent before testing it on them [21].

The 1972 Devonport, UK, incident resulted in at least five deaths when drug products designed to be sterile became contaminated and recipients developed infections. Root cause for this incident on investigation was found an unwritten change to autoclave operation. This change was made orally between operators and was communicated from one operator to other orally, resulting in dextrose IV solutions that were not uniformly sterile. Along with this the Clothier inquiry, which examined the causes and contributing factors, also identified several other violations of what we now consider basic GMP [2]. The current requirement of "Documented Evidence" may be driven by this event.

In 1979 more than 100 infants were made seriously ill by a lack of chlorides in two soy-based formulas. This incident bound the manufacturers to analyze each batch of formula for nutrient levels and make safety checks, conduct stability tests, code each container with a lot number, keep detailed records of production and analysis, and so on. The food GMPs [27], which include special provisions for infant formulas, were finalized in the 1980s [21]. In 1980, congress passed the Infant Formula Act giving FDA authority to create and enforce standards and specify nutritional requirements for commercial infant formulas.

In 1982, several consumers of over-the-counter Tylenol capsules suddenly died of cyanide poisoning. An intensive investigation of the production records showed that this was not the result of a raw materials mix-up during manufacturing. Rather, tampering apparently occurred on store shelves. A new vulnerability was identified in the supply chain. The manufacturer, Johnson and Johnson, notified the public and voluntarily recalled its entire product in what is now a textbook case of how to respond to a health disaster. Their development scientists went into overdrive to re-design the capsule to make tampering more difficult and more detectable. The industry as a whole re-evaluated the means of delivering over-the-counter medicines.

Regulations were started updating in 1982, and they now require tamper-resistant packaging that aids in the detection of tampering. Without these steps, over-the-counter pharmaceuticals could have become an unacceptable safety risk[2].

In 1989, an outbreak of toxic reactions to over-the-counter l-tryptophan, a dietary supplement, resulted in 38 deaths and probably thousands of less severe reactions. The event was the result of a manufacturing process change that increased the level of a harmful by product. Doses that had previously been safe now caused toxicity. One response to this event was the clarification of requirements for characterizing drug impurities and new requirements for evaluation of minor impurities. In the biological products area, extensive policy and guidances have been issued on how to establish comparability when process, facility, or other changes are made[2].

EVOLUTION OF GMP

World Health Organization (WHO) prepared first draft text on good manufacturing practices (GMP) in 1967 after consulting with a group of expert consultants at the request of the Twentieth World Health Assembly (resolution WHA20.34). Subsequently, "Draft requirements for good manufacturing practice in the manufacture and quality control of medicines and pharmaceutical specialities" was submitted and accepted by the Twenty first World Health Assembly. Thereafter, in 1968 WHO expert committees on specifications for pharmaceutical preparation discussed the revised text and published as an annex to its twenty-second report. In 1971, after some revisions the text was in the Supplement to the second edition of The International Pharmacopoeia.

World Health Assembly recommended the first version of the WHO Certification Scheme on the quality of pharmaceutical products moving in international commerce in resolution WHA22.50 in 1969. In the same assembly it got approval and accepted the GMP text as an integral part of the Scheme. In 1975 under resolution WHA28.65, both the Certification Scheme and the GMP text were revised and adopted. Since then, the Certification Scheme has been extended to include the certification of:

- Veterinary products administered to food-producing animals;
- Starting materials for use in dosage forms, when they are subject to control by legislation in both the exporting Member State and the importing Member State;
- Information on safety and efficacy (resolution WHA41.18, 1988).

In 1992, the revised draft requirements for GMP were presented in three parts [27] as follows:

1. "Quality management in the medicines industry: philosophy and essential elements", outlines the general concepts of quality assurance (QA) as well as the principal components or subsystems of GMP, which are joint responsibilities of top management and of production and quality control management. These include hygiene, validation, self-inspection, personnel, premises, equipment, materials and documentation.
2. "Good practices in production and quality control", provides guidance on actions to be taken separately by production and by quality control personnel for the implementation of the general principles of QA. These two parts were subsequently supplemented by further guidelines which are integral parts of these GMP for pharmaceutical products.
3. Documents

With change and developments in technology, several other guidelines and revisions in existing guidelines with intention to help manufacturers in implementing modern quality systems and risk management approaches to meet the requirements of current good manufacturing practice (CGMP) regulations took place and appeared[28-33]. These guidelines described comprehensive quality systems (QS) model, highlighting the model's consistency with the CGMP regulatory requirements for manufacturing human and veterinary drugs, including biological drug products. They also explained how manufacturers implementing such quality systems can be in full compliance with them. These guiding documents, do not establish legally enforceable responsibilities, instead, described the current thinking of agency on a topic and should be viewed only as recommendations *i.e.* the agency recommend or suggest, but not necessarily required unless specific regulatory or statutory requirements are cited.

Originally, the PIC/S GMP Guide ("PIC Basic Standards" of 1972) was derived from the WHO GMP Guide but was further developed in order to comply with stringent manufacturing and health requirements in PIC/S countries,[34] and to cover new areas *(e.g.* biological, radiopharmaceutical etc.) and to adapt to scientific and industrial technology *(e.g.* biotech, parametric release etc.). These improvements were made with the aim to ensure high quality medicines were produced in line with the PIC Convention and then the PIC Scheme. In 1989, the EU adopted its own GMP Guide, which – in terms of GMP requirements – was equivalent to the PIC/S GMP Guide. Since that time, the EU and the PIC/S GMP Guides have been developed in parallel and whenever a change has been made to one, the other has been amended so that both Guides are practically identical.

During these changes it was observed that the concept of validation is required to be incorporated in the main basic principles. Among other items of feedback discussed during the consultation on WHO guidelines for medicines quality assurance, quality control (QC) laboratories and transfer of technology on 27–31 July 2009, the need was identified to incorporate a new section on "Product quality review" under Chapter 1: "Quality assurance". In addition, several updates and revisions were suggested to further enhance and empower the guidelines. These included the introduction of concept of risk management, replacing "drugs" by the term "medicines" and introducing the concept of a "quality unit". During 2012, the Secretariat was made aware that the current Good manufacturing practices (GMP) for pharmaceutical products: main principles, published as Annex 3 in the WHO Technical Report Series, No. 961, 2011, would need updating.[35]

As many pharmaceutical manufacturers have already implemented comprehensive, modern quality systems and risk management approaches, thus with an intention to encourage manufactures to implement modern quality systems and risk management approaches to meet the requirements of the USFDA's CGMP regulations, in August 2002, the agency announced the Pharmaceutical CGMPs for the 21st Century Initiative. In that announcement, the Agency explained its intention to integrate quality systems and risk management approaches into its existing programs with the goal of encouraging industry to adopt modern and innovative manufacturing technologies.

The CGMP initiative was spurred by the fact that since 1978, when the last major revision of the CGMP regulations was published, there have been many advances in manufacturing technology and in understanding of quality systems. The Agency also saw a need to harmonize the CGMPs with other non-U.S. pharmaceutical regulatory systems and with FDA's own medical device quality systems regulations. The revised guidance supports these goals. It also supports the objectives of the Critical Path Initiative, which intends to make the development of innovative medical products more efficient so that safe and effective therapies can reach patients sooner.

The CGMPs for the 21st Century Initiative steering committee created a Quality System Guidance Development working group (QS working group) to compare the current CGMP regulations, which call for some specific quality management elements, to other existing quality management systems. The QS working group mapped the relationship between CGMP regulations and various quality system models, such as the Drug Manufacturing Inspections Program (*i.e.*, systems-based inspectional program), [36] the Environmental Protection Agency's Guidance for Developing Quality Systems for Environmental Programs, ISO Quality Standards, other quality publications, and experience from regulatory cases. The QS working group determined that, although the CGMP regulations do provide great flexibility, they do not incorporate explicitly all of the elements that today constitute most quality management systems.

The CGMP regulations and other quality management systems differ somewhat in organization and in certain constituent elements; however, they are very similar and share underlying principles. For example, the CGMP regulations stress quality control. More recently developed quality systems stress quality management, quality assurance, and the use of risk management tools, in addition to quality control. The QS working group decided that it would be very useful to examine exactly how the CGMP regulations and the elements of a modern, comprehensive quality system fit together in today's manufacturing world. This guidance is the result of that examination.

The WHO Expert Committee on Specifications for Pharmaceutical Preparations discussed the need for an update during its forty-seventh meeting and agreed to pursue the matter accordingly. The following sections were updated in the newly revised version and, after the usual consultation process, were presented to the forty-eighth Expert Committee for adoption:

Section: Pharmaceutical quality system

Section 2: 2. Good manufacturing practices for pharmaceutical products

Section 7: Contract production, analysis and other activities

Section 17: 17. Good practices in quality control

Chronological Development of GMP regulations has been summarized in Table 1.

ROLE OF WHO IN PHARMACEUTICAL REGULATION

WHO is the directing and coordinating authority for health within the United Nations system [37]. It is responsible for providing leadership on global health matters, shaping the health research agenda, setting norms and standards, articulating evidence-based policy options, providing technical support to countries and monitoring and assessing health trends. In the 21st century,health is a shared responsibility, involving equitable access to essential care and collective defence against transnational health threats. WHO's role in drug regulation is fourfold.

First: issuing necessary norms and standards (see examples above) through its Expert Committees (such as WHO Expert Committee on Specifications for Pharmaceutical Preparations and WHO Expert Committeeon Biological Standardization) and Expert Committee like bodies (such as International Non-proprietary Names Expert Group and International Working Group for Drug Statistics Methodology – issuing Anatomical, Therapeutic and Chemical or ATC codes and Daily Defined Doses or DDDs for drug utilization research).

Table 1: Chronological development of GMP

Year	***Major amendments***
1902	Biologics Control Act
1906	Pure Food and Drug Act
1938	Federal Food, Drug and Cosmetic (FD & C) Act
1941	Two Unrelated Events Insulin Amendment requires FDA to test and certify purity and potency of insulin. Tragedy: nearly 300 deaths and injuries from distribution of sulfathiazole tablets tainted with Phenobarbital. Result: FDA revises manufacturing and quality controls drastically, the beginning of what will later be called GMPs.
1944	Public Health Services Act
1946	Publication by the Pharmaceutical Manufacturers Association of America lf a "Guideline for Good Manufacturing Practices for Pharmaceuticals"
1962	The "Thalidomide Tragedy" leads the US Congress to add GMP to the Food, Drugs and Cosmetic Act.The FDA publishes their first Regulation on Good Manufacturing Practices" – A drug which is not made following GMP is adulterd (Contaminated)
1969	The World Health Organization publishes the first universal guideline "Basic Rules for the Manufacture of Pharmaceuticals and the Assurance of their Quality"
1972	The Daily Telegraph published as its main news the recall of 5% Dextrose Infusion Solution after 5 patients die at Devonport Hospital ("The Devonport Hospital Affair")
1974	Allergic reaction due to extremely small traces of penicillin in other drug products leads to demands for separation of penicillin and non-penicillin production.
1974	FDA Starts investigating some US toxicology laboratories and finds evidence of widespread mis-management and even fraud.
1976	FDA publishes their proposals for "Good Laboratory Practices for Non-Clinical Studies"
1975	The EU Directive 75/319 lays down the basic procedures (approximatations) for the registration, trade and compensation for damages for "Medicinal Products" with the EU.
1978	CGMPs Final Rules for Drugs (21 CFR Parts 210–211)
1979	Infant Formula Act
1982	Temper-Resistant Packaging Regulations Issued for OTC Products
1983	The Guide to the Inspection of Computerized Systems in Drug Processing initiates tighter controls on computers and computer validation.
1986	Microbial contamination of an API for veterinary use later causes the deaths of several hundred cattle in Germany.
1987	Guideline on General Principles of Process Validation
1989	FDA discovers mis-management and even fraud in the applications by US generic drug manufacturers in trying to get approval for the sale of their products. (One company even tested not its own product, but the competitor's product against the competitor's products in order to get approval for sale from the FDA.) This leads to Pre-Approval Inspections (PAIs)
1989	The inspectors of the EU agree on a Guideline for GMP and the EU publishes its Directive on the "Approximation of provisions for GMP in the European Community", *i.e.* a legal basis is established for pharmaceutical GMP within the European Community.
1991	FDA publishes their "Guide to the Inspection of Bulk Pharmaceuticals" which

Table 1: *(Contd...)*

Year	*Major amendments*
	strongly influences the way in which Starting Materials for pharmaceuticals are produced.
1994	The EU and the FDA open negotiations on the mutual recognition of GMP inspections. (Agreement was finally reached and a DRAFT was signed).
1996	PIC accepts the European industry's GMP Guide
1998	"GMPs for Starting Materials" is added to the ICH work programme to be decided by an Expert Working Group.
2001	ICH Q7A API Guidance ICH's "Good Manufacturing Practice Guidance for Active Pharmaceutical Ingredients (APIs)"

Second: supporting regulatory capacity building leading to implementation of drug regulation on national level and its harmonization on regional and Global level. This activity involves assessment of regulatory activities on country level and various technical training courses (such as GMP and GCP, how to assess generic medicines, bioequivalence, safety monitoring and pharmacovigilance, quality assurance and quality control) and customized technical assistance (in cooperation with numerous WHO collaborating centers and other partners) to the countries.

Third: in selected areas of essential products, ensuring the quality, safety and efficacy of limited high public health value essential medicines (such as antiretrovoirals to treat HIV/AIDS, or medicines to treat malaria) and vaccines (used in national vaccination programs) through "prequalification". De facto prequalification, although primarily meant for UN procurement and international donors, is a regulatory activity mimicking medicines registration (marketing authorization) in its all elements to ensure that products prequalified meet all international standards for quality, safety and efficacy. Prequalification program has also a very strong capacity building element built into it.

Fourth: WHO plays a very important role in facilitating exchange of regulatory information for which it has developed a number of tools. Since 1980 WHO convenes every second year International Conference of Drug Regulatory Authorities (ICDRA) and publishes their proceedings. These conferences provide drug regulatory authorities of WHO Member States with a forum to meet and discuss ways to strengthen collaboration. The ICDRAs have been instrumental in guiding through its recommendations regulatory authorities, WHO and interested stakeholders and in determining priorities for action in national and international regulation of medicines, vaccines, biomedicines and herbals.

WHO manages also a system for regular exchange of information between Member States on the safety and efficacy of pharmaceutical products, using a network of designated national drug information officers. WHO ensures the prompt transmission to national health authorities of new information on serious adverse effects of pharmaceutical products and it also responds to individual requests for information. These goals are achieved by the regular publication of regulatory information in the *WHO Pharmaceuticals Newsletter* [38] and by the dissemination of one-page *Drug Alerts* on an *ad-hoc* basis. Relevant restrictive regulatory decisions are ultimately compiled in the United Nations Consolidated List of Products Whose Consumption and/ or Sale have been banned, withdrawn, severely restricted or not Approved by Governments. WHO publishes updates to this list: Pharmaceuticals: Restrictions in use and availability. WHO publishes also quarterly WHO Drug Information [39] journal which provides an overview of topics of current relevance relating to drug development, safety and regulation. Latest lists of proposed and recommended International Non-proprietary Names (INN) for Pharmaceutical Substances are also published in this journal.

WHO cooperates very actively with national regulatory authorities of all of its Member States. It tries to facilitate spreading best practices and experience. Through its observer role in the international Conference of Harmonization (ICH) WHO is liaising between ICH and non-ICH countries trying to ensure that information exchange between highly industrialized and less resourced countries is taking place.

CURRENT SCENARIO

Concept of GMP evolved on the basis of the recognition that end-point analysis done by the quality control is not sufficient to assure the quality of the individual medication unit (the tablet, the capsule, the vial) dispensed to the patient, but rather it is required that quality is needed to be assured at each step of the manufacturing process to be as certain as possible that each dosage unit met its quality specifications more specifically the main concept is that quality cannot be built by testing but is required to build through manufacturing. Before the emergence of GMP, pharmaceutical product quality was analysed against the specification laid down in the pharmacopoeia.

Good Manufacturing Practices (GMPs) forms that component of quality assurance system which ensures that products produced meet the quality standards appropriate to their intended use consistently and continuously as required by the Marketing Authorization or product specification. GMP is concerned with both production (manufacturing) and quality control (analysis). Worldwide, various official regulatory statements and guidelines on Good Manufacturing Practices for pharmaceutical (or "drug" or "medicinal") products exist. Their names may differ like regulations (as in the US, Japan or Korea), directives (as in the EU), guides (as in the UK), codes (as in Australia), or WHO code (as in many Southeast Asia Countries).

Out of them, following stands out as being the most influential and most frequently referenced:

- The US Current Good Manufacturing Practices for Finished Pharmaceuticals regulations (the "US cGMPs")
- The Guide to Good Manufacturing Practice for Medicinal Products of the European Union (the "EC GMP Guide") (Eudralex)
- ICH Q7 Good Manufacturing Practice Guide for Active Pharmaceutical Ingredients (ICH, 2000).
- WHO good manufacturing practices (GMP, 2003).

The other regulation referred by the Indian pharmaceutical manufacturers is Schedule M "Good Manufacturing Practices and Requirements of Premises, Plant and Equipment for Pharmaceutical Products" The Drugs And Cosmetics Act And Rules, India (Schedule, 2005). The glance of major GMP regulatory agencies or guidelines is highlighted in Tables 2 and 3 respectively.

FUTURE PROSPECTS

Regulatory requirements for the pharmaceutical industry have been developing together with the sciences involved in developing new drugs and pharmaceutical products. Developments in health delivery systems have also played role as those involved in health service delivery are interested in safe and effective treatments which would be cheaper, effective, safer and affordable. With the increase in regulatory requirements, costs of research and development and regulatory assessment of products during registration for marketing are also increasing. There is likely no alternative for harmonization amongst international, regional and sub-regional regulatory requirements along with work sharing and information sharing between different national regulatory authorities. Smaller regulatory authorities could not afford the cost of full assessment for a new drug as it is increasingly day by day thus the need of harmonization increased for better information exchange and gradual trust building in each other's decisions leading to recognition instead of duplication. Although even quality issues related to products are still a problem (starting materials including active pharmaceutical ingredients, finished dosage forms, spreading of counterfeit medicines), it is likely that new technologies and new products will create new regulatory challenges.

For example, increased public attention and expectations on medicines safety or using new technologies or product formulation such as nanotechnologies change the medicines regulation or issues relating to the understanding of how the nanoparticles are presented to organs, cells and organelles are of the different mechanisms for intracellular trafficking and

Table 2: Major GMP regulation agencies

Country	***Regulatory body***
India	CDSCO
USA	US-FDA
UK	MHRA
European Union	EMEA (EU-GMP)
Ukraine	SAUMP
Brazil	ANVISA
Kenya	PPB
Nigeria	NAFDAQ
South Africa	MCC
Zimbabwe	MCAZ
Australia	TGA
Canada	Health Canada
Germany	Ministry of Health, Labour and Welfare
China	SFDA
Korea	KFDA
Japan	MHLW
New Zealand	Medsafe
Denmark	Danish Medicines Agency
Costa Rica	Ministry of Health
Sweden	Medical Products Agency (MPA)
Netherlands	Medicines Evaluation Board
Ireland	Irish Medicines Board
Italy	Italian Pharmaceutical Agency
Singapore	Centre for Pharmaceutical Administration Health Sciences Authority
Hong Kong	Department of Health: Pharmaceutical Services
Paraguay	Ministry of Health
Sweden	Medical Products Agency (MPA)
Thailand	Ministry of Public Health
Malaysia	National Pharmaceutical Control Bureau, Ministry of Health
Philippines	Philippines FDA
Pakistan	Drugs Control Organization, Ministry of Health
Sri Lanka	SPC, Ministry of Health
Switzerland	Swissmedic, Swiss Agency for Therapeutic Products
Uganda	Uganda National Council for Science and Technology (UNCST)

Table 3: Global/ Multinational Regulatory authority

WHO	***World Health Organisation***
PICS	Pharmaceutical Inspection Co-operation Scheme
PAHO	Pan American Health Organisation
WIPO	World Intellectual Property Organisation
ICH	International Conference on Harmonisation
ASEAN	Association of South East Asian nations

use their full the highest importance when trying to understand therapeutic potential. Those aspects cannot be established without improving appropriate basic knowledge of cell and molecular biology at the intracellular level.

However, at the same time important quality problems can also rise. In order to assure quality physical and chemical properties of such products, including residual solvents, processing variables, impurities and excipients, should all be well known. There will be a need for well-established standard tools to be used in the characterization of novel drug products, including availability of validated assay methods to detect nanoparticles in tissues, medicinal products qualitatively and quantitatively. Toxicological aspects of these products have also been highlighted with focus on long-term toxicity. Carbon nanotubes, quantum dots and other nonbiodegradable and potentially harmful materials should be given closer attention weather associated with medicines or diagnostics.

Pharmaceuticals will have an increasingly prominent role in the health care of the future. The health of citizens of the any country depends on the availability of safe, effective and affordable medicines. In the future, pharmaceutical manufacturing will need to employ innovation, cutting edge scientific and engineering knowledge, and the best principles of quality management to respond to the challenges of new discoveries and ways of doing business such as individualized therapies or genetically tailored treatments. Regulation of the future will also need to meet these challenges, by incorporating new scientific information into regulatory standards and policies. Both industry and regulatory practices will need to be informed by the best techniques of risk assessment and management. "Pharmaceutical cGMPs for the 21st Century" is intended to jump-start progress into this future.

The last few years has seen the FDA steer industry further in the direction of a quality-by-design (QbD) approach, and away from the quality-by-testing (QbT) approach traditionally taken by the pharmaceuticals sector. This move has largely been lauded by business as a sensible move likely to ensure consistent quality of the end product. The shift in focus is expected to bring about a well-needed modernization to the sector and allow new ideas the breeding ground needed to flourish. As pharmaceutical manufacturing evolves from an art to science and engineering based activity, application of this enhanced science and engineering knowledge in regulatory decision–making, establishment of specifications, and evaluation of manufacturing processes should improve the efficiency and effectiveness of both manufacturing and regulatory decision–making, A Process and Analytical Technology (PAT) initiative has been initiated by the FDA and designed to revolutionize and improve many pharmaceutical processes. A regulatory framework, PAT discusses possible routes and opportunities to promote and encourage opportunities for innovation. The FDA has outlined the guidelines of the initiative in a document entitled "Guidance for Industry PAT – A Framework for Innovative Pharmaceutical, Development, Manufacturing and Quality Assurance".

Effectively using this knowledge in regulatory decisions in establishing specifications and evaluating manufacturing processes can substantially improve the efficiency of both manufacturing and regulatory processes. This initiative is designed to do just that through an integrated systems approach to product quality regulation founded on sound science and engineering principles for assessing and mitigating risks of poor product and process quality in the context of the intended use of pharmaceutical products. In this regard, the desired future state of pharmaceutical manufacturing may be characterized as:

- Product quality and performance achieved and assured by design of effective and efficient manufacturing processes
- Product specifications based on mechanistic understanding of how formulation and process factors impact product performance
- Continuous "real time" assurance of quality
- Regulatory policies and procedures tailored to recognize the level of scientific knowledge supporting product applications, process validation, and process capability
- Risk based regulatory scrutiny that relates to the level of scientific understanding of how formulation and manufacturing process factors affect product quality and performance and the capability of process control strategies to prevent or mitigate risk of producing a poor quality product (Summary Progress Report).

CONCLUSIONS

To conclude, and as a final reminder to readers of this chapter, the contents emphasised on the recommended practices and principles of GMP which are required to be instituted by the pharmaceutical industry to supplement current GMPs and should be interpreted to provide maximum flexibility to manufacturers to adapt programs to their unique product, processes and facilities to ensure product quality, safety and efficacy. This industry have seen some extremely dark phases but it is the courage and confidence of this sector which helped the manufacturers to overcome these setbacks and to reach this milestone. Although we have reach a quite far distance but it is not the end. It is just a new start. We all have a long journey ahead which will lead to some new developments.

REFERENCES

[1] "Diphtheria — Timelines — History of Vaccines"
[2] "Drug Abuse Control Amendments of 1965". *NEJM*. 273 (22): 1222–1223. 1965-11-25
[3] "Maurice R. Hilleman, 85; Scientist Developed Many Vaccines That Saved Millions of Lives - Los Angeles Times"
[4] "Nobel Prize Facts" (https://www.nobelprize.org/nobel_prizes/facts/)

[5] "Sedative-Hypnotic Drugs — The Barbiturates — I". *NEJM*. 255 (24): 1150–1151. 1956.
[6] "www.cdc.gov"
[7] 21 CFR Part 110
[8] 2l CFR parts 210 and 211
[9] Aminov RI (2010). "A brief history of the antibiotic era: Lessons learned and challenges for the future" *Front Microbiol*. 1: 134.
[10] CPGM 7356.002 Compliance Program – Drug Manufacturing Inspections http://www.fda.gov/cder/dmpq/compliance_guide.htm
[11] Cutler, David; Meara, Ellen (October 2001). "Changes in the Age Distribution of Mortality Over the 20th Century". NBER Working Paper No. 8556.
[12] *EudraLex* – Volume 4. *Good manufacturing practice (GMP) Guidelines. European Commission*. (http://ec.europa.eu/health/documents/eudralex/vol-4/ index_en.htm).
[13] FDA (1995) Milestones in U.S. Food and Drug Law History. FDA Backgrounder: Current and Useful Information from the Food and Drug Administration (FDA, Rockville, MD, August 1995). Available from: www.fda.gov/opacom/backgrounders/miles.html.
[14] FDA (2000) Office of Women's Health, FDA Milestones in Women's Health: Looking Back as We Move into the New Millennium (FDA, Rockville, MD). Available from: www.fda.gov/womens/milesbro.html.
[15] FDA (overview) An Overview of FDA. Available from: http://www.fda.gov/oc/opacom/fda101/sld013.html
[16] Good manufacturing practices for pharmaceutical products. *In*: WHO Expert Committee on Specifications for Pharmaceutical Preparations. Thirty-seventh report. Geneva, World Health Organization, 2003 (WHO Technical Report Series, No. 908), Annex 4.
[17] Hager, Thomas (2006). The demon under the microscope: From battlefield hospitals to Nazi labs, one doctor's heroic search for the world's first miracle drug (*1st ed.*). New York: Harmony Books. ISBN 1-4000-8213-7
[18] http://www.who.int/medicines/areas/quality_safety/quality_assurance/production/en/index.html " Quality assurance of pharmaceuticals: A compendium of guidelines and related materials
[19] http://www.who.int/medicines/publications/newsletter/en/index.html
[20] Immel BK (2005) A Brief History of the GMPs, Regulatory Compliance Newsletter, Winter 2005. Available from: http://www.gmplabeling.com/catalog/news1105.pdf
[21] John Parascandola (1980). The History of antibiotics: a symposium. American Institute of the History of Pharmacy No. 5
[22] Klein, Herbert (2012). A Population History of the United States. Cambridge University Press. p. 167
[23] Learoyd P (2005) Good Manufacturing Practices or 'GMP' A Brief Guide, NBS-Scientific and Technical Training STT-040, Sept 2005.
[24] López-Muñoz F, Ucha-Udabe R, Alamo C (December 2005). "The history of barbiturates a century after their clinical introduction". *Neuropsychiatr Dis Treat*. 1 (4): 329–43
[25] Pharmaceutical Inspection Convention, Pharmaceutical Inspection Co-operation Scheme (PIC/S). In: *Guide to good manufacturing practice for medicinal plants*. Geneva, PIC/S Secretariat, 2000.
[26] PIC/S "Guide to good manufacturing practice for medicinal products" PE 009-11 (Intro). 01 Mar, 2014.
[27] *Quality assurance of pharmaceuticals. WHO guidelines, related guidance and GXP training modules*. Geneva, World Health Organization, 2013 (CD-ROM).
[28] Rasmussen, Nicolas (2006) "Making the First Anti-Depressant: Amphetamine in American Medicine, 1929-1950". *J Hist Med Allied Sci*. 61 (3): 288–323.

[29] Rosenfeld L (December 2002). "Insulin: Discovery and controversy". *Clin. Chem.* 48 (12): 2270–88.
[30] see more on web site: http://www.who.int/en/
[31] Sepkowitz KA (July 2011). "One hundred years of Salvarsan". *N. Engl. J. Med.* 365 (4): 291–3
[32] Shadle PJ (2004) Overview of GMPs, *BioPharm International*, Nov 15, 2004.
[33] Stehlin IB (1995) How FDA Works to Ensure Vaccine Safety. Available from: http:/ /www.fda.gov/fdac/features/095_vacc.html
[34] Time Line: Chronology of Drug Regulation in the United States. Available from: http://www.fda.gov/cder/about/history/time1.htm.
[35] Top Pharmaceuticals: Introduction: Emergence Of Pharmaceutical Science And Industry: 1870-1930
[36] Validation of analytical procedures used in the examination of pharmaceutical materials. In: *WHO Expert Committee on Specifications for Pharmaceutical Preparations. Thirty-second report.* Geneva, World Health Organization, 1992 (WHO Technical Report Series, No. 823), Annex 5.
[37] Walter Sneader (31 October 2005). Drug Discovery: A History (https:// books.google.com/books?id=jglFsz5EJR8C). John Wiley & Sons. pp. 155–156. ISBN 978-0-470-01552-0.3], [Rasmussen, Nicolas (2006)
[38] www.who.int/druginformation/
[39] Yasiry Z, Shorvon SD (December 2012). "How phenobarbital revolutionized epilepsy therapy: the story of phenobarbital therapy in epilepsy in the last 100 years". *Epilepsia.* 53 Suppl 8: 26–39.

2

Quality Assurance

ABSTRACT

Quality is the most important attribute to assess any product. Quality of the product also helps in assessing the quality system of the manufacturers. While a consumer receives a defective product, he / she will eventually prepare a negative image of the manufacturer in his / her brain. It also stands for medicinal products. Any defective medicine with any type of defect in terms of effect or quality ultimately brings losses to the manufacturers. To overcome these quality issues, manufacturers have established quality systems. This quality system includes quality assurance and quality control. While quality assurance comprises administrative and procedural activities to achieve product quality, quality control mainly deals with the analysis of the product. In this chapter we are going to learn about the quality assurance, its history, approaches, activities and requirements. Along with this, chapter shall also emphasise on aspect of quality and quality assurance with respect to pharmaceutical industry and various aspects of pharmaceutical quality attributes.

INTRODUCTION

Quality assurance (QA) is a way of preventing mistakes and defects in manufactured products and avoiding problems when delivering solutions or services to customers; which ISO 9000 defines as "part of quality management focused on providing confidence that quality requirements will be fulfilled" [1]. This defect prevention in quality assurance differs subtly from defect detection and rejection in quality control, and has been referred to as a shift left as it focuses on quality earlier in the process *i.e.* to the left of a linear process diagram reading left to right [2]. The terms "quality assurance" and "quality control" are often used interchangeably to refer to ways of ensuring the quality of a service or product [3]. For instance, the term "assurance" is often used as follows: Implementation of inspection and structured testing as a measure of quality assurance in a television set software project at Philips Semiconductors is described [4]. The term "control", however, is used to describe the fifth phase of the Define, Measure, Analyze, Improve, Control (DMAIC) model. DMAIC is a data-driven quality strategy used to improve processes [5].

Quality assurance comprises administrative and procedural activities implemented in a quality system so that requirements and goals for a product, service or activity will be fulfilled. It is the systematic measurement, comparison with a standard, monitoring of processes and an associated feedback loop that confers error prevention [6]. This can be contrasted with quality control, which is focused on process output. Quality assurance includes two principles: "Fit for purpose" (the product should be suitable for the intended purpose); and "right first time" (mistakes should be eliminated). QA includes management of the quality of raw materials, assemblies, products and components, services related to production, and management, production and inspection processes [7]. The two principles also manifest before the background of developing (engineering) a novel technical product: The task of engineering is to make it work once, while the task of quality assurance is to make it work all the time [8]. Historically, defining what suitable product or service quality means has been a more difficult process, determined in many ways, from the subjective user-based approach that contains "the different weights that individuals normally attach to quality characteristics," to the value-based approach which finds consumers linking quality to price and making overall conclusions of quality based on such a relationship [9]. Duties of Quality assurance unit are illustrated in Fig. 1.

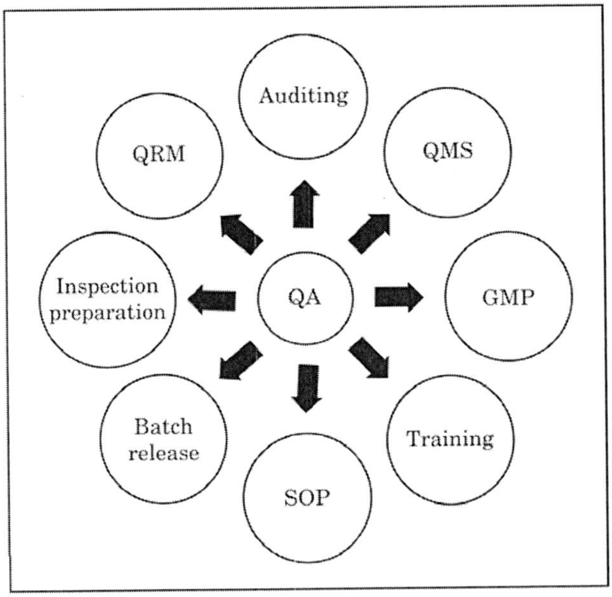

Fig. 1: Duties of quality assurance section

HISTORY

Initial Efforts to Control the Quality of Production

During the Middle Ages, guilds adopted responsibility for the quality of goods and services offered by their members, setting and maintaining certain standards for guild membership. Royal governments purchasing material were interested in quality control as customers. For this reason, King John of England appointed William de Wrotham to report about the construction and repair of ships. Centuries later, Samuel Pepys, Secretary to the British Admiralty, appointed multiple such overseers to standardize sea rations and naval training. Prior to the extensive division of labor and mechanization resulting from the Industrial Revolution, it was possible for workers to control the quality of their own products. The Industrial Revolution led to a system in which large groups of people performing a specialized type of work were grouped together under the supervision of a foreman who was appointed to control the quality of work manufactured [10, 11, 12].

Wartime Production

During the time of the First World War, manufacturing processes typically became more complex, with larger numbers of workers being supervised. This period saw the widespread introduction of mass production and piece work, which created problems as workmen could now earn more money by the production of extra products, which in turn occasionally led to poor quality workmanship being passed on to the assembly lines. Pioneers such as Frederick Winslow Taylor and Henry Ford recognized the limitations of the methods being used in mass production at the time and the subsequent varying quality of output. Taylor, utilizing the concept of scientific management, helped separate production tasks into many simple steps (the assembly line) and limited quality control to a few specific individuals, limiting complexity. Ford emphasized standardization of design and component standards to ensure a standard product was produced, while quality was the responsibility of machine inspectors, "placed in each department to cover all operations ... at frequent intervals, so that no faulty operation shall proceed for any great length of time."Out of this also came statistical process control (SPC), which was pioneered by Walter A. Shewhart at Bell Laboratories in the early 1920s. Shewhart developed the control chart in 1924 and the concept of a state of statistical control. Statistical control is equivalent to the concept of exchangeability developed by logician William Ernest Johnson also in 1924 in his book Logic, Part III: The Logical Foundations of Science. Along with a team at AT&T that included Harold Dodge and Harry Romig, he worked to put sampling inspection on a rational statistical basis as well. Shewhart consulted with Colonel Leslie E. Simon in the application of control charts to munitions manufacture at the Army's Picatinny Arsenal in 1934. That successful application helped convince Army

Ordnance to engage AT&T's George Edwards to consult on the use of statistical quality control among its divisions and contractors at the outbreak of World War II [13-19].

Postwar

In the period following World War II, many countries' manufacturing capabilities that had been destroyed during the war were rebuilt. General Douglas MacArthur oversaw the re-building of Japan. During this time, General MacArthur involved two key individuals in the development of modern quality concepts: W. Edwards Deming and Joseph Juran. Both individuals, as well as others, promoted the collaborative concepts of quality to Japanese business and technical groups, and these groups utilized these concepts in the redevelopment of the Japanese economy. Although there were many individuals trying to lead United States industries towards a more comprehensive approach to quality, the U.S. continued to apply the Quality Control (QC) concepts of inspection and sampling to remove defective product from production lines, essentially unaware of or ignoring advances in QA for decades [20, 21].

APPROACHES

Following approaches are applied to enforce quality assurance system [22-27]

Failure Testing

A valuable process to perform on a whole consumer product is failure testing or stress testing. In mechanical terms this is the operation of a product until it fails, often under stresses such as increasing vibration, temperature, and humidity. This exposes many unanticipated weaknesses in a product, and the data are used to drive engineering and manufacturing process improvements. Often quite simple changes can dramatically improve product service, such as changing to mold-resistant paint or adding lock-washer placement to the training for new assembly personnel.

Statistical Control

Statistical control is based on analysis of objective and subjective data. Many organizations use statistical process control as a tool in any quality improvement effort to track quality data. Any product can be statistically charted as long as they have a common cause variance or special cause variance to track. Walter Shewart of Bell Telephone Laboratories recognized that when a product is made, data can be taken from scrutinized areas of a sample lot of the part and statistical variances are then analyzed and charted. Control can then be implemented on the part in the form of rework or scrap, or control can be implemented on the process that made the part, ideally eliminating the defect before more parts can be made like it.

Total Quality Management

The quality of products is dependent upon that of the participating constituents, some of which are sustainable and effectively controlled while others are not. The process(es) which are managed with QA pertain to Total Quality Management. If the specification does not reflect the true quality requirements, the product's quality cannot be guaranteed. For instance, the parameters for a pressure vessel should cover not only the material and dimensions but operating, environmental, safety, reliability and maintainability requirements.

Models and Standards

ISO 17025 is an international standard that specifies the general requirements for the competence to carry out tests and or calibrations. There are 15 management requirements and 10 technical requirements. These requirements outline what a laboratory must do to become accredited. Management system refers to the organization's structure for managing its processes or activities that transform inputs of resources into a product or service which meets the organization's objectives, such as satisfying the customer's quality requirements, complying with regulations, or meeting environmental objectives. WHO has developed several tools and offers training courses for quality assurance in public health laboratories. The Capability Maturity Model Integration (CMMI) model is widely used to implement Process and Product Quality Assurance (PPQA) in an organization. The CMMI maturity levels can be divided into 5 steps, which a company can achieve by performing specific activities within the organization.

Company Quality

During the 1980s, the concept of "company quality" with the focus on management and people came to the fore in the U.S. It was considered that, if all departments approached quality with an open mind, success was possible if management led the quality improvement process. The company-wide quality approach places an emphasis on four aspects (enshrined in standards such as ISO 9001).

- Elements such as controls, job management, adequate processes, performance and integrity criteria and identification of records
- Competence such as knowledge, skills, experiences, qualifications

- Soft elements, such as personnel integrity, confidence, organizational culture, motivation, team spirit and quality relationships
- Infrastructure (as it enhances or limits functionality)

The quality of the outputs is at risk if any of these aspects is deficient. QA is not limited to manufacturing, and can be applied to any business or non-business activity, including: design, consulting, banking, insurance, computer software development, retailing, investment, transportation, education, and translation. It comprises a quality improvement process, which is generic in the sense that it can be applied to any of these activities and it establishes a behavior pattern, which supports the achievement of quality. This in turn is supported by quality management practices which can include a number of business systems and which are usually specific to the activities of the business unit concerned. In manufacturing and construction activities, these business practices can be equated to the models for quality assurance defined by the International Standards contained in the ISO 9000 series and the specified Specifications for quality systems. In the system of Company Quality, the work being carried out was shop floor inspection which did not reveal the major quality problems. This led to quality assurance or total quality control, which has come into being recently.

PHARMACEUTICAL QUALITY

As in most manufacturing processes, the quality of a final pharmaceutical product is determined by the starting materials, equipment, and technical know-how that go into producing and packaging it. Unlike a steel bolt or a tailored suit, however, a medicine is a dynamic product whose color, consistency, weight, and even chemical identity can change between manufacture and ultimate consumption. A medicine that passes all laboratory tests upon receipt may be useless within a few months if the packaging, storage, and transportation conditions are not maintained properly. The purpose of quality assurance in pharmaceutical supply systems is to help ensure that each medicine reaching a patient is safe, effective, and of appropriate quality. The quality of pharmaceutical products is ensured by the technical and managerial activities of the quality system, which includes evaluating pharmaceutical product documentation, performing or reviewing quality-control laboratory tests, and monitoring product performance. Managerial activities include selecting reliable suppliers, preparing contract terms, monitoring supplier performance, and performing inspection procedures throughout the distribution network.

PHARMACEUTICAL QUALITY ASSURANCE FRAMEWORK

The following five elements are critical to achieving the expected treatment outcome using a pharmaceutical product to treat a patient presumes that the—

1. Active pharmaceutical ingredient (API) has been shown to be safe and effective for this treatment
2. Product is of suitable quality to provide an effective outcome
3. Prescriber has accurately identified the need for the treatment
4. Prescriber or dispenser has properly instructed the patient on how to use the product
5. Patient complies with the prescribed regimen correctly

The first two items are product-specific issues, which are the most easily addressed technically, whereas items three and four are practitioner-specific and depend on the practitioners' education, knowledge, and skill as well as the rigorous enforcement of performance standards. Item five is a patient-specific issue that depends on the patient's knowledge and commitment and the patient's access to services. The safety and effectiveness of an API may be established either through a review of historical usage, such as in the case of digoxin's evolution from the foxglove plant (*Digitalis purpurea*), or through complex procedures established for new chemical entities, such as those described by the International Conference on Harmonisation of Technical Requirements for Registration of Pharmaceuticals for Human use (ICH).

After the safety and effectiveness of an API has been approved for marketing in an ICH market region, other regions of the world follow with little or no additional assessment. The ICH economic zones (european union, Japan, united States) perform almost 100 percent of the pharmaceutical research and consume over 85 percent (by value) of the pharmaceutical products in the world. These regions allocate large amounts of resources to ensure the safety and effectiveness of APIs granted market authorization in their zones. Once the safety and efficacy have been established through these procedures, other regions do not have to expend the same level of resources to establish these attributes. However, other product-quality issues, including bioavailability and bioequivalence, content uniformity, impurities and degradation, and medicine safety (pharmacovigilance), should be monitored on an ongoing basis in all market zones.

The complexity of globalized pharmaceutical markets and the difficulty in ensuring quality of imported products, including API, have been illustrated in headlines about deaths caused by adulterated products such as cough syrup in Peru and heparin in the United States both tied to ingredients from China. As a result, the U.S. Food and Drug Administration seeks to increase its global presence to make monitoring foreign manufacturers easier and to strengthen its involvement with harmonization of pharmaceutical standards. In addition, the FDA wants to help build regulatory capacity in foreign counterparts. As part of that international effort, the agency has opened permanent offices in a number of cities around the world and has entered into dozens of agreements with other drug regulatory authorities (DRAs) to share inspection reports and other private information that can help improve the quality of pharmaceutical products worldwide. The pharmaceutical regulatory and quality assurance processes that should be addressed by a country's DRA include:

- Product registration: assessing and authorizing products for market entry and monitoring their safety and effectiveness after entry
- Regulation of manufacturing, importation, and distribution
  - Quality of manufacturing (good manufacturing practices)
  - Procurement integrity (assuring the qualifications of suppliers)
  - Quality of medicines in the distribution system (including product and premises inspection and product screening and testing)
- Regulation of medicine promotion and information: including post-marketing pharmacovigilance and consumer education

Of course, a country's quality assurance system is only as effective as its ability to monitor and enforce regulations. A country should address all issues at some level as part of a basic pharmaceutical quality assurance infrastructure; however, in a resource-constrained setting, the risks to patients for each process must be assessed so resources can be allocated to focus on the most significant health threats.

DEFINING AND ASSESSING PHARMACEUTICAL QUALITY

Pharmaceutical quality can be defined and tested in many ways. Quality standards are published periodically in pharmacopoeias and in some government publications, which provide detailed descriptions of pharmaceutical characteristics and analytical techniques. Standards may vary slightly from one pharmacopoeia to another, so a particular pharmaceutical may meet the standards of one pharmacopoeia and not those of another. When public standards have not been established, as is generally the case for newly marketed pharmaceuticals, analytical methods developed by the manufacturer and submitted as a part of the tender or marketing authorization requirements are usually applied.

The major pharmaceutical manufacturing and exporting countries publish their own pharmacopoeias, and on a regional basis, the European Pharmacopoeia establishes standards that are enforced by the governments of the European Union and others that adopt them. The International Pharmacopoeia, published by the World Health Organization, the U.S. Pharmacopeia, and the British Pharmacopoeia are used frequently by public-sector pharmaceutical supply programs in developing countries. One important limitation of the European Pharmacopoeia is that it provides few specifications for individual dosage forms. The WHO International Pharmacopoeia includes monographs on finished dosage forms, including antiretrovirals and newly developed antimalarial medicines. Analytical procedures in the U.S. Pharmacopeia tend to use complex and expensive technology, which may be beyond the reach of many developing countries. The European, Japanese, and U.S. pharmacopoeias are engaged in ongoing efforts to harmonize some of their standards, but progress is slow. Until common standards are finally achieved, purchasers must specify which dosage form standards are acceptable. For pharmaceutical procurement organizations, pharmaceutical quality is assessed as the product's compliance with specifications concerning identity, purity, strength, potency, and other characteristics. Uniformity of the dosage form, bioavailability, and stability are important characteristics that are also considered in the specifications.

Identity

The identity test should confirm the existence of the active ingredient(s) indicated on the label. This characteristic is generally the easiest to check.

Purity

In addition to the API, most pharmaceuticals are made with ingredients added for bulk, consistency, or color that should not contain potentially harmful contaminants or microorganisms. The product should not have significant quantities of other products from cross-contamination.

Strength or potency

The medicine should contain the declared amount of API. Harmful by-products of degradation must be absent or should be below defined limits. Most pharmacopoeias specify an average content range, such as 90 to 110 percent of the amount written on the label, rather than an exact amount. To ensure a long shelf life, manufacturers often produce pharmaceuticals with the maximum allowable amount (for example, 110 mg rather than 95 mg), which provides a margin of safety for slight losses in strength or potency over time.

Uniformity of dosage form

The consistency, color, shape, and size of tablets, capsules, creams, and liquids should not vary from one dose to the next. Any lack of uniformity may suggest problems with other quality parameters such as identity, purity, or strength or potency. Lack of dosage uniformity may not influence the safety or effectiveness of a medicine, but it does reflect a lack of good manufacturing practices, which could influence the acceptability of a product to pharmacists, medical practitioners, and patients.

Bioavailability

Bioavailability refers to the speed and completeness with which a pharmaceutical administered in a specific form (tablet, capsule, intramuscular injection, subcutaneous injection) enters the bloodstream. The bio- availability of a product may depend on the other ingredients used in the formulation, such as solvents, binders, coloring agents, and coatings, or how ingredients are combined. The comparative bioavailability of two pharmaceuticals is particularly important when a product that is usually purchased from one manufacturer is replaced with a product containing the same drug substance in the same dosage form, and in the same amount, but manufactured by a different firm. Even though the products both contain the correct amount of the API, the preparations may not give the expected therapeutic result if the API is released too quickly, too slowly, or incompletely when they are compared. Two pharmaceuticals are said to be bioequivalent and may be used interchangeably if both are absorbed into the blood- stream at the same rate and to the same extent. Human bioequivalence studies are required for a number of medicines. Guidelines are available for the study of bioavailability, as well as specific bioavailability protocols for a small number of medicines. If purchasing is done through established and reliable suppliers, the bioavailability of most brand-name and generic medicines used in primary health care is sufficient to ensure that the patient receives the intended effect. Deciding which pharmaceuticals have a potential bioavailability problem is important, because manufacturers cannot supply clinical studies for all products, and government procurement programs generally cannot perform bioequivalence testing. The Biopharmaceutical Classification System can help identify potential bioavailability problem products. Where pharmaceutical registration systems exist, manufacturers or suppliers should be required to supply data on clinical studies whenever needed. Procurement agencies should also work with country DRAs and use their information in making decisions.

Stability

To be useful, a pharmaceutical must retain its properties within specified limits, such as particular storage conditions. The manufacturer and, in some cases, a country's DRA establish the time that a pharmaceutical's stability is under warranty, which ends with the expiration date. A product's stability depends on the active ingredient, which can be affected by its formulation and packaging. Improper storage and distribution can lead to physical deterioration and chemical decomposition, reduced potency, and occasionally, formation of toxic by-products of degradation. These effects are more likely to occur under tropical conditions of high temperature and humidity. WHO has published a list of pharmaceutical substances that are less stable and therefore require particular attention. However, few data are available on the stability of medicines under true field conditions. The ICH, whose members comprise experts from the major pharmaceutical manufacturing countries, has established guidelines on quality testing and storage in tropical regions. WHO has been updating its stability guidelines with input from member country DRAs and in cooperation with ICH. Several studies have examined the stability of a small number of essential medicines under tropical conditions of excessive temperature (over 40°C), high humidity, and inappropriate storage conditions.

CONSEQUENCES OF POOR PHARMACEUTICAL QUALITY

A poor-quality medicine is one that does not meet specifications. The use of poor-quality products may have undesirable clinical and economic effects, as well as affect the credibility of the health delivery system. Clinical effects can include prolonged illness or death or adverse reactions. On the economic side, limited financial resources may be wasted on poor-quality medicines. Lack of therapeutic effect may lead to prolonged illness or death. Poor pharmaceutical quality can sometimes lead to serious health consequences and death—for example, the use of poor-quality cardiac medicines and medicines for seizures and asthma. With others, such as cold remedies and minor painkillers, a reduction of up to 50 percent in the content of the active ingredient may not have serious consequences apart from ineffectiveness, although the best procurement policy requires all products to meet specifications. Poor-quality pharmaceuticals may induce toxic or adverse reactions. When some products expire or are exposed to adverse climatic conditions (for example, excessive heat and humidity), they may undergo physical or chemical changes that can result in the formation of possibly toxic degradation products. Although fear of toxic pharmaceutical degradation in tropical climates is prevalent, tetracycline is the only common medicine in which it is known to occur. Excessive active ingredients may also lead to toxic or adverse reactions. A much more frequent problem is contamination with microorganisms, usually bacteria or fungi. The consequences of this lack of sterility can be quite severe, particularly in the case of injectable medicines or in patients who are immunocompromised. Contamination of creams, syrups, and other medicines in jars and tubes is especially common in tropical environments, but the consequences vary, depending on the type of organism and the pharmaceutical involved. Errors in formulation and product contamination are uncommon with manufacturers who strictly comply with internationally accepted procedures and good manufacturing practices (GMPs). In practice, however, adherence to GMPs may vary from country to country, from manufacturer to manufacturer, or even between production runs at the same manufacturer. When contaminants are highly toxic or when toxic substances are inadvertently included in the product, the result can be catastrophic.

- Poor pharmaceutical quality wastes money. Ineffective care or the need to treat adverse drug reactions resulting from poor product quality leads to more costly treatments. Poor pharmaceutical packaging casts doubts on product quality, leading to rejection by health personnel and patients. These products will then expire on the medical stores' shelves, wasting limited financial resources.

- Poor pharmaceutical quality may seriously affect health system credibility. Patients and providers may suspect the quality of medicines when therapeutic failure or adverse drug reactions occur. Changes in product appearance, such as discoloration, crumbling of tablets, and hardening of oral suspensions, or changes in taste and smell rightly influence patients' perceptions of product quality. Patients may be discouraged from using health facilities, and worker morale may be affected, particularly if medicine shortages are also common.

DETERMINANTS OF PHARMACEUTICAL QUALITY

The quality of a medicine product coming off the production line is determined by the start-up materials, plant environment, manufacturing equipment, and technical know-how invested in developing and manufacturing the pharmaceutical. The medicine that ultimately reaches the patient, however, is further affected by packaging and by transportation and storage conditions.

These influences, especially factors in the manufacturing process, can be cumulative. For example, the excipient substances used to give tablets bulk and consistency may not affect the color, texture, or chemical quality of a pharmaceutical until the immediate container is opened in a hot, humid environment. Then, depending on the ingredients, the tablet may remain firm and dry or become moist and crumble within a matter of days. Factory humidity during packaging may also affect quality. If oral rehydration sachets are not packaged in a very low-humidity environment, moisture enters the sachet and may result in chemical or physical changes in the mixture that make it difficult to use. Similarly, the amount of grinding, thoroughness of mixing, choice of packaging, maintenance of packaging equipment, and other factors can have an effect that may not appear until the medicine reaches the point of consumption. The dynamic nature of pharmaceuticals and the cumulative effects of the production process, right through to packaging, handling, transport, and storage conditions, require quality assurance at all levels in the pharmaceutical supply system.

PREVALENCE OF POOR-QUALITY PHARMACEUTICALS

In recent years, national and international authorities have recognized the emergence of counterfeit medicines as a serious problem. In most industrialized countries with effective regulatory systems and market control, the incidence of counterfeit medicines is an estimated 1% of market value. Therefore, most counterfeiting cases occur in developing countries—especially in Asia, where many of the counterfeit medicines are produced, and in Africa, where poverty and loose regulatory oversight make marketing of counterfeit products easier. However, counterfeiting is an increasing problem in all countries, including developed countries, where Internet purchases are popular. Over half of Internet medicine purchases from illegal websites are counterfeit.

GLOBAL QUALITY-MONITORING OPTIONS

Currently, no global pharmaceutical quality standards exist, even for the APIs used in worldwide pharmaceutical product formulation, which are produced by only a few countries. However, the ICH processes to establish GMPs for APIs were more inclusive than any of the previous pro- cesses; for example, besides the usual ICH parties, representatives from the generics industry, the self-medication industry, and the Pharmaceutical Inspection Convention and Pharmaceutical Inspection Co-operation Scheme were included in the deliberations.

These GMP standards are the world's first harmonized standards and have been adopted by the ICH regions and the Pharmaceutical Inspection Convention and Pharmaceutical Inspection Co-operation Scheme, in addition to WHO and many other countries. This harmonization implies that any DRA could perform an inspection of an API manufacturer and expect it to conform to these consensus GMPs. However, because almost all sovereign nations or market zones protect their local production of pharmaceutical products through selective tariffs and other mechanisms, no incentive exists for the development of a worldwide quality standard for APIs. Some pharmacopoeias, including the European Pharmacopoeia and WHO's International Pharmacopoeia, have regional quality standards for many APIs; however, these pharmacopoeial standards have not been harmonized, resulting in varying specifications for APIs among regions. Because of the lack of harmonized standards, no basis exists for a pharmaceutical product common market with universal recognition of quality standards. The dearth of internationally recognized specifications leaves each market zone to establish its own specifications. Among the major pharmacopoeias, only the British Pharmacopoeia and the U.S. Pharmacopeia have standards for a significant number of products, and even they have essentially no specifications for products under patent protection in their markets.

PRACTICAL APPROACHES TO QUALITY ASSURANCE

The procedures to establish a comprehensive quality assurance program can be divided into three categories—

1. Procedures to ensure that only medicine products that meet current standards for quality are bought. These include—

- Careful product selection
- Careful supplier selection
- Certificate of analysis for each batch of product
- Certification of good manufacturing practices
- Batch certification (WHO-type certificate of a pharmaceutical product)
- Inclusion of detailed product-quality specifications in the contract

2. Procedures to verify that shipped goods meet the specifications. These include—
   - Pre- and post shipment inspection
   - Analytical pharmaceutical testing
3. Procedures to monitor and maintain the quality of pharmaceuticals from the moment they are received until the medicine is finally consumed by the patient. These involve—
   - Proper storage and distribution procedures
   - Appropriate dispensing
   - Instructions to the patient on proper use of medications
   - Product defect and pharmacovigilance reporting programs

Few pharmaceutical management programs can effectively manage all the possible quality assurance activities for all the medicines that are procured. Consequently, realistic goals must be set to identify the combination of managerial and technical quality assurance activities that will be most effective under existing conditions. Because resources are limited, countries should target priorities for quality assurance activities. The VEN (vital, essential, nonessential) method helps identify a small group of medicines that have the greatest health impact. Vital life-saving medicines (antibiotics, cardiac medications, and intravenous solutions) warrant greater attention than other important but not life-saving medications, such as analgesics. ABC analysis can be used to identify those medicines that have the greatest budgetary effect if their quality is unacceptable. The choice of medicines to monitor closely is based on the following criteria—

- Medicines with a narrow therapeutic window
- Medicines with inherent bioavailability problems
- Modified-release preparations
- Products from new suppliers and suppliers with problems in the past
- Medicines that require stable dosage forms and appearance

OBTAINING GOOD QUALITY PHARMACEUTICALS

Obtaining medicines of good quality involves careful selection of suppliers and products, compliance with GMPs, reliance on appropriate pharmaceutical product or batch certificates, and detailed contract specifications.

Careful Product Selection

In many systems, therapeutic medicine formulary committees first assess the safety and efficacy of selected medicines on the basis of evidence from clinical trials. Specific product selection involves assessing the technical documentation provided by the supplier on the pharmaceutical characteristics of the dosage form. Dosage forms that may offer longer shelf life include—

- Powders for reconstitution instead of injectable liquids
- Powders for reconstitution instead of oral suspensions
- Tablets instead of capsules

When appropriate, request and review product-specific stability studies from the manufacturer. For a few medicines, such as certain heart, asthma, and seizure medicines, studies that demonstrate bioequivalence among different manufacturers' products may also be necessary. Select products with packaging that can withstand rough transport and extreme climatic conditions. Plastic containers may be better than glass bottles for intravenous solutions, oral liquids, and disinfectants. Avoid metal tins that will rust. In some countries, unit-of-use packages (blister packs) and containers with smaller quantities (for example, 100 tablets rather than 1,000 tablets) may be cost-effective. These measures aim to avoid quality loss after the containers are opened or as a result of frequent handling. The increased costs should be weighed against the wastage and contamination that may occur with bulk containers, plus the costs of any repackaging.

Careful Supplier Selection

This step may be the most critical in quality assurance. Suppliers can be selected competitively by restricted tender with prequalification, through open tender with post award qualification, or in some cases, through less formal procedures. Standard procedures should include requiring certifications, gathering information on supplier reliability and product quality, inspecting product samples, and if necessary, conducting laboratory testing of pharmaceuticals with high potential for bioavailability or stability problems. Country procurement offices obtained a major resource for helping assure quality pharmaceutical purchases when WHO launched its medicine prequalification program in 2001. Contacts with DRAs and purchasing groups (for example, the United Nations Children's Fund and IDA Foundation) and product-quality testing laboratories can help with reference checks and exchanges of information on problem products. Publications by medicine information services and professional organizations, such as the U.S.

Pharmacopeia, the FDA, and the American Society of Health-System Pharmacists, provide information on the bioequivalence of pharmaceuticals as well as on pharmaceutical recalls.

A procurement office or agency needs to analyze information on suppliers' performance and develop and apply operational definitions and criteria to assess the reliability of suppliers and avoid subjectivity. Lack of explicit definitions and criteria provides rejected suppliers with the opportunity to question the integrity of the procurement process. For products from new suppliers, visual inspection of samples of the product, packaging, and labelling is important. Some programs send samples for laboratory testing on a routine basis; others do so only when concerns arise about specific products. Although prepurchase testing may detect defective products, bear in mind that the samples are provided by the supplier, which will make every effort to ensure that the samples meet the standards. The samples may not, however, be representative of what is actually delivered. Keeping a record of condition of received goods, compliance with contract terms, and timeliness of delivery is essential. This information, and that from the adverse drug reaction and product-quality reporting system, should be considered when assessing offers and awarding supply contracts.

Product Certification

WHO has established GMPs for pharmaceutical products, similar to those enforced by the national pharmaceutical control agencies in industrialized countries. They include criteria for personnel, facilities, equipment, materials, manufacturing operations, labelling, packaging, quality control, and in most cases, stability testing. In countries with effective pharmaceutical control agencies, adherence to GMPs is enforced by a system of inspections and regulatory controls, often specific to individual medicine dosage forms. A manufacturer may have acceptable standards for solid dosage forms but not for sterile injectable preparations. Recent reports of GMP inspections and pharmaceutical recall histories can be obtained by writing to national pharmaceutical control agencies. Often, a supplier must approve or at least expedite requests for performance reports from national pharmaceutical control agencies, and failure to obtain such reports for the buyer makes past performance suspect.

Buyers with pharmaceutical staff trained in GMP inspection may perform their own inspections of local manufacturers that are potential suppliers, if funds are available to do so. Countries that participate in the scheme agree to certify that pharmaceuticals are registered in the exporting country and that manufacturers' facilities have been inspected and comply with GMPs. However, a WHO study (1995) showed that very few importing countries actually request pharmaceutical product certificates for registration or procurement purposes. This certification scheme provides some assurance, based on inspection of the manufacturing facilities for GMPs by the competent authority of the exporting country. For the procurement office, it is an inexpensive means to help ensure the quality of purchased products. Through the certification scheme, the procurement office should be able to obtain the following information—

- Whether a product is legally marketed in the exporting country, and if not, the reasons why
- Whether the supplier manufactures the dosage forms, packages, and/or labels a finished dosage form manufactured by an independent company, or is involved in none of these activities
- Whether the manufacturer of the product has been inspected and the periodicity of inspection
- Whether the certificate is provisional, pending technical review
- Whether the information submitted by the supplier satisfies the certifying authority on all aspects of manufacture of the product undertaken by another party

The reliability of the pharmaceutical product certificates issued under the WHO scheme and access to them depend largely on the—

- Reliability and responsiveness of the exporting country's authority
- Capability of the exporting country's authority to make adequate GMP inspections
- Capability of the importing country's authority to assess the authenticity or validity of the certificate of a pharmaceutical product submitted, especially when it is submitted through the manufacturer or importing agent

Therefore, product certification under the WHO scheme is only as reliable as the agency performing it, and WHO estimates that only about 20 percent of member countries have a national drug regulatory system that can ensure the quality of medicines circulating in their national markets. For this reason, certificates should be accepted with caution unless the national DRA's competence to fulfil the scheme is known. In addition, although national pharmaceutical control agencies in the major pharmaceutical-exporting countries are generally conscientious in their assessments, receiving reports may take some time. Agencies in some countries have been found to be less reliable and responsive. WHO recognizes that today's pharmaceutical manufacturing sector looks much different from when the scheme was formulated decades ago under the assumption that a pharmaceutical product would be sold directly from the country of manufacture to the country of final destination. Pharmaceutical manufacturing and trade have become far more globalized in that different stages of manufacturing take place in different countries before the product reaches the final destination. Because of this evolution and other identified problems, WHO has proposed revising the scheme.

Product Pedigrees

The purpose of a pharmaceutical pedigree is to establish a chain of custody from the manufacturer to the dispenser by documenting all parties that have handled a particular unit of a pharmaceutical as it travels through each step in the supply chain. Pharmaceutical wholesalers who provide fraudulent or no product pedigrees may help divert counterfeits into legitimate distribution systems. Failure to comply with the pedigree requirements is against the law in the United States. Implementing a pharmaceutical pedigree process can be done with paper or electronic records. For example, affixing radio frequency identification (RFID) or bar codes to packaging would help maintain supply chain integrity and improve inventory control. Although electronic tracking is likely more efficient and secure, it requires expensive technology and training. Paper-based systems may be executed quickly but in the long run may be more time-consuming and more susceptible to forgery.

Batch Certificates

Reliable pharmaceutical manufacturers may comply with GMPs by routinely conducting batch analyses. Local manufacturers that do not have their own quality control laboratories may contract quality-control testing services from other manufacturers, private testing facilities, or national reference laboratories. Some pharmaceutical procurement offices request other certificates, such as the certificate of free sale, the certificate of origin, or the certificate of licensing status. These certificates do not provide important information regarding compliance with GMPs, or results of laboratory testing of samples from individual batches. For this reason, the WHO-type certificate of a pharmaceutical product and batch certificate are preferred.

DRAs and the Procurement Market Today

In many countries, DRAs and procurement offices do not work together effectively, nor are integrated information systems in place. Ideally, when a DRA exists and the medicine registration system is operational, procurement by government agencies should be limited to medicines registered by the DRA. Procurement offices should seek information from the DRA and strive for closer cooperation with the authority. To facilitate registration of generic medicines, the evaluation and approval process should not be complicated. Clinical trial data, except for bioequivalence data, are not normally required, allowing the submission of an abbreviated application by the manufacturer or distributor. WHO recommends that all medicines on the public or private market in a country, whether they are imported or locally manufactured, be subject to the same standard of control, including medicine registration.

The standard of control varies from country to country. In some exporting countries, medicines are registered and freely sold but not rigorously evaluated for efficacy. In other countries, which do evaluate efficacy, certain medicines may have been registered before evidence of efficacy was legally required. Moreover, in some countries, manufacturers may produce exclusively for export; the exporting country's DRA may not closely scrutinize these manufacturing plants. Procurement offices still need to request certificates from the DRA of the exporting country, as recommended by WHO.

Contract Specifications

Detailed specifications to help ensure that high-quality products are bought and received include the following—

- Analytical methods and source of reference materials or documented evidence of suitability for the material used to assess product-quality attributes and certificate of analysis.
- Portions of manufacturers' reference materials to be used in product-quality assessments.

For these reference materials, the manufacturers will supply either the API used in the manufacture of the product or a purified portion of the API. Because the reference material is used to assign qualitative and quantitative properties, its identity must be assured and its purity must be suitable to perform the assessments at an appropriate confidence level for the intended use of the material. The identity of a reference material is generally assessed by infrared spectral comparisons and quantitative assessments performed by ultraviolet-visible spectral measures, either directly or in conjunction with chromatographic procedures. However, for most pharmaceutical measurements, the identity and quality of solid materials can be assessed by melting point/mixed melting point measurements, while liquids can be assessed by refractive index measurements.

- Language for the product label and package insert, which should be the language or languages common to the country.
- Minimum information required on the label (generic or International Non-proprietary Name, dosage form, strength, quantity, expiration date, manufacturer, batch number).
- Additional information, such as the product registration number and date of manufacture.

- Standards for packaging that will withstand the specific storage and transport conditions (for example, corrugated boxes with specifications for dividers, maximum size, and maximum weight).

To reduce theft and resale, some programs may require labelling and logos to indicate that the product is solely for distribution within a particular health care program (*for example*, Ministry of Health, Social Security Fund).

Verifying the Quality of Shipped Products

The quality of products received should be verified as soon as possible by physically inspecting each shipment and testing selected products in the laboratory as required by regulation. In addition, more advanced product-tracking technologies have been introduced to help ensure the integrity of the pharmaceutical supply chain.

Product Identification Technology

The traditional approach to assuring product integrity is labelling with batch number and expiration date. Unfortunately, this labelling is easily duplicated. To make fraud more difficult, several approaches are available that use overt or covert systems. Overt technologies are visible to the eye, and covert technologies require devices for detection. Because each step up in identification technology costs more, the most advanced technologies are used on high- value products or in large-quantity inventory control.

Bar coding

The simplest and least expensive technology for product tracking is the bar code, which has been adopted widely in many industries. Its uses range from tracking shipping containers to individual dosage units. The airline industry makes extensive use of this technology to track and direct baggage, and the retail industry has made bar coding the standard to track inventory and sales. Because of their widespread use and simplicity, bar-code detection devices are relatively inexpensive.

Radiofrequency identification

The RFID tag is a radio- frequency transponder chip with a permanent unique identification code and the ability to be programmed with product information, such as batch number and expiration date. The combination of product information and identification code provides a high level of security against counterfeiting. RFID can be used overtly or covertly—either visible on the product or hidden in the packaging. Another advantage of the RFID technology is the ability to detect several different items at the same time, unlike visual bar-code readers, which must have each tag visible and separate for reading. However, until this RFID technology matures and becomes more widespread, it will remain much more expensive than the traditional bar-code technology.

Holograms

Hologram technology provides visual authentication that can be very difficult to counterfeit or remove (although instances of fake holograms have been found on counterfeit antimalarial products in Southeast Asia). However, the technology is not easily automated and optimally requires an authentic label or accurate image for visual comparison.

Other technologies that have been developed for product authentication include color-shifting inks, ultraviolet printing, and embedded chemical markers and infrared tags. As the technologies mature, several will likely be used to assure different aspects of the supply chain. The continuing adoption of these authentication technologies will make product counterfeiting more difficult and expensive, but unfortunately will not likely eliminate it.

Inspection of Shipments

Regardless of other quality assurance procedures in use, each pharmaceutical shipment should be physically inspected. This means verifying adherence to contract specifications and order completeness as well as inspecting samples of all items to spot any major problems. Training competent receiving staff can be an economical means of ensuring pharmaceutical quality and reducing losses from supplier negligence or fraud. Inspection in the exporting country before shipment can be arranged through an independent agency for early detection of noncompliance with contract terms or defective products.

Tiered Pharmaceutical Quality Assessments

The safety and efficacy of an API is the most critical attribute of a pharmaceutical product. The safety and efficacy of new APIs in the European union, Japan, and the united States are determined in accordance with exhaustive ICH consensus guidelines that have been incorporated into the laws and regulations of those sovereign areas. When the safety and efficacy of an API have been established, the dosage regimen is set so the minimum therapeutic level is attained without exceeding the maximum tolerated dose. That level of efficacy is called the "therapeutic window". Pharmaceutical quality assessments may include bioavailability testing to ensure that the API falls within the therapeutic window. Three tiers of product-quality assessment differ by cost and levels of precision, accuracy, and sensitivity—

1. *Minilab® screening assessments:* The Global Pharma Health Fund developed the Minilab to rapidly assess whether products are grossly substandard and to detect counterfeit products with no API or the wrong ingredients. The Minilab uses a thin layer chromatography method that does not require standard laboratory resources, so it can be used in the field, such as at ports of entry, while providing a good level of quality assurance. The Minilab has methods available for more than fifty pharmaceutical products and is regularly incorporating more.
2. *Validated laboratory assessments or legal reference method assessments:* These methods are used to assess assays, content uniformity, known impurities, and API dosage release. For medicines with a narrow therapeutic index, such as warfarin sodium, or for pharmaceuticals that fail the first-tier screening assessment, more accurate laboratory assessment technologies are required to support litigation concerning quality standards violations. Legal reference methods are methods of analysis that have been adopted into law and are suitable for use in litigation; however, Minilab screening and validated assessments are generally quicker, less labor intensive, and less expensive than legal reference methods, which are the gold standard.
3. *Specialized instruments:* Methods such as high- performance liquid chromatography coupled with mass spectrometry may be used to determine unknown impurities and metabolites. Generally, these technologies are expensive and require highly trained individuals to operate them and interpret the data.

In summary, wide-therapeutic-index products may be screened rapidly to assess their quality clearance with minimal risk of compromising their safety and efficacy. Narrow- therapeutic-index products and those that fail the rapid screening technologies should be assessed by validated technologies that are fast and efficient. Products that fail the validated technologies may require further assessments by the legal reference methods of the sovereign state to support litigation or with specialized instrumentation to litigate untoward or unexpected contamination.

Laboratory Testing

Upon arrival after shipment, batch samples may be laboratory tested routinely or "by exception." Most programs test selected samples from only some of the batches. Testing by exception means that analyses are done only when a supplier or a particular product is suspect. Laboratory testing is costly in terms of technical human resources, equipment, and reagents. Guidelines should target sampling to products that:

a. Have the greatest potential for bioavailability and stability problems,
b. Are from new or questionable suppliers, and
c. Have been the source of complaints.

Supplier's whose failure rates are unacceptable are dropped from future tenders. Sampling from well-established suppliers is done much less frequently, often only for at-risk products. Programs that require routine testing of samples for all products prior to distribution to health facilities often produce significant delays in product availability at the health facility level. The need for laboratory testing of products reported to have problems should be carefully assessed; many problems with quality are detectable on visual inspection and do not require laboratory testing. For example, verified observations of tablets that crumble before their expiry date, oral suspensions that harden, or injectable solutions that contain particles are enough to justify recalling the product without testing. The tests that should be performed depend on the pharmaceutical and the reason for testing. Basic chemical analyses are done to verify the identity of the medicine and under extenuating circumstances to look for degradation, chemical contamination, or adulteration. WHO advocates a system of economical, less technically demanding basic tests for commonly used medicines that can be done in simple laboratories. A complete analysis of tablet and capsule forms includes tests for identity, strength or potency, uniformity, impurities, disintegration, and dissolution.

Biological testing is more specialized and can be performed only in established facilities with staff trained to use microbiological and pharmacological methods. Microbiological tests include sterility tests for injectable medicines and eye preparations and microbiological assays of antibiotics and vitamins. Pharmacological tests include the pyrogen test; toxicity tests; hormone assays, such as for insulin and pituitary derivatives; and tests to determine the bioavailability of selected pharmaceuticals. Construction of a quality-control laboratory where one does not already exist should be considered with caution. It may not be cost-effective for some countries to establish a sophisticated national pharmaceutical control laboratory for a number of reasons, including—

- Low projected volume of work
- Insufficient financial resources for land purchase, facility construction, testing equipment, furniture, supplies, equipment maintenance, salaries, training, and other operating costs
- Lack of trained personnel, such as microbiologists, pharmacologists, laboratory technicians, and animal caretakers
- Lack of local capacity for maintenance and repair of equipment, difficulty in obtaining spare parts, irregular and unstable power supply

In some countries, a college of pharmacy or an independent laboratory may have some of the required testing facilities. Also, many international quality-control laboratories provide pharmaceutical analyses at a relatively reasonable price. If analyses are performed by foreign laboratories, foreign exchange and billing problems may be reduced by requiring the suppliers to pay the laboratory directly, with the arrangement clearly described in the purchase contract. In addition, chain-of-custody and legal standing of the testing laboratory in the importing country may be at issue.

Maintaining Pharmaceutical Quality

Maintaining medicine quality requires careful attention to storage conditions and transport, as well as to dispensing practices and use.

Appropriate Storage and Transport

Procedures to help maintain pharmaceutical quality begin with proper storage conditions at the port and prompt release.

Appropriate Dispensing and Use

Inappropriate dispensing procedures contribute to pharmaceutical product deterioration and contamination or medication errors. The following procedures help maintain the quality of pharmaceutical products—

- Use only proper dispensing containers (for example, airtight containers, light-resistant bags or vials).
- Require clear labelling of dispensed medicines, and enforce procedures to label products with the name, strength, expiration date, and instructions for its use and storage.
- Write information and instructions in the local language, avoiding the use of abbreviations, or use symbolic instructions.

The prescriber and the dispenser should counsel the patient on the proper use of medications, explaining what the medicine is, why the patient needs it, how to take it, and where and how to store it until treatment is completed, in addition to possible contraindications and adverse reactions.

Monitoring Pharmaceutical Quality

Despite every effort, defective products occasionally slip through, and the quality of even the best-manufactured product may deteriorate. Furthermore, health care personnel and patients alike may have erroneous perceptions that only brand-name products from innovator firms are of good product quality, especially when generic products are not well known and accepted.

Product Problem Reporting System

Establishing a national product problem reporting system is important so that health workers can report suspected or confirmed problems with specific pharmaceutical products. Product problem reporting should be part of an overall pharmacovigilance system, which also includes monitoring and reporting adverse drug events and medication errors. Standard procedures for product problem reporting should specify—

- Who should report the perceived product quality problem
- How to fill in the reporting form
- Where and to whom the reporting form should be sent
- What additional measures need to be taken, such as sending samples or information concerning the quantities involved
- What follow-up information should be provided to the person or facility that reported the problem

Quality assurance program staff should carefully analyze all reports, using laboratory testing as required, and take appropriate actions. The reporter should be informed about the results and the actions taken, even if products are not defective, to encourage continued participation in the program. Product problem reports and results should be recorded to provide information for future procurement.

Product Recalls

Pharmaceutical products found to be defective should be recalled quickly. The quality assurance unit in the country's DRA should develop standard procedures for carrying out the recall. Rapid action helps avoid unnecessary exposure once the problem has been detected. The central distributor's inventory control system should include information on all batches that have been received. Because tracking individual batches to the health facility is often either impractical or fraught with uncertainty, recall notices have to be sent to all health facilities that received any of the products in question to check their shelves and return the products to the central distribution point.

Recalls may be classified according to the degree of risk to the consumer:

a. Serious illness or death,
b. Temporary or mild illness, or
c. No adverse clinical effect.

The level of recall is determined by both the degree of risk and the extent of distribution of the product and may be directed at the patient, the health facility, or the medical stores level. After issuing a recall, the quality assurance program should monitor its progress to ensure complete compliance. The supplier should be notified and required to replace defective products. The procurement office should pursue other remedies specified in the contract, such as withholding payment or obtaining reimbursement for or replacement of the defective products.

Personnel and Training in the Supply System

Central to the operation of most well-run pharmaceutical supply systems is at least one qualified pharmacist with some training or experience in industrial pharmacy and procurement. Such an individual can be invaluable in establishing and overseeing quality-control practices suited to local requirements. This person should participate in—

- Selecting medicines
- Setting technical specifications for pharmaceutical contracts
- Reviewing supply offers and selecting suppliers
- Reviewing storage and transportation facilities
- Coordinating any pharmaceutical quality testing and helping to train the inspectors who check pharmaceutical shipments

In some government systems, qualified pharmacists are employed at all levels, including the district hospitals, and they are expected to oversee local storage and transportation conditions. In addition, they report problems or questions concerning individual medicines to the main office. In other countries, locally trained dispensers are responsible for much of the day-to-day work and must be trained to detect and report quality problems. Some countries must rely on staff that has not received any technical training in pharmaceutical management. In addition to pharmacists and pharmaceutical assistants, other staff members involved in quality assurance need training and supervision as a part of quality assurance efforts.

- Physicians, health administrators, and health system officials must know about the factors that influence pharmaceutical quality to make informed decisions about supply sources and to monitor and promote quality assurance in their facilities.
- Port-clearing personnel should be trained to identify the categories of pharmaceuticals requiring special storage and transport conditions.
- Clerks responsible for inspecting pharmaceutical shipments should receive formal training in inspection procedures.
- Pharmaceutical inspectors must be familiar enough with pharmaceutical labelling and packaging materials to determine whether contract conditions regarding pharmaceutical dosage, packaging, and labelling have been met.
- Staff involved with local repackaging should be trained to ensure pharmaceutical quality and to follow good practices, especially regarding label control.

- Physicians, nurses, and paramedical personnel handling pharmaceuticals throughout the health system need to know about the factors that influence pharmaceutical quality and what they can do to ensure that the medicines dispensed to patients are safe and effective.

CONCLUSIONS

Quality assurance is a widely shared responsibility. With-in a supply system, the organizational structure needs to establish the responsibilities for the review and preservation of pharmaceutical quality at all levels. If a pharmaceutical becomes ineffective or unsafe by the time it reaches the patient, then all the other activities of the supply system have been in vain. A holistic approach of QA process optimization and organization can generate a quality culture across a pharmaceutical organization and help to overcome the challenges faced. The purpose of process optimization is to focus on value adding activities so that value and responsiveness to the customer are maximized and waste and delays are eliminated. Globally the implementation of quality assurance presents many advantages. The major constraint that any QA organization has to face is that a tremendous effort of standardization has to be provided in order to obtain meaningful documents and information. The standardization however must not be seen as a limit to the system, which must remain flexible enough to accept changes in the standard tables without greatly affecting the output.

REFERENCES

[1] "ASQ – Practical Quality Assurance for Embedded Software".
[2] "Define, Measure, Analyze, Improve, Control (DMAIC Approach) – ASQ".
[3] "Leslie E. Simon 1924". West Point Association of Graduates. Retrieved 29 November 2017.
[4] "Quality Assurance vs Quality Control – Learning Resources – ASQ".
[5] "Quality tools and training". www.euro.who.int. 10 August 2018.
[6] "Samuel Pepys and the Navy". Royal Museums Greenwich. Retrieved 29 November 2017.
[7] "Statistical Process Control & Process Control Tools – ASQ".
[8] "Total Quality". Learn About Quality. American Society for Quality. Retrieved 29 November 2017.
[9] ASQ – History of Quality. Retrieved 17 November 2014
[10] Barlow, R.E.; Irony, T.Z. (1992). "Foundations of statistical quality control". Current Issues in Statistical Inference: Essays in Honor of D. Basu. Institute of Mathematical Statistics Lecture Notes - Monograph Series. 17: 99–112. doi:10.1214/lnms/1215458841. ISBN 0-940600-24-2.
[11] Bergman, B. (2008). "Conceptualistic Pragmatism: A framework for Bayesian analysis?". *IEEE Transactions*. 41 (1): 86–93. doi:10.1080/07408170802322713.
[12] Brooks, F.W. (1925). "William de Wrotham and the Office of Keeper of the King's Ports and Galleys". *The English Historical Review*. 40 (160): 570–579. doi:10.1093/ehr/XL.CLX.570.

[13] Evans, James R. (1994) Introduction to Statistical Process Control Archived October 29, 2013, at the Wayback Machine., Fundamentals of Statistical Process Control, pp 1–13
[14] Garvin, D.A. (15 October 1984). "What Does "Product Quality" Really Mean?". MIT Sloan Management Review. Massachusetts Institute of Technology. Retrieved 29 November 2017.
[15] http://www.nctr.usf.edu/jpt/pdf/JPT%208-2%20Smith_Chaudhry.pdf
[16] ISO 9000:2005, Clause 3.2.11
[17] Larry, Smith (2001). "Shift-Left Testing".
[18] Littauer, S.B. (1950). "The Development of Statistical Quality Control in the United States". *The American Statistician*. 4 (5): 14–20. doi:10.2307/2681449. JSTOR 2681449.
[19] Milakovich, M. (1995). Improving Service Quality: Achieving High Performance in the Public and Private Sectors. CRC Press. p. 280. ISBN 978-1-884015-45-8.
[20] Papp, J. (2014). Quality Management in the Imaging Sciences. Elsevier Health Sciences. p. 372. ISBN 978-0-323-26199-9.
[21] Prause, Christian; Bibus, Markus; Dietrich, Carsten; Jobi, Wolfgang (2016). "Software Product Assurance at the German Space Agency". *Journal of Software: Evolution fand Process*. 28 (9): 744–761.
[22] Praxiom Research Group Limited (16 August 2017). "ISO 9001 Translated Into Plain English". Praxiom Research Group Limited. Retrieved 29 November 2017.
[23] Stebbing, L. (1993). Quality Assurance: The Route to Efficiency and Competitiveness (3rd ed.). Prentice Hall. p. 300. ISBN 978-0-13-334559-9.
[24] Thareja, Mannu; Thareja, Priyavrat (February 2007). "The Quality Brilliance Through Brilliant People". Quality World. 4 (2). SSRN 1498550/ Freely accessible.
[25] The Marketing Accountability Standards Board (MASB) endorses this definition as part of its ongoing Common Language in Marketing Project.
[26] Wood, J.C.; Wood, M.C., eds. (2003). Henry Ford: Critical Evaluations in Business and Management. 1. Taylor and Francis. p. 384. ISBN 978-0-415-24825-9.
[27] Zabell, S.L. (1992). "Predicting the unpredictable". Synthese. 90 (2): 205–232. doi:10.1007/BF00485351.

FURTHER READINGS

Ahmad, K. 2004. Antidepressants are sold as Antiretrovirals in DR Congo. Lancet 363:713.
Bogdanich, W. 2007. "Chinese Chemicals Flow unchecked onto World Drug Market." New York Times,
CPM (Center for Pharmaceutical Management). 2003a. Access to Essential Medicines: Cambodia, 2001. Prepared for the Strategies for enhancing Access to Medicines Program. Arlington, Va.: Management Sciences for Health.
2003b. Access to Essential Medicines: El Salvador, 2001. Prepared for the Strategies for enhancing Access to Medicines Program. Arlington, Va.: Management Sciences for Health.
2003c. Access to Essential Medicines: Ghana, 2001. Prepared for the Strategies for enhancing Access to Medicines Program. Arlington, Va.: Management Sciences for Health.
2003d. Access to Essential Medicines: Minas Gerais, Brazil, 2001. Prepared for the Strategies for enhancing Access to Medicines Program. Arlington, Va.: Management Sciences for Health.
2003e. Access to Essential Medicines: Rajasthan, India, 2001. Prepared for the Strategies for enhancing Access to Medicines Program. Arlington, Va.: Management Sciences for Health.
2003f. Access to Essential Medicines: Tanzania, 2001. Prepared for the Strategies for enhancing Access to Medicines Program. Arlington, Va.: Management Sciences for Health.

CPM/MSH (Center for Pharmaceutical Management/Management Sciences for Health). 2011. Center for Pharmaceutical Management: Technical Frameworks, Approaches, and Results. Arlington, Va.: CPM. FDA (U.S. Food and Drug Administration).

2007. "FDA Warns Consumers about Counterfeit Drugs from Multiple Internet Sellers." FDA news release P07-76,

Gammon, D. L., S. Su, J. Jordan, R. Patterson, P. J. Finley, C. Lowe, andR. Huckfeldt. 2008. Alteration in Prehospital Drug Concentration after Thermal exposure. *American Journal of Emergency Medicine* 26(5):566–73.

Hogerzeil, H. V., G. J. A. Walker, and M. J. de Goeje. 1993. Stability of Injectable Oxytocics in Tropical Climates: Results of Field Surveys and Simulation Studies on Ergometrine, Methylergometrine and Oxytocin. Geneva: World Health Organization.

Hogerzeil, H. V., A. Battersby, V. Srdanovic, and N. E. Stjernstrom. 1992. Stability of essential Drugs during Shipment to the Tropics. *British Medical Journal* 304:210–2.

Hogerzeil, H. V., A. Battersby, V. Srdanovic, L. V. Hansen, O. Boye, B. Lindren, G. Everitt, and N. E. Stjernstrom. 1991. WHO/UNICEF Study on the Stability of Drugs during International Transport.

Hussain, K., P. Ibrahim, Z. Ismail, M. T. Majeed, and A. Sadikun. 2009. Traditional and Complementary Medicines: Quality Assessment

ICH (International Conference on Harmonisation of Technical Requirements for Registration of Pharmaceuticals for Human use). 2003. ICH Harmonised Tripartite Guideline Stability Testing of New Drug Substances and Products Q1A(R2)

2000. ICH Harmonised Tripartite Guideline: Good Manufacturing Practice Guide for Active Pharmaceutical Ingredients Q7: Current Step 4

Kasim, N. A., M. Whitehouse, C. Ramachandran, M. Bermejo,H. Lennerna, A. S. Hussain, H. e. Junginger, *et al.* 2004. Molecular Properties of WHO essential Drugs and Provisional Biopharmaceutical Classification. *Molecular Pharmaceutics* 1(1):85–96.

Newton, P. N., F. M. Fernández, A. Plançon, D. C. Mildenhall, M. D. Green, L. Ziyong, e. M. Christophel, *et al.* 2008. A Collaborative epidemiological Investigation into the Criminal Fake Artesunate Trade in South east Asia. *PLoS Medicine* 5(2):e32.

Pau, A. K., N. K. Moodley, D. T. Holland, H. Fomundam, G. u. Matchaba, and e. V. Capparelli. 2005. Instability of Lopinavir/ Ritonavir Capsules at Ambient Temperatures in Sub-Saharan Africa:

Relevance to WHO Antiretroviral Guidelines. AIDS 19(11):1233–4. Promoting the Quality of Medicines Program. 2010. Matrix of Medicine Quality Reports Affecting USAID-Assisted Countries. (updatedregu-larly.) Rockville, Md.: united States Pharmacopeial Convention.

Product Quality Assurance Program. Arlington, Va.: Management Sciences for Health.

Quality assurance of pharmaceuticals. WHO guidelines, related guidance and GXP training modules. Geneva, World Health Organization, 2013 (CD-ROM).

Seiter, A. 2005a. Pharmaceuticals: Counterfeits, Substandard Drugs and Drug Diversion. HNP Brief #2. Washington, D.C.: World Bank.

Strategies and Safe usage. *Southern Med Review* 2(1):19–23.

2005b. Pharmaceuticals: Quality Assurance in the Distribution Chain. Washington, D.C.: World Bank.

USP (United States Pharmacopeia). No date. US Pharmacopeia– National Formulary. updated annually. Rockville, Md.: United States Pharmacopeial Convention.

2007. Ensuring the Quality of Medicines in Resource-Limited Countries: An Operational Guide. Rockville, Md.: united States Pharmacopeial Convention.

USP and USAID (U.S. Pharmacopeia and U.S. Agency for International Development). 2009. Survey of the Quality of Selected Antimalarial Medicines Circulating in Madagascar, Senegal, and Uganda. Rockville, Md.: united States Pharmacopeial Convention.

WHO (World Health Organization). 2010a. Guidelines for Implementation of the WHO Certification Scheme on the Quality of Pharmaceutical Products Moving in International Commerce.
2010b. Medicines: Counterfeit Medicines. Fact sheet 275. Geneva: WHO.
2010c. Prequalification of Medicines Success in 2009. *WHO Drug Information* 24(1):3–6.
2010d. WHO Expert Committee on Specifications for Pharmaceutical Preparations. 44th Report. Geneva: WHO.
2009a. Prequalification of Quality Control Laboratories. *WHO Drug Information* 23(4): 300–5.
2009b. Stability Testing of Active Pharmaceutical Ingredients and Finished Pharmaceutical Products. Annex 2 to WHO Expert Committee on Specifications for Pharmaceutical Preparations. 43rd Report. Geneva: WHO.
2008a. The International Pharmacopoeia. 4th ed. Geneva: WHO.
2008b. WHO Certification Scheme on the Quality of Pharmaceutical Products Moving in International Commerce. *WHO Drug Information* 22(3):211–9.
2007a. General Guidelines for the establishment, Maintenance and Distribution of Chemical Reference Substances. Revision. Annex 3 to WHO Expert Committee on Specifications for Pharmaceutical Preparations. 41st Report. Geneva: WHO.
2007b. Quality Assurance of Pharmaceuticals: A Compendium of Guidelines and Related Materials. Good Manufacturing Practices and Inspection, 2nd updated ed. Vol. 2. Geneva: WHO.
2004a. Stability Testing for Hot and Humid Climates. *WHO Drug Information* 18(2): 113–6.
2004b. The World Medicines Situation. Geneva: WHO.
2003. Regulation of Fixed-Dose Combination Products.
WHO Drug Information 17(3):174–7.
1998. Basic Tests for Drugs: Pharmaceutical Substances, Medicinal Plant Materials and Dosage Forms. Geneva: WHO.
1997a. Certification Scheme on the Quality of Pharmaceutical Products Moving in International Commerce. Geneva: WHO.
1997b. Quality Assurance of Pharmaceuticals: A Compendium of Guidelines and Related Materials. Vol. 1. Geneva: WHO.
1995. Use of the WHO Certification Scheme on the Quality of Pharmaceutical Products Moving in International Commerce. Geneva: WHO.
1994. WHO Guidelines on Stability Testing of Pharmaceutical Products Containing Well-Established Drug Substances in Conventional Dosage Forms. Geneva: WHO.
1990. WHO Expert Committee on Specifications for Pharmaceutical Preparations. 31st Report. Geneva: WHO.
1986. Accelerated Stability Studies of Widely Used Pharmaceutical Substances under Simulated Tropical Conditions. Geneva: WHO.
WHO/euRO (World Health Organization Regional Office for europe). 1988. The Investigation of Bioavailability and Bioequivalence. (Draft.) Copenhagen

3

Good Manufacturing Practices: A Review

ABSTRACT

In the previous chapters we learned about the pharmaceutical industry and quality assurance. We had also covered about what the Good Manufacturing Practices or GMP is? As we already learned that GMP is a part of quality management system to regulate pharmaceutical manufacturing which helps to ensure that products are consistently and continuously produced and controlled according to the quality standards appropriate to their intended use and as required by the marketing authorization, clinical trial authorization or product specification. We also covered in the previous chapter the scope and subjects covered by the GMP. In this chapter we are going to deal with the basic parts of the GMP. The term GMP was introduced to standardize manufacturing and packaging operations in the pharmaceutical industry.

INTRODUCTION

Manufacturing practices that follow a rigorous cGMP system, designed to produce materials that meet all finished product specifications, is the only acceptable way to ensure consistent quality products. Finished product testing alone will not provide a sufficient level of quality. At best, only a very limited number of samples can be tested and this small sampling may or may not provide a true representation of the actual quality. In fact, if a product is "not manufactured using good manufacturing practices," the FDA can classify a product as adulterated even if it complies with all finished product specifications. Also, any product with USP/NF on the label can result in a mandate from the FDA for a formal audit. While this is important, the ultimate assurance of quality comes from our all-inclusive system of cGMPs. This formalized system ensures that every aspect of our manufacturing process contributes to a final product that consistently and reproducibly satisfies all requirements for strength, identity, purity, potency, quality, and regulatory compliance [1].

In United States, the first GMP regulations were issued in 1963 and described the GMP to be followed in the manufacture, packaging, and storage of finished pharmaceutical products [2]. GMP regulations were developed by the US FDA and issued the United States CFR Chapter 21 in 1978 [3]. In the 1980, US FDA began publishing series of guidance documents that have a major effect on our interpretation of current GMP (cGMP). US congress passed the Federal Anti-tempering Act in 1983, making it a crime to tamper with packaged consumer products. A "Guide to Inspection of Computerized Systems in Drug Processing" was published in 1983 and "Guideline on General Principles of Process Validation" was published in 1987. March 1997, the US FDA issued 21 CFR Part 11 which dealt with the use of electronic records and signatures. In 2000, US FDA introduced a guidance document on the incorporation of risk management into device development[4-8].

Orange book was compiled by The Medicine Inspector of the Department of Health and Social Security of England, in consultation with other interested bodies with an expectation to act as the guide to the GMP. The first edition of the guide was published in 1971, the manufacturing of drug carried out under the Medicines Act. It was a relatively light volume of 20 pages, and was reissued as third impression in 1972, with the addition of a 2-page appendix on sterile medicinal products. Due to the colour of its cover, it was later known as the Orange Guide. The second edition (52 pages, including five appendices) was published in 1977. The third edition (110 pages, five appendices) was published in 1983. The Medicines and Healthcare products Regulatory Agency (MHRA) has published new edition of the Orange Guide in 2007. The regulation was similar in concept to the Orange Guide, but enforceable by law whereas the UK guide as an advisory [9].

The World Health Organization (WHO) version of GMP is used by pharmaceutical regulators and the pharmaceutical industry in over one hundred countries worldwide, primarily in the developing world including country like Nepal [10]. The European Union's GMP (EU-GMP) enforces similar requirements to WHO GMP, as does the Food and Drug Administration's version in the US [11]. Similar GMPs are used in other countries, with Australia, Japan, Canada, Singapore and others having highly developed/sophisticated GMP requirements. In the United Kingdom, the Medicines Act (1968) covers most aspects of GMP commonly referred to as "The Orange Guide", which is officially known as Rules and Guidance for Pharmaceutical Manufacturers and Distributors [9].

GMP inspections are performed in the United Kingdom by the Medicines and Healthcare Products Regulatory Agency (MHRA); in the Republic of Korea (South Korea) by the Korea Food and Drug Administration (KFDA); in Australia by the Therapeutically Goods Administration (TGA); in South Africa by the Medicines Control Council (MCC); in Brazil by the Agencia

Nacional de Vigilancia Sanitaria (National Health Surveillance Agency Brazil) (ANVISA). In India GMP inspections are carried out by state Food and Drug Administration (FDA) and these FDA report to Central Drugs Standard Control Organization: in Nepal, GMP inspections are carried out by the Department of Drug Administration (DDA) and in Pakistan by the Ministry of Health. Nigeria has National Agency for Food and Drug Administration and Control (NAFDAC).

GOOD MANUFACTURING PRACTICES (GMP) GUIDELINES

Many countries have legislated that pharmaceutical and medical device companies created their own GMP guidelines that correspond with their legislation. Basic concepts of GMP guidelines goal of safeguarding the health of the patient as well as producing good quality medicine, medical devices or active pharmaceutical products. The formalization of GMP commenced in the 1960s and their effect were observed in over 100 countries ranging from Afghanistan to Zimbabwe. Examples of these include the following.

(a) *Pharmaceutical Inspection Convention (PIC)*:- Guide to GMP for pharmaceutical products-Australia, Austria, Belgium, Canada, Italy, Latvia, Liechtenstein, Denmark, Finland, France, Hungary, Ireland, Malaysia, The Netherlands, Norway, Poland, Portugal, Romania, Singapore, Slovak Republic, Spain, Sweden, Switzerland, and the United Kingdom [12, 13].

(b) *Association of South-East Asia Nations (ASEAN)*:- General guidelines for Brunei Darussalam, Indonesia, Lao PDR, Malaysia, Cambodia, Myanmar, Philippines, Singapore, Thailand, and Vietnam [14].

(c) *European Economic Community (EEC)*:- Guide to GMP for medicinal products Austria, Belgium, Denmark, Ireland, Italy, Luxembourg, the Netherlands, Finland, France, Germany, Greece, Portugal, Spain, Sweden, and the United Kingdom [11].

In general, GMP has been issued guides to the achievement of consistent product quality, with interpretation and individual variations being accepted. GMP enforced in the United States by the US FDA, under Section 501(B) of the 1938 Food, Drug, and Cosmetic Act (21 USCS § 351). The regulations use the phrase "current Good Manufacturing Practices" (cGMP) and it describes the guidelines [15].

QUALITY MANAGEMENT

Quality Management is a wide-ranging concept, covering all matters, which individually or collectively influence the quality of a product. It is the sum total of the organised arrangements made with the aim to ensure that medicinal products are of the quality required for their intended use. Quality Management therefore incorporates Good Manufacturing Practice [10].

The holder of a manufacturing authorization must manufacture medicinal products so as to ensure that they are fit for their intended use, comply with the requirements of the marketing authorization and do not place patients at risk due to inadequate safety, quality or efficacy. The attainment of this quality objective is the responsibility of senior management and requires the participation and commitment by staff in many different departments and at all levels within the company, by the company's suppliers and by the distributors. In the pharmaceutical industry at large, quality management is usually defined as the aspect of management function that determines and implements the "quality policy", *i.e.* the overall intention and direction of an organization regarding quality, as formally expressed and authorized by top management [16-19].

The Pharmaceutical Quality System should be defined and documented. A Quality Manual or equivalent documentation should be established and should contain a description of the quality management system including management responsibilities [10].

QUALITY ASSURANCE (QA)

QA is a wide ranging concept, which covers all matters, which individually or collectively influence the quality of a product. It is the sum total of the organized arrangements made with the objective of ensuring that pharmaceutical products are of the quality required for their intended use. QA, therefore, incorporates GMP and other factors such as product design and development [10]. The system of QA appropriate for the manufacture of pharmaceutical products should ensure that:

(a) Pharmaceutical products are designed and developed in a way that takes account of the requirements of GMP and other associated codes such as those of Good Laboratory Practice (GLP) and Good Clinical Practice (GCP).

(b) Production and control operations are clearly specified in a written form and GMP requirements are adopted.

(c) Arrangements are made for the manufacture, supply and use of the correct starting and packaging materials.

(d) All necessary controls on starting materials, intermediate products, and bulk products and other in-process controls, calibrations, and validations are carried out.

(e) The finished product is correctly processed and checked, according to the defined procedures, pharmaceutical products are not sold or supplied before the authorized persons have certified that each production batch has been produced and controlled in accordance with the requirements of the marketing authorization and any other regulations relevant to the production, control and release of pharmaceutical products.

(f) Satisfactory arrangements exist to ensure, as far as possible, that the pharmaceutical products are stored by the manufacturer, distributed, and subsequently handled so that quality is maintained throughout their shelf-life;

(g) Deviations are reported, investigated and recorded.

(h) Regular evaluations of the quality of pharmaceutical products should be conducted with the objective of verifying the consistency of the process and ensuring its continuous improvement.

The manufacturing practices used by these companies must comply with certain standards, identified in the Act as current good manufacturing practices (CGMP). If a company's practices do not conform with CGMPs, the finished products are considered adulterated, even if the products are technically perfect. The purpose of CGMPs is to assure the safety and efficacy of the finished products. CGMP represents a process-oriented regulation (a regulation which focuses on the technology and/or practices used in production, rather than on the output). By managing the process, the regulatory agency can also control the quality and impacts of the completed product [19]. This chapter reviews the basic aspects of the CGMP requirement and considers whether government agencies should be involved in regulating the process as well as the final product. In addressing the process-product distinction, the paper compares the CGMP regulations to a similar process-oriented regulation found in the Clean Air Act {the requirement that certain permitted facilities use the best available control technology} [20, 21]. Main aspects of GMP are illustrated in Fig. 1.

GOOD MANUFACTURING PRACTICE (GMP) FOR MEDICINAL PRODUCTS

GMP applies to the lifecycle stages from the manufacture of investigational medicinal products, technology transfer, commercial manufacturing through to product discontinuation. However the Pharmaceutical Quality System can extend to the pharmaceutical development lifecycle stage as described in ICH Q10, which while optional, should facilitate innovation and continual improvement and strengthen the link between pharmaceutical development and manufacturing activities [22]. The current Good Manufacturing Practices formalize, through documented systems and procedures, the quality requirements and attributes of all systems, operations, equipment, and personnel. These procedures are often referred to as Standard Operating Procedures or SOPs [19]. The term "manufacture" is very inclusive and refers not only to the actual production of a substance but also to all aspects of the manufacturing process including:

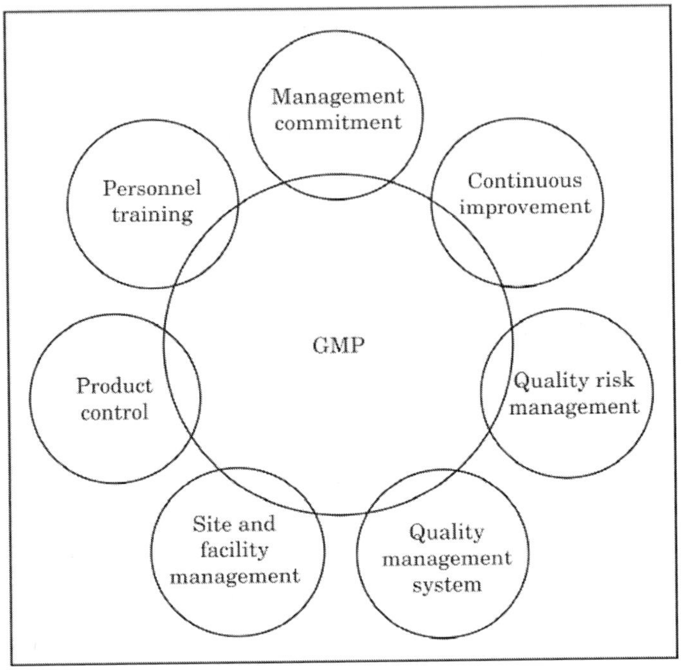

Fig. 1: Aspects of GMP

- Organizational and Personnel Requirements
- Facilities/Equipment/Systems Qualification
- Receipt and Approval of Raw Materials
- Production and Processing Controls
- Packaging and Labelling Control
- Quality Control of Materials and Systems
- Systems and Process Validation
- Laboratory Controls and Release of Finished Products
- Product Stability Testing
- Storage and Distribution

GMP is a part of QA which ensures that products are consistently produced and controlled to the quality standards appropriate to their intended use and as required by the marketing authorizations or product specification[10]. GMP is aimed primarily at diminishing the risks inherent in any pharmaceutical production. The basic requirements of GMP are that:

a. All manufacturing processes are clearly defined, systematically reviewed in the light of experience, and shown to be capable of consistently manufacturing pharmaceutical products of the required quality that comply with their specifications.

b. Qualification and validation are performed.
c. All necessary resources are provided.
d. Instructions and procedures are written in clear and unambiguous language, specifically applicable to the facilities provided.
e. Operators are trained to carry out procedures correctly.
f. Records are made during manufacture to show that all the steps required by the defined procedures and instructions have in fact been taken and that the quantity and quality of the product are as expected; any significant deviations are fully recorded and investigated.
g. Records manufacture and distribution, which enable the complete history of a batch to be traced, are retained in a comprehensible and accessible form.
h. The proper storage and distribution of the products minimizes any risk to their quality.
i. A system is available to recall any batch of product from sale or supply.
j. Complaints about marketed products are examined, the causes of investigated, and appropriate measures taken in respect of the defective products to prevent recurrence .

QUALITY CONTROL (QC)

QC is a part of GMP, concerned with sampling, specifications and testing, and with the organization, documentation and release procedures which ensure that the necessary and relevant tests are actually carried out and that materials are not released for use, nor products released for sale or supply, until their quality has been judged to be satisfactory. QC is not confined to laboratory operations, but may be involved in many decisions concerning the quality of the product. QC establish, validate and implement all QC procedures, to evaluate, maintain, and store the reference standards for substances, to ensure the correct labelling of containers of materials and products, to ensure that the stability of the active pharmaceutical ingredients (APIs) and products is monitored, to participate in the investigation of complaints related to the quality of the product, and to participate in environmental monitoring [10]. The basic requirements of Quality Control are that:

(i) Adequate facilities, trained personnel and approved procedures are available for sampling and testing starting materials, packaging materials, intermediate, bulk, and finished products, and where appropriate for monitoring environmental conditions for GMP purposes;
(ii) Samples of starting materials, packaging materials, intermediate products, bulk products and finished products are taken by approved personnel and methods;
(iii) Test methods are validated;

(iv) Records are made, manually and/or by recording instruments, which demonstrate that all the required sampling, inspecting and testing procedures were actually carried out. Any deviations are fully recorded and investigated;

(v) The finished products contain active ingredients complying with the qualitative and quantitative composition of the Marketing Authorisation or Clinical Trial Authorisation, are of the purity required, and are enclosed within their proper containers and correctly labelled;

(vi) Records are made of the results of inspection and that testing of materials, intermediate, bulk, and finished products is formally assessed against specification.

(vii) Product assessment includes a review and evaluation of relevant production documentation and an assessment of deviations from specified procedures;

(viii) No batch of product is released for sale or supply prior to certification by an Authorised Person that it is in accordance with the requirements of the relevant authorisations;

(ix) Sufficient reference samples of starting materials and products to permit future examination of the product if necessary and that the sample is retained in the final pack.

PRODUCT QUALITY REVIEW

Regular periodic or rolling quality reviews of all authorised medicinal products, including export only products, should be conducted with the objective of verifying the consistency of the existing process, the appropriateness of current specifications for both starting materials and finished product, to highlight any trends and to identify product and process improvements [10-22]. Such reviews should normally be conducted and documented annually, taking into account previous reviews, and should include at least:

(i) A review of starting materials including packaging materials used in the product, especially those from new sources and in particular the review of supply chain traceability of active substances;

(ii) A review of critical in-process controls and finished product results;

(iii) A review of all batches that failed to meet established specification(s) and their investigation;

(iv) A review of all significant deviations or non-conformances, their related investigations, and the effectiveness of resultant corrective and preventive actions taken;

(v) A review of all changes carried out to the processes or analytical methods;

(vi) A review of Marketing Authorisation variations submitted, granted or refused, including those for third country (export only) dossiers;

(vii) A review of the results of the stability monitoring programme and any adverse trends;

(viii) A review of all quality-related returns, complaints and recalls and the investigations performed at the time;

(ix) A review of adequacy of any other previous product process or equipment corrective actions;

(x) For new Marketing Authorisations and variations to Marketing Authorisations, a review of post-marketing commitments;

(xi) The qualification status of relevant equipment and utilities, *e.g.* HVAC, water, compressed gases, etc;

(xii) A review of any contractual arrangements to ensure that they are up to date.

The manufacturer and, where different, marketing authorisation holder should evaluate the results of the review and an assessment made as to whether corrective and preventive action or any revalidation should be undertaken, under the Pharmaceutical Quality System. There should be management procedures for the ongoing management and review of these actions and the effectiveness of these procedures verified during self-inspection. Quality reviews may be grouped by product type, *e.g.* solid dosage forms, liquid dosage forms, sterile products, etc. where scientifically justified[10].

Where the marketing authorisation holder is not the manufacturer, there should be a technical agreement in place between the various parties that defines their respective responsibilities in producing the product quality review.

QUALITY RISK MANAGEMENT

Quality risk management is a systematic process for the assessment, control, communication and review of risks to the quality of the active substance. It can be applied both proactively and retrospectively [10]. The quality risk management system should ensure that:

- The evaluation of the risk to quality is based on scientific knowledge, experience with the process and ultimately links to the protection of the patient through communication with the user of the active substance.
- The level of effort, formality and documentation of the quality risk management process is commensurate with the level of risk.

BASIC COMPONENTS OF THE GMP

GMP requires that the manufacturing process is fully defined before being initiated and all the necessary facilities are provided. In practice, personnel must be adequately trained, suitable premises and equipment used, correct materials used, approved procedures adopted, suitable storage and transport facilities available, and appropriate records made. Indian schedule M for GMP and requirements of premises, plant and equipment for pharmaceutical products includes general requirements, Warehousing area, Production area, Quality control area, Personnel, Ancillary area, Health, clothing and sanitation of workers, Manufacturing operations and controls, Sanitation in the manufacturing premises, Raw materials, Equipment, Documentation and Records, Labels and other printed materials, Quality assurance, Self inspection and quality audit, Quality control system, Specification, Master formula records, Packing records, Batch packaging records, Batch processing records, Standard operating procedures (SOPs) and records, Reference samples, Reprocessing and recoveries, Distribution records, Validation and process validation, Product recalls, Complaints and adverse reactions and Site-master file. It also mentioned about the specific requirements for manufacture of different products and specific requirements of premises, plant and materials for manufacture of active pharmaceutical ingredients (bulk drugs). It also described the requirement of plant and equipments for various dosage forms. GMP is broadly analysed on the basis of following parts. These each single part consists of several sub parts [19]. These include:

1. Sanitation and hygiene
2. Qualification and validation
3. Complaints and product recalls
4. Contact production and analysis
5. Self inspection, quality audits and supplier audits/approval
6. Personnel, training and personal hygiene
7. Premises
8. Equipment
9. Material
10. Packaging material
11. Documentation
12. Holding and distribution

In the later sections, we shall discuss these parts in details.

SANITATION AND HYGIENE

Sanitation is an essential component of any quality system needed to ensure that the manufacturing environment and equipment are free from pathogens and other unwanted microorganisms that could potentially contaminate the product. In order to maintain good sanitation practices, sanitation programs should be written and include the sanitation objective, sanitizing procedures, schedules, monitoring programs, corrective action processes and documentation. A high level of sanitation and hygiene should be practiced in every aspect of the manufacture of medicine products. The scope of sanitation and hygiene covers personnel, premises, equipment and apparatus, production materials and containers, products for cleaning and disinfection, and anything that could become a source of contamination to the product. Potential sources of contamination should be eliminated through an integrated comprehensive programme of sanitation and hygiene. The areas, surfaces, and equipment in and on which products are made must be kept clean. Dirt, and the microbes that it can harbor, must not get into or on products. Disinfectants can be inactivated by dirt. Dirt (particularly oily or greasy films and protein like matter) can also protect microorganisms against the action of disinfectants. So, before disinfection, it is important to first clean surfaces. Where gross amounts of dirt are present, it may be necessary to first remove most of it by scrubbing. Then surfaces may be cleaned by the application of a cleaning agent, followed by rinsing [10-19].

QUALIFICATION AND VALIDATION

Qualification is an action of providing that any premises, systems and items of equipment work correctly and actually lead to the expected results. Validation is defined as the establishing of documented evidence which provides a high degree of assurance that a planned process will consistently perform according to the intended specified outcomes. Validation studies should reinforce GMP and be conducted in accordance with defined procedures. Results and conclusions should be recorded. When any new manufacturing formula or method of preparation is adopted, steps should be taken to demonstrate its suitability for routine processing [23-26]. Qualification and validation should establish and provide documented evidence that:

a. The premises, supporting utilities, equipment and processes have been designed in accordance with the requirements for GMP (Design qualification or DQ).
b. The premises, supporting utilities and equipment have been built and installed in compliance with their design specifications (Installation qualification or IQ).
c. The premises, supporting utilities and equipment operate in accordance with their design specifications (Operational qualification or OQ).
d. A specific process will consistently produce a product meeting its predetermined specifications and quality attributes (Process validation or PV, also called performance qualification or PQ).

COMPLAINTS AND PRODUCT RECALLS

QA and GMP are about preventing errors. However, in this imperfect universe there is no such thing as an infallibly perfect system, and an essential feature of any QA system is a plan for dealing with complaints, or reports of faulty products, if they do occur. A requirement to cover this occurs in all notable GMP guidelines. Complaints received from consumers, professionals and the trade serves as a primary means of obtaining feedback about product quality after distribution. It is necessary, therefore, that each complaint or inquiry be evaluated by knowledgeable and responsible personnel. The records of packaging, production and distribution of drug and the retained samples provide the basis for assessing the validity and seriousness of the alleged deviations that precipitated the complaint. The complaint file itself also plays an important role in determining whether any other similar complaints have been received on the lot in question, or on any other lots of the same product. The evaluation of complaints serves several valuable purposes. First, there is the urgent need to confirm whether consumers are potentially at risk and to initiate any appropriate action. A second value is the review of the product and its production process to establish whether any modifications are required. Third is the need to rapidly respond to the customer, thereby attempting to maintain confidence in the product and company. [10]

CONTRACT PRODUCTION AND ANALYSIS

The global industry is changing its shape through rationalization, mergers and acquisitions. Companies are increasingly considering the use of other manufacturers to produce or manufacture their products. Companies are also finding that they do not have the technology or expertise to manufacture certain new special dosage forms. In some cases, financial targets mean that companies are not using manufacturing as a core business process. This means that the importance of contract manufacturing and testing of products is also increasing. The main principle underlying contract production and analysis is very simple. The work has to be clearly defined, agreed and controlled to avoid misunderstandings. The simplest way to avoid such misunderstandings is to have a written contract, setting out the duties of all parties to the contract and the standards that must be met [10-19].

SELF INSPECTION, QUALITY AUDITS AND SUPPLIER'S AUDITS/ APPROVAL

The purpose of self-inspection is to evaluate the manufacturer's compliance with GMP in all aspects of production and quality control. The self-inspection programme should be designed to detect any shortcomings in the implementation of GMP and to recommend the necessary corrective actions. Self-inspections should be performed routinely, and may be, in addition, performed on special occasions, *e.g.* in the case of product recalls or repeated rejections, or when an inspection by the health authorities is announced. The team responsible for self inspection should consist of personnel who can evaluate the implementation of GMP objectively. Management appoints a self-inspection team consisting of experts in their respective fields and familiar with GMP [10-19].

PERSONNEL, TRAINING AND PERSONAL HYGIENE

The establishment and maintenance of a satisfactory system of quality assurance and the correct manufacture and control of pharmaceutical products and active ingredients is a cGMP requirement. For this reason there must be sufficient qualified personnel to carry out all the tasks for which the manufacturer is responsible. Individual responsibilities should be clearly defined and understood by the persons concerned and recorded as written job descriptions. Personnel should be aware of the principles of GMP that affect them and receive initial and continuing training, including hygiene instructions, relevant to their need. In order to effectively monitor and control virtually all GMP documents/activities in a facility, the quality professional should have a very high level of skills, knowledge and experience. Peoples are the most important factor in the assurance of quality. This is true of all levels within an organization, from company president and managing director to the most-junior employee. It may well be possible for high-quality, well-trained, dedicated personnel to compensate for a lack or deficiency in the other elements. Nothing, not even the finest equipment, premises, materials, or procedures can compensate for the quality hazard represented by low-standard, ill-trained, or poorly motivated staff. Self-responsible, well-motivated staff will produce more goods, with a greater assurance of the quality of those goods, than will poorly motivated staff. Conversely, in the special context of medicines manufacture, poorly motivated staff can represent a hazard to themselves, to the public, and to company profits [10-19].

Proper and adequate employee training is an utmost requirement for GMP implementation. Without effective training, safe production of product is jeopardized. The approach companies may take for training on GMPs is to work in partnership with industry, academia and government so that issues remain current and data are relevant and up-to-date. GMP training should focus less on providing specific content and standards and rather assure that the knowledge and expertise necessary to produce safe products is provided to supervisors and workers in a manner appropriate for the intended audience. The training content, comprehension and attendance should be documented [27].

PREMISES

Premises must be located, constructed, adapted, designed, and maintained to suit the operations to be carried out. The layout and design of premises must aim to minimize the risk of errors and permit effective cleaning and maintenance in order to avoid cross contamination, build-up of dust or dirt, and in general, any adverse effect on the quality of products [10-19]. The choices of materials of construction for manufacturing facilities are numerous. Some examples are presented subsequently.

a. ***Walls:*** Walls in manufacturing areas, packaging areas and corridors should be of plaster finish on high-quality concrete blocks or gypsum board. The finish should be smooth, usually with enamel or epoxy paint. They should be washable and able to resist repeated applications of cleaning and disinfecting agents.

b. ***Floors:*** Floor covering should be selected for durability as well as for clean ability and resistance to the chemicals with which it is likely to come into contact. Epoxy flooring provides a durable and readily cleanable surface.

c. ***Ceilings:*** Suspended ceilings may be provided in office areas, toilets, laboratories and cafeterias. They usually consist of lay-in acoustical panels of non brittle, non friable, non asbestos and non combustible material. Manufacturing areas require a smooth finish, often of seamless plaster or gypsum board. All ceiling fixtures such as light fittings, air outlets and returns should be designed to assure ease of cleaning and to minimize the potential for accumulation of dust.

d. ***Services:*** In the building design, provisions must be made for drains, steam, electricity, water and other services to allow for ease of maintenance. Access should, ideally, be possible without disruption of activity within the actual rooms provided with the services. Doors and window-frames should all have a hard, smooth, impervious finish, and should close tightly. Window and door frames should be fitted flush, at least on sides facing inward to processing areas. Doors, except emergency exits, should not open directly from production areas to the outside world. Any emergency exit doors should be kept shut and sealed, and designed so as to be open able only when emergency demands.

EQUIPMENT

Manufacturing equipment should be capable of producing materials, products and intermediates that are intended and that conform to the required or specified quality characteristics. The equipment must be designed and built so that it is possible to clean it thoroughly. Surfaces that come into contact with products should have polished finishes, smooth with no recesses, crevices, difficult corners, uneven joints, dead-legs, projections, or rough welds to harbor contamination or make cleaning difficult. Equipment must also be capable of withstanding repeated, thorough cleaning. Traces of previous product, at levels that might be acceptable in other industries, are totally unacceptable in the manufacture of medicines. Between batches all manufacturing equipment must be thoroughly cleaned and disinfected or sterilized [10-19].

MATERIALS

The purchasing department orders the material on the basis of a starting material specification provided to them by the QC. Purchasing department sends the order to an approved supplier, which is a company that has been approved, jointly by the QA, QC and production to supply the material in question. Different suppliers batches within one delivery are to be segregated, one from another, with a different internal lot number for each entered on the QUARANTINE label, which is applied to each container. If all the containers in the delivery appear to be correct and in good condition, the goods inwards departments then place on each container a QUARANTINE label with the entries for "Code Number," "Name of Material," "Lot Number," and "Date Received" are completed [28].

Notes:

a. It is useful to have the QUARANTINE label and the RELEASED and REJECTED labels printed in different colors, for example, for QUARANTINE, black print on a yellow background, for RELEASED green print on a white background, and for REJECTED red print on a white background.

b. In the examples shown, the intention is that, when the QC decision is made, the RELEASED (or REJECTED) label should be applied just over the lower QUARANTINE panel. This may seem an infringement of the golden rule about not applying new labels over old ones, but here (if the, say, RELEASED label falls off, or is removed) the labeled status of the material reverts to QUARANTINE, *i.e.,* it is fail-safe. The benefit of the labelling system illustrated is the elimination of any possible error in transcribing the information originally entered on the QUARANTINE label.

Life cycle for any vendor selection and material management in pharmaceutical industry is as Fig. 2.

PACKAGING MATERIALS

The purchase, sampling, release, receipt and control of printed packaging materials and primary packaging materials (that is packaging materials

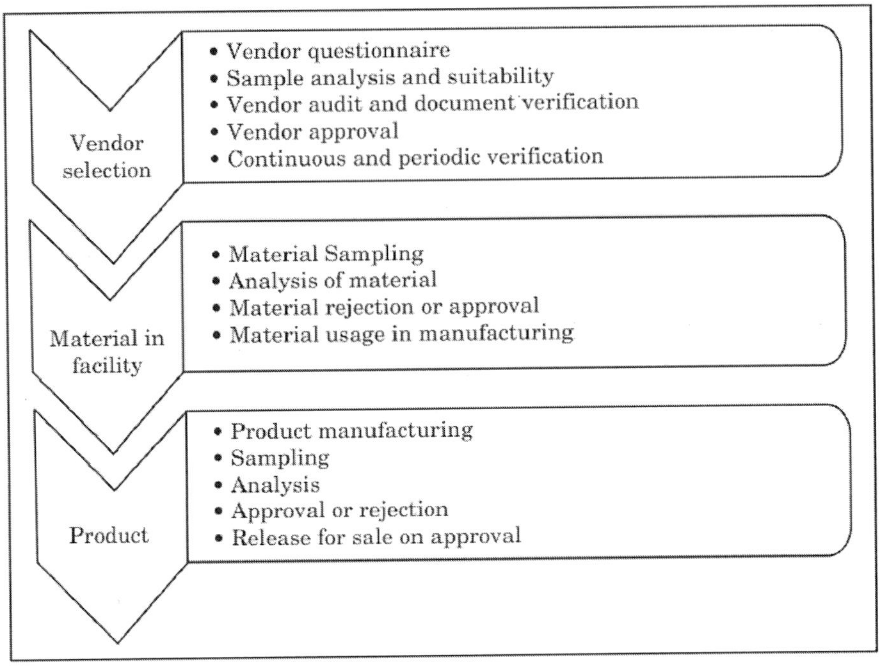

Fig. 2: Material management in pharmaceutical industry

that come into direct contact with the product, as compared with secondary packaging materials, which do not) need to be accorded the same level of attention as given to starting materials. Documents, records, and procedures analogous to those outlined above should be employed. All the regulatory requirements are in agreement that components or (starting materials) and containers, etc. should be storage is to "permit batch segregation and stock rotation" [FEFO, "first expiry, first out" or FIFO "first in, first out"]. It also permits wet-cleaning of floors, without the risk of wetting the materials [10-19]. Classification of packing material is as per Fig. 3.

DOCUMENTATION

Good documentation is an essential part of the QA system and GMP. The various types of documents used should be fully defined in the manufacturer's quality management system (QMS). The main objective of the system of documentation utilized must be to establish, control, monitor and record all activities which directly or indirectly impact on all aspects of the quality of medicinal products [10-19, 29]. Given below is a list of the most common types of documents along with a brief description of each.

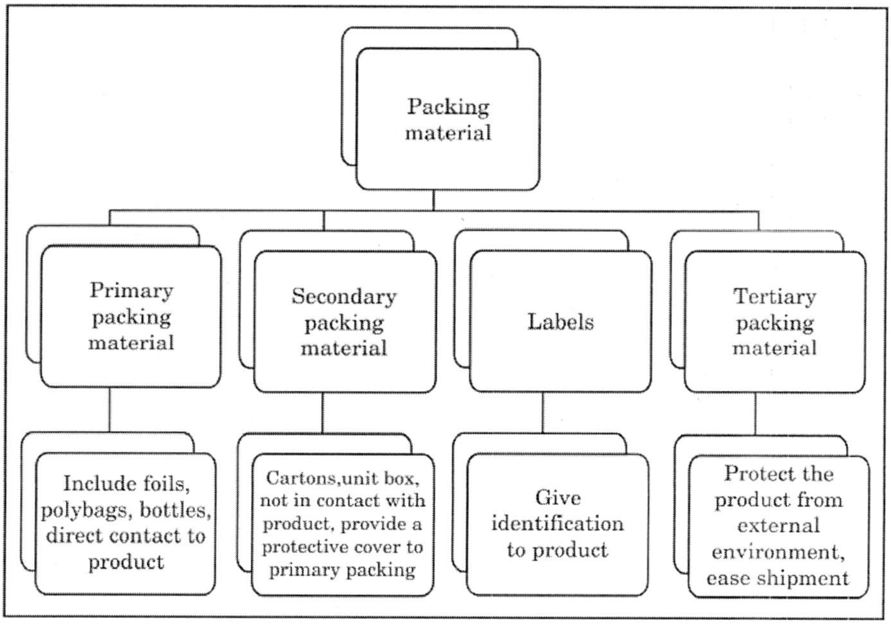

Fig. 3: Classification of packing material

a. ***Site Master File:*** A document describing the GMP related activities of the manufacturer.

b. ***Quality Manual:*** A global company document that describes, in paragraph form, the regulations and/or parts of the regulations that the company is required to follow.

c. ***Policies:*** Documents that describe in general terms, and not with step-by-step instructions, how specific GMP aspects (such as security, documentation, health, and responsibilities) will be implemented.

d. ***Standard Operating Procedures (SOPs):*** Step-by-step instructions for performing operational tasks or activities.

e. ***Batch Records:*** These documents are typically used and completed by the manufacturing department. Batch records provide step-by-step instructions for production-related tasks and activities, besides including areas on the batch record itself for documenting such tasks.

f. ***Test Methods:*** These documents are typically used and completed by the quality control (QC) department. Test methods provide step-by-step instructions for testing supplies, materials, products, and other production-related tasks and activities, *e.g.*, environmental monitoring of the GMP facility.

g. ***Logbooks:*** Logbooks are used for documenting the operation, maintenance, and calibration of a piece of equipment. Logbooks are also used to record critical activities, *e.g.*, monitoring of clean rooms, solution preparation, recording of deviation, change controls and its corrective action assignment.

h. ***Batch processing record:*** A batch processing record should be kept for each batch processed. It should be based on the relevant parts of the currently approved manufacturing formula and processing instructions, and should contain the following information:

(i) The name and batch number of the product.

(ii) Dates and times of commencement, of significant intermediate stages and of completion of production.

(iii) Identification of the operator who performed each significant step of the process and, where appropriate, the name of any person who checked these operations.

(iv) The batch number and analytical control number as well as the quantities of each starting material actually weighed.

(v) A record of the in-process controls and the initials of the person(s) carrying them out, and the results obtained.

(vi) The product yield obtained at different and pertinent stages of manufacture.

(vii) Notes on special problems including details, with signed authorization for any deviation from the manufacturing formula and processing instructions.

(viii) Approval by the person responsible for the processing operations.

i. ***Batch packaging record-*** A batch packaging record should be kept for each batch or part batch processed. The batch packaging record should contain the following information:

(i) The name and batch number of the product.

(ii) The date and times of the packaging operations.

(iii) Identification of the operator who performed each significant step of the process and, where appropriate, the name of any person who checked these operations.

(iv) Records of checks for identity and conformity with the packaging instructions, including the results of in-process controls.

(v) Details of the packaging operations carried out, including references to equipment and the packaging lines used.

(vi) Whenever possible, samples of printed packaging materials used, including specimens of the batch coding, expiry dating and any additional overprinting.

(vii) The quantities and reference number or identification of all printed packaging materials and bulk product issued, used, destroyed or returned to stock and the quantities of obtained product, in order to provide for an adequate reconciliation.

(viii) Approval by the person responsible for the packaging operations.

HOLDING AND DISTRIBUTION

The goods hold stage is where it is necessary to ensure that the goods remain in good condition, and do not become harmed or damaged through incorrect or unsuitable storage conditions or bad handling. All goods must be stored in a clean, neat, orderly way, in conditions that will not affect their quality or cause them to deteriorate in any way.

Goods out might well be the last chance of checking and ensuring that everything is in order before the goods leave a manufacturer's hands, to the next step in the distribution chain, on their way to the consumer [10-19]. It is necessary to make, and keep, a record of each order that is dispatched, which shows:

- Date of dispatch of goods
- Customer's name and address
- Quantity, name, batch number, and expiry date of each product dispatched

The manufacturer must maintain records of all distribution transactions involving in process or finished goods. All distribution records should be maintained for a minimum 3-year period after the distribution process for any control number has been completed. If expiration dating is used for a product, distribution records must be maintained at least for one year past the expiration date of the product.

CONCLUSIONS

GMP is a production and testing practice that helps to ensure in built quality product. Many countries have legislated that pharmaceutical companies must follow GMP procedures, and have created their own GMP guidelines that correspond with their legislation. Basic concepts of all of these guidelines remain more or less similar to the ultimate goals of safeguarding the health of the patient as well as producing good quality medicines.

Quality objective can be achieved only through careful planning and implementation of QA system and practical implementation of GMP. The effective implementation of GMP requires extensive care and knowledge about the different components of GMP that should be incorporated form the inception of the manufacturing building and product development till the production.

REFERENCES

[1] 21 CFR parts 110, 210 and 211
[2] ASEAN: ASEAN operational manual for implementation of GMP, Indonesian national GMP team Asean, 2000.
[3] Chaloner-Larsson, G. Anderson, R. Filho, M.A.F.C. and Herrera, J.F.G.: Validation In: A WHO guide to good manufacturing practice (GMP) requirements, World Health Organization, Geneva, 1997.
[4] CPGM 7356.002 Compliance Program – Drug Manufacturing Inspections http://www.fda.gov/cder/dmpq/compliance_guide.htm
[5] *EudraLex* – Volume 4. *Good manufacturing practice (GMP) Guidelines. European Commission.* (http://ec.europa.eu/health/documents/eudralex/vol-4/ index_en.htm).
[6] FDA (1995) Milestones in U.S. Food and Drug Law History. FDA Backgrounder: Current and Useful Information from the Food and Drug Administration (FDA, Rockville, MD, August 1995).
[7] FDA (2000) Office of Women's Health, FDA Milestones in Women's Health: Looking Back as We Move into the New Millennium (FDA, Rockville, MD). Available from: www.fda.gov/womens/milesbro.html.
[8] FDA (overview) An Overview of FDA. Available from: http://www.fda.gov/oc/opacom/fda101/sld013.html
[9] Good manufacturing practices for pharmaceutical products. *In*: WHO Expert Committee on Specifications for Pharmaceutical Preparations. Thirty-seventh report. Geneva, World Health Organization, 2003 (WHO Technical Report Series, No. 908), Annex 4.
[10] Huber, L. (2012). Validation of analytical methods and procedures, 25.03.2012, labcompliance.com/tutorial/methods/default.aspx.
[11] ICH Q10
[12] Immel BK (2005) A Brief History of the GMPs, Regulatory Compliance Newsletter, Winter 2005. Available from: http://www.gmplabeling.com/catalog/news1105.pdf
[13] Learoyd P (2005) Good Manufacturing Practices or 'GMP' A Brief Guide, NBS-Scientific and Technical Training STT-040, Sept 2005.
[14] Lund, W.: Good manufacturing practices. The pharmaceutical codex: principle and practice of pharmaceutics. London, Edition 12, The Pharmaceutical Press, 1994, 362-397.
[15] Nally J. and Kieffer R.G.: GMP compliance, productivity and quality, Interpharm, 1998, 465-466.
[16] Nally J.D.: Good manufacturing practices for pharmaceuticals, Informa healthcare USA, Inc., ISBN 10:0-8593-3972-3 and ISBN13:, Edition 6, New York, 2007, 978-0-8493-3972- 1.
[17] Patel K.T. and Chotai N.P. (2011) Documentation and records: Harmonized GMP requirements, *Journal of young pharmacists,* 3:138-150.
[18] Pharmaceutical Inspection Convention, Pharmaceutical Inspection Co-operation Scheme (PIC/S). In: *Guide to good manufacturing practice for medicinal plants.* Geneva, PIC/S Secretariat, 2000.
[19] PIC/S "Guide to good manufacturing practice for medicinal products" PE 009-11 (Intro). 01 Mar, 2014.
[20] Schedule M. Good manufacturing practices and requirements of premises, plant and equipment for pharmaceutical products,
[21] Shadle PJ (2004) Overview of GMPs, BioPharm International, Nov 15, 2004.
[22] Sharp J.: Wider aspects of GMP. Good manufacturing practice: philosophy and applications. Illinois, Interpharm Press, 1991, 71-79.
[23] Sharp, J.: Quality in the manufacture of medicines and other healthcare products, pharmaceutical press, ISBN London, 2000, 0-85369-431-1.

[24] Stehlin IB (1995) How FDA Works to Ensure Vaccine Safety. Available from: http://www.fda.gov/fdac/features/095_vacc.html
[25] Time Line: Chronology of Drug Regulation in the United States. Available from: http://www.fda.gov/cder/about/history/time1.htm.
[26] US FDA.: Guidance for industry, Quality systems approach to pharmaceutical current good manufacturing practice regulations, Food and drug administration, Center for drug evaluation and research (CDER), Center for biologics evaluation and research (CBER), Center for veterinary medicine, office of regulatory affairs (ORA), Rockville, MD, 2004, fda.gov/cvm /guidance/published.html.
[27] Validation of analytical procedures used in the examination of pharmaceutical materials. *In*: *WHO Expert Committee on Specifications for Pharmaceutical Preparations. Thirty-second report*. Geneva, World Health Organization, 1992 (WHO Technical Report Series, No. 823), Annex 5.
[28] WHOTRS: Annex 2 Supplementary guidelines on good manufacturing practices for heating, ventilation and airconditioning systems for non-sterile pharmaceutical dosage forms, In; WHO expert committee on specifications for pharmaceutical preparations Fortieth report WHO technical report series 937, Geneva, 2006, 45-84.
[29] WHOTRS: Annex 3 WHO good manufacturing practices: Main principles for pharmaceutical products, *In*; WHO expert committee on specifications for pharmaceutical preparations Forty-fifth report WHO Technical report series 961, PP. 94-147, ISBN 978 92 4 120961 8, ISSN, Geneva, 2011, 0512-3054.

FURTHER READINGS

Immel, B. K.: 2005, A brief history of the GMPs, Regulatory compliance newsletter, The MP labeling system, (25.03.2012).
PIC/S Secretariat *(Ed.)*: guide to good manufacturing practice for medicinal products, Pharmaceutical inspection convention/ pharmaceutical inspection co-operation scheme PE 009-2 1 July 2004, Geneva.
Sharp, J.: Good Pharmaceutical manufacturing practice rationale and compliance, CRC Press, ISBN Washington, D.C., 2005, 0-8493-1994-3.
Signore, A. A. and Jacobs, T.: Good design practices for GMP pharmaceutical facilities, Taylor & Francis group, ISBN Boca Raton, 2005, 10: 0-8247-5463-8 & ISBN 13: 978-0-247-5463-1.
US FDA: Improving public health through human drugs, CDER 2001 Report to the nation, Food and drug administration, Center for drug evaluation and research, 2001.
WHOTRS: Annex 3 WHO Good manufacturing practices: water for pharmaceutical use, In; WHO expert committee on specifications for pharmaceutical preparations Thirty-ninth report WHO technical report series 929, 40-58, ISBN 92 4 120929 1, ISSN Geneva, 2005, 0512-3054.

4

Quality Risk Management

ABSTRACT

This chapter is intended to provide a holistic briefing on the field of quality risk management (QRM). The chapter will provide background information to the QRM discipline and will explore topics including the various types of risks associated with medicinal products, the role of risk management in pharmaceutical and biopharmaceutical regulation, QRM principles and practices, the role of QRM across the product life cycle, primary literature sources for QRM, and common challenges associated with QRM implementation. Risk is commonly defined as the chances of getting hazard in common language but while going in technical language it includes aspects of severity, probability of occurrence of hazard and measures to detect. It specifically provides guidance on the principles and some of the tools of quality risk management that can enable more effective and consistent risk based decisions, both by regulators and industry, regarding the quality of drug substances and drug (medicinal) products across the product lifecycle. It is not intended to create any new expectations beyond the current regulatory requirements. It serves as a foundation or resource document that is independent of, yet supports, other ICH Quality documents and complements existing quality practices, requirements, standards, and guidelines within the pharmaceutical industry and regulatory environment.

INTRODUCTION

Risk is defined as the combination of the severity of harm, probability of occurrence and detectability of that event [1]. Risk management principles are effectively utilized in many areas of production, marketing, business and government [2]. Although there are some examples of the use of quality risk management in the pharmaceutical industry today, they are limited and do not represent the full contributions that risk management has to offer. In addition, the importance of quality management system has been recognized in the pharmaceutical industry and it is becoming evident that quality risk management is a important component of an effective quality management system. In relation to pharmaceuticals, although there are a variety of stakeholders, including patients and medical practitioners as well as government and industry, the protection of the patient by managing the risk to quality should be considered of prime importance [3-5].

The manufacturing and use of a medicinal product, including its components, necessarily entail some degree of risk. The risk to its quality is just one component of the overall risk. It is significant to understand that product quality should be maintained throughout the lifecycle such that the attributes that are important to the quality of the medicinal product remain consistent with those used in the clinical studies [2, 6]. An effective quality risk management approach can further ensure the high quality of the drug (medicinal) product to the patient by providing a proactive means to identify and control potential quality issues during development and manufacturing. Additionally, use of quality risk management can improve the decision making if a quality problem arises. Effective quality risk management can facilitate better and more informed decisions, can provide regulators with greater assurance of a company's ability to deal with potential risks and can beneficially affect the extent and level of direct regulatory oversight [3-5].

It is neither always appropriate nor always necessary to use a formal risk management process (using recognized tools and/ or internal procedures *e.g.*, standard operating procedures). The use of informal risk management processes (using empirical tools and/ or internal procedures) can also be considered acceptable [7-8]. Appropriate use of quality risk management can facilitate but does not obviate industry's obligation to comply with regulatory requirements and does not replace appropriate communications between industry and regulators. In most countries compliance with good manufacturing practices (GMP, including validation), drug regulatory activities and inspections together provide good assurance that risks are largely controlled. However, in countries where control is less effective, patients may be put at risk through the production of drugs of inadequate quality. The assessment of individual risks related to specific products and starting materials and the recognition of hazards at specific stages of production or distribution should permit regulatory authorities to improve control of medicines by increasing the effectiveness of their activities within the limits of the available resources.

Hazard analysis and critical control point (HACCP) methodology, traditionally a food safety management system but subsequently applied to other industries, has been the basis of WHO risk management (RM) guidance to the pharmaceutical industry [5]. The aim has been to assist the development and implementation of effective RM plans covering activities such as research and development, sourcing of materials, manufacturing, packaging, testing and distribution. HACCP is science-based and systematic and identifies specific hazards and measures for their control, as well as providing information on environmental protection and labour safety. HACCP is a tool to assess hazards and establish control systems that focus on prevention rather than relying on corrective action based on end-product testing. All HACCP systems are capable of accommodating changes, such as advances in equipment design and processing procedures or technological developments [1].

However, recent international guidance has emerged that is of specific relevance to the pharmaceutical industry and which addresses the full scope of pharmaceutical industry RM more effectively than HACCP principles, including how to structure regulatory filings using a risk-based approach. Consequently, WHO guideline has been developed as an update of WHO advice to the pharmaceutical industry, taking account of this new guidance[5]. International medicines regulatory authorities (MRAs) are encouraging pharmaceutical manufacturers to adopt a risk-based approach to the development of drug products. In return for using this approach, there are potential opportunities for both MRAs and pharmaceutical manufacturers as summarized in the following sections [1-8].

a) Quality risk management (QRM) principles can be applied to both MRAs and pharmaceutical manufacturers and MRAs
   1. *MRAs:* Systematic and structured planning of reviews and inspections. The submission review and inspection programmes can also operate in a coordinated and synergistic manner.
   2. *Manufacturers:* Development, manufacture, distribution of medicines. RM can be an integral element of organizational culture.

b) Science-based decision-making can be embedded into practice
   1. *MRAs:* Company decisions easier to scrutinize. Acceptance of residual risks through understanding the RM decisions involved.
   2. *Manufacturers:* Quality decisions and filing commitments can be based on science-based process understanding and RM (quality by design). Process control focused on critical attributes. Uncertainty can be addressed explicitly.

c) Resources can be focused on risks to patients
   1. *MRAs:* RM can be used to determine best allocation of inspection resource, both in terms of product types and for specific areas of focus for a given inspection. This enables the most efficient and effective scrutiny of the most significant health risks. Those manufacturers with poor histories of GMP compliance can also be more closely and frequently evaluated by on-site inspection than those manufacturers with better records.
   2. *Manufacturers:* Evaluation of quality risk through science-based decisions can be linked ultimately to protection of the patient. Supports a corporate culture to focus on the patient as a primary stakeholder in all activities.

d) Restrictive and unnecessary practices can be avoided
   1. *MRAs:* Regulatory scrutiny adjusted to level of process understanding. Improvement and innovation by manufacturers is encouraged.
   2. *Manufacturers:* Instead of having systems designed to inhibit change and minimize business risk, changes can be managed within a company's quality management system. Real-time batch release is feasible. Innovation and the adoption of latest scientific advances in manufacturing and technology are supported.

e) Communication and transparency are facilitated
   1. *MRAs:* Facilitated dialogue with pharmaceutical manufacturers and tailoring of the inspection programme. Improved clarity of a company's decision-making process and judgement on critical issues.
   2. *Manufacturers:* Matrix team approach, stakeholders kept informed *via* science-based decisions. Culture of trust and "one-team" mindset with focus on product and patient. QRM is the overall and continuing process of minimizing risks to product quality throughout its life-cycle in order to optimize its benefit/risk balance. It is a systematic process for the assessment, control, communication and review of risks to the quality of the medicinal product.

QRM can be applied both proactively and retrospectively. QRM should ensure the evaluation of risk to quality based on scientific knowledge and experience that ultimately links to the protection of the patient.

QUALITY RISK MANAGEMENT

Quality risk management is a systematic process for the assessment, control, communication and review of risks to the quality of the active substance. The quality risk management system should ensure that:

- The evaluation of the risk to quality is based on scientific knowledge, experience with the process and ultimately links to the protection of the patient through communication with the user of the active substance.
- The level of effort, formality and documentation of the quality risk management process is commensurate with the level of risk.

The International Conference on Harmonization (ICH) Q9 Quality Risk Management Guidance for Industry states "it is becoming evident that quality risk management is a valuable component of an effective quality system." It goes on to say "Quality risk management supports a scientific and practical approach to decision making". It provides documented, transparent, and reproducible methods to accomplish steps of the quality risk management process based on current knowledge about assessing the probability, severity, and, sometimes, detectability of the risk." The document provides a quality risk management process. The model is comprised of three primary areas — risk assessment, risk control, and risk review — contained in a framework of using risk management tools and risk communications [1].

To establish a quality risk management program and ensure that the appropriate types of risks remain at the forefront of subsequent QRM efforts, it is necessary for QRM practitioners to understand the breadth of risks to which the patient might be exposed. Within the realm of medicinal products, two general categories of risk to the patient can be identified: intrinsic risk and extrinsic risk [9-11].

Intrinsic risks

Intrinsic risks are those inherent to a drug, given the nature of certain biochemical reactions within the body when exposed to the drug or its constituent parts. Intrinsic risks generally surface during research and development and in the clinic and are weighed against the overall medical benefits of the product when determining whether the drug is suitable for commercial sale. For example, while the risk of suicidal thoughts or feelings might be considered acceptable in the context of an antidepressant medication where such underlying urges may already be present that same risk would be unacceptable if it were to accompany a mild pain reliever such as ibuprofen. The acceptability of intrinsic risks is therefore relative, based on the therapeutic benefits a drug delivers. While intrinsic risks are rarely discussed within the realm of commercial pharmaceutical manufacturing and the chemistry, manufacturing, and controls (CMC) portion of the product life cycle, QRM practitioners should possess adequate knowledge of these risks to understand the underlying relationship between these and the quality risks that are the focuses of QRM [12-14].

Understanding Intrinsic Risks

Generally, intrinsic risks are communicated to patients and their healthcare providers through product labelling so that patients, in consultation with their medical teams, can make informed decisions regarding the course of their care. While requirements for drug product labelling vary by region, in most instances the communication of intrinsic risks can be subdivided into categories, including adverse reactions, warnings and precautions, and contraindications. Adverse reactions (known in some regions as side effects or undesirable effects) are conditions that are undesirable in nature that the patient might reasonably expect to occur during use of the medicinal product. These may include (but are certainly not limited to) dry mouth, drowsiness, stomach pain, nausea, vomiting, or diarrhoea. Side effects are often discovered over the course of clinical trials and may be further refined through data from adverse event reporting, complaints, and pharmacovigilance activities that occur in the commercial phase of the product life cycle.

Warnings and precautions are extensions of adverse reactions that might threaten the patient's health and well-being, either because the adverse reaction is severe enough to impact decisions regarding a patient's care or because the adverse reaction might require more specific precautions to be communicated to the patient. For example, the common analgesic and fever reducer paracetamol (called acetaminophen in the U.S.) comes with a warning regarding liver failure in doses in excess of recommendations. Intrinsic risks grouped within warnings and precautions are often discovered during drug development but may also be included to highlight logical consequences of known side effects (as is the case, for example, when drugs that cite drowsiness as an adverse reaction also include a precaution against driving and operating heavy machinery). Warnings and precautions, therefore, are derived from risk assessments in which the gravity of the risk (likelihood of harm, severity of the harm, or a combination thereof) or consequences of drug administration might pose a threat to the patient in an unintended way.

Contraindications are an additional class of intrinsic risk in which a causal relationship between the drug and some other physiological condition (a disease condition or cohort of the patient population) exists and may result in an adverse reaction. For example, certain drugs may be contraindicated for use in children, pregnant or lactating women, or the elderly, while others may be ill-advised for administration when the patient is immunocompromised due to a coexisting condition. In addition, certain drugs may interact with other drugs, resulting in serious consequences that jeopardize the patient's overall health, as is the case when two classes of antidepressant drugs (monoamine oxidase inhibitors, or MAOIs, and selective serotonin reuptake inhibitors, or SSRIs) are used simultaneously [9-17].

Balancing Intrinsic Risks, Medicinal Benefits

Regulatory authorities around the world base product approval decisions on a variety of factors, the most important of which is the benefit-risk profile (also referred to as "risk-benefit"). This evaluation weighs the intrinsic risks of the product (such as the nature of adverse reactions that may occur, the relative severity of the reactions, and their estimated or confirmed rate of occurrence in the target patient population) against the medical benefits of the product. In most cases, the benefits of the product must clearly outweigh the risks in order to be considered appropriate for commercial use; panels of experts are often used to guide the final decision, though quantitative risk assessment models may be employed to calibrate the scientific judgment of decision makers. In some cases, however, the data may reveal that the benefits outweigh the risks only in certain circumstances, or certain risks are severe enough to warrant additional management to ensure the benefit-risk profile remains favorable. In these instances, a regulatory authority may call for the proposal and enactment of a risk management plan (RMP) to manage these risks in a commercial setting.

Risk management plans (referred to as risk evaluation and mitigation strategies, or REMS, in the U.S.) manage intrinsic risk through the application of targeted controls. The nature of the controls varies based on the risk and are intended to assure that the medical benefits of the drug product continue to outweigh the risks. For example, the medication isotretinoin (originally marketed under the brand name Accutane) offers significant relief to patients with severe acne, a painful condition that can negatively impact patients' self-confidence. Isotretinoin is incredibly effective in the treatment of acne, in most cases eliminating the condition altogether; however, it can also cause severe birth defects. Despite the fact that the drug's labelling documents a contraindication for pregnant women, a risk management plan was deemed necessary to ensure that women would not become pregnant while using the product. The REMS for isotretinoin, called iPledge, includes a medication guide, a certification program for prescribing physicians and dispensing pharmacies, and mandatory enrolment of patients in the iPledge program. Risk controls associated with the iPledge program include limited prescribing allowances (no more than 30 days of medication with no refills at any time), contraception counselling between the healthcare provider and patient, two pregnancy tests performed prior to drug administration with monthly follow-up tests thereafter, certification from the patient that she will use two forms of contraception throughout the treatment period, and other similar controls These additional risk controls are intended to ensure that the benefits of isotretinoin (the treatment and potential elimination of severe acne) outweigh the risks (severe birth defects) by preventing fetal exposure to the drug. Regulators and industry acknowledge that the data obtained during drug development and clinical testing may not be sufficient to reveal all intrinsic risks. As a result, ongoing pharmacovigilance is required. Pharmacovigilance is "the science and activities relating to the detection, assessment, understanding and prevention of adverse effects or any other possible drug-related problems." Conducted in a post-market environment, these programs enable the identification of signals that might indicate a new intrinsic risk, or provide additional data regarding the frequency and severity of known risks that can further inform the benefit-risk balance. New information gleaned from pharmacovigilance may result in the discontinuation of a product. For example, the popular weight loss drug fenfluramine was discontinued in 1997 after pharmacovigilance activities revealed a correlation with heart valve disease and pulmonary hypertension, conditions not previously identified in clinical trials [18-19].

Historically, pharmacological research and drug approval regulation have focused primarily on these intrinsic risks; as such, intrinsic risks garnered the most industry and regulatory scrutiny However, intrinsic risks are only a portion of the total risk a patient may be exposed to during their use of a medicinal product. The other category of risks, extrinsic risks, may have similarly grave consequences, yet they have been comparatively neglected until recent times [9, 20-24].

Quality Risk Management Focuses On Extrinsic Risks

Extrinsic risks can be defined as unintended risks to the patient arising from events or circumstances unrelated to the drug product itself; for example, dosing errors, counterfeiting or tampering, drug shortages, or risks introduced during manufacturing, packaging, labelling, distribution, or storage. A critical subset of these are quality risks — risks to patients that are associated with the quality of the medicinal product. These are the risks that constitute the focus of quality risk management. Quality risks are a nefarious bunch. Because quality problems often manifest as failures to meet specifications, and because drug specifications address chemical and biochemical attributes of the product, quality problems are often invisible to the patient. Quality problems can vary by manufacturer and batch — as such, the same drug might expose patients to different quality risks, depending on the brand or product lot number. Patients are rarely informed of the potential quality risks associated with a given product, limiting their ability to make informed choices about their healthcare. Finally, quality risks may greatly affect the benefit-risk balance of product, since products are approved for sale based on a favourable benefit-risk ratio, and quality risks introduce new considerations into that equation. Patients and healthcare providers make an inherent assumption that a product's intrinsic risk has been accepted through regulatory approval and that the drug they administer or receive is both safe and effective. Regulators and industry acknowledge, of course, that deviations from cGMP and product-specific quality attributes could threaten the critical link between an individual dose of a medicinal product and its marketing authorization, thereby rendering the drug "adulterated." In other words, any quality risk imposed in addition to the drug's intrinsic risk upsets the benefit-risk balance and should therefore be identified and controlled [1, 3-6].

When patients take a medicine, they exercise their trust in the pharmaceutical industry. They trust that the product is as it is labelled and that no external circumstance might put them at risk beyond that disclosed in the labelling. They trust that drug manufacturers have produced the product in a safe and consistent way and that their health and safety are protected. The market does not distinguish between high- or low-quality drugs, because acceptable quality is presumed to be present. Those familiar with quality-related recalls and GMP-related warning letters understand that this assumption is far from the truth. While the sources of quality problems, consequences of poor quality drug products, and the resultant patient impacts have been well documented, a rigorous inquiry into a methodological approach to the resolution of these issues was notably absent until the advent of the discipline of quality risk management [6].

UNDERSTANDING THE ICH Q9

International Conference on Harmonisation (ICH) guideline Q9, Quality Risk Management, represents the first internationally recognized guideline specifically addressing QRM for the pharmaceutical and biopharmaceutical industries. Published in June 2005, the guideline offers an overview of general quality risk management principles, an example of a risk management life cycle, discussion around the activities that occur in each life cycle phase and a list of risk tools and quality system areas to which QRM can be applied [1]. This section discusses ICH Q9 in detail, including generally accepted interpretations of the intent and application of the guideline.

In the introduction to the guideline, ICH acknowledges that risk management has been used with much success in other industries, as well as to measure and monitor the intrinsic risk of pharmaceuticals, as discussed in the first article in this series. The introduction describes the gap the guideline seeks to fulfill — that of a risk management framework addressing quality risks that could ultimately impact the patient. Rightly so, ICH Q9 positions the patient at the heart of all QRM activities by acknowledging that, despite the diversity of stakeholder interests (*e.g.*, regulators, industry, healthcare providers, etc.), the interests of the patient are paramount. In practice, industry often uses product quality as a surrogate for the patient, since the impacts of quality risks are easier and more scientifically and statistically valid to measure. Provided product quality is defined with an appropriate link to patient, as in quality by design (QbD), the application of such a proxy is fitting.

ICH Q9 moves on to immediately dispel a myth that had taken hold in prior industry and regulatory cultures — the concept of zero risk. In older quality paradigms, drug manufacturers sought to eliminate risk from their products and processes, taking their cue from regulators who implied, through regulatory publications and inspections, that no degree of risk was acceptable. ICH, however, acknowledges that "the manufacturing and use of a drug (medicinal) product, including its components, necessarily entail some degree of risk." This perspective shifts the industry-regulator conversation from one of absolutes, where quality was a black and white concept of right and wrong, to one focused on balance, where the level of risk is managed to protect product quality and patient safety. The challenge therefore transitions from achieving an esoteric concept of "perfect" quality to understanding what constitutes acceptable risk and striving to achieve that state — perhaps the most significant paradigm shift to occur in the history of drug manufacturing and regulation.

Some other misconceptions regarding risk management are addressed in ICH Q9. For example, many associate risk management with the use of rigorous, detailed tools such as failure modes and effects analysis (FMEA; one of the most common tools employed by industry). However, Q9 is careful to apply the principles of risk management to the practice of risk management itself; using formal or less formal approaches is acceptable, provided the effort is proportionate to the risk of the product, process, or system being assessed. This enables industry to embed risk management in all measures of activities, without the need to undertake a formal, resource intensive exercise. In addition, Q9 is quite clear that the "appropriate use of quality risk management can facilitate but does not obviate industry's obligation to comply with regulatory requirements and does not replace appropriate communications between industry and regulators." Compliance with all applicable laws, of course, is mandatory; risk management may not be used to justify noncompliance or to argue why a specific regulatory requirement need not be fulfilled in a specific instance. Rather, QRM can be used to offer perspectives on how best to comply with statutes and to characterize the aspects of quality that are not specifically associated with compliance.

The benefits of a QRM approach are many, ICH Q9 continues. Better assurance of product quality, for example, may be achieved through the proactive identification and avoidance or minimization of quality risks, as well as the identification of sources of variability in the product and manufacturing process that may be targeted for continuous improvement. The decision making process can be enhanced, as QRM provides a lens through which scientific data and information can be viewed to better weigh options and understand potential outcomes of a given decision. Finally, QRM can "beneficially affect the extent and level of direct regulatory oversight," ostensibly by increasing regulators' trust in a company's self-awareness through transparency of QRM efforts.

Per ICH Q9, the benefits of risk management are to be achieved through the application of a QRM life cycle, an example of which is depicted in Fig. 1. The QRM life cycle is an iterative process consisting of four primary phases: risk assessment, risk control, risk review, and risk communication, each of which is facilitated by the application of risk management tools. While ICH Q9 acknowledges that other life cycle models might be used, the majority of the industry has adopted the exact life cycle model described in the guideline.

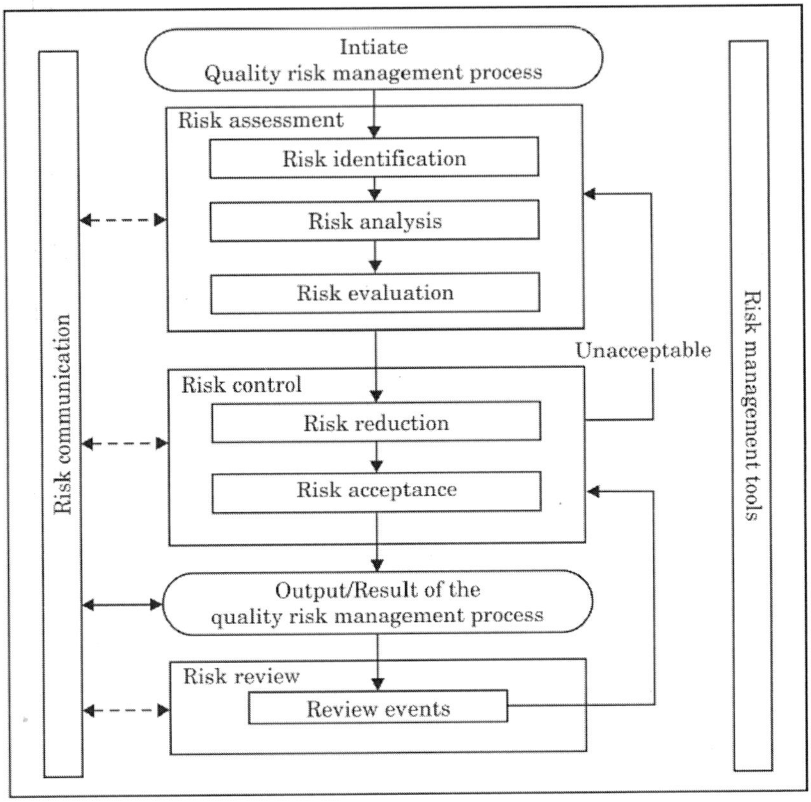

Fig. 1: Quality risk management life cycle, per ICH Q9

Unsurprisingly, the first step in the QRM life cycle is the initiation of the process. ICH Q9 describes activities that might be performed during this initiation step, including the identification of resources, leadership, and timelines; specifying the problem statement (also referred to as the risk question); outlining expected deliverables; and gathering applicable data and information that will serve as inputs into the risk management effort. However, Q9 fails to describe when or under what circumstances the QRM process should be initiated; that is, what triggers might exist that should invoke this critical first step.

After initiation, a risk assessment is performed. This phase of the QRM life cycle seeks to determine which risks associated with the product, process, or system under review are unacceptable — a determination made in three general steps. First, hazards are identified as applicable to the problem statement/risk question (risk identification). Each hazard is then analyzed to determine its relative criticality (risk analysis), using the risk equation (likelihood x severity = risk). Finally, the identified and analyzed risks are compared with predefined criteria to determine their acceptability (risk evaluation). The risk assessment phase of the QRM life cycle typically draws most heavily upon the use of risk management tools, which allow for a methodical, structured way to identify and analyze risks.

The next phase in the QRM life cycle, risk control, focuses on reducing risks to an acceptable level. This phase is perhaps the most important of the QRM life cycle, as it is the point in the process in which control strategies are identified, implemented, and continuously improved; risk control is the phase that assures adequate protection of the patient. There are two general activities that occur in risk control: the first is a concerted reduction in risk through the application of risk mitigation techniques (risk reduction), and the second includes a confirmation that the risk mitigation actions did not adversely affect the overall risk profile through the introduction of new risks or an increase in risk levels, the risks are adequately controlled (*i.e.,* that the risk mitigation actions and other risk controls are effective), and that the resultant risks are therefore acceptable (risk acceptance). In the event the risk remains unacceptable following risk reduction, the QRM life cycle returns to the risk assessment phase, allowing the practitioner to repeat the process.

Following risk control, there is an output. Though included in the QRM life cycle, ICH Q9 does not devote any narrative description regarding what such an output or result might entail. Typically, this portion of the life cycle is interpreted as a documentation point — the point where the results of the risk assessment and risk control outcomes are drafted into a report that describes the risk assessment outcomes (often formatted to align with the risk management tool employed), risk reduction efforts undertaken, and acceptability of the residual risk.

Once risk control is complete and the results have been documented, the risk review phase of the QRM life cycle begins. The objective of this phase is to ensure that prior activities and associated deliverables remain accurate, relevant, and complete in light of changing conditions. Knowledge gained over the product life cycle, ongoing activities such as changes to the product, process, or system, unplanned events such as deviations and customer complaints, and changes in the internal and external business and regulatory climate have the potential to impact decisions made in the risk assessment and risk acceptance phases of the life cycle. Risk review, therefore, entails a periodic or event-driven review of these changes to determine whether the original risk assessment should be updated (as might be the case when new or previously unrecognized hazards emerge or the original estimates of likelihood and severity have changed) and whether the acceptability of the risk may be affected as a result. In this sense, ICH Q9 positions risk review as an opportunity to confirm the continued validity of decisions made within the QRM process; it does not address a mechanism to determine whether the QRM process (and encompassing program) itself has been effective with respect to reducing risk to the patient.

A critical and often overlooked element of the QRM life cycle is risk communication. Risk communication aims to ensure all applicable stakeholders are aware of risk information, including such aspects as the "existence, nature, form, probability, severity, acceptability, control, treatment, detectability or other aspects of risks to quality." Such communication most commonly occurs at the output stage of the QRM life cycle, leveraging the documentation associated with the risk assessment and control activities as the primary mechanism to communicate; however, risk communication can, and should, occur at other stages of the QRM life cycle, based on the nature and criticality of the identified risks. Risk communication can occur between varieties of "interested parties," as depicted in Fig. 2.

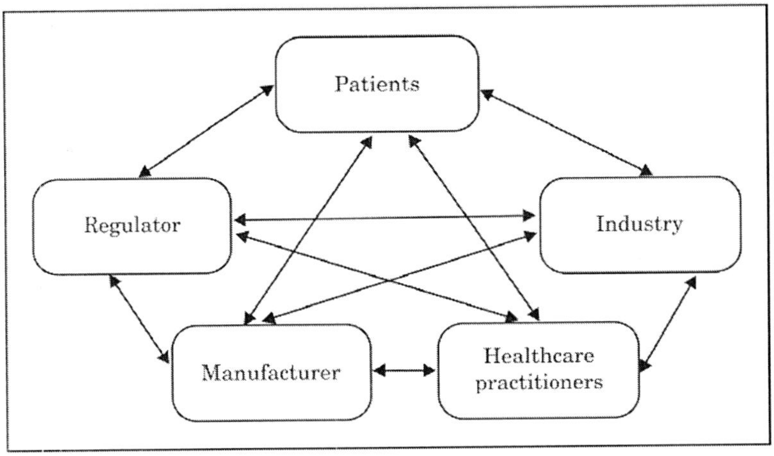

Fig. 2: Potential channels for risk communication

A significant challenge in the communication of quality risks lies in the relatively limited options for communication between QRM practitioners and decision makers and the patient. Unlike intrinsic risks (such as known adverse reactions), which are typically communicated through product labeling, extrinsic risks, including quality risks, have no defined mechanism for communication. ICH Q9 concludes with two annexes: the first describing common risk management tools that may be used to execute the QRM life cycle, and the second describing potential areas for QRM application within the quality system and product life cycle. These annexes are of pivotal importance to the effective implementation of QRM. Despite ICH's insistence that the Q9 guideline "is not intended to create any new expectations beyond the current regulatory requirements," regulatory bodies the world over embraced QRM and have since integrated it at the regional level. Some examples are:

- Inclusion of a new annex to the EU GMPs (Annex 20, which has since been retired and the QRM requirements moved to Chapter 3 of the GMPs), as well as revisions to other directives, annexes, and guidelines to incorporate the principles and practices of quality risk management[3]

- Inclusion of a new annex to the PIC/S GMP guide (also Annex 20) to adopt ICH Q9 for all member countries [4]
- Publication of the WHO guidelines on quality risk management [5]

In this way, QRM has become an integral part of current good manufacturing practices (cGMPs) for pharmaceuticals and biopharmaceuticals, as well as a precision tool to add value to both the pharmaceutical manufacturer and the patient [25-27].

Brainstorming, Affinity Diagrams, and Multi-Voting

Before presenting some of the tools used for risk management, it should be stated that risk management tools are the most useful and complete when applied using a team-based approach. Brainstorming is one tool to generate lists of ideas on what risks may be present and how to manage and mitigate those risks. Brainstorming involves a group of individuals generating ideas without consideration for whether the idea is good or bad. The technique relies on the free flow of ideas; those ideas will typically trigger additional ideas that an individual working alone may not have thought about. A good method for brainstorming is to write the ideas on sticky notes. Once the list of ideas is generated an affinity diagram can be completed to group ideas into logical categories. The process involves having the individuals place the brainstorming session's sticky notes into logical groups. The process usually works best when a set time limit is used. The last step is to prioritize the groups generated from the affinity diagram. One technique that can be used to prioritize the groups is multi-voting, in which each participant ranks the groups. For example, there may be 10 groups, so each person would rank each group 10, 9, 8, 7, etc. by assigning the most important group the highest number. After that, the scores for each group are tallied and the groups are prioritized by the average ranking they received [28].

Benchmarking

Benchmarking can be used to measure your organization's performance against that of other companies that are successful, determine what makes those companies successful, and use the information to improve performance. The benchmarking process, which can be used to assess other organizations, systems, processes, services, and products, can be competitive or technical. Competitive benchmarking measures how an organization is performing as compared to its competitors. Technical benchmarking is conducted to determine the features of products or services. The output of the benchmarking process can be used to perform a strengths, weaknesses, opportunities, and threats (SWOT) analysis or a political, social, economic, and technological (PEST) analysis[28].

Failure Mode and Effects Analysis

Failure mode and effects analysis (FMEA) is a step-by-step approach to identify all possible failures in a design or in a manufacturing or assembly process, or in a product or service. It methodically breaks down the analysis of complex products and processes into manageable steps; risk reduction can then be used to eliminate, contain, reduce, or control failures and risks. The potential areas of use for FMEA are to prioritize risks and monitor the effectiveness of risk control activities. It can be applied to user needs, products (design and manufacture), processes (quality and service), equipment, facilities, and can even be used to analyze a manufacturing operation and its effect on product or process. FMEA identifies elements/ operations within the system that render it vulnerable to risks [1-5]. The output or results of FMEA can be used as a basis for:

- Design and development activities
- Inspection activities (incoming, in-process, and release)
- Commissioning and validation activities
- Supplier management
- Audit findings (internal and external)
- Complaints
- Nonconformances
- Corrective and preventive action (CAPA)

Generally, use of three levels of risk outputs that can be provided by a FMEA: high, medium, and low is preferable. Using three levels provides separation between each level, which facilitates the determination of the risk level. It should also be stated that when determining the risk level, it is generally best practice to be conservative and when in doubt assign a higher level. The use of FMEA is fundamental to the application of management policies, procedures, and practices to the tasks of analyzing, evaluating, controlling, and monitoring risk. The output of the FMEA process is the basis for risk-based thinking that can be readily applied throughout the QMS.

Strengths, Weaknesses, Opportunities, and Threats Analysis

Strengths, weaknesses, opportunities, and threats (SWOT analysis is a planning tool that can be used to identify internal and external strengths and weaknesses. SWOT can be used for short term tactical planning such as processes and systems, and for long-term strategic organizational planning[28].

Strengths

What do you do well?
What unique resources can you draw on?
What do others see as your strengths?

Weaknesses

What could you improve?
Where do you have fewer resources than others?
What are others likely to see as weaknesses?

Opportunities

What opportunities are open to you?
What trends could you take advantage of?
How can you turn your strengths into opportunities?

Threats

What threats could harm you?
What is your competition doing?
What threats do your weaknesses expose you to?

Political, Social, Economic, and Technological Analysis

Political, social, economic, and technological (PEST) analysis is a planning tool that is like the SWOT analysis but is more focused on long-term strategic organizational planning rather than short-term tactical planning [28].

Political

What are the political factors that are likely to affect the business? (Consider risks and opportunities.)

Economic

What are the economic factors that will affect the business? (Consider risks and opportunities.)

Social

What social/cultural aspects are likely to affect the business? (Consider risks and opportunities.)

Technological

What technological changes may affect the business? (Consider risks and opportunities.)

A variation of PEST analysis is the PESTLE analysis. PESTLE analysis is simple PEST analysis with the additional topics of legal and environmental.

Legal

What current and impending legislation will affect the business? (Consider risks and opportunities.)

Environmental

What are the environmental considerations that may affect the business? (Consider risks and opportunities.)

Fault Tree Analysis

Fault tree analysis (FTA) evaluates system (or subsystem) failures individually, represented pictorially in the form of a branching tree of various fault modes. Each level of the tree represents combinations of fault modes that are described with logical operators (*e.g.*, AND, OR). A potential area of use for FTA can be to establish the pathway to the root cause of the failure. FTA can be used to investigate complaints or deviations to fully understand their root cause and to ensure that intended improvements will resolve the issue and not lead to other issues. FTA is an effective tool for evaluating how multiple factors affect a given issue. The output of an FTA includes a visual representation of failure modes. It is useful both for risk assessment and in developing monitoring programs [1-5].

Hazard Analysis and Critical Control Points

Hazard analysis and critical control points (HACCP) is used to manage risks with physical, chemical, and biological hazards. HACCP has seven steps: Conduct

1. A hazard analysis
2. Determine the critical control points
3. Establish critical limits
4. Establish a system to monitor the critical control points
5. Establish corrective actions
6. Establish a system to verify that the HACCP system is working effectively
7. Establish a record-keeping system

HACCP principles can used be to identify, mitigate, and manage risks. HACCP is useful when product and process understanding is sufficiently comprehensive to support identification of critical control points. The output of an HACCP analysis is risk management information that facilitates monitoring of critical points not only in the manufacturing process but also in other life cycle phases [1-5, 29, 30].

Preliminary Hazard Analysis

Preliminary hazard analysis (PHA) is a simple, inductive method of analysis whose objective is to identify the hazards that can cause harm for a given activity, facility, or system. It is usually carried out early in the development of a product or process, when there is little information on design details or operating procedures. It can be used to help identify the hazards or risks for the development of FMEAs and facilitate specification development activities [1-5]. The tool consists of:

- Identification of the likelihood that the risk event will happen
- Qualitative evaluation of the extent of possible injury or damage to health that could result
- A relative ranking of the hazard using a combination of severity and likelihood of occurrence
- Identification of possible remedial measures

HISTORY OF QRM

Those new to the field of quality risk management (QRM) should be familiar with the history of risk management for pharmaceutical and biopharmaceutical products and the role of risk management as a regulatory tool. This section reviews the origins of pharmaceutical risk management and regulatory thinking that led to the establishment of QRM as a unique discipline in pharmaceutical development and manufacturing [1-5].

Early Pharmaceutical Risk Management

Risk management has been a foundational element of the regulation of healthcare products since the inception of related regulatory bodies; indeed, one could argue that the primary reason such regulatory bodies exist is to protect the public from health and safety risks associated with medicinal product use.

Some sources date early formularies, known as pharmacopoeias, back to first century AD Greek texts (such as Pliny's catalogue of medicinal herbs in Naturalis Historae) [31]. The earliest known regulation for such pharmacopoeia was the Salerno Medical Edict issued by Frederick II of

Sicily in 1240, which required apothecaries to prepare their medicinal remedies in the same way. Such laws, which became increasingly pervasive throughout the European continent during medieval times, recognized that consistency across drug formulations was necessary to assure the intended effects of the product, thereby minimizing risk to the patient. The late 19 century saw additional drug legislation come into effect. In the U.S., the first such legislation occurred following the Mexican-American War of 1846-1848, during which American soldiers were administered various drugs for a host of maladies (including malaria, yellow fever, and cholera). Many of these drugs were imported, and some proved to lack the safety and efficacy needed to fully protect the troops. The large number of deaths that occurred in that period can be attributed not only to the typical slaughter seen in wartime, but also to these faulty drugs. The U.S. Import Drug Act of 1848 was sanctioned to ensure that imported drugs were subject to purity and quality testing prior to crossing the border. The Import Drug Act established a theme for drug regulation the world over — advances in pharmaceutical regulation generally occur as a consequence of tragedy in the public eye, seeking to manage risk to patient safety and health reactively [31, 32].

In the U.S., which represents the world's largest population of drug consumers, the growth in both scope and statute of the FDA was borne of several highly publicized tragedies. This pattern of reactivity, where healthcare disaster is antecedent to advances in regulatory science, continues to the present day. For example, the heparin scandal of 2008 led to many dozens of deaths followed by a surge in attention to the management of active pharmaceutical ingredients (APIs) and control over the increasingly complex supply chain. While this reactive process serves to prevent future injury and death, one is left with regret at the prospect that such tragedies could have been anticipated and avoided with the application of the right tools and the right conviction [32].

The Precautionary Principle

The precautionary principle represents one of the first proactive risk management mindsets to reach the public sphere. Originally discussed in the context of environmental law, the principle asserts that when faced with uncertainty regarding a given risk, particularly when the consequences of the risk may have serious and lasting effects, an abundance of caution must be used to provide the desired level of protection to society. The principle serves as a decision making guideline for regulators, to be invoked in circumstances when scientific evidence regarding a certain risk is lacking. In these cases, a failure to actively avoid the risk could lead to an incredible amount of damage, both of person and of cost; therefore, the only appropriate response is to implement the appropriate measures (such as banning a given substance) to protect the public while simultaneously seeking to increase understanding of the risks. As a decision aid, the precautionary principle can be viewed as a rudimentary risk management process. The proactive nature of the precautionary principle stems from the early identification of sources of uncertainty, combined with the concerted effort to avoid the associated risk until the uncertainty can be reduced or eliminated. In this way, the concept of risk is linked with scientific knowledge, such that appropriate risk management can only be effectively applied where there is sufficient understanding upon which sound conclusions can be drawn [15-17, 32].

Modern Inquiries into The Role of Risk Management in Pharmaceutical Regulation

Modern exploration of risk management for drugs and biologics arose with a 1999 report to the FDA commissioner from the Task Force on Risk Management. This task force, established by then-commissioner Dr. Jane Henney, was tasked with determining the technical soundness, consistency, and validity of risk management activities ongoing within the FDA at the time and the development of recommendations to improve the effectiveness and efficiency of these activities. The final report from the task force, Managing the Risks from Medical Product Use: Creating a Risk Management Framework, focused on the premarket benefit-risk assessments performed in support of new drug applications (NDAs) for pharmaceuticals, biological license applications (BLAs) for biopharmaceuticals and biologics, and premarket approvals (PMAs) for medical devices, as well as post-market surveillance activities. The report did not explore quality-related risk management, explaining that "injury from product defects is unusual in the United States because of the great attention paid to product quality control and quality assurance during manufacturing." Despite this claim, the report goes on to cite several case studies of injury and death that, through a contemporary understanding of product quality, could be traced to a lack of QRM.

One example describes a spate of product mix-ups that led to the administration of the wrong drug in a hospital setting, leading to three injuries and one death. The distributor, Burroughs Wellcome, packaged the implicated product in a manner similar to other products — including a foil overlay with a transparent window through which the original product labelling could be viewed. The design of this foil overlay allowed for movement of the product within, allowing the product label to slip below the viewing window, rendering the contents of the package difficult to determine. Sadly, this was the root cause of the injuries and death, as the incorrect product was administered to unwitting patients. The report did not acknowledge that the application of QRM to the foil overlay design might have allowed for the anticipation and avoidance of such use errors[32].

Despite the (perhaps myopic) scope of the report, several recommendations were proposed to improve risk communication and early intervention in the event a potential risk is realized. These recommendations ultimately contributed to the implementation of several successful programs at the FDA, such as formalization of risk evaluation and mitigation strategies (REMS) and the Sentinel adverse event tracking system, serving the agency's goal to leverage improved data collection and risk management to better protect public health [23].

While the 1999 report marked one of the first contemporary explicit inquiries into the existence and effectiveness of risk management and risk-based decision making from regulatory authorities, the topic of quality risk management was not addressed. A fully formed concept for proactive risk management, including the management of both intrinsic and extrinsic risks, emerged in August 2002 with the announcement of a new FDA initiative titled Pharmaceutical cGMPs for the 21 Century – A Risk-Based Approach [8]. The objectives of this initiative were as follows:

- "Encourage the early adoption of new technological advances by the pharmaceutical industry
- Facilitate industry application of modern quality management techniques, including implementation of quality systems approaches, to all aspects of pharmaceutical production and quality assurance
- Encourage implementation of risk-based approaches that focus both industry and Agency attention on critical areas
- Ensure that regulatory review, compliance, and inspection policies are based on state of the-art pharmaceutical science
- Enhance the consistency and coordination of FDA's drug quality regulatory programs, in part, by further integrating quality systems approaches into the Agency's business processes and regulatory policies concerning review and inspection activities"

The final report on the initiative, issued in September 2004, laid out the framework through which the FDA intended to meet or encourage these objectives. While only one of the goals explicitly listed risk management as a focus area, a careful reading of the final report reveals that risk principles underpin the plan. The report foretold the adoption of a quality systems model for quality management and regulation, to be applied by both industry and the FDA alike. While the quality systems concept had been implemented for some time within medical device regulation (for example, within ISO 13485, Medical devices – quality management systems – requirements for regulatory purposes, and 21 CFR 820, Quality System Regulation), the idea of such a system within pharmaceutical and biopharmaceutical circles was novel.

Several advances in regulatory science had been made under the umbrella of the 21 Century initiative, combining knowledge gained through state-of-the art science and technology with a risk-based orientation. These include, for example: Creation of a risk-based model for inspectional oversight Issuance of a new guidance on 21 CFR, Part 11, Electronic Records, Electronic Signatures, to encourage the use of risk-based approaches in the adoption of the requirements Issuance of a new guidance on aseptic processing, Sterile Drug Products Produced by Aseptic Processing – Current Good Manufacturing Practice, to emphasize the need to proactively prevent contamination during sterile product manufacturing and to further encourage the adoption of risk management principles in the assurance of sterility.

The 21 Century initiative marked a paradigm shift in pharmaceutical regulation: a transition away from rule-based compliance (in which the emphasis was on following statute, often at the expense of developing a deep understanding of products, processes, and associated risks) toward a risk-based view of quality and compliance. In the context of this research, perhaps the most interesting emphasis throughout the 21 Century initiative final report is the repeated use of the phrase efficient risk management. The implications here are, of course, that risk management, if not performed properly, can be inefficient. This is quite a curious prospect, given that one of the reasons a risk-based framework would be employed for a given problem is to ensure that resources are efficiently allocated to the things that matter most. The concept that risk management should be performed in an efficient and effective manner to yield an efficient and effective outcome for the patient is one that, while coveted by industry, remains elusive.

QRM AND THE PRODUCT LIFE CYCLE

Quality risk management (QRM) is not a concept to be applied in a vacuum. Rather, QRM is a discipline that provides the most value when used throughout the product life cycle, from the design and development of products, manufacturing process, equipment, and facilities, to the application of the quality system that provides oversight over pharmaceutical production, to the change and life cycle management associated with the product and process. This chapter reviews each of the areas in turn, providing an overview of the key concepts and how QRM can enhance efforts throughout the product life cycle [29].

Quality Risk Management and Quality by Design: ICH Q8 And ICH Q11

ICH Q8, Pharmaceutical Development (currently in its second revision), outlines the process for the development of new pharmaceutical and biopharmaceutical products, based on the principles of quality by design (QbD) — a concept originally introduced by Joseph Juran in his 1992 book Juran on Quality by Design: The New Steps for Planning Quality into Goods and Services. QbD, as described in ICH Q8, is considered by many to have brought drug development into the modern era. In traditional developmental models, a candidate molecule was identified, formulated based on preexisting knowledge of chemistry and pharmacology (or in the case of biopharmaceuticals, standard cell culture and purification processes), scaled to ensure manufacturing processes could serve anticipated demand, and maintained over the commercial life of the product. In many cases, manufacturers, marketing authorization holders (MAHs), and regulators possessed little knowledge of why the product worked and how the associated manufacturing processes supported the clinical effects of the product. As a result, change was demonized; significant efforts were made to keep the manufacturing process static, since the potential implications of change were largely unknown. Over time, this led to antiquated products and associated manufacturing processes, a general reluctance to harness the newest available manufacturing technology, and stalled efforts toward continuous improvement. In QbD development models, the emphasis is on understanding the linkages between the product and its clinical effects in the patient, the manufacturing process and the product it delivers, and manufacturing systems and the processes they support. Quality risk management plays a pivotal role in a QbD development model, by helping to improve the breadth and depth of product and process knowledge and enabling this knowledge to serve as an input into manufacturing process design. The application of QbD (and by extension, QRM) ensures that the manufacturing process delivers a product that consistently meets its specifications, that the defined specifications have meaning in a clinical context. The first step in applying QbD principles to drug development is to define the quality target product profile (QTPP); that is, the overarching quality characteristics of the product to ensure quality, safety, efficacy, and usability. A list of product attributes can be created from the QTPP and preliminary developmental studies. Through the application of QRM principles and tools, the product attributes can be further triaged to identify those that are critical to the patient (critical quality attributes or CQAs) and those that are not. This distinction allows for the focused application of resources (for example, technical and toxicological studies, preclinical and clinical protocol development, and experimental design) to gain knowledge where it matters. The identified CQAs are used as the input into manufacturing process development and characterization. Given the large number of variables that exist in even the simplest manufacturing process, the need to distinguish between those variables that are critical to ensure the CQAs are met and those that are not becomes clear. Process parameters or variables that have a direct link to CQAs are deemed critical process parameters, or CPPs, and are identified through the application of QRM. Manufacturing systems, including facilities, utilities, and equipment, are not discussed in detail in ICH Q8. However, these crucial components are often included in the overarching QbD model, driven by necessity, since manufacturing processes are, by definition, run on equipment, using associated utilities, within a specific-purpose facility. Where a manufacturer chooses to extend its development efforts to manufacturing systems, a similar philosophy applies; the equipment, utilities, and facilities are designed to ensure the CPPs of the associated process are sufficiently controlled. The attributes of manufacturing systems that are linked to CPPs are often referred to as critical aspects (CAs). ICH Q11, Development and Manufacture of Drug Substances (Chemical Entities and Biotechnological/ Biological Entities), was published in 2012 and reiterates the general concepts of QbD devised in ICH Q8 as applied to drug substances. The novel aspects of ICH Q11, when compared with ICH Q8, surround the discussion of how scientific knowledge and QRM can facilitate intended results in a drug development landscape. ICH Q11 directs attention toward a number of applications of QRM in product and process development, including:

- The evaluation of options for the design of the manufacturing process
- The identification of CQAs and CPPs
- The identification of material attributes (*e.g.*, starting materials, raw materials, reagents, etc.) that may have an impact on CQAs
- The identification of functional relationships that link material attributes and process parameters to the CQAs
- The prioritization of attributes or parameters for further study
- The characterization of how downstream processing could affect the acceptability of risk in upstream unit operations (*e.g.*, how impurities present early in the manufacturing process might be acceptable given the process capability of downstream clearance and purification activities), and
- The definition and continuous improvement of the control strategy and associated monitoring program

However, based on the relatively limited descriptions of how to employ QRM in ICH Q11, inconsistencies and confusion may result. For example, ICH Q11 notes that "either formal or informal risk management tools… can be used." This statement could violate the tenants of ICH Q9, which notes that the level of formality of QRM should be commensurate with the level of risk. Indeed, it is difficult to envision how the use of an informal risk tool could be sufficient to characterize the critical elements of a product and process and ensure their control as these are perhaps the highest risk aspects of the product life cycle. In addition, ICH Q11 notes that "the risk assessment can also identify CQAs for which there are inherent limitations in detectability in the drug substance (*e.g.*, viral safety). In these cases, such CQAs should be controlled at an appropriate point upstream in the process," and "when developing a control strategy, a manufacturer can consider implementing controls for a specific CQA at single or multiple locations in the process, depending on the risk associated with the CQA and the ability of individual controls to detect a potential problem." These quotes conflict with the very tenet they seek to explain — that quality cannot be tested into the product, rather it must be built into the product by design. These clauses from ICH Q11 imply that preventive controls should be explored only in the event detection controls are insufficient. Example 2 of ICH Q11 illustrates the risk ranking of process parameters, indicating how QRM could be used to propose that low-risk parameters be changed without prior regulatory authorization, whereas changes to high-risk parameters would be subject to pre-approval. The use of risk ranking is curious in this context, since it is not the level of risk that would enable this determination but rather the severity of the impact a process parameter might have on a CQA — one-half of the risk equation. For example, a process parameter would be considered critical in the event it exhibits a strong statistical correlation with a given CQA — that is, if variation in the process parameter has been demonstrated to lead to variation in one or more CQAs. However, risk is not a measure of the likelihood that this correlation exists, but rather the likelihood that unacceptable variation will occur, given the control strategy. The ideal state, of course, is that all process parameters deemed critical based on their functional relationship with a given CQA are well-controlled — meaning, have a low probability of affecting a CQA in the context of the process and associated control strategy. The objective is to ensure that all CPPs are likewise low risk. It is possible that ambiguities of language and imprecision of examples in the regulatory sphere, such as those illustrated above, could result in a reluctance to apply QRM, or worse, incorrect application [33].

QRM as an Enabler: ICH Q10

ICH Q10, Pharmaceutical Quality System, was published in June 2008 and combined the concepts of QbD, QRM, and GMP into an overarching quality management system to be employed throughout the product life cycle. This document was developed based on existing requirements and guidance, such as ICH Q7, Good Manufacturing Practice Guide for Active Pharmaceutical Ingredients, ISO 9000, Quality Management Systems, and regional GMP requirements. ICH Q10 is often grouped with ICH Q8 and ICH Q9 when describing the fundamental paradigm shift that occurred in the pharmaceutical and biopharmaceutical industries in the late 2000s. The objectives of ICH Q10 are to:

- Achieve product realization, including the definition and attainment of quality specifications as appropriate for the product and patient
- Establish and maintain a state of control, including the definition of what this state of control entails

- Facilitate continual improvement by enhancing the level of control and knowledge of the behaviors of the product and process interface

In order to facilitate these goals, ICH Q10 reintroduced industry to the product life cycle and described how four primary quality system elements (process performance and product quality monitoring, CAPA, change management, and management review) should be employed over the various life cycle stages. A sizable emphasis is placed on management responsibilities, including ultimate accountability for the quality system and its effectiveness. In addition, ICH Q10 squarely positioned QRM and knowledge management as the two enablers of the quality system. The product life cycle begins with drug development, a topic discussed in detail in ICH Q8. Following technology transfer, the product is manufactured at commercial scale for sale — products spend the majority of their life cycle in this stage. The final stage of the life cycle is product discontinuation, which may be done for any number of (usually business-driven) reasons, such as the expiration of patent protection or the commercial availability of newer products for the target disease indication. Quality risk management, knowledge management, and the four primary quality system elements facilitate all aspects of the product life cycle, from development through discontinuation. Risk management principles and practices are embedded in all aspects of the quality system. The intersection of each quality system element (column) and product life cycle stage (row) identifies the benefits of applying QRM at that stage. As an enabler of the quality system, QRM is the "engine" that drives the quality system over the product life cycle, transforming information into knowledge and facilitating the identification of opportunities to improve the product and associated processes to better serve the patient [29,30,33].

Quality Risk Management and Life Cycle Management: ICH Q12

In September 2014, ICH announced a new effort to expand the portfolio of quality guidelines with the addition of ICH Q12, Technical and Regulatory Considerations for Pharmaceutical Product Lifecycle Management. In the final concept paper for this guideline, ICH acknowledged that, true its original name of the International Conference on the Harmonisation of Technical Requirements for Registration of Pharmaceuticals for Human Use, the majority of deliverables had focused on premarket requirements. There was a clear need, however, to extend the scope of the group into later stages of the product life cycle, since "the envisioned post-approval 'operational flexibility' [outlined in ICH Q8 through Q11] has not been achieved." In order to better facilitate this objective, the Q12 guideline will attempt to:

"...provide a framework to facilitate the management of post-approval Chemistry, Manufacturing and Controls (CMC) changes in a more predictable and efficient manner across the product life cycle. Adoption of this guideline will promote innovation and continual improvement, and strengthen quality assurance and reliable supply of product, including proactive planning of supply chain adjustments. It will allow regulators (assessors and inspectors) to better understand, and have more confidence and trust in, a firm's Pharmaceutical Quality System (PQS) for management of post-approval CMC changes."

ICH later changed its name to the International Council on Harmonization to better align with the newly envisioned scope of influence. The announcement of this effort was lauded by industry, as the challenges associated with regional differences in post-approval change management are many. Each country has a distinct set of requirements and expectations regarding how such changes may be handled, whether through a firm's change management program within its quality system (with post implementation communication to regulators), or through rigorous pre-implementation regulatory approval. This poses logistical difficulties, as companies must juggle inventory manufactured with different variations of change, directing product to specific markets based on the CMC approval status of the applicable regulatory authority. This often requires firms to continue manufacturing product under an older manufacturing scheme to ensure consistent supply of product to patients under the jurisdiction of regulatory bodies requiring pre-implementation approval of the change. Because of this, many have noted that the global complexity associated with manufacturing change has discouraged innovation and continual improvement. Among other benefits, ICH Q12 is expected to more clearly link change management with QRM and knowledge management, the two enablers of the quality system as described in ICH Q10. In addition, minimization of the regulatory hurdles associated with product and process life cycle management and post-approval change management should spur renewed focus on improvement and innovation [29, 30. 33].

CONCLUSIONS

Risk management is a process to detect, assess, control, communicate and review the risk. It is a systematic process for evaluation, control, communication and review of risks to the quality of the drug product across the product lifecycle. Every effective quality system includes some form of risk assessment, whether it has been expressly identified as such or not. However, evaluating actions stemming from a risk assessment is not always clear. When a specific risk has been identified, it usually leads to a clear statement of what will happen if certain actions are not taken. When preventive actions based on possible but not proven risks are implemented, however, the results are often difficult to verify. That's because of the absence of objective evidence that the actions taken are directly responsible for preventing the risk from occurring. Effective Quality Risk Management can facilitate better and more informed decisions, can provide regulators with greater assurance of a company's ability to deal with potential risks, and might affect the extent and level of direct regulatory oversight.

REFERENCES

[1] American Academy for Dermatology. Isotretinoin: Treatment for severe acne. Acne and Rosacea. [Online] [Cited: Sep 25, 2016.] www.aad.org/public/diseases/acne-and-rosacea/isotretinoin-treatment-for-severe-acne.
[2] Dunner, D.L. Combining antidepressants. : Shanghai Archives of Psychiatry, 26 (6). Dec 2014.
[3] EC. COM(2000) 1. On the precautionary principle.
[4] EC. The EU pharmacovigilance system. [Online] [Cited: Sep 24, 2016.] http://ec.europa.eu/health/human-use/pharmacovigilance/index_en.htm.
[5] Elliot, W.T. and J. Chan. Fenfluramine and dexfenfluramine withdrawn from market. AHC Media. Nov 1, 1997.
[6] EMA, Committee for Medicinal Products for Human Use. Reflection Paper on Benefit-Risk Assessment Methods in the Context of the Evaluation of Marketing Authorisation Applications for Medicinal Products for Human Use. Mar 2008.
[7] Eudralex. Annex 20: Quality Risk Management. s.l.: Volume 4, EU Guidelines to Good Manufacturing Practice, Medicinal Products for Human and Veterinary Use, Feb 2008.
[8] FDA. A Brief Overview of Risk Evaluation and Mitigation Strategies (REMS). [Online] [Cited: Sep 25, 2016.] http://www.fda.gov/AboutFDA/Transparency/Basics / ucm325201.htm.
[9] FDA. A History of the FDA and Drug Regulation in the United States. [Online] [Cited: Aug 20, 2016.] http://www.fda.gov/centennial/history/history.html.
[10] FDA. Guidance for Industry: Adverse Reactions Section of Labeling for Human Prescription Drug and Biological Products - Content and Format. Jan 2006.
[11] FDA. Guidance for Industry: Warnings and Precautions, Contraindications, and Boxed Warning Sections of Labeling for Human Prescrption Drug and Biological Products - Content and Format. Oct 2011.
[12] FDA. Managing the Risks from Medical Product Use: Creating a Risk Management Framework. May 1999.
[13] FDA. Pharmaceutical cGMPs for the 21st Century — A Risk Based Approach. Final Report. Sep 2004.
[14] FDA. Risk Evaluation and Mitigation Strategies (REMS): The iPledge Program – Single Shared System for Isotretinoin. Apr 2012.
[15] Feb 2000. WHO. The precautionary principle: protecting public health, the environment, and the future of our children. 2004.
[16] Greenemeier, L. Heparin Scare: Deaths from Tainted Blood-Thinner Spur Race for Safe Replacement. Scientific American. [Online] Nov 4, 2008. [Cited: Aug 20, 2016.] http://www.scientificamerican.com/article/heparin-scare-deaths/.
[17] ICH. Final business plan - Q12: Technical and Regulatory Considerations for Pharmaceutical Product Lifecycle Management. Jul 2014.
[18] ICH. Final concept paper - Q12: Technical and Regulatory Considerations for Pharmaceutical Product Lifecycle Management. Jul 2014.
[19] ICH. How ICH Q8, Q9, Q10 guidelines are working together throughout the product lifecycle. Nov 2010.
[20] ICH. ICH Q10: Pharmaceutical Quality System. Jun 2008.
[21] ICH. ICH Q11: Development and Manufacture of Drug Substances (Chemical Entities and Biotechnological/Biological Entities). May 2012.

[22] ICH. ICH Q8(R2): Pharmaceutical Development. 1. Aug 2009.
[23] International Conference on Harmonisation, (ICH) Harmonised Tripartite Guideline, June 2006, ICH Q9: Quality Risk Management, http://www.ich.org.
[24] Pew Health Group. After Heparin: Protecting Consumers from the Risks of Substandard and Counterfeit Drugs. 2011.
[25] PIC/S. Annex 20, Quality Risk Management. Guide to Good Manufacturing Practice for Medicinal Products, Annexes. Oct 2015.
[26] Rago, L. and Santoso, B. Drug Regulation: History, Present and Future. [ed.] C.J. van Boxtel, B. Santoso and I.R. Edwards. Drug Benefits and Risks: International Textbook of Clinical Pharmacology, 2nd edition. s.l.: IOS Press, 2008.
[27] Ranhalker, H. Historical Overview of Pharmaceutical Industry and Drug Regulatory Affairs. Pharmaceutical Regulatory Affairs. S11-002, 2012.
[28] United Nations Education, Science, and Cultural Organization (UNESCO), World Commission on the Ethics of Scientific Knowledge and Technology. The Precautionary Principle. Mar 2005.
[29] van Tellingen, C. Pliny's pharmacopoeia or the Roman treat. *Netherlands Heart Journal,* 15 (3). Mar 2007.
[30] Waldron, K. Quality Risk Management 101: Risks Associated with Medicinal Products. Pharmaceutical Online, Jan 2018.
[31] WHO. The Safety of Medicines in Public Health Programmes: Pharmacovigilance an essential tool.
[32] WHO. WHO guidelines on quality risk management. WHO Technical Report Series 981, Annex 2. 2013.
[33] Wilkins Parker, J. Risk Management in the United States. [Online] [Cited: Aug 20, 2016.] http://www.fda.gov/downloads/Drugs/ResourcesForYou/HealthProfessionals/UCM473163.pdf.

5

Quality Management System

ABSTRACT

This chapter establishes a new ICH model for an effective quality management system for the pharmaceutical industry, referred to as the Pharmaceutical Quality System. Throughout this chapter, the term "pharmaceutical quality system" refers to the ICH Q10 model. This document outlines the quality system requirements for GMP Pharmaceutical Inspectorates. It is intended that each GMP Pharmaceutical Inspectorate uses the document as the basis for developing and implementing its own quality system and for preparing its own quality manual. In addition to providing a basis for self-assessment and a reference document for use by external assessors, establishing and maintaining an effective quality system will generate confidence within and between GMP National Pharmaceutical Inspectorates in the assessment of compliance with good manufacturing practice and/or good wholesale distribution practice. A quality management system (QMS) is a set of policies, processes and procedures required for planning and execution (production/development/service) in the core business area of an organization. (i.e. areas that can impact the organization's ability to meet customer requirements.) ISO 9001 is an example of a Quality Management System. This chapter will show you what a documented Quality Management System (QMS) looks like and how the documents all flow together.

INTRODUCTION

Quality Management System a set of interacting elements based on procedures, policies, resources, and objectives that are established collectively to guide an organization. Quality Management System takes into account all applicable guidelines and regulations that are designed to maintain its robustness. Some people generically refer to the group of documents as a QMS, but specifically it refers to the entire system – the documents just describe it. A QMS integrates the various internal processes within the organization and intends to provide a process approach for project execution. A process based QMS enables the organizations to identify, measure, control and improve the various core business processes that will ultimately lead to improved business performance. A complete Quality Management System must address all the requirements of ISO 9001, including the documentation requirements.

Further, the system provides assurance of continued suitability as well as the capability of processes that are useful in identifying the monitoring and controlling systems. The system is designed to meet the needs of life science and other regulated companies. Companies globally streamline, automate as well as manage efficiently their processes through the regulation of quality management systems. The pharmaceutical company is ultimately responsible for ensuring processes are in place to assure the control of outsourced activities and quality of purchased activities.

Quality Management System stems key regulations for the pharmaceutical industry. It designs a product and its manufacturing process for pharmaceutical organizations to consistently deliver the intended performance as well as meet the needs of healthcare professionals and patients. These approaches transfer product and production process knowledge between development and manufacturing so that to achieve product utilization. Companies establish control strategy that attributes to drug substance and drug product materials that facilitate timely and appropriate corrective action as well as preventive measures. This approach helps the pharmaceutical industries to identify resources of variation affecting process presentation and product quality for possible improvement measures to reduce variation. Additionally, quality management systems provide the tools for measurement in the pharmaceutical industry for analysis as parameters that attribute to the control strategy. A well-defined scheme for process presentation and product superiority assures pharmaceutical industries performance and identifies improvement areas.

ICH Q10 describes one comprehensive model for an effective pharmaceutical quality system that is based on International Standards Organisation (ISO) quality concepts, includes applicable Good Manufacturing Practice (GMP) regulations and complements ICH Q8 "Pharmaceutical Development" and ICH Q9 "Quality Risk Management". ICH Q10 is a model for a pharmaceutical quality system that can be implemented throughout the different stages of a product lifecycle. Much of the content of ICH Q10 applicable to manufacturing sites is currently specified by regional GMP requirements. ICH Q10 is not intended to create any new expectations beyond current regulatory requirements. Consequently, the content of ICH Q10 that is additional to current regional GMP requirements is optional.

ICH Q10 demonstrates industry and regulatory authorities' support of an effective pharmaceutical quality system to enhance the quality and availability of medicines around the world in the interest of public health. Implementation of ICH Q10 throughout the product lifecycle should facilitate innovation and continual improvement and strengthen the link between pharmaceutical development and manufacturing activities.

PRINCIPLE

The holder of a Manufacturing Authorisation must manufacture medicinal products so as to ensure that they are fit for their intended use, comply with the requirements of the Marketing Authorisation or Clinical Trial Authorisation, as appropriate and do not place patients at risk due to inadequate safety, quality or efficacy. The attainment of this quality objective is the responsibility of senior management and requires the participation and commitment by staff in many different departments and at all levels within the company, by the company's suppliers and by its distributors. To achieve this quality objective reliably there must be a comprehensively designed and correctly implemented Pharmaceutical Quality System1 incorporating Good Manufacturing Practice and Quality Risk Management. It should be fully documented and its effectiveness monitored. All parts of the Pharmaceutical Quality System should be adequately resourced with competent personnel, and suitable and sufficient premises, equipment and facilities. There are additional legal responsibilities for the holder of the Manufacturing Authorisation and for the Qualified Person(s).

The basic concepts of Quality Management, Good Manufacturing Practice and Quality Risk Management are inter-related. They are described here in order to emphasise their relationships and their fundamental importance to the production and control of medicinal products. The primary purpose of a quality system is to ensure that adequate quality standards are maintained. The purpose of adopting a common standard for quality system requirements is to achieve consistency in inspection standards between GMP National Pharmaceutical Inspectorates and thus to facilitate mutual recognition of and mutual confidence between those Inspectorates. This standard should help facilitate the implementation of the EEA Joint Audit Programme and PIC/S Joint Re-assessment Programme.

This guideline applies to the systems supporting the development and manufacture of pharmaceutical drug substances (*i.e.,* API) and drug products, including biotechnology and biological products, throughout the product lifecycle. The elements of ICH Q10 should be applied in a manner that is appropriate and proportionate to each of the product life-cycle stages, recognising the differences among, and the different goals of each stage. For the purposes of this guideline, the product lifecycle includes the following technical activities for new and existing products:

- *Pharmaceutical Development*
- Drug substance development;

- Formulation development (including container/closure system);
- Manufacture of investigational products;
- Delivery system development (where relevant);
- Manufacturing process development and scale-up;
- Analytical method development.
- *Technology Transfer*
- New product transfers during Development through Manufacturing;
- Transfers within or between manufacturing and testing sites for marketed products.
- *Commercial Manufacturing*
- Acquisition and control of materials;
- Provision of facilities, utilities, and equipment;
- Production (including packaging and labelling);
- Quality control and assurance;
- Release;
- Storage;
- Distribution (excluding wholesaler activities).
- *Product Discontinuation*
- Retention of documentation;
- Sample retention;
- Continued product assessment and reporting.

Where wholesale inspections are required by national legislation to be carried out by GMP National Pharmaceutical Inspectorate Service, this document specifies the quality system requirements for National Pharmaceutical Inspection Services competent for the inspection of good wholesale distribution practice of medicinal products.

PHARMACEUTICAL QUALITY SYSTEM

Quality Management is a wide-ranging concept, which covers all matters, which individually or collectively influence the quality of a product. It is the sum total of the organised arrangements made with the objective of ensuring that medicinal products are of the quality required for their intended use. Quality Management therefore incorporates Good Manufacturing Practice. GMP applies to the lifecycle stages from the manufacture of investigational medicinal products, technology transfer, commercial manufacturing through to product discontinuation. However the Pharmaceutical Quality System can extend to the pharmaceutical development lifecycle stage as described in ICH Q10, which while optional, should facilitate innovation and continual improvement and strengthen the link between pharmaceutical development and manufacturing activities. ICH Q10 is reproduced in Part III of the Guide and can be used to supplement the contents of this chapter.

The size and complexity of the company's activities should be taken into consideration when developing a new Pharmaceutical Quality System or modifying an existing one. The design of the system should incorporate appropriate risk management principles including the use of appropriate tools. While some aspects of the system can be company-wide and others site-specific, the effectiveness of the system is normally demonstrated at the site level. A Pharmaceutical Quality System appropriate for the manufacture of medicinal products should ensure that:

1. Product realisation is achieved by designing, planning, implementing, maintaining and continuously improving a system that allows the consistent delivery of products with appropriate quality attributes;
2. Product and process knowledge is managed throughout all lifecycle stages;
3. Medicinal products are designed and developed in a way that takes account of the requirements of Good Manufacturing Practice;
4. Production and control operations are clearly specified and Good Manufacturing Practice adopted;
5. Managerial responsibilities are clearly specified;
6. Arrangements are made for the manufacture, supply and use of the correct starting and packaging materials, the selection and monitoring of suppliers and for verifying that each delivery is from the approved supply chain;
7. Processes are in place to assure the management of outsourced activities.
8. A state of control is established and maintained by developing and using effective monitoring and control systems for process performance and product quality.
9. The results of product and processes monitoring are taken into account in batch release, in the investigation of deviations, and, with a view to taking preventive action to avoid potential deviations occurring in the future.
10. All necessary controls on intermediate products, and any other in-process controls and validations are carried out;
11. Continual improvement is facilitated through the implementation of quality improvements appropriate to the current level of process and product knowledge.
12. Arrangements are in place for the prospective evaluation of planned changes and their approval prior to implementation taking into account regulatory notification and approval where required;

13. After implementation of any change, an evaluation is undertaken to confirm the quality objectives were achieved and that there was no unintended deleterious impact on product quality;
14. An appropriate level of root cause analysis should be applied during the investigation of deviations, suspected product defects and other problems.

    This can be determined using Quality Risk Management principles. In cases where the true root cause(s) of the issue cannot be determined, consideration should be given to identifying the most likely root cause(s) and to addressing those. Where human error is suspected or identified as the cause, this should be justified having taken care to ensure that process, procedural or system based errors or problems have not been overlooked, if present. Appropriate corrective actions and/or preventative actions (CAPAs) should be identified and taken in response to investigations. The effectiveness of such actions should be monitored and assessed, in line with Quality Risk Management principles.
15. Medicinal products are not sold or supplied before a Qualified Person has certified that each production batch has been produced and controlled in accordance with the requirements of the Marketing Authorisation and any other regulations relevant to the production, control and release of medicinal products;
16. Satisfactory arrangements exist to ensure, as far as possible, that the medicinal products are stored, distributed and subsequently handled so that quality is maintained throughout their shelf life;
17. There is a process for self-inspection and/or quality audit, which regularly appraises the effectiveness and applicability of the Pharmaceutical Quality System.

Senior management has the ultimate responsibility to ensure an effective Pharmaceutical Quality System is in place, adequately resourced and those roles, responsibilities, and authorities are defined, communicated and implemented throughout the organisation. Senior management's leadership and active participation in the Pharmaceutical Quality System is essential. This leadership should ensure the support and commitment of staff at all levels and sites within the organisation to the Pharmaceutical Quality System. There should be periodic management review, with the involvement of senior management, of the operation of the Pharmaceutical Quality System to identify opportunities for continual improvement of products, processes and the system itself. The Pharmaceutical Quality System should be defined and documented. A Quality Manual or equivalent documentation should be established and should contain a description of the quality management system including management responsibilities.

The overall idea of the quality management system is to support the quality manual and achievement of the short and long-term objectives of the pharmaceutical industry. The procedures help to establish and maintain a clear line of communication to ensure customer requirement is well understood. Subsequently, management reviews in the pharmaceutical industry contributed to determining the stability and the quality of the product. Quality Management Systems assist the design and development process in the pharmaceutical industry to ensure that the resulting product meets the agreed specification. The industry can achieve this by establishing as well as maintaining documented procedures to verify and control the design and development of the product.

BASIC CONCEPT

Monitoring for the duration of scale-up activities can offer a preliminary sign-off process presentation and the thriving integration into manufacturing. Ideally, knowledge obtained at some point in the transfer, and scale-up actions can be valuable in further increasing the control policy. Stability testing of the product in the pharmaceutical industry continues to be executed according to the regulations set by the Quality Management Systems. Activities in the pharmaceutical industry through the quality management system is systematically planned as well as documented. This help to ensure consistency of performance and provide greater assurance that the ending will be suitable. A Quality Management System in its basic concept is quite simple. It seeks to,

- Recognize interested party requirements including Licenses to Trade, guidelines, customer requirements, and the chosen management system standard(s).
- Ensure that all requirements have been met.
- Confirm that employees receive applicable training in the quality system requirements.
- Determine processes, their interaction, inputs and outputs.
- Produce records or evidence that system requirements have been met.
- Measure, monitor and report the performance of the QMS.
- Plan changes to the QMS and take actions to address risks and opportunities as a result of changes.
- Perform internal audit to analyze the QMS and correct nonconformities.
- Continually improve the QMS.

WHAT A QUALITY MANAGEMENT SYSTEM IS NOT?

There are many definitions for general quality management systems. Most of them emphasize the use of some type of system that is repeatable, measurable and constantly improving. In an ISO 9001 (or other ISO standards) quality system, this structured way of delivering a better service or product is supported by documented information such as procedures, work instructions, policies and forms. The key is to provide all those who must execute the quality system with documented, understandable and workable instructions which define both expectations, responsibilities and actions to achieve the stated quality goals. Most of the systems include some type of external and internal auditing process which ensures that the system is in compliance with requirements.

At its core, a quality management system is an integrative element, uniting diverse aspects of a company into a unified purpose of delivering products/services in their best form. Rather than be seen as a cost burden, an effective quality management system is viewed as key component of success. Quality management systems focus on:

- Being centered on the customer or consumer of the good or service, actively providing that customer with the best value possible.
- Some type of continuous improvement program, which implies that there is not a "perfect" state, all processes can be continually improved upon.
- An efficiency imperative that says waste must be reduced and all resources maximized.
- Top management is to support and provide adequate resources to achieve goals.
- It aids or facilitates a clear understanding of expectations between all participants.
- Measurement and accurate data collection are incorporated to support data-driven decision making.
- Documentation of QMS processes is maintained and controlled.

RELATIONSHIP OF ICH Q10 TO REGIONAL GMP REQUIREMENTS, ISO STANDARDS AND ICH Q7

Regional GMP requirements, the ICH Q7 Guideline, "Good Manufacturing Practice Guide for Active Pharmaceutical Ingredients", and ISO quality management system guidelines form the foundation for ICH Q10. To meet the objectives described below, ICH Q10 augments GMPs by describing specific quality system elements and management responsibilities. ICH Q10 provides a harmonised model for a pharmaceutical quality system throughout the lifecycle of a product and is intended to be used together with regional GMP requirements.

The regional GMPs do not explicitly address all stages of the product lifecycle (*e.g.*, Development). The quality system elements and management responsibilities described in this guideline are intended to encourage the use of science and risk based approaches at each lifecycle stage, thereby promoting continual improvement across the entire product lifecycle.

RELATIONSHIP OF ICH Q10 TO REGULATORY APPROACHES

Regulatory approaches for a specific product or manufacturing facility should be commensurate with the level of product and process understanding, the results of quality risk management, and the effectiveness of the pharmaceutical quality system. When implemented, the effectiveness of the pharmaceutical quality system can normally be evaluated during a regulatory inspection at the manufacturing site.

ICH Q10 OBJECTIVES

Implementation of the Q10 model should result in achievement of three main objectives which complement or enhance regional GMP requirements.

Achieve Product Realisation

To establish, implement and maintain a system that allows the delivery of products with the quality attributes appropriate to meet the needs of patients, health care professionals, regulatory authorities (including compliance with approved regulatory filings) and other internal and external customers.

Establish and Maintain a State of Control

To develop and use effective monitoring and control systems for process performance and product quality, thereby providing assurance of continued suitability and capability of processes. Quality risk management can be useful in identifying the monitoring and control systems.

Facilitate Continual Improvement

To identify and implement appropriate product quality improvements, process improvements, variability reduction, innovations and pharmaceutical quality system enhancements, thereby increasing the ability to fulfil quality needs consistently. Quality risk management can be useful for identifying and prioritising areas for continual improvement.

ENABLERS: KNOWLEDGE MANAGEMENT AND QUALITY RISK MANAGEMENT

Use of knowledge management and quality risk management will enable a company to implement ICH Q10 effectively and successfully. These enablers will facilitate achievement of the objectives described above by providing the means for science and risk based decisions related to product quality.

Knowledge Management

Product and process knowledge should be managed from development through the commercial life of the product up to and including product discontinuation. For example, development activities using scientific approaches provide knowledge for product and process understanding. Knowledge management is a systematic approach to acquiring, analysing, storing and disseminating information related to products, manufacturing processes and components. Sources of knowledge include, but are not limited to prior knowledge (public domain or internally documented); pharmaceutical development studies; technology transfer activities; process validation studies over the product lifecycle; manufacturing experience; innovation; continual improvement; and change management activities.

Quality Risk Management

Quality risk management is integral to an effective pharmaceutical quality system. It can provide a proactive approach to identifying, scientifically evaluating and controlling potential risks to quality. It facilitates continual improvement of process performance and product quality throughout the product lifecycle. ICH Q9 provides principles and examples of tools for quality risk management that can be applied to different aspects of pharmaceutical quality.

DESIGN AND CONTENT CONSIDERATIONS

(a) The design, organisation and documentation of the pharmaceutical quality system should be well structured and clear to facilitate common understanding and consistent application.

(b) The elements of ICH Q10 should be applied in a manner that is appropriate and proportionate to each of the product lifecycle stages, recognising the different goals and knowledge available for each stage.

(c) The size and complexity of the company's activities should be taken into consideration when developing a new pharmaceutical quality system or modifying an existing one. The design of the pharmaceutical quality system should incorporate appropriate risk management principles. While some aspects of the pharmaceutical quality system can be company-wide and others site-specific, the effectiveness of the pharmaceutical quality system is normally demonstrated at the site level.

(d) The pharmaceutical quality system should include appropriate processes, resources and responsibilities to provide assurance of the quality of outsourced activities and purchased materials.
(e) Management responsibilities, should be identified within the pharmaceutical quality system.
(f) The pharmaceutical quality system should include the following elements, process performance and product quality monitoring, corrective and preventive action, change management and management review.
(g) Performance indicators, should be identified and used to monitor the effectiveness of processes within the pharmaceutical quality system.

QUALITY MANUAL

A Quality Manual or equivalent documentation approach should be established and should contain the description of the pharmaceutical quality system. The description should include:

(a) The quality policy;
(b) The scope of the pharmaceutical quality system;
(c) Identification of the pharmaceutical quality system processes, as well as their sequences, linkages and interdependencies. Process maps and flow charts can be useful tools to facilitate depicting pharmaceutical quality system processes in a visual manner;
(d) Management responsibilities within the pharmaceutical quality system.

The Pharmaceutical Inspectorate should prepare and maintain a quality manual covering the elements described in this document. It is for each Pharmaceutical Inspectorate to decide on the format and style of their quality manual, but it must include, or make reference to, the quality system procedures which define the activities of the Inspectorate and the arrangements for maintaining the quality system. The reference used to complete it must be quoted too.

ADMINISTRATIVE STRUCTURE

The structure, membership and operation of the GMP Pharmaceutical Inspectorate should be such as to enable it to meet the objectives of quality management and to ensure that impartiality is safeguarded. The personnel of the inspection service, including sub-contracted personnel and experts, should be free from any commercial, financial and other pressures which might affect their judgement and freedom to act. The Pharmaceutical

Inspectorate should ensure that persons or organisations external to the inspection organisation cannot influence the result of inspections. The system for obtaining fees should not improperly influence the inspection procedure. Rules for deontology, ethics, conflict of interest and improper influence should be clearly defined. The relationship of the Pharmaceutical Inspectorate to other agencies and to other organisations within and outside the Inspectorate should be described where relevant. The Pharmaceutical Inspectorate should implement a policy which distinguishes between the process of inspection and that of issuing a manufacturing licence. Where relevant, the Pharmaceutical Inspectorate should implement a policy which distinguishes between the process of inspection and that of providing an advisory service. This service should be of benefit to all of industry and not solely to individual organisations.

ORGANISATION AND MANAGEMENT

Senior management of the Pharmaceutical Inspectorate should make a formal commitment to support the recommended principles embodied in this document by ensuring that the quality policy of the Inspectorate is documented, that it is relevant to the objectives of that organisation and that it is implemented. The responsibility, authority and reporting structure of the Pharmaceutical Inspectorate should be clearly defined and documented. The structure should be defined in organisation charts and should be supported by written job descriptions for each member of staff.

There should be nominated an appropriately qualified and experienced person or persons with responsibility to carry out the quality assurance function, including implementing and maintaining the quality system. This person should have direct access to senior management. The Pharmaceutical Inspectorate should have sufficient resources at all levels to enable it to meet its objectives effectively and efficiently. Senior management should ensure that all personnel are competent and qualified to carry out their assigned duties and that they receive appropriate training. Such training should be documented and its effectiveness assessed periodically. There should be a system for periodic management review of the quality system. Such reviews should be documented and records should be retained for a defined period.

MANAGEMENT RESPONSIBILITY

Leadership is essential to establish and maintain a company-wide commitment to quality and for the performance of the pharmaceutical quality system.

Management Commitment

(a) Senior management has the ultimate responsibility to ensure an effective pharmaceutical quality system is in place to achieve the quality objectives, and that roles, responsibilities, and authorities are defined, communicated and implemented throughout the company.

(b) Management should:

(1) Participate in the design, implementation, monitoring and maintenance of an effective pharmaceutical quality system;

(2) Demonstrate strong and visible support for the pharmaceutical quality system and ensure its implementation throughout their organisation;

(3) Ensure a timely and effective communication and escalation process exists to raise quality issues to the appropriate levels of management;

(4) Define individual and collective roles, responsibilities, authorities and inter-relationships of all organisational units related to the pharmaceutical quality system. Ensure these interactions are communicated and understood at all levels of the organisation. An independent quality unit/structure with authority to fulfil certain pharmaceutical quality system responsibilities is required by regional regulations;

(5) Conduct management reviews of process performance and product quality and of the pharmaceutical quality system;

(6) Advocate continual improvement;

(7) Commit appropriate resources.

QUALITY POLICY

(a) Senior management should establish a quality policy that describes the overall intentions and direction of the company related to quality.

(b) The quality policy should include an expectation to comply with applicable regulatory requirements and should facilitate continual improvement of the pharmaceutical quality system.

(c) The quality policy should be communicated to and understood by personnel at all levels in the company.

(d) The quality policy should be reviewed periodically for continuing effectiveness.

QUALITY PLANNING

(a) Senior management should ensure the quality objectives needed to implement the quality policy are defined and communicated.

(b) Quality objectives should be supported by all relevant levels of the company.

(c) Quality objectives should align with the company's strategies and be consistent with the quality policy.

(d) Management should provide the appropriate resources and training to achieve the quality objectives.

(e) Performance indicators that measure progress against quality objectives should be established, monitored, communicated regularly and acted upon as appropriate.

RESOURCE MANAGEMENT

(a) Management should determine and provide adequate and appropriate resources (human, financial, materials, facilities and equipment) to implement and maintain the pharmaceutical quality system and continually improve its effectiveness.

(b) Management should ensure that resources are appropriately applied to a specific product, process or site.

INTERNAL COMMUNICATION

The size of the company determines the level of management and the timely communication to raise related quality issues.

(a) Management should ensure appropriate communication processes are established and implemented within the organisation.

(b) Communications processes should ensure the flow of appropriate information between all levels of the company.

(c) Communication processes should ensure the appropriate and timely escalation of certain product quality and pharmaceutical quality system issues.

MANAGEMENT REVIEW

(a) Senior management should be responsible for pharmaceutical quality system governance through management review to ensure its continuing suitability and effectiveness.

(b) Management should assess the conclusions of periodic reviews of process performance and product quality and of the pharmaceutical quality system.

MANAGEMENT OF OUTSOURCED ACTIVITIES AND PURCHASED MATERIALS

The pharmaceutical quality system, including the management responsibilities described in this section, extends to the control and review of any outsourced activities and quality of purchased materials. The pharmaceutical company is ultimately responsible to ensure processes are in place to assure the control of outsourced activities and quality of purchased materials. These processes should incorporate quality risk management and include:

(a) Assessing prior to outsourcing operations or selecting material suppliers, the suitability and competence of the other party to carry out the activity or provide the material using a defined supply chain (*e.g.*, audits, material evaluations, qualification);
(b) Defining the responsibilities and communication processes for quality-related activities of the involved parties. For outsourced activities, this should be included in a written agreement between the contract giver and contract acceptor;
(c) Monitoring and review of the performance of the contract acceptor or the quality of the material from the provider, and the identification and implementation of any needed improvements;
(d) Monitoring incoming ingredients and materials to ensure they are from approved sources using the agreed supply chain.

MANAGEMENT OF CHANGE IN PRODUCT OWNERSHIP

When product ownership changes, (*e.g.*, through acquisitions) management should consider the complexity of this and ensure:

(a) The ongoing responsibilities are defined for each company involved;
(b) The necessary information is transferred.

CONTINUAL IMPROVEMENT OF PROCESS PERFORMANCE AND PRODUCT QUALITY

This section describes the lifecycle stage goals and the four specific pharmaceutical quality system elements that augment regional requirements to achieve the ICH Q10 objectives. It does not restate all regional GMP requirements.

Lifecycle Stage Goals

The goals of each product lifecycle stage are described below.

Pharmaceutical Development

The goal of pharmaceutical development activities is to design a product and its manufacturing process to consistently deliver the intended performance and meet the needs of patients and healthcare professionals, and regulatory authorities and internal customers' requirements. Approaches to pharmaceutical development are described in ICH Q8. The results of exploratory and clinical development studies, while outside the scope of this guidance, are inputs to pharmaceutical development.

Technology Transfer

The goal of technology transfer activities is to transfer product and process knowledge between development and manufacturing, and within or between manufacturing sites to achieve product realisation. This knowledge forms the basis for the manufacturing process, control strategy, process validation approach and ongoing continual improvement.

Commercial Manufacturing

The goals of manufacturing activities include achieving product realisation, establishing and maintaining a state of control and facilitating continual improvement. The pharmaceutical quality system should assure that the desired product quality is routinely met, suitable process performance is achieved, the set of controls are appropriate, improvement opportunities are identified and evaluated, and the body of knowledge is continually expanded.

Product Discontinuation

The goal of product discontinuation activities is to manage the terminal stage of the product lifecycle effectively. For product discontinuation, a pre-defined approach should be used to manage activities such as retention of documentation and samples and continued product assessment (*e.g.*, complaint handling and stability) and reporting in accordance with regulatory requirements.

Pharmaceutical Quality System Elements

The elements described below might be, required in part under regional GMP regulations. However, the Q10 model's intent is to enhance these elements in order to promote the lifecycle approach to product quality. These four elements are:

- Process performance and product quality monitoring system;
- Corrective action and preventive action (CAPA) system;
- Change management system;

- Management review of process performance and product quality.
- Complaints

These elements should be applied in a manner that is appropriate and proportionate to each of the product lifecycle stages, recognising the differences among, and the different goals of, each stage. Throughout the product lifecycle, companies are encouraged to evaluate opportunities for innovative approaches to improve product quality.

Each element is followed by a table of example applications of the element to the stages of the pharmaceutical lifecycle.

Process Performance and Product Quality Monitoring System

Pharmaceutical companies should plan and execute a system for the monitoring of process performance and product quality to ensure a state of control is maintained. An effective monitoring system provides assurance of the continued capability of processes and controls to produce a product of desired quality and to identify areas for continual improvement. The process performance and product quality monitoring system should:

(a) Use quality risk management to establish the control strategy. This can include parameters and attributes related to drug substance and drug product materials and components, facility and equipment operating conditions, in-process controls, finished product specifications, and the associated methods and frequency of monitoring and control. The control strategy should facilitate timely feedback / feed-forward and appropriate corrective action and preventive action;

(b) Provide the tools for measurement and analysis of parameters and attributes identified in the control strategy (*e.g.*, data management and statistical tools);

(c) Analyse parameters and attributes identified in the control strategy to verify continued operation within a state of control;

(d) Identify sources of variation affecting process performance and product quality for potential continual improvement activities to reduce or control variation;

(e) Include feedback on product quality from both internal and external sources, *e.g.*, complaints, product rejections, non-conformances, recalls, deviations, audits and regulatory inspections and findings;

(f) Provide knowledge to enhance process understanding, enrich the design space (where established), and enable innovative approaches to process validation.

Corrective Action and Preventive Action (CAPA) System

Through the quality management system, pharmaceutical industry focuses on correcting as well as preventing problems within the sector. It is evident that preventing problems is cheaper as compared to fixing them after they occur. As such the range and the nature of manufacturing by-product, inherent variability in biological products are likely to be variable. The quality management system principles help the pharmaceutical industry in the verification of its activities. The pharmaceutical company should have a system for implementing corrective actions and preventive actions resulting from the investigation of complaints, product rejections, non-conformances, recalls, deviations, audits, regulatory inspections and findings, and trends from process performance and product quality monitoring. A structured approach to the investigation process should be used with the objective of determining the root cause. The level of effort, formality, and documentation of the investigation should be commensurate with the level of risk, in line with ICH Q9. CAPA methodology should result in product and process improvements and enhanced product and process understanding. The procedure should include the prescribing, implementation and verification of corrective action. The procedure should cover also corrective actions arising from the investigation of complaints and other observations relating to the activities of the Inspectorate. The system should include a description of the steps to be taken in assessing the need for quality improvement and preventive action. Corrective and preventive actions should be documented and records should be retained for a defined period.

Change Management System

Innovation, continual improvement, the outputs of process performance and product quality monitoring and CAPA drive change. In order to evaluate, approve and implement these changes properly, a company should have an effective change management system. There is generally a difference in formality of change management processes prior to the initial regulatory submission and after submission, where changes to the regulatory filing might be required under regional requirements. The changes to the quality management systems in the pharmaceutical industry have evaluated the marketing authorization contributing the appropriate expertise and knowledge from relevant areas. The change management system ensures continual improvement is undertaken in a timely and effective manner. It should provide a high degree of assurance there are no unintended consequences of the change. The change management system should include the following, as appropriate for the stage of the lifecycle:

(a) Quality risk management should be utilised to evaluate proposed changes. The level of effort and formality of the evaluation should be commensurate with the level of risk;

(b) Proposed changes should be evaluated relative to the marketing authorisation, including design space, where established, and/or current product and process understanding. There should be an assessment to determine whether a change to the regulatory filing is required under regional requirements. As stated in ICH Q8, working within the design space is not considered a change (from a regulatory filing perspective). However, from a pharmaceutical quality system standpoint, all changes should be evaluated by a company's change management system;

(c) Proposed changes should be evaluated by expert teams contributing the appropriate expertise and knowledge from relevant areas (*e.g.*, Pharmaceutical Development, Manufacturing, Quality, Regulatory Affairs and Medical), to ensure the change is technically justified. Prospective evaluation criteria for a proposed change should be set;

(d) After implementation, an evaluation of the change should be undertaken to confirm the change objectives were achieved and that there was no deleterious impact on product quality.

Management Review of Process Performance and Product Quality

Management review should provide assurance that process performance and product quality are managed over the lifecycle. Depending on the size and complexity of the company, management review can be a series of reviews at various levels of management and should include a timely and effective communication and escalation process to raise appropriate quality issues to senior levels of management for review.

(a) The management review system should include:
  (1) The results of regulatory inspections and findings, audits and other assessments, and commitments made to regulatory authorities;
  (2) Periodic quality reviews, that can include:
    (i) Measures of customer satisfaction such as product quality complaints and recalls;
    (ii) Conclusions of process performance and product quality monitoring;
    (iii) The effectiveness of process and product changes including those arising from corrective action and preventive actions.
  (3) Any follow-up actions from previous management reviews.

(b) The management review system should identify appropriate actions, such as:
  (1) Improvements to manufacturing processes and products;
  (2) Provision, training and/or realignment of resources;
  (3) Capture and dissemination of knowledge.

Complaints

The Pharmaceutical Inspectorate should establish and maintain a procedure for dealing with complaints relating to its activities, or those of its personnel, and any contracted persons or organisations. The procedure should describe the application and verification of corrective action arising from the investigation of complaints.

Records should be maintained of all complaints received and actions taken and should be retained for a defined period.

Inspection

The Pharmaceutical Inspectorate should conduct repeated inspections of manufacturers and/ or wholesale distributors and should issue inspection reports in accordance with National or European Community requirements as appropriate. The Pharmaceutical Inspectorate should have the documented procedures and resources to enable inspection of manufacturing and wholesale distribution operations to be carried out in accordance with the official guidelines and National legislation and in accordance with a formal inspection plan. All instructions, standards or written procedures, worksheets, check lists and reference data relevant to the work of the Pharmaceutical Inspectorate should be maintained up-to-date and be readily available to staff. When more than one inspector is involved in an inspection, a lead inspector should be appointed to co-ordinate inspection activities. The inspection report should normally be prepared by the lead inspector and should be agreed by all participating inspectors.

Inspection report format should be in compliance with the PIC/S procedure or European model. Report should follow the procedure above. The inspection report should be sent to the responsible person of the inspected company (preferably the authorised person or qualified person). The lead inspector and all concerned inspectors should participate in assessing the eventual reply or replies to determine the appropriateness of corrective actions and the GMP status of the company. Observations and/ or data obtained in the course of inspections should be recorded in a timely manner to prevent loss of relevant information. Completed inspections should be reviewed to ensure that the requirements are met.

Internal Audit

The Pharmaceutical Inspectorate should carry out and document periodic internal audits of its operations to assess compliance with the requirements of the quality system. Results of internal audits and associated corrective actions should be reviewed as part of the management review process. Internal audit processes and documents, auditors qualifications should be clearly defined. Internal audit records should be retained for a defined period.

CONTINUAL IMPROVEMENT OF THE PHARMACEUTICAL QUALITY SYSTEM

This section describes activities that should be conducted to manage and continually improve the pharmaceutical quality system.

Management Review of the Pharmaceutical Quality System

Management should have a formal process for reviewing the pharmaceutical quality system on a periodic basis. The review should include:

(a) Measurement of achievement of pharmaceutical quality system objectives;

(b) Assessment of performance indicators that can be used to monitor the effectiveness of processes within the pharmaceutical quality system, such as:

  (1) Complaint, deviation, CAPA and change management processes;

  (2) Feedback on outsourced activities;

  (3) Self-assessment processes including risk assessments, trending, and audits;

  (4) External assessments such as regulatory inspections and findings and customer audits.

Monitoring of Internal and External Factors Impacting the Pharmaceutical Quality System

Factors monitored by management can include:

(a) Emerging regulations, guidance and quality issues that can impact the Pharmaceutical Quality System;

(b) Innovations that might enhance the pharmaceutical quality system;

(c) Changes in business environment and objectives;

(d) Changes in product ownership.

Outcomes of Management Review and Monitoring

The outcome of management review of the pharmaceutical quality system and monitoring of internal and external factors can include:

(e) Improvements to the pharmaceutical quality system and related processes;

(f) Allocation or reallocation of resources and/or personnel training;

(g) Revisions to quality policy and quality objectives;

(h) Documentation and timely and effective communication of the results of the management review and actions, including escalation of appropriate issues to senior management.

CONCLUSIONS

Pharmaceutical market has undergone significant change forcing pharmaceutical companies to focus on the needs and internal efficiency to continue to compete effectively. Therefore, QMS supports pharmaceutical industry to enhance the quality and availability of medicines around the globe in the interest of public health. Through the regulation of quality management system, organizations facilitate innovation along with continual improvement as well as strengthen the link between pharmaceutical development and manufacturing activities. The areas of continual improvement in pharmaceutical industry include enhancements of the pharmaceutical quality system, identifying and prioritizing the quality of the products as well as consistently fulfilling the quality of drug manufacturers. Quality Management System in the pharmaceutical industry helps to develop an effective monitoring control based on the performance as well as product quality. Further, the system provides assurance of continued suitability as well as the capability of processes that are useful in identifying the monitoring and controlling systems. The system is designed to meet the needs of life science and other regulated companies. Companies globally streamline, automate as well as manage efficiently their processes through the regulation of quality management systems. The pharmaceutical company is ultimately responsible for ensuring processes are in place to assure the control of outsourced activities and quality of purchased activities. It is evident that control parameters will be required to give the necessary level of confidence in the eminence of the end product in the drug industry. Therefore, the involvement of quality management systems in the industry has ensured that equipment is maintained to a standard sufficient capable of performing its intended functions.

FURTHER READINGS

ICH. How ICH Q8, Q9, Q10 guidelines are working together throughout the product life-cycle. Nov 2010.

ICH. ICH Q10: Pharmaceutical Quality System. Jun 2008

PIC/S Recommendation on Quality System Requirements for Pharmaceutical inspectorates. PI002-3, 2007

6

Documentation: Control and Practice

ABSTRACT

'If it's not written down, then it didn't happen!' The basic rules in any good manufacturing practice (GMP) regulations specify that the pharmaceutical manufacturer must maintain proper documentation and records. Documentation helps to build up a detailed picture of what a manufacturing function has done in the past and what it is doing now and, thus, it provides a basis for planning what it is going to do in the future. Regulatory inspectors, during their inspections of manufacturing sites, often spend much time examining a company's documents and records. Effective documentation enhances the visibility of the quality assurance system. Good Documentation Practice (GDP or GDocP), a term used in the pharmaceutical industry, is essential for the integrity of data collection and reporting for supporting development, registrations, commercialization, and life-cycle management of pharmaceutical products. Adhering to the GDPs assures preventing errors within the manufacturing environment and during the analysis of pharmaceutical products which could otherwise impact product quality, and safety of the patients, state of manufacturing facilities, and related activities. Compliance to GDPs is required by both the US and the European regulatory authorities, i.e., FDAs CFR (Code of Federal Regulations) and EMA (European Medicines Agency). In addition to the United States of Pharmacopeia (USP) issuing a general chapter <1029>, the World Health Organization (WHO), Health Canada, and EudraLex (the collection of rules and regulations governing medicinal products in European Union) have published specific guidance related to GDPs. On the other hand GDP is an important part of current Good Manufacturing Practices (cGMPs) in the US. In addition to regulatory requirements, it is also important to maintain accurate records and documentations of activities in the pharmaceutical industry for business reasons which allow one to critically evaluate the internal procedures for improvement of processes and products and spending less time in repeating studies, if needed, rather than starting from the beginning.

INTRODUCTION

Document is any written statement or proof of any activity in pharmaceuticals. Documentations are to define the manufacturers system of information and control, to minimize the risk of misinterpretation and errors inherent in oral or casually written communication, to provide unambiguous procedures to be followed to provide confirmation of performance, to allow calculations to be checked and to allow tracing of batch history. Due to the importance given to documentation in pharma "good documentation practices" is required. Good documentation is a systematic procedure of preparation, checking, verifying, issuing, storing and reviewing of any documents. Batch record is an important document kept along with reserve sample until one year of expiry of the product, and final products are release only after proper review of BMR, even after testing of Product from QC, product would not be released without review and completing of BMR and other documents .every activity should be available written form as SOPs is a requirements of GMP. Control of document is also an important part of GDP to reduce error and misuses of any documents. Master copy for all activity should be prepared such as SOPs started from Draft copy and finalizes after checking and reviewing and Approved by QA documentation. Final copy should be printed as Master copy and stamped as "master copy" by red ink. A photocopy of master copy should be issued to concern department with stamped "control copy". A record should be maintained for issuing any documents with sign and date. Every document should have effective date, review date and revision no.

The GDP can be defined as "Good documentation practice is an essential part of the quality assurance and such, related to all aspects of GMP" this definition is based on WHO. Clearly written documents prevent errors of various activities in pharma each and every activity is written in specific documents such as SOPs and strictly followed. Spoken communications may be create errors so that all important documents such as Master formula record, procedure and record must be free from errors and Documented. It is difficult to make a list of required documents and totally depend upon Companies activity or environment. Followings are the activity factors considered during designing of any documents.

1. Type of formulation
2. Country requirements
3. Availability of ERP or SAP system

PRINCIPLE OF DOCUMENTATION

Good data and record management are critical elements of the pharmaceutical quality system and a systematic approach should be implemented to provide a high level of assurance that across the product life cycle all G x P records and data are accurate, consistent, trustworthy and reliable. The data governance programme should include policies and governance procedures that address the general principles listed below for a good data management program. These principles are clarified with additional detail in sections below.

Applicability to both paper and electronic data

The requirements for good data and record management that assure robust control of data validity apply equally to paper and electronic data. Organizations subject to G x P should be fully aware that reverting from automated/ computerized to manual/paper-based systems does not in itself remove the need for robust management controls.

Applicability to contract givers and contract acceptors

The principles of these guidelines apply to contract givers and contract acceptors. Contract givers are ultimately responsible for the robustness of all decisions made on the basis of G x P data, including those that are made on the basis of data provided to them by contract acceptors. Contract givers therefore should perform due diligence to assure themselves that contract acceptors have in place appropriate programmes to ensure the veracity, completeness and reliability of provided data.

Good documentation practices

To achieve robust decisions and data sets based need to be reliable and complete. Good documentation practices (GDP) should be followed in order to ensure all records, both paper and electronic, allow the full reconstruction of the related activities.

Management governance

To establish a robust and sustainable good data management system it is important that senior management ensure that appropriate data management governance programmes are in place.

Quality culture

Management, together with the quality unit, should establish and maintain a working environment often referred to as a quality culture that minimizes the risk of noncompliant records and erroneous records and data. An essential element is the transparent and open reporting of deviations, errors, omissions and aberrant results at all levels of the organization. Steps should be taken to prevent and detect and correct weaknesses in systems and procedures that may lead to data errors so as to continually improve scientific robustness of decision making of the organization.

Quality risk management and sound scientific principles

Assuring robust decision making requires valid and complete data, appropriate quality and risk management systems, adherence to sound scientific and statistical principles. For example, the scientific principle of being an objective, unbiased observer regarding the outcome of a sample analysis requires that suspect results be investigated and rejected from the reported results only if they are clearly due to an identified cause. Adhering to good data and record-keeping principles requires that any rejected results be recorded, together with a documented justification for their rejection, and that this documentation is subject to review and retention.

Data life cycle

Continual improvement of products to ensure and enhance their safety, efficacy and quality requires a data governance approach to ensure management of data integrity risks throughout all phases of the process by which data are recorded, processed, reviewed, reported, retained, retrieved and subject to ongoing review. In order to ensure that the organization, assimilation and analysis of data into information facilitates evidence based and reliable decision-making, data governance should address data ownership and accountability for data process(es) and risk management of the data lifecycle.

Design of record-keeping methodologies and systems

Record-keeping methodologies and systems, whether paper or electronic, should be designed in a way that encourages compliance with the principles of data integrity.

Maintenance of record-keeping systems

The systems implemented and maintained for both paper and electronic record-keeping should take account of scientific and technical progress. Systems, procedures and methodology used to record and store data should be periodically reviewed and updated as necessary.

PURPOSE OF DOCUMENTATIONS

Pharmaceutical regulatory systems worldwide have always depended upon the knowledge of organizations that develop, manufacture and package, test, distribute and monitor pharmaceutical products. Implicit in the assessment and review process is a trust between the regulator and the regulated that the information submitted in dossiers and used in day-to-day decision-making is comprehensive, complete and reliable. Data on which these decisions are based should therefore be complete as well as being accurate, legible, contemporaneous, original and attributable;

commonly referred to as "ALCOA". These basic ALCOA principles and the related good practice expectations that assure data reliability are not new. The reasons for this increased level of authority concern regarding data reliability are undoubtedly multi-factorial and include increased regulatory awareness and concern regarding gaps between industry choices and appropriate and modern control strategies. Contributing factors include failures by organizations to apply robust systems that inhibit data risks, to improve the detection of situations where data reliability may be compromised, and/ or to investigate and address root causes when failures do arise. Documents and documentation control system assure that the organization have a robust system. Along with this document accomplish following purposes:

- Defines specifications and procedures for all materials and methods of manufacture and control
- Ensures all personnel know what to do and when to do it
- Ensure that authorized persons have all information necessary for release of product
- Ensures documented evidence, traceability, provide records and audit trail for investigation
- Ensures availability of data for validation, review and statistical analysis.

CLASSIFICATION OF DOCUMENTATION

Following are the classification of Documents

- Policy documents
- Commitment documents
- Instructive documents
- Executive documents

PREPARATION, ISSUES AND USES OF DOCUMENTS

Documents should be carefully and logically specify to prevent wrong uses. All necessary information's are written unambiguously. Each document includes:

1. Company name
2. Purpose and title of documents
3. Identification No and revision No.
4. Date of authorization
5. Date of review

6. Signature of prepared by, checked and authorized by.
7. Distribution list
8. Page no.
9. Reason for revision should be documented.
10. Abbreviation and reference

Each document is clear and computerized so that it is readable, issued documents signed by a concern person to indicate a verified issue. Any correction is made by cutting with single line with signature and date, do not overwrite. Document to filled have a sufficient space, ball ink pen should be used for hand written filling.

DOCUMENT CONTROL

The process by which a manufacturer ensures that all procedures used and documents generated in cGMP – related actions are current, accurate and approved.

Purpose of document control to control issuance, possession, use and revision of master documents including:

Standard Operating Procedures
Data collection forms
Validation Protocols
Master formulae
Batch records
Function of Quality Assurance Unit

Initially document is prepared by concern department as draft and draft is reviewed by dept. head and final draft is send to QA department that convert a draft to a final documents checked and approved by authorize person. Control copies are issued to concern department and issuance records are maintained. After approval of documents such as sops quality assurance must ensure that all users/ concerned department gets training before the implementation of the sops record of such training must be maintained. A training co-coordinator preferably the head of user department or any designated individuals shall be responsible for organizing the training. After successful implementation of training on any sops, the sops become effective. Original sops are stamped as "MASTER COPY" with red ink, master copy are stored under supervision and photocopy of master copy duly stamped as "CONTROL COPY" in blue color. Sops distribution list should be maintained for issuance records, change in sops need to initiated change request and all issue copies are retrieve and new one implemented with training.

Why is the control of records important?

- Evidence of activities performed;
- Evidence of compliance with GMP requirements and company policies, procedures and work instructions;
- Effectiveness of Pharmaceutical QMS;
- Traceability;
- Process authenticity and consistency ;
- Evidence of the good quality attributes of the medicinal products manufactured; and
- In case of complaints, records could be used for investigational purposes.

GENERATION, DISTRIBUTION AND CONTROL OF TEMPLATE RECORDS

Managing and controlling master records is necessary to ensure that the risk of someone inappropriately using and/or falsifying a record 'by ordinary means' (*i.e.* not requiring the use of specialist fraud skills) is reduced to an acceptable level. The following expectations (Table 1) should be implemented using a quality risk management approach, considering the risk and criticality of data recorded. An index of all the template records should be maintained by QA organisation. This index should mention for each type of template record at least the following information: title, reference number including version number, location (*e.g.*, documentation data base, effective date, next review date, etc. Table 1 gives an insight for the expectations during documentation process and risks associated if these expectations are not met.

Table 1: Expectations and potential risks failing these expectations:

Expectation Generation	***Potential risk if not meeting expectation***
All documents should have a unique identification number (including the version number) and should be checkcked, approved, signed and dated. The use of uncontrolled documents should be prohibited by local procedures. The use of temporary recording practices, *e.g.* scraps of paper should be prohibited.	Uncontrolled documents increase the potential or omission or loss of critical data as these documents may not be designed to correctly record critical data. It may be easier to falsify uncontrolled records. Risk of using superseded forms if there is no version control or controls for issuance.
The document design should provide sufficient space for manual data entries.	Handwriting data may not be clear and legible if the spaces provided for data entry are not sufficiently sized. If additional pages of the documents are added to allow complete documentation, the number of, and reference to

Table 1: (*Contd...*)

Table 1: *(Contd...)*

Expectation Generation	***Potential risk if not meeting expectation***
	any pages added should be clearly documcumented on the main record page and signed.
The document design should make it clear what data is to be provided in entries.	Ambiguous instructions may lead to inconsistent/ incorrect recording of data. Ensures clear, contemporaneous and indelible/ durable completion of entries.
Documents should be stored in a manner which ensures appropriate version control.Master copy (in soft copy) should be prevented from unauthorised or inadvertent changes.	Inappropriate storage conditions can allow unauthorised modification, use of expired and/ or draft documents or cause the loss of master documents. The processes of implementation and the effective communication are just as important as the document. Master copies should contain distinctive marking so to distinguguish the master from a copy, *e.g.* use of colored papers or inks so as to prevent inadvertent use.
Distribution and control Updated versions should be distributed in a timely manner.Obsolete master documents and files should be archived and their access restricted. Any issued and unused physical documents retrieved and destroyed accordingly.	There may be a risk that obsolete versions can be used by mistake if available for use.
Issue should be controlled by written procedures that include the following controls: - using of a secure stamp, or paper color code not available in the working areas or another appropriate system. -ensuring that only the current approved version is available for use. - allocating a unique identifier to each blank document issued and the issue of each document in a register. - numbering every distributed copy and sequential numbering of issued pages in bound books. - Where the re-issue of additional copies of the blank template is necessary, a controlled process regarding re-issue should be followed. All distributed copies should be maintained and a justification and approval for the need of an extra copy. should be recorded, *e.g.*: "the original template record was damaged". - All issued records should be reconciled following use to ensure the accuracy and completenessof records.	Without the use of security measures, there is a risk that rewriting or falsification of data may be made after photocopying or scanning the template record (which gives the user another template copy to use). Obsolete version can be used intentionally or by error. A filled record with an anomalous data entry could be replaced by a new rewritten template. All unused forms should be accounted for, and either defaced and destroyed, or returned for secure filing.

USE AND CONTROL OF RECORDS WITHIN PRODUCTION AREAS

Records should be appropriately controlled in the production areas by designated persons or processes. These controls should be carried out to minimize the risk of damage or loss of the records and ensure data integrity. Where necessary, measures must be taken to protect records from being soiled (*e.g.* getting wet or stained by materials, etc).

Table 2: Expectations while filling documents

Expectation Completion of records	*Potential risk of not meeting expectation*
Handwritten entries must be made by the person who executed the task. Unused, blank fields within documents should be crossed-out, dated and signed. Handwritten entries should be made in clear and legible writing. The completion of date fields should be done in the format defined for the site. *e.g.* dd/mm/yyyy or mm/dd/yyyy.	Check that handwriting is consistent for entries made by the same person. Check the entry is legible and clear (*i.e.* unambiguous; and does not include the use of unknown symbols /abbreviation, *e.g.* use of ditto (") marks. Check for completeness of data recorded. Check correct pagination of the records and are all pages present.
Filling out operations should be contemporaneous.	Verify that records are available within the immediate areas in which they are used, *i.e* Inspectors should expect that sequential recording can be performed at the site of operations.If the form is not available at the point of use, this will not allow operators to fill in records at the time of occurrence.
Records should be indelible.	Check that written entries are in ink, which is not erasable and/or will not smudge or fade (during the retention period).Check that the records were not filled out using pencil prior to use of pen (overwriting).Note that some paper printouts from systems may fade over time, *e.g.* thermal paper.
Records should be signed and dated using a unique identifier that is attributable to the author.	Check that there are signatures and initials logs, that are controlled and current and that demonstrate the use of unique examples, not just standardized printed letters.Ensure that all key entries are signed and dated, particularly if steps occur over time, *i.e.* not just signed at the end of the page and/or process.The use of personal seals is generally not encouraged; however, where used, seals must be controlled for access.There should be a log which clearly shows traceability between an individual and their personal seal. Use of personal seals must be dated (by the owner), to be deemed acceptable.

FILLING OUT RECORDS

The items listed in the Table 2 should be controlled to assure that a record is properly filled out.

MAKING CORRECTIONS ON RECORDS

Corrections to the records must be made in such way that full traceability is maintained. Table 3 gives detailed process of making corrections.

Table 3: How to make corrections?

How to make correction?	*Specific elements that should be checked when reviewing records:*
Cross out what is to be changed with a single line.Where appropriate, the reason for the correction must be clearly recorded and verified if critical. Initial and datethe change made.	Check that the original data are readable not obscured (*e.g.*: not obscured by use of liquid paper; overwriting is not permitted). If changes have been made to critical data entries, verify that a valid reason for the change has been recorded and that supporting evidence for the change is available.Check for unexplained symbols or entries in records
Corrections must be made in indelible ink.	Check that written entries are in ink, which is not erasable and/or will not smudge or fade (during the retention period). Check that the records were not filled out using pencil prior to use of pen (overwriting).

VERIFICATION OF DOCUMENTS

During verification of the documents consideration should be made that it should be verified by a different person than the person who filled it. Table 4 gives detailed information for the elements to be verified during document review.

MAINTAINING A DOCUMENT

Document management include retrieval and archival of the filled documents. This archival should be in such a way that document could be presented to any person at the time of need. Table 5 gives basic information regarding expectations made by the inspectors for document archival and management.

Direct print-outs from electronic systems

Paper records generated by very simple electronic systems, *e.g.* balances, pH meters or simple processing equipment which do not store data provide

Table 4: Document verification process

Expectation	***Specific elements that should be checked when reviewing records:***
When and who should verify the records? A- Batch production records of critical process steps should be: - reviewed/witnessed by designated pers-onnel (*e.g.*: production supervisor) at the time of operations occurring;and - reviewed by an authorised person wit-hin production before sending them to the QC department; and - reviewed and approved by the Quality Assurance Unit (*e.g.* Authorised Person / Qualified Per-son) before release or distribution of the batch produced. B- Batch production records of non-criti-cad process steps is generally reviewed by prouction personnel according to an proved procedure. This verification must be conducted after performing production-related tasks and activities. This verifica-tion mustbe signed or initiated and dated by the appropriate persons. Local SOPs must be in place to describe the process for review of written documents.	Verify the process for the handling of prod-uction records within processing areas to ensure they are readily available to the cor-rect personnel at the time of performing the activity to which the record relates. Verify that any secondary checks perform-ed during processing were performed by appropriately qualified and independent personnel, *e.g.* production supervisor or QA. Check that documents were reviewed by production and then quality personnel following completion of operational activi-ties.
How should records be double checked? Check that all the fields have been com-pleted correctly using the current (appro-ved) templates, and that the data were critically compared to the acceptance criteria.	Inspectors should review company proced-ures for the review of manual data to det-ermine the adequacy of processes. Check that the secondary reviews of data include a verification of any calculations used. View original data (where possible) to confirm that the correct data were transcribed for the calculation.

limited opportunity to influence the presentation of data by (re-) processing,changing of electronic date/time stamps. In these circumstances, the original record should be signed and dated by the person generating the record and the original should be attached to batch processing records.

True copies

Copies of original paper records (*e.g.* analytical summary reports, validation reports etc.) are generally very useful for communication purposes, *e.g.* between companies operating at different locations. These records must be controlled during their life cycle to ensure that the data received from another site (sister company, contractor etc.) are maintained as "true copies"

Table 5: Document management

How to maintain a document?	*Specific elements to be reviewed*
Companies should implement a defined system(s) for storage and recovery of records. All records must be stored in the specified location in a traceable and accessible manner. Systems should ensure that all GMP/GDP relevant records are stored for periods that meet GMP/GDP requirements	Check if the records are stored in an orderly manner and are easily identifiable.
All records should be protected from damage or destruction by: - fire; - liquids (*e.g.* water,solvents and buffer solution); - rodents; - hygrometry etc.- unauthorised personnel access, who may attempt to amend, destroy or replace records	Check if there are systems in place to protect records (*e.g.* pest control and sprinklers). Note: Sprinkler systems can be implemented provided that they are designed to prevent damage documents, *e.g.* documents are protected from water (*e.g.* by covering them with plastic film).
Strategy for disaster recovery	Check for system is in place for the recovery of records in a disaster situation

where appropriate, or used as a "summary report" where the requirements of a "true copy" are not met (*e.g.* summary of complex analytical data). It is conceivable for raw data generated by electronic means to be retained in an acceptable paper or pdf format, where it can be justified that a static record maintains the integrity of the original data. However, the data retention process must be shown to include verified copies of all raw data, metadata, relevant audit trail and result files, software / system configuration settings specific to each analytical run, and all data processing runs (including methods and audit trails) necessary for reconstruction of a given raw data set. It would also require a documented means to verify that the printed records were an accurate representation. This approach is likely to be onerous in its administration to enable a GMP compliant record. Many electronic records are important to retain in their dynamic (electronic) format, to enable interaction with the data. Data must be retained in a dynamic form where this is critical to its integrity or later verification. This should be justified based on risk. At the receiving site, these records (true copies) may either be managed in a paper or electronic format (*e.g.*, PDF) and should be controlled according to an approved QA procedure. Care should be taken to ensure that documents are appropriately authenticated as "true copies" either through the use of handwritten or digital signatures. Table 6 gives the information for the document control and review factors to be checked by the inspectors.

A quality agreement should be in place to address the responsibilities for the generation and transfer of "true copies" and data integrity controls.The system for the issuance and control of "true copies" should be

Table 6: Document control

How should the "true copy" be issued and controlled?	***Specific elements that should be checked when reviewing records:***
Creating a "true copy" of a paper document. At the company who issues the true copy: - Obtain the original of the document to be copied - Photocopy the original document ensuring that no information from the original copy is lost; - Verify the authenticity of the copied document and sign and date the new hardcopy as a "true copy"; The "True Copy" may now be sent to the intended recipient.Creating a "true copy"of a electronic document.A 'true copy' of an electronic record should be created by electronic means (electronic file copy) including all required metadata. Creating pdf versions of electronic data should be discouraged, as this is equivalent to a printout from the electronic system, which risks loss of metadata.The "True Copy" may now be sent to the intended recipient.A distribution list of all issued "true copies" (soft/ hard) should be maintained.	Verify the procedure for the generation of true copies.Check that true copies issued are identical (complete and accurate) to original records. Copied records should be checked against the original document records to make sure there is no tampering of the scanned image.Check that scanned or saved records are protected to ensure data integrity. After scanning paper records and verifying creation of a 'true copy', it may be possible to permit destruction of the original documents from which the scanned images have been created. There should be a documented approval process for this destruction.
At the company who receives the true copy: - The paper version, scanned copy or electronic file should be reviewed and filed according to good document management processes.The document should clearly indicate that it is a true copy and not an original record.	Check that received records are checked and retained appropriately.A system should be in place to verify the authenticity of "true copies" *e.g.* through verification of the correct signatories.

audited by the contract giver and receiver to ensure the process is robust and meets data integrity principles.

LIMITATIONS OF REMOTE REVIEW OF SUMMARY REPORTS

The remote review of data within summary reports is a common necessity; however, the limitations of remote data review must be fully understood to enable adequate control of data integrity. Summary reports of data are often supplied between physically remote manufacturing sites, Market Authorisation Holders and other interested parties. However, it must be acknowledged that summary reports are essentially limited in their nature, in that critical supporting data and metadata is often not included and therefore original data cannot be reviewed. It is therefore essential that summary reports are viewed as but one element of the process for the transfer of data and that interested parties and inspectorates do not place sole reliance on summary report data. Prior to acceptance of summary data, an evaluation of the supplier's quality system and compliance with data integrity principles should be established through on-site inspection when considered important in the context of quality risk management. The inspection should ensure the veracity of data generated by the company, and include a review of the mechanisms used to generate and distribute summary data and reports.

DOCUMENT RETENTION

The retention period of each type of records should (at a minimum) meet those periods specified by GMP/GDP requirements. Consideration should be given to other local or national legislation that may stipulate longer storage periods. The records can be retained internally or by using an outside storage service subject to quality agreements. A risk assessment should be available to demonstrate retention systems/ facilities/ services are suitable and that the residual risks are understood. It is important and essential to establish procedures for archiving and safeguarding of documents so that these are available during repeat of studies, if needed, during product registrations, and during inspections by the regulatory agencies. The organizations should establish appropriate infrastructure, written policies and procedures, and systems to prevent any loss or damage to the documentations during archival, retrieval, and transfer from one department to another. Table 7 gives a basic information for the document retention and archival.

Table 7: Document archival

Where and how should records be archived?	***Specific elements that should checked be when reviewing records:***
A system should be in place describing the different steps for archiving records (identification of archive boxes, list of records by box, retention period, archiving location etc.).	Check that the system implemented for retrieving archived records is effective and traceable.Check that access to archived documents is restricted to authorised personnel ensuring integrity of the stored records.The storage methods used should permit efficient retrieval of documents when required.
All hardcopy quality records should be archived in: - secure locations to prevent damage or loss; - such a manner that it is easy retrievable. - Ensure that records likely durable for are their archived life	Check for the outsourced archived operations if there is a quality agreement in place and if the storage location was audited. Ensure there is some assessment of ensuring that documents will still be legible/ available for the entire archival period. Check that access to archived documents is restricted to authorised personnel ensuring integrity if the stored records. The storage methods used should permit efficient retrieval of documents when required.

DISPOSAL OF ORIGINAL RECORDS

A documented process for the disposal of records should be in place to ensure that the correct original records are disposed of after the defined retention period. The system should ensure that current records are not destroyed by accident and that historical records do not inadvertently make their way back into the current record stream (*e.g*. Historical records confused/mixed with existing records.) A record/ register should be available to demonstrate appropriate and timely destruction of retired records. Measures should be in place to reduce the risk of deleting the wrong documents. The access rights allowing deletion of records should be limited to few persons. In case of printouts which are not permanent (*e.g.* thermo transfer paper) a verified ('true') copy may retained, and it is possible to discard the non- permanent original Paper records may be replaced by Scans provided that the principles of 'true copy' are addressed.

QUALITY RISK MANAGEMENT TO ENSURE DOCUMENT MANAGEMENT

All organizations performing work subject to G x P are required by applicable existing WHO guidance to establish, implement and maintain an appropriate quality management system, the elements of which should be documented in their prescribed format such as a quality manual or other appropriate documentation. The quality manual, or equivalent documentation, should include a quality policy statement of management's commitment to an effective quality management system and good professional practice. These policies should include expected ethics and proper code of conduct to assure the reliability and completeness of data, including mechanisms for staff to report any questions or concerns to management.

Within the quality management system, the organization should establish the appropriate infrastructure, organizational structure, written policies and procedures, processes and systems to both prevent and detect situations that may impact data integrity and in turn the risk-based and scientific robustness of decisions based upon that data. Quality risk management is an essential component of an effective data and record validity program. The effort and resource assigned to data and record governance should be commensurate with the risk to product quality. The risk-based approach to record and data management should ensure that adequate resources are allocated and that control strategies for the assurance of the integrity of G x P data are commensurate their potential impact on product quality and patient safety and related decision-making.

Control strategies that promote good practices and prevent record and data integrity issues from occurring are preferred and are likely to be the most effective and cost-effective. For example, security controls that prevent persons from altering a master processing formula will reduce the probability of invalid and aberrant data occurring. Such preventive measures, when effectively implemented, also reduce the degree of monitoring required to detect uncontrolled change. Record and data integrity risks should be assessed, mitigated, communicated and reviewed throughout the data life cycle in accordance with the principles of quality risk management. Example approaches that may enhance data reliability are given in these guidelines but should be viewed as recommendations. Other approaches may be justified and shown to be equally effective in achieving satisfactory control of risk. Organizations should therefore design appropriate tools and strategies for management of data integrity risks based upon their specific G x P activities, technologies and processes. A document management program developed and implemented, based upon sound quality risk management principles, is expected to leverage existing technologies to their full potential, streamline data processes in a manner that not only improves good data management but also the business process efficiency and effectiveness, thereby reducing costs and facilitating continual improvement.

Training in Document Management

Personnel should be trained in data integrity policies and agree to abide by them. Management should ensure personnel are trained to understand and distinguish between proper and improper conduct, including deliberate falsification and potential consequences. In addition, key personnel, including managers, supervisors and quality unit personnel, should be trained in measures to prevent and detect data issues. This may require specific training in evaluating the configuration settings and reviewing electronic data and metadata, such as audit trails, for individual computerized systems used in the generation, processing and reporting of data. For example, the quality unit should learn how to evaluate configuration settings that may intentionally or unintentionally allow data to be overwritten or obscured through the use of hidden fields or data annotation tools; supervisors responsible for reviewing electronic data should learn which audit trails in the system track significant data changes and how these might be most efficiently accessed as part of their review. Management should also ensure that, at the time of hire and periodically afterwards as needed, all personnel are trained in procedures to ensure GDP for both paper and electronic records. The quality unit should include checks for adherence to GDP for both paper records and electronic records in their day-to-day work, system and facility audits and self-inspections and report any opportunities for improvement to management.

CONCLUSIONS

Documents are a mirror to show actual image of any pharmaceutical company. Documents and products are produced in pharmaceuticals but regulatory bodies are interested to see documents first. Different documents can describe the different activity in pharma and its actual image. Pharmaceutical manufacture and regulation is clearly an international business. With the increasing emphasis on harmonization efforts and standard setting, as well as mutual recognition agreements, knowledge of foreign regulations is a must both for understanding the future direction of these efforts as well as for international supply of drug products. It is anticipated that the approach described here will be a useful reference work for those personnel preparing and using documents for pharmaceutical manufacture. It can serve as a tool for training staff and may prove to be useful for quality assurance professionals for assessment of compliance during self-inspection. It is again emphasized that documentation is a very important aspect of GMP and will enhance the visibility of the quality assurance function.

In summary, as a good practice and to be compliant with the expectations of the regulatory authorities, it is important that an organization.

a. Provides enough resources to create and complete documentation,
b. Ensures that the documents follow ALCOA
c. Conducts a thorough gap analysis of existing documentation,
d. Provides resources for initial and ongoing training to the personnel, involved in development and manufacturing of the pharmaceutical products, in documents creation, management, and security of documents during lifecycle management of products.
e. Finally, an oversight of Quality Assurance is needed to ensure that personnel are following good documentation practices.

FURTHER READINGS

Computerised systems. *In*: The rules governing medicinal products in the European Union. Vol. 4. Good manufacturing practice (GMP) guidelines. Annex 11

EudreaLex-European Commission (2011) Good Manufacturing Practices for Medicinal Products for Human and Veterinary Use.

European Commission Health and Consumers Directorate-General, Belgium 4: 1-9.

Good automated manufacturing practice (GAMP) Good Practice Guides: Validation of laboratory computerized systems. International Society for Pharmaceutical Engineering (ISPE), 2005.

Good automated manufacturing practice (GAMP) Good Practice Guides: Electronic data archiving. International Society for Pharmaceutical Engineering (ISPE), 2007.

Health Canada (2015) Good Manufacturing Practices Guidance Document. Health, Canada.

Official Medicines Control Laboratories Network of the Council of Europe, Quality Assurance Documents: PA/PH/OMCL (08) 69 3R — Validation of computerised systems — core document

Supplementary guidelines in good manufacturing practice: validation. Validation of computerized systems. *In*: WHO Expert Committee on Specifications for Pharmaceutical Preparations. Fortieth report. Geneva, World Health Organization, 2006, Annex 4, Appendix 5 (WHO Technical Report Series, No. 937).

Title 21 Code of Federal Regulations (21 CFR Part 11): Electronic records; electronic signatures. US Food and Drug Administration. The current status of 21 CFR Part 11

USP (2015) Good Documentation Guidelines, US Pharmacopeial Convention, USA.

WHO (2016) Guidance on Good Data and Record Management Practices, World Health Organization, Switzerland, pp. 165-210.

WHO Good manufacturing practices for active pharmaceutical ingredients, Annex 2, WHO Technical Report Series, No. 957, 2010.

WHO good manufacturing practices for Pharmaceutical products: main principles, Annex 2, WHO Technical Report Series 986, 2014.

WHO good practices for pharmaceutical quality control laboratories, WHO Technical Report Series, No. 957, 2010.

7

Data Integrity

ABSTRACT

This chapter is designed to help the user facilitate compliance through education, whilst clarifying the regulatory interpretation of existing requirements. Readers should ensure their efforts are balanced when safeguarding data from risk with their other compliance priorities. This chapter should be considered as a means of understanding data integrity and the minimum expectation to achieve compliance. Main aim of this chapter is to promote a risk-based approach to data management that includes data risk, criticality and lifecycle. Readers need to understand their data processes (as a lifecycle) to identify data with the greatest G x P impact. From that, the identification of the most effective and efficient risk-based control and review of the data can be determined and implemented. This chapter primarily addresses data integrity and not data quality since the controls required for integrity do not necessarily guarantee the quality of the data generated. This chapter should be read in conjunction with the applicable regulations and the general guidance specific to each G x P. Where G x P-specific references are made within this document, consideration of the principles of these documents may provide guidance and further information.

INTRODUCTION

Authorities regularly undertake inspections of manufacturers and distributors of API and medicinal products in order to determine the level of compliance with GMP/GDP principles. These inspections are commonly performed on-site however may be performed through the remote or off-site evaluation of documentary evidence, in which case the limitations of remote review of data should be considered. The effectiveness of these inspection processes is determined by the veracity of the evidence provided to the inspector and ultimately the integrity of the underlying data. It is critical to the inspection process that inspectors can determine and fully rely on the accuracy and completeness of evidence and records presented to them. Good data management practices influence the integrity of all data generated and recorded by a manufacturer and these practices should ensure that data are accurate, complete and reliable. While the main focus of this document is in relation to data integrity expectations, the principles herein should also be considered in the wider context of good data management.

Data integrity enables good decision-making by pharmaceutical manufacturers and regulatory authorities. It is a fundamental requirement of the pharmaceutical quality system, applying equally to manual (paper) and electronic systems. Promotion of a quality culture together with implementation of organisational and technical measures which ensure data integrity is the responsibility of senior management. It requires participation and commitment by staff at all levels within the company, by the company's suppliers and by its distributors. Senior management should ensure that data integrity risk is assessed, mitigated and communicated in accordance with the principles of quality risk management. The effort and resource assigned to data integrity measures should be commensurate with the risk to product quality, and balanced with other quality assurance resource demands. Where long term measures are identified in order to achieve the desired state of control, interim measures should be implemented to mitigate risk, and should be monitored for effectiveness.

BACKGROUND

The way regulatory data are generated has continued to evolve in line with the ongoing development of supporting technologies such as the increasing use of electronic data capture, automation of systems and use of remote technologies; and the increased complexity of supply chains and ways of working, for example, *via* third party service providers. Systems to support these ways of working can range from manual processes with paper records to the use of fully computerised systems. The main purpose of the regulatory requirements remains the same, *i.e.*, having confidence in the quality and the integrity of the data generated (to ensure patient safety and quality of products) and being able to reconstruct activities.

THE PRINCIPLES OF DATA INTEGRITY

Data Integrity is defined as "the extent to which all data are complete, consistent and accurate, throughout the data lifecycle" and is fundamental in a pharmaceutical quality system which ensures that medicines are of the required quality. Poor data integrity practices and vulnerabilities undermine the quality of records and evidence, and may ultimately undermine the quality of medicinal products. Data integrity applies to all elements of the Quality Management System and the principles herein apply equally to data generated by electronic and paper-based systems. The responsibility for good practices regarding data management and integrity lies with the manufacturer or distributor undergoing inspection. They have full responsibility and a duty to assess their data management systems for potential vulnerabilities and take steps to design and implement good data governance practices to ensure data integrity is maintained. Data integrity is the degree to which data are complete, consistent, accurate, trustworthy, reliable and that these characteristics of the data are maintained throughout the data life cycle. The data should be collected and maintained in a secure manner, so that they are attributable, legible, contemporaneously recorded, original (or a true copy) and accurate. Assuring data integrity requires appropriate quality and risk management systems, including adherence to sound scientific principles and good documentation practices.

The organisation needs to take responsibility for the systems used and the data they generate. The organisational culture should ensure data are complete, consistent and accurate in all its forms, *i.e.,* paper and electronic. Arrangements within an organisation with respect to people, systems and facilities should be designed, operated and, where appropriate, adapted to support a suitable working environment, *i.e.,* creating the right environment to enable data integrity controls to be effective. The impact of organisational culture, the behaviour driven by performance indicators, objectives and senior management behaviour on the success of data governance measures should not be underestimated. The data governance policy (or equivalent) should be endorsed at the highest levels of the organisation. Organisations are expected to implement, design and operate a documented system that provides an acceptable state of control based on the data integrity risk with supporting rationale. An example of a suitable approach is to perform a data integrity risk assessment (DIRA) where the processes that produce data or where data are obtained are mapped out and each of the formats and their controls are identified and the data criticality and inherent risks documented. Organisations are not expected to implement a forensic approach to data checking on a routine basis. Systems should maintain appropriate levels of control whilst wider data governance measures should ensure that periodic audits can detect opportunities for data integrity failures within the organisation's systems. The effort and resource applied to assure the integrity of the data should be commensurate with the risk and impact of a data integrity failure to the patient or environment. Collectively these arrangements fulfil the concept of data governance. Organisations should be aware that reverting from automated or computerised systems to paper-based manual systems or *vice-versa* will not in itself remove the need for appropriate data integrity controls. Where data integrity weaknesses are identified, companies should ensure that appropriate corrective and preventive actions are implemented across all relevant activities and systems and not in isolation. Appropriate notification to regulatory authorities should be made where significant data integrity incidents have been identified.

The guidance refers to the acronym ALCOA rather than 'ALCOA+'. ALCOA being Attributable, Legible, Contemporaneous, Original, and Accurate and the '+' referring to Complete, Consistent, Enduring, and Available. ALCOA was historically regarded as defining the attributes of data quality that are suitable for regulatory purposes. The '+' has been subsequently added to emphasise the requirements. There is no difference in expectations regardless of which acronym is used since data governance measures should ensure that data are complete, consistent, enduring and available throughout the data life-cycle.

The Pharmaceutical Quality Management System (QMS) should be implemented throughout the different stages of the life cycle of the Active Pharmaceutical Ingredients and medicinal products and should encourage the use of science and risk-based approaches. To ensure that decision making is well informed and to verify that the information is reliable, the events or actions that informed those decisions should be well documented. As such, Good Documentation Practices (GDocPs) are key to ensuring data integrity, and a fundamental part of a well designed Pharmaceutical Quality Management System.

The application of GDocPs may vary depending on the medium used to record the data (*i.e.,* physical *vs.* electronic records), but the principles are applicable to both. Some key concepts of GDocPs are summarised by the acronym ALCOA: Attributable, Legible, Contemporaneous, Original, Accurate. To this list can be added the following: Complete, Consisitent, Enduring and Available (ALCOA+). Together, these expectations ensure that events are properly documented and the data can be used to support informed decisions. Table 1 gives detailed information on all the attributes of GDocPs (ALCOA+) for better understanding of the readers.

If these elements are appropriately applied to all applicable areas of GMP and GDP-related activities, along with other supporting elements of a Pharmaceutical Quality Management System, the reliability of the information used to make critical decisions regarding drug products should be adequately ensured.

ESTABLISHING DATA CRITICALITY AND INHERENT INTEGRITY RISK

Data have varying importance to quality, safety and efficacy decisions. Data criticality may be determined by considering how the data are used to influence the decisions made. The risks to data are determined by the potential to be deleted, amended or excluded without authorisation and the opportunity for detection of those activities and events. The risks to data may be increased by complex, inconsistent processes with open-ended and subjective outcomes, compared to simple tasks that are undertaken

Table 1: Basic DI principles applicable to both paper and electronic systems (ALCOA +):

Abbreviations	***Attribute***	***Requirements***
A	Attributable	It should be possible to identify the individual who performed the recorded task. The need to document who performed the task / function, is in part to demonstrate that the function was performed by trained and qualified personnel. This applies to changes made to records as well: corrections, deletions, changes, etc.
L	Legible	All records must be legible – the information must be readable in order for it to be of any use. This applies to all information that would be required to be considered Complete, including all Original records or entries. Where the 'dynamic' nature of electronic data (the ability to search, query, trend, etc) is important to the content and meaning of the record, the ability to interact with the data using a suitable application is important to the 'availability' of the record.
C	Contemporaneous	The evidence of actions, events or decisions should be aneous recorded as they take place. This documentation should serve as an accurate attestation of what was done, or what was decided and why, *i.e.,* what influenced the decision at that time.
O	Original	The original record can be described as the first-capture of information, whether recorded on paper (static) or electronically (usually dynamic, depending on the complexity of the system). Information that is originally captured in a dynamic state should remain available in that state.
A	Accurate	Ensuring results and records are accurate is achieved through many elements of a robust Pharmaceutical Quality Management System. This can be comprised of: - Equipment related factors such as qualification, calibration, maintenance and computer validation. - Policies and procedures to control actions and behaviours, including data review procedures to verify adherence to procedural requirements - Deviation management including root cause analysis, impact assessments and CAPA - Trained and qualified personnel who understand the importance of following established procedures and documenting their actions and decisions. - Together, these elements aim to ensure the accuracy of information, including scientific data, that is used to make critical decisions about the quality of products.
C	Complete	All information that would be critical to recreating an event is important when trying to understand the event. The level of detail required for an information set to be considered complete would depend on the criticality of the information. A complete record of data generated electronically includes relevant metadata.
C	Consistent	Good Documentation Practices should be applied throughout any process, without exception, including deviations that may occur during the process. This includes capturing all changes made to data.

Table 1: *Contd...*

Abbreviations	***Attribute***	***Requirements***
E	Enduring	Part of ensuring records are available is making sure they exist for the entire period during which they might be needed. This means they need to remain intact and accessible as an indelible/ durable record.
A	Available	Records must be available for review at any time during the required retention period, accessible in a readable format to all applicable personnel who are responsible for their review whether for routine release decisions, investigations, trending, annual reports, audits or inspections.

consistently, are well defined and have a clear objective. Data may be generated by:

- Recording on paper, a paper-based record of a manual observation or of an activity or
- Electronically, using equipment that range from simple machines through to complex highly configurable computerised systems or
- By using a hybrid system where both paper-based and electronic records constitute the original record or
- By other means such as photography, imagery, chromatography plates, etc.

Paper

Data generated manually on paper may require independent verification if deemed necessary from the data integrity risk assessment or by another requirement. Consideration should be given to risk-reducing supervisory measures. The effective management of paper based documents is a key element of GMP/ GDP. Accordingly the documentation system should be designed to meet GMP/ GDP requirements and ensure that documents and records are effectively controlled to maintain their integrity. Paper records must be controlled and must remain attributable, legible, indelible/ durable, contemporaneous, original and accurate (ALCOA) throughout the data lifecycle. Procedures outlining good documentation practices and arrangements for document control should be available within the QMS. These procedures should specify:

- How master documents and procedures are created, reviewed and approved for use;
- Generation, distribution and control of templates used to record data (master, logs, etc.);
- Retrieval and disaster recovery processes regarding records.

- The process for generation of working copies of documents for routine use, with specific emphasis on ensuring copies of documents, *e.g.,* SOPs and blank forms are issued and reconciled for use in a controlled and traceable manner.
- Guidance for the completion of paper based documents, specifying how individual operators are identified, data entry formats and amendments to documents are recorded.
- How completed documents are routinely reviewed for accuracy, authenticity and completeness;
- Processes for the filing, retrieval, retention, archival and disposal of records.
- How data integrity is maintained throughout the lifecycle of the data.

Electronic Generated

The inherent risks to data integrity relating to equipment and computerised systems may differ depending upon the degree to which the system generating or using the data can be configured, and the potential for manipulation of data during transfer between computerised systems during the data lifecycle. The use of available technology, suitably configured to reduce data integrity risk, should be considered. Simple electronic systems with no configurable software and no electronic data retention (*e.g.,* pH meters, balances and thermometers) may only require calibration, whereas complex systems require 'validation for intended purpose'. Validation effort increases with complexity and risk (determined by software functionality, configuration, the opportunity for user intervention and data lifecycle considerations). It is important not to overlook systems of apparent lower complexity. Within these systems, it may be possible to manipulate data or repeat testing to achieve the desired outcome with limited opportunity for detection (*e.g.,* stand-alone systems with a user-configurable output such as ECG machines, FTIR, UV spectrophotometers).

Computer Generated

A large variety of computerised systems are used by companies to assist in a significant number of operational activities. These range from the simple stand-alone to large integrated and complex systems, many of which have an impact on the quality of products manufactured. It is the responsibility of each regulated entity to fully evaluate and control all computerised systems and manage them in accordance with G x P requirements.

Organisations should be fully aware of the nature and extent of computerised systems utilised, and assessments should be in place that describes each system, its intended use and function, and any data integrity risks or vulnerabilities that may be susceptible to manipulation. Particular emphasis should be placed on determining the criticality of computerised systems and any associated data, in respect of product quality.

All computerised systems with potential for impact on product quality should be effectively managed under a mature quality management system which is designed to ensure that systems are protected from acts of accidental or deliberate manipulation, modification or any other activity that may impact on data integrity. When determining data vulnerability and risk, it is important that the computerised system is considered in the context of its use within the business process. For example, data integrity of an analytical method with computerised interface is affected by sample preparation, entry of sample weights into the computerised system, use of the computerised system to generate data, and processing/recording of the final result using that data.

Hybrid

Where hybrid systems are used, it should be clearly documented what constitutes the whole data set and all records that are defined by the data set should be reviewed and retained. Hybrid systems should be designed to ensure they meet the desired objective.

Other

Where the data generated is captured by a photograph or imagery (or other media), the requirements for storage of that format throughout its lifecycle should follow the same considerations as for the other formats, considering any additional controls required for that format. Where the original format cannot be retained due to degradation issues, alternative mechanisms for recording (*e.g.,* photography or digitisation) and subsequent storage may be considered and the selection rationale documented (*e.g.,* thin layer chromatography).

Reduced effort and/ or frequency of control measures may be justified for data that has a lesser impact to product, patient or the environment if those data are obtained from a process that does not provide the opportunity for amendment without high-level system access or specialist software/ knowledge. The data integrity risk assessment (or equivalent) should consider factors required to follow a process or perform a function. It is expected to consider not only a computerised system but also the supporting people, guidance, training and quality systems. Therefore, automation or the use of a 'validated system' (*e.g.,* e-CRF; analytical equipment) may lower but not eliminate data integrity risk. Where there is human intervention, particularly influencing how or what data are recorded, reported or retained, an increased risk may exist from poor organisational controls or data verification due to an overreliance on the system's validated state. Where the data integrity risk assessment has highlighted areas for remediation, prioritisation of actions (including acceptance of an appropriate level of residual risk) should be documented, communicated to management, and subject to review. In situations where long-term remediation actions are identified, risk-reducing short-term measures should be implemented to provide acceptable data governance in the interim.

Senior management is responsible for the implementation of systems and procedures to minimise the potential risk to data integrity, and for identifying the residual risk, using the principles of ICH Q9. Contract Givers should perform a similar review as part of their vendor assurance programme. The effort and resource assigned to data governance should be commensurate with the risk to product quality, and should also be balanced with other quality resource demands. Manufacturers and analytical laboratories should design and operate a system which provides an acceptable state of control based on the data integrity risk, and which is fully documented with supporting rationale. Where long term measures are identified in order to achieve the desired state of control, interim measures should be implemented to mitigate risk, and should be monitored for effectiveness. Where interim measures or risk prioritisation are required, residual data integrity risk should be communicated to senior management, and kept under review. Reverting from automated / computerised to paper-based systems will not remove the need for data governance. Not all data or processing steps have the same importance to product quality and patient safety. Risk management should be utilised to determine the importance of each data/processing step. An effective risk management approach to data governance will consider:

- Data criticality (impact to decision making and product quality) and
- Data risk (opportunity for data alteration and deletion, and likelihood of detection / visibility of changes by the manufacturer's routine review processes).

From this information, risk proportionate control measures can be implemented.

Data Criticality

The decision that data influences may differ in importance, and the impact of the data to a decision may also vary. Points to consider regarding data criticality include:

- Which decision does the data influence? For example: when making a batch release decision, data which determines compliance with critical quality attributes is of greater importance than warehouse cleaning records.

- What is the impact of the data to product quality or safety? For example: for an oral tablet, active substance assay data are of generally greater impact to product quality and safety than tablet friability data.

Data Risk

Data risk assessment should consider the vulnerability of data to involuntary or deliberate alteration, falsification, deletion, loss or re-creation, and the likelihood of detection of such actions. Consideration should also be given to ensuring complete data recovery in the event of a disaster. Control measures which prevent unauthorised activity, and increase visibility / detectability can be used as risk mitigating actions. Examples of factors which can increase risk of data integrity failure include complex, inconsistent processes with open ended and subjective outcomes. Simple tasks which are consistent, well defined and objective lead to reduced risk. Risk assessments should focus on a business process (*e.g.,* production, QC), evaluate data flows and the methods of generating data, and not just consider IT system functionality or complexity. Factors to consider include:

- Process complexity;
- Methods of generating, storing and retiring data and their ability to ensure data accuracy, legibility, indelibility;
- Process consistency and degree of automation / human interaction;
- Subjectivity of outcome / result (*i.e.,* is the process open-ended or well defined?); and
- The outcome of a comparison between of electronic system data and manually recorded events could be indicative for malpractices (*e.g.,* apparent discrepancies between analytical reports and raw-data acquisition times).

For computerised systems, manual interfaces with IT systems should be considered in the risk assessment process. Computerised system validation in isolation may not result in low data integrity risk, in particular when the user is able to influence the reporting of data from the validated system. Critical thinking skills should be used by inspectors to determine whether control and review procedures effectively achieve their desired outcomes. An indicator of data governance maturity is an organisational understanding and acceptance of residual risk, which prioritises actions. An organisation which believes that there is 'no risk' of data integrity failure is unlikely to have made an adequate assessment of inherent risks in the data lifecycle. The approach to assessment of data lifecycle, criticality and risk should therefore be examined in detail. This may indicate potential failure modes which can be investigated during an inspection.

DESIGNING SYSTEMS AND PROCESSES TO ASSURE DATA INTEGRITY; CREATING THE 'RIGHT ENVIRONMENT'

Systems and processes should be designed in a way that facilitates compliance with the principles of data integrity. Enablers of the desired behaviour include but are not limited to:

- At the point of use, having access to appropriately controlled/ synchronised clocks for recording timed events to ensure reconstruction and traceability, knowing and specifying the time zone where these data are used across multiple sites.
- Accessibility of records at locations where activities take place so that informal data recording and later transcription to official records does not occur.
- Access to blank paper proformas for raw/source data recording should be appropriately controlled. Reconciliation, or the use of controlled books with numbered pages, may be necessary to prevent recreation of a record. There may be exceptions such as medical records (GCP) where this is not practical.
- User access rights that prevent (or audit trail, if prevention is not possible) unauthorised data amendments. Use of external devices or system interfacing methods that eliminate manual data entries and human interaction with the computerised system, such as barcode scanners, ID card readers, or printers.
- The provision of a work environment (such as adequate space, sufficient time for tasks, and properly functioning equipment) that permit performance of tasks and recording of data as required.
- Access to original records for staff performing data review activities.
- Reconciliation of controlled print-outs.
- Sufficient training in data integrity principles provided to all appropriate staff (including senior management).
- Inclusion of subject matter experts in the risk assessment process.
- Management oversight of quality metrics relevant to data governance.

The use of scribes to record activity on behalf of another operator can be considered where justified, for example:

- The act of contemporaneous recording compromises the product or activity *e.g.,* documenting line interventions by sterile operators.
- Necropsy (GLP)
- To accommodate cultural or literacy/language limitations, for instance where an activity is performed by an operator but witnessed and recorded by a second person.

Consideration should be given to ease of access, usability and location whilst ensuring appropriate control of the activity guided by the criticality of the data. In these situations, the recording by the second person should be contemporaneous with the task being performed, and the records should identify both the person performing the task and the person completing the record. The person performing the task should countersign the record wherever possible, although it is accepted that this countersigning step will be retrospective. The process for supervisory (scribe) documentation completion should be described in an approved procedure that specifies the activities to which the process applies.

DATA

Facts, figures and statistics collected together for reference or analysis. All original records and true copies of original records, including source data and metadata and all subsequent transformations and reports of these data, that are generated or recorded at the time of the G x P activity and allow full and complete reconstruction and evaluation of the G x P activity. Data governance measures should also ensure that data are complete, consistent, enduring and available throughout the lifecycle.

RAW DATA

Raw data are defined as the original record (data) which can be described as the first-capture of information, whether recorded on paper or electronically. Information that is originally captured in a dynamic state should remain available in that state. Raw data must permit full reconstruction of the activities. Where this has been captured in a dynamic state and generated electronically, paper copies cannot be considered as 'raw data'. In the case of basic electronic equipment that does not store electronic data, or provides only a printed data output (*e.g.,* balances or pH meters), then the printout constitutes the raw data. Where the basic electronic equipment does store electronic data permanently and only holds a certain volume before overwriting; this data should be periodically reviewed and where necessary reconciled against paper records and extracted as electronic data where this is supported by the equipment itself.

METADATA

Metadata are data that describe the attributes of other data and provide context and meaning. Typically, these are data that describe the structure, data elements, inter-relationships and other characteristics of data *e.g.,* audit trails. Metadata also permit data to be attributable to an individual. Metadata form an integral part of the original record. Without the context provided by metadata, the data have no meaning.

DATA GOVERNANCE

Data governance is the sum total of arrangements which provide assurance of data integrity. These arrangements ensure that data, irrespective of the process, format or technology in which it is generated, recorded, processed, retained, retrieved and used will ensure a complete, consistent and accurate record throughout the data lifecycle. The data lifecycle refers to how data are generated, processed, reported, checked, used for decision-making, stored and finally discarded at the end of the retention period. Data relating to a product or process may cross various boundaries within the lifecycle. This may include data transfer between manual and IT systems, or between different organisational boundaries; both internal (*e.g.,* between production, QC and QA) and external (*e.g.,* between service providers or contract givers and acceptors).

Data governance should address data ownership and accountability throughout the lifecycle, and consider the design, operation and monitoring of processes/systems to comply with the principles of data integrity including control over intentional and unintentional changes to data. Data Governance systems should include staff training in the importance of data integrity principles and the creation of a working environment that enables visibility, and actively encourages reporting of errors, omissions and undesirable results.

Senior management should be accountable for the implementation of systems and procedures to minimise the potential risk to data integrity, and for identifying the residual risk, using risk management techniques such as the principles of ICH Q9. Contract Givers should ensure that data ownership, governance and accessibility are included in any contract/ technical agreement with a third party. The Contract Giver should also perform a data governance review as part of their vendor assurance programme. Data governance systems should also ensure that data are readily available and directly accessible on request from national competent authorities. Electronic data should be available in human-readable form.

DATA GOVERNANCE SYSTEMS

Data governance systems should be integral to the pharmaceutical quality system. It should address data ownership throughout the lifecycle, and consider the design, operation and monitoring of processes/ systems in order to comply with the principles of data integrity, including control over intentional and unintentional changes to, and deletion of information. The data governance system should ensure controls over data lifecycle which are commensurate with the principles of quality risk management. These controls may be:

Organisational

- Procedures, *e.g.,* instructions for completion of records and retention of completed paper records;
- Training of staff and documented authorisation for data generation and approval;
- Tata governance system design, considering how data are generated recorded, processed retained and used, and risks or vulnerabilities are controlled effectively;
- Routine data verification;
- Periodic surveillance, *e.g.,* self-inspection processes seek to verify the effectiveness of the data governance policy.

Technical

- Computerised system control,
- Cutomation

An effective data governance system will demonstrate Management's understanding and commitment to effective data governance practices including the necessity for a combination of appropriate organisational culture and behaviours and an understanding of data criticality, data risk and data lifecycle. There should also be evidence of communication of expectations to personnel at all levels within the organisation in a manner which ensures empowerment to report failures and opportunities for improvement. This reduces the incentive to falsify, alter or delete data. The organisation's arrangements for data governance should be documented within their Quality Management System and regularly reviewed.

DATA GOVERNANCE SYSTEM REVIEW

The effectiveness of data integrity control measures should be assessed periodically as part of self-inspection (internal audit) or other periodic review processes. This should ensure that controls over the data lifecycle are operating as intended. In addition to routine data verification checks, self-inspection activities should be extended to a wider review of control measures, including:

- A check of continued personnel understanding of data integrity in the context of protecting of the patient, and ensuring the maintenance of a working environment which is focussed on quality and open reporting of issues, *e.g.,* by review of continued training in data integrity principles and expectations.
- A review for consistency of reported data/outcomes against raw data entries.

- In situations where routine computerised system data are reviewed by a validated 'exception report'4, a risk-based sample of computerised system logs / audit trails to ensure that information of relevance to GMP activity is reported as expected

An effective review process will demonstrate understanding regarding importance of interaction of company behaviours with organisational and technical controls. The outcome of data governance system review should be communicated to senior management, and be used in the assessment of residual data integrity risk.

DATA LIFECYCLE

All phases in the life of the data from generation and recording through processing (including analysis, transformation or migration), use, data retention, archive/retrieval and destruction. Data governance, as described in the previous section, must be applied across the whole data lifecycle to provide assurance of data integrity. Data can be retained either in the original system, subject to suitable controls, or in an appropriate archive.

RECORDING AND COLLECTION OF DATA

Organisations should have an appropriate level of process understanding and technical knowledge of systems used for data collection and recording, including their capabilities, limitations and vulnerabilities. The selected method should ensure that data of appropriate accuracy, completeness, content and meaning are collected and retained for their intended use. Where the capability of the electronic system permits dynamic storage, it is not appropriate for static (printed / manual) data to be retained in preference to dynamic (electronic) data. As data are required to allow the full reconstruction of activities the amount and the resolution (degree of detail) of data to be collected should be justified.

When used, blank forms (including, but not limited to, worksheets, laboratory notebooks, and master production and control records) should be controlled. For example, numbered sets of blank forms may be issued and reconciled upon completion. Similarly, bound paginated notebooks, stamped or formally issued by a document control group allow detection of unofficial notebooks and any gaps in notebook pages.

DATA TRANSFER / MIGRATION

Data transfer is the process of transferring data between different data storage types, formats, or computerised systems. Data migration is the process of moving stored data from one durable storage location to another.

This may include changing the format of data, but not the content or meaning. Data transfer is the process of transferring data and metadata between storage media types or computerised systems. Data migration where required may, if necessary, change the format of data to make it usable or visible on an alternative computerised system.

Data transfer/ migration procedures should include a rationale, and be robustly designed and validated to ensure that data integrity is maintained during the data lifecycle. Careful consideration should be given to understanding the data format and the potential for alteration at each stage of data generation, transfer and subsequent storage. The challenges of migrating data are often underestimated, particularly regarding maintaining the full meaning of the migrated records.

Data transfer should be validated. The data should not be altered during or after it is transferred to the worksheet or other application. There should be an audit trail for this process. Appropriate Quality procedures should be followed if the data transfer during the operation has not occurred correctly. Any changes in the middle layer software should be managed through appropriate Quality Management Systems. Electronic worksheets used in automation like paper documentation should be version controlled and any changes in the worksheet should be documented/ verified appropriately.

DATA PROCESSING

A sequence of operations performed on data to extract, present or obtain information in a defined format. Examples might include: statistical analysis of individual patient data to present trends or conversion of a raw electronic signal to a chromatogram and subsequently a calculated numerical result. There should be adequate traceability of any user-defined parameters used within data processing activities to the raw data, including attribution to who performed the activity. Audit trails and retained records should allow reconstruction of all data processing activities regardless of whether the output of that processing is subsequently reported or otherwise used for regulatory or business purposes. If data processing has been repeated with progressive modification of processing parameters this should be visible to ensure that the processing parameters are not being manipulated to achieve a more desirable result.

EXCLUDING DATA

Data may only be excluded where it can be demonstrated through valid scientific justification that the data are not representative of the quantity measured, sampled or acquired. In all cases, this justification should be documented and considered during data review and reporting. All data (even if excluded) should be retained with the original data set, and be available for review in a format that allows the validity of the decision to exclude the data to be confirmed.

ORIGINAL RECORD

The first or source capture of data or information *e.g.,* original paper record of manual observation or electronic raw data file from a computerised system, and all subsequent data required to fully reconstruct the conduct of the G x P activity. Original records can be Static or Dynamic.

A static record format, such as a paper or electronic record, is one that is fixed and allows little or no interaction between the user and the record content. For example, once printed or converted to static electronic format chromatography records lose the capability of being reprocessed or enabling more detailed viewing of baselines. Records in dynamic format, such as electronic records, allow an interactive relationship between the user and the record content. For example, electronic records in database formats allow the user to track, trend and query data; chromatography records maintained as electronic records allow the user or reviewer (with appropriate access permissions) to reprocess the data and expand the baseline to view the integration more clearly.

Where it is not practical or feasibly possible to retain the original copy of source data, (*e.g.,* MRI scans, where the source machine is not under the study sponsor's control and the operator can only provide summary statistics) the risks and mitigation should be documented. Where the data obtained requires manual observation to record (for example results of a manual titration, visual interpretation of environmental monitoring plates) the process should be risk assessed and depending on the criticality, justify if a second contemporaneous verification check is required or investigate if the result could be captured by an alternate means.

TRUE COPY

A copy (irrespective of the type of media used) of the original record that has been verified (*i.e.,* by a dated signature or by generation through a validated process) to have the same information, including data that describe the context, content, and structure, as the original. A true copy may be stored in a different electronic file format to the original record if required, but must retain the metadata and audit trail required to ensure that the full meaning of the data are kept and its history may be reconstructed. Original records and true copies must preserve the integrity of the record. True copies of original records may be retained in place of the original record (*e.g.,* scan of a paper record), if a documented system is in place to verify and record the integrity of the copy. Organisations should consider any risk associated with the destruction of original records.

It should be possible to create a true copy of electronic data, including relevant metadata, for the purposes of review, backup and archival. Accurate and complete copies for certification of the copy should include the meaning of the data (*e.g.,* date formats, context, layout, electronic signatures and authorisations) and the full G x P audit trail. Consideration should be given to the dynamic functionality of a 'true copy' throughout the retention period. Data must be retained in a dynamic form where this is critical to its integrity or later verification. If the computerised system cannot be maintained *e.g.,* if it is no longer supported, then records should be archived according to a documented archiving strategy prior to decommissioning the computerised system. It is conceivable for some data generated by electronic means to be retained in an acceptable paper or electronic format, where it can be justified that a static record maintains the integrity of the original data. However, the data retention process must be shown to include verified copies of all raw data, metadata, relevant audit trail and result files, any variable software/ system configuration settings specific to each record, and all data processing runs (including methods and audit trails) necessary for reconstruction of a given raw data set. It would also require a documented means to verify that the printed records were an accurate representation. To enable a G x P compliant record this approach is likely to be demanding in its administration. Where manual transcriptions occur, these should be verified by a second person or validated system.

COMPUTERISED SYSTEM TRANSACTIONS

A computerised system transaction is a single operation or sequence of operations performed as a single logical 'unit of work'. The operation(s) that makes a transaction may not be saved as a permanent record on durable storage until the user commits the transaction through a deliberate act (*e.g.,* pressing a save button), or until the system forces the saving of data. The metadata (*e.g.,* username, date, and time) are not captured in the system audit trail until the user saves the transaction to durable storage. In computerised systems, an electronic signature may be required for the record to be saved and become permanent.

A critical step is a parameter that must be within an appropriate limit, range, or distribution to ensure the safety of the subject or quality of the product or data. Computer systems should be designed to ensure that the execution of critical steps is recorded contemporaneously. Where transactional systems are used, the combination of multiple unit operations into a combined single transaction should be avoided, and the time intervals before saving of data should be minimised. Systems should be designed to require saving data to permanent memory before prompting users to make changes. The organisation should define during the development of the system (*e.g., via* the user requirements specification) what critical steps are appropriate based on the functionality of the system and the level of risk associated. Critical steps should be documented with process controls that consider system design (prevention), together with monitoring and review processes. Oversight of activities should alert to failures that are not addressed by the process design.

AUDIT TRAIL

The audit trail is a form of metadata containing information associated with actions that relate to the creation, modification or deletion of G x P records. An audit trail provides for secure recording of life-cycle details such as creation, additions, deletions or alterations of information in a record, either paper or electronic, without obscuring or overwriting the original record. An audit trail facilitates the reconstruction of the history of such events relating to the record regardless of its medium, including the "who, what, when and why" of the action. Where computerised systems are used to capture, process, report, store or archive raw data electronically, system design should always provide for the retention of audit trails to show all changes to, or deletion of data while retaining previous and original data. It should be possible to associate all data and changes to data with the persons making those changes, and changes should be dated and time stamped (time and time zone where applicable). The reason for any change, should also be recorded. The items included in the audit trail should be those of relevance to permit reconstruction of the process or activity.

Audit trails (identified by risk assessment as required) should be switched on. Users should not be able to amend or switch off the audit trail. Where a system administrator amends, or switches off the audit trail a record of that action should be retained. The relevance of data retained in audit trails should be considered by the organisation to permit robust data review/ verification. It is not necessary for audit trail review to include every system activity (*e.g.,* user log on/off, keystrokes etc.). Where relevant audit trail functionality does not exist (*e.g.,* within legacy systems) an alternative control may be achieved for example defining the process in an SOP, and use of log books. Alternative controls should be proven to be effective. Where add-on software or a compliant system does not currently exist, continued use of the legacy system may be justified by documented evidence that a compliant solution is being sought and that mitigation measures temporarily support the continued use.

Routine data review should include a documented audit trail review where this is determined by a risk assessment. When designing a system for review of audit trails, this may be limited to those with G x P relevance. Audit trails may be reviewed as a list of relevant data, or by an 'exception reporting' process. An exception report is a validated search tool that identifies and documents predetermined 'abnormal' data or actions that require further attention or investigation by the data reviewer. Reviewers should have sufficient knowledge and system access to review relevant audit trails, raw data and metadata. Where systems do not meet the audit trail and individual user account expectations, demonstrated progress should be available to address these shortcomings. This should either be through add-on software that provides these additional functions or by an upgrade to a compliant system. Where remediation has not been identified or subsequently implemented in a timely manner a deficiency may be cited.

ELECTRONIC SIGNATURES

A signature in digital form (bio-metric or non-biometric) that represents the signatory. This should be equivalent in legal terms to the handwritten signature of the signatory. The use of electronic signatures should be appropriately controlled with consideration given to:

- How the signature is attributable to an individual.
- How the act of 'signing' is recorded within the system so that it cannot be altered or manipulated without invalidating the signature or status of the entry.
- How the record of the signature will be associated with the entry made and how this can be verified.
- The security of the electronic signature *i.e.,* so that it can only be applied by the 'owner' of that signature.

It is expected that appropriate validation of the signature process associated with a system is undertaken to demonstrate suitability and that control over signed records is maintained. Where a paper or pdf copy of an electronically signed document is produced, the metadata associated with an electronic signature should be maintained with the associated document.

The use of electronic signatures should be compliant with the requirements of international standards. The use of advanced electronic signatures should be considered where this method of authentication is required by the risk assessment. Electronic signature or E-signature systems must provide for "signature manifestations" *i.e.,* a display within the viewable record that defines who signed it, their title, and the date (and time, if significant) and the meaning of the signature (*e.g.,* verified or approved). An inserted image of a signature or a footnote indicating that the document has been electronically signed (where this has been entered by a means other than the validated electronic signature process) is not adequate. Where a document is electronically signed then the metadata associated with the signature should be retained. For printed copies of electronically signed documents refer to True Copy section.

DATA REVIEW AND APPROVAL

The approach to reviewing specific record content, such as critical data and metadata, cross-outs (paper records) and audit trails (electronic records) should meet all applicable regulatory requirements and be risk-based. There should be a procedure that describes the process for review and approval of data. Data review should also include a risk-based review of relevant metadata, including relevant audit trails records. Data review should be documented and the record should include a positive statement regarding whether issues were found or not, the date that review was performed and the signature of the reviewer.

A procedure should describe the actions to be taken if data review identifies an error or omission. This procedure should enable data corrections or clarifications to provide visibility of the original record, and traceability of the correction, using ALCOA principles. Where data review is not conducted by the organisation that generated the data, the responsibilities for data review must be documented and agreed by both parties. Summary reports of data are often supplied between organisations (contract givers and acceptors). It must be acknowledged that summary reports are limited and critical supporting data and metadata may not be included. Many software packages allow configuration of customised reports. Key actions may be incorporated into such reports provided they are validated and locked to prevent changes. Automated reporting tools and reports may reduce the checks required to assure the integrity of the data. Where summary reports are supplied by a different organisation, the organisation receiving and using the data should evaluate the data provider's data integrity controls and processes prior to using the information.

- Routine data review should consider the integrity of an individual data set *e.g.,* is this the only data generated as part of this activity? Has the data been generated and maintained correctly? Are there indicators of unauthorised changes?
- Periodic audit of the data generated (encompassing both a review of electronically generated data and the broader organisational review) might verify the effectiveness of existing control measures and consider the possibility of unauthorised activity at all interfaces, *e.g.,* have there been IT requests to amend any data post review? Have there been any system maintenance activities and has the impact of that activity been assessed?

COMPUTERISED SYSTEM USER ACCESS/SYSTEM ADMINISTRATOR ROLES

Full use should be made of access controls to ensure that people have access only to functionality that is appropriate for their job role, and that actions are attributable to a specific individual. Companies must be able to demonstrate the access levels granted to individual staff members and ensure that historical information regarding user access level is available. Where the system does not capture this data, then a record must be maintained outside of the system. Access controls should be applied to both the operating system and application levels. Individual login at operating system level may not be required if appropriate controls are in place to ensure data integrity (*e.g.,* no modification, deletion or creation of data outside the application is possible).

For systems generating, amending or storing G x P data shared logins or generic user access should not be used. Where the computerised system design supports individual user access, this function must be used. This may require the purchase of additional licences. Systems (such as MRP systems) that are not used in their entirety for G x P purposes but do have elements within them, such as approved suppliers, stock status, location and transaction histories that are G x P applicable require appropriate assessment and control. It is acknowledged that some computerised systems support only a single user login or limited numbers of user logins. Where no suitable alternative computerised system is available, equivalent control may be provided by third-party software or a paper-based method of providing traceability (with version control). The suitability of alternative systems should be justified and documented. Increased data review is likely to be required for hybrid systems because they are vulnerable to non-attributable data changes. It is expected that companies should be implementing systems that comply with current regulatory expectations.

System administrator access should be restricted to the minimum number of people possible taking account of the size and nature of the organisation. The generic system administrator account should not be available for routine use. Personnel with system administrator access should log in with unique credentials that allow actions in the audit trail(s) to be attributed to a specific individual. The intent of this is to prevent giving access to users with potentially a conflict of interest so that they can make unauthorised changes that would not be traceable to that person. System Administrator rights (permitting activities such as data deletion, database amendment or system configuration changes) should not be assigned to individuals with a direct interest in the data. Individuals may require changes in their access rights depending on the status of clinical trial data. For example, once data management processes are complete, the data are 'locked' by removing editing access rights. This should be able to be demonstrated within the system.

DATA RETENTION

Data retention may be for archiving (protected data for long-term storage) or backup (data for the purposes of disaster recovery). Data and document retention arrangements should ensure the protection of records from deliberate or inadvertent alteration or loss. Secure controls must be in place to ensure the data integrity of the record throughout the retention period and should be validated where appropriate. Data (or a true copy) generated in paper format may be retained by using a validated scanning process provided there is a documented process in place to ensure that the outcome is a true copy. Procedures for destruction of data should consider data criticality and where applicable legislative retention requirements.

ARCHIVE

A designated secure area or facility (*e.g.,* cabinet, room, building or computerised system) for the long term, retention of data and metadata for the purposes of verification of the process or activity. Archived records may be the original record or a 'true copy' and should be protected so they cannot be altered or deleted without detection and protected against any accidental damage such as fire or pest. Archive arrangements must be designed to permit recovery and readability of the data and metadata throughout the required retention period. In the case of archiving of electronic data, this process should be validated, and in the case of legacy systems the ability to review data periodically verified (*i.e.,* to confirm the continued support of legacy computerised systems). Where hybrid records are stored, references between physical and electronic records must be maintained such that full verification of events is possible throughout the retention period.

When legacy systems can no longer be supported, consideration should be given to maintaining the software for data accessibility purposes (for as long possible depending upon the specific retention requirements). This may be achieved by maintaining software in a virtual environment. Migration to an alternative file format that retains as much as possible of the 'true copy' attributes of the data may be necessary with increasing age of the legacy data. Where migration with full original data functionality is not technically possible, options should be assessed based on risk and the importance of the data over time. The migration file format should be selected considering the balance of risk between long-term accessibility *versus* the possibility of reduced dynamic data functionality (*e.g.,* data interrogation, trending, re-processing etc). It is recognised that the need to maintain accessibility may require migration to a file format that loses some attributes and/or dynamic data functionality.

BACKUP

A copy of current (editable) data, metadata and system configuration settings maintained for recovery including disaster recovery. Backup and recovery processes should be validated and periodically tested. Each back up should be verified to ensure that it has functioned correctly *e.g.,* by confirming that the data size transferred matches that of the original record. The backup strategies for the data owners should be documented. Backups for recovery purposes do not replace the need for the long term, retention of data and metadata in its final form for the purposes of verification of the process or activity.

FILE STRUCTURE

Data Integrity risk assessment requires a clear understanding of file structure. The way data are structured within the G x P environment will depend on what the data will be used for and the end user may have this dictated to them by the software/computerised system(s) available. There are many types of file structure, the most common being flat files and relational databases. Different file structures due to their attributes may require different controls and data review methods and may retain meta data in different ways.

VALIDATION - FOR INTENDED PURPOSE

Computerised systems should comply with regulatory requirements and associated guidance. These should be validated for their intended purpose which requires an understanding of the computerised system's function within a process. For this reason, the acceptance of vendor-supplied validation data in isolation of system configuration and users intended use is not acceptable. In isolation from the intended process or end-user IT infrastructure, vendor testing is likely to be limited to functional verification only and may not fulfil the requirements for performance qualification.

Functional verification demonstrates that the required information is consistently and completely presented. Validation for intended purpose ensures that the steps for generating the custom report accurately reflect those described in the data checking SOP and that the report output is consistent with the procedural steps for performing the subsequent review.

IT SUPPLIERS AND SERVICE PROVIDERS

Where 'cloud' or 'virtual' services are used, attention should be paid to understanding the service provided, ownership, retrieval, retention and security of data. The physical location where the data are held, including the impact of any laws applicable to that geographic location, should be considered. The responsibilities of the contract giver and acceptor should be defined in a technical agreement or contract. This should ensure timely access to data (including metadata and audit trails) to the data owner and national competent authorities upon request. Contracts with providers should define responsibilities for archiving and continued readability of the data throughout the retention period. Appropriate arrangements must exist for the restoration of the software/system as per its original validated state, including validation and change control information to permit this restoration. Business continuity arrangements should be included in the contract, and tested. The need for an audit of the service provider should be based upon risk.

ORGANISATIONAL INFLUENCES ON SUCCESSFUL DATA INTEGRITY MANAGEMENT

It may not be appropriate or possible to report an inspection citation relating to organisational behaviour. An understanding of how behaviour influences

(i) The incentive to amend, delete or falsify data and

(ii) The effectiveness of procedural controls designed to ensure data integrity, can provide the inspector with useful indicators of risk which can be investigated further.

An effective 'quality culture' and data governance may be different in its implementation from one location to another. Depending on culture, an organisation's control measures may be:

- 'Open' (where hierarchy can be challenged by subordinates, and full reporting of a systemic or individual failure is a business expectation)
- 'Closed' (where reporting failure or challenging a hierarchy is culturally more difficult)

Good data governance in 'open' cultures may be facilitated by employee empowerment to identify and report issues through the quality system. In 'closed' cultures, a greater emphasis on oversight and secondary review may be required to achieve an equivalent level of control due to the social barrier of communicating undesirable information. The availability of anonymous escalation to senior management may also be of greater importance in this situation. The extent of Management's knowledge and understanding of data integrity can influence the organisation's success of data integrity management. Management must know their legal and moral obligation (*i.e.,* duty and power) to prevent data integrity lapses from occurring and to detect them, if they should occur.

Lapses in data integrity are not limited to fraud or falsification, they can be unintentional and still pose risk. Any potential for compromising the reliability of data is a risk that should be identified and understood in order for appropriate controls to be put in place. Direct controls usually take the form of written policies and procedures, but indirect influences on employee behaviour (such as incentives for productivity in excess of process capability) should be understood and addressed as well.

Data integrity breaches can occur at any time, by any employee, so management needs to be vigilant in detecting issues and understand reasons behind lapses, when found, to enable investigation of the issue and implementation of corrective and preventative actions. There are consequences of data integrity lapses that affect the various stakeholders (patients, regulators, customers) including directly impacting patient safety and undermining confidence in the organisation and its products. Employee awareness and understanding of these consequences can be helpful in fostering an environment in which quality is a priority.

Management should establish controls to prevent, detect and correct data integrity breaches, as well as verify those controls are performing as intended to assure data integrity. To achieve success with data integrity, Management should address the following:

Code of Ethics and Policies

A Code of Values and Ethics should reflect Management's philosophy on quality, achieved through policies (*i.e.,* a Code of Conduct) that are aligned to the quality culture and develop an environment of trust, where all individuals are responsible and accountable for ensuring patient safety and product quality. The company's general ethics and integrity standards need to be established and known to each employee and these expectations should be communicated frequently and consistently. Management should make personnel aware of the importance of their role in ensuring data integrity and the implication of their activities to assuring product quality and protecting patient safety. Code of Conduct policies should clearly define the expectation of ethical behaviour, such as honesty. This should be communicated to and be well understood by all personnel. The communication should not be limited only to knowing the requirements, but also why they were established and the consequences of failing to fulfill the requirements. Unwanted behaviours, such as deliberate data falsification, unauthorised changes, destruction of data, or other conduct that compromises data integrity should be addressed promptly. Disciplinary action may be taken, when warranted. Similarly, conforming behaviours should be recognised appropriately.

There should be a confidential escalation program supported by company policy and procedures whereby it encourages personnel to bring instances of possible breaches to the Code of Conduct to the attention of management without consequence.

Quality Culture

Management should aim to create a work environment (*i.e.,* quality culture) that is transparent and open, one in which personnel are encouraged to freely communicate failures and mistakes, including potential data reliability issues, so that corrective and preventative actions can be taken. Organisational reporting structure should permit the information flow between personnel at all levels.

It is the collection of values, beliefs, thinking, and behaviours demonstrated consistently by management, team leaders, quality personnel and all personnel that contribute to creating a quality culture to assure data integrity.

Management can foster quality culture:

- Ensure awareness and understanding of expectations (*e.g.,* Code of Ethics and Code of Conduct)
- Lead by example, management should demonstrate the behaviours they expect to see ;
- Ensure accountability for actions and decisions;
- Stay continuously and actively involved;
- Set realistic expectations, consider the limitations that place pressures on employees;
- Allocate resources to meet expectations;
- Implement fair and just consequences and rewards; and
- Be aware of regulatory trends to apply lessons learned to your organisation.

Modernising the Pharmaceutical Quality Management System

The application of modern quality risk management principles and good data management practices to the current pharmaceutical quality management system serves to modernize the System to meet the challenges that come with the generation of complex data. The company's Quality Management System should be able to prevent, detect and correct weaknesses in the system or their processes that may lead to data integrity lapses. The company should know their data life cycle and integrate the appropriate controls and procedures such that the data generated will be valid, complete and reliable. Specifically, such control and procedural changes may be in the following areas:

- Risk assessment and management,
- Investigation programs,
- Data review practices,
- Computer software validation,
- Vendor/ contractor management,
- Training program to include company's data integrity policy and data integrity SOPs ,

- Self-inspection program to include data integrity, and
- Quality metrics and reporting to senior management.

Regular Management Review of Quality Metrics

There should be regular management reviews of quality metrics, including those related to data integrity, such that significant issues are identified, escalated and addressed in a timely manner. Caution should be taken when key performance indicators are selected so as not to inadvertently result in a culture in which data integrity is lower in priority. The head of the Quality unit should have direct access to the highest level of management in order to directly communicate risks so that senior management is aware and can allocate resources to address any issues. Management can have an independent expert periodically verify the effectiveness of their systems and controls.

Resource Allocation

Management should allocate appropriate resources to support and sustain good data integrity management such that the workload and pressures on those responsible for data generation and record keeping do not increase the likelihood of errors or the opportunity to deliberately compromise data integrity. There should be sufficient number of personnel for quality and management oversight, IT support, conduct of investigations, and management of training program that are commensurate with the operations of the organisation. There should be provisions to purchase equipment, software and hardware that are appropriate for their needs, based on the criticality of the data in question.

Personnel must be qualified and trained for their specific duties, with appropriate segregation of duties, including the importance of good documentation practices. There should be evidence of the effectiveness of training on critical procedures, such as electronic data review. The concept of data integrity applies to all functional departments that play a role in GMP, including areas such as IT and engineering. Data integrity should be familiar to all, but data integrity experts from various levels (SMEs, supervisors, team leaders) may be called upon to work together to conduct/ support investigations, identify system gaps and drive implementation of improvements. Introduction of new roles in an organisation relating to data integrity such as a data custodian or Chief Compliance Officer might be considered.

Dealing with Data Integrity Issues Found Internally

In the event that data integrity lapses are found, they should be handled as any deviation would be according to the Quality Management System. It is important to determine the extent of the problem as well as its root cause, then correcting the issue to its full extent and implement preventative measures. This may include the use of a third party for additional expertise or perspective, which may involve a gap assessment to identify weaknesses in the system. When considering the impact on product, any conclusions drawn should be supported by sound scientific evidence. Corrective actions may include product recall, client notification and reporting to regulatory authorities.

DATA INTEGRITY CONSIDERATIONS FOR OUTSOURCED ACTIVITIES

Data integrity plays a key part in ensuring the security and integrity of supply chains. Data governance measures by a contract giver may be significantly weakened by unreliable or falsified data or materials provided by supply chain partners. This principle applies to all outsourced activities, including suppliers of raw materials or contract manufacture / analytical services. Initial and periodic re-qualification of supply chain partners and outsourced activities should include consideration of data integrity risks and appropriate control measures. It is important for an organisation to understand the data integrity limitations of information obtained from the supply chain (*e.g.,* summary records and copies / printouts), and the challenges of remote supervision. This will help to focus resources towards data integrity verification and supervision using a quality risk management approach.

Routine Document Verification

The supply chain relies upon the use of documentation and data passed from one organisation to another. It is often not practical for the contract giver to review all raw data relating to reported results. Emphasis should be placed upon robust supplier and contractor qualification, using the principles of quality risk management.

Strategies for Assessing Data Integrity in the Supply Chain

Companies should conduct regular risk reviews of supply chains and outsourced activity that evaluate the extent of data integrity controls required. Information considered during risk reviews may include:

- The outcome of site audits, with focus on data governance measures
- Review of data submitted in routine reports, for example:

Quality agreements should be in place in place between manufacturers and suppliers/ contract manufacturing organisations (CMOs) with specific

Area for review	*Rationale*
Comparison of analytical data reported by the contractor or supplier *vs* in-house data from analysis of the same material	To look for discrepant data which may be an indicator of falsification

provisions for ensuring data integrity across the supply chain. This may be achieved by setting out expectations for data governance, and transparent error/deviation reporting by the contract acceptor to the contract giver. There should also be a requirement to notify the contract giver of any data integrity failures identified at the contract acceptor site. Audits of suppliers and manufacturers of APIs, critical intermediate suppliers and service providers conducted by the manufacturer (or by a third party on their behalf) should include a verification of data integrity measures at the contract organisation.

Contract givers may work with the contract acceptor to ensure that all client confidential information is encoded to de-identify clients. This would facilitate review of source electronic data and metadata at the contract giver's site, without breaking confidentiality obligations to other clients. By reviewing a larger data set, this enables a more robust assessment of the contract givers data governance measures. It also permits a search for indicators of data integrity failure, such as repeated data sets or data which does not demonstrate the expected variability. Care should be taken to ensure the authenticity and accuracy of supplied documentation. The difference in data integrity and traceability risks between 'true copy' and 'summary report' data should be considered when making contractor and supply chain qualification decisions.

REMEDIATION OF DATA INTEGRITY FAILURES

Consideration should be primarily given to resolving the immediate issues identified and assessing the risks associated with the data integrity issues. The response by the company in question should outline the actions taken. Responses should include:

- A comprehensive investigation into the extent of the inaccuracies in data records and reporting, to include:
  - A detailed investigation protocol and methodology; a summary of all laboratories, manufacturing operations, and systems to be covered by the assessment; and a justification for any part of the operation that the regulated user proposes to exclude;
  - Interviews of current and former employees to identify the nature, scope, and root cause of data inaccuracies. These interviews may be conducted by a qualified third party;

- An assessment of the extent of data integrity deficiencies at the facility. Identify omissions, alterations, deletions, record destruction, non-contemporaneous record completion, and other deficiencies;
- Determination of the scope and extent and timeframe for the incident, with justification for the time-boundaries applied;
- Data, products, processes and specific batches implicated in any investigations;
- A description of all parts of the operations in which data integrity lapses occur, additional consideration should be given to global corrective actions for multinational companies or those that operate across multiple differing sites;
- A comprehensive retrospective evaluation of the nature of the testing and manufacturing data integrity deficiencies, and the potential root cause(s). The services of a qualified third-party consultant with specific expertise in the areas where potential breaches were identified may be necessary;
- A risk assessment of the potential effects of the observed failures on the quality of the drugs involved. The assessment should include analyses of the risks to patients caused by the release of drugs affected by a lapse of data integrity, risks posed by ongoing operations, and any impact on the veracity of data submitted to regulatory agencies, including data related to product registration dossiers;

- Corrective and preventative actions taken to address the data integrity vulnerabilities and timeframe for implementation, and including:
  - Interim measures describing the actions to protect patients and to ensure the quality of the medicinal products, such as notifying customers, recalling product, conducting additional testing, adding lots to the stability program to assure stability, drug application actions, and enhanced complaint monitoring.
  - Long-term measures describing any remediation efforts and enhancements to procedures, processes, methods, controls, systems, management oversight, and human resources (*e.g.*, training, staffing improvements) designed to ensure the data integrity.
- Whenever possible, inspectorates should meet with senior representatives from the implicated companies to convey the nature of the deficiencies identified and seek written confirmation that the company commits to full disclosure of issues and their prompt resolution. A management strategy should be submitted to the regulatory authority that includes the details of the global corrective action and preventive action plan. The strategy should include:
  - A detailed corrective action plan that describes how the regulated user intends to ensure the reliability and completeness of all of

the data generated, including analytical data, manufacturing records, and all data submitted to the Competent Authority.

- A comprehensive description of the root causes of your data integrity lapses, including evidence that the scope and depth of the current action plan is commensurate with the findings of the investigation and risk assessment. This must indicate if individuals responsible for data integrity lapses remain able to influence GMP/ GDP-related or drug application data.

- Inspectorates should implement policies for the management of significant data integrity issues identified at inspection in order to manage and contain risks associated with the data integrity breach.

Indicators of Improvement

An on-site inspection is required to verify the effectiveness of actions taken to address data integrity issues. Some indicators of improvement are:

- Evidence of a thorough and open evaluation of the identified issue and timely implementation of effective corrective and preventative actions;
- Evidence of open communication of issues with clients and other regulators.
- Transparent communication should be maintained throughout the investigation and remediation stages.
- Regulators should be aware that further data integrity failures may be reported as a result of the detailed investigation.
- Any additional reaction to these notifications should be proportionate to public health risks, to encourage continued reporting;
- Evidence of communication of data integrity expectations across the organisation, incorporating processes for open reporting of potential issues and opportunities for improvement without repercussions;
- The regulated user should ensure that an appropriate evaluation of the vulnerability of any sophisticated electronic systems to data manipulation takes place to ensure that follow-up actions have fully resolved all the violations, third party expertise may be required;
- Implementation of data integrity policies in line with the principles of this guide;
- Implementation of routine data verification practices.

SPECIFIC DATA INTEGRITY CONSIDERATIONS FOR COMPUTERISED SYSTEMS

A large variety of computerised systems are used by companies to assist in a significant number of operational activities. These range from the simple standalone to large integrated and complex systems, many of which have an impact on the quality of products manufactured. It is the responsibility of each regulated entity to fully evaluate and control all computerised systems and manage them in accordance with GMP and GDP requirements. Organisations should be fully aware of the nature and extent of computerised systems utilised, and assessments should be in place that describes each system, its intended use and function, and any data integrity risks or vulnerabilities that may be susceptible to manipulation. Particular emphasis should be placed on determining the criticality of computerised systems and any associated data, in respect of product quality.

All computerised systems with potential for impact on product quality should be effectively managed under a mature quality management system which is designed to ensure that systems are protected from acts of accidental or deliberate manipulation, modification or any other activity that may impact on data integrity. When determining data vulnerability and risk, it is important that the computerised system is considered in the context of its use within the business process. For example, data integrity of an analytical method with computerised interface is affected by sample preparation, entry of sample weights into the computerised system, use of the computerised system to generate data, and processing / recording of the final result using that data.

CONCLUSIONS

Development, registration and manufacturing of medicines for commercial purposes involves multiple activities, one of them is linked to the robustness and accuracy of the data. These data must be comprehensive, complete, reliable, accurate and true to assure the quality of studies supporting applications and must comply with a number of standards, *i.e.,* Good Manufacturing Practices (GMP), Good Documentation Practices (GDP), and Good Laboratory Practices (GLP). Establishing robust Quality Assurance and Control systems a quality culture that encourages personnel to be transparent about failures can minimize data risks and improve the situations where data reliability may be compromised. This enables to investigate and address root causes when data integrity issues arise. The number of computerized data acquisition and processing systems in the pharmaceutical industry is growing quickly and with it the number of records generated that are inextricably linked with the regulated products manufactured by the industry. The situation is complicated by the integration of systems, interfaces between the systems, and conversions, calculations, and compression of information that may take place during transmission. The knowledge generated from these data and information is directly used in the manufacture of drugs. Data integrity and its practical maintenance are therefore crucial to the safety of patients and the quality of healthcare products. To control data integrity, it is necessary to develop a corporate ethics program that includes clear policy statement and expectation for employee conduct improvement. 'Health' of operating environment includes:

- Periodic trainings
- Disciplinary action against unethical practices
- Risk assessment for identifying gaps
- Company management should be committed to provide necessary training, resources, support and work culture.

FURTHER READINGS

Computerised systems. *In*: The rules governing medicinal products in the European Union. Volume 4: Good manufacturing practice (GMP) guidelines: Annex 11. Brussels: European Commission.

Good Clinical Practice (GCP) ICH E6(R2) November 2016

Good Practices for Data Management and Integrity in Regulated GMP/GDP Environments – PIC/S; PI041-1(draft 2); August 2016.

Guidance on good data and record management practices; World Health Organisation, WHO Technical Report Series, No.996, Annex 5; 2016.

MHRA GMP data integrity definitions and guidance for industry. London: Medicines and Healthcare Products Regulatory Agency; March 2015.

MHRA/HRA DRAFT Guidance on the use of electronic consent

OECD series on principles of good laboratory practice (GLP) and compliance monitoring. Paris:

Organisation for Economic Co-operation and Development.

The Human Medicines Regulations 2012 (Statutory Instrument 2012 No. 1916):

8

Validation: Basic Preview

ABSTRACT

The prime objective of any pharmaceutical plant is to manufacture products of requisite attribute and quality consistently, at the lowest possible cost. Although validation studies have been conducted in the pharmaceutical industry for a long time, there is an ever increasing interest in validation owing to their industry's greater emphasis in recent years on quality assurance program and is fundamental to an efficient production operation. Validation is a concept that has evolved in United States in 1978. The concept of validation has expanded through the years to embrace a wide range of activities from analytical methods used for the quality control of drug substances and drug products to computerized systems for clinical trials, labelling or process control. Validation means assessment of validity or action of proving effectiveness. Validation is a team effort where it involves people from various disciplines of the plant. This chapter will make an attempt to describe the principles of validation which are applicable to the facilities, equipment, utilities, manufacturing process and cleaning processes used during the pharmaceutical operations. It is binding requirements of the GMP that manufacturer's control the critical aspects of their particular operations through qualification and validation over the life cycle of the product and process. Any planned or unplanned changes to the facilities, equipment, utilities and processes, which may or may not affect the quality, safety and efficacy of the product, should be formally documented and the impact on the validated status or control strategy assessed. Computerised systems used for the manufacture of medicinal products should be validated. The relevant concepts and guidance presented in various guidelines (EU-GMP Volume 4Annex 15, WHO TRS, ICH Q8, Q10 and Q11) should also be taken into account.

INTRODUCTION

Validation is a method of quality assurance and an important part of the GMP. The European GMP guideline defines validation as the following:

"Action of proving, in accordance with the principles of Good Manufacturing Practice, that any Procedure, process, equipment, material, or activity. Actually leads to the expected results." European GMP Guideline Part 1 The FDA´s definition requires manufacturers a clear understanding of the manufacturing process: *"Process validation*: The collection and evaluation of data, from the process design stage through to commercial production, which establishes scientific evidence that a process is capable of consistently delivering quality products." *Guidance for Industry: Process Validation: General Principles and Practices, FDA.*

Both definitions promote the manufacturers understands and controls all quality relevant processes including their risks assessment and is eager to maintain the validated status. Validation is required by GMP guidelines, however what and how to validate, is not explicitly mentioned in detail. Validation is an essential part of cGMP system and good clinical practices. Thus it also becomes an element of the pharmaceutical quality system which eventually deals with any equipment, utility, facility, product or process. Validation, as a concept, incorporates qualification and should be applied over the life cycle of, *e.g.* the applicable product, process, system, equipment or utility. The basic principles of quality assurance have as their goal the production of products that are fit for their intended use.

These principles are as follows:

- Quality, safety and efficacy must be designed and built into the product.
- The execution of validation should be in compliance with regulatory expectations;
- Quality cannot be inspected or tested into the product.
- Each critical step of the manufacturing process must be validated.
- Other steps in the process must be under control to maximize the probability that the finished product consistently and predictably meets all quality and design specifications.
- Quality risk management principles should be applied in determining the need, scope and extent of validation;
- Ongoing review should take place to ensure that the validated state is maintained and opportunities for continuing improvement are identified.

Validation of processes and systems is fundamental to achieving these goals. It is by design and validation that a manufacturer can establish confidence that the manufactured products will consistently meet their product specifications.

The implementation of validation work requires considerable resources such as:

- *Time:* generally validation work is subject to rigorous time schedules.
- *Financial:* validation often requires the time of specialized personnel and expensive technology.
- *Human:* validation requires the collaboration of experts from various disciplines (*e.g.* a multidisciplinary team, comprising quality assurance, engineering, manufacturing and other disciplines, depending on the product and process to be validated).

Qualification and validation are essentially the same. The term qualification is normally used for equipment and utilities, and validation for systems and processes. In this sense, qualification can be seen as part of validation. Manufacturers should plan validation in a manner that will ensure regulatory compliance and ensuring that product quality, safety and consistency are not compromised. A quality risk management approach should be applied throughout the lifecycle of a medicinal product. As part of a quality risk management system, decisions on the scope and extent of validation and qualification should be based on a justified and documented risk assessment of the facilities, equipment, utilities and processes. The principles in ICH Q8, Q9, Q10 and Q11 or other systems guaranteeing at least the same level of product quality and security should be used to support validation and qualification activities. Data supporting qualification and/or validation studies which were obtained from sources outside of the manufacturers own validation programme may be used provided that this approach has been justified and that there is adequate assurance that controls were in place throughout the acquisition of such data.

The overview of the validation activities shows that validation is used as the overall term but also describes stand-alone activities like process validation or computer validation. For facilities, equipment and staff the term qualification is exclusively used. There is no official unified terminology but it is generally agreed that qualification refers to everything that is physical and validation refers to methods, procedures and processes. The approach to validation and qualification are the same. The validation of a process requires the qualification of each of the important elements of the process. The relative importance of an element may vary from process to process. Fig. 1 is given a basic layout for various aspects of validation.

HISTORY

The concept of validation was first proposed by two Food and Drug Administration (FDA) officials, Ted Byers and Bud Loftus, in 1979 in USA, to improve the quality of pharmaceuticals. It was proposed in direct response to several problems in the sterility of large volume parenteral market. The first validation activities were focused on the processes involved in making these products, but quickly spread to associated processes including environmental control, media fill, and equipment sanitization and purified water production.

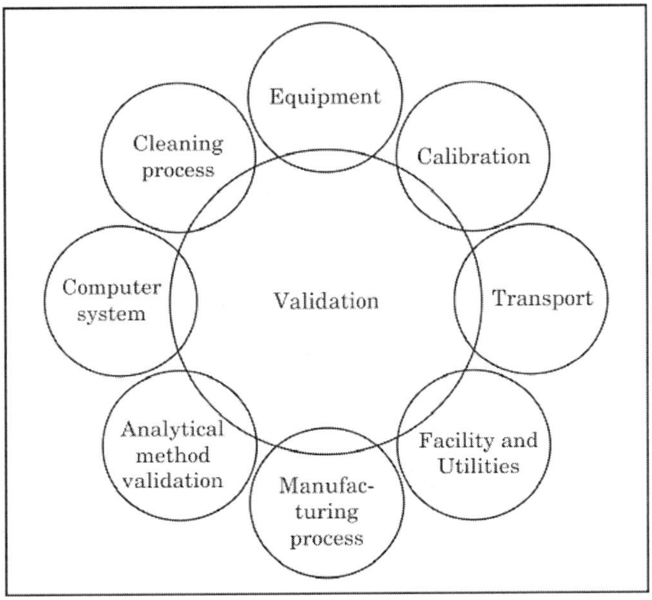

Fig. 1: Aspects of validation

The concept of validation was first developed for equipment and processes and derived from the engineering practices used in delivery of large pieces of equipment that would be manufactured, tested, delivered and accepted according to a contract. The use of validation spread to other areas of industry after several large-scale problems highlighted the potential risks in the design of products. The most notable is the Therac-25 incident. Here, the software for a large radiotherapy device was poorly designed and tested. In use, several interconnected problems led to several devices giving doses of radiation several thousands of times higher than intended, which resulted in the death of three patients and several more being permanently injured. In 2005 an individual wrote a standard by which the transportation process could be validated for cold chain products. This standard was written for a biological manufacturing company and was then written into the PDA's Technical Report # 39, thus establishing the industry standard for cold chain validation. This was critical for the industry due to the sensitivity of drug substances, biologics and vaccines to various temperature conditions. The FDA has also been very focused on this final area of distribution and the potential for a drug substances quality to be impacted by extreme temperature exposure.

APPROACH TO VALIDATION

Qualification and validation activities should be done in accordance with predetermined protocols, and the results appropriately documented, *e.g.* in reports. Statistical calculations should be applied, where appropriate, and provide scientific evidence that the process, system or other related aspect is appropriately validated. Manufacturer should ensure that an appropriate and effective quality system is present to organise and manage validation activities. This system shall also ensure that there are sufficient resources to perform validation in a timely manner. Management and persons responsible for quality assurance should be actively involved in the process and authorization of protocols and reports. There should be a specific programme or schedule to support planning and execution of validation activities. Validation should be performed in a structured way according to the documented protocols and procedures.

Qualification and validation should be performed:

- For new premises, equipment, utilities and systems, and processes and procedures;
- When changes are made, depending on the outcome of risk assessment;
- Where necessary or indicated based on the outcome of periodic review.

A written report on the outcome of the validation should be prepared. The scope and extent of validation should be based on knowledge and experience, and the outcome of quality risk management principles. Where necessary worst-case situations or specific challenge tests should be considered for inclusion in the validation, for example, stress load and volume verification in computer system validation.

Validation may include:

- Extensive product testing, which may involve extensive sample testing (with the estimation of confidence limits for individual results) and the demonstration of intra- and inter-batch homogeneity;
- Simulation process trials;
- Challenge/worst case tests, which determine the robustness of the process;
- Control of process parameters being monitored during normal production runs to obtain additional information on the reliability of the process.

SCOPE OF VALIDATION

There should be an appropriate and sufficient system including organizational structure and documentation infrastructure, sufficient personnel and financial resources to perform validation tasks in a timely manner. Management and persons responsible for quality assurance should be involved. Personnel with appropriate qualifications and experience should be responsible for performing validation. They should represent different departments depending on the validation work to be performed. There should be a clear distinction between in-process controls and validation. In-process tests are performed during the manufacture of each batch according to specifications and methods devised during the development phase. Their objective is to monitor the process continuously. When a new manufacturing formula or method is adopted, steps should be taken to demonstrate its suitability for routine processing. The defined process, using the materials and equipment specified, should be shown to result in the consistent yield of a product of the required quality. Manufacturers should identify what validation work is needed to prove that critical aspects of their operations are appropriately controlled. Significant changes to the facilities or the equipment, and processes that may affect the quality of the product should be validated. A risk assessment approach should be used to determine the scope and extent of validation required.

ORGANISATION AND PLANNING

All qualification and validation activities should be planned and take the life cycle of equipment, process and product into consideration. Validation activities should only be performed by suitably trained personnel who follow approved validation procedures. Validation personnel should report as defined in the pharmaceutical quality system although this may not necessarily be to a quality management or a quality assurance function, however there should be appropriate oversight over the whole validation life cycle. The key elements of the site validation programme should be clearly defined and documented in a validation master plan (VMP) or equivalent document. The VMP should be a summary document which is brief, concise, clear and contain data on at least the following:

- Validation policy.
- The organisational structure for validation activities.
- Summary of the facilities, systems, equipment, processes on site and the current validation status.
- Template formats to be used for protocols and reports.
- Planning and scheduling.
- Change control and deviation management for validation.
- Handling of acceptance criteria
- References to existing documents.
- An assessment of the resources required.

- The ongoing validation strategy, including revalidation and / requalification, where applicable.
- Confirmation that the materials used for validation are of the required quality and suppliers are qualified to the appropriate level.

For large and complex projects, planning takes on added importance and it may be necessary to create a separate VMP. A quality risk management approach should be used for validation activities with risk assessments repeated, as required, in light of increased knowledge and understanding from any changes during the project phase or during commercial production. The way in which risk assessments are used to support validation activity should be clearly documented.

VALIDATION SET-UP

Critical quality attributes include physical as well as chemical characteristics. Acceptance specifications for the product should be established in order to attain uniformity and consistently the desired product attributes, and the specifications should be derived from testing and challenge of the system on sound statistical basis during the initial development and production phases and continuing through subsequent routine production. The process and equipment should be selected to achieve the product specification. For example; design engineers; production and quality assurance people may all be involved. The process should be defined with a great deal of specificity and each step of the process should be challenged to determine its adequacy. These aspects are important in order to assure products of uniform quality, purity and performance.

VALIDATION TEAM

A multidisciplinary team is primarily responsible for conducting and supervising validation studies. Personnel qualified by training and experience in a relevant discipline may conduct such studies.

Responsibilities of Validation Team

- Creates updates and reviews/ approves individual project validation plans and validation deliverables.
- Ensures validation compliance with the company validation master plan and project validation plan.
- Coordinates, implements, verify elements of VMP.
- Consults on, evaluates and approves changes.
- Reviews and approves IQ/ OQ/ PQ procedures and plans.

- Reviews test results and makes recommendations regarding release.
- Assess risks and develops contingency plan.

DOCUMENTATION

Good documentation practices are important to support knowledge management throughout the validation lifecycle. All documents generated during validation should be approved and authorised by appropriate personnel as defined in the pharmaceutical quality system. The relationship between documents in complex validation projects should be clearly defined and any inter-relationships documented. A written validation protocol should be prepared which defines the critical systems, attributes and parameters which are important and the acceptance criteria for each. Where validation protocols are supplied by a third party, the manufacturer should confirm suitability and compliance with company procedures before approval. Any changes to the approved protocol during execution should be documented as a deviation and be scientifically justified. Results which fail to meet the pre-defined acceptance criteria should be recorded as a deviation, be fully investigated and any implications for the validation discussed in the report. The conclusions of the validation should be reported and the results obtained summarised against the acceptance criteria. Any subsequent changes to acceptance criteria should be scientifically justified and a final recommendation made as to the outcome of the validation. A formal release for the next step in the validation process should be authorised by the relevant responsible personnel either as part of the validation report approval or as a separate summary document. Conditional approval to proceed to the next stage can be given where certain acceptance criteria or deviations have not been fully addressed and there is a documented assessment that there is no significant impact on the next activity.

Documents associated with qualification and validation includes:

- Validation master plan (VMP);
- Standard operating procedures (SOPs);
- Specifications;
- Protocols and reports;
- Risk assessment outcomes;
- Process flow charts;
- Operator manuals;
- Training records;
- Calibration procedures and records;
- Sampling plans;
- Testing plans and methods;
- Statistical methods and results;

- History of qualification or validation;
- Plan for ensuring review of validation status;
- Plan for ensuring maintaining a validated state.

VALIDATION MASTER PLAN

A manufacturer should have a VMP which reflects the key elements of validation. This VMP shall be based on a policy that defines what the validation and qualification process is and its purpose. The policy must make a commitment to maintaining critical processes, equipment, facilities and systems in a valid state and should mention applicable regulations, standards and guidelines that underpin approach to validation. This policy shall also include a commitment to documenting what process, equipment, facilities and systems are subject to validation and how they will be validated in the form of a VMP supported by written validation procedures or protocols and validation records.

VMP should be concise and clear and contain at least the following:

- Title page and authorization (approval signatures and dates);
- Table of contents;
- Abbreviations and glossary;
- Validation policy;
- Philosophy, intention and approach to validation;
- Roles and responsibilities of relevant personnel;
- Resources to ensure validation is done;
- Outsourced services (selection, qualification, management through life cycle);
- Deviation management in validation;
- Change control in validation;
- Risk management principles in validation;
- Training;
- Scope of validation;
- Documentation required in qualification and validation such as procedures, certificates, protocols and reports;
- Premises qualification;
- Utilities qualification;
- Equipment qualification;
- Process validation;
- Cleaning validation;
- Personnel qualification such as analyst qualification;

- Analytical method validation;
- Computerized system validation;
- Establishing acceptance criteria;
- Life-cycle management including retirement policy;
- Requalification and revalidation;
- Relationship with other quality management elements;
- Validation matrix;
- References

The VMP should be reviewed at regular intervals and kept up to date according to current GMP. Prior to each validation activity there is a Validation Master Plan (VMP). This governing document contains information about the company, describes the validation project and names the persons in charge. Further it contains the validation policy and states the general approach of how to validate. The Validation Master Plan includes all validation protocols and validation reports as a requirement of Good Documentation Practice. It is possible to reference existing documents as well as norms and standards.

QUALIFICATION AND VALIDATION PROTOCOLS

There should be qualification and validation protocols describing the qualification and validation to be performed. As a minimum the protocols should include the following significant background information:

- The objectives;
- The site;
- The responsible personnel
- Description of the standard operating procedures (SOPs) to be followed;
- Equipment or instruments to be used;
- Standards and criteria as appropriate;
- The stage of validation or qualification;
- The processes and/or parameters;
- Sampling, testing and monitoring requirements;
- Stress testing where appropriate;
- Calibration requirements;
- Predetermined acceptance criteria for drawing conclusions;
- Review and interpretation of results;
- Change control, deviations;
- Archiving and retention.

There should be a description of the way in which the results will be analysed, including statistical analysis where appropriate. The protocol should be approved prior to use. Any changes to a protocol should be approved prior to implementation of the change.

QUALIFICATION AND VALIDATION REPORTS

There should be written reports on the qualification and validation performed. Reports should reflect the protocols and procedures followed and include at least the title and objective of the study; make reference to the protocol; reference to the appropriate risk assessment; details of materials, equipment, programmes and cycles used; procedures and test methods with appropriate traceability. Results should be recorded and be in compliance with good data and record management practices. Results should be reviewed, analysed and compared against the justified predetermined acceptance criteria, interpreted and statistically analysed where appropriate. Results should meet the acceptance criteria. Deviations, out-of-specification and out-of-limit results should be documented and investigated according to appropriate procedures. If these deviations are accepted, this should be justified. Where necessary, further studies should be performed.

The conclusion of the report should state whether or not the outcome of the qualification and/or validation was considered successful, and should make recommendations for future monitoring and setting of alert and action limits where applicable. The departments responsible for the qualification and validation work should approve the completed report. The quality assurance department should approve the report after the final review. The criteria for approval should be in accordance with the company's quality assurance system. Any deviations found during the validation process should be 498 managed and documented. Corrective actions should be considered.

PRODUCT LIFE CYCLE APPROACH

Validation process efforts must account for the complete product life cycle, including developmental procedures adapted for qualification of a drug product commencing with its research and development phase, rationale for adapting a best fit formula which represents the relationship between required outputs and specified inputs, and procedure for manufacturing. Each step is required to be justified and monitored in order to provide a good quality food and drug product. The FDA emphasizes the product life cycle approach in its evaluation of manufacturer regulatory compliance as well.

VALIDATION PROCESS

The validation scope, boundaries and responsibilities for each process or groups of similar processes or similar equipment's must be documented and approved in a validation plan. These documents, terms and references for the protocol authors are for use in setting the scope of their protocols. It must be based on a Validation Risk Assessment (VRA) to ensure that the scope of validation being authorised is appropriate for the complexity and importance of the equipment or process under validation. Within the references given in the VP the protocol authors must ensure that all aspects of the process or equipment under qualification; that may affect the efficacy, quality and or records of the product are properly qualified. Fig. 2 is giving a flow diagram for various processes to be performed during any validation activities. Qualification includes the following steps:

- Design qualification (DQ)- Demonstrates that the proposed design (or the existing design for an off-the-shelf item) will satisfy all the requirements that are defined and detailed in the User Requirements Specification (URS). Satisfactory execution of the DQ is a mandatory requirement before construction (or procurement) of the new design can be authorised.
- Installation qualification (IQ) – Demonstrates that the process or equipment meets all specifications, is installed correctly, and all required components and documentation needed for continued operation are installed and in place.
- Operational qualification (OQ) – Demonstrates that all facets of the process or equipment are operating correctly.
- Performance qualification (PQ) – Demonstrates that the process or equipment performs as intended in a consistent manner over time.
- Component qualification (CQ) – is a relatively new term developed in 2005. This term refers to the manufacturing of auxiliary components to ensure that they are manufactured to the correct design criteria. This could include packaging components such as folding cartons, shipping cases, labels or even phase change material. All of these components must have some type of random inspection to ensure that the third party manufacturer's process is consistently producing components that are used in the world of GMP at drug or biologic manufacturer.

There are instances when it is more expedient and efficient to transfer some tests or inspections from the IQ to the OQ, or from the OQ to the PQ. This is allowed for in the regulations, provided that a clear and approved justification is documented in the Validation Plan (VP). This combined testing of OQ and PQ phases is sanctioned by the European Commission Enterprise Directorate-General within 'Annex 15 to the EU Guide to Good

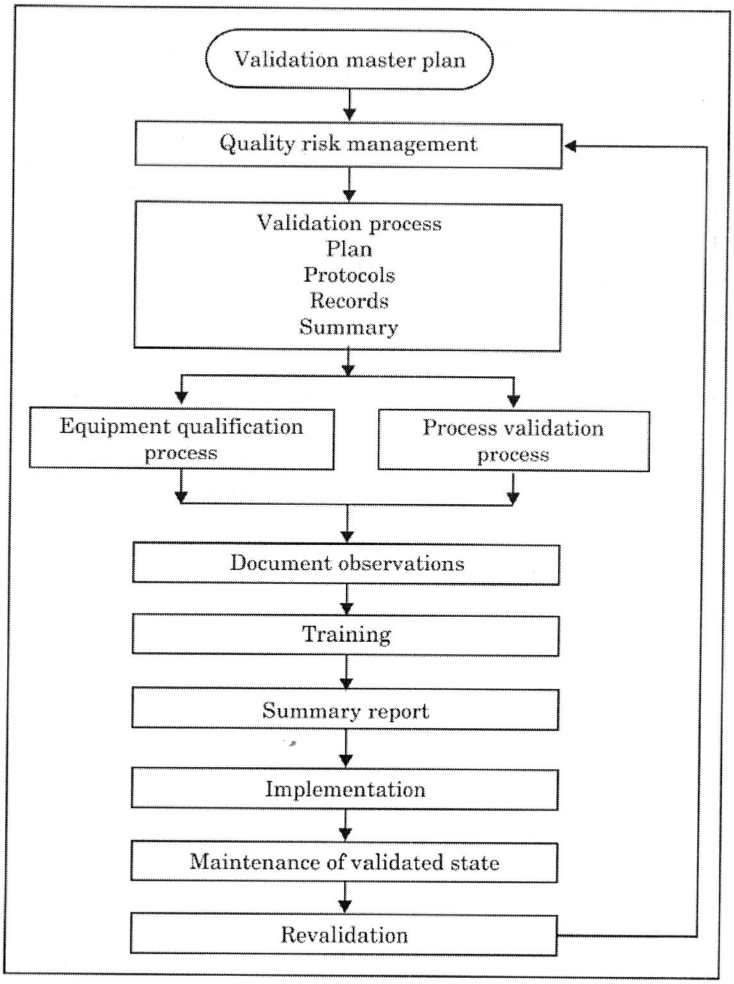

Fig. 2: Validation process

Manufacturing Practice guide' (2001, p. 6) which states that: "*Although PQ is described as a separate activity, it may in some cases be appropriate to perform it in conjunction with OQ.*"

REVALIDATION

Processes and procedures should be revalidated to ensure that they remain capable of achieving the intended results. There should be periodic revalidation, as well as revalidation after changes. Revalidation should be done in accordance with a defined schedule. The frequency and extent of revalidation should be determined using a risk-based approach together with a review of historical data.

Periodic Revalidation

Periodic revalidation should be performed to assess process changes that may occur gradually over a period of time, or because of wear of equipment. The following should be considered when periodic revalidation is performed:

- Master formulae and specifications;
- SOPs;
- Records (*e.g.* of calibration, maintenance and cleaning); and
- Analytical methods.

Revalidation After Change

Revalidation should be performed following a change that could have an effect on the process, procedure, quality of the product and /or the product characteristics. Revalidation should be considered as part of the change control procedure.

The extent of revalidation will depend on the nature and significance of the change(s). Changes should not adversely affect product quality or process characteristics. Changes requiring revalidation should be defined in the validation plan and may include:

- Changes in starting materials (including physical properties, such as density, viscosity or particle size distribution that may affect the process or product);
- Change of starting material manufacturer;
- Transfer of processes to a different site (including change of facilities and installations which influence the process);
- Changes of primary packaging material (*e.g.* substituting plastic for glass);
- Changes in the manufacturing process (*e.g.* mixing times or drying temperatures);
- Changes in the equipment (*e.g.* addition of automatic detection systems, installation of new equipment, major revisions to machinery or apparatus and breakdowns);
- Production area and support system changes (*e.g.* rearrangement of areas, or a new water treatment method);
- Appearance of negative quality trends;
- Appearance of new findings based on current knowledge, *e.g.* new technology;
- Support system changes.

Changes of equipment which involve the replacement of equipment on a "like-for-like" basis would not normally require a revalidation. For example, installation of a new centrifugal pump to replace an older model would not necessarily require revalidation.

CONCLUSIONS

Validation is the most widely used word in the areas of drug development, manufacturing and specification of finished products. The consistency and reliability of a validated system to enable production of a quality product is very important for an industry. Pharmaceutical Validation is the most important and recognized parameters of cGMP. Validation is intended to assist manufacturers in understanding quality management system (QMS) requirements concerning validation and has general applicability to manufacturing process. In general, pharmaceutical validation and process control provide a certain assurance of batch uniformity and integrity of the product manufactured.

FURTHER READINGS

EU-GMP Volume 4: EU Guidelines for Good Manufacturing Practice for Medicinal Products for Human and Veterinary Use, Annex 15
ICH. ICH Q10: Pharmaceutical Quality System. Jun 2008.
ICH. ICH Q11
ICH. ICH Q8
WHO TRS 937

9

Validation Master Plan

ABSTRACT

In the previous chapter we studied regarding validation and various documents for the validation activities. Validation master plan or VMP is a document which will explain or give a basic introduction regarding validation activities performed in the organisation. It will give approaches for validation activities, different type of validations performed in the organisations and introduction regarding and eligibility requirements for the validation team members. The Validation Master Plan (VMP) must present an overall picture of the company facility, organization and capability. It must give a clear and concise overview of how the company has integrated all applicable current Good Manufacturing Practice (cGMP) requirements into its operations.

INTRODUCTION

The Validation Master Plan (VMP); also known as Master Validation Plan (MVP) is a document, used to represent an overall picture to visiting auditors, investigators or inspectors, of how the company has integrated cGMP into its day to day activities. Even sometimes although not mandatory; it inevitably will be the first document, auditors will ask to review. Although there is no strict format for the VMP to follow; still they have projected an expectation that they expect to be able to review such a document and that such a document must project a picture of how your company has integrated "Current Good Manufacturing Practices" (cGMP); as promulgated in 21 CFR Part 820 and 211, into all aspects of the manufacture of a regulatory controlled product. This is because they expect this document to clearly and concisely illustrate to them how management has delegated responsibilities, designed product processes, planned resources usage and established a fully trained competent work force. On the basis of review to document they will look for evidence to convince them that there is sufficient ongoing training to maintain these standards and sufficient auditing to prove it.

Quality engineering services are geared towards the management, development, operation and maintenance of quality attributes, and are essential for companies of all sizes, since they can help make sure that quality standards and requirements are met across the board. Validation of products, processes and facilities is an important part of a company's QMS (Quality Management System), especially for pharmaceutical, biotechnology or medical device manufacturing. While there is no formal need for a Validation Master Plan according to FDA rules, it is often included in quality engineering services for these sectors.

As part of GMPs (Good Manufacturing Practices) for pharmaceutical, biotech and medical device companies, a Validation Master Plan (or VMP) is document that outlines and defines which processes and equipment are to be validated, the priority and order in which this will be done, as well as who is responsible for the validation process, etc. Validation Master Plan can help companies overcome challenges faced in heavily regulated sectors, since FDA inspectors may request documentation summarizing an organization's process/ equipment validation plan. As mentioned above, it's part of industry GMPs and not a formal requirement, but can help reduce the chances of receiving an FDA warning letter.

VMP must define validation activities and allot responsibilities for authoring, reviewing, approving, and executing validation documentation and tasks. It must comply with all the appropriate requirements documented in 21 Code of Federal Regulation Part 11, 210, 211 and 820 legislation. Validation provides evidence of state of control to third party auditors. The VMP creates a disciplined approach to the development and release of products and processes:

- Serves to ensure the identification of all necessary elements and their relationship in the manufacture of products and development of processes.
- Creates an understanding of the entire process.
- The plan forces a structured and standardized approach to validation across the organization, for example, it forces equivalent approval authority levels across different organizational departments.
- It is good business practice, as it ensures a balanced consistent approach to product and process quality, reliability and safety.

While not directly called out as required in the Food and Drug Administration's (FDA) Quality System Regulation (21 CFR 820), a good Validation Master Plan (VMP) is critical to executing a solid process validation program. A Validation Master Plan provides medical device manufacturers with a roadmap, by outlining the process validation requirements and providing justification for these requirements. Therefore, manufacturers should understand what makes for a good Validation Master Plan.

PURPOSE OF VMP

The Validation Master Plan is intended to represent the manufacturing validation life cycle. It should be created concurrently with the design and development effort and can be used as a tool for project planning. Pharmaceutical manufacturers would not begin a product realization effort without a Design and Development Plan. Similarly, a manufacturing effort should not begin without a VMP. The VMP is beneficial for planning purposes because it identifies anticipated resource needs and provides key input into scheduling of project timelines. It documents the scope of the validation effort, including impacted product, processes, procedures, facilities, equipment, and utility systems. The VMP allows companies to agree upon and document an overall validation strategy, which can be provided to regulators to serve as clear justification for the validation effort. The VMP allows medical device manufacturers to show that they are in control of their quality system and producing devices with a focus on product quality.

IMPORTANCE OF VMP

VMP is a roadmap of validation activity like facility qualification and also define system and area to be validated. VMP justifies the strategy, documenting the necessary program. It's a "high level" document which provides a written program to ensure a continuing state of validation. We can say VMP is achieving and maintaining qualified facility. All Validation program is mention in VMP. In simple language we can describe the major element of "Validation program"-

- Tell them what are you going to do
- Do it
- Tell them what you did

Validation in general requires a meticulous preparation and careful planning of the various steps in the process. In addition, all work involved should be carried out in a structured way according to formally authorised standardised working and administrative procedures. In addition validation is characterised by:

Multidisciplinary approach

A specific characteristic of validation work is that it requires the collaboration of experts of various disciplines such as pharmacists, technologists, metrologists, chemical analysts, microbiologists, engineers, experts on Q.A. validation etc.

Time constraints

Generally validation work is submitted to rigorous time schedules. These studies are always the last stage prior to taking new processes, facilities into routine operation.

Costs

Validation studies are costly as they require time of highly specialised personnel and expensive technology. The above factors require a well organised and structured approach that should be adequately described in a Validation Master Plan (VMP).

Purpose

The VMP should present an overview of the entire validation operation, its organisational structure, its content and planning. The core of the VMP being the list/ inventory of the items to be validated and the planning schedule. A VMP helps management:

- To know what the validation programme involves with respect to time, people and money, and
- To understand the necessity for the programme;

A VMP helps all members of the validation team to know their tasks and responsibilities. A VMP helps GMP inspectors to understand the firm's approach to validation and the set up an organisation of all validation activities. A Validation Master Plan is a document that summarises the firm's overall philosophy, intentions and approach to be used for establishing performance adequacy. All validation activities relating to critical technical operations, relevant to product and process controls within a firm should be included in a VMP. This includes qualification of critical manufacturing and control equipment. It should comprise all types of validation activities including Re-validations. In case of large projects like the construction of a new facility, often the best approach is to create a separate VMP.

VMP AND VP DIFFERENT CONTEXT

While writing and reviewing VMP extremely important commitments and decisions have to be made. Program conceptions have to be mated to the User Requirements Specifications (URS). These specifications have to be mated to the VMP. From these plans the User Requirements Specification (URS), the Validation Risk Assessment (VRA), the Design Qualification (DQ), the Installation Qualification (IQ), the Operational Qualification (OQ), and the Performance Qualifications (PQ) have to be authorized, authored, approved for content, and issued for execution. The completed documentation has to be reviewed and accepted as complete by persons authorised to execute this role. All of these functions must be detailed in the VMP, when the project concept demands that a VMP is required or the Validation Plan (VP) where it does not. Responsibilities have to be declared, people have to be nominated, and everyone involved is duly served with a copy that carries the full authority of the company. Fig. 1 gives a basic layout for the planning processes for a validation activity.

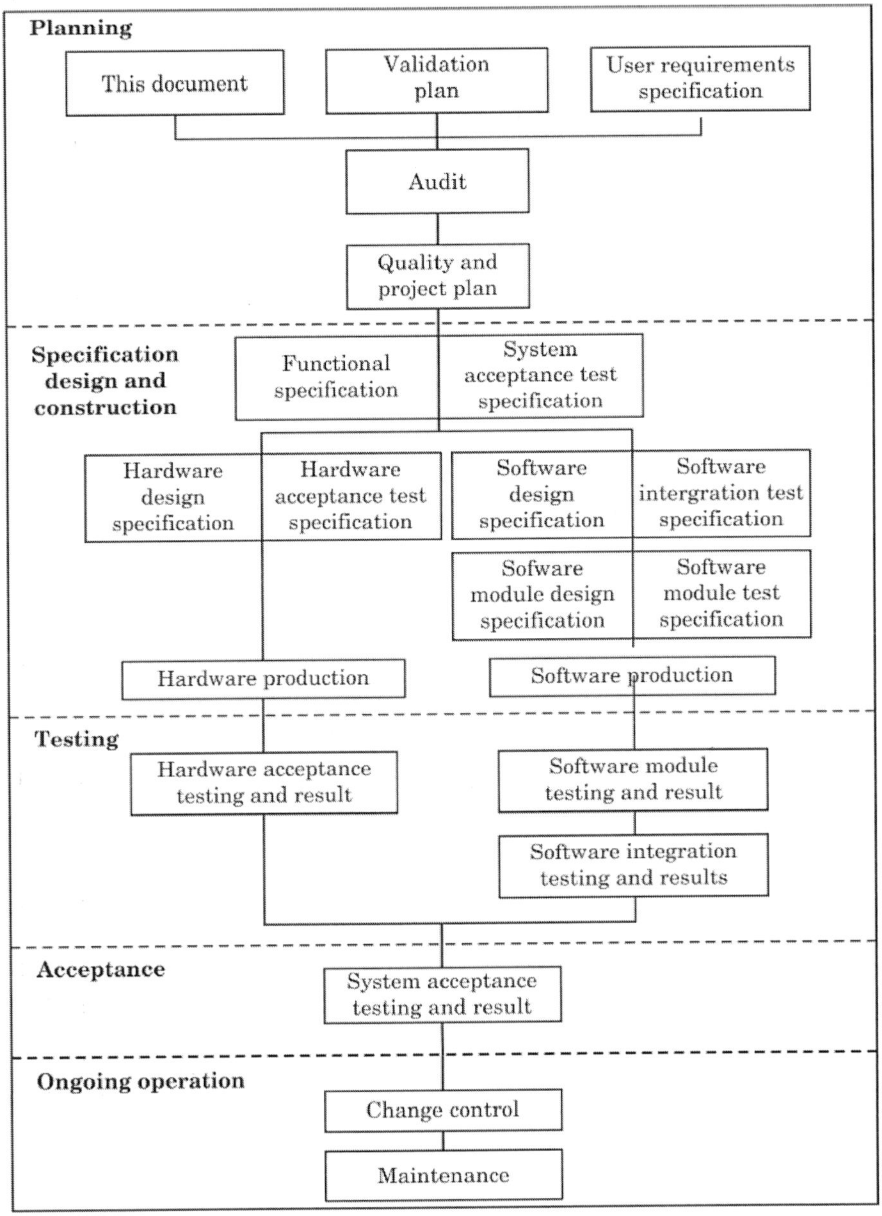

Fig. 1: VMP plan and process

VMP INTEGRATION

The Validation Master Plan is a top layer document and should not go into specific detail; but present an overall picture of the company facility, organisation and capability. It must give a clear and concise overview, to a reviewer, of how the company has integrated all the applicable cGMP requirements into every aspect of its operations. It must define validation activities and allot responsibilities for authoring, reviewing, approving, and executing validation documentation and tasks.

It must define the range of documentation spreading from the VMP to the VP, URS, DQ, IQ, OQ and PQ. It must explain and detail the company's approach to risk based validation and the interaction of the VRA, VA, and 21 CFR Part 11. Facilities are portrayed with the use of layered drawings; where different layers show individual systems and equipment lists give equipment type and identity details. It is normal to include layered drawings to enable a clear and easily observed presentation of the following systems.

1) Facility building overall location and access.
2) Facility production/ clerical/ storage/ controlled areas, rooms or zones.
3) Raw material ingress and finished product egress routes.
4) Personnel ingress and egress routes, along with changing areas.
5) Utility Layouts
6) Electrical layouts
7) Controlled areas along with air flow directions and pressure regimes.
8) Dressing codes for these controlled areas.

CONTENTS OF VALIDATION MASTER PLAN

From a risk perspective, the VMP should include an overall assessment of the potential impact of the manufacturing processes on product quality. By using a risk-based approach, the VMP will identify which processes to validate and in what order to perform the validations. This risk assessment may also identify processes that do not need validated. In the VMP, each manufacturing process should be broken down and assessed to understand the impact each could have on the final product. This assessment serves as a strong justification for the scope and requirements included in process validation protocols. Overall, the VMP describes the activities and requirements for a validation program and mandates the methods for continuous monitoring. While VMPs are not listed in the Code of Federal Regulations, appropriate "Guidance for Industry" recommendations say that they should include details of:

- All validation activities
- Time, location, priority and order of validation activities

- A statement describing the validation policy of the company
- An overview of the organization's scope of operations,
- Describing the facilities, products and processes
- Facility management/personnel who have agreed upon the plan
- Details or copies of any corresponding validation plans,
- Existing SOPs,
- Relevant policy documents
- Validation reports/protocols, etc.
- Persons who are responsible and provide approval for SOPs, protocols and the VMP, as well as any review and reference tracking systems
- References to or appendices detailing any plans for validation training programs

Format and Content

The VMP should be a summary document and should therefore be brief, concise and clear. It should not repeat information documented elsewhere but refer to existing documents such as Policy Documents, SOP's and Validation Protocols/ Reports. The VMP should be agreed by management.

Validation Master Plan: Sections

A VMP should contain data on the following subjects / proposed chapters.

Introduction

A brief overview of the project, (name, address, type of products and market) which includes the company's name, location, any applicable division/ subsidiary name, the sector/industry it serves, and references to the company's Quality Assurance Policy. It shall describe the approach of the company and details the company vision for the validation.

Objective

This section details the objectives of the VMP and the way or pathway to fulfil these objectives. VMP describes the company's intentions. This Validation Master Plan (VMP) describes the company's intentions regarding the validation of equipment, instruments, systems, utilities, facilities, materials, analytical methods, processes and personnel.

Scope

An outline defining the range and extent of the organization's validation activities, whether single/multiproduct, the installation as well as equipment installed (both existing and new).

Validation policy

This section lays down the company policies and mission statement.

Validation Team

This section shall describe the details of the department and personnel responsible for the validation activities. The team members shall plan for the validation, sampling plan.

Organization and Responsibilities

It shall elaborate department name and responsibility assigned. It shall mention Organizational Structure of Validation Team. This section shall clarify organisational structure of all validation activities like personnel responsibility for

- The VMP,
- Protocols of individual validation projects,
- Validation work,
- Report and document preparation and control,
- Approval / authorisation of validation protocols and reports in all stages of validation processes,
- Tracking system for reference and review,
- Training needs in support of validation.

Facility Description

The facility's characteristics (whether the building is new, or an extension/ remodel), *e.g.,* number of floors, isolation means, access between process and utility systems, clean room certification levels, special surfaces/finishes that affect product quality, etc. The focus is on facility design, and personnel flow, raw material, waste flow and design product characteristics need to be studied to reduce cross-contamination risks. This section shall mention critical and non-critical classification. A common principle in validation studies is to challenge processes, systems etc. The rationale behind any challenge and or "worst case" situation should be explained. Consideration can be given to the grouping of products / processes for the purpose of validating "worst case" situations. Where "worst case" situations cannot be simulated, the rationale for the groupings made should be defined.

Commissioning

While commissioning of equipment, utilities and support systems is not FDA-regulated and typically not part of validation, this section should list the selection criteria used to determine which systems will be tested. This explains to the FDA why certain utilities are not validated (if they don't affect product quality) and shows that each support system has been thoroughly tested within the anticipated OQ operating range to check for impact on product quality.

Definition of validation concept

This section defines the type of validation activities carried out in the facility. This section also includes possible reason for starting the revalidation including periodic revalidation.

Qualification

Selection criteria used to decide which equipment and utilities will go through qualification, as well as published guidelines, regulatory references and company policies that affect the selection process. This section may also include final report and protocol formats (with a description of the format or references to existing protocol development procedures), individual IQ/OQ/PQ definitions, and final reports.

List of Products / Processes / Systems to be Validated

All validation activities comprised in the VMP should be summarised and compiled in a matrix format. Such matrix should provide an overview and contain:

- All items covered by the VMP that are subject to validation describing the extent of validation required [*i.e.,* IQ, OQ and/or PQ].
- It should include validation of analytical techniques which are to be used in determining the validation status of other processes or systems, the validation approach,
- Re-validation activities,
- Actual status and future planning.

Process Validation

Selection criteria used to decide which equipment and utilities will go through process validation, as well as published guidelines, regulatory references and company policies that affect the selection process, any cleaning validations needed to verify inter-campaign/intra-campaign cleaning methods, and packaging and sterility validation for finished products.

Specific Process Considerations

Under this heading specific characteristics / requirements of the plant / process etc. that are critical for yielding a quality product and need extra attention may be briefly outlined here.

Computer System Validation

Details of computer validation through an installed control system (Distributed Control System/DCS or Programmable Logic Controller/ PLC), the selection criteria used to decide which computer systems will go through validation, and the control system's 21 CFR 11 compliance details (authority checks, secure audit trails, etc.).

List of Required Protocols and Procedures

Equipment and utilities represented in a table (which can be used as a "deliverables list" for external validation), as well as the required procedures and protocols. This section defines validation requirements and resource loading for the project, forming the core of the VMP.

List of Standard Operating Procedures

Equipment and utilities represented in a table, as well as required standard operating procedures (SOPs), like the section for "protocols and procedures" above. This section can be used to pinpoint the SOP levels (typically operation, maintenance, and cleaning SOPs) that need to be generated for validation.

Along with the above mentioned parts VMP document shall also contains following information:

Approval page

It indicates agreement with the qualification and validation annual plan. Quality assurance shall prepare VMP and checked by Production, Quality Control, ware house and engineering personal. Document shall be reviewed by QA and approved by QA Head.

Acceptance criteria

A list of the general acceptance criteria for the validation tasks must comply to concisely define the completion of validation tasks. If possible, at this stage of project, specific acceptance criteria should be developed for each unit to be validated.

Element of Equipment Validation

This section mention:

- Facility Qualification,
- Equipment Qualification (DQ, IQ, OQ, PQ),
- Computer system Qualification/ Validation,
- Calibration,

- Calibration Policy,
- Preventive maintenance program,
- Process Validation,
- Criteria of Process Validation,
- Process Validation Parameter,
- Variable parameters,
- Evaluation parameters,
- Acceptance criteria,
- Approach, General Protocol,
- Cleaning Validation and approach,
- Heating Ventilation Air Conditioning (HVAC system) qualification,
- Pharmaceutical compressed Air test function and acceptance criteria,
- Water generation and distribution system,
- Media fill,
- Control of validation document.

Planning and Scheduling

Validation schedule is the last but not the least important component of overall validation activity. This section should include:

- An estimate of staffing (including training needs),
- Equipment and other specific requirements to complete the validation effort,
- A time plan of the project with detailed planning of subprojects,

Due to this reason a VMP requires regular updating.

Qualification/ Validation Report

A report that cross-references the qualification and/or validation protocol should be prepared, summarising the results obtained, commenting on any deviations observed, and drawing the necessary conclusions, including recommending changes necessary to correct deficiencies. Any changes to the plan/procedure as defined in the protocol should be documented with appropriate justification.

Deviation

Any deviations/ critical changes to the approved protocol during the execution of process validation shall be handled as per handling of deviation procedure. Details of deviation shall be documented in the report with details such as, description of deviation, reason/ cause, corrective and preventive action, and status of the deviation. All the deviations shall be closed or resolution shall be specified prior to release of product for intended purpose.

Deficiency (If any) and Corrective Action Report

During validation or qualification if any deficiency shall be observed, then following things must be recorded such as

1. Description of deficiency and date observed
2. Person, Responsible for corrective action and date assigned
3. Corrective actions taken and date conducted:

These are always approved by HOD of Quality Assurance.

Addendums to Protocols

Addendums are used during execution of a protocol in following instances:

- Addendums are utilized to record additional data/ test not initially written into the protocol, but will enhance the validation of the System/ Equipment.
- Addendums are utilized when a test was inadvertently left out of the initial protocol writing and the test is necessary to enhance the validation of the System/Equipment.
- Addendums are utilized if a test initially written into the protocol cannot be performed or must be changed.
- The Addendum is utilized for detailing the new test and recording the data.
- Use of the Addendum in this manner requires approval by the Validation Taskforce leader prior to implementation and execution.
- Addendums are utilized when more space is required to completely record data and/or comments.
- The Addendums require the protocol name, protocol number, execution date, signature of the preparer, date, and signature of the approver and date.

Conditional Final Report (CFR)

The conditional Final Report (CFR) is utilized in a circumstance when the portion of the validation effort impacting equipment, systems, and/or processes needed to complete scheduling deadlines is completed within the acceptance criteria limits, but the entire protocol is not completed and approved.

The CFR provides conditional approval for use of the specific area of the equipment, system, or process required by the schedule. The CFR summarizes the observations, data, deviations, conclusions, and recommended actions resulting from execution of the specific area of the appropriate protocols for the equipment, system, or process being following departments or their designees as applicable: Engineering, Production, Quality Assurance, Quality Control, and/ or Research and Development. The conditional review of the validation testing, take place during "sign off" of results. CFR or FR is only a compilation of the signed off results.

Attachments

Site Plan, Process flow chart, Qualification Matrix, URS Protocol, IQ, OQ and PQ Protocol, PQ Variable, Validation Activities (Validation Planner), Process Validation Protocol, Process Validation Parameter, SOP list and Validation deliverables/responsibilities for equipment's and utilities other than QC instrument.

Change Control

A statement of the company's commitment to controlling critical changes to materials, facilities, equipment or processes (including analytical techniques), should be included. The VMP is a controlled document. It should be reviewed on regular basis either periodic or as and when required. Layouts should be generated by drawing software and any changes in VMP should be made through document control.

NEED TO MAINTAIN A VALIDATION MASTER PLAN

To assure product quality

To assure that all the elements necessary to support product processing are qualified and proven as capable prior to commencement of any processing activities.

Regulatory compliance

Validation is a requirement of many regulatory bodies, for example:

- The US FDA,
- The European Competent Authorities,
- The UK's Medical Healthcare Regulatory Agency,
- The Australia New Zealand Therapeutic Products Agency (ANZTPA),
- Health Canada, etc.

CONCLUSIONS

In the US, a Validation Master Plan is not technically a regulatory requirement; in the EU, it is. For the US, the actual regulatory requirement is that you have a clearly defined and documented validation program. In

EU, you are subject to receiving a note of deficiency if you don't have a Validation Master Plan in place. In both areas, even if you have documents that are equivalent to a Validation Master Plan, it's preferred to have them in a master document.

EU GMP Vol. 4 Annex 15 says: "The key elements of a validation programme should be clearly defined and documented in a validation master plan (VMP) or equivalent documents." However, a Validation Master Plan is an extremely good idea (even in the US) simply because it helps give sense and organization to your validation efforts and an understanding of how it supports the goals of your facility. And during an inspection this type of planning document is going to make auditors happy. This chapter shall act as recommendation, for a starting point, is to do a web search on "validation project plan" and "validation master plan." Here are some nice documents that can give detailed guidance and samples.

Essentially a VMP must outline the processes and equipment that require validation and the job roles responsible for executing validation. A regulatory inspector wants to see a summary of the validation practices, listed by priority. Check out these sources of information:

The Pharmaceutical Inspection Co-operation Scheme has published a document called: "Recommendations on the Validation Master Plan, Installation and Operational Qualification, Non-Sterile Process Validation/ Cleaning Validation". This document, in combination with the PIC/s's "Good Practices for Computerised Systems in Regulated 'G x P' Environments" briefly outlines a Validation Master plan like so:

1. A list of all validation activities:
2. A list or copies of any parallel Validation Plans
3. References to existing documents such as Policy Documents, SOP's and Validation Protocols/ Reports
4. A list of facility management who have agreed upon the master plan
5. A statement of the firm's validation policy
6. General description of the scope of the operations of the firm which describes the facilities, processes and products
7. The time and location of validation activities (ideally prioritized)
8. A list of personnel responsible for the VMP, SOPs and protocols
9. A list relevant validation reports and documents
10. A list of personnel (roles) who provide approval
11. Description of any tracking systems used for reference and review
12. Validation training program plans - either the plans as appendices or references to the plans as separate documents

FURTHER READINGS

EU-GMP Volume 4: EU Guidelines for Good Manufacturing Practice for Medicinal Products for Human and Veterinary Use, Annex 15
ICH. ICH Q10: Pharmaceutical Quality System. Jun 2008.
ICH. ICH Q11
ICH. ICH Q8
WHO TRS 937

10

Equipment Qualification

ABSTRACT

This chapter describes the general approach to qualifications for, example, premises, systems, utilities and equipment. The principles in this chapter may also be applied to the qualification of instruments, analytical instruments and testing devices; where appropriate. It may include and are not limited to: certain rooms; water purification systems; cleaning systems; heating, ventilation and air conditioning systems; compressed air systems; gas systems; steam systems; as well as production equipment and analytical instruments.

INTRODUCTION

Equipment qualification is a term used to describe a set of independent procedures that are used to check if a product meets the specifications and requirements of its intended purposes. Regulatory agencies around the world have strict requirements for quality, procedures, performance testing, safety checks and the like, for a wide range of products.

THE IMPORTANCE OF EQUIPMENT VALIDATION

In precision instruments, lab equipment or specialized machinery, even minor inaccuracies can cause problems and lead to inaccurate or incomplete results. Equipment validation ensures your product will consistently perform within a given range. Most consumers look for certification from quality management systems, like ISO, before they even consider buying a product; so an incorrect system of validating your equipment can threaten your adherence to industry norms, as well as your certifications and compliances.

PRINCIPLE

In principle, premises, systems, utilities and equipment should be appropriately designed, located, installed, operated, cleaned, maintained and qualified to suit their intended purpose. Quality management systems should be in place to ensure that these remain in a qualified state throughout their life cycle. Products should be manufactured on qualified equipment.

GENERAL

The remainder of the text in this chapter will refer to utilities and equipment as examples, even though the principles may be applicable to others such as premises and systems. The validation master plan, or other relevant document, should specify the policy, organization, planning, scope and stages applied in qualification on site, and should cover, *e.g.*, production, quality control and engineering. Quality risk management principles should be applied in qualification. The scope and extent of qualification and requalification should be determined based on the principles of impact assessment and risk management principles. Qualification should be executed by trained personnel. Training records should be maintained.

Where appropriate, new premises, systems, utilities and equipment should be subjected to all stages of qualification. This includes the preparation of user requirement specifications (URS), design qualification (DQ), installation qualification (IQ), operational qualification (OQ) and performance qualification (PQ). Fig. 1 is presenting the V model to be considered during equipment qualification activity. This figure presents relations between different stages of the qualification process. Justification should be provided where it is decided that not all stages of qualification are required. Qualification should be done in accordance with predetermined and approved qualification protocols. The results of the qualification should be recorded and reflected in qualification reports. There should be a logical sequence for executing qualification including such as premises (rooms), then utilities and equipment. Normally, qualification stages should be sequential. (For example, operational qualification should follow after the successful completion of installation qualification). In some cases, different stages of qualification may be executed concurrently. Equipment should be released for routine use only once there is documented evidence that the qualification has been successful. Certain stages of the qualification may be done by a supplier or a third party, subject to the conditions and responsibilities as defined in a written agreement between the parties. The contract giver remains responsible to ensure that the qualification is done in accordance with the principles of good manufacturing practices (GMP). The relevant documentation associated with qualification, including standard operating procedures (SOPs), specifications and acceptance criteria, certificates and manuals, should be available. Utilities and equipment should be maintained in a qualified state and should be periodically reviewed for the need for requalification. Requalification should be considered when changes are made.

All relevant SOPs for operation, maintenance and calibration should be prepared during qualification. Training should be provided to operators and training records should be maintained. Normally, qualification should be completed before process validation is performed. The process of qualification should be a logical, systematic process and should follow a logical flow from the premises, followed by utilities, equipment, to procedures and processes. Stages of qualification should normally start with the preparation of user requirement specifications (URS). Depending on the function and operation of the utility, equipment or system, this is followed by, as appropriate, different stages in qualification such as a factory acceptance test (FAT), site acceptance test (SAT), design qualification (DQ), installation qualification (IQ), operational qualification (OQ) and performance qualification (PQ).

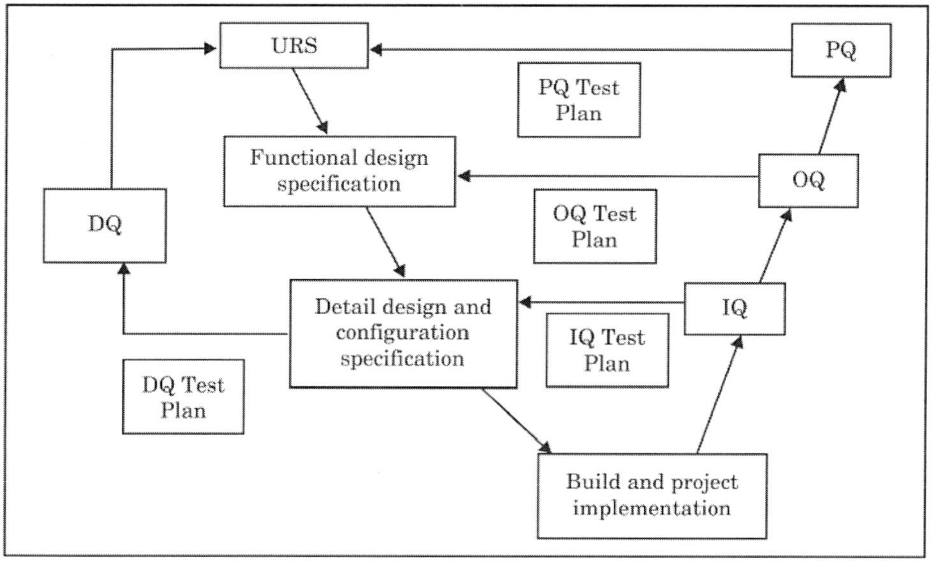

Fig. 1: V Model for direct impact system

DIFFERENT ASPECTS OF EQUIPMENT VALIDATION

Equipment qualification through DQ, IQ, OQ and PQ practices is a part of Good Manufacturing Practice (GMP), through which manufacturers and laboratories can ensure that their equipment delivers consistent quality. It reduces the margin for errors, so the product quality can be maintained within industry standards or regulatory authority requirements. When qualification of equipment is not needed very frequently, performing it in-house might not be feasible, so smaller laboratories might benefit from scheduling external equipment validation services on a regular basis instead. Here are some of the protocols that need to be kept in mind for successful equipment validation:

Documentation Availability

All the documentation that is required should be verified and made available. This includes electrical schematics, mechanical and instrument drawings, utility and supply ratings, spare parts lists, and such.

Component and Design Verification

The design of the equipment and its components should be verified in accordance with specifications and verification norms.

Electrical Connections and Supply

All the electrical connections and the power supply to the equipment needs to be checked thoroughly before you begin the validation process.

Utility Supply

Hydraulic, pneumatic, and other input supplies, as well as the connections, should be verified for quality and checked for leaks.

Safety Compliance

Safety checks should be tested and noise levels should be within applicable standards. Electrical connections and fail-safes need to be checked and tested, and the wiring needs to be checked for leaks. Radiation and interference levels should be within acceptable limits too.

Critical Instrument Calibration

Any sensors or monitoring instruments need to be calibrated correctly. The accuracy of primary monitoring instruments and controls should be within the limits of traceable standards, and the resolution should be within the required range.

Environmental Verification

Instruments need to be checked for operation in various environments. This includes testing within the required ranges of temperature, humidity, light, electrostatic discharge isolation, and other conditions.

Standard Operating Procedures

SOPs for various procedures should be available, like cleaning, periodic maintenance, software configuration, disaster recovery, etc.

Instrumentation for Validation

The instruments used to validate the installation qualification should be listed and should be within the due date for re-calibration

These are just a few things that almost every validation process should incorporate. Depending on the industry the instruments are built for and the individual requirements of the validation, other aspects might also need to be taken into account.

VALIDATION PROCESS

Instrument validation begins with a validation master plan that defines the steps in each process. Traditionally, these steps can be categorized into 5 separate qualification categories (URS, DQ, FAT, IQ, OQ, PQ), which include:

One stage of qualification should be successfully completed before the next stage is initiated, *e.g.,* from IQ to OQ. In some cases, only IQ and OQ may be required, as the correct operation of the equipment, utility or system could be considered to be a sufficient indicator of its performance. Major equipment and critical utilities and systems, however, may require URS, DQ, IQ, OQ and PQ.

Computerized systems, including equipment with software component(s), require user and functional requirements specifications, design and configuration specifications, development of SOPs, training programmes for system use and administration, and an appropriate level of IQ, OQ and PQ verification testing. This includes tests such as stress, load, volume and other performance verification tests that mimic the live production environment. It also includes user acceptance testing according to draft SOPs and training as well as end-to-end business processes for intended use. Equipment qualification process is illustrated in Fig. 2.

USER REQUIREMENT SPECIFICATIONS

Manufacturers should prepare a document that describes, for example, the utility or equipment to be sourced. The requirements and specifications for the utility or equipment should be defined by the user and documented in the URS. The URS should be used when selecting the required utility or equipment from an approved supplier, and to verify suitability throughout the subsequent stages of qualification. A well-written URS provides several specific benefits, as it:

- Serves as a reference against which off-the-shelf commercial products are selected, evaluated in detail, and any enhancements are defined. You are less likely to be seduced by technology or buy a poor system using this approach.

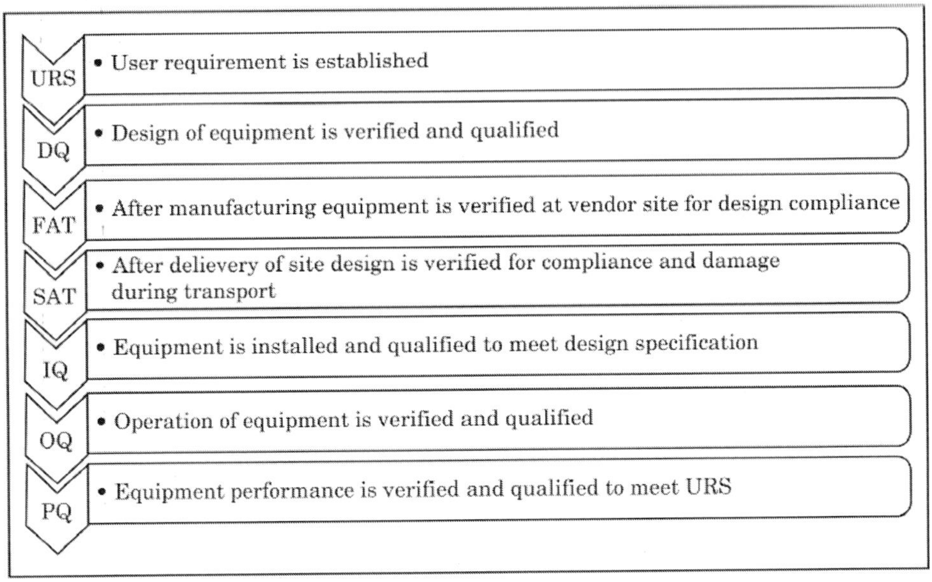

Fig. 2: Equipment qualification process

- Reduces the total system effort and costs, since careful review of the document should reveal omissions, misunderstandings and/or inconsistencies in the specification and this means that they can be corrected easily before you purchase the system.
- Provides the input to user acceptance test specifications and/or qualification of the system.

A URS defines clearly and precisely, what the customer (*i.e.*, you) wants the system to do, and should be understood by both the customer and the instrument vendor. The URS is a living document, and must be kept updated, *via* a change control procedure, throughout the computer system life cycle. After purchase, if and when you upgrade the software, the URS is also updated to reflect the changes and new functions in the latest version. A URS defines the functions to be carried out, the data on which the system will operate, and the operating environment. Ideally, the emphasis is on the required functions and not the method of implementation as this focuses on the "what" rather than the "how".

If you are selecting any new equipment, then the main purpose of a URS from a business rationale is to select a system based on your defined requirements. This avoids the user community from being seduced by technology as the system selection is based on documented requirements and what the users actually want. Furthermore, it allows the selection to be based on objective requirements that will allow you to cut through the marketing literature and focus on your specific requirements. As the URS defines what the system can do, it provides a platform to assess if any system can provide the required functionality.

URS should be prepared for but not limited to, utilities and equipment, as appropriate. URS should be used at later stages in qualification to verify that the purchased and supplied utility or equipment is in accordance with the user's needs. The function of a User Requirement document is to serve as the mandate or terms of reference for the design, development and realisation of the technical component of a system or subsystem within a Project. Usually there is only one User Requirement document for every equipment, even when the required development encompasses more than one development contract.

User Requirement document is produced as a result of appropriate Requirements Analysis activity, based on the stipulations of the Project Definition document and the Implementation Plan. All specific requirements in the User Requirement document must be consistent with similar statements in higher-level specifications, if they exist. The User Requirement document is the primary input to subsequent System Design work and to the procurement specifications for pertinent system development contracts.

From the V model shown it is evident that the user requirements are related to the tests carried out in the qualification phase (typically either the OQ or the PQ). Therefore, it is important to define the requirements for the basic functions of the equipment, the adequate size, 21 CFR 11 requirements and consistent intended performance in the URS that will be tested before the system goes live. The main elements in a URS are:

- Corporate requirements for hardware, work stations and operating systems, *e.g.,* terminal emulation such as Citrix.
- Overall system requirements such as number of users, locations where the system will be used and the instruments connected to the system.
- Compliance requirements from the predicate rule and 21 CFR 11 such as: Open or closed system definition
- Security and access configuration of the software application including user types Data integrity, Time and date stamp requirements, Electronic signature requirements
- Defined data system functions, which should be based on the workflow outlined for writing a URS.
- In addition, include requirements for system capacity such as maximum number of samples to be run, custom calculations and reports for the initial implementation and roll-out, etc.
- IT Support requirements. These include backup and recovery, off-line archive and restore.
- Interface requirements. For example, will the CDS be a standalone system or will it interface with a LIMS and if so how?

Requirements Analysis will generally include

- Review of all relevant documents,
- Establishment of an initial system concept, if not already done
- Consultation of users
- Consolidation of inputs
- Negotiation of a definitive statement of User Requirements.

All users, both end-users and operators/maintainers, should be consulted. Consultation may be by any expedient means, including interviews, workshops, questionnaires, and e mail. The "user" in the title of this document is a deliberately vague term intended to encompass all parties who have a legitimate interest in the system envisaged, including even customers who will never see it. They are thus sometimes called "stakeholders". They may include, for example

- Those who will actually operate the equipment
- Those who will operate or manage the processes which the equipment will support
- The external "customers" of those processes
- Those who will support the system or its users, or provide the platforms on which it runs.

It must be recognised, however, that users are generally not directly consulted in the course of Requirements Analysis, but only through designated representatives. Some representatives are more closely linked to the population they represent than others are, of course. Nor are all designated representatives fully enfranchised within the development process. In particular, only a limited number have the power to accept or reject the specifications which are produced.

It is important that the nature of the entire user population, the manner in which they were represented during consultation and negotiation, and the way in which specification of User Requirements was (or will be) approved, be spelt out as completely as possible in the User Requirement document.

There may be a conflict of requirements, where there are multiple stakeholders and users. These must be resolved before this document is finalised.

The final decision on approval of the specification of User Requirements should be with the pertinent authority. Therefore:

- The User Requirement document should not be circulated as other than an unauthorised draft until that approval has been given;

- The User Requirement document should be in all respects presented at a level and in a manner suitable for evaluation and approval.

FACTORY ACCEPTANCE TEST AND SITE ACCEPTANCE TEST

Where appropriate, FAT and SAT should be performed to verify the suitability of the system at site, prior to the subsequent stages of qualification. This should be appropriately documented. Where a utility or equipment is assembled, or partially assembled at a site other than that of the purchaser or end-user, testing and verification may be done, based on quality risk management principles, to ensure that it is appropriate and ready for dispatch. The checks and tests during factory acceptance test (FAT) should be recorded. The acceptability of the assembly and overall status of the utility or equipment should be described in a conclusion of the report for the FAT, prior to shipment.

Tests, based on quality risk management principles, may be performed to verify the acceptability of the utility or equipment when it is received at the end-user. This is a site acceptance test (SAT). The results of the tests should be recorded and the outcome of the acceptability of the utility or equipment should be recorded in the conclusion section of the report for the SAT.

DESIGN QUALIFICATION

It is the first step is to demonstrate whether the proposed design of the instrument can cope with the functional requirements of the end user. A proposed design must satisfy the DQ before construction and procurement of parts. DQ should demonstrate that the system, as designed, is appropriate for its intended use as defined in the URS. A suitable supplier should be selected and approved for the relevant utility or equipment.

How Should Design Qualification Be Performed?

Designing equipment to meet specific requirements always has an element of risk, but proper equipment validation and qualification can reduce that tremendously. IQ OQ PQ protocols are pretty straightforward. However, design qualification (DQ) can be a bit of a handful.

Regulatory authorities don't specify the process too well, using terms like "could", "typically" and "should", leaving the implementation open to interpretation. Additionally, there's no defined requirement for DQ standards or what purpose it serves.

Why is Design Qualification Required?

Regulatory authorities in the EU, USA and Japan have together established the ICH (International Conference on Harmonization of Technical Requirements for Registration of Pharmaceuticals for Human Use).

The project established the ICH Q7A, a GMP (Good Manufacturing Practice) standard for governing Active Pharmaceutical Ingredients (APIs). Even the US FDA has accepted its relevance and stated that it superseded its own draft API.

- Under this guidance, DQ protocol is defined as documented verification of a proposed design's ability to meet the requirements it needs to fulfill.
- Bear in mind, this is only a guidance, not a requirement for procedure or regulation, so there's a lot of leeway.
- Most companies involved in tightly controlled and monitored industries, like drug and pharmaceutical manufacturing, treat even FDA guidelines like a regulatory requirement.
- Guidance documentation traditionally have a heavy weightage in "risk-averse" environments.

When Should DQ Be Performed?

Along with process validation, when to perform DQ is a critical decision pharmaceutical manufacturers should take while the project is still in the initial stages. The ICH Q7A uses "proposed design" in the definition, which points to the status of the product design when DQ is performed. That's not very well-defined, so here are some pointers to follow:

1. For your DQ to be considered valid, other qualifications need to be implemented on each instrument and the system as a whole, like:
   - Installation qualification (IQ)
   - Operational qualification (OQ)
   - Performance qualification (PQ)
2. DQ at various points during design conceptualization allows manufacturers to make changes and corrections as they're needed, reducing costs and delays.
3. Changes made to the design can be documented as part of DQ, which makes DQ on the finalized design easier and less prone to errors.
4. From the standpoint of a project, waiting till the design has been finalized before verifying that the equipment can meet the user requirement specification isn't very practical.

5. At the very least, DQ should be performed once the final design has been created.

User Requirements

User requirement specifications are a kin to a checklist which defines DQ, and ensures:

- Performance parameters of the equipment or facility being designed are met.
- You understand what is needed, why it's needed and how it can be implemented in the design.
- The equipment or facility you're designing will be suitable for its intended application.
- All the products (that it's used to manufacture) meet quality assurance requirements.
- Legal and technical requirements are met, like CGMP, employee protection, safety, calibration and validation, etc.

Technical Specifications

Technical specifications are charted to translate the list of operational requirements in the user requirements into binding requirements and technical specifications for the supplier. In some cases, like procuring HPCL facilities as off-the-shelf equipment, these technical specifications can be replaced by a detailed proposal. After the equipment has been delivered, technical specifications and user requirements are important documents for legal purposes like legally prescribed acceptance.

Risk Analysis

Traditionally, equipment validation services and tests were carried out to measure the criticality of almost every feature or function. Nowadays, a lot of companies are shifting towards analyzing most technical systems through risk analysis.

- This is a crucial step which can reduce the time, cost and effort needed for performance testing and re-qualification.
- Suppliers and pharmaceutical manufacturers must be able to reach a consensus on the actual risk rating and levels a technical system has.
- A risk-based approach must be able to differentiate functions on the basis of criticality to the quality or process.
- You can refer to a trace matrix which compares user requirements and technical specifications

INSTALLATION QUALIFICATION

The instrument, with all its components and documentation, is placed correctly and checked for performance according to the requirements. Any new equipment is first validated to check if it is capable of producing the desired results through Design Qualification (DQ), but its performance in a real-world scenario depends on the installation procedure that is followed. Installation Qualification (IQ) verifies that the instrument or equipment being qualified, as well as its sub-systems and any ancillary systems, have been delivered, installed and configured in accordance with the manufacturer's specifications or installation checklist.

In addition to this, any cGMP requirements that pertain to the IQ and the approach used for IQ is thoroughly-documented in the Validation Master Plan (VMP).

For successful qualification, the installation must meet manufacturer requirements, like:

- Installation location and floor space
- Power, gas supply and other energy sources
- Environmental and operating conditions
- Unpacking instruments and checking for damage
- Cross-checking contents against the packing list
- Documentation of computer-controlled instrumentation
- Checking software-installation and basic accessibility
- Installation ancillary instruments and options
- Verifying connections and communication with peripheral units
- Recording firmware versions and serial numbers
- Tagging instruments with IQ stickers
- Recording calibration and validation dates of equipment used for IQ
- Gathering all manuals and certificates of conformity

Utilities and equipment should be correctly installed, in an appropriate location. There should be documented evidence of the installation. This should be in accordance with the IQ protocol which contains all the relevant details. IQ should include identification, verification and installation of relevant components identified, *e.g.,* services, controls and gauges. Identified measuring, control and indicating devices, should be calibrated on site unless otherwise appropriately justified. The calibration should be traceable to national or international standards. Traceable certificates should be available. The execution of the protocol should be recorded in the report. The report should include, *e.g.,*

- The title,
- Objective,
- Site,
- Details of the supplier and manufacturer,
- System or equipment name and unique identification number,
- Model and serial number,
- Date of installation,
- Tests executed,
- Components and their identification numbers or codes and material of construction,
- Actual results of tests and measurements,
- Relevant procedures followed for tests and certificates as applicable.

Deviations and non-conformances including those from URS, DQ and acceptance criteria specified and observed during installation should be recorded, investigated, and corrected or justified. Normally, the outcome of the IQ should be recorded in the conclusion of the report, before OQ is started. Requirements and procedures for calibration, maintenance and cleaning should normally be prepared during IQ or OQ.

OPERATIONAL QUALIFICATION

All the major parts of the instrument are tested to ensure they all perform correctly and are in sync with the entire system. Once each protocol of the IQ phase has been met, Operational qualification (OQ) is performed to check that the equipment's performance is consistent with the user requirement specification, within the manufacturer-specified operating ranges. During the OQ phase, all the items in the test plan are tested individually and their performance documented. This is a prerequisite for technical acceptance of the equipment and the facility, so it can only be performed once the IQ has been successful. Apart from qualification after the initial installation, requalification also needs to be carried out after any major maintenance work or modifications have been made to equipment, or as part of a regular quality assurance schedule. The main purpose of OQ is to identify and inspect features of the equipment that can influence final product quality, like:

- Display units and signalling LEDs
- Temperature controls and fluctuations
- Overheating and low-temperature protection systems and alarms
- Pressure/Vacuum controlling systems
- Controlling systems
- Humidity measuring and controlling systems

- Fan and fan-speed controllers
- Servo motors and air flap controllers
- Card readers and access controllers
- Temperature distribution

Utilities and equipment should operate correctly and their operation should be verified in accordance with an OQ protocol. OQ normally follows IQ but depending on the complexity of utility or equipment, it may be performed as a combined installation/operation qualification (IOQ).

OQ should include but is not limited to the following:

- Tests that have been developed from the knowledge of processes, systems and equipment to ensure the utility or equipment is operating as designed;
- Tests to confirm upper and lower operating limits, and/or "worst case" conditions.
- Training of operators for the utilities and equipment should be provided and training records maintained.
- Calibration, cleaning, maintenance, training and related tests and results should be verified to be acceptable.
- Deviations and non-conformances observed should be recorded, investigated and corrected or justified.

The results for the verification of operation should be documented in the OQ report. The outcome of the OQ should be recorded in the conclusion of the report, normally before PQ is started.

How to Perform Operational Qualification?

IQ OQ PQ Protocols are used at different stages with the same common goal – the system being designed should be able to perform the job it's designed for. Operational Qualification (OQ) is the process of verifying that each system and its subsystems are able to perform as intended, throughout the operating range which is anticipated. It is somewhat related to the other protocols (DQ IQ OQ PQ), and is often mistakenly clubbed with them, but they are all in fact very different.

Why is Operational Qualification Needed?

Operational Qualification is performed to assess if performance is consistent, within the parameters of the user requirement specification. Some companies combine OQ, PQ and equipment validation after installation into a single activity, often termed OPQ.

How Often Operational Qualification is done?

Before creating an OQ procedure schedule, you should consider the intended use of the equipment. If it is going to be used for different applications and will cater to high performance demands, the tests may need to be quite extensive and frequent.

Conversely, if it's used rarely or for just one application, the acceptance criteria of performance parameters can be limited. Before-and-after performance should be recorded with detailed documentation to track the adequacy of the regimen. Typically, a periodic frequency is considered appropriate for general equipment and conditions, but the actual schedule can vary based on factors like:

- The type of instrument
- Stability of the parameters
- The specific acceptance criteria for the device or equipment
- How often the equipment is used

You should aim for a time interval that establishes a high probability of the performance remaining within acceptable limits. Timely OQ and process validation increases dependability on the analytical results gathered, which directly results in higher quality assurance.

How is OQ Performed?

Operational Qualification is quite similar in implementation to design qualification (DQ), except it tests physical equipment. Most equipment is accompanied by an SOP (standard operating procedures) document which outlines the procedures for OQ. Here are some questions you should ask yourself before designing a protocol for OQ:

- Which standards and procedures should you use?
- Should you follow manufacturer's specifications?
- Will you perform in-house qualification?
- Does preventive maintenance need to be carried out before OQ?
- Is OQ required every time the instrument is relocated?
- For software products, will you need OQ after upgrades?
- Do you need OQ if the instrument is only going to be used for one application?

OQ is a part of cGMP guidelines, so if you are unsure about how you should proceed, it might be wise to get a professional opinion. Equipment validation services can help you establish a schedule and offer other guidance too.

Scope of OQ

OQ inspections and tests should include tests for at least the following factors:

- Loop installations
- Brief description of the validated product process.
- Loop test verification
- Alarms
- Permissive conditions and interlocks
- Database and data storage integrity
- Event chronicle and report generation
- Equipment functionality
- High-load dry-runs of the software, if required
- System functionality (for compliance with 21 CFR Part 11)
- Verification of 21 CFR Part 11 compliance, if needed
- Security levels (for unauthorized access)
- Power loss recovery system
- All interfaces
- Effects and the ability of equipment to handle electromagnetic interference

PERFORMANCE QUALIFICATION

The instrument is monitored over a period of time to check if it consistently delivers results within the required parameters. PQ is the final step in qualification processes for equipment, and this step involves verifying and documenting that the equipment is working reproducibly within a specified working range. Rather than testing each instrument individually, they are all tested together as part of a partial or overall process. Before the qualification begins, a detailed test plan is created, based on the process description.

Process Performance Qualification (PPQ) protocol is a vital part of process validation and qualification, which is used to ensure ongoing product quality by documenting performance over a period of time for a certain process.

FDA guidelines recommend including the following criteria as part of PQ and PPQ protocols:

- Manufacturing conditions like equipment limits, operating parameters and component inputs
- A list of the data that should be recorded or analyzed during tests, calibration and validation

- Tests that need to be performed to ensure consistent quality at various steps of production
- A sampling plan which outlines the sampling methods used during and in between production batches
- Analysis methodology for making data, scientific and risk-oriented decisions based on statistical data
- Defining variability limits and contingency plans for handling non-conformance
- Approval of the PPQ protocol by relevant departments

PQ should normally follow the successful completion of IQ and OQ. In some cases it may be appropriate to perform PQ in conjunction with OQ or process validation. PQ should include, but is not limited to the following:

- Tests, using production materials,
- Qualified substitutes or simulated products proven to have equivalent behaviour under normal operating conditions with worst case batch sizes where appropriate;
- Tests should cover the operating range.

Utilities and equipment should consistently perform in accordance with their design specifications and URS. The performance should be verified in accordance with a PQ protocol. There should be records (*e.g.,* PQ report) for the PQ to indicate the satisfactory performance over a predefined period of time. Manufacturers should justify the period over which PQ is done.

PERIODIC REVIEW AND REQUALIFICATION

Utilities and equipment should be maintained in a qualified state through the life cycle of the utility or equipment. Utilities and equipment should be reviewed periodically to confirm that they remain in a qualified state and to determine the need for requalification. Where the need for requalification is identified, this should be performed.

Risk management principles should be applied in the review and requalification and the possible impact of small changes over a period of time should further be considered. Risk management principles may include factors such as calibration, verification, maintenance data and other information.

The qualification status and requalification due dates should be documented, *e.g.,* in a qualification matrix, schedule or plan. In case a utility or equipment in use is identified, where it had not been subjected to qualification, a qualification protocol should be prepared where elements of URS, design specifications, operation and performance are verified for acceptability. The outcome of this qualification should be recorded in a report.

Auxiliary components and parts that are sourced from a third-party manufacturer are periodically subjected to random tests for quality and performance to ensure they are manufactured to the right specifications and won't hamper the performance of the instrument.

BENEFITS OF EQUIPMENT VALIDATION SERVICES

Creating a calibration process that encompasses all the requirements can be time-consuming and cumbersome. Validation services can help you save both time and money by streamlining your validation procedures. Let's look at the detailed benefits of validation services below:

- Validation and quality checking processes may include unnecessary tests and procedures, which add to your delivery time and waste labour resources.
- A validation service can provide a standardized methodology to optimize the validation lifecycle to cover only the required steps and checks.
- Equipment validation services can provide documented independent verification and validation of your system's performance.
- Purchasing equipment for validating products can be a costly venture. A validation service can offset the cost, without jeopardizing the end results. Experienced and qualified staff for managing your validation process is also expensive.

Validating your products might seem like a long, drawn-out process, but there's a good reason for it. If you can ensure your products perform consistently and meet all the requirements of the industry, the value of both the product and your brand increases, and that's always a good thing!

CONCLUSIONS

Pharmaceutical manufacturers have increasingly faced increasing research costs, compounded by the expiry of blockbuster patents and the limited profit margins. Therefore they need to minimize process complexity and reduce costs, which have often led to the closure of manufacturing plants. Concurrently, pharmaceutical manufacturers faced a concomitant increase in GMP requests by regulatory bodies. As a result of these, one scenario is the establishment of new equipment/machines. The need to keep the company's internal structure flexible and contain personnel costs leads to pharmaceutical companies outsourcing. However, the supervision and responsibility of GMP activities is ultimately the company's responsibility.

In order to comply with regulatory requirements, companies need to perform complete qualification of the equipment. To comply with these demands pharmaceutical manufacturers must keep in mind certain considerations during equipment qualification. Companies are typically driven by high quality standards to meet the needs of their challenging requirements. Therefore, for ideal equipment qualification service should:

- Adopt a strong Quality Management System
- Establish properly trained staff, technicians and engineers
- Possess an adequate number of equipment, managed and routinely checked as required by GMP
- Assure high quality standards, both in technical competencies and in documentation
- Ensure personnel have expertise and a thorough understanding and methodology in IT Compliance and Validation in Compliance with 21 CFR part 11.

FURTHER READINGS

See WHO TRS 992, 2015, Annex 3 for aspects to be considered in process validation.

WHO TRS 1010, 2018, Annex 8 for aspects to be considered for inclusion in qualification of heating, ventilation and air-conditioning (HVAC) systems.

WHO TRS 970, 2012, Annex 2 for aspects to be considered for inclusion in qualification of water purification systems.

11

Non-Sterile Process Validation

ABSTRACT

Validation is an integral part of quality assurance; which involves the systematic study of systems, facilities and processes aimed at determining whether they perform their intended functions adequately and consistently as specified. A validated process is one which has been demonstrated to provide a high degree of assurance that uniform batches will be produced consistently and continuously which will meet the required specifications and has therefore been formally approved. Validation in itself does not improve processes but confirms that the processes have been properly developed and are under control. Process Validation is the most important and recognized parameters to determine the state of CGMPs in pharmaceutical industry. The goal of a quality system is to consistently produce products that are fit for their intended use. Process validation is a key element in assuring that these principles and goal are met. The process validation is standardization of the validation documents that must be submitted with the submission file for marketing authorization. The process validation is intended to assist manufacturers in understanding quality management system (QMS) requirements concerning process validation and has general applicability to manufacturing process. According to FDA, assurance of product quality is derived from careful and systemic attention to a number of importance factors, including: selection of quality process through in-process and end-product testing.

INTRODUCTION

Process Validation is a means of ensuring that manufacturing processes are capable of consistently producing a finished product of the required quality. It involves providing documentary evidence that key steps in the manufacturing process are consistent and reproducible. A validated manufacturing process is one that has been proven to do what it purports or is presented to do.

USFDA defines validation as: "Validation is establishing documented evidence which provides a high degree of assurance that a specific process will consistently produce a product meeting its pre-determined specifications and quality characteristics.

According to European commission: Validation is defined as "Action providing in accordance with the principles of GMP, that any procedure, process, equipment, material, activity or system actually lead to the expected results.

Process validation establishes the flexibility and constraints in the manufacturing process controls in the attainment of desirable attributes in the drug product while preventing undesirable properties. This is an important concept, since it serves to support the underlying definition of validation, which is a systematic approach to identifying, measuring, evaluating, documenting, and re-evaluating a series of critical steps in the manufacturing process that require control to ensure a reproducible final product.

Before any batch from the process is commercially distributed for use by consumers, a manufacturer should have gained a high degree of assurance in the performance of the manufacturing process such that it will consistently produce APIs and drug products meeting those attributes relating to identity, strength, quality, purity, and potency. The assurance should be obtained from objective information and data from laboratory-, pilot-, and/or commercial-scale studies. Information and data should demonstrate that the commercial manufacturing process is capable of consistently producing acceptable quality products within commercial manufacturing conditions.

A successful validation program depends upon information and knowledge from product and process development. This knowledge and understanding is the basis for establishing an approach to control of the manufacturing process that result in products with the desired quality attributes. Manufacturers should:

- Understand the sources of variation
- Detect the presence and degree of variation
- Understand the impact of variation on the process and ultimately on product attributes
- Control the variation in a manner commensurate with the risk it represents to the process and product

Process validation is defined as the collection and evaluation of data, from the process design stage through commercial production, which establishes scientific evidence that a process is capable of consistently delivering quality product. Process validation involves a series of activities taking place over the lifecycle of the product and process. Each manufacturer should judge whether it has gained sufficient understanding to provide a high degree of assurance in its manufacturing process to justify commercial distribution of the product. Focusing exclusively on qualification efforts without understanding the manufacturing process and associated variations may not lead to adequate assurance of quality. After establishing and confirming the process, manufacturers must maintain the process in a state of control over the life of the process, even as materials, equipment, production environment, personnel, and manufacturing procedures change.

GENERAL CONSIDERATIONS FOR PROCESS VALIDATION

In all stages of the product lifecycle, good project management and good archiving that capture scientific knowledge will make the process validation program more effective and efficient. The following practices should ensure uniform collection and assessment of information about the process and enhance the accessibility of such information later in the product lifecycle.

- An integrated team approach to process validation that includes expertise from a variety of disciplines (*e.g.,* process engineering, industrial pharmacy, analytical chemistry, manufacturing, and quality assurance). Project plans, along with the full support of senior management, are essential elements for success.
- Throughout the product lifecycle , various studies can be initiated to discover, observe, correlate, or confirm information about the product and process
- All studies should be planned and conducted according to sound scientific principles, appropriately documented, and approved in accordance with the established procedure appropriate for the stage of the lifecycle.
- Many products are single-source or involve complicated manufacturing processes. Homogeneity within a batch and consistency between batches are goals of process validation activities. Validation offers assurance that a process is reasonably protected against sources of variability that could affect production output, cause supply problems, and negatively affect public health.
- The terms attribute(s) (*e.g.,* quality, product, component) and parameter(s) (*e.g.,* process, operating, and equipment) are not categorized with respect to criticality in this guidance.

While each organization may have its own mechanism for process validation, there are some general considerations which can be taken into account while devising these systems:

- One of the key aspects is an "all hands" approach wherein all the stakeholders across disciplines and subject matter experts are roped in along with clear project planning and buy in from the senior management is a taken into account.

- Process validation must be a way of life throughout the product development life cycle and thereafter too. An acute evaluation through regular studies is a must for successful process validation.
- Clear sense of direction and a standard set of evaluation criteria are important for an effective process validation, to maintain consistency and standardization of products if they are being released batch-wise.

BACKGROUND

Emphasis to process validation was raised in late 70s. In the Federal Register of May 11, 1987 (52 FR 17638), FDA issued a notice announcing the availability of a guidance entitled Guideline on General Principles of Process Validation (the 1987 guidance). Since then, we have obtained additional experience through our regulatory oversight that allows us to update our recommendations to industry on this topic. This revised guidance conveys FDA's current thinking on process validation and is consistent with basic principles first introduced in the 1987 guidance. The revised guidance also provides recommendations that reflect some of the goals of FDA's initiative entitled "Pharmaceutical CGMPs for the 21st Century ¯ A Risk-Based Approach," particularly with regard to the use of technological advances in pharmaceutical manufacturing, as well as implementation of modern risk management and quality system tools and concepts. This revised guidance replaces the 1987 guidance.

FDA has the authority and responsibility to inspect and evaluate process validation performed by manufacturers. The CGMP regulations for validating pharmaceutical (drug) manufacturing require that drug products be produced with a high degree of assurance of meeting all the attributes they are intended to possess (21 CFR 211.100(a) and 211.110(a)). Chronological development in the field of process validation is explained in the Table 1.

Similar requirements are included in the World Health Organization (WHO), the Pharmaceutical Inspection Co-operation Scheme (PIC/S), and the European Union (EU) requirements, along with those of Australia, Canada, Japan, India and other international authorities.

PRINCIPLES AND IMPORTANCE OF PROCESS CONTROL SYSTEM VALIDATION

Process control system validation as the name suggests is a set of activities which are carried out to check the efficacy of a process control system. It could be a piece of software or hardware which has been introduced to

Table 1: Chronological regulatory development for process validation

Year	**:**	***Development***
1962	:	The Kefauver-Harris Amendments to the FD&C Act were approved - Section 501(a)(2)(B)
1963	:	Requirement has been aroused as per CGMP regulations for finished pharmaceutical products
1963	:	The first CGMP regulations, based on the Pharmaceutical Manufacturers Association's manufacturing control guidelines, were published and became effective
1974	:	Paper presented by Ted Byers, entitled "Design for Quality"- paper described an increased attention to adequacy of processes for the pharmaceutical products
1978	:	Bernard Loftus in Parenteral Drug Association presented paper entitled "Validation and Stability" discussing the legal basis for the requirement that processes be validated
11 May 1987	:	Guideline on General Principles of Process Validation was written for the pharmaceutical, device, and veterinary medicine industries.
1992-93	:	One injunction case filed in 1992, was contested in court and led to a lengthy written order and opinion by the U.S. District Court in February of 1993
Feb, 1993	:	Court ordered the defendants to perform process validation studies on certain drug products, as well as equipment cleaning validation studies
03 May 1996	:	FDA drafted revisions to several parts of regulations. The proposed revisions were published in the *Federal Register.*
Aug, 2002	:	FDA launched new initiative entitled "Pharmaceutical CGMP for the 21st Century: A risk based approach"
Sept, 2004	:	FDA printed new guideline entitled "PAT- A framework for innovative pharmaceutical development, manufacturing and quality assurance
Jan, 2011	:	FDA revised the guidelines for process validation

automate a certain process, which needs validation. Alternately, it could be a set of steps established to execute a certain process. Process validation is a mechanism which is put in place to run regular checks and to execute the principles of quality assurance.

THE BASIC PRINCIPLE OF QUALITY ASSURANCE

Quality assurance is the process of ensuring that the manufactured goods and the services provided are adherent to the quality standards, as per specifications laid down in the quality policy and guidelines. It ensures that the organization stays focused on good manufacturing practice consistently. Quality assurance is one of the founding pillars of pharmaceutical CGMP, since quality is centered on the efficacy of the drug not at the final stage but at each stage of the drug development life cycle. The core principles of quality assurance are suitability of a product and first time accuracy to minimize the need for iterations.

In the parlance of pharmaceutical industry, it has a direct impact on the pharmaceutical quality since it must assure how suitable a drug is for the ailment. It does not remain limited to drugs alone but it extended to other pharmaceutical products such as diagnostic kits and medical equipment too.

APPROACH TO PROCESS VALIDATION

Process validation is implemented by evaluating data at all stages of product development to ensure that it is meeting the necessary quality standards. Process validation is typically undertaken in stages:

- At the design stage the product fitment is evaluated.
- At the next stage, the commercial scalability of the product is validated.
- Once the rollout is completed, a continued ongoing routine review is conducted at timely intervals to ensure consistent and improved quality of the product.

The success of a process validation is determined by the accuracy of the knowledge gathered, which in turn becomes the basis for determining the efficacy of the product. This is particularly true for the pharmaceutical industry which, even though it is a manufacturing segment in nature, but is knowledge-intensive since its products are a derivate of core research.

IMPORTANCE OF PROCESS VALIDATION

Process control validation is an essential mechanism to implement quality assurance. This is especially important considering that quality assurance must be executed from time to time, process control validation enables a company to maintain quality standards and also bring in any variations in line with changes in the compliance environment and market forces.

Implementing systems once and for all with no looking back is not an option anymore, especially in today's dynamic environment (of rapidly developing newer products, changing quality standards and stringent CGMPs). Hence, process control validation is more imperative than ever in the current scheme of things.

Assurance of Quality

Validation is an extension of the concepts of quality assurance since close control of the process is necessary to assure product quality and it is not possible to control a process properly without thorough knowledge of the capabilities of that process without validated and controlled processes, it is impossible to produce quality products consistently. End product testing, in the absence of validation, gives little assurance of quality for variety reasons, among which are.

1. Very limited sample size.
2. The limited number of tests performed on a sample. For example, it is impractical to test for all potential impurities or contaminants.
3. The limited sensitivity of the test.

Process Optimization

The optimization of a process for maximum efficiency, while maintaining quality standards, is a consequence of validation. Literal meaning of word to optimize is "To make as effective, perfect or useful as possible". The optimization of the facility, equipment, systems, and processes results in a product that meets quality requirements at the lowest cost.

Reduction of Quality Costs

Quality costs are divided in to four categories. They are:

a) Preventive costs.
b) Appraisal costs.
c) Internal failure costs.
d) External failure costs *e.g.,* of internal failure costs: Any validated and controlled process will result in fewer internal failures like;
   - Fewer rejects
   - Reworks
   - Re-tests
   - Re-inspection

REGULATORY REQUIREMENT OF PROCESS VALIDATION

FDA regulation describing current good manufacturing practices (CGMPs) for finished pharmaceuticals are provided in 21 CFR parts 210 and 211. The CGMP regulations require that manufacturing processes be designed and controlled to assure that in-process materials and the finished product meet predetermined quality requirements and do so consistently and reliably. Process validation is required, in both general and specific terms, by the CGMP regulations in parts 210 and 211. The foundation for process validation is provided in § 211.100(a), which states that "here shall be written procedures for production and process control designed to assure that the drug products have the identity, strength, quality, and purity they purport or are represented to possess". The CGMP regulations regarding sampling set forth a number of requirements for validation: samples must represent the batch under analysis (§ 211.160(b) (3)); the sampling plan must result in statistical confidence (§ 211.165(c) and (d)); and the batch must meet its predetermined specifications (§ 211.165(a)). The CGMP regulations also provide norms for establishing in-process specifications as an aspect of process validation. Section 211.110(b) establishes two follow when establishing in-process specifications.

The first principle is that "in-process specifications for such characteristics [of in-process material and the drug product] shall be consistent with drug product final specifications". The second principle is this regulation further requires that in-process specifications "shall be derived determined by the application of suitable statistical procedures were appropriate". The CGMP regulations require that facilities in which drugs are manufactured be of suitable size, construction, and location to facilitate proper operations (§ 211.42). Equipment must be of appropriate design, adequate size, and suitable located to facilitate operations for its intended use (§ 211.63). Automated, mechanical and electronic equipment must be calibrated, inspected, or checked according to the written program designed to assure proper performance (§ 211.68).

In summary, the CGMP regulations require that manufacturing processes be designed and controlled to assure that in-process material and finished product meet predetermined quality requirements and do so consistently and reliability throughout product lifecycle .

VALIDATION LIFE CYCLE

Validation is a continuing and evolving process. Validation process which extends from very basic to a very broad theological and methodical investigation to determine how the system and processes perform. Its scope encompasses documentation revision control, training and maintenance of the system and process. Evidence of validation should be seen at the corporate level, and be reflected in the management structure. Validation is a method for building and maintaining quality.

Each manufacturer should judge whether it has gained sufficient understanding to provide a high degree of assurance in its manufacturing process to justify commercial distribution of the product. Focusing exclusively on qualification efforts without also understanding the manufacturing process and associated variations may not lead to adequate assurance of quality. After establishing and confirming the process, manufacturers must maintain the process in a state of control over the life of the process, even as materials, equipment, production environment, personnel, and manufacturing procedures change. Fig. 1 is giving basic information regarding the lifecycle for the validation.

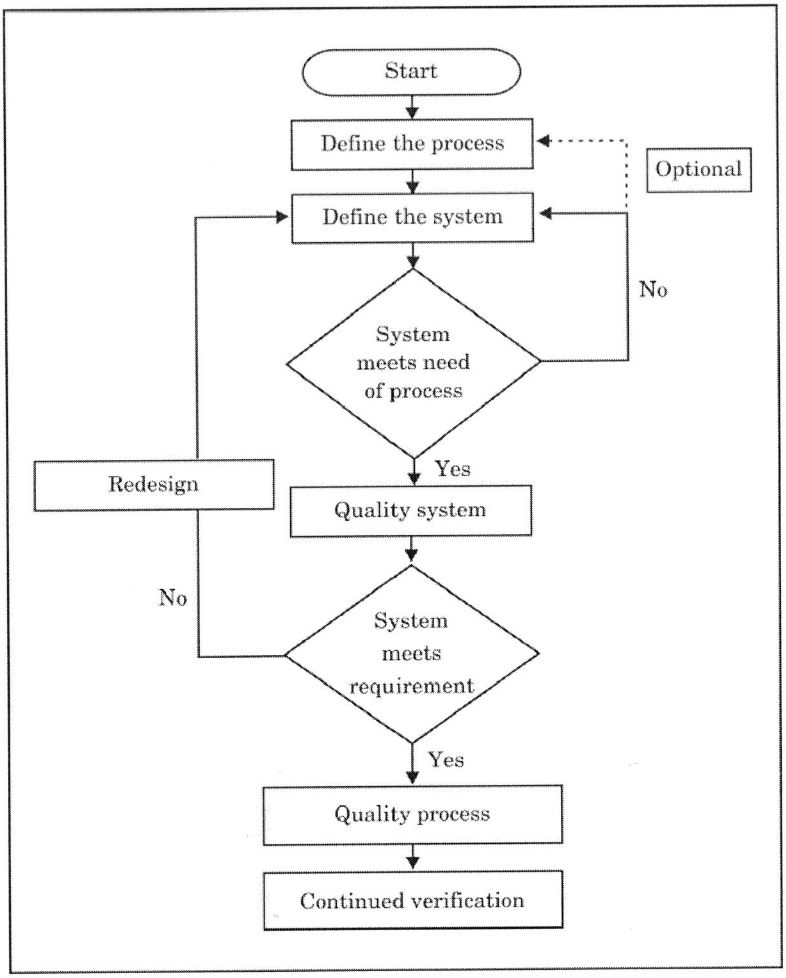

Fig. 1: Validation life cycle

PROCESS VALIDATION WITHIN THE QUALITY MANAGEMENT SYSTEM

Process validation is part of the integrated requirements of a quality management system. It is conducted in the context of a system including design and development control, quality assurance, process control, and corrective and preventive action. The product should be design robustly enough to withstand variations in the manufacturing process and the manufacturing process should be capable and stable to assure continued safe products that perform adequately. Corrective actions often identify inadequate processes/process validations. Each corrective action applied to a manufacturing process should include the consideration for conducting process validation/ revalidation.

Process Validation Decision

The following model (Fig. 2) may be useful in determining whether or not a process should be validated:

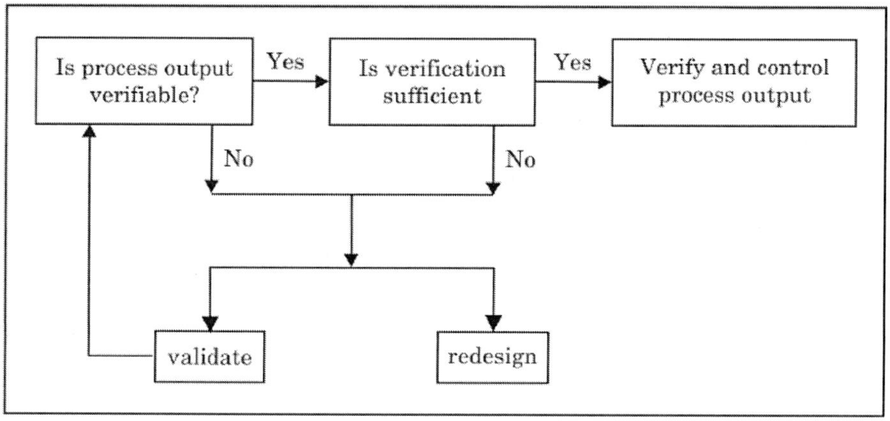

Fig. 2: Validation decision tree

The manufacturer should consider whether the output can be verified by subsequent monitoring or measurement (A). If the answer is positive, then the consideration should be made as to whether or not verification alone is sufficient to eliminate unacceptable risk and is a cost effective solution (B). If yes, the output should be verified and the process should be appropriately controlled (C). If the output of the process is not verifiable then the decision should be to validate the process (D). Alternatively, it may become be apparent that the product or process should be redesigned to reduce variation and improve the product or process (E).

STAGES OF PROCESS VALIDATION

Manufacturers should use ongoing programs to collect and analyze product and process data to evaluate the state of control of the process. These programs may identify process or product problems or opportunities for process improvements that can be evaluated and implemented through some of the activities described in Stages 1 and 2.

Manufacturers of legacy products can take advantage of the knowledge gained from the original process development and qualification work as well as manufacturing experience to continually improve their processes. Implementation of the recommendations in this guidance for legacy products and processes would likely begin with the activities described in Stage 3.

Process Validation is defined as the collection and evaluation of data, from the process design stage through commercial production, which establishes scientific evidence that a process is capable of consistently delivering quality product. Process Validation involves a series of activities taking place over the lifecycle of the product and process. The activities relating to validation studies may be classified into three stages as depicted in Fig. 3:

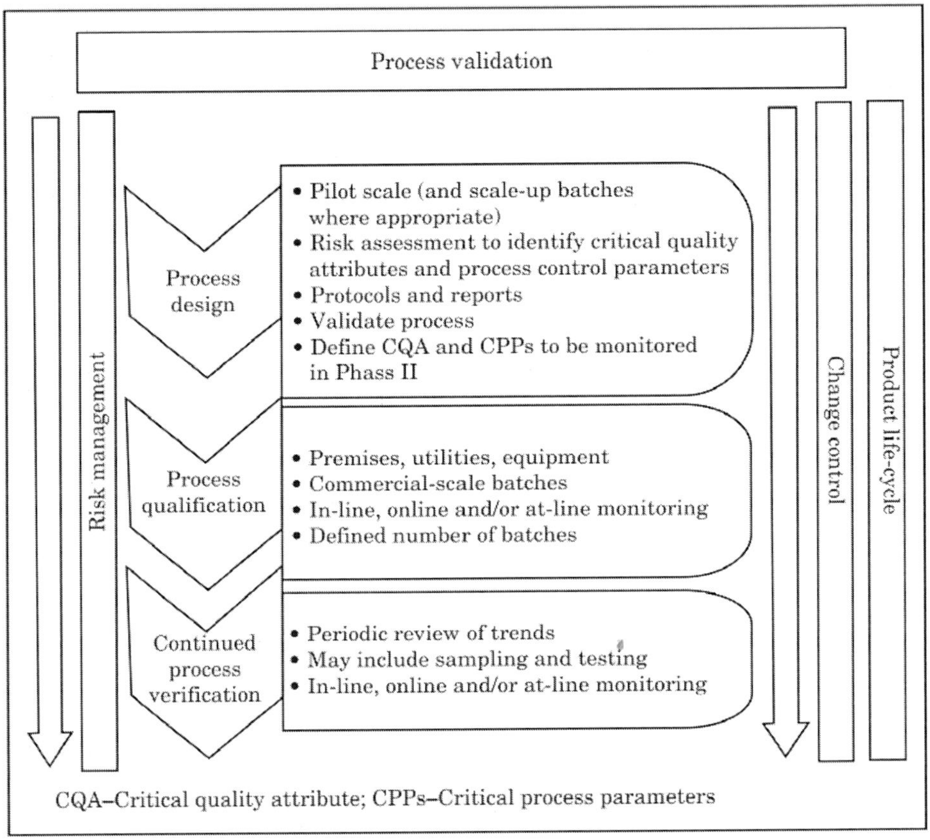

Fig. 3: Stages of process validation

Stage 1 – Process Design

"Focussing exclusively on qualification efforts without also understanding the manufacturing process is defined during this stage based on knowledge gained through development and scale-up activities. It covers all activities relating to product research and development, formulation, pilot batch studies, scale-up studies, transfer of technology to commercial scale batches, establishing stability conditions, storage and handling of in-process and finished dosage forms, equipment qualification, installation qualification, master production documents, operational qualification, process capability. Also this is the stage in which the establishment of a strategy for process control is taking place using accumulation knowledge and understanding of the process."

Building and Capturing Process Knowledge and Understanding

Generally, early process design experiments do not need to be performed under the CGMP conditions required for drugs intended for commercial distribution that are manufactured during Stage 2 (process qualification) and Stage 3 (continued process verification). They should, however, be conducted in accordance with sound scientific methods and principles, including good documentation practices. This recommendation is consistent with ICH Q10 Pharmaceutical Quality System. Decisions and justification of the controls should be sufficiently documented and internally reviewed to verify and preserve their value for use or adaptation later in the lifecycle of the process and product.

Although often performed at small-scale laboratories, most viral inactivation and impurity clearance studies cannot be considered early process design experiments. Viral and impurity clearance studies intended to evaluate and estimate product quality at commercial scale should have a level of quality unit oversight that will ensure that the studies follow sound scientific methods and principles and the conclusions are supported by the data.

Product development activities provide key inputs to the process design stage, such as the intended dosage form, the quality attributes, and a general manufacturing pathway. Process information available from product development activities can be leveraged in the process design stage. The functionality and limitations of commercial manufacturing equipment should be considered in the process design, as well as predicted contributions to variability posed by different component lots, production operators, environmental conditions, and measurement systems in the production setting. However, the full spectrum of input variability typical of commercial production is not generally known at this stage. Laboratory or pilot-scale models designed to be representative of the commercial process can be used to estimate variability.

Designing an efficient process with an effective process control approach is dependent on the process knowledge and understanding obtained. Design of Experiment (DOE) studies can help develop process knowledge by revealing relationships, including multivariate interactions, between the variable inputs (*e.g.,* component characteristics or process parameters) and the resulting outputs (*e.g.,* in-process material, intermediates, or the final product). Risk analysis tools can be used to screen potential variables for DOE studies to minimize the total number of experiments conducted while maximizing knowledge gained. The results of DOE studies can provide justification for establishing ranges of incoming component quality, equipment parameters, and in-process material quality attributes.

Other activities, such as experiments or demonstrations at laboratory or pilot scale, also assist in evaluation of certain conditions and prediction of performance of the commercial process. These activities also provide information that can be used to model or simulate the commercial process. Computer-based or virtual simulations of certain unit operations or dynamics can provide process understanding and help avoid problems at commercial scale. It is important to understand the degree to which models represent the commercial process, including any differences that might exist, as this may have an impact on the relevance of information derived from the models.

It is essential that activities and studies resulting in process understanding be documented. Documentation should reflect the basis for decisions made about the process. For example, manufacturers should document the variables studied for a unit operation and the rationale for those variables identified as significant. This information is useful during the process qualification and continued process verification stages, including when the design is revised or the strategy for control is refined or changed.

Establishing a strategy for process control

Process knowledge and understanding is the basis for establishing an approach to process control for each unit operation and the process overall. Strategies for process control can be designed to reduce input variation, adjust for input variation during manufacturing (and so reduce its impact on the output), or combine both approaches. Process controls address variability to assure quality of the product. Controls can consist of material analysis and equipment monitoring at significant processing points (§ 211.110(c)). Decisions regarding the type and extent of process controls can be aided by earlier risk assessments, then enhanced and improved as process experience is gained.

It is expected controls to include both examination of material quality and equipment monitoring. Special attention to control the process through operational limits and in-process monitoring is essential in two possible scenarios:

- When the product attribute is not readily measurable due to limitations of sampling or detectability (*e.g.,* viral clearance or microbial contamination) or
- When intermediates and products cannot be highly characterized and well-defined quality attributes cannot be identified.

These controls are established in the master production and control records (see § 211.186(a) and (b) (9)). More advanced strategies, which may involve the use of process analytical technology (PAT), can include timely analysis and control loops to adjust the processing conditions so that the output remains constant. Manufacturing systems of this type can provide a higher degree of process control than non-PAT systems. In the case of a strategy using PAT, the approach to process qualification will differ from that used in other process designs. Further information on PAT processes can be found in FDA's guidance for industry on *PAT ¯ A Framework for Innovative Pharmaceutical Development, Manufacturing, and Quality Assurance.*

The planned commercial production and control records, which contain the operational limits and overall strategy for process control, should be carried forward to the next stage for confirmation.

Input

- Type of information during the design phase
- Information to ensure that product is produced consistently every time
- Knowledge of process / product
- Technology Transfer Package

Output

- Verification/ determination of the limits for the critical process parameters.
- The limits/ process boundary have been validated.
- Knowledge of process variable is gained, enabling the establishment of control strategy

Stage 2 – Process Qualification

During this stage, the process design is evaluated to determine if the process is capable of reproducible commercial manufacturing. It confirm that all established limits of the Critical Process Parameters are valid and that satisfactory products can be produced even under "worst case" conditions. GMP compliant procedures must be followed in this stage and successful completion of this stage is necessary before commercial distribution of a product. During Stage 2, CGMP-compliant procedures must be followed. Successful completion of Stage 2 is necessary before commercial distribution. Products manufactured during this stage, if acceptable, can be released for distribution. There are two aspect of process qualification:

a) Design of facilities and qualification of equipment and utilities

- Proper design of manufacturing facility is desired under 21 CFR part 211, subpart C, of the CGMP regulation on Buildings and Facilities.
- Activities performed to assure proper facility design and that the equipment and utilities are suitable for their intended use and perform properly.
- Selecting utilities and equipment construction materials, operating principles, and performance characteristics based on whether they are appropriate for their specific uses.
- Verifying that utility systems and equipment are built and installed in compliance with the design specifications (*e.g.,* built as designed with proper materials, capacity, and functions, and properly connected and calibrated).
- Verifying that utility systems and equipment operate in accordance with the process requirements in all anticipated operating ranges. This should include challenging the equipment or system functions while under load comparable to that expected during routine production. It should also include the performance of interventions, stoppage, and start-up as is expected during routine production. Operating ranges should be shown capable of being held as long as would be necessary during routine production.

Qualification of utilities and equipment can be covered under individual plans or as part of an overall project plan. The plan should consider the requirements of use and can incorporate risk management to prioritize certain activities and to identify a level of effort in both the performance and documentation of qualification activities. The plan should identify the following items:

1. The studies or tests to use,
2. The criteria appropriate to assess outcomes,
3. The timing of qualification activities,
4. The responsibilities of relevant departments and the quality unit, and
5. The procedures for documenting and approving the qualification.

The project plan should also include the firm's requirements for the evaluation of changes. Qualification activities should be documented and summarized in a report with conclusions that address criteria in the plan. The quality control unit must review and approve the qualification plan and report (§ 211.22).

(b) Process performance qualification

The process performance qualification (PPQ) is the second element of Stage 2, process qualification. The PPQ combines the actual facility, utilities, equipment (each now qualified), and the trained personnel with the commercial manufacturing process, control procedures, and components to produce commercial batches. A successful PPQ will confirm the process design and demonstrate that the commercial manufacturing process performs as expected.

Success at this stage signals an important milestone in the product lifecycle. A manufacturer must successfully complete PPQ before commencing commercial distribution of the drug product. The decision to begin commercial distribution should be supported by data from commercial-scale batches. Data from laboratory and pilot studies can provide additional assurance that the commercial manufacturing process performs as expected.

The approach to PPQ should be based on sound science and the manufacturer's overall level of product and process understanding and demonstrable control. The cumulative data from all relevant studies (*e.g.,* designed experiments; laboratory, pilot, and commercial batches) should be used to establish the manufacturing conditions in the PPQ. To understand the commercial process sufficiently, the manufacturer will need to consider the effects of scale. However, it is not typically necessary to explore the entire operating range at commercial scale if assurance can be provided by process design data. Previous credible experience with sufficiently similar products and processes can also be helpful. In addition, we strongly recommend firms employ objective measures (*e.g.,* statistical metrics) wherever feasible and meaningful to achieve adequate assurance.

In most cases, PPQ will have a higher level of sampling, additional testing, and greater scrutiny of process performance than would be typical of routine commercial production. The level of monitoring and testing should be sufficient to confirm uniform product quality throughout the batch. The increased level of scrutiny, testing, and sampling should continue through the process verification stage as appropriate, to establish levels and frequency of routine sampling and monitoring for the particular product and process. Considerations for the duration of the heightened sampling and monitoring period could include, but are not limited to, volume of production, process complexity, level of process understanding, and experience with similar products and processes.

The extent to which some materials, such as column resins or molecular filtration media, can be re-used without adversely affecting product quality can be assessed in relevant laboratory studies. The usable lifetimes of such materials should be confirmed by an ongoing PPQ protocol during commercial manufacture.

A manufacturing process that uses PAT (Process and analytical technologies) may warrant a different PPQ approach. PAT processes are designed to measure in real time the attributes of an in-process material and then adjust the process in a timely control loop so the process maintains the desired quality of the output material. The process design stage and the process qualification stage should focus on the measurement system and control loop for the measured attribute. Regardless, the goal of validating any manufacturing process is the same: to establish scientific evidence that the process is reproducible and will consistently deliver quality products.

- Criteria and process performance indicators that allow for a science and risk-based decision about the ability of the process to consistently produce quality products.
- Criteria and process performance indicators that allow for a science and risk based decision about the ability of the process to consistently produce quality products.
- Part of the planning for stage 2 involves defining performance criteria and deciding what data to collect when, how much data, and appropriate analysis of the data.
- Likely consist of planned comparisons and evaluations of some combination of process measures as well as in-process and trial product attributes.
- Manufacturer must scientifically determine suitable criteria and justify it.
- Objective measures, where possible.
- May be possible to leverage earlier study data if relevant to the commercial scale.

(c) PPQ protocol

A written protocol that specifies the manufacturing conditions,controls, testing, and expected outcomes is essential for this stagne of process validation. We recommend that the protocol discuss the following elements:

- The manufacturing conditions, including operating parameters, processing limits, and component (raw material) inputs.
- The data to be collected and when and how it will be evaluated.
- Tests to be performed (in-process, release, characterization) and acceptance criteria for each significant processing step.
- The sampling plan, including sampling points, number of samples, and the frequency of sampling for each unit operation and attribute.
- The number of samples should be adequate to provide sufficient statistical confidence of quality both within a batch and between batches.
- The confidence level selected can be based on risk analysis as it relates to the particular attribute under examination.

- Sampling during this stage should be more extensive than is typical during routine production.
- Criteria and process performance indicators that allow for a science- and risk-based decision about the ability of the process to consistently produce quality products. The criteria should include:
  - A description of the statistical methods to be used in analyzing all collected data (*e.g.*, statistical metrics defining both intra-batch and inter-batch variability).
  - Provision for addressing deviations from expected conditions and handling of nonconforming data. Data should not be excluded from further consideration in terms of PPQ without a documented, science-based justification.
- Design of facilities and the qualification of utilities and equipment, personnel training and qualification, and verification of material sources (components and container/closures), if not previously accomplished.
- Status of the validation of analytical methods used in measuring the process, in-process materials, and the product.
- Review and approval of the protocol by appropriate departments and the quality unit.

(d) PPQ protocol execution and report

Execution of the PPQ protocol should not begin until the protocol has been reviewed and approved by all appropriate departments, including the quality unit. Any departures from the protocol must be made according to established procedure or provisions in the protocol. Such departures must be justified and approved by all appropriate departments and the quality unit before implementation (§ 211.100).

The commercial manufacturing process and routine procedures must be followed during PPQ protocol execution (§§ 211.100(b) and 211.110(a)). The PPQ lots should be manufactured under normal conditions by the personnel routinely expected to perform each step of each unit operation in the process. Normal operating conditions should include the utility systems (*e.g.*, air handling and water purification), material, personnel, environment, and manufacturing procedures.

A report documenting and assessing adherence to the written PPQ protocol should be prepared in a timely manner after the completion of the protocol. This report should:

- Discuss and cross-reference all aspects of the protocol.
- Summarize data collected and analyze the data, as specified by the protocol.

- Evaluate any unexpected observations and additional data not specified in the protocol.
- Summarize and discuss all manufacturing non-conformances such as deviations, aberrant test results, or other information that has bearing on the validity of the process.
- Describe in sufficient detail any corrective actions or changes that should be made to existing procedures and controls.
- State a clear conclusion as to whether the data indicates the process met the conditions established in the protocol and whether the process is considered to be in a state of control.
- If not, the report should state what should be accomplished before such a conclusion can be reached.
- This conclusion should be based on a documented justification for the approval of the process, and release of lots produced by it to the market in consideration of the entire compilation of knowledge and information gained from the design stage through the process qualification stage.
- Include all appropriate department and quality unit review and approvals.

Input

- Design of the facility, utility
- Qualification of equipment
- Personnel
- Performance qualification
- Process performance qualification protocol and report

Output

- Confidence in manufacturing process
- Evidence to assure that process is capable of consistently delivering quality product
- Demonstrate that process works as intended

Stage 3 – Continued Process Verification

It is a science and risk-based real-time approach to verify and demonstrate that a process that operates within the predefined specified parameters consistently produces material which meets all its critical quality attributes (CQAs) and control strategy requirements. In order to enable continuous process verification, companies should perform, as relevant, extensive in-line, on-line or at-line controls and monitor process performance and product quality on each batch. Relevant data on quality attributes of incoming materials or components, in-process material and finished products should be collected. This should include the verification of attributes, parameters and end points, and assessment of CQA and critical process parameter (CPP) trends. Process analytical technology (PAT) applications such as NIR spectroscopy with or without feedback loop (*e.g.,* end point determination of blend homogeneity, determination of granules surface area, determination of content uniformity with large sample size) and Multivariate Statistical Process Control (MSPC) can be viewed as enablers for continuous process verification.

Ongoing assurance is gained during routine production that the process remains in a state of control. The validation maintenance stage requires frequent review of all process related documents, including validation audit reports to assure that there have been no changes, deviations, failures, modifications to the production process, and that all SOPs have been followed, including change control procedures. A successful validation program depends on the knowledge and understanding and the approach to control manufacturing processes. These include the source of variation, the limitation of the detection of the variation, and the attributes susceptible of the variation.

The goal of the third validation stage is continual assurance that the process remains in a state of control (the validated state) during commercial manufacture. A system or systems for detecting unplanned departures from the process as designed is essential to accomplish this goal. Adherence to the CGMP requirements, specifically, the collection and evaluation of information and data about the performance of the process, will allow detection of undesired process variability. Evaluating the performance of the process identifies problems and determines whether action must be taken to correct, anticipate, and prevent problems so that the process remains in control (§ 211.180(e)).

An ongoing program to collect and analyze product and process data that relate to product quality must be established (§ 211.180(e)). The data collected should include relevant process trends and quality of incoming materials or components, in-process material, and finished products. The data should be statistically trended and reviewed by trained personnel. The information collected should verify that the quality attributes are being appropriately controlled throughout the process.

It is recommended that a statistician or person with adequate training in statistical process control techniques develop the data collection plan and statistical methods and procedures used in measuring and evaluating process stability and process capability. Procedures should describe how trending and calculations are to be performed and should guard against overreaction to individual events as well as against failure to detect unintended process variability. Production data should be collected to evaluate process stability and capability. The quality unit should review this information. If properly carried out, these efforts can identify variability in the process and/or signal potential process improvements.

Good process design and development should anticipate significant sources of variability and establish appropriate detection, control, and/or mitigation strategies, as well as appropriate alert and action limits. However, a process is likely to encounter sources of variation that were not previously detected or to which the process was not previously exposed. Many tools and techniques, some statistical and others more qualitative, can be used to detect variation, characterize it, and determine the root cause. We recommend that the manufacturer use quantitative, statistical methods whenever appropriate and feasible. Scrutiny of intra-batch as well as inter-batch variation is part of a comprehensive continued process verification program under § 211.180(e).

We recommend continued monitoring and sampling of process parameters and quality attributes at the level established during the process qualification stage until sufficient data are available to generate significant variability estimates. These estimates can provide the basis for establishing levels and frequency of routine sampling and monitoring for the particular product and process. Monitoring can then be adjusted to a statistically appropriate and representative level. Process variability should be periodically assessed and monitoring adjusted accordingly.

Variation can also be detected by the timely assessment of defect complaints, out-of-specification findings, process deviation reports, process yield variations, batch records, incoming raw material records, and adverse event reports. Production line operators and quality unit staff should be encouraged to provide feedback on process performance. We recommend that the quality unit meet periodically with production staff to evaluate data, discuss possible trends or undesirable process variation, and coordinate any correction or follow-up actions by production.

Data gathered during this stage might suggest ways to improve and/or optimize the process by altering some aspect of the process or product, such as the operating conditions (ranges and set-points), process controls, component, or in-process material characteristics. A description of the planned change, a well-justified rationale for the change, an implementation plan, and quality unit approval before implementation must be documented (§ 211.100). Depending on how the proposed change might affect product quality, additional process design and process qualification activities could be warranted.

Maintenance of the facility, utilities, and equipment is another important aspect of ensuring that a process remains in control. Once established, qualification status must be maintained through routine monitoring, maintenance, and calibration procedures and schedules (21 CFR part 211, subparts C and D). The equipment and facility qualification data should be assessed periodically to determine whether re-qualification should be performed and the extent of that re-qualification. Maintenance and calibration frequency should be adjusted based on feedback from these activities. Sufficient knowledge and understanding of the process is required in order to support continuous process verification. However, the scope and extent of continuous process verification will be influenced by a number of factors including:

- Prior development and manufacturing knowledge from similar products and/or processes;
- The extent of process understanding gained from development studies and commercial manufacturing experience;
- The complexity of the product and/or manufacturing process;
- The level of process automation and analytical technologies used;
- For legacy products, with reference to the product lifecycle , process robustness and manufacturing history since point of commercialization as appropriate.

A discussion on the appropriateness and feasibility of the continuous process verification strategy should be included in the development section of the dossier and should be supported with data from at least laboratory or pilot scale batches. A description of the continuous process verification strategy including the process parameters and material attributes that will be monitored, as well as the analytical methods that will be employed, should be included as described in Annex 1, with cross-reference to the validation section of the dossier. Actual data generated during continuous process verification at production scale should be available at the site for inspection. The applicant should define the stage at which the process is considered to be under control and the validation exercise completed prior to release of the product to the market, and the basis on which that decision will be made. The discussion should include a justification for the number of batches to be used based on the complexity and expected variability of the process and existing manufacturing experience of the manufacturing site. Continuous process verification would be considered the most appropriate method for validating continuous processes. Continuous process verification can be introduced at any time in the lifecycle of the product. It can be used for the initial commercial production, to re-validate commercialised products as part of process changes or to support continual improvement. Continuous process verification is dependent on compliance with GMP principles and requirements. Pharmaceutical quality systems (PQS) as described in ICH Q10 can complement GMP requirements. However, GMP matters and PQS should not be included in the submission as they are assessed and handled by GMP inspectors as appropriate.

Input

- Knowledge of process
- Data collected
- Data reviewed and information gathered
- Trends
- Sample quantity and plan

Output

- Allow detection of process drift.
- Helps in getting feedback about product performance
- Helps in process maintenance
- Helps in determining need of new process

CONSIDERATION OF PROCESS VALIDATION

Process validation should confirm that the control strategy is adequate to the process design and the quality of the product. The validation should cover all manufactured strengths and all manufacturing sites used for production of the marketed product. A bracketing approach may be acceptable for different strengths, batch sizes and pack sizes. However, validation must cover all proposed sites. Process validation data should be generated for all products to demonstrate the adequacy of the manufacturing process at each site of manufacture. Validation should be carried out in accordance with GMP and data should be held at the manufacturing location and made available for inspection if not required in the dossier.

Process validation can be performed in a traditional way, as described below, regardless of the approach to development taken. However, there is also the possibility to implement continuous process verification if an enhanced approach to development has been performed or where a substantial amount of product and process knowledge and understanding has been gained through historical data and manufacturing experience. A combination of traditional process validation and continuous process verification may be employed. The in-line, on-line or at-line monitoring that is often utilised for continuous process verification provides substantially more information and knowledge about the process and might facilitate process improvements. In all stages of the product lifecycle, good project management and good archiving that capture scientific knowledge will make the process validation program more effective and efficient. The following practices should ensure uniform collection and assessment of information about the process and enhance the accessibility of such information later in the product lifecycle.

- An integrated team approach to process validation that includes expertise from a variety of disciplines (*e.g.,* process engineering, industrial pharmacy, analytical chemistry, microbiology, statistics, manufacturing, and quality assurance).
- Project plans, along with the full support of senior management, are essential elements for success.
- Throughout the product lifecycle, various studies can be initiated to discover, observe, correlate, or confirm information about the product and process.
- All studies should be planned and conducted according to sound scientific principles, appropriately documented, and approved in accordance with the established procedure appropriate for the stage of the lifecycle.
- The terms attribute(s) (*e.g.,* quality, product, component) and parameter(s) (*e.g.,* process, operating, and equipment) are not categorized with respect to criticality in this guidance.
- With a lifecycle approach to process validation that employs risk based decision making throughout that lifecycle, the perception of criticality as a continuum rather than a binary state is more useful.
- All attributes and parameters should be evaluated in terms of their roles in the process and impact on the product or in-process material, and re-evaluated as new information becomes available.
- The degree of control over those attributes or parameters should be commensurate with their risk to the process and process output. In other words, a higher degree of control is appropriate for attributes or parameters that pose a higher risk.
- Many products are single-source or involve complicated manufacturing processes.
- Homogeneity within a batch and consistency between batches are goals of process validation activities.
- Validation offers assurance that a process is reasonably protected against sources of variability that could affect production output, cause supply problems, and negatively affect public health.

PRE-REQUISITE OF PROCESS VALIDATION

- Process Development Designee shall review the product development report, data from pilot scale, scale up batch and proposed master formula document of product intended for manufacturing.
- Process Development Designee shall review/ ensure the availability analytical method transfer report to the plant and plant preparedness for conducting validation testing and routine testing; function shall co-ordinate with QC/QA in this regards.

- Process Development Designee shall prepare commercial/ exhibit batch production and control records which include the operational limits and overall strategy for process control based on development report.
- The Process Validation is performed after the facility, utility, and equipment, and laboratory test methods have been validated and released fir process validation activities. Where compendia method is used only limited analytical method validation shall be conducted.
- All raw material and packaging material specification shall be from approved vendors and shall be approved by quality control.
- All the equipment and instrument to be utilized are calibrated and preventive maintenance programs are in place.
- Relevant SOPs are in place and training is completed on equipment, operation, manufacturing instruction and sampling strategy.
- Key process steps and process variables are identified and their operating ranges have been established.
- All the master formula, manufacturing instruction, packaging instruction, testing procedure and specification shall be approved before execution of process validation batches.
- The cleaning of the area and equipment has been completed prior to the initiation of process validation.
- The validation team and operational team shall be trained from process engineer.

VALIDATION SAMPLING PROCEDURE AND ACCEPTANCE CRITERIA

A validation plan shall be specific to be the requirement of validation run of a particular product. A detailed plan of sampling procedure of samples which shall be analyzed/ monitored during the validation run shall be outlined systematically. The sampling plan including sampling points, number of samples and the frequency of sampling for each stage operation shall be decided based on characteristics of the product and deed or critical points of equipments. The number of samples should be adequate to provide sufficient statistical confidence of quality both within a batch and between batches. Quality of sample to be drawn from each sampling point shall be decided based on 1x – 3x formula in case of blend sample on case to case basis. As per USFDA sampling size can be increased from 1x – 10x provided on scientifically justified.

The acceptance criteria for each testing can be obtained from a particular pharmacopoeia reference/ laid specifications/ predetermined acceptance criteria and wherever sampling is done for the academic interest for future reference in product life cycle. Sampling location is to be clearly indicated by diagram for any equipment from which the sample are withdrawn (where ever application). This shall be help process validation team. Sampling in case of revalidation and process validation: following sampling plan is applicable for drug products which are already validated and or subjected to limited process validation or revalidation. The limited process validation/ revalidation is generally carried out on one commercial batch which include following situations:

- When the source of excipient (s) is changed, with no change in physical and chemical parameters.
- When the source of excipient (s) is changed, with significant change in physical and chemical parameters.
- One process validation batch with the excipient from the new source shall be manufactured. Complete validation batch of one batch as per individual process protocol of that product shall be followed.

Acceptance Criteria and Inference

The validation test and the results obtained there by will be discussed against by the acceptance criteria of test or specification and the conformance to the same will be discussed to support the validation activity. Recommendations for limits, frequencies and action to be taken in the event of the limits being exceeded shall be specified in the report together with recommendations on the extent of monitoring and the in-process controls necessary for routine production. Further the overall review of results should be checked for consistency and reproducibility. Results should demonstrate the control on the manufacturing process throughout all stages of manufacturing and the collected data to indicate the process consistency and reproducibility to yield a product which meets predetermined attributes. Based on the results generated during the study performed as per approved validation protocol, a validation report shall be prepared.

Failure and Deviation

Any test during process validation shall investigate to determine the case of failure. Where the case of failure is not obvious, it may useful to us an investigation procedure to ensure that all the possible areas of potential failure are covered. Once the case of the process validation failure has been identified, the failure shall classified into the following categories.

Type I: where the failure can be attributed to an occurrence which is not intrinsic to the process for example, an equipment failure raw material that it can be agreed to complete the validation exercise substituting another batch for the one that failed. This investigation and the subsequent action shall be included in the validation report.

Type II: where the failure may be attribute failure or where the investigation is inconclusive than the validation exercise has failed. In this case the validation terms decide and justify the course of action to be taken, recording its justification and recommendations.

This decision shall consider:

- Re-testing - if investigation of the analytical results supports the decision.
- Introduction a change in operation parameters, process steps.
- Changing the process equipment or the procedure for using the equipment.
- Suspension of the process validation exercise until further technical evaluation and/ or development has been carried out.
- Changing the sampling regime.
- Review of historical data.
- Change of the process validation acceptance criteria.
- Change to an analytical procedure.

CONCURRENT RELEASE OF PPQ BATCHES

In most cases, the PPQ study needs to be completed successfully and a high degree of assurance in the process achieved before commercial distribution of a product. In special situations, the PPQ protocol can be designed to release a PPQ batch for distribution before complete execution of the protocol steps and activities, *i.e.,* concurrent release. FDA expects that concurrent release will be used rarely. Concurrent release might be appropriate for processes used infrequently for various reasons, such as to manufacture drugs for which there is limited demand (*e.g.,* orphan drugs, minor use and minor species veterinary drugs) or which have short half lives (*e.g.,* radiopharmaceuticals, including positron emission tomography drugs). Concurrent release might also be appropriate for drugs that are medically necessary and are being manufactured in coordination with the Agency to alleviate a short supply.

Conclusions about a commercial manufacturing process can only be made after the PPQ protocol is fully executed and the data are fully evaluated. If Stage 2 qualification is not successful (*i.e.,* does not demonstrate that the process as designed is capable of reproducible performance at commercial scale), then additional design studies and qualification may be necessary. The new product and process understanding obtained from the unsuccessful qualification study (ies) can have negative implications if any lot was already distributed. Full execution of Stages 1 and 2 of process validation is intended to preclude or minimize that outcome. Circumstances and rationale for concurrent release should be fully described in the PPQ protocol. Even when process performance assessment based on the PPQ protocol is still outstanding, any lot released concurrently must comply with all CGMPs, regulatory approval requirements, and PPQ protocol lot release criteria. Lot release under a PPQ protocol is based upon meeting confidence levels appropriate for each quality attribute of the drug.

When warranted and used, concurrent release should be accompanied by a system for careful oversight of the distributed batch to facilitate rapid customer feedback. For example, customer complaints and defect reports should be rapidly assessed to determine root cause and whether the process should be improved or changed. Concurrently released lots must also be assessed in light of any negative PPQ study finding or conclusions and appropriate corrective action must be taken (§§ 211.100(a), 211.180(e), and 211.192). We recommend that each batch in a concurrent release program be evaluated for inclusion in the stability program. It is important that stability test data be promptly evaluated to ensure rapid detection and correction of any problems.

SCALE-UP

In order to avoid the repetition of lengthy and costly tests, it is necessary to gather information during properly designed development and process optimisation studies, when scaling up from laboratory through pilot to production scale. Such information provides the basis for justification that scale-up can be achieved without a consequent loss in quality. Those parts of the process likely to be critical in scale-up should be identified. Where ranges of batch sizes are proposed, it should be justified that variations in batch size would not adversely alter the CQAs of the finished product. It is envisaged that those parameters listed in the process validation scheme will need to be re-validated once further scale-up is proposed post-authorisation unless the process has been proven to be scale independent or continuous process verification is employed.

REVALIDATION

Revalidation is needed to ensure that changes in the process and/or in the process environment, whether intentional or unintentional, do not adversely affect process characteristics and product quality. Revalidation may be divided into two broad categories:

- Revalidation after any change having a bearing on product quality.
- Periodic revalidation carried out at scheduled intervals.

Revalidation after Changes

Revalidation must be performed on introduction of any changes affecting a manufacturing and/or standard procedure having a bearing on the established product performance characteristics. Such changes may include those in starting material, packaging material, manufacturing processes, equipment, in-process controls, manufacturing areas, or support systems (water, steam, etc.). Every such change requested should be reviewed by a qualified validation group, which will decide whether it is significant enough to justify revalidation and, if so, its extent. Revalidation after changes may be based on the performance of the same tests and activities as those used during the original validation, including tests on sub processes and on the equipment concerned. Some typical changes which require revalidation include the following:

- ***Changes in the starting material(s):*** Changes in the physical properties, such as density, viscosity, particle size distribution, and crystal type and modification, of the active ingredients or excipients may affect the mechanical properties of the material; as a consequence, they may adversely affect the process or the product.
- ***Changes in the packaging material:*** *For example,* replacing plastics by glass, may require changes in the packaging procedure and therefore affect product stability.
- ***Changes in the process:*** *For example,* changes in mixing time, drying temperature and cooling regime, may affect subsequent process steps and product quality.
- ***Changes in equipment:*** including measuring instruments, may affect both the process and the product; repair and maintenance work, such as the replacement of major equipment components, may affect the process.
- ***Changes in the production area and support system:*** *For example,* the rearrangement of manufacturing areas and/or support systems, may result in changes in the process. The repair and maintenance of support systems, such as ventilation, may change the environmental conditions and, as a consequence, revalidation/requalification may be necessary, mainly in the manufacture of sterile products.
- ***Unexpected changes and deviations may be observed during self-inspection or audit, or during the continuous trend analysis of process data.***

Periodic Revalidation

It is well known that process changes may occur gradually even if experienced operators work correctly according to established methods. Similarly, equipment wear may also cause gradual changes. Consequently, revalidation at scheduled times is advisable even if no changes have been deliberately made. The decision to introduce periodic revalidation should be based essentially on a review of historical data, *i.e.,* data generated during in-process and finished product testing after the latest validation, aimed at verifying that the process is under control. During the review of such historical data, any trend in the data collected should be evaluated. In some processes, such as sterilization, additional process testing is required to complement the historical data. The degree of testing required will be apparent from the original validation.

Additionally, the following points should be checked at the time of a scheduled revalidation:

- Have any changes in master formula and methods, batch size, etc., occurred? If so, has their impact on the product been assessed?
- Have calibrations been made in accordance with the established programme and time schedule?
- Has preventive maintenance been performed in accordance with the programme and time schedule?
- Have the standard operating procedures (SOPs) been properly updated?
- Have the SOPs been implemented?
- Have the cleaning and hygiene programmes been carried out?
- Have any changes been made in the analytical control methods?

POST APPROVAL CHANGE CONTROL

Clearly defined procedures are needed to control changes proposed in production processes. These procedures are part of GMP and would not normally be specified in the dossier. Such procedures should control planned changes, ensure that sufficient supporting data are generated to demonstrate that the revised process will result in a product of the desired quality, consistent with the approved control strategy and ensure that all aspects are thoroughly documented and approved including whether regulatory approval is needed by way of variation.

DOCUMENTATION

Documentation at each stage of the process validation lifecycle is essential for effective communication in complex, lengthy, and multidisciplinary projects. Documentation is important so that knowledge gained about a product and process is accessible and comprehensible to others involved in each stage of the lifecycle. Information transparency and accessibility are fundamental tenets of the scientific method. They are also essential to enabling organizational units responsible and accountable for the process to make informed, science-based decisions that ultimately support the release of a product to commerce.

The degree and type of documentation required by CGMP vary during the validation lifecycle. Documentation requirements are greatest during Stage 2, process qualification, and Stage 3, continued process verification. Studies during these stages must conform to CGMPs and must be approved by the quality unit in accordance with the regulations (see §§ 211.22 and 211.100). Viral and impurity clearance studies, even when performed at small scale, also require quality unit oversight.

CGMP documents for commercial manufacturing (*i.e.,* the initial commercial master batch production and control record (§ 211.186) and supporting procedures) are key outputs of Stage 1, process design. We recommend that firms diagram the process flow for the full-scale process. Process flow diagrams should describe each unit operation, its placement in the overall process, monitoring and control points, and the component, as well as other processing material inputs (*e.g.,* processing aids) and expected outputs (*i.e.,* in-process materials and finished product). It is also useful to generate and preserve process flow diagrams of the various scales as the process design progresses to facilitate comparison and decision making about their comparability.

ANALYTICAL METHODOLOGY

Process knowledge depends on accurate and precise measuring techniques used to test and examine the quality of drug components, in-process materials, and finished products. Validated analytical methods are not necessarily required during product- and process-development activities or when used in characterization studies. Nevertheless, analytical methods should be scientifically sound (*e.g.,* specific, sensitive, and accurate) and provide results that are reliable. There should be assurance of proper equipment function for laboratory experiments. Procedures for analytical method and equipment maintenance, documentation practices, and calibration practices supporting process-development efforts should be documented or described. New analytical technology and modifications to existing technology are continually being developed and can be used to characterize the process or the product. Use of these methods is particularly appropriate when they reduce risk by providing greater understanding or control of product quality. However, analytical methods supporting commercial batch release must follow CGMPs in parts 210 and 211. Clinical supply production should follow the CGMPs appropriate for the particular phase of clinical studies.

CONCLUSIONS

Validation is a widely used word in the areas of drug development, manufacturing and specification of finished products. The consistency and reliability of a validated process to produce a quality product is important for an industry. Pharmaceutical Process Validation is important and recognized parameters of cGMP. The process validation is intended to assist manufacturers in understanding quality management system (QMS) requirements and has general applicability to manufacturing process. This chapter generally outlines the principles and approaches that consider appropriate elements of process validation for the manufacture of drugs products and it incorporates principles and approaches that all manufacturers can use to validate manufacturing process. It can be stated that Process validation is a major requirement of cGMP regulation for finished pharmaceutical products and it helps in setting specification limits as a basis for releasing or rejecting product. It will carry out programs to determine whether or not the new information indicates the changes in product or process has occurred. All the process steps should be validated according to the protocol prepared by the validation team. One has to select consecutive batches for the execution of process validation. Sampling has to be done and the samples are sent to quality control department for analysis to ensure that the dosage form comply with the standards\ specifications. Process validation helps in building quality into the product as it is an important tool for quality management of pharmaceutics.

FURTHER READINGS

Agalloco J. The validation life cycle. *J Parenter Sci Technol*. 1993; 47(3):142-147.

ASTM E2281-03 Standard Practice for Process and Measurement Capability Indices.

ASTM E2474-06 Standard Practice for Pharmaceutical Process Design Utilizing Process Analytical Technology.

ASTM E2476-09 Standard Guide for Risk Assessment and Risk Control as it Impacts the Design, Development, and Operation of PAT Processes for Pharmaceutical Manufacture.

ASTM E2500-07 Standard Guide for Specification, Design, and Verification of Pharmaceutical and Biopharmaceutical Manufacturing Systems and Equipment.

ASTM E2709-10 Standard Practice for Demonstrating Capability to Comply with a Lot Acceptance Procedure.

Britain H.G pharmaceutical technology., July 2002; 68 to 70.

British Pharmacopoeia 2002, Department of Health, Scottish Home and Health department, Volume I,736.

Carleton FJ and Agalloco JP. Validation of pharmaceutical processes, sterile products., second edition., 1 to 16.

Chapman KG, Amer G, Brower G, GreenC, Hall WE and Harpaz D. *Journal of Validation Technology*. 2000;6:505-506.

European Commission Enterprise Directorate General Single market, regulatory environment, industries under vertical legislation Pharmaceuticals and Cosmetics Brussels, July 2001. EU Guide to Good Manufacturing Practice, Qualification and validation.

FDA guidelines on General Principles of Process Validation (May 1987)

FDA, (CDER), Investigating Out-of-Specification (OOS) Test Results for Pharmaceutical Production, guidance for industry, October 2006.

FDA, (CDER, CBER, CVM, and ORA), Quality Systems Approach to Pharmaceutical Current Good Manufacturing Practice Regulations, guidance for industry, September 2006.

FDA, (CDER, CVM, and ORA), PAT — A Framework for Innovative Pharmaceutical Development, Manufacturing, and Quality Assurance, guidance for industry, September 2004.

FDA/ICH (CDER and CBER) Q10 Pharmaceutical Quality System, guidance for industry, April 2009.

FDA/ICH, (CDER and CBER), Q7 Good Manufacturing Practice for Active Pharmaceutical Ingredients, guidance for industry, August 2001.

FDA/ICH, (CDER and CBER), Q8(R2) Pharmaceutical Development, guidance for industry, November 2009.

FDA/ICH, (CDER and CBER), Q9 Quality Risk Management, guidance for industry, June 2006.

Guidance for Industry: Process Validation: General Principles and Practices. U.S. Department of Health and Human Services, Food and Drug Administration, Centre for Drug Evaluation and Research (CDER), Centre for Biologics Evaluation and Research (CBER), Centre for Veterinary Medicine (CVM), January 2011.

Guidance on process Validation: Rev 1- EMA/CHMP/CVMP/QWP/7027/2012.

Guide to Inspections of Oral Solid Dosage Forms pre/post Approval Issue for Development and Validation; issue (1/94); January, 2010.

Guidelines for Process Validation of Pharmaceutical Dosage Form – Saudi Food & Drug Authority; Version 2; February, 1992.

Health Canada / Health Products and Food Branch Inspectorate Validation Guidelines for Pharmaceutical Dosage Forms (GUI – 0029) / December, 2009.

Health Products and Food Branch Inspectorate, Guidance Document Validation, Guidelines for Pharmaceutical Dosage Forms.

Howard T. Fuller Six Sigma for Validation, *Journal of Validation Technology*. 2000; 6(4):749-765,751.

Kathiresan K, Moorthi C, Prathyusha Y, Gade B. R, Reddy B. K, Manavalan R, ; An overview of pharmaceutical validation; *Research Journal of Pharmaceutical, Biological and Chemical Sciences*; ISSN: 0975-8585; October – December 2010; RJPBCS 1(4); Page No. 1026.

Kiffer,R.G, *J. Pharma. Sci. Tec.,* 1995, 44, 5, p. 249.

Kumar NL, MoorthyDG, Kumar RS, Sekaran CS. An overview of pharmaceutical validation: quality assurance view point, 2011; 1(4): 1003-1014.

Nash R. A and Wachter A. H, Pharmaceutical Process Validation an International Third Edition. Revised and Expended, Marcel Dekkar, Inc., New York, 2003; 17 – 40.

Nash RA and Berry IR. Pharmaceutical Process Validation., second edition, Marcel Dekker inc., 167-188,200-202,205.

Note for Guidance on Process Validation – The Europe Agency fro Evaluation of Medicinal Products; CPMP/QWP/848/96; EMEA/CVMP/598/99;

Oechslein C, Lazar M. S – Process Validation from view report of the FDA, Maas & Peither AG – GMP Publishing, LOGFILE No. 3/ February 2012.

Patel R. C, Bhuva C. K, singh R. P, Dadhich A, Sharma A., - Pharmaceutical Process Validation, Pharmatutor – ART – 1053.

Quality Management System – Process Validation Guidance GHTF/SG3/N99-10:2004 (Edition 2).

Satyabratajena, Arjun G, Anil kumarravipati N V, Satishkumar D, Vinod K R, David banji, Industrial Process Validation of Solid Dosage Forms–An Overview *International Journal of Pharmaceutical Sciences Review and Research*. 2010, 4(2).

The European agency for evaluation of medical products, London Note for Guidance on Process Validation, 2001.

Validation Master Plan Installation and Operational Qualification – Pharmaceutical Inspection Convention; Pharmaceutical Inspection Co-Operation Scheme; PI 006 – 2; July, 2004.

Validation Master Plan, www.labcompliance.com.

12

Sterile Process Validation

ABSTRACT

In the previous chapter we learnt about the non-sterile process validation. Although most of the validation parameters and attributes are same in non-sterile and sterile validations but some additional process are required to be validated in sterile processes. In this chapter we shall emphasize on those additional validation activities to be performed for sterile processes like sterilization. Sterilization process validation data, however, should be generated using procedures and conditions that are fully representative and descriptive of the procedures and conditions proposed for manufacture of the product in the application. This chapter is intended to provide guidance for the submission of information and data in support of the efficacy of sterilization processes in drug applications.

INTRODUCTION

According to the GMP regulations, to avoid microbiological contamination on aseptic products, a manufacturer must set up and exactly comply with the documented manufacture process. This documentation must include the validation of all sterilization process. The efficacy of a given sterilization process for a specific drug product is evaluated on the basis of a series of protocols and scientific experiments designed to demonstrate that the sterilization process and associated control procedures can reproducibly deliver a sterile product.

Regardless of whether the applicant uses terminal sterilization or aseptic processing to manufacture a drug product that is purported to be sterile, the information about the validation of that process should be submitted for all types of sterilization. Whether a product is sterilized by a terminal sterilization process or by an aseptic filling process, the efficacy of the sterilization process may be validated without the manufacture of three production batches.

GENERAL CONSIDERATIONS

The production of sterile preparations should be carried out in clean areas, entry to which should be through airlocks for personnel and/or for equipment and materials. Clean areas should be maintained to an appropriate standard of cleanliness and supplied with air that has passed through filters of the required efficiency. The various operations of component preparation (such as those involving containers and closures), product preparation, filling and sterilization should be carried out in separate areas within the clean area. These areas are classified into four grades. Manufacturing operations are divided here into two categories:

- First, those where the product is terminally sterilized; and
- Second, those which are conducted aseptically at some or all stages.

QUALITY CONTROL

The sterility test applied to the finished product should only be regarded as the last in a series of control measures by which sterility is assured. The test should be validated for the product(s) concerned. Samples taken for sterility testing should be representative of the whole of the batch but should, in particular, include samples taken from parts of the batch considered to be most at risk of contamination, for example:

- For products that have been filled aseptically, samples should include containers filled at the beginning and end of the batch and after any significant interruption of work;
- For products that have been heat sterilized in their final containers, consideration should be given to taking samples from that part of the load that is potentially the coolest.

The sterility of the finished product is assured by validation of the sterilization cycle in the case of terminally sterilized products, and by "media simulation" or "media fill" runs for aseptically processed products. Batch-processing records and, in the case of aseptic processing, environmental quality records, should be examined in conjunction with the results of the sterility tests. The sterility test procedure should be validated for a given product. Pharmacopoeial methods should be used for the validation and performance of the sterility test. In those cases where parametric release has been authorized in place of sterility testing special attention should be paid to the validation and the monitoring of the entire manufacturing process.

For injectable products the water for injection and the intermediate, if appropriate, and finished products should be monitored for endotoxins, using an established pharmacopoeial method that has been validated for each type of product. For large-volume infusion solutions, such monitoring of water or intermediates should always be done, in addition to any tests required by an approved monograph for the finished product. When a sample fails a test, the cause of the failure should be investigated and necessary action should be taken. Alternative methods to those in the pharmacopoeias may be used if they are validated, justified and authorized.

The use of rapid microbiological methods to replace the traditional microbiological methods, and to obtain earlier results on the microbiological quality of, for example, water, the environment or bioburden, could be considered if appropriately validated and if a comparative assessment of the proposed rapid method is performed against the pharmacopoeial method.

SANITATION

The sanitation of clean areas is particularly important. They should be cleaned frequently and thoroughly in accordance with an approved written programme. Where disinfectants are used, more than one type should be employed. Monitoring should be regularly undertaken to detect contamination or the presence of an organism against which the cleaning procedure is ineffective. Interactions between different cleaning materials should be validated. Appropriate cleaning validation should be carried out to ensure disinfectant residuals can be detected and are removed by the cleaning process.

Disinfectants and detergents should be monitored for microbial contamination; dilutions should be kept in previously cleaned containers and should only be stored for defined periods unless sterilized. Disinfectants and detergents used in Grade A and B areas should be sterile before use. A disinfectant programme should also include a sporicidal agent since many common disinfectants are ineffective against spores. The effectiveness of cleaning and disinfectant procedures should be demonstrated. Fumigation of clean areas may be useful for reducing microbial contamination in inaccessible places.

MANUFACTURE OF STERILE PREPARATIONS

Clean areas for the manufacture of sterile products are classified according to the required characteristics of the environment. Each manufacturing operation requires an appropriate level of environmental cleanliness in the operational state to minimize the risks of particulate or microbial contamination of the product or materials being handled. Detailed information on methods for determining the microbiological and particulate cleanliness of air, surfaces, etc., is not given in these guidelines. ISO 14644-

1 should be used for classification of cleanliness according to concentration of airborne particles (determination of number of sample locations, calculation of sample size and evaluation of classification from the data obtained). Table 1 should also be used to define the levels to be used as the basis for monitoring clean areas for airborne particles. For the manufacture of sterile pharmaceutical preparations, four grades of clean areas are distinguished as follows:

- *Grade A:* The local zone for high-risk operations, *e.g.,* filling and making aseptic connections. Normally such conditions are achieved by using a unidirectional airflow workstation. Unidirectional airflow systems should provide a homogeneous air speed of 0.36–0.54 m/s (guidance value) at a defined test position 15–30 cm below the terminal filter or air distributor system. The velocity at working level should not be less than 0.36 m/s. The uniformity and effectiveness of the unidirectional airflow should be demonstrated by undertaking airflow visualization tests.
- *Grade B:* In aseptic preparation and filling, this is the background environment for the Grade A zone.
- *Grades C and D:* Clean areas for carrying out less critical stages in the manufacture of sterile products or carrying out activities during which the product is not directly exposed (*i.e.,* aseptic connection with aseptic connectors and operations in a closed system).

A unidirectional airflow and lower velocities may be used in closed isolators and glove boxes.

In order to reach the B, C and D air grades the number of air changes should be appropriate for the size of the room and the equipment and personnel present in it. High-efficiency particulate air (HEPA) filters should be subjected to an installed filter leakage test in accordance with ISO 14644-3 at a recommended interval of every 6 months, but not exceeding 12 months. The purpose of performing regular leak tests is to ensure the filter media, filter frame and filter seal are free from leaks. The aerosol selected for HEPA leak testing should not support microbial growth and should be composed of a sufficient number or mass of particles. HEPA filter patching is allowed at the filter manufacturer and in situ operation provided that the patch sizes and procedures follow the recommendations of ISO 1822-4.

CLEAN ROOM AND CLEAN-AIR DEVICE CLASSIFICATION

Clean rooms and clean-air devices should be classified in accordance with ISO 14644. Classification should be clearly differentiated from operational process environmental monitoring. The maximum permitted airborne particle concentration for each grade is given in Table 1.

Table 1: Maximum permitted airborne particle concentration

	Maximum permitted number of particles per m^3 greater than or equal to the tabulated size	
Grade	***0.5 µm***	***5.0 µm***
A	3520	0
B	35200	29
C	352000	290
D	3520000	2900

For classification purposes in Grade A zones, a minimum sample volume of $1m^3$ should be taken per sample location. Referring to Table 1,

- For Grade A the airborne particle classification is ISO 4.8 dictated by the limit for particles ≥ 5.0µm.
- For Grade B (at rest) the airborne particle classification is ISO 5 for both particle sizes considered.
- For Grade C (at rest and in operation) the airborne particle classification is ISO 7 and ISO 8, respectively.
- For Grade D (at rest) the airborne particle classification is ISO 8.

For classification purposes ISO 14644-1 methodology defines both the minimum number of sample locations and the sample size based on the class limit of the largest particle size considered and the method of evaluation of the data collected. The sample volume should be determined according to ISO 14644-1 clause B.4.2. However, for lower grades (Grade C in operation and Grade D at rest) the sample volume per location should be at least 2 litres and the sample time per location should be not less than 1 minute. Portable particle counters with a short length of sample tubing should be used for classification purposes to avoid the loss of particles ≥ 5.0 µm. Isokinetic sample heads should be used in unidirectional airflow systems. "In operation" classification may be demonstrated during normal operations, simulated operations or during media fills as worst-case simulation is required for this. ISO 14644-2 provides information on testing to demonstrate continued compliance with the assigned cleanliness classification.

Clean Room and Clean-Air Device Monitoring

Clean rooms and clean-air devices should be routinely monitored while in operation and the monitoring locations based on a formal risk analysis study and the results obtained during the classification of rooms and/or clean-air devices. For Grade A zones, particle monitoring should be undertaken for the full duration of critical processing, including equipment assembly, except where justified by contaminants in the process that would damage the particle counter or present a hazard, for example, live organisms and radiological hazards. In such cases monitoring during routine equipment set-up operations should be undertaken before exposure to the risk. Monitoring during simulated operations should also be performed. The Grade A zone should be monitored at a frequency and sample size such that all interventions, transient events and any system deterioration would be captured and alarms triggered if alert limits are exceeded. It is accepted that it may not always be possible to demonstrate low levels of ≥ 5.0 µm particles at the point of fill when filling is in progress, due to the generation of particles or droplets from the product itself.

It is recommended that a similar system be used for Grade B zones, although the sample frequency may be decreased. The importance of the particle monitoring system should be determined by the effectiveness of the segregation between the adjacent Grade A and B zones. The Grade B zone should be monitored at a frequency and with a sample size such that changes in levels of contamination and any deterioration of the system would be captured and alarms triggered if alert limits are exceeded. Airborne particle monitoring systems may consist of independent particle counters; a network of sequentially accessed sampling points connected by manifold to a single particle counter; or multiple small particle counters located near monitoring points and networked to a data acquisition system. Combinations of systems can also be used. The system selected should be appropriate for the particle size considered.

Where remote sampling systems are used, the length of tubing and the radii of any bends in the tubing should be considered in the context of particle losses in the tubing. The selection of the monitoring system should take account of any risk presented by the materials used in the manufacturing operation, for example, those involving live organisms or radiopharmaceuticals. The sizes of samples taken for monitoring purposes using automated systems will usually be a function of the sampling rate of the system used. It is not necessary for the sample volume to be the same as that used for formal classification of clean rooms and clean-air devices.

The airborne particle conditions given in Table 1 for the "at rest" state should be achieved in the absence of the operating personnel after a short "clean-up" or "recovery" period of about 15–20 minutes (guidance value), after completion of the operations. The particulate conditions given in Table 1 for Grade A "in operation" should be maintained in the zone immediately surrounding the product whenever the product or open container is exposed to the environment. The "clean-up" or "recovery" test should demonstrate a change in particle concentration by a factor of 100 within the prescribed time (ISO 14644-3 clause B.12).

In order to demonstrate control of the cleanliness of the various clean areas during operation, they should be monitored for airborne particles and microbial contamination. In addition to "at rest" and "in operation" classification, airborne particles should be monitored periodically "in operation" at critical locations. The sampling plan need not be the same as that used for classification. Locations and sample sizes should be determined based on an assessment of the process and contamination risk. The monitoring of Grade C and D areas in operation should be performed in accordance with the principles of quality risk management. The requirements and alert/action limits will depend on the nature of the operations carried out, but the recommended "clean-up period" should be attained. Other characteristics such as temperature and relative humidity depend on the product and nature of the operations carried out. These parameters should not interfere with the defined cleanliness standard. Examples of operations to be carried out in the various grades are given in Table 2.

Table 2: Examples of operations to be carried out in the various grades

Grade	*Operations*
A	Aseptic manufacturing Aseptic Filling
C	Preparation of solution (usually to be filtered)
D	De-cartoning, washing, preparation of solution to be sterilised.

To control the microbiological cleanliness of Grades A–D in operation the clean areas should be monitored. Where aseptic operations are performed, monitoring should be frequent using methods such as settle plates, volumetric air and surface sampling (*e.g.,* swabs and contact plates). Sampling methods used in operation should not interfere with zone protection. Results from monitoring should be considered when reviewing batch documentation for finished product release. Surfaces and personnel should be monitored after critical operations. Additional microbiological monitoring is also required outside production operations, *e.g.,* after validation of systems, cleaning and sanitization.

Levels of detection of microbial contamination should be established for the purpose of setting alert and action limits and for monitoring the trends in environmental cleanliness in the facility. Limits expressed in colony-forming units (CFU) for the microbiological monitoring of clean areas in operation are given in Table 3. The sampling methods and numerical values included in the table are not intended to represent specifications, but are for information only.

Appropriate alert and action limits should be set for the results of particulate and microbiological monitoring. If the action limits are exceeded or a trend is identified in the alert limits, investigation should be initiated and the appropriate corrective actions should be taken, as prescribed in the operating procedures. The area grades as specified in sections 4.12 to 4.20 should be selected by the manufacturer on the basis of the nature of the process operations being performed and validation runs (*e.g.,* aseptic media fills or others types of process simulations) are used to establish processing hold times and a maximum fill duration. The determination of an appropriate process area environment and a time limit should be based on the microbial contamination (bioburden) found.

Table 3: Recommended limits for microbial contamination

Grade	*Air sampling (Active sampling) Cfu/m³*	*Settle plate (Passive sampling) Cfu/4h*	*Contact plate Cfu/plate*	*Glove print (5 Fingers) Cfu/gloves*
A	<1	<1	<1	<1
B	10	5	5	5
C	100	50	25	–
D	200	100	50	–

Terminally Sterilized Products

Components and most products should be prepared in at least a Grade D environment to ensure low microbial bioburden and particulate counts prior to filtration and sterilization. Where the product is at unusual risk of microbial contamination (*e.g.,* because it actively supports microbial growth, must be held for a long period before sterilization, or is necessarily processed mainly in open vessels), the preparation should generally be done in a Grade C environment. The filling of products for terminal sterilization should generally be done in at least a Grade C environment.

Where the product is at unusual risk of contamination from the environment (*e.g.,* because the filling operation is slow, the containers are wide necked or are necessarily exposed for more than a few seconds before sealing), the filling should be done in a Grade A zone with at least a Grade C background. The preparation and filling of ointments, creams, suspensions and emulsions should generally be done in a Grade C environment before terminal sterilization.

Aseptic Preparation

Components after washing should be handled in at least a Grade D environment. The handling of sterile starting materials and components, unless subjected to sterilization or filtration through a microorganism retaining filter later in the process, should be undertaken in a Grade A environment with a Grade B background. The preparation of solutions which are to be sterile-filtered during the process should be undertaken in a Grade C environment (unless a closed system is used, in which case a Class D environment may be justifiable). If not sterile-filtered (therefore an aseptic manipulation) the preparation of materials and products should be undertaken in a Grade A environment with a Grade B background.

The handling and filling of aseptically prepared products, as well as the handling of exposed sterile equipment, should be undertaken in a Grade A environment with a Grade B background.

The transfer of partially closed containers, as used in freeze-drying, before stoppering is completed, should be undertaken either in a Grade A environment with a Grade B background or in sealed transfer trays in a Grade B environment. The preparation and filling of sterile ointments, creams, suspensions and emulsions should be undertaken in a Grade A environment with a Grade B background when the product is exposed and is not subsequently filtered.

Processing

Precautions to minimize contamination should be taken during all processing stages, including the stages before sterilization. In general, preparations containing live microorganisms should not be made, nor should containers be filled in areas used for the processing of other pharmaceutical products. However, if the manufacturer can demonstrate and validate effective containment and decontamination of the live microorganisms, the use of multiproduct facilities may be justifiable. Vaccines consisting of dead organisms or of bacterial extracts may be dispensed into containers in the same premises as other sterile pharmaceutical products, provided that the inactivation procedure has been properly validated. When multiproduct facilities are used to manufacture sterile preparations containing live microorganisms and other sterile pharmaceutical products, the manufacturer should demonstrate and validate the effective decontamination of the live microorganisms, in addition to precautions taken to minimize contamination.

Care should be taken to ensure that any validation does not compromise the processes. Water sources, water-treatment equipment and treated water should be monitored regularly for chemicals, biological contamination and contamination with endotoxins to ensure that the water complies with the specifications appropriate to its use. Records should be maintained of the results of the monitoring and of any action taken.

Activities in clean areas, especially when aseptic operations are in progress, should be kept to a minimum and the movement of personnel should be controlled and methodical, so as to avoid excessive shedding of particles and organisms due to over-vigorous activity. As far as possible, personnel should be excluded from Grade A zones. The ambient temperature and humidity should not be uncomfortably high because of the nature of the garments worn and to reduce the risk of contamination liberated from the personnel.

The presence of containers and materials liable to generate fibers should be minimized in clean areas and avoided completely when aseptic work is in progress. Components, bulk-product containers and equipment should be handled after the final cleaning process in such a way as to ensure that they are not re-contaminated. The stage of processing of components as well as the bulk-product containers and equipment should be properly identified. The interval between the washing and drying and the sterilization of components, bulk-product containers and equipment, as well as between sterilization and use, should be as short as possible and subject to a time limit appropriate to the validated storage conditions. The time between the start of the preparation of a solution and its sterilization or filtration through a bacteria-retaining filter should be as short as possible. A maximum permissible time should be set for each product that takes into account its composition and the prescribed method of storage.

Any gas that is used to purge a solution or blanket a product should be passed through a sterilizing filter. The bioburden should be monitored before sterilization. There should be working limits on contamination immediately before sterilization, which are related to the efficiency of the method to be used. Bioburden assay should be performed on each batch for both aseptically filled products and terminally sterilized products. Where overkill sterilization parameters are set for terminally sterilized products, bioburden might be monitored only at suitable scheduled intervals. For parametric release systems, bioburden assay should be performed on each batch and considered as an in-process test. Where appropriate, the level of endotoxins should be monitored. All solutions, in particular large-volume infusion fluids, should be passed through a microorganism-retaining filter, if possible sited immediately before filling.

Components, bulk-product containers, equipment, and any other articles required in a clean area where aseptic work is in progress, should be sterilized and wherever possible passed into the area through double ended sterilizers sealed into the wall. Other procedures that prevent the introduction of contamination may be acceptable in some circumstances. The efficacy of any new processing procedure should be validated and the validation should be repeated at regular intervals thereafter or when any significant change is made in the process or equipment.

Sterilization

Whenever possible products intended to be sterile should be terminally sterilized by heat in their final container. Where it is not possible to carry out terminal sterilization by heating due to the instability of a formulation or incompatibility of a pack type (necessary to the administration of the product, *e.g.*, plastic eye-dropper bottles), a decision should be taken to use an alternative method of terminal sterilization following filtration and/or aseptic processing.

Sterilization can be achieved by the use of moist or dry heat, by irradiation with ionizing radiation (noting that ultraviolet irradiation is not normally an acceptable method of sterilization), by ethylene oxide (or other suitable gaseous sterilizing agents), or by filtration with subsequent aseptic filling of sterile final containers. Each method has its advantages and disadvantages. Where possible and practicable, heat sterilization is the method of choice. In any case the sterilization process must be in accordance with the marketing and manufacturing authorizations. The microbial contamination of starting materials should be minimal and their bioburden should be monitored before sterilization. Specifications should include requirements for microbiological quality when the need for this has been indicated by monitoring. All sterilization processes should be validated. Particular attention should be paid when the adopted sterilization method is not in accordance with pharmacopoeial standards or other national standards, or when it is used for a preparation that is not a simple aqueous or oily solution, for example, colloidal suspensions.

Before any sterilization process is adopted, its suitability for the product and its efficacy in achieving the desired sterilizing conditions in all parts of each type of load to be processed should be demonstrated by physical measurements and by biological indicators, where appropriate. The validity of the process should be verified at scheduled intervals, at least annually, and whenever significant modifications have been made to the equipment. Records should be kept of the results. For effective sterilization the whole of the material should be subjected to the required treatment and the process should be designed to ensure that this is achieved.

Biological indicators should be considered only as an additional method of monitoring the sterilization process. They should be stored and used according to the manufacturer's instructions, and their quality checked by positive controls. If they are used, strict precautions should be taken to avoid any transfer of microbial contamination from them. There should be a clear means of differentiating products that have not been sterilized from those which have. Each basket, tray, or other carrier of products or components should be clearly labeled with the name of the material, its batch number and an indication of whether or not it has been sterilized. Indicators such as autoclave tape may be used where appropriate to indicate whether or not a batch (or sub-batch) has passed through a sterilization process, but they do not give a reliable indication that the batch is in fact sterile. Validated loading patterns should be established for all sterilization processes. Sterilization records should be available for each sterilization run. They should be approved as part of the batch-release procedure.

TERMINAL STERILIZATION

Sterilization by Heat

Each heat-sterilization cycle should be recorded by means of appropriate equipment of suitable accuracy and precision, *e.g.*, on a time/ temperature chart with a suitably large scale. The temperature should be recorded by a probe situated at the coolest part of the load or loaded chamber, this point having been determined during the validation; the temperature should preferably be checked against a second independent temperature probe located at the same position. Sterilization records should be available for each sterilization run and should be approved as part of the batch release procedure. Chemical or biological indicators may also be used but should not take the place of physical controls.

Sufficient time should be allowed for the whole of the load to reach the required temperature before measurement of the sterilizing time is started. This time should be determined for each type of load to be processed. After the high-temperature phase of a heat sterilization cycle, precautions should be taken against contamination of a sterilized load during cooling. Any cooling fluid or gas in contact with the product should be sterilized.

Sterilization by Moist Heat

Both temperature and pressure should be used to monitor the process. Control instrumentation should normally be independent of monitoring instrumentation and recording charts. Where automated control and monitoring systems are used for these applications they should be validated to ensure that critical process requirements are met. System and cycle faults should be registered by the system and observed by the operator. The reading of the independent temperature indicator should be routinely checked against the reading on the chart recorder during the sterilization period. For sterilizers fitted with a drain at the bottom of the chamber, it may also be necessary to record the temperature at this position throughout the sterilization period. There should be regular leak tests on the chamber when a vacuum phase is part of the cycle. The items to be sterilized, other than products in sealed containers, should be wrapped in a material that allows the removal of air and the penetration of steam but prevents recontamination after sterilization. Specially designed autoclavable stainless steel containers, that allow steam to enter and air to leave, can also be used. All parts of the load should be in contact with water or saturated steam at the required temperature for the required time.

Care should be taken to ensure that the steam used for sterilization is of suitable quality (chemical, microbiological and endotoxin analysis of condensate and physical examination of steam (such as dryness, superheat, and non-condensable gases) and does not contain additives at a level that could cause contamination of the product or equipment. Steam used for sterilization should be tested regularly.

Description of the Process and Product

1. *The Drug Product and Container-Closure System:* Descriptions of the drug product and the container-closure system (s) to be sterilized (*e.g.,* size (s), fill volume, or secondary packaging).
2. *The Sterilization Process:* A description of the sterilization process used to sterilize the drug product in its final container-closure system, as well as a description of any other sterilization process(es) used to sterilize delivery sets, components, packaging, bulk drug substance or bulk product, and related items.
3. Information and data in support of the efficacy of these processes should also be submitted.
4. *The Autoclave Process and Performance Specifications:* A description of the autoclave process, including pertinent information such as cycle type (*e.g.,* saturated steam, water immersion, and water spray), including the manufacturer and model, of the autoclave. A description of performance specifications (*e.g.,* temperature, pressure, time, and minimum and maximum FO). Identify the autoclave(s) to be used for production sterilization.
5. *Autoclave Loading Patterns:* A description of representative autoclave loading patterns should be provided.
6. *Methods and Controls to Monitor Production Cycles:* Methods and controls used to monitor routine production cycles (*e.g.,* thermocouples, pilot bottles, and biological indicators) should be described, including the number and location of each as well as acceptance and rejection specifications.
7. *Requalification of Production Autoclaves:* A description of the program for routine and unscheduled requalification of production autoclaves, including frequency, should be provided.
8. *Reprocessing:* A description and validation summary of any program that provides for reprocessing (*e.g.,* additional thermal processing) of product should be provided. Please note that the stability program is also affected by additional thermal processing.

Thermal Qualification of the Cycle

1. *Heat Distribution and Penetration Studies:* Heat distribution and penetration study protocols and data summaries that demonstrate the uniformity, reproducibility, and conformance to specifications of the production sterilization cycle should be provided.

2. Results from a minimum of three consecutive, successful cycles should be provided to ensure that the results are consistent and meaningful.
3. *Thermal Monitors:* The number of thermal monitors used and their location in the chamber should be described. A diagram is helpful.
4. *The Effects of Loading on Thermal Input:* Data should be generated with minimum and maximum load to demonstrate the effects of loading on thermal input to product. Additional studies may be necessary if different fill volumes are used in the same container line. Data summaries are acceptable for these purposes.
5. A summary should consist of, for example, high and low temperatures (range), average temperature during the dwell period, minimum and maximum F0 values, and dwell time, run date and time, and identification of the autoclave(s) used.
6. These data should have been generated from studies carried out in production autoclave(s) that will be used for sterilization of the product that is the subject of the application.

Microbiological Efficacy of the Cycle

1. Validation studies that demonstrate the efficacy (lethality) of the production cycle should be provided. A sterility assurance of 10^{-6} or better should be demonstrated for any terminal sterilization process. This level of sterility assurance should be demonstrated for all parts of the drug product (including the container and closure, if applicable), which are claimed to be sterile.
2. The specific type of study and the methods used to carry out the study (or studies) are product and process specific and may vary from manufacturer to manufacturer. In general, the following types of information and data should be provided.
3. *Identification and Characterization of Bioburden Organisms:* The amount and type of information supplied may be dependent on the validation strategy chosen. For example, more information may be needed for bioburden-based autoclave processes than for overkill processes.
4. Information concerning the number, type, and resistance of bioburden organisms may be necessary, including those organisms associated with the product solution and the container and closure.
5. Describe the methods and results from studies used to identify and characterize bioburden organisms. It may be necessary to identify the most heat-resistant bioburden organisms.
6. *Specifications for Bioburden:* Specifications (alert and action levels) for bioburden should be provided. A description should be included of the program for routinely monitoring bioburden to ensure that validated and established limits are not exceeded (*e.g.,* frequency of analysis and methods used in bioburden screening).

7. *Identification, Resistance, and Stability of Biological Indicators:* Information and data concerning the identification, resistance (D and Z values), and stability of biological indicators used in the biological validation of the cycle should be provided. If biological indicators are purchased from a commercial source, it may be necessary to corroborate the microbial count and resistance, and provide performance specifications.
8. *The Resistance of the Biological Indicator Relative to That of Bioburden:* A description of characterizing the resistance of the biological indicator relative to that of bioburden may be necessary. Resistance in or on the product (*i.e.*, in the product solution or on the surface of container or closure parts or interfaces) should be determined as necessary. If spore carriers are used the resistance of spores on the carrier relative to that of directly inoculated product should be determined, if necessary.
9. *Microbiological Challenge Studies:* Microbiological validation studies should be submitted that demonstrate the efficacy of the minimum cycle to provide a sterility assurance of 10-6 or better to the product under the most difficult to sterilize conditions (*e.g.,* the most difficult to sterilize load with biological indicators at microbiological master sites or in master product or both). Use of a microbiological master product or site should be supported by scientific data. Microbiological master sites or solutions are those sites or solutions in which it is most difficult to kill the biological indicator under sterilization cycles that simulate production conditions.

Microbiological Monitoring of the Environment

The establishment of scientifically sound and appropriate specifications, standards, sampling plans, and test procedures designed to ensure that components, drug product containers, closures, in-process materials, and drug products conform to appropriate quality standards. Therefore, a microbiological monitoring program for production areas along with a bioburden-monitoring program for components and process water should be established. Process water includes autoclave-cooling water. Applicants should provide information concerning this program. Frequency, methods used, action levels, and data summaries should be included. A description of the actions taken when specifications are exceeded should be provided.

Container-Closure and Package Integrity

1. *Simulation of the Stresses from Processing:* Experimental designs should simulate the stresses of the sterilization process, handling, and storage of the drug and their effects on the container-closure system. Physical, chemical, and microbiological challenge studies may be necessary.

2. *Demonstrate Integrity Following the Maximum Exposure:* Container-closure integrity should be demonstrated on product units that have been exposed to the maximum sterilization cycle(s). If a product is exposed to more than one process, then exposure to the maximum cycle of all processes should be incorporated into the study design.
3. *Multiple Barriers:* Each barrier that separates areas of the drug product claimed to be sterile should be separately evaluated and validated.
4. *The Sensitivity of the Test:* The sensitivity of the experimental method used for container-closure integrity testing should be specified and provided.
5. *Integrity over the Product Shelf Life:* Microbial integrity of the container-closure system should be demonstrated over the shelf life of the product.

Bacterial Endotoxins Test and Method

The bacterial endotoxins test used for the product should be described. The description should include qualification of the laboratory, inhibition and enhancement tasting and results, determination of non-inhibitory concentration and maximum valid dilution.

Sterility Testing Methods and Release Criteria

1. Sterility test methods should be described and should include the protocol for the selection of representative units during production.
2. Testing performed within barrier systems should be described.
3. Information concerning validation of the barrier system may be necessary.

Sterilization by Dry Heat

Sterilization by dry heat may be suitable for non-aqueous liquids or dry-powder products. The process used should include air circulation within the chamber and the maintenance of a positive pressure to prevent the entry of non-sterile air. If air is supplied it should be passed through a microorganism-retaining filter (*e.g.,* a HEPA filter). Where sterilization by dry heat is also intended to remove pyrogens, challenge tests using endotoxins are required as part of the validation.

OTHER TERMINAL STERILIZATION PROCESSES

Although the information above directly addresses moist heat processes, the same type of information would pertain to other terminal sterilization processes used singly or in combination to sterilize a drug product. The types of information outlined are, in general, also applicable to ethylene oxide and radiation (gamma and electron beam). These other processes should be addressed as each applies to the drug product, sterile packaging and in-process sterilization of components. Examples of such information might include: descriptions of loading configurations; qualification and validation of master load configurations; determination and validation of the efficacy of the minimum cycle to provide sterility assurance at the product master sites; requalification of the cycle; provisions for re-sterilization; specifications and monitoring program for product bioburden; and container-closure integrity. Additional information relating to the effects of the sterilization process on the chemical and physical attributes of the drug substance or drug product may be applicable.

Sterilization by Radiation

Sterilization by radiation is used mainly for heat-sensitive materials and products. Many pharmaceutical products and some packaging materials are radiation-sensitive, so this method is permissible only when the absence of deleterious effects on the product has been confirmed experimentally. Ultraviolet irradiation is not an acceptable method for terminal sterilization. If sterilization by radiation is done by an outside contractor, the manufacturer is responsible for ensuring that the requirements of section 6.8 are met and that the sterilization process is validated. During the sterilization procedure the radiation dose should be measured. The dosimeters used for this purpose should be independent of the dose rate and should provide a quantitative measurement of the dose received by the product itself. Dosimeters should be inserted in the load in sufficient number and close enough together to ensure that there is always a dosimeter in the chamber. Where plastic dosimeters are used they should be used within the time-limit of their calibration. Dosimeter absorbance should be read shortly after exposure to radiation. Radiation-sensitive colour discs may be used to differentiate between packages that have been subjected to irradiation and those that have not; they are not indicators of successful sterilization. The information obtained should constitute part of the batch record.

Validation procedures should ensure that consideration is given to the effects of variations in the density of the packages. Material-handling procedures should prevent any mix-up of irradiated and non-irradiated materials. Each package should carry a radiation-sensitive indicator to show whether or not it has been subjected to radiation treatment. The total radiation dose should be administered within a predetermined period.

The Facility and the Process

1. The radiation facility should be identified (A diagram is helpful).
2. The radiation source, method of exposure (*i.e.*, movement through the irradiator), and the type and location of dosimeters used to monitor routine production loads should be described. If the low dose site is

not used for routine monitoring, data that shows the dose relationship between the two sites should be provided.

The Packaging of the Product

The packaging of the drug product within the shipping carton and within the carrier should be described.

Multiple-Dose Mapping Studies

Multiple-dose mapping studies for identification of low and high dose sites and demonstration of uniformity and reproducibility of the process should be described.

Microbiological Methods and Controls

The microbiological methods and controls used to establish, validate, and audit the efficacy of the cycle should be described.

Monitoring Stability

The program for monitoring the stability of packaging and the integrity of the container-closure system barrier over the claimed shelf life should be described.

Sterilization by Gases and Fumigants

Sterilization by gases and fumigants should only be used for finished products where there is no suitable alternative. Various gases and fumigants may be used for sterilization (*e.g.,* ethylene oxide and hydrogen peroxide vapour). Ethylene oxide should be used only when no other method is practicable. During process validation it should be shown that the gas has no damaging effect on the product and that the conditions and time allowed for degassing are such as to reduce any residual gas and reaction products to defined acceptable limits for the type of product or material concerned. These limits should be incorporated in the specifications.

Direct contact between gas and microorganisms is essential; precautions should, therefore, be taken to avoid the presence of organisms likely to be enclosed in materials such as crystals or dried protein. The nature and quantity of packaging materials can significantly affect the process. Before exposure to the gas, materials should be brought into equilibrium with the humidity and temperature required by the process. This requirement should be balanced against the need to minimize the waiting time before sterilization.

Each sterilization cycle should be monitored with suitable biological indicators, using the appropriate number of test pieces distributed throughout the load. The information thus obtained should form part of the batch record. Biological indicators should be stored and used according to the manufacturer's instructions and their performance checked by positive controls. For each sterilization cycle, records should be made of the time taken to complete the cycle, of the pressure, temperature and humidity within the chamber during the process and of the gas concentration. The pressure and temperature should be recorded on a chart throughout the cycle. The records should form part of the batch record. After sterilization, the load should be stored in a controlled manner in ventilated conditions to allow concentrations of residual gas and reaction products to fall to their prescribed levels. This process should be validated.

Ethylene Oxide

1. *Sterilizer:* The sterilizer(s) and controlled site(s) for pre-humidification and aeration of the product load should be described.
2. *Cycle Parameters:* The parameters and limits for all phases of the cycle, *e.g.,* pre-humidification, gas concentration, vacuum and gas pressure cycles, exposure time and temperature, humidity, degassing, aeration, and determination of residuals should be specified. Specific procedures used to monitor and control routine production cycles to assure that performance is within validated limits should be provided.
3. *Microbiological Methods:* The microbiological methods (growth medium, incubation temperature, and time interval) for cultivating spores from inoculated samples during validation experiments should be described as well as the microbiological methods used as part of routine production cycles.
4. *Stability:* The program for monitoring the stability of packaging and the integrity of the container-closure system barrier over the claimed shelf life should be described.

Aseptic Processing and Sterilization by Filtration

The objective of aseptic processing is to maintain the sterility of a product that is assembled from components, each of which has been sterilized by one of the above methods. The operating conditions should be such as to prevent microbial contamination. In order to maintain the sterility of the components and the product during aseptic processing, careful attention needs to be given to:

- The environment;
- Personnel;
- Critical surfaces;
- Container/closure sterilization and transfer procedures;
- The maximum holding period of the product before filling into the final container; and
- The sterilizing filter.

Certain solutions and liquids that cannot be sterilized in the final container can be filtered through a sterile filter of nominal pore size 0.22 micron (or less), or with at least equivalent microorganism-retaining properties, into a previously sterilized container. Such filters can remove bacteria and moulds, but not all viruses or mycoplasmas. Consideration should be given to complementing the filtration process with some degree of heat treatment. Filtration alone is not considered sufficient when sterilization in the final container is possible. Of the methods currently available, steam sterilization is preferred.

Owing to the potential additional risks of the filtration method as compared with other sterilization processes, a double-filter layer or second filtration through a further sterilized microorganism-retaining filter immediately prior to filling may be advisable. The final sterile filtration should be carried out as close as possible to the filling point. The fiber-shedding characteristics of filters should be minimal (virtually zero). Asbestos-containing filters should not be used under any circumstances.

The integrity of the sterilized filter should be verified before use and should be confirmed immediately after use by an appropriate method such as a bubble point, diffusive flow or pressure hold test. The time taken to filter a known volume of bulk solution and the pressure difference to be used across the filter should be determined during validation and any significant differences from these during routine manufacturing should be noted and investigated. Results of these checks should be included in the batch record. The integrity of critical gas and air vent filters should be confirmed after use. The integrity of other filters should be confirmed at appropriate intervals. Consideration should be given to increase monitoring of filter integrity in processes that involve harsh conditions, *e.g.,* the circulation of high-temperature air.

The same filter should not be used for more than one working day unless such use has been validated. The filter should not affect the product either by removing ingredients from it or by releasing substances into it.

Isolator Technology

The use of isolator technology to minimize human interventions in processing areas may result in a significant decrease in the risk of microbial contamination of aseptically manufactured products from the environment. There are many possible designs of isolators and transfer devices. The isolator and the background environment should be designed so that the required air quality for each zone can be realized. Isolators are constructed of various materials more or less prone to puncture and leakage. Transfer devices may vary from single-door to double-door designs to fully-sealed systems incorporating sterilization mechanisms.

The transfer of materials into and out of the unit is one of the greatest potential sources of contamination. In general the area inside the isolator is the local zone for high-risk manipulations, although it is recognized that unidirectional airflow may not exist in the working zone of all isolators and transfer devices. The air classification required for the background environment depends on the design of the isolator and its application. It should be controlled, and for aseptic processing it should be at least Grade D.

Isolators should be introduced only after appropriate validation. Validation should take into account all critical factors of isolator technology, for example, the quality of the air inside and outside (background) the isolator, sanitization of the isolator, the transfer process and isolator integrity. Monitoring should be done routinely and should include frequent leak testing of the isolator and the glove/sleeve system.

Blow/ Fill/ Seal Technology

Blow/ fill/ seal units are purpose-built machines in which, in one continuous operation, containers are formed from a thermoplastic granulate, filled and then sealed, all by the one automatic machine. Blow/ fill/ seal equipment used for aseptic production which is fitted with an effective Grade A air shower may be installed in at least a Grade C environment, provided that Grade A or B clothing is used. The environment should comply with the viable and non-viable limits at rest and the viable limit only when in operation. Blow/fill/seal equipment used for the production of products which are terminally sterilized should be installed in at least a Grade D environment. Because of this special technology, particular attention should be paid to at least the following:

- Equipment design and qualification;
- Validation and reproducibility of cleaning-in-place and sterilization-in place;
- Background clean room environment in which the equipment is located;
- Operator training and clothing; and
- Interventions in the critical zone of the equipment including any aseptic assembly prior to the commencement of filling.

PERSONNEL

Only the minimum number of personnel required should be present in clean areas; this is particularly important during aseptic processes. As far as possible, inspections and controls should be conducted from outside such areas. All personnel (including those concerned with cleaning and maintenance) employed in such areas should receive initial and regular training in disciplines relevant to the correct manufacture of sterile products, including hygiene and the basic elements of microbiology. When outside staff who have not received such training (*e.g.,* building or maintenance contractors) need to be brought in, particular care should be taken over their instruction and supervision.

Staff who have been engaged in the processing of animal-tissue materials or of cultures of microorganisms other than those used in the current manufacturing process should not enter sterile-product areas unless rigorous and clearly defined decontamination procedures have been followed. High standards of personal hygiene and cleanliness are essential and personnel involved in the manufacture of sterile preparations should be instructed to report any conditions that may cause the shedding of abnormal numbers or types of contaminants; periodic health checks for such conditions are desirable. The action to be taken in respect of personnel who might be introducing undue microbial hazards should be decided by a designated competent person.

Changing and washing should follow a written procedure designed to minimize the contamination of clean-area clothing or the carry-through of contaminants to clean areas. The clothing and its quality should be appropriate for the process and the grade of the working area. It should be worn in such a way as to protect the product from contamination. Outdoor clothing should not be brought into changing rooms leading to Grade B and C rooms. For every worker in a Grade A/B area, clean sterile (sterilized or adequately sanitized) protective garments should be provided at each work session. Gloves should be regularly disinfected during operations. Masks and gloves should be changed at least every working session. Operators working in Grade A and B areas should wear sanitized goggles.

Wrist-watches, cosmetics and jewellery should not be worn in clean areas. The clothing required for each grade is as follows:

- *Grade D:* The hair and, where relevant, beard and moustache should be covered. Protective clothing and appropriate shoes or overshoes should be worn. Appropriate measures should be taken to avoid any contamination from outside the clean area.
- *Grade C:* The hair and, where relevant, beard and moustache should be covered. A one-piece jumpsuit, gathered at the wrists and with a high neck, and appropriate shoes or overshoes should be worn. The clothing should shed virtually no fibres or particulate matter.
- *Grades A and B:* Entry of personnel into Grade A areas should be minimized. Headgear should totally enclose the hair and, where relevant, beard and moustache. A one-piece jumpsuit, gathered at the wrists and with a high neck, should be worn. The headgear should be tucked into the neck of the suit. A face-mask should be worn to

prevent the shedding of droplets. Sterilized, non-powdered gloves of appropriate material and sterilized or disinfected footwear should be worn. Trouser-bottoms should be tucked inside the footwear and garment sleeves into the gloves. The protective clothing should shed virtually no fibres or particulate matter and should retain particles shed by the body.

Clothing used in clean areas should be laundered or cleaned in such a way that it does not gather additional particulate contaminants that can later be shed. Separate laundry facilities for such clothing are desirable. If fibers are damaged by inappropriate cleaning or sterilization, there may be an increased risk of shedding particles. Washing and sterilization operations should follow standard operating procedures.

PREMISES

All premises should as far as possible be designed to avoid the unnecessary entry of supervisory or control personnel. Grade A and B areas should be designed so that all operations can be observed from outside. In clean areas all exposed surfaces should be smooth, impervious and unbroken to minimize the shedding or accumulation of particles or microorganisms and to permit the repeated application of cleaning agents and disinfectants, where used. To reduce the accumulation of dust and to facilitate cleaning, there should be no un-cleanable recesses and a minimum of projecting ledges, shelves, cupboards and equipment. Doors should be carefully designed to avoid un-cleanable recesses; sliding doors may be undesirable for this reason. Swing doors should open to the high-pressure side and be provided with self-closers. Exceptions are permitted based on egress and site environmental, health and safety containment requirements. False ceilings should be sealed to prevent contamination from the void space above them.

Pipes and ducts and other utilities should be installed so that they do not create recesses, unsealed openings and surfaces that are difficult to clean. Sanitary pipes and fittings should be used and threaded pipe connections should be avoided. Sinks and drains should be avoided wherever possible and should be excluded from Grade A and B areas where aseptic operations are carried out. Where installed they should be designed, located and maintained so as to minimize the risks of microbial contamination; they should be fitted with effective, easily cleanable traps and with air breaks to prevent backflow. Any floor channels should be open and easily cleanable and be connected to drains outside the area in a manner that prevents the ingress of microbial contaminants.

Changing rooms should be designed as airlocks and used to provide physical separation of the different stages of changing and so minimize microbial and particulate contamination of protective clothing. They should be flushed effectively with filtered air. The final stage of the changing room should, in the at-rest state, be the same grade as the area into which it leads. The use of separate changing rooms for entering and leaving clean areas is sometimes desirable. In general hand-washing facilities should be provided only in the first stage of the changing rooms. There should not be a change of more than one grade between airlocks or passages and changing rooms, *i.e.,* a Grade D passage can lead to a Grade C airlock, which leads to a Grade B changing room, which leads to a Grade B clean room. Changing rooms should be of a sufficient size to allow for ease of changing. Changing rooms should be equipped with mirrors so that personnel can confirm the correct fit of garments before leaving the changing room.

Airlock doors should not be opened simultaneously. An interlocking system and a visual and/or audible warning system should be operated to prevent the opening of more than one door at a time. A filtered air supply should be used to maintain a positive pressure and airflow relative to surrounding areas of a lower grade under all operational conditions; it should flush the area effectively. Adjacent rooms of different grades should have a pressure differential of approximately 10–15 Pascals. Particular attention should be paid to the protection of the zone of greatest risk, *i.e.,* the immediate environment to which the product and the cleaned components in contact with it are exposed. The recommendations regarding air supplies and pressure differentials may need to be modified where it becomes necessary to contain certain materials, *e.g.,* pathogenic, highly toxic, radioactive or live viral or bacterial materials or products. The decontamination of the facilities and the treatment of air leaving a clean area may be necessary for some operations.

It should be demonstrated that airflow patterns do not present a contamination risk; for example, care should be taken to ensure that particles from a particle-generating person, operation or machine are not conveyed to a zone of higher product risk. A warning system should be operated to indicate failure in the air supply. Indicators of pressure differentials should be fitted between areas where this difference is important, and the pressure differentials should be regularly recorded and failure alarmed. Consideration should be given to restricting unnecessary access to critical filling areas, *e.g.,* Grade A filling zones, by means of a physical barrier.

Buildings and Facilities

A brief description of the manufacturing building and facilities should be provided. The following information should be included:

1. *Floor Plan:* A floor plan of the areas holding the aseptic filling facilities including preparation and holding areas, filtering and filling areas, and gowning rooms should be included. Class 100, Class 10,000, Class

100,000 should be identified. Isolators or barrier systems should be identified.

2. *Location of Equipment:* The placement of all critical equipment, including, but not limited to, laminar flow hoods, autoclaves, lyophilizers, and filling heads, should be identified. Equipment within barrier or isolation systems should be noted.

Overall Manufacturing Operation

The overall manufacturing operation including, for example, material flow, filling, capping, and aseptic assembly, should be described.

The normal flow (movement) of product and components from formulation to finished dosage form should be identified and indicated on the floor plan described above. The following information should be considered when describing the overall manufacturing operation:

1. *Drug Product Solution Filtration:* The specific bulk product solution filtration processes, including tandem filter units, prefilter, and bacterial retentive filters, should be described.
2. A summary should be provided containing information and data concerning the validation of the retention of microbes and compatibility of the filter used for the specific product. Any effects of the filter on the product formulation should be described, *e.g.,* adsorption of preservatives or active drug substance, or extractable

Specifications Concerning Holding Periods

1. GMP Regulations requires, in part, when appropriate, the establishment of time limits for completing each phase of production to ensure the quality of the drug product. Therefore, specifications concerning any holding periods between the compounding of the bulk drug product and its filling into final containers should be provided.
2. These specifications should include, for example, holding tanks, times, temperatures, and conditions of storage.
3. Procedures used to protect microbiological quality of the bulk drug during these holding periods should be indicated.
4. Maintenance of the microbiological quality during holding periods may need verification.

Critical Operations

1. The critical operations that expose product or product contact surfaces to the environment (such as transfer of sterilized containers or closures to the aseptic filling areas) should be described.
2. Any barrier or isolation systems should be described.

Sterilization and Depyrogenation of Containers, Closures, Equipment, and Components

1. The sterilization and depyrogenation processes used for containers, closures, equipment, components, and barrier systems should be described.
2. A description of the validation of these processes should be provided including, where applicable, heat distribution and penetration summaries, biological challenge studies (microbiological indicators and endotoxin) and routine monitoring procedures.
3. Validation information for sterilization processes other than moist heat should also be included.
4. Methods and data (including controls) demonstrating distribution and penetration of the sterilant and microbiological efficacy of each process should be submitted.
5. *Bulk Drug Solution Components That are Sterilized Separately:* If the bulk drug solution is aseptically formulated from components that are sterilized separately, information and data concerning the validation of each of these separate sterilization processes should be provided.
6. *Sterilization Information in the Batch Records:* The completed batch record supplied with the application should identify the validated processes to be used for sterilization and depyrogenation of any container-closure components. This information may be included in the batch record by reference to the validation protocol or SOP.

Procedures and Specifications for Media Fills

1. The procedures and specifications used for media fills should be described.
2. Summaries of results for validation using the same container- closure system and filling process that is to be used for the product should be described.
3. Any procedural differences between the media fill and the production process should be indicated.
4. A summary of recent media fill results, including failures, should be provided.
5. These data should be obtained using the same filling line(s) that are to be used for the drug product.
6. The following are recommended to be included with the data summary for each media fill run described
   - The filling room: Identify the aseptic filling area used and relate this to the floor plan.

- Container-closure type and size
- Volume of medium used in each container
- Type of medium used
- Number of units filled
- Number of units incubated
- Number of units positive
- Incubation parameters
- The incubation time and temperature for each group of units incubated and specifications for any group of units subjected to two (or more) different temperatures should be specified.
- Date of each media fill
- *Simulations:* The procedures used to simulate any steps of a normal production fill should be described. This might include, for example, slower line speed, personnel shift changes, equipment failure and repair, mock lyophilization and substitution of vial headspace gas.
- *Microbiological monitoring:* The microbiological monitoring data obtained during the media fill runs should be provided (see Chapter 4 section 6 of this guidance).
- *Process parameters:* The parameters used for production filling and for media fills (*e.g.,* line speed, fill volume, number of containers filled, or duration of fill) should be compared.

Actions Concerning Product When Media Fills Fail

The disposition of product made before and after a failed media fill should be described. The description should include details of investigations, reviews, and how decisions are made to reject or release product.

Microbiological Monitoring of the Environment

The microbiological monitoring program used during routine production and media fills should be described. The frequency of monitoring, type of monitoring, sites monitored, alert and action level specifications and precise descriptions of the actions taken when specifications are exceeded should be included.

1. *Microbiological Methods:* The microbiological materials and methods used in the environmental monitoring program should be described. Methods may include sample collection, transport, and neutralization of sanitizers, incubation, and calculation of results.
2. The following are sources of microbial contamination and their monitoring that should be addressed, including specifications:

   Airborne microorganisms

Microorganisms on inanimate surfaces

Microorganisms on personnel

Water systems

Product component bioburden

3. *Yeasts, Molds, and Anaerobic Microorganisms:* A description of periodic or routine monitoring methods used for yeasts, molds, and anaerobes should be provided.
4. *Exceeded Limit:* A description of the actions taken when specifications are exceeded should be provided.

Container-Closure and Package Integrity

1. The methods and results demonstrating the integrity of the microbiological barrier of the container-closure system should be summarized. This should include testing for initial validation. The procedures used for the stability protocol also should be described. For initial validation of microbiological integrity of container-closure systems, product sterility testing is not normally considered sufficient.
2. The sensitivity of the experimental method used for container-closure integrity testing should be specified and provided.

Bacterial Endotoxins Test and Method

1. The bacterial endotoxin test used for the product should be described, if applicable. This description should include qualification of the laboratory, inhibition and enhancement testing and results, determination of non-inhibitory concentration and maximum valid dilution.

Sterility Testing Methods and Release Criteria

1. Sterility test methods should be described and should include the protocol for the selection of representative units during production.
2. For a drug product represented to be a drug recognized in an official compendium, when test methods differ significantly from official compendial test methods, a demonstration of the equivalency to the official compendial method should be provided.
3. Testing performed within barrier systems should be discussed, and information concerning validation of the barrier system may be necessary.

EQUIPMENT

A conveyor belt should not pass through a partition between a Grade A or B clean area and a processing area of lower air cleanliness, unless the belt itself is continuously sterilized (*e.g.,* in a sterilizing tunnel). Whenever possible, equipment used for processing sterile products should be chosen so that it can be effectively sterilized by steam or dry heat or other methods. As far as possible, equipment fittings and services should be designed and installed so that operations, maintenance and repairs can be carried out outside the clean area. Equipment that has to be taken apart for maintenance should be re-sterilized after complete reassembly, wherever possible. When equipment maintenance is carried out within a clean area, clean instruments and tools should be used and the area should be cleaned and disinfected again, where appropriate, before processing recommences, if the required standards of cleanliness and/or asepsis have not been maintained during the maintenance work.

All equipment such as sterilizers, air-handling and filtration systems, air vent and gas filters, water treatment, generation, storage and distribution systems should be subject to validation and planned maintenance; their return to use should be approved. Water-treatment plants and distribution systems should be designed, constructed and maintained so as to ensure a reliable source of water of an appropriate quality. They should not be operated beyond their designed capacity. Consideration should be given to including a testing programme in the maintenance of a water system. Water for injection should be produced, stored and distributed in a manner which prevents the growth of microorganisms, *e.g.,* by constant circulation at a temperature above 70°C or not more than 4°C.

FINISHING OF STERILE PRODUCTS

Containers should be closed by appropriately validated methods. Containers closed by fusion, *e.g.,* glass or plastic ampoules, should be subject to 100% integrity testing. Samples of other containers should be checked for integrity according to appropriate procedures. The container closure system for aseptically filled vials is not fully integral until the aluminum cap has been crimped into place on the stoppered vial. Crimping of the cap should, therefore, be performed as soon as possible after stopper insertion.

As the equipment used to crimp vial caps can generate large quantities of non-viable particulates, the equipment should be located at a separate station equipped with adequate air extraction. Vial capping can be undertaken as an aseptic process using sterilized caps or as a clean process outside the aseptic core. Where this latter approach is adopted, vials should be protected by Grade A conditions up to the point of leaving the aseptic processing area, and thereafter stoppered vials should be protected with a Grade A air supply until the cap has been crimped. Vials with missing or displaced stoppers should be rejected prior to capping. Where human intervention is required at the capping station, appropriate technology should be used to prevent direct contact with the vials and to minimize microbial contamination.

Restricted access barriers and isolators may be beneficial in assuring the required conditions and minimizing direct human interventions into the capping operation. Containers sealed under vacuum should be tested for maintenance of that vacuum after an appropriate, predetermined period. Filled containers of parenteral products should be inspected individually for extraneous contamination or other defects. When inspection is carried out visually this should be done under suitable and controlled conditions of illumination and background. Operators doing the inspection should pass regular eyesight checks, using personal corrective lenses (*e.g.,* spectacles or contact lenses) as required, and be allowed frequent breaks from inspection. Where other methods of inspection are used, the process should be validated and the performance of the equipment checked at intervals. Results should be recorded.

MAINTENANCE OF MICROBIOLOGICAL CONTROL AND QUALITY

Container-Closure Integrity

The ability of the container-closure system to maintain the integrity of its microbial barrier, and, hence, the sterility of a drug product throughout its shelf life, should be demonstrated. As previously stated, sterility testing at the initial time point is not considered sufficient to demonstrate the microbial integrity of a container-closure system. Documentation of the sensitivity of the container-closure integrity test should be provided.

Preservative Effectiveness

1. The efficacy of preservative systems inadvertently introduced during drug product use should be demonstrated at the minimum concentration specified for drug product release or at the minimum concentration specified for the end of the expiration dating period, whichever is less.
2. Since the efficacy of preservative systems is judged by their effect on microorganisms, microbial challenge assays should be performed.
3. For purposes of the stability protocol, the stability protocol, the first three production lots should be tested with a microbial challenge assay at the beginning and end of the stability period.
4. Chemical assays to monitor the concentration of preservatives should be performed at all test intervals.
5. For subsequent lots placed on stability, chemical assays may be adequate to demonstrate the presence of specified concentrations of preservatives, and such testing should be carried out according to the approved stability study protocol.

Pyrogen or Endotoxin Testing

For drug products purporting to be pyrogen free, it is recommended that pyrogen or endotoxin tests be carried out at the beginning and end of the stability period as part of the approved stability study protocol.

CONCLUSIONS

Quality is always an imperative prerequisite when we consider any product and when it comes with sterile products, risks value increases. Therefore, sterile drug products must be manufactured to the highest quality levels. End-product testing by itself does not guarantee the quality of the product. Quality assurance techniques must be used to build the quality into the product at every step and not just tested for at the end. In pharmaceutical industry, sterile process validation performs this task to build the quality into the product because, it had been proven to be an important tool for quality management of pharmaceuticals. This chapter has attempted to summarize, and to provide commentary where appropriate, on the most significant parameters to be validated for sterile products. It is not possible, or even necessarily productive, for a single chapter to go through each of the clauses point by point. It is important to re-emphasize that the document is suggestive and that its contents might differ from actual regulatory requirements.

FURTHER READINGS

FDA Guidance for Industry. Sterile drug products produced by aseptic processing — cGMP. US Food and Drug Administration, 2004.

Good manufacturing practices for pharmaceutical products: Water for pharmaceutical use. *In:* WHO Expert Committee on Specifications for Pharmaceutical Preparations. Thirty-ninth report. Geneva, World Health Organization, 2005 (WHO Technical Report Series, No. 929), Annex 3; and in Quality assurance of pharmaceuticals. A compendium of guidelines and related materials. Vol. 2. 2nd updated ed. Good manufacturing practices and inspection. Geneva, World Health Organization, 2007.

Good manufacturing practices for sterile pharmaceutical products. *In*: WHO Expert Committee on Specifications for Pharmaceutical Preparations. Thirty-sixth report. Geneva, World Health Organization, 2002 (WHO Technical Report Series, No. 902), Annex 6; and in Quality assurance of pharmaceuticals. A compendium of guidelines and related materials. Vol. 2. 2nd updated ed. Good manufacturing practices and inspection. Geneva, World Health Organization, 2007; and in Quality Assurance of Pharmaceuticals. A compendium of guidelines and related materials. Geneva, World Health Organization, 2010 (CD-ROM).

Guidance for industry. Sterile drug products produced by aseptic processing. Japan, 2005.

ISO 14644-1. Clean rooms and associated controlled environments. Part 1: Classification of airborne particles. Geneva, International Organization for Standardization.

ISO 14644-2. Clean rooms and associated controlled environments. Part 2: Monitoring for continued compliance with ISO 14644-1. Geneva, International Organization for Standardization.

ISO 14644-3. Clean rooms and associated controlled environments. Part 3: Test methods. Geneva, International Organization for Standardization.
ISO 14644-4. Clean rooms and associated controlled environments. Part 4: Design, construction and start-up. Geneva, International Organization for Standardization.
ISO 14644-5 Clean rooms and associated controlled environments. Part 5: Cleanroom operations. Geneva, International Organization for Standardization.
ISO 1822-4. High efficiency air filters (HEPA and ULPA). Determining leakage of filter elements.
Manufacture of sterile medicinal products. *In:* The rules governing medicinal products in the European Union Vol. 4. EU guidelines to good manufacturing practice medicinal products for human and veterinary use. Annex 1, Brussels, 2008.

13

Media Fill (Sterile Simulation) Study

ABSTRACT

According to all guidelines the process simulation with media fill is state of the art for the validation of aseptic manufacturing process. Media fill means that a microbiological nutrient media will be filled into a container / closure system (ampoule, vials etc) instead of the product under simulation of aseptic standard procedure. The filled container closure systems are incubated under defined parameters and finally checked for microbiological contamination. This is to demonstrate that rooms, equipment and personnel are able to manufacture a product with very low contamination rate. In this chapter we shall learn about the media fill study and its importance in sterile industry.

INTRODUCTION

All manufacturing procedures in pharmaceutical industry must be validated. This requirement is stated in the European Pharmacopoeia:18 "Process validation include checks on the process are regularly carried out by means of process simulation tests using microbial growth media which are then incubated and examined for microbial contamination (media fill tests).[1]" The EU GMP Guide provides more details on this issue: – "Validation of aseptic processing should include a process simulation test using a nutrient medium (media fill).[2] The process simulation test should imitate as closely as possible the routine manufacturing process and include all the critical subsequent manufacturing steps.

GENERAL CONSIDERATIONS

Validation of aseptic processing should include a process simulation test using a nutrient medium (media fill). Selection of the nutrient medium should be made based on dosage form of the product and selectivity, clarity, concentration and suitability for sterilization of the nutrient medium. The process simulation test should imitate as closely as possible the routine aseptic manufacturing steps except where the activity may lead to any potential microbial contamination. Process simulation tests should be performed as part of validation by running three consecutive satisfactory simulation tests. These tests should be repeated at defined intervals and after any significant modification to the heating, ventilation and air-conditioning (HVAC) system, equipment or process. Process simulation tests should incorporate activities and interventions known to occur during normal production as well as the worst-case situation. The process simulation tests should be representative of each shift and shift changeover to address any time-related and operational features.

The number of containers used for media fills should be sufficient to enable a valid evaluation. For small batches the number of containers for media fills should at least equal the size of the product batch. The target should be zero growth and the following should apply:

- When filling fewer than 5000 units, no contaminated units should be detected.
- When filling 5000–10 000 units:
  - One contaminated unit should result in an investigation, including consideration of a repeat media fill;
  - Two contaminated units are considered cause for revalidation following investigation;
- When filling more than 10 000 units:
  - One contaminated unit should result in an investigation;
  - Two contaminated units are considered cause for revalidation following investigation.

For any run size, intermittent incidents of microbial contamination may be indicative of low-level contamination that should be investigated. Investigation of gross failures should include the potential impact on the sterility assurance of batches manufactured since the last successful media fill.

DESCRIPTION OF MEDIA FILL

Choice of the Media Fill

A microbiologically appropriate nutrient is to be used. Within pharmaceutical industries Soya-bean casein digest medium (aerobe microorganisms) and thioglycollate (anaerobe microorganisms) have been verified. Both media relate to the quality control of pharmaceutical medicinal products because of their use in sterility testing. The growth promotion proprieties for a lot of microorganisms such as bacteria, yeasts and moulds have been proved very often. The anaerobe simulation is restricted for filling lines which are used for products filled in an atmosphere where oxygen is excluded. The absence of germs of Bovine Spongiforme Encephalopathy (BSE) is to be mandatorily demonstrated in case of every nutrient.

Media Fill and Filling Volume

Some points regarding the filling volume have to be considered:-

- All surfaces and stoppers must be wetted;
- Microbiological growth must be ensured;
- This means that at least half of the nominal volume of the container should be used,
- The filling volume has to be taken into account the physiological preconditions of the microorganisms

Preparation of Media Fill

The nutrient medium must be processed, handled, and filled in a manner that precisely simulates the normal manufacturing process. Thus, the normal manufacturing process has to be analysed. In media fill validation, dried nutrient medium base and Water for Injection (WFI) are used as the compounding starting materials. Bioburden counts and determinations of endotoxin content, as well as analysis of pathogenic contaminants, for *e.g., Pseudomonas aeruginosa* or *Echerichia coli*, are performed as in-process controls on the raw materials. Media fill should be prepared considering the instructions of the manufacturer regarding the usual manufacturing process (for example using the sterile filter systems as appropriate). The preparation should be performed analogously as the drug product (facility, monitoring activities, equipment, materials, personnel).

Environmental monitoring, comprising

- Airborne counts,
- Particle counts, and
- Hygiene status of personnel and materials.

Prior to filtration, the pH-value of the nutrient broth is checked and in-process controls (IPC) on identity, clarity, and bioburden are conducted. Samples are controlled for analytical and microbiological controls like that of any other product. Holding and process times are documented and may be prolonged for validation purposes. The bulk solution is sterile-filtered using the same filter material as in normal aseptic processing.

- Filter integrity is checked prior to and after use.
- Environmental monitoring is conducted at this processing step.

- Prior to filling, primary containers are sterilised and depyrogenized, the filling line is cleaned and sterilised or transfer lines and dosage pumps are sterilised separately.
- Environmental monitoring is performed during the filling procedure.
- A change in personnel is carried out during filling, as are several, pre-defined investigation and in process controls, for *e.g.*, filling volume.

Worst Case Simulation

The simulation should consider such conditions which simulate the highest risk (worst case) of maximum expected and permitted loads. Examples for worst case conditions are defined in ISO 13408.28 PIC/S 26 requires simulation of all interventions which may occur during a shift (refilling of closures, adjustments of filling needles) Not only should these kinds of interventions be regarded, but also their frequency [3, 4]. For vial dimension and filling speed the worst condition is the biggest vial with the longest filling time, the widest-neck vial and the smallest vial with the highest speed.

Interventions

All interventions and measures of the usual process should be simulated in media fill. For example manual control of the filling volume, interventions in class A / 100, change in personnel, performance of environmental monitoring. Even technical interruptions should be considered (lack of air system, stopping of the machine). The approach is done during risk analysis with cooperation from the following departments: production, quality, validation, quality assurance.

Number of Filled Units and Duration of the Filling Process

According to FDA Guidance 24 the minimum number of filled units of media fill is 3,000 units (to reach a confidence level of 95% for demonstration of a contamination rate of less than 0.1%) [5]. For batch sizes smaller than 3,000 units, smaller numbers are acceptable (requirements are given in ISO 13408.28 and EU GMP Guide Annex 111). For small batch sizes (for example products used for clinical trials) at least the actual batch size should be simulated during media fill [2, 6]. For very large batches, it is recommended to simulate media fill with 1% till 10% of the actual daily batch size. The vials with the smallest and the biggest size should be regarded in media fill. The units in media fill shall be enough to simulate worst case conditions.

Duration of Process, Holding Times and Stopping Times

Time limits should be established for each phase of aseptic processing. Time limits should include for example the period between the start of bulk product, compounding and its filtration, filtration processes, product exposure while on the processing line, and storage of sterilised equipment, containers and closures. Bioburden and endotoxin load should be assessed when establishing time limits for stages such as formulation processing stage. The total duration of the procedure consists of the time needed for the preparation of the bulk, time between the beginning of the preparation and the end of the sterile filtration. PIC/S26 recommendation gives information about the duration of a media fill run. The whole filling time should be simulated, but it is possible to stop the machine to avoid excessive numbers of filled units. PIC/S26 recommends simulating the process per shift and per filling line and not only per filling line. This is integrated in the EU GMP guide Annex 111 and also in the FDA Draft Guidance 2003 [4, 6, 7].

Holding times (*e.g.*, materials, bulk, equipment) up to the beginning of the filling process etc. are usually defined within the manufacturing process. The validation of such times is performed during media fill and then simulates worst case conditions. For small batch sizes (for example products for clinical trial) at least the actual batch size should be simulated during media fill (GMP Guide Annex 111) [7]. ISO 13408-128 requires at least 5,000 units for the primary qualification of the process with three or more runs [3]. The number of units for media fill is increased in FDA draft Guidance12 (at least 5,000 units) compared with the current FDA Guidance [8].

Selection of Units

It is recommendable to incubate all units of media fill. In any case the thorough documentation of all filled units is necessary. It is possible to select damaged units prior to incubation according to routine processing. But the accurate reconciliation of all units is a general requirement. It is not acceptable to select positive units after incubation because the checking reveals defects for example in the container closure system. The FDA draft Guidance 12 clarifies that intervention in the aseptic manufacturing process during media; that is to say an interruption of the aseptic barrier does not mean that those units have to be incubated, but it must be assured (SOP) that during routine manufacturing process such units are rejected [8]. Although no guideline mentions that the samples for fertility testing should not be taken prior to incubation of media fill, it is recommended to perform the fertility test after the evaluation of the media fill.

Acceptance Criteria in Media Fill

Warning Limits and Action Limits

All guidelines regard any positive unit during media fill as a potential problem and the source of contamination should be evaluated thoroughly. ISO 13408-128 contains a table which gives a statistical approach of the evaluation of media fill [3]. Warning limits and action limits have to be defined. Acceptance criteria for the successful validation of an aseptic manufacturing process is a contamination rate of 0.1% in at least 3,000 filled units with a confidential level of 95%. The sterilisation assurance level SAL is 10^{-3}. The current discussion of the contamination rate aims at negative detection of contaminated units. A contamination rate of 0.1% will no longer be tolerated by FDA's inspectors. Any positive unit has to be examined thoroughly and could be a reason for the failed media fill. FDA's acceptance of this probability in test results (0.1% contamination rate) does not mean that an aseptically processed lot of drug product purporting to be sterile may contain one non-sterile unit per thousand count. According to PIC/S 26 the contamination rate should be ideally zero but the statistic approach refers to ISO 13408-1 [3, 4].

Action Limits / Procedure in the Case of Failed Simulations

Measures for analysing the cause of contamination and an investigation thereafter have to be established. On exceeding the action limit, a requalification is immediately required. According to ISO 13408-128 an investigation should be performed in case of exceeding the warning limit (1 contaminated unit up to 10, 250 units) and the run has to be repeated [3]. If the warning limit is exceeded again, it implies that the media fill has failed and the complete primary qualification has to be repeated (three consecutive runs of media fill must be successful). In the case of requalification (usually every 6 months one successful media fill) exceeding of the warning limit in two consecutive runs has to be evaluated as exceeding the action limit. This is clearly said in the ISO 13408-128 and in PIC/S 26 "Exceeding the action limit means that a thorough investigation into the failure has to be performed and a complete requalification must be initiated [3, 4]. All produced batches since the failure must be quarantined until the cause for failure of the media fill is identified." PIC/S 26 recommends that all produced batches since the last successful process simulation have to be taken into account [4].

First Qualification and Requalification

1. Warning and Action Limits in Media Fill According to ISO 13408-128 [3].
2. In case of any contamination, it is necessary to identify the corresponding microorganism. The FDA Draft Guidance 12 recommends the following [8]:-

- 5,000 – 10,000 filling units in media fill: 1 contaminated unit (investigation required including consideration of a repeat media fill)
- < 10,000 filling units in media fill: 1 contaminated unit (investigation required 2 contaminated units are considered as cause for revalidation following investigation

Incubation Conditions

The container filled with media fill shall be incubated for 14 days at temperatures which allow the growth of a wide microbiological spectrum. The FDA Draft Guidance 12 recommends a temperature range from 20 to 35°C and maintenance within 2.5°C of the target temperature [8]. A link to sterility testing is recommendable so as to have a rationale for the choice of these temperatures. Usually the containers are stored for 7 days at 20 to 25°C followed by 7 days at 30 to 35°C (the temperatures are defined in the European Pharmacopoeia). The incubation conditions have to be documented.[9] The change in incubation temperature requires a change in storing of the filled containers. Here, during change in storing it is recommendable to inspect the containers and to wet the whole surface of the container with media fill.

CONCLUSIONS

We believe that aseptic processing in our industry has improved including

- Improved clean room garments and a better understand of modes of contamination
- Improved clean room designs and operational performance
- More comprehensive employee training and qualification programs
- Improved aseptic processing equipment requiring fewer line interventions
- Well-established validation programs incorporating sound change-control practices to ensure continuing reliability of the processes
- Implementation of advanced contamination control technologies.

The industry as a whole has earned an enviable safety record in aseptic processing over the years. In 1988, aseptic technologies operating in compliance with industry and regulatory guidelines resulted in product that was unquestionably and unequivocally safe with respect to microbial contamination. Today, as in 1988, the weakest link in the sterile and aseptic product delivery pathway is at the level of administration rather than manufacturing. Logically, those concerned with patient safety would seem better advised to focus their energies where they are likely to have the greatest effect.

There have, of course, been recent reports of firms releasing aseptically processed products that purportedly lack sterility assurance. We do not doubt that in very rare instances product has been made in a manner contrary to good contamination control practice. However, it is inappropriate to punish the many for the sins of a very few. Those firms lacking the commitment to manufacture "sterile" products in an appropriate manner should have known better. Successful production of "sterile" products using aseptic processing can certainly be made possible if the precepts outlined within this chapter are ascribed to. Perfection in aseptic processing is not currently achievable, because an absolute demonstration of unequivocal sterility assurance is not possible. However, safety is both possible and routinely attained, and for that industry can be proud. Industry understands that continuous process improvement in our performance, especially in the production of "sterile" products is not just desirable, but essential. We have no doubt that in the coming decades risks from microbial contamination will be even better controlled than they are today. After all, the only significant source of contamination is widely recognized, and there are superb methods for minimizing this risk even further than is possible today.

REFERENCES

[1] EU GMP Guide 11
[2] EU GMP Guide 111
[3] European Pharmacopoeia 18
[4] FDA Draft Guidance 12
[5] FDA Draft Guidance 2003
[6] FDA Guidance 24
[7] ISO 13408
[8] PDA32
[9] PIC/S 26

14

Cleaning Validation

ABSTRACT

Cleaning is a risk reducing measure and carry-over limits for cleaning validation studies are widely used in the pharmaceutical industry. A variety of approaches are taken in order to establish these limits and often do not take account of the available pharmacological and toxicological data. Hence, a more scientific case by case approach is warranted for risk identification and to support risk reduction measures for all classes of pharmaceutical substances. The subject of cleaning validation in active pharmaceutical ingredient manufacturing plants has continued to receive a large amount of attention from regulators, companies and customers alike. The integration of Cleaning Validation within an effective Quality System supported by Quality Risk Management Processes should give assurance that API Manufacturing Operations are performed in such a way that Risks to patients related to cleaning validation are understood, assessed for impact and are mitigated as necessary.

INTRODUCTION

During manufacturing of pharmaceutical products accidental cross-contamination can result from the uncontrolled release of dust, gases, vapours, aerosols, genetic material or organisms from active substances, other starting materials, and other products being processed concurrently, as well as from residues on equipment, and from operators' clothing. Due to the perceived risk, certain classes of medicinal product are required to be manufactured in dedicated or segregated self-contained facilities including, "certain antibiotics, hormones, cytotoxics and certain highly active drugs". Contamination and Cross contamination must be avoided in the Pharmaceutical industry at all costs and successful cleaning validation ensures that patients are not put at risk due to cross contamination. The process can be divided into a number of sections each of which must be fully understood and areas of concern addressed to ensure a successful outcome across the entire process. This spans both the manufacturing and subsequent analytical and microbiological support. The data used to confirm a positive/ successful cleaning validation is underpinned by the results of validated analytical methods. It is essential that these results are truly representative as patient safety is based upon the absence of equipment residues. So what are those areas of concern, what affects your ability to get a successful outcome and what do you need to consider when carrying out a Cleaning Validation exercise?

It is important that the requirements for the finished manufacturing companies are not transferred back in the process to active pharmaceutical ingredient manufacturers without consideration for the different processes that take place at this stage. For example, higher limits may be acceptable in chemical production compared to pharmaceutical production because the carry-over risk is much lower for technical and chemical manufacturing reasons. The document reflects the outcome of discussions between APIC member companies on how cleaning validation requirements could be fulfilled and implemented as part of routine operations.

In addition, APIC is aligning this guidance with the ISPE Risk MaPP Guide that follows the Quality Risk Management Processes as described in the ICH Q9 Guidance on Quality Risk Management. The criteria of Acceptable Daily Exposure (ADE) is now recommended to be used by companies to decide if Dedicated Facilities are required or not and to define the Maximum Acceptable Carry Over (MACO) of API's in particular, in Multi-Purpose Equipment. The PDA Technical Report No. 29 – Points to Consider for Cleaning Validation [4] is also recommended as a valuable guidance document from industry. The following topics are discussed in the PDA document: Cleaning process (CIP/COP): design and qualification

- Types of residues, setting acceptance criteria, sampling and analytical methods
- Maintenance of the validated state: critical parameters measurements, process alarms, change control, trending and monitoring, training and periodic review
- Documentation

OBJECTIVES

The objective of Cleaning Validation is to establish cleaning procedures and residue limits that are practical, achievable, and verifiable and assure safety. Cleaning of the equipment train, individual equipment, utensil and / or components are carried out separately and clubbed with a pre-wash and inspection program. The cleaning procedure comprise of thorough cleaning with Sodium Lauryl Sulphate and soft water in suitable combination followed by final rinsing with Purified Water. The objective of this chapter is to recommend an approach to review and evaluate pharmacological and toxicological data of individual active substances and thus enable determination of threshold levels as referred to in the GMP guideline. These levels can be used as a risk identification tool and can also be used to justify carry over limits used in cleaning validation.

GENERAL CONSIDERATION

A detailed study of all the equipment to be cleaned must be carried out by a qualified team to ensure the chosen cleaning method will be successful. This is colloquially known as "Walking the plant". It is important to understand what can affect your cleaning results and to either engineer out those areas of concern or include them in your cleaning procedure. FDA expects firms to have written procedures (SOP's) detailing the cleaning processes used for various pieces of equipment. If firms have one cleaning process for cleaning between different batches of the same product and use a different process for cleaning between product changes, we expect the written procedures to address these different scenarios. Similarly, if firms have one process for removing water soluble residues and another process for non-water soluble residues, the written procedure should address both scenarios and make it clear when a given procedure is to be followed. Bulk pharmaceutical firms may decide to dedicate certain equipment for certain chemical manufacturing process steps that produce tarry or gummy residues that are difficult to remove from the equipment. Fluid bed dryer bags are another example of equipment that is difficult to clean and is often dedicated to a specific product. Any residues from the cleaning process itself (detergents, solvents, etc.) also have to be removed from the equipment.

FDA expects firms to have written general procedures on how cleaning processes will be validated. FDA expects the general validation procedures to address who is responsible for performing and approving the validation study, the acceptance criteria, and when revalidation will be required. FDA expects firms to prepare specific written validation protocols in advance for the studies to be performed on each manufacturing system or piece of equipment which should address such issues as sampling procedures, and analytical methods to be used including the sensitivity of those methods. FDA expects firms to conduct the validation studies in accordance with the protocols and to document the results of studies. FDA expects a final validation report which is approved by management and which states whether or not the cleaning process is valid. The data should support a conclusion that residues have been reduced to an "acceptable level."

BACKGROUND

For FDA to require that equipment be clean prior to use is nothing new, the 1963 GMP Regulations (Part 133.4) stated as follows "Equipment shall be maintained in a clean and orderly manner" A very similar section on equipment cleaning (211.67) was included in the 1978 CGMP regulations. Of course, the main rationale for requiring clean equipment is to prevent contamination or adulteration of drug products. Historically, FDA investigators have looked for gross insanitation due to inadequate cleaning and maintenance of equipment and/ or poor dust control systems. Also, historically speaking, FDA was more concerned about the contamination of non-penicillin drug products with penicillins or the cross-contamination of drug products with potent steroids or hormones. A number of products have been recalled over the past decade due to actual or potential penicillin cross-contamination.

One event which increased FDA awareness of the potential for cross contamination due to inadequate procedures was the 1988 recall of a finished drug product, Cholestyramine Resin USP [1]. The bulk pharmaceutical chemical used to produce the product had become contaminated with low levels of intermediates and degradants from the production of agricultural pesticides. The cross-contamination in that case is believed to have been due to the reuse of recovered solvents. The recovered solvents had been contaminated because of a lack of control over the reuse of solvent drums. Drums that had been used to store recovered solvents from a pesticide production process were later used to store recovered solvents used for the resin manufacturing process. The firm did not have adequate controls over these solvent drums, did not do adequate testing of drummed solvents, and did not have validated cleaning procedures for the drums.

Some shipments of this pesticide contaminated bulk pharmaceutical were supplied to a second facility at a different location for finishing. This resulted in the contamination of the bags used in that facility's fluid bed dryers with pesticide contamination. This in turn led to cross contamination of lots produced at that site, a site where no pesticides were normally produced.

FDA instituted an import alert in 1992 on a foreign bulk pharmaceutical manufacturer which manufactured potent steroid products as well as non-steroidal products using common equipment. This firm was a multi-use bulk pharmaceutical facility. FDA considered the potential for cross-contamination to be significant and to pose a serious health risk to the public. The firm had only recently started a cleaning validation program at the time of the inspection and it was considered inadequate by FDA [2]. One of the reasons it was considered inadequate was that the firm was only looking for evidence of the absence of the previous compound. The firm had evidence, from TLC tests on the rinse water, of the presence of residues of reaction byproducts and degradants from the previous process.

EVALUATION OF CLEANING VALIDATION

The first step is to focus on the objective of the validation process, and we have seen that some companies have failed to develop such objectives. It is not unusual to see manufacturers use extensive sampling and testing programs following the cleaning process without ever really evaluating the effectiveness of the steps used to clean the equipment. Several questions need to be addressed when evaluating the cleaning process. For example, at what point does a piece of equipment or system become clean? Does it have to be scrubbed by hand? What is accomplished by hand scrubbing rather than just a solvent wash? How variable are manual cleaning processes from batch to batch and product to product? The answers to these questions are obviously important to the inspection and evaluation of the cleaning process since one must determine the overall effectiveness of the process. Answers to these questions may also identify steps that can be eliminated for more effective measures and result in resource savings for the company.

Determine the number of cleaning processes for each piece of equipment. Ideally, a piece of equipment or system will have one process for cleaning, however this will depend on the products being produced and whether the cleanup occurs between batches of the same product (as in a large campaign) or between batches of different products. When the cleaning process is used only between batches of the same product (or different lots of the same intermediate in a bulk process) the firm need only meet a criteria of, "visibly clean" for the equipment. Such between batch cleaning processes do not require validation.

1. Equipment Design

Examine the design of equipment, particularly in those large systems that may employ semi-automatic or fully automatic clean-in-place (CIP) systems since they represent significant concern. For example, sanitary type piping without ball valves should be used. When such non-sanitary ball valves are used, as is common in the bulk drug industry, the cleaning process is more difficult. When such systems are identified, it is important that operators performing cleaning operations be aware of problems and have special training in cleaning these systems and valves. Determine whether the cleaning operators have knowledge of these systems and the level of training and experience in cleaning these systems. Also check the written and validated cleaning process to determine if these systems have been properly identified and validated. In larger systems, such as those employing long transfer lines or piping, check the flow charts and piping diagrams for the identification of valves and written cleaning procedures. Piping and valves should be tagged and easily identifiable by the operator performing the cleaning function. Sometimes, inadequately identified valves, both on prints and physically, have led to incorrect cleaning practices. Always check for the presence of an often critical element in the documentation of the cleaning processes; identifying and controlling the length of time between the end of processing and each cleaning step. This is especially important for topicals, suspensions, and bulk drug operations. In such operations, the drying of residues will directly affect the efficiency of a cleaning process. Whether or not CIP systems are used for cleaning of processing equipment, microbiological aspects of equipment cleaning should be considered. This consists largely of preventive measures rather than removal of contamination once it has occurred. There should be some evidence that routine cleaning and storage of equipment does not allow microbial proliferation. For example, equipment should be dried before storage, and under no circumstances should stagnant water be allowed to remain in equipment subsequent to cleaning operations. Subsequent to the cleaning process, equipment may be subjected to sterilization or sanitization procedures where such equipment is used for sterile processing, or for non-sterile processing where the products may support microbial growth. While such sterilization or sanitization procedures are beyond the scope of this guide, it is important to note that control of the bioburden through adequate cleaning and storage of equipment is important to ensure that subsequent sterilization or sanitization procedures achieve the necessary assurance of sterility. This is also particularly important from the standpoint of the control of pyrogens in sterile processing since equipment sterilization processes may not be adequate to achieve significant inactivation or removal of pyrogens.

2. Cleaning Process Written Procedure and Documentation

Examine the detail and specificity of the procedure for the (cleaning) process being validated, and the amount of documentation required. We have seen general SOPs, while others use a batch record or log sheet system that requires some type of specific documentation for performing each step. Depending upon the complexity of the system and cleaning process and the ability and training of operators, the amount of documentation necessary for executing various cleaning steps or procedures will vary. When more complex cleaning procedures are required, it is important to document the critical cleaning steps (for example certain bulk drug synthesis processes). In this regard, specific documentation on the equipment itself which includes information about who cleaned it and when is valuable. However, for relatively simple cleaning operations, the mere documentation that the overall cleaning process was performed might be sufficient. Other factors such as history of cleaning, residue levels found after cleaning, and variability of test results may also dictate the amount of documentation required. For example, when variable residue levels are detected following cleaning, particularly for a process that is believed to be acceptable, one must establish the effectiveness of the process and operator performance. Appropriate evaluations must be made and when operator performance is deemed a problem, more extensive documentation (guidance) and training may be required.

3. Analytical Methods

Determine the specificity and sensitivity of the analytical method used to detect residuals or contaminants. With advances in analytical technology, residues from the manufacturing and cleaning processes can be detected at very low levels. If levels of contamination or residual are not detected, it does not mean that there is no residual contaminant present after cleaning. It only means that levels of contaminant greater than the sensitivity or detection limit of the analytical method are not present in the sample. The firm should challenge the analytical method in combination with the sampling method(s) used to show that contaminants can be recovered from the equipment surface and at what level, *i.e.,* 50% recovery, 90%, etc. This is necessary before any conclusions can be made based on the sample results. A negative test may also be the result of poor sampling technique (see below).

4. Sampling

There are two general types of sampling that have been found acceptable. The most desirable is the direct method of sampling the surface of the equipment. Another method is the use of rinse solutions.

- ***Direct Surface Sampling***

  Determine the type of sampling material used and its impact on the test data since the sampling material may interfere with the test. For example, the adhesive used in swabs has been found to interfere with the analysis of samples. Therefore, early in the validation program, it is important to assure that the sampling medium and solvent (used for extraction from the medium) are satisfactory and can be readily used. Advantages of direct sampling are that areas hardest to clean and which are reasonably accessible can be evaluated, leading to establishing a level of contamination or residue per given surface area. Additionally, residues that are "dried out" or are insoluble can be sampled by physical removal.

- ***Rinse Samples***

  Two advantages of using rinse samples are that a larger surface area may be sampled and inaccessible systems or ones that cannot be routinely disassembled can be sampled and evaluated. A disadvantage of rinse samples is that the residue or contaminant may not be soluble or may be physically occluded in the equipment. An analogy that can be used is the "dirty pot." In the evaluation of cleaning of a dirty pot, particularly with dried out residue, one does not look at the rinse water to see that it is clean; one looks at the pot. Check to see that a direct measurement of the residue or contaminant has been made for the rinse water when it is used to validate the cleaning process. For example, it is not acceptable to simply test rinse water for water quality (does it meet the compendia tests) rather than test it for potential contaminates.

- ***Routine Production In-Process Control Monitoring***

  Indirect testing, such as conductivity testing, may be of some value for routine monitoring once a cleaning process has been validated. This would be particularly true for the bulk drug substance manufacturer where reactors and centrifuges and piping between such large equipment can be sampled only using rinse solution samples. Any indirect test method must have been shown to correlate with the condition of the equipment. During validation, the firm should document that testing the uncleaned equipment gives a not acceptable result for the indirect test.

AREAS OF CONCERN

All product contact pipe work should be thoroughly evaluated. The geometry of the pipe work can play a vital role in a successful outcome. Multiple bends, flanges, angles of pipe-work and dead ends, can all result in product retention and possible cross contamination. There are recorded cases in the industry of minor changes to pipe-work geometry resulting in cross contamination issues. If you change the shape of a piece of pipe-work it may no longer clean as well.

Specific areas to be mindful of are:

1. **Service lines**

   These are small bore lines and very difficult to clean. There have been a number of cases over the years where investigations into cross contamination issues have concluded that the service lines were at fault. Ensure that you have adequate safeguards in place (*e.g.*, non return valves and filters) to ensure these lines do not get contaminated.

2. **Gaskets**

   The microscopic nature of materials used to make gaskets result in product retention and possible swab failure. It is recognized that gaskets are necessary but a study should be carried out to ensure that there are not gaskets in the system that are no longer required and that all gaskets in the plant are in good condition to reduce the risks.

3. **Filter meshes**

   These are designed to retain product and therefore can also result in cross contamination if not carefully cleaned.

4. **Valves**

   Material can be drawn into valve housings and returned to the product stream at a later date resulting in cross contamination. All valves in the product stream should be investigated, a cross section dismantled and tested during validation to ensure that they do not present a risk to the outcome.

5. **Pumps and samplers**

   These pieces of equipment are very difficult to clean successfully. It should be determined if they are really necessary. Can the geometry of the plant be altered to avoid their usage? If not they must be included in your cleaning exercise.

6. **Process investigations**

   It is important that an understanding of what can go wrong in a process is obtained. Sometimes a process error at an earlier date can result in product being deposited in an area of the plant where it normally would not reach. This can then result in swab failures during cleaning or more critically Product contamination at a later date. *e.g.,* Over-heating of a vessel can result in product being deposited in condenser return lines.

7. **Packaging lines**

   It should be determined that there are no areas in the line where tablets could bounce and get stuck *e.g.* on the top of sensors etc. These may then fall off later into a different product and cause cross-contamination, patient injury or even death. Screens should be erected at these areas to ensure this cannot ever happen.

DESIGN AND CONTROL OF CLEANING METHODS

A procedure that has been used for years may not necessarily be the best. A review of the methods should be carried out at validation to determine their suitability and effectiveness. Procedures should include factors such as:

1. Operation of valves during cleaning
2. Filling pipe-work with solvent and allowing dissolution time
3. Refluxing solvent around system and through condenser return lines

Manual cleaning is very subjective. Two different operators may not necessarily clean to the same degree. In order to achieve reproducibility it is critical that all operators carry out the procedure in the same way. Very detailed procedures and training are required to ensure the successful outcome of a manual cleaning exercise. It is sometimes easier to alter plant layout so that Clean in Place (CIP) can be performed in place of manual cleaning, *e.g.,* moving a pan filter from beside the vessel to the floor below can result in a double bonus. The pan filter can then be washed using a CIP procedure and the move also results in a loss of a pump and extra pipework. This sort of rearrangement should be considered as it reduces risks of error.

Ensure that:

- Written procedures will deal with the outcome of a process failure based on knowledge of what can go wrong in your process. Often what can go wrong in a process is more critical to the cleaning than what can go right.
- All process operators are fully trained and their records are up to date. Validation exercises have failed in the past, during audits, due to failure to ensure that operators' training records were complete and up to date.

ISSUES WITH SAMPLING AND TESTING

A considerable proportion of the testing failures experienced in the industry are not related to the ability to clean the equipment or perform the analysis. They are solely related to the skills of the person taking the swabs. It is easy to write and train a procedure on how to carry out a swab test but it is a different thing being able to perform a test correctly and reproducibly. So what can be done to reduce this risk and help secure a successful validation outcome?

1. A number of issues can be identified related to the swabbing procedure and these must all be addressed if success is to be guaranteed.
2. Control of swab equipment – It is essential that all the equipment used to carry out a swab test is reliably controlled. It is extremely easy to contaminate a swab and put your whole cleaning validation exercise at risk of failure. The swab material, the solvent used, any disposable gloves etc. must be very carefully controlled to reduce the risk of possible false results.
3. Test the ability of the operator to perform not only the swab procedure itself but also their skill in:
   - Being able to determine the correct area to be swabbed even when they cannot visually see where the task is being performed. Failure to swab the required area will result in either a failed swab or worse still, from a cross contamination viewpoint, a passed result which should really fail.
   - Their reproducibility in being able to repeat this exercise 4 times in exactly the same place.

It has been demonstrated that a swab taken using 4 wipes of the same area results in maximum recovery (>90%) from a given surface. However the ability to do this requires considerable skill and training.

All of the above require considerable skill and extensive training of the operator. However, techniques have been developed that will test these skills and give assurance that the final test results reflect the actual plant cleanliness and not the ability of the swab operator to perform the task.

ESTABLISHMENT OF LIMITS

FDA does not intend to set acceptance specifications or methods for determining whether a cleaning process is validated. It is impractical for FDA to do so due to the wide variation in equipment and products used throughout the bulk and finished dosage form industries. The firm's rationale for the residue limits established should be logical based on the manufacturer's knowledge of the materials involved and be practical, achievable, and verifiable. It is important to define the sensitivity of the analytical methods in order to set reasonable limits. Some limits that have been mentioned by industry representatives in the literature or in presentations include analytical detection levels such as 10 PPM, biological activity levels such as 1/1000 of the normal therapeutic dose, and organoleptic levels such as no visible residue.

Check the manner in which limits are established. Unlike finished pharmaceuticals where the chemical identity of residuals are known (*i.e.*, from actives, inactives, detergents) bulk processes may have partial reactants and unwanted by-products which may never have been chemically identified. In establishing residual limits, it may not be adequate to focus only on the principal reactant since other chemical variations may be more difficult to remove. There are circumstances where TLC screening, in addition to chemical analyses, may be needed. In a bulk process, particularly for very potent chemicals such as some steroids, the issue of by-products needs to be considered if equipment is not dedicated. The objective of the inspection is to ensure that the basis for any limits is scientifically justifiable.

OTHER ISSUES

(a) Placebo Product

In order to evaluate and validate cleaning processes some manufacturers have processed a placebo batch in the equipment under essentially the same operating parameters used for processing product. A sample of the placebo batch is then tested for residual contamination. However, we have documented several significant issues that need to be addressed when using placebo product to validate cleaning processes.

One cannot assure that the contaminate will be uniformly distributed throughout the system. For example, if the discharge valve or chute of a blender is contaminated, the contaminant would probably not be uniformly dispersed in the placebo; it would most likely be concentrated in the initial discharge portion of the batch. Additionally, if the contaminant or residue is of a larger particle size, it may not be uniformly dispersed in the placebo. Some firms have made the assumption that a residual contaminant would be worn off the equipment surface uniformly; this is also an invalid conclusion. Finally, the analytical power may be greatly reduced by dilution of the contaminate. Because of such problems, rinse and/or swab samples should be used in conjunction with the placebo method.

DEVELOPMENT AND VALIDATION OF ANALYTICAL TEST METHODS

Alongside the product manufacture, the analytical method is of critical importance when assessing the cleanliness of pharmaceutical manufacturing equipment. In order to satisfy this requirement, it is key to ensure a high level of confidence in the generation of results derived through the use of the method. This, in turn, is underpinned by the development of a suitable, fit-for purpose analytical method, designed not only to be specific to the analyte, but also able to ensure its ability to quantify at the prescribed residue limits.

On the subject of residue limits, this is very much a subject in its own right. The regulatory authorities do not set limits for specific products. The key factors to bear in mind when approaching this with respect to a given pharmaceutical product:

- Defined limits should be logical
- They should be practical and achievable (in terms of method sensitivity)
- Verifiable

An approach for limit setting should be identified early on since this will have a direct impact on the analytical test method and its ability to detect the analyte(s) at the required level.

Determining cleanliness can prove to be a very challenging task, with the aim being to measure trace residues (target analytes) on the surfaces. The residue must initially be extracted from a surface, recovered from the extraction matrix and then suitably quantified. Note that sampling is usually performed *via* direct methods (swabbing), however indirect strategies (such as rinse samples) may also be used, though the latter is not a preferred approach.

Very often, the starting point in the development of a cleaning method would be based upon a previously developed assay method. The main aspects to be borne in mind are:

1) Attainment of suitable sensitivity to quantify at the limits,
2) Specificity (between the target analyte and other matrix components)
3) A curtailed run time to allow the requisite high sample throughput that is generally needed when analyzing swab samples.

In many respects, the requirements for validating cleaning methods are closely aligned with a standard assay, evaluating factors such as specificity, accuracy (recovery), linearity, sensitivity, precision, robustness and solution stability. However, one area that does require some time is the swabbing technique itself. A large part of the development procedure itself is focused upon deriving a swabbing procedure that allows acceptable recovery of API residues from the required surface types. Furthermore, the choice of swab surface used will be dictated by conducting a plant walk-around and subsequent risk assessment of the manufacturing plant and determination of the key 'risk' areas where residues are most likely to remain following manufacture. It should be noted that there is currently an increasing shift towards the use of Total Organic Carbon (TOC) Analysis to determine residues following cleaning of the manufacturing plant. The increasing view is that apart from looking at specific active traces, a 'crude' evaluation of contamination should be considered. The advantages of TOC over more traditional HPLC methods are:

1) The ability to evaluate the overall contamination,
2) Reduced time and cost for the development, validation and subsequent analysis.

This can potentially have very real positives from a manufacturing perspective as it will enable much more rapid turn-around time for the analytics, thereby reducing down-time for the plant. Whilst TOC may be suitable in certain cases, these would be limited to manufacturing lines that have proven control of the cleaning process and hence where TOC results (*i.e.,* non-specific, gross contamination) are determined to be well below the specified residue limits. If this is not the case, then it would be necessary to develop specific methods (such as HPLC) to determine the levels of a given active(s).

SWABBING

Often, insufficient time is invested in the actual swabbing regime, which can ultimately lead to a less than robust final method. Each of the surface types identified (discussed previously) should be spiked with the API (at the calculated residue limit) and experiments performed to demonstrate that acceptable recovery is repeatedly obtained. This can involve the evaluation of a number of different swabbing solvents and swab types together with optimization of the actual swab technique. This combined with the need to be able to repeatedly detect residues at very low levels, can contribute significantly towards the time required for successful method development and validation.

Recovery experiments essentially underpin all other validation parameters since the residue must be:

1. Successfully extracted from a surface
2. Recovered from the extraction matrix
3. Appropriately quantified

If the method is shown to have sufficient accuracy, then all of these parameters can be evaluated as a single entity. If inadequate results are obtained then each of the steps would need to be investigated individually to identify which of the component steps is responsible for the poor recovery, and allow screening of other solvents or swab material that may improve recovery. It should provide assurance that an analyte can be analysed in a matrix, which, for a finished product, would include excipients, impurities or perhaps solvents used in the manufacture of the actual API. If a cleaning agent is used, its composition should also be considered. An evaluation of specificity should first be conducted to ensure the absence of any interference between matrix components and the target analyte.

Another key factor to be considered throughout the development process is the stability of the analytical samples; that is, the ability of the active substance to degrade once in the extraction solvent. If appropriate expiry dates are not set, significant degradation could occur, leading to apparent low swab levels, which could actually be attributable to the instability of the active and not representative of the levels actually swabbed from the equipment surfaces potentially giving a result that "passed" which should actually fail.

There is such an array of validation parameters that could be discussed, however this article cannot possibly do each of these justice. However, In terms of analytical method validation, there should be no unexpected surprises. All of the critical parameters to be assessed should be identified and evaluated prior to commencement of the formal validation. The method development should therefore be used to obtain the initial information to set the limits stipulated within a validation protocol and hence build in Quality by Design.

MICROBIOLOGICAL CONTAMINATION

Aside from the manufacturing and analytical aspects, it is also paramount to consider cleaning validation from a microbiology point of view. This focuses on contamination control in pharmaceutical and healthcare facilities.

Pharmaceutical manufacturing process can be subjected to microbial contamination. Therefore a good cleaning and disinfection process is necessary to maintain a good hygiene in facilities. Disinfectants are used to prevent microbial contamination of pharmaceutical products. Where chemical disinfectants are used as part of contamination control, it is important to evaluate the efficacy of the disinfectants to ensure they are fit for purpose. So why do you have to evaluate the efficacy of your disinfectant?

Apart from being a regulatory requirement, you need to establish whether your disinfectants are effective under the conditions they are used. Factors such as the surfaces they are used on, contact time, concentration and so on will alter the effectiveness of disinfectants. The test performed by the disinfectant manufacturer before release does not mimic the way you use them, and therefore does not establish they are fit for purpose.

CHOOSING A DISINFECTANT

Disinfectants are usually chosen based on their chemical properties and expected effectiveness against microorganisms. Before evaluating the efficacy of your disinfectant, it is important to consider a few points and ask do I have the right disinfectants in place?

- *Bactericidal and fungicidal agents* – It is important to use disinfectants that are effective against bacteria and fungi. This will ensure that bacteria and fungi on surfaces are killed.
- *Sporicidal agents* – It is important to have disinfectant that is effective against bacteria and fungi but some disinfectants are only effective against vegetative microorganisms. Not all disinfectants are effective against spores, therefore a sporicide should be added to the disinfectant rotation.
- *Sterile disinfectant* – If disinfectants are used in a cleanroom (Grade A and B) environment, they should be sterile prior to use. Where disinfectants are transferred into spray bottles before use, then the bottles should also be sterilised.
- *Available data* – Disinfectant manufacturers that supply to the pharmaceutical and healthcare industries perform various tests that evaluates the efficacy of their disinfectants.

Ask the manufacturer for the available data to help you establish if the selected disinfectants are good enough.

Note – The test results cannot be taken in place of a validation. This is because they do not represent how the disinfectants are used in practice against your surfaces and organisms present in your facilities.

VALIDATING DISINFECTANT

The effectiveness of a disinfectant would depend on the biocidal properties of the disinfectant. However, a number of factors can affect the effectiveness depending on the way it is used. The following factors most be considered in the validation process to help establish if your disinfectants are fit for purpose.

- *Contact time* – Apply contact times that are practical and are actually followed in the disinfection process. Shorter contact times can be validated to cover a worst case scenario. Consider a practical contact time when testing alcohol as it evaporates within a short period of time. Some sporicidal agents might need an extended contact time depending on prior knowledge provided by the manufacturer.
- *Surface* – Make sure the disinfectants are validated against the surfaces they are used on. In some cases, not all surfaces can be included in the cleaning validation, therefore a risk assessment approach most be adopted to determine the most appropriate surfaces to use.

Use the exact surface present in your facility as a slight modification might affect the efficacy of the disinfectant. For example if you have a coated vinyl floor within your facilities, then the exact vinyl surface should be used.

- *Condition* – The validation process should apply interfering substances to create a clean or a dirty condition. Substances like Bovine Serum Albumin can be added to mimic the amount of soiling present on surfaces. Select the most appropriate condition that mimics where disinfectants are used.
- *Temperature* – Validation should be performed under the same temperature the disinfectants are used.
- *Organisms* – Ensure the organisms used covers a variety so that the bactericidal, fungicidal and sporicidal ability of the disinfectants can be determined.
- *Environmental isolates* – Environmental isolates should be added to the validation process to help prove that the disinfectants are effective against organisms they would encounter on your facilities.
- *In use state* – Disinfectants should be validated at their in use state. If they are transferred to a spray bottle, then it should be validated at that state.

They should also be validated at the end of their hold time to cover a worst case scenario. The concentration at which the disinfectant are used must also be applied in the validation process.

MICROBIOLOGICAL PRACTICAL TEST

The efficacy of a disinfectant can be demonstrated with a suspension test or a surface test. Suspension test can be used to determine if the concentration at which a disinfectant is used is effective. Since the disinfectant is tested in a suspension, it does not mimic the way it is used in practice. A surface test is designed to mimic a possible contamination on a surface which can be found in a pharmaceutical or healthcare facility in the presence of an interfering substance.

The Quantitative Surface Test EN 13697 can be used to validate the efficacy of a chemical disinfectant. Test process – A known level of test organisms are dried on the surfaces then the disinfectant is added to the surface and left for the standard contact time used during disinfection.

The effect of the disinfectant is neutralized after the contact time and the recovery of surviving organisms will be used to evaluate the efficacy of the disinfectant. Numerous controls are used to ensure that the result is due to the effect of the disinfectant.

VALIDATE ENVIRONMENTAL MONITORING MEDIA

To have confidence that selected disinfectants are not influencing the recovery of organisms on media used to perform routine environmental monitoring, it is important to verify the process. This validation will enable pharmaceutical and healthcare facilities to implement the use of adequate contact plates and swabs containing the appropriate neutralizers in the environmental monitoring process.

THE MATRIX APPROACH

Where there are multiple medicinal drug products coming into contact with equipment surfaces there is the opportunity to apply the matrix approach. This approach evaluates the overall cleaning requirements of the product range and concentrates the validation efforts on 'worst case' situations. A matrix approach will result in an overall reduction of validation work performed, when compared to products validated on an individual basis. There is however a requirement for ongoing review of the matrix approach once it has been agreed to ensure that the documented rational upon which it is based remains valid.

Generating a Matrix

A rational must be generated to support the matrix, clearly stating the justification for use of a matrix approach for the cleaning validation exercise.

The rationale would typically refer to areas of equivalence to justify application of a matrix approach. A matrix approach can only be used where there is a common cleaning procedure. Once the use of a matrix has been justified the rationale would then typically target the worst case scenarios for the equipment/ products to be validated.

A number of factors may define the worst case products(s) to use within a matrix. A bias of the cleaning validation exercise towards a certain product(s) may consider the following factors:

- *Toxicity* – one product significantly worse than other(s)
- *Acceptance limit* – one product limit significantly more stringent than others
- *Physical characteristics* – least soluble, known cleanability
- *Usage* – high usage of product (*i.e.,* will be cleaned most often)
- *Concentration of active* – high quantity of active in formulation (*i.e.* high challenge)
- *Previous results* – difficulty/ ease in meeting acceptance criteria

A matrix table may be a useful aid in highlighting those product/ equipment combinations to be defined as worst case and hence subjected to cleaning validation. There is a requirement to ensure that the rationale and matrix remain valid. Likely events leading to change would be:

- Introduction of new products
- Modifications to cleaning procedures/ equipment/ staff
- Changes in regulatory requirements

A change to the rationale/ matrix would be formally recorded and appropriate validation performed. The responsibility for maintaining the rationale and matrix should be defined. This aspect may be considered as part of validation review/maintenance.

DETERMINATION OF HEALTH BASED EXPOSURE LIMITS

Calculation of a Permitted Daily Exposure (PDE)

The procedure proposed in this document for determination of health based exposure limits for a residual active substance is based on the method for establishing the so-called Permitted Daily Exposure (PDE). The PDE represents a substance-specific dose that is unlikely to cause an adverse effect if an individual is exposed at or below this dose every day for a 1lifetime.

Determination of a PDE involves

(i) Hazard identification by reviewing all relevant data,

(ii) Identification of "critical effects",

(iii) Determination of the no-observed-adverse-effect level (NOAEL) of the findings that are considered to be critical effects,

(iv) Use of several adjustment factors to account for various uncertainties.

Following equation could be used for the derivation of the PDE:

PDE = NOAEL X Weight adjustment/ F1 x F2 x F3 x F4 x F5

Where NOAEL is No observed adverse effect level, F1, F2, F3, F4 and F5 are factors.

It is considered pragmatic that PDEs should be derived assuming human exposure. The level of contamination that can be accepted is then calculated from the human PDE. This is considered to represent a pragmatic approach and is in line with the approach to calculate residual solvent limits applied for medicinal products.

The derivation of limits will need to take account of the dose to be administered, which will be influenced by the body weight of the species to be treated. In order to facilitate this, the PDE should be calculated on a mg/ kg body weight basis rather than on a per person basis. When the product that may become contaminated with a residual active substance is a veterinary medicinal product for administration to food producing animals, the carryover limit applied must take account of both target animal safety considerations and consumer safety considerations. It should therefore be demonstrated, based on worst case exposure scenarios, that neither the target animal nor the consumer will be exposed to residual active substance levels exceeding the PDE.

Alternative approaches to the NOAEL such as the Benchmark dose may also be used. The use of other approaches to determine health based exposure limits could be considered acceptable if adequately and scientifically justified.

Data Requirements for Hazard Identification

Hazard identification is the qualitative appraisal of the inherent property of a substance to produce adverse effects. For hazard identification, a review of all available animal and human data should be performed for each compound. Data for hazard identification would include non-clinical pharmacodynamic data, repeat-dose toxicity studies, carcinogenicity studies, *in vitro* and *in vivo* genotoxicity studies, reproductive and developmental toxicity studies as well as clinical data (therapeutic and adverse effects).

The availability of data for an active substance will vary depending on the stage of development and indication. If data sets are incomplete, the identified gaps will need to be critically assessed with regard to the impact this might have on deriving a reliable health based exposure limit.

Identification of Critical Effects

Critical effects would include the most sensitive indicator of an adverse effect seen in non-clinical toxicity studies unless there is clear evidence (*e.g.,* from mechanistic studies, pharmacodynamic data etc.) that such findings are not relevant to humans or the target animal. A critical effect would also include any clinical therapeutic and adverse effect.

Establishing NOAEL(s)

For all critical effects identified, a NOAEL should be established. The NOAEL is the highest tested dose at which no "critical" effect is observed. If the critical effect is observed in several animal studies, the NOAEL occurring at the lowest dose should be used for calculation of the PDE value. If no NOAEL is obtained, the lowest-observed-adverse-effect level (LOAEL) may be used. A NOAEL based on clinical pharmacodynamic effects should correspond to the highest dose tested which is considered therapeutically inefficacious.

Application of Adjustment Factors

The PDE is derived by dividing the NOAEL for the critical effect by various adjustment factors (also referred to as safety-, uncertainty-, assessment- or modifying factors) to account for various uncertainties and to allow extrapolation to a reliable and robust no-effect level in the human or target animal population. F1 to F5 are addressing the following sources of uncertainty:

- F1: A factor (values between 2 and 12) to account for extrapolation between species
- F2: A factor of 10 to account for variability between individuals
- F3: A factor 10 to account for repeat-dose toxicity studies of short duration, *i.e.,* less than 4-weeks
- F4: A factor (1-10) that may be applied in cases of severe toxicity, *e.g.,* non-genotoxic carcinogenicity, neurotoxicity or teratogenicity
- F5: A variable factor that may be applied if the no-effect level was not established. When only an LOEL is available, a factor of up to 10 could be used depending on the severity of the toxicity.

The use of additional modifying factors to address residual uncertainties not covered by the above factors may be accepted provided they are well supported with literature data and an adequate discussion is provided to support their use *e.g.,* lack of data for reproductive and developmental toxicity.

Investigator may refer to Appendices 3 of the ICH Q3C (R4) guideline for further guidance on the choice of adjustment factors F1 and F4. The use and choice of adjustment factors should be justified. A restriction to use of F2 and potentially F5 may be acceptable when deriving a PDE on the basis of human end points. Deviations from the default values for the adjustment factors presented above can be accepted if adequately and scientifically justified.

Selection of Final PDE

If several critical effects have been identified resulting in calculation of more than one PDE value, a decision with respect to the most appropriate PDE to be used for the cleaning validation process should be made with an appropriate justification. Usually, by default the lowest PDE value will be used.

Use of Clinical Data

The aim of determining a health-based exposure limit is to ensure human safety, and consequently it is considered that good quality human clinical data are highly relevant. Unintended pharmacodynamic effects in patients caused by contaminating active substances may constitute a hazard thus clinical pharmacological data should be considered when identifying the critical effect. Consideration should be given to what extent the active substance in question has been associated with critical adverse effects in the clinical setting.

If the most critical effect identified to determine a health-based exposure limit is based on pharmacological and/or toxicological effects observed in humans rather than animals, the use of the PDE formula may be inappropriate and a substance-specific assessment of the clinical data may be used for this purpose.

Extrapolation to Other Routes of Administration

While the PDE value derived for an active substance (contaminant) generally is based on studies applying the intended clinical route of administration, a different route of administration may be applied for the active substance or medicinal product subsequently produced in the shared facility. Changing the route of administration may change the bioavailability; hence correction factors for route-to-route extrapolation should be applied if there are clear differences (*e.g.*, > 40%) in route-specific bioavailability. As bioavailability may vary between species, the correction factors for route-to-route extrapolation should preferably be based on human data or in the case of veterinary medicinal products, data in the relevant target animal.

In case human or target animal bioavailability data are not available for other routes and it is to be expected that the change in route of administration may result in an increase in systemic exposure for the contaminant (*e.g.*, oral to inhalation), a conservative extrapolation can be performed by assuming 100% bioavailability of the contaminant. For example, in the case of oral-to-inhalation extrapolation, the PDE derived on basis of oral data can be corrected by multiplying with the following correction factor:

Correction factor (oral-to-inhalation): % oral absorption/ 100% respirable absorption.

In cases where human or target animal bioavailability data are not available for other routes and it can be expected that the systemic exposure to the contaminant will be lower *via* the route applied for the contaminated active substance/medicinal product, there is no need to apply a correction factor to the PDE calculation. It is expected that the route-to-route extrapolation will be performed on a case-by-case basis.

SPECIFIC CONSIDERATIONS

Active Substances with a Genotoxic Potential

For genotoxic active substances for which there is no discernible threshold, it is considered that any level of exposure carries a risk. However, a pre-defined level of acceptable risk for non-threshold related genotoxicants has been established in the EMA Guideline on the Limits of Genotoxic Impurities in the form of the Threshold of Toxicological Concern (TTC) of 1.5 µg/ person/ day. The TTC represents the genotoxic impurity exposure level associated with a theoretical cancer risk of 1 additional cancer in 100,000 patients when exposed over a life time. Given the fact that exposure duration to residual active substances will be much more restricted (for example because, in practice, levels of residual active substance carryover can be expected to diminish on a batch by batch basis), limits based on a maximum, exposure to 1.5 µg/person/day in this case would not exceed a theoretical 1×10^{-6} excess cancer risk. Hence, in the case of residual active substances without a threshold, a limit dose of 1.5 µg/person/day may be applied. When the product that may become contaminated with a residual active substance is a veterinary medicinal product the same TTC should be used, but expressed on a 'per kg bodyweight' basis (*i.e.,* the TTC is 0.03 µg/kg bw/day). When the contaminated product is for administration to food producing animals, the carryover limit applied must take account of both target animal safety considerations and consumer safety considerations. It should therefore be demonstrated, based on worst case exposure scenarios, that neither the target animal nor the consumer will be exposed to residual active substance levels exceeding the TTC.

For genotoxic active substances where sufficient carcinogenicity data exists, compound-specific risk assessments to derive acceptable intakes should be applied instead of the TTC-based acceptable intake approach. For genotoxic pharmaceutical substances with sufficient evidence of a threshold related mechanism, safe exposure levels without appreciable risk of genotoxicity can be established by using the PDE approach.

Active Substances with a Highly Sensitising Potential

Drug-induced immune-mediated hypersensitivity reactions may develop in sensitive individuals. The observed reactions may range from mild cases of contact sensitisation to potentially lethal anaphylactic reactions. Dedicated facilities are required for manufacturing active substances and medicinal products with a high sensitising potential for which scientific data does not support an acceptable level of exposure or the risk associated with the handling the product at the facility cannot be adequately controlled by organisational or technical measures. Classification of an active substance or medicinal product with a high sensitising potential should consider whether the substance shows a high frequency of sensitising occurrence in humans; or a probability of occurrence of a high sensitisation rate in humans based on animal data or other validated tests. Severity of these reactions should also be considered and should be included in a weight of evidence assessment.

Therapeutic Macromolecules and Peptides

Therapeutic macromolecules and peptides are known to degrade and denature when exposed to pH extremes and/or heat, and may become pharmacologically inactive. The cleaning of biopharmaceutical manufacturing equipment is typically performed under conditions which expose equipment surfaces to pH extremes and/or heat, which would lead to the degradation and inactivation of protein-based products. In view of this, the determination of health based exposure limits using PDE limits of the active and intact product may not be required. Where other potential routes of cross-contamination exist, the risks posed should be considered on a case-by-case basis.

Lack of Animal Data on Reproductive and Developmental Toxicity

In order to ensure protection of all populations, the presence of residual active substance should be reduced to a level that will not pose a risk for effects on reproductive and developmental parameters. However, in the early phases of development, non-clinical data to assess the potential of the new active substance to cause reproductive and developmental toxicity may not yet have been generated. Gaps in scientific knowledge may also exist for authorised medicinal products, *e.g.,* the potential for a male-specific drug to cause adverse effects on embryo-foetal development. In these cases, the NOAEL of a sub-chronic/chronic study may be used in the calculation of a PDE with application of an additional adjustment factor (*e.g.,* 10) if adequately justified. In cases where appropriate data from reproductive and developmental toxicity studies of related compounds are available a class-specific profile may be used for hazard identification of the not tested contaminant through application of a read across approach.

Investigational Medicinal Products

For early development (Phase I/II) investigational medicinal products (IMPs) estimation of PDEs may be difficult based on their limited data sets. Where this is apparent, an alternative approach using categorisation into specific default value categories *e.g.,* based on low/high expected pharmacological potency, low/high toxicity, genotoxicity/carcinogenicity, similar to the tiered Threshold of Toxicological Concern approaches proposed by Kroes *et.al.,* [5], Munro *et.al.,* [6], and Dolan *et.al.,* [7], can be considered to derive health-based exposure limits if adequately justified. Since most default limits are defined for chronic exposure durations, a higher limit may be justified if a drug substance shares equipment with another that is intended for short-term clinical trials [8]. With the availability of more pharmacological and toxicological data, compound-specific limits should be calculated as described above for the derivation of health-based exposure limits.

REPORTING OF THE PDE DETERMINATION STRATEGY

The identification of a “critical effects” in the establishment of a PDE as outlined in section 4 should be based on a comprehensive literature search including handbook and monographs as well as searches in electronic scientific databases. The search strategy and the results of the search must be clearly documented. Following an expert review, the company should provide a discussion with respect to the critical endpoints of concern and their rationale for the choice of endpoints and dose that is to be used in the derivation of the PDE. The pivotal animal and human studies used for the derivation of the PDE should be sourced to the original reference and reviewed regarding their quality (study design, description of finding, accuracy of the report etc.). The PDE determination strategy should provide a clear rationale regarding the adjustment factors that were applied in deriving the PDE. Moreover, in order to provide an overview to the GMP inspectors, the initial page of any prepared PDE determination strategy document should be a summary of the assessment process (please see Annex for template example).

IMPLEMENTATION

This guideline has been developed as a risk identification tool to facilitate the implementation of a science and risk based approach to manufacture of medicinal products using shared manufacturing facilities. To allow manufacturers to adapt accordingly the date of coming into effect will be phased in as follows: For medicinal products already produced in shared manufacturing facilities the guidance will take effect, or existing arrangements should be scientifically justified, within:

- 1 year after publication of the guideline for manufacturers of products for human use including those who manufacture human and veterinary medicines using shared manufacturing facilities.
- 2 years after publication of the guideline for manufacturers solely producing products for veterinary use.

CLEANING AND EXTENT OF CLEANING

Drug Products / Formulations

In manufacturing process, two different cleaning situations arise and each situation are described as follows;

Cleaning between batch-to-batch changeover.

Cleaning between product-to-product changeover.

In our non-dedicated drug product manufacturing facility different cleaning procedures are developed depending upon the change over situations.

Type A Cleaning

Used only when cleaning between different batches of the same product; *i.e.,* batch to batch cleaning. Example – In manufacturing of product X, there are 2 Batches to be manufactured one after another as shown in the following flow chart (Fig. 1). For a particular equipment and/ or equipment train, if batch A is to be followed by Batch B, then a type A cleaning is required.

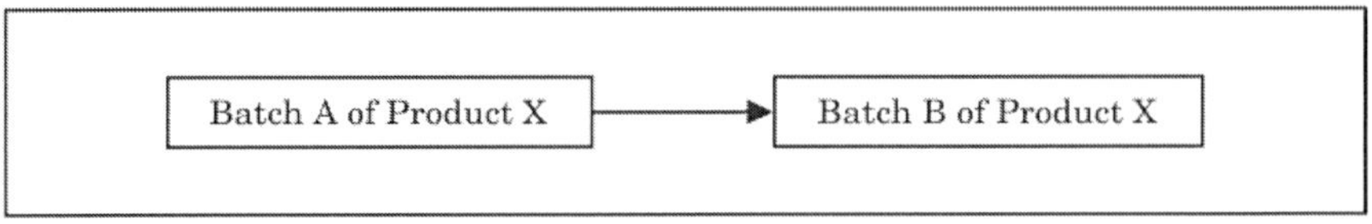

Fig. 1: Type a cleaning

Type B Cleaning

Used when cleaning between different Product-Batches; *i.e.,* product to product cleaning.

Example – In manufacturing of product X followed by product Y as shown in the following flow diagram (Fig. 2).

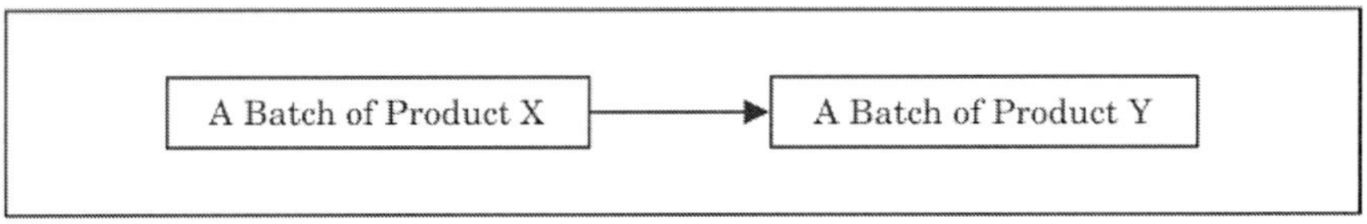

Fig. 2: Type B cleaning

The two different types of cleaning (Level A and Level B) differ in thoroughness of the cleaning process, cleaning conditions, the level of verification of cleaning and degree of risk associated with contamination, as shown in the following order. Table 1 depicts risks involved in cleaning process.

Table 1: Risks involved in cleaning process

	Type A	*Type B*
Risk	Lowest	Highest
Acceptance Limit	Highest	Lowest
Extent of Cleaning	Less Extensive	More Extensive
Verification of Cleaning	Visual Inspection	Visual and Analytical Testing

DEVELOPMENT OF CLEANING VALIDATION PROGRAM

Only B cleaning is subjected to be validated. A systematic cleaning validation program shall be followed which are described in the following sub-sections.

Identification of Potential Contaminants

The contaminants in pharmaceutical product manufacturing may be of different types like the active substances of previously manufactured drug product, cleaning agents, microorganisms, lubricants, solvents, equipment related, etc. Among these the potential contaminants are active of previously manufactured drug product and microorganisms, which shall be considered in cleaning validation.

Product Grouping and Worst Case Selection

During development of cleaning validation program the products shall be grouped to identify that particular product which will represent the worst case and making the cleaning validation program manageable. The philosophy behind product grouping is as follows:

All products having same dosage form.

All products having same active ingredients.

All products shall be listed in the form of a matrix, showing corresponding batch size, dosage strength, amount of active ingredients, minimum daily dose (of active), maximum daily dose (of drug product), water solubility, preferable swab medium and step by step calculated results. The product(s) that shows the highest dosage strength and lowest acceptance criteria with respect to less water solubility can be considered as the product of worst case. It is common that practically the perfect worst case may not come in a single product; in that case more than one product shall be selected as worst case. Bracketing concept can be used to show the extremity of cleaning procedure.

Manufacturing Equipment Grouping and Worst Case Selection

All processing equipments shall be arranged in train as per the manufacturing flow of product. This comes right from the dispensing of raw materials to primary packaging. The equipment train having highest product contact surface area shall be considered as worst case.

Selection of Cleaning Procedure

Same cleaning procedure shall be followed for all the manufacturing equipments and utensils irrespective of the product. There are following two types of cleaning procedures used in our manufacturing facility.

Automated Cleaning Procedure

Cleaning of the equipment is performed in place without disassembling.

Cleaning process may be controlled by an automated program.

Very consistent in nature.

Manual Cleaning Procedure

Cleaning of the disassembled equipment is performed

Effectiveness largely depends upon the person performing the cleaning operation.

For any type of cleaning method used, cleaning validation is a basic requirement, samples shall be taken, analyzed and results documented.

After Validation of the cleaning method, suitable reports shall be prepared to demonstrate that critical parameters such as the temperature, cycle time and sequence, quantity of detergent used etc. are still being achieved and / or followed on a routine basis. These records shall be incorporated in the Cleaning Validation Report.

Once the cleaning method is validated, it shall be ensured that the method is not changed. If required any change in the validated cleaning method shall be governed as per the company's existing change control policy and the need for re-validation shall be evaluated.

Selection of Sampling Method

There are two kinds of sampling method shall be followed during validation; *e.g.,* Swab (Direct Surface) Sampling method and Rinse (Wash Water) Sampling Method. Direct surface monitoring should be used for validation as well as regular cleaning verification. All samples shall adequately be identified by their identification numbers, provided in the individual cleaning validation protocols.

Swab (Direct Surface) Sampling Method

Absorbent cotton swab of 5 cm. × 5 cm. (25 cm^2) shall be used.

Residue shall be collected by physical rubbing of swab on the cleaned equipment / utensil surface. The swab shall be wet by the solvent, specified in the preferable swab medium column in the product matrix. Finally the sampled swab shall be desorbed in the glass bottle containing 20 ml. of that specific solvent. Most difficult to clean locations shall be selected for swab sampling. It is recommended to collect swabs at least from 5 locations (in case of swab taken for chemical residue) of each major processing equipment. The sampling locations along with the drawing shall be specified in the cleaning validation protocol(s).

Readymade Sterile swab shall be used for microbiological sampling.

Rinse (Wash Water) Sampling Method

Large surface area can be easily sampled by this method. Strongest preferred method for difficult to access parts of equipment. Rinse sample shall be collected in conjunction with swab samples. 2 litres of purified water, representing total equipment (product contact area) surface area shall be used for final rinsing.

Finally 100 ml. of water shall be collected in glass bottle as rinse sample. Details of sampling procedure shall be described in individual cleaning validation protocols.

Selection of Analytical Method

It is important to select an appropriate method for detection of the residue in the cleaning sample. Analytical method shall be selected as per the applicability depends on the residue of the active to be analyzed. Methods shall be validated for accuracy, precision, linearity, ruggedness, robustness, sensitivity and recovery.

Specific Analytical Test Methods

Specific analytical test methods shall be applicable for identification and quantitative analysis of microbes / active residue in swab / rinse samples. Some common examples of specific analytical methods are given;

High Performance Liquid Chromatography (HPLC).

Ultra violate Spectrophotometer (UV).

Microbial Test.

Non-Specific Analytical Methods

Although it is expected to follow specific analytical test methods for the cleaning samples, but many of the non-specific methods are preferable because these are simple, fast and ability to provide overall contamination level of cleaning. Some examples are mentioned below;

Visual Examination

pH

Total Organic Carbon (TOC)

Conductivity

Non-specific analytical methods shall be utilized to analyze the rinse water sample during cleaning validation / cleaning verification.

ANALYTICAL METHOD VALIDATION

The analytical method used for evaluation of cleaning efficacy shall be validated prior execution. Analytical method shall be validated on the basis of following validation parameters [3].

Limit of detection (LOD)

Limit of Detection is the lowest amount of the analyte in the sample that can be detected qualitatively. The analytical method should be sensitive enough to detect the active residue present in the sample. The limit of detection shall be established during the validation of analytical method.

Limit of Quantification (LOQ)

Limit of Quantification is the lowest amount of the analyte in the sample that can be detected qualitatively. The analytical method shall be validated not on the basis of L2* but rather on the L3* basis. This fourfold factor in limit of quantification is significant for successful cleaning validation.

Determination of Recovery Factor and Limit

The recovery studies shall be a part of cleaning validation studies. The limit L3 is the acceptance limit in the analyzed sample. It shall be adjusted by swab recovery factor and the ultimate outcome will be L4*. Typically a recovery study comprises of the following:

Deliberately contaminating the subjected equipment surface and/ or similar coupon surface (predefined area) with known concentration of the molecule of interest. The interested molecule residue shall be recovered form the same surface by using the same sampling techniques (rinse / swab), which would be used during the validation studies.

The recovered quantity shall be determined by using the same validated analytical methods, which would be used during the validation studies. A recovery factor shall be established based on statistical evaluation of the results. Table 2 may be used for determination of recovery factor(s);

ESTABLISHMENT OF LIMITS AND ACCEPTANCE CRITERIA

The equipment and utensil surface are should be visually clean. The rationale for the residue limit shall be scientific, logical and based upon the knowledge of the material. It shall also be practical, achievable and verifiable. The quantitative acceptance criteria shall be considered as the best for the determination of residue limits. In cleaning validation, two types of residues

Table 2: Calculation of recovery factor

Initial Quantity (contamination) in µg (A)		_____ (#value)
Actual Recovered Quantity in µg	1.	_____ (#value)
	2.	_____ (#value)
	3.	_____ (#value)
	4.	_____ (#value)
	5.	_____ (#value)
Average (B)		_____ (#value)
Standard Deviation		_____ (#value)
Recovery Factor = (B) / (A)		_____ (#value)

and microbiological consideration shall be of prime importance as these have major impact on equipment cleanliness and processing product quality. These residues and their acceptance limits are as follows;

Residue of the previously manufactured product

Mainly the active ingredient(s) are concern. The acceptance criterion shall be based on the therapeutic dose and safety factor of the active being used in the previously manufactured drug product at the same equipment. Safety factor is the allowing not more than a fraction of a therapeutic dose to be present in the subsequent product. The safety factors may vary, as the degree of risks is different for different dosage forms as listed in Table 3.

Table 3: Dosage form and safety factor

Dosage Form	***Safety Factor***
Research Compounds	1 / 100, 000 – 1 / 10, 000
Oral Dosage Forms	1 / 1000
Topical Products	1 / 100 – 1 / 10

Limit Calculation on The Basis of Therapeutic Dose

The step-by-step approach shall be followed for the determination of limit. The following formula shall be used;

Step – 1

Purpose: To calculate the limit of active agent in any subsequently manufactured product (LSP).

Information required

Minimum daily dose of the active being cleaned (TD).

Maximum daily dose of the subsequently manufactured drug product (LDD). (iii) Safety factor of the active being cleaned (SF).

Formula

LSP = (SF × TD)/LD

Step – 2

***Purpose*:** To determine the residue limit of active contamination level per area of equipment (L2*).

Information required

LSP from 1st stage.

The batch size of the subsequent product (BSSP in kg.)

The shared equipment surface area (SESA in cm^2).

Formula

L2 = (LSP x BSSP x 1000)/ SESA

Step – 3

***Purpose*:** To determine the residue limit for the analytical sample (L3*).

Information required

The surface area residue limit (L2).

The surface area swabbed (in cm^2).

The amount of solvent the swab is desorbed (in gm.).

Formula

L3 = (L2 × Swabbed surface area)/ Amt. of desorption solvent

Step – 4

***Purpose*:** To determine the residue limit for the analytical sample considering swab recovery factor (L4*).

Information required

Residue limit for the analytical sample (L3).

Swab recovery factor determined by practical experiment.

Formula

L4 = L3/ Swab Recovery Factor

Limit Determination on the Basis of 10 ppm Criterion

As per cGMP, the highest allowable residue of active should not exceed 10 ppm level. On that basis the 10 ppm limit shall be considered conservatively in place of the dosage criterion limit on those case(s) where calculated limit will be greater than 10 ppm.

Residue of Cleaning Agent

The cleaning program shall be designed to demonstrate the removal of cleaning agent below the acceptance level. As per the established cleaning procedure, sodium lauryl sulphate is used to clean the processing equipments and utensils. Not more than 10 ppm of the detergent residue shall be considered as acceptance criteria.

Microbiological Consideration

Sufficient documented evidence shall be established to demonstrate that the routine cleaning and storage of the cleaned equipment does not allow microbial growth, beyond the defined limit. Any equipment cleaned shall be dried and protected to ensure that, there will be no microbial proliferation and microbial contamination of the cleaned equipment.

Practically it cannot expect equipment free from all microorganisms. Setting of the microbial limit is important and required because even a single organism in the equipment could possibly result in significantly higher contamination level in the product manufactured using that equipment. Three kind of microbiological limit can be categorized;

The first criteria with respect to the microbial contamination limit of the equipment surface, is absence of pathogenic organisms such as *E. coli*, *Enterococcus*, *Salmonella*, etc (commonly known as USP indicator organisms).

Not more than 10 cfu / 25 cm^2 is recommended as swab limit.

Rinse samples shall not be exceeding 100 cfu / ml.

CLEANING VALIDATION STRATEGY

The manufacturing equipments shall be cleaned as per the preestablished Standard Operating Procedures (SOPs) on equipment cleaning. The whole cleaning validation study shall be divided into two phases; first phase is the Introductory Phase and second phase is Confirmatory Phase. In the Introductory Phase, three consecutive batches of considered product(s) shall be taken for cleaning validation study in which 100 % swab sampling shall be done in conjunction with rinse water collections. In the Confirmatory Phase, only rinse water sampling shall be conducted for next three batches of same product(s).

Data Interpretation and Drawing Conclusion

All test results shall be verified in accordance with the established acceptance criteria. Data generated during cleaning validation shall be systematically documented to facilitate sound understanding regarding the effectiveness of existing cleaning methods. Analytical results complying the established acceptance criteria shall be considered as the root of a successful cleaning validation study. A correlation shall be estimated in between the result obtained from swab sample analysis and result obtained from rinse water analysis.

Equipment wise, comparative graphical representation of analytical test results can be used as a tool of showing relation between two types of samples. The test results of rinse water samples of next three batches shall be served as a confirmatory evaluation of the cleaning efficacy. In these cases, the analytical results should not give rise an unexpected result. If the outcomes of all six batches are consistent with the predetermined limits, the cleaning validation can be considered as successful. Any deviation or nonconformity of the cleaning process, sampling method, analytical method and test results, shall be fully investigated and decision may be taken for further consideration of cleaning validation.

Step by step approach of Cleaning Validation

The following Flow Chart (Fig. 3) represents development of Cleaning Validation program;

ONGOING VERIFICATION OF CLEANING

Verification of cleaning shall be conducted regularly after completion of cleaning validation. It involves the performance of visual inspection of cleaned equipments and / utensils and testing of collected samples. However additional verification may be necessary depending on the complexity of the equipment / product being cleaned.

Visual Verification

The cGMP regulations require visual inspection of each piece of equipment immediately before use to ensure its cleanliness. No traces of contaminants should remain on the equipment and utensil surface. After successful completion of cleaning validation (for both Introductory Stage and Confirmatory stage), visual inspection shall be considered as vital tool for verification of cleaning effectiveness. The visual inspection procedure is mentioned bellow;

The visual inspection is subjected to follow for each and every batch of product being cleaned. It is applicable for both types of cleaning A and B. Cleaned equipment surfaces shall be inspected with naked eye at a distance of approximately 25cm. Adequate quantity and intensity of light should be present in the area during visual inspection. Visual inspection shall be

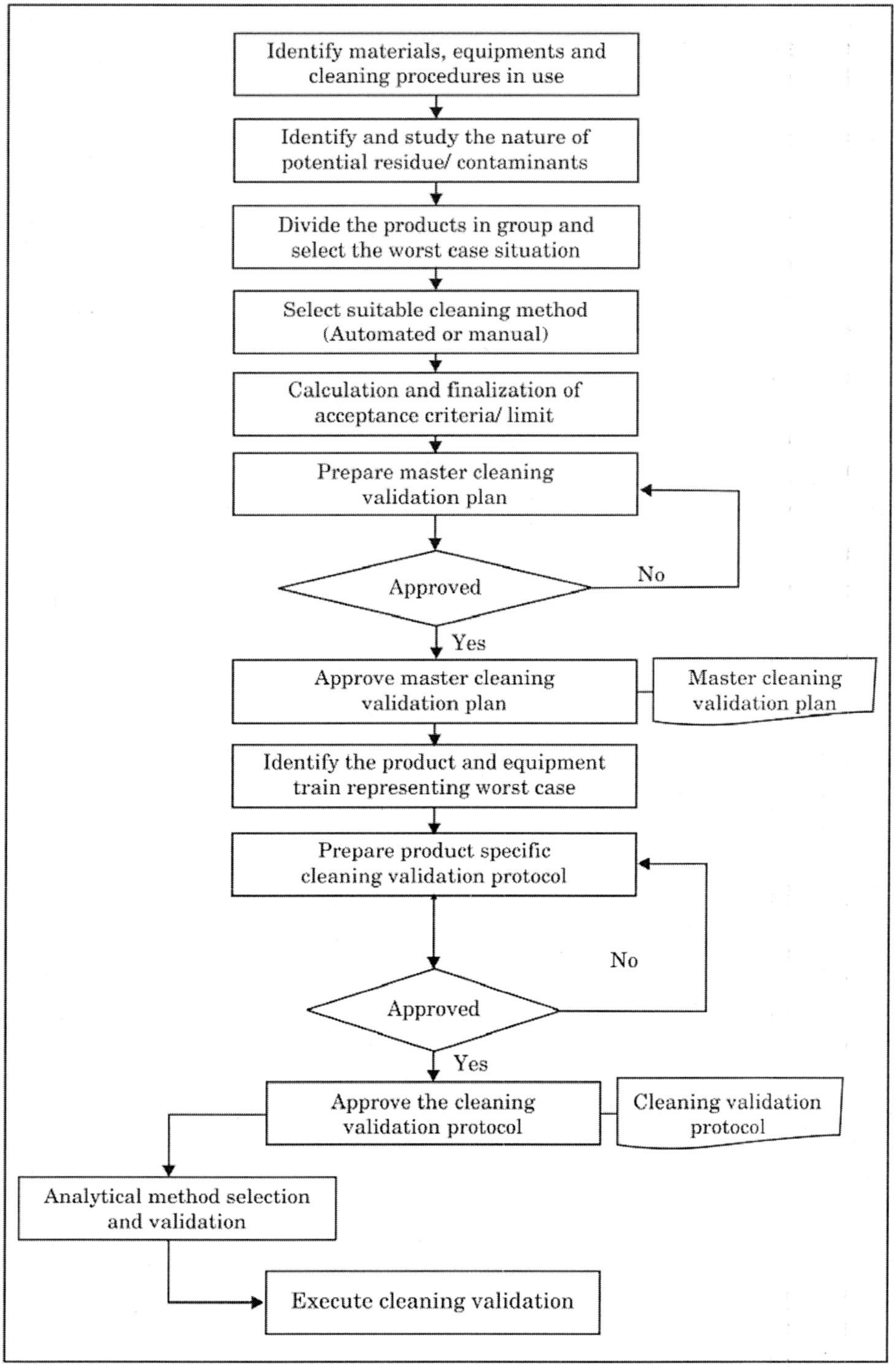

Fig. 3: Cleaning validation program

conducted just before the use of cleaned equipments/ utensils for processing of next batch / product. The results of visual inspection shall be documented in the respective BMR/ BPR. Any deviation from the anticipated result shall be mentioned in the respective BMR/ BPR and subjected to investigation.

Verification by Testing

The validated cleaning method shall be verified with analytical testing during periodic revalidation. The procedure of verification by testing is described as follows;

Rinse (Wash Water) shall be considered as the preferred sampling method for cleaning verification. Non-Specific Analytical Testing Methods (*e.g.*, TOC, Conductivity, pH) shall be used for the quantitative analysis of residue. Test results shall be documented in accordance with acceptance criteria in the periodic revalidation report followed by conclusion.

Any deviation from the anticipated result shall be mentioned in the respective cleaning validation protocol and subjected to investigation.

REVALIDATION

Revalidation shall be conducted to demonstrate that the existing cleaning procedure is in the state of validation. There are two different types of Cleaning Revalidation can be conducted depending upon the situation arises and consideration of the cleaning validation team members.

Revalidation due to Change

The degree of revalidation due to Change should be based on the risk assessment of the change/ observation regarding the cleaning efficacy. The list of changes is mentioned below which may affect the existing cleaning validation status.

Modification in the existing equipment design.

Changes in the equipment / utensil cleaning method.

Changes in the analytical sample testing method.

Changes in detergent used for cleaning.

Changes in sampling method / tool regarding cleaning.

New product in the facility that challenges the existing worst-case consideration. Addition of new equipment(s) in the processing line which increases the total surface area of entire equipment train and challenges the pre-considered surface area of largest equipment train.

Revalidation due to change can be partial validation / full validation depending upon the situation on which revalidation will be considered. It is the responsibility of cleaning validation team to determine the effect of proposed changes on the current state of cleaning. The major changes in the existing equipments, critical cleaning procedure and analytical method shall be subjected to go through the company's change control procedure. A new cleaning validation protocol shall be prepared, followed by preparation of report.

DOCUMENTATION FOR CLEANING VALIDATION

Further documentation shall be prepared for each cleaning validation study, which will be product specific. The documentation for cleaning validation comprises of Protocol and Report. The details of protocol and report are specified as follows;

Cleaning Validation Protocol

An authorized product specific validation protocol shall be prepared prior to conducting the cleaning validation study. The product representing the worst case shall be subjected to get validated. The cleaning validation protocol shall contain the following heads but may not be limited to this;

Objective

Scope

Description of the process

Identification of critical monitoring parameter (for the cleaning procedure).

Test Functions (Tests to be utilized for validation of cleaning procedure).

Sampling Locations and Procedures (with relevant drawing).

Analytical Test Methods

Limit and Acceptance Criteria

Cleaning Validation Report

Cleaning Validation Report shall be prepared in accordance with the established protocol. It may contain the following fields;

Inprocess Observations and Visual Inspection results.

Analytical Observations and results.

Data interpretations and statistical evaluation of results.

Relationship of test results between swab and rinse sample analysis.

Any Deviations Observed.

CONCLUSIONS

Cleaning validation is a process of attaining and documenting sufficient evidence to prove the effectiveness of cleaning process. Cleaning is directly related to safety and purity of the pharmaceutical product therefore it becomes important and primary activity. So, it is necessary to have effective cleaning program in place because of the regulatory requirement.

REFERENCES

[1] Bercu JP & Dolan DG, (2013). Application of the threshold of toxicological concern concept when applied to pharmaceutical manufacturing operations intended for short-term clinical trials. *Regul Toxicol Pharmacol.* 2013 Feb;65(1):162-7.

[2] Dolan DG, Naumann BD, Sargent EV, Maier A, Dourson M (2005). Application of the threshold of toxicological concern concept to pharmaceutical manufacturing operations. *Regul Toxicol Pharmacol*, 43, 1-9.

[3] FDA Guide to Inspections Validation of Cleaning Processes, http://www.fda.gov/ICECI/Inspections/InspectionGuides/ucm074922.htm

[4] ICH Q2 (R1), Validation of Analytical Procedures: Text and Methodology, November 2005.

[5] Kroes R, Renwick A, Cheeseman M, Kleiner J, Mangelsdorf I, Piersma A, Schilter B, Schatter J, van Schothorst F, Vos JG, Würtzen G. (2004). Structure-based thresholds of toxicological concern (TTC): guidance for application to substances present at low levels in the diet. *Fd Chem Toxicol* 42, 65-83.

[6] Munro IC, Renwick AG, Danielewska-Nikiel B (2008). The threshold of toxicological concern (TTC) in risk assessment. *Toxicol Lett* 180, 151-156.

[7] Parenteral Drug Association (PDA) Guidance for Industry.Technical Report No. 29 (Revised 2012) Points to Consider for Cleaning Validation, Destin A. LeBlanc, Gretchen Allison, Jennifer L. Carlson, Koshy George, Igor Gorsky, Irwin S. Hirsh, Jamie Osborne, Greg Randall, Pierre-Michel Riss, George Verghese, Jenn Walsh, Vivienne Yankah.

[8] USP 24, The United States Pharmacopoeia, United States Pharmacopeial Convention, Inc., 12601 Twinbrook Parkway, Rockville, MD 20852.

FURTHER READING

[1] Active Pharmaceutical Ingredients Committee (Apic) "Guidance On Aspects of Cleaning Validation in Active Pharmaceutical Ingredient Plants" May 2014

15

Analytical Method Validation

ABSTRACT

Validation of analytical methods acts as a documented evidence that the method is suitable for its purpose. Analytical methods need to be validated prior to their introduction into routine analyses. The overarching philosophy in cGMPs of the 21st century and robust modern quality systems is the quality has to be built into the product, and testing alone cannot be relied to ensure the quality of the product. From the analytical perspective, it will mean that analytical methods used to test products should have quality attributes built into them. In order to apply quality attributes into the analytical method, fundamental quality attributes have to be applied by the bench - level scientist. This is a paradigm shift that requires the bench - level scientist to have a scientific and technical understanding, product knowledge, process knowledge, and / or risk assessment ability to appropriately execute the quality functions of analytical method validation. In addition, it requires the following procedures: (a) an appropriate training of the bench - level scientist to understand the principles involved with method validation, validate an analytical method, and understand the principles involved with the method validation, (b) proper documentation and understanding and interpreting data, and (c) cross – an understanding functional of the effect of their activities on the product and to customers (the patient). This chapter gives a review and strategy for the validation of analytical methods in-house, recommendation in documentation and completion of method validation in the pharmaceutical environmental.

INTRODUCTION

Test procedures for assessment of the quality levels of pharmaceutical articles are subject to various requirements. The Current Good Manufacturing Practice regulations [21 CFR 211.194(a)] [1] require that test methods, which are used for assessing compliance of pharmaceutical articles with established specifications, must meet proper standards of accuracy and reliability. Also, according to these regulations [21 CFR 211.194(a) [2]], users of analytical methods described in USP–NF [2] are not required to validate the accuracy and reliability of these methods, but merely verify their suitability under actual conditions of use. Recognizing the legal status of USP and NF standards, it is essential, therefore, that proposals for adoption of new or revised compendial analytical procedures be supported by sufficient laboratory data to document their validity. The text of this chapter harmonizes, to the extent possible, with the Tripartite International Council for Harmonisation (ICH) documents Validation of Analytical Procedures and the Methodology extension text, which are concerned with analytical procedures included as part of registration applications submitted within the EC, Japan, and the USA [3]. Information may vary depending upon the type of method involved. However, in most cases a submission will consist of the following sections.

1. ***Rationale:*** This section should identify the need for the procedure and describe the capability of the specific procedure proposed and why it is preferred over other types of determinations. For revised procedures, a comparison should be provided of limitations of the current compendial procedure and advantages offered by the proposed procedure.
2. ***Proposed Analytical Procedure:*** This section should contain a complete description of the analytical procedure sufficiently detailed to enable persons "skilled in the art" to replicate it. The write-up should include all important operational parameters and specific instructions such as preparation of reagents, performance of system suitability tests, description of blanks used, precautions, and explicit formulas for calculation of test results.
3. ***Data Elements:*** This section should provide thorough and complete documentation of the validation of the analytical procedure. It should include summaries of experimental data and calculations substantiating each of the applicable analytical performance characteristics. These characteristics are described in the following section.

VALIDATION

Validation of an analytical procedure is the process by which it is established, by laboratory studies, that the performance characteristics of the procedure meet the requirements for the intended analytical applications. Because opinions may differ with respect to terminology and use, each of the performance characteristics is defined in the next section of this chapter, along with a delineation of a typical method or methods by which it may be measured. The definitions refer to "test results". The description of the analytical procedure should define what the test results for the procedure are. As noted in ISO 5725-1 [4] and 3534-1 [5], a test result is "the value of a characteristic obtained by carrying out a specified test method. The test method should specify that one or a number of individual measurements be made, and their average, or another appropriate function (such as the median or the standard deviation), be reported as the test result. It may also require standard corrections to be applied, such as correction of gas volumes to standard temperature and pressure. Thus, a test result can be a result calculated from several observed values. In the simple case, the test result is the observed value itself." A test result also can be, but need not be, the final, reportable value that would be compared to the acceptance criteria of a specification. Validation of physical property methods may involve the assessment of chemometric models. However, the typical analytical characteristics used in method validation can be applied to the methods derived from the use of the chemometric models. Typical Analytical Characteristics Used in Method Validation is as enlisted below:

- Accuracy
- Precision
- Specificity
- Detection limit
- Quantitation limit
- Linearity
- Range
- Robustness

The effects of processing conditions and potential for segregation of materials should be considered when obtaining a representative sample to be used for validation of procedures. In the case of compendial procedures, revalidation may be necessary in the following cases: a submission to the USP of a revised analytical procedure or the use of an established general procedure with a new product or raw material. The ICH documents give guidance on the necessity for revalidation in the following circumstances: changes in the synthesis of the drug substance, changes in the composition of the drug product, and changes in the analytical procedure. This chapter is intended to provide information that is appropriate to validate a wide range of compendial analytical procedures. The validation of compendial procedures may use some or all of the suggested typical analytical characteristics used in method validation and categorized by type of analytical method in Table 1. For some compendial procedures the fundamental principles of validation may extend beyond characteristics suggested in this chapter. For these procedures theW user is referred to the individual compendial chapter for those specific analytical validation characteristics and any specific validation requirements.

Table 1: Data Elements Required for Validation

Analytical performance characteristic	*Category I*	*Category II*		*Category III*	*Category IV*
		Quantitative	*Limit test*		
Accuracy	√	√	√*	√*	X
Precision	√	√	X	√	X
Specificity	√	√	√	√*	√
Detection limit	X	X	√	√*	X
Quantitation limit	X	√	X	√*	X
Linearity	√	√	X	√*	X
Range	√	√	√*	√*	X

*May be required, depending on the nature of the specific test

ANALYTICAL PERFORMANCE CHARACTERISTICS

Accuracy

Definition: The accuracy of an analytical procedure is the closeness of test results obtained by that procedure to the true value. The accuracy of an analytical procedure should be established across its range. [A note on T*erminology*: The definition of accuracy in this chapter and ICH Q2 corresponds to unbiasedness only. In the International Vocabulary of Metrology (VIM) and documents of the International Organization for Standardization (ISO), "accuracy" has a different meaning. In ISO, accuracy combines the concepts of unbiasedness (termed "trueness") and precision.] *Determination:* In the case of the assay of a drug substance, accuracy may be determined by application of the analytical procedure to an analyte of known purity (*e.g.,* a Reference Standard) or by comparison of the results of the procedure with those of a second, well-characterized procedure, the accuracy of which has been stated or defined. In the case of the assay of a drug in a formulated product, accuracy may be determined by application of the analytical procedure to synthetic mixtures of the drug product components to which known amounts of analyte have been added within the range of the procedure. If it is not possible to obtain samples of all drug product components, it may be acceptable either to add known quantities of the analyte to the drug product (*i.e.,* "to spike") or to compare results with those of a second, well characterized procedure, the accuracy of which has been stated or defined. In the case of quantitative analysis of impurities, accuracy should be assessed on samples (of drug substance or drug product) spiked with known amounts of impurities. Where it is not possible to obtain samples of certain impurities or degradation products, results should be compared with those obtained by an independent procedure. In the absence of other information, it may be necessary to calculate the amount of an impurity based on comparison of its response to that of the drug substance;

the ratio of the responses of equal amounts of the impurity and the drug substance (relative response factor) should be used, if known. Accuracy is calculated as the percentage of recovery by the assay of the known added amount of analyte in the sample, or as the difference between the mean and the accepted true value, together with confidence intervals. The ICH documents recommend that accuracy should be assessed using a minimum of nine determinations over a minimum of three concentration levels, covering the specified range (*i.e.,* three concentrations and three replicates of each concentration).

Assessment of accuracy can be accomplished in a variety of ways, including evaluating the recovery of the analyte (percent recovery) across the range of the assay, or evaluating the linearity of the relationship between estimated and actual concentrations. The statistically preferred criterion is that the confidence interval for the slope be contained in an interval around 1.0, or alternatively, that the slope be close to 1.0. In either case, the interval or the definition of closeness should be specified in the validation protocol. The acceptance criterion will depend on the assay and its variability and on the product. Setting an acceptance criterion based on the lack of statistical significance of the test of the null hypothesis that the slope is 1.0 is not an acceptable approach. Accuracy of physical property methods may be assessed through the analysis of standard reference materials, or alternatively, the suitability of the above approaches may be considered on a case-by-case basis.

Precision

Definition: The precision of an analytical procedure is the degree of agreement among individual test results when the procedure is applied repeatedly to multiple samplings of a homogeneous sample. The precision of an analytical procedure is usually expressed as the standard deviation or relative standard deviation (coefficient of variation) of a series of measurements. Precision may be a measure of either the degree of reproducibility or of repeatability of the analytical procedure under normal operating conditions. In this context, reproducibility refers to the use of the analytical procedure in different laboratories, as in a collaborative study. Intermediate precision (also known as ruggedness) expresses within-laboratory variation, as on different days, or with different analysts or equipment within the same laboratory. Repeatability refers to the use of the analytical procedure within a laboratory over a short period of time using the same analyst with the same equipment.

Determination: The precision of an analytical procedure is determined by assaying a sufficient number of aliquots of a homogeneous sample to be able to calculate statistically valid estimates of standard deviation or relative standard deviation (coefficient of variation). Assays in this context are independent analyses of samples that have been carried through the complete analytical procedure from sample preparation to final test result. The ICH documents recommend that repeatability should be assessed using a minimum of nine determinations covering the specified range for the procedure (*i.e.*, three concentrations and three replicates of each concentration) or using a minimum of six determinations at 100% of the test concentration.

Specificity

Definition: The ICH documents define specificity as the ability to assess unequivocally the analyte in the presence of components that may be expected to be present, such as impurities, degradation products, and matrix components. Lack of specificity of an individual analytical procedure may be compensated by other supporting analytical procedures. For the tests discussed below, the above definition has the following implications.

Identification tests: Ensure the identity of the analyte.

Purity tests: Ensure that all of the analytical procedures performed allow an accurate statement of the content of impurities of an analyte (*e.g.*, related substances test, heavy metals limit, or organic volatile impurities).

Assays: Provide an exact result, which allows an accurate statement on the content or potency of the analyte in a sample.

Determination: In the case of qualitative analyses (identification tests), the ability to select between compounds of closely related structure that are likely to be present should be demonstrated. This should be confirmed by obtaining positive results (perhaps by comparison to a known reference material) from samples containing the analyte, coupled with negative results from samples that do not contain the analyte and by confirming that a positive response is not obtained from materials structurally similar to or closely related to the analyte. In the case of analytical procedures for impurities, specificity may be established by spiking the drug substance or product with appropriate levels of impurities and demonstrating that these impurities are determined with appropriate accuracy and precision. In the case of the assay, demonstration of specificity requires that it can be shown that the procedure is unaffected by the presence of impurities or excipients. In practice, this can be done by spiking the drug substance or product with appropriate levels of impurities or excipients and demonstrating that the assay result is unaffected by the presence of these extraneous materials. If impurity or degradation product standards are unavailable, specificity may be demonstrated by comparing the test results of samples containing impurities or degradation products to a second well-characterized procedure (*e.g.*, a pharmacopeial or other validated procedure). These comparisons should include samples stored under relevant stress conditions (*e.g.,* light, heat, humidity, acid/base hydrolysis, and oxidation). In the case of the assay, the results should be compared; in the case of chromatographic impurity tests, the impurity profiles should be compared. The ICH documents state that when chromatographic procedures are used, representative chromatograms should be presented to demonstrate the degree of selectivity, and peaks should be appropriately labeled. Peak purity tests (*e.g.,* using diode array or mass spectrometry) may be useful to show that the analyte chromatographic peak is not attributable to more than one component. For validation of specificity for qualitative and quantitative determinations by spectroscopic methods, chapters related to topics such as near-infrared spectrophotometry, Raman spectroscopy, and X-ray powder diffraction should be consulted.

Detection Limit

Definition: The detection limit is a characteristic of limit tests. It is the lowest amount of analyte in a sample that can be detected, but not necessarily quantitated, under the stated experimental conditions. Thus, limit tests merely substantiate that the amount of analyte is above or below a certain level. The detection limit is usually expressed as the concentration of analyte (*e.g.,* percentage or parts per billion) in the sample.

Determination: For noninstrumental procedures, the detection limit is generally determined by the analysis of samples with known concentrations of analyte and by establishing the minimum level at which the analyte can be reliably detected. For instrumental procedures, the same approach may be used as for non-instrumental procedures. In the case of procedures submitted for consideration as official compendial procedures, it is almost never necessary to determine the actual detection limit. Rather, the detection limit is shown to be sufficiently low by the analysis of samples with known concentrations of analyte above and below the required detection level. For example, if it is required to detect an impurity at the level of 0.1%, it should be demonstrated that the procedure will reliably detect the impurity at that level. In the case of instrumental analytical procedures that exhibit background noise, the ICH documents describe a common approach, which is to compare measured signals from samples with known low concentrations of analyte with those of blank samples. The minimum concentration at which the analyte can reliably be detected is established. Typically acceptable signal to noise ratios are 2:1 or 3:1. Other approaches depend on the determination of the slope of the calibration curve and the standard deviation of responses. Whatever method is used, the detection limit should be subsequently validated by the analysis of a suitable number of samples known to be near, or prepared at, the detection limit.

Quantitation Limit

Definition: The quantitation limit is a characteristic of quantitative assays for low levels of compounds in sample matrices, such as impurities in bulk drug substances and degradation products in finished pharmaceuticals. It is the lowest amount of analyte in a sample that can be determined with acceptable Precision and Accuracy under the stated experimental conditions. The quantitation limit is expressed as the concentration of analyte (*e.g.,* percentage or parts per billion) in the sample.

Determination: For non-instrumental procedures, the quantitation limit is generally determined by the analysis of samples with known concentrations of analyte and by establishing the minimum level at which the analyte can be determined with acceptable Accuracy and Precision. For instrumental procedures, the same approach may be used as for non-instrumental procedures. In the case of procedures submitted for consideration as official compendial procedures, it is almost never necessary to determine the actual quantitation limit. Rather, the quantitation limit is shown to be sufficiently low by the analysis of samples with known concentrations of analyte above and below the quantitation level. For example, if it is required that an analyte be assayed at the level of 0.1 mg/tablet, it should be demonstrated that the procedure will reliably quantitate the analyte at that level. In the case of instrumental analytical procedures that exhibit background noise, the ICH documents describe a common approach, which is to compare measured signals from samples with known low concentrations of analyte with those of blank samples. The minimum concentration at which the analyte can reliably be quantified is established. A typically acceptable signal-to-noise ratio is 10:1. Other approaches depend on the determination of the slope of the calibration curve and the standard deviation of responses. Whatever approach is used, the quantitation limit should be subsequently validated by the analysis of a suitable number of samples known to be near, or prepared at, the quantitation limit.

Linearity and Range

Definition of linearity: The linearity of an analytical procedure is its ability to elicit test results that are directly, or by a well-defined mathematical transformation, proportional to the concentration of analyte in samples within a given range. Thus, in this section, "linearity" refers to the linearity of the relationship of concentration and assay measurement. In some cases, to attain linearity, the concentration and/or the measurement may be transformed. Possible transformations may include log, square root, or reciprocal, although other transformations are acceptable. If linearity is not attainable, a nonlinear model may be used. The goal is to have a model, whether linear or nonlinear, that describes closely the concentration–response relationship.

Definition of range: The range of an analytical procedure is the interval between the upper and lower levels of analyte (including these levels) that have been demonstrated to be determined with a suitable level of precision, accuracy, and linearity using the procedure as written. The range is normally expressed in the same units as test results (*e.g.,* percent or parts per million) obtained by the analytical procedure.

Determination of linearity and range: Linearity should be established across the range of the analytical procedure. It should be established initially by visual examination of a plot of signals as a function of analyte concentration of content. If there appears to be a linear relationship, test results should be established by appropriate statistical methods (*e.g.,* by calculation of a regression line by the method of least squares). Data from the regression line itself may be helpful to provide mathematical estimates of the degree of linearity. The correlation coefficient, y-intercept, slope of the regression line, and residual sum of squares should be submitted. The range of the procedure is validated by verifying that the analytical procedure provides acceptable precision, accuracy, and linearity when applied to samples containing analyte at the extremes of the range as well as within the range. ICH recommends that, for the establishment of linearity, a minimum of five concentrations normally be used. It is also recommended that the following minimum specified ranges should be considered:

Assay of a drug substance (or a finished product): From 80% to 120% of the test concentration

Determination of an impurity: From 50% to 120% of the acceptance criterion

For content uniformity: A minimum of 70%–130% of the test concentration, unless a wider or more appropriate range based on the nature of the dosage form (*e.g.,* metered-dose inhalers) is justified

For dissolution testing: ±20% over the specified range (*e.g.,* if the acceptance criteria for a controlled-release product cover a region from 30% after 1 h, and up to 90% after 24 h, the validated range would be 10%–110% of the label claim).

The traditional definition of linearity, *i.e.,* the establishment of a linear or mathematical relationship between sample concentration and response, is not applicable to particle size analysis. For particle size analysis, a concentration range is defined (instrument and particle size-dependent) such that the measured particle size distribution is not affected by changes in concentration within the defined concentration range. Concentrations below the defined concentration range may introduce an error due to poor signal-to-noise ratio, and concentrations exceeding the defined concentration range may introduce an error due to multiple scattering.

Robustness

Definition: The robustness of an analytical procedure is a measure of its capacity to remain unaffected by small but deliberate variations in procedural parameters listed in the procedure documentation and provides an indication of its suitability during normal usage. Robustness may be determined during development of the analytical procedure.

System Suitability

If measurements are susceptible to variations in analytical conditions, these should be suitably controlled, or a precautionary statement should be included in the procedure. One consequence of the evaluation of Robustness and ruggedness should be that a series of system suitability parameters is established to ensure that the validity of the analytical procedure is maintained whenever used. Typical variations are the stability of analytical solutions, different equipment, and different analysts. In the case of liquid chromatography, typical variations are the pH of the mobile phase, the mobile phase composition, different lots or suppliers of columns, the temperature, and the flow rate. In the case of gas chromatography, typical variations are different lots or suppliers of columns, the temperature, and the flow rate. System suitability tests are based on the concept that the equipment, electronics, analytical operations, and samples to be analyzed constitute an integral system that can be evaluated as such. System suitability test parameters to be established for a particular procedure depend on the type of procedure being evaluated. They are especially important in the case of chromatographic procedures. Submissions to the USP should make note of the requirements in Chromatography <621>, System Suitability.

Data Elements Required for Validation

Compendial test requirements vary from highly exacting analytical determinations to subjective evaluation of attributes. Considering this broad variety, it is only logical that different test procedures require different validation schemes. This chapter covers only the most common categories of tests for which validation data should be required. These categories are as follows:

Category I

Analytical procedures for quantitation of major components of bulk drug substances or active ingredients (including preservatives) in finished pharmaceutical products.

Category II

Analytical procedures for determination of impurities in bulk drug substances or degradation compounds in finished pharmaceutical products. These procedures include quantitative assays and limit tests.

Category III

Analytical procedures for determination of performance characteristics (*e.g.*, dissolution, drug release, and others).

Category IV

Identification tests: For each category, different analytical information is needed. Listed in Table 1 are data elements that are normally required for each of these categories. Already established general procedures (*e.g.*, titrimetric determination of water or bacterial endotoxins) should be verified to establish their suitability for use, such as their accuracy (and absence of possible interference) when used for a new product or raw material. When validating physical property methods, consider the same performance characteristics required for any analytical procedure. Evaluate use of the performance characteristics on a case-by-case basis, with the goal of determining that the procedure is suitable for its intended use. The specific acceptance criteria for each validation parameter should be consistent with the intended use of the method. Physical methods may also be classified into the four validation categories. For example, validation of a quantitative spectroscopic method may involve evaluation of Category I or Category II Analytical Performance Characteristics, depending on the method requirements. Qualitative physical property measurements, such as particle size, surface area, bulk and tapped density, which could impact performance characteristics, often best fit in Category III. Category IV Analytical Performance Characteristics usually applies to validation of qualitative identification spectroscopic methods. However, the various techniques may be used for different purposes, and the specific use of the method and characteristics of the material being analyzed should be considered when definitively applying a category to a particular type of method. The validity of an analytical procedure can be verified only by laboratory studies. Therefore, documentation of the successful completion of such studies is a basic requirement for determining whether a procedure is suitable for its intended application(s). Current compendial procedures are also subject to regulations that require demonstration of suitability under actual conditions of use. Appropriate documentation should accompany any proposal for new or revised compendial analytical procedures.

VERIFICATION OF COMPENDIAL PROCEDURES

The intent of this general information chapter is to provide general information on the verification of compendial procedures that are being performed for the first time to yield acceptable results utilizing the personnel, equipment, and reagents available. Verification consists of assessing selected analytical performance characteristics, to generate appropriate, relevant data rather than repeating the validation process. Users of compendial analytical procedures are not required to validate these procedures when first used in their laboratories, but documented evidence of suitability should be established under actual conditions of use. In the United States, this requirement is established in 21 CFR 211.194(a) of the current Good Manufacturing Practice regulations, which states that the "suitability of all testing methods used shall be verified under actual conditions of use." [7]

Verification Process

The verification process for compendial test procedures is the assessment of whether the procedure can be used for its intended purpose, under the actual conditions of use for a specified drug substance and/or drug product matrix. Users should have the appropriate experience, knowledge, and training to understand and be able to perform the compendia procedures as written. Verification should be conducted by the user such that the results will provide confidence that the compendial procedure will perform suitably as intended. If the verification of the compendial procedure is not successful, it may be concluded that the procedure may not be suitable for use with the article being tested in that laboratory. It may then be necessary to develop and validate an alternate procedure as allowed in the General Notices. The alternate procedure may be submitted to USP, along with the appropriate data, to support a proposal for inclusion or replacement of the current compendial procedure.

Verification Requirements

Verification requirements should be based on an assessment of the complexity of both the procedure and the material to which the procedure is applied. Although complete revalidation of a compendial method is not required to verify the suitability of a procedure under actual conditions of use, some of the analytical performance characteristics listed in, Table 1, may be used for the verification process. Only those characteristics that are considered to be appropriate for the verification of the particular procedure need to be evaluated. The process of assessing the suitability of a compendial analytical test procedure under the conditions of actual use may or may not require actual laboratory performance of each analytical performance characteristic. The degree and extent of the verification process may depend on the level of training and experience of the user, on the type of procedure and its associated equipment or instrumentation, on the specific procedural steps, and on which article(s) are being tested. Verification should assess whether the compendial procedure is suitable for the drug substance and/or the drug product matrix, taking into account the drug substance's synthetic route, the method of manufacture for the drug product, or both, if applicable. Verification should include an assessment of elements such as the effect of the matrix on the recovery of impurities and drug substances from the drug product matrix, as well as the suitability of chromatographic conditions and column, the appropriateness of detector signal response, etc. As an example, an assessment of specificity is a key parameter in verifying that a compendial procedure is suitable for use in assaying drug substances and drug products. For instance, acceptable specificity for a chromatographic method may be verified by conformance with system suitability resolution requirements (if specified in the procedure). However, drug substances from different suppliers may have different impurity profiles that are not addressed by the compendial test procedure. Similarly, the excipients in a drug product can vary widely among manufacturers and may have the potential to directly interfere with the procedure or cause the formation of impurities that are not addressed by the compendial procedure. In addition, drug products containing different excipients, antioxidants, buffers, or container extractives may affect the recovery of the drug substance from the matrix. In these cases, a more thorough assessment of the matrix effects may be required to demonstrate suitability of the procedure for the particular drug substance or product. Other analytical performance characteristics such as an assessment of the limit of detection or quantitation and precision for impurities procedures may be useful to demonstrate the suitability of the compendial procedure under actual conditions of use. Verification is not required for basic compendial test procedures that are routinely performed unless there is an indication that the compendial procedure is not appropriate for the article under test. Examples of basic compendial procedures include, but are not limited to, loss on drying, residue on ignition, various wet chemical procedures such as acid value, and simple instrumental determinations such as pH measurements. However, for the application of already established routine procedures to compendial articles tested for the first time, it is recommended that consideration be given to any new or different sample handling or solution preparation requirements.

CONCLUSIONS

Analytical method validation plays a fundamental role in pharmaceutical industry for releasing the commercial batch and stability data therefore; the data must be produced to acceptable scientific standards. For this reason and the need to satisfy regulatory authority requirements, all analytical methods should be properly validated and documented. Primary aim of this chapter is to provide simple to use approaches with a appropriate scientific background to improve the quality of the analytical method validation process. This chapter attempted to provide an idea how to perform analytical method validation process. It also described the fundamentals and figures of importance for analytical method validation in pharmaceutical industry for analysis purposes. The validation process acts as documented evidence to confirm that the analytical method is suitable for its anticipated purpose and to prove the capabilities of the analytical method. The definitions of method validation parameters are well explained by health authorities. Although the requirements of validation have been clearly documented by regulatory authorities, the approach to validation is varied and opened to interpretation, and validation requirements differ during the development process of pharmaceuticals.

REFERENCES

[1] 21 CFR Part 211
[2] ICH Q2 (R1), Validation of Analytical Procedures: Text and Methodology, November 2005.
[3] ISO 3534-1
[4] ISO 5725-1
[5] USP 40/ NF 35, General Information / <1225> Validation of Compendial Procedures, The United States Pharmacopoeia, United States Pharmacopeial Convention, Inc., 12601 Twinbrook Parkway, Rockville, MD 20852.
[6] USP 40/ NF 35, General Information / <1226> Verification of Compendial Procedures, The United States Pharmacopoeia, United States Pharmacopeial Convention, Inc., 12601 Twinbrook Parkway, Rockville, MD 20852.
[7] USP 40/ NF 35, General Information / <621> Chromatography, The United States Pharmacopoeia, United States Pharmacopeial Convention, Inc., 12601 Twinbrook Parkway, Rockville, MD 20852.

FURTHER READINGS

G. A. Shabir, Step by step method validation and protocol in quality system and compliance industry; Institute of Validation Technology
Guidance for industry; Analytical procedures and method validation for drugs and biologics; USFDA July 2015
WHO TRS, Guidelines on validation; Appendix 4: Analytical method validation; Draft copy; June 2016;

16

Computer System Validation

ABSTRACT

The FDA mandates that software used for the design, manufacture, packaging, labeling, storage, installation, and servicing of all finished devices intended for human use shall be validated. While ISO (International Organization for Standardization) and SOX (Sarbanes-Oxley) regulations are not as clear about the validation process, they do require that software development lifecycle processes be followed in areas where they apply because software validation demonstrates evidence which provides a high degree of assurance that a specific process will consistently produce the expected result. Initial system assessment should provide you with the list of your systems which require validation. Below are eight of the most common systems. All of these systems fall under FDA regulation, but you can see from the connecting lines that ISO and SOX controls, also apply. The systems in red typically affect multiple business units within the organization, most of which are Configurable-off-the-Shelf (COTS) software systems. These systems allow you to configure the software to meet your business needs. This chapter mainly deals with the considerations to be made during computer system validation.

INTRODUCTION

In August 1997, the FDA's regulation on electronic signatures and electronic record-keeping became effective. The Regulation, at 21 CFR Part 11, describes the technical and procedural requirements that must be met if a firm chooses to maintain records electronically and/or use electronic signatures. Part 11 works in conjunction with other FDA regulations and laws that require recordkeeping [1]. Those regulations and laws ("predicate rules') establish requirements for record content, signing, and retention. Certain older electronic systems may not have been in full compliance with Part 11 by August 1997 and modification to these so called "legacy systems" may take more time. Part 11 does not grandfather legacy systems and FDA expects that firms using legacy systems are taking steps to achieve full compliance with Part 11. If a firm is keeping electronic records or using electronic signatures, determine if they are in compliance with 21 CFR Part 11. Determine the depth of part 11 coverage on a case by case basis, in light of initial findings and program resources. At a minimum ensure that:

(1) The firm has prepared a corrective action plan for achieving full compliance with part 11 requirements, and is making progress toward completing that plan in a timely manner;
(2) Accurate and complete electronic and human readable copies of electronic records, suitable for review, are made available; and
(3) Employees are held accountable and responsible for actions taken under their electronic signatures.

If initial findings indicate the firm's electronic records and/ or electronic signatures may not be trustworthy and reliable, or when electronic recordkeeping systems inhibit meaningful FDA inspection, a more detailed evaluation may be warranted. Districts should consult with center compliance officers and the Office of Enforcement (HFC-240) in assessing the need for, and potential depth of, more detailed part 11 coverage. When substantial and significant part 11 deviations exist, FDA will not accept use of electronic records and electronic signatures to meet the requirements of the applicable predicate rule.

COMPUTER SYSTEM VALIDATION

Computer system validation (sometimes called computer validation or CSV) is the process of documenting that a computer system meets a set of defined system requirements. Validation of computer systems to ensure accuracy, reliability, consistent intended performance, and the ability to discern invalid or altered records is a critical requirement of electronic record compliance [1, 2].

- Software Validation – Computer systems validation services for SAP, LIMS, Salesforce, Trackwise, and other business and laboratory data management systems
- Web Based Applications – Specialized validation services for web, cloud, and mobile applications
- MS Excel Spreadsheets – Spreadsheet security and compliance with 21 CFR 11
- MS Access Databases – Your internally-created databases made compliant with FDA requirements
- Computer System Validation – Scalable training classes on computer validation. Learn computer system validation principles and ensure compliance.

- Spreadsheet Compliance and Validation – Online training classes that discuss specific validation requirements for spreadsheet validation
- Review of Computer System Validation Documentation and Techniques – Web-based classes that provide an overview of the validation process and best practices
- Automatic manufacturing apparatus
- Control systems
- Laboratory data capture devices
- Automated laboratory equipment
- Manufacturing execution systems
- Laboratory, clinical or manufacturing database systems

Computerized systems should be validated at the level appropriate for their intended use and in accordance with quality risk management principles. This applies to systems used in all good (anything) practices (G x P) activities (*e.g.*, good clinical practice (GCP), good laboratory practice (GLP) and good manufacturing practices (GMP). The purpose of validation of a computerized system is to ensure an acceptable degree of documented evidence that establishes confidence in the accuracy, reliability and consistency in performance of the system in accordance with predetermined specifications. The validation data should meet the principles of being attributable, legible, contemporaneous, original and accurate (ALCOA) throughout the data life cycle.

Computerized system validation should ensure that all necessary technical and procedural controls are implemented ensuring compliance with good documentation practices for electronic data generated by the system [3]. System elements that need to be considered in computerized system validation include computer hardware and software, related equipment and network components and operating system environment, procedures and systems documentation including user manuals and people (such as, but not limited to, users, data reviewers, system application administrators, network engineers, database administrators and people involved in archiving). Computerized system validation activities should address both system configuration as well as any custom-developed elements.

Computerized systems should be maintained in the validated state with risk-based controls appropriate to the different stages of the system life cycle. These stages include system planning, specification, programming and configuration, system testing, preparation and verification of standard operating procedures (SOPs) and training programmes, system operation and maintenance including handling of software and hardware updates, monitoring and review, followed by system retirement.

Depending on the types of systems or typical applications such as process control systems (distributed control system (DCS), programmable logic controller (PLC), supervisory control and data acquisition (SCADA)), laboratory information management systems (LIMS), laboratory instrument control systems and business systems (enterprise resource planning (ERP), manufacturing resource planning (MRP II)) used by the manufacturer, a document covering (but not limited to) the following information should be available on-site:

- Purpose and scope;
- Roles and responsibilities;
- Validation approach;
- Risk management principles;
- System acceptance criteria;
- Vendor selection and assessment;
- Computerized system validation steps;
- Configuration management and change control procedures;
- Back-up and recovery;
- Error handling and corrective action;
- Contingency planning and disaster recovery;
- Maintenance and support;
- System requirement;
- Validation deliverables and documentation;
- Template, formats, annex; examples.

A typical model for computerized systems validation is the V-model. The lifecycle development model (or V-model for short), is a framework or structure for undertaking the design, execution and commissioning of a design project baseline: a risk based approach to compliant G x P computerized systems GAMP). The left-hand edge of the V is where the project is defined and specified in greater detail. The bottom point of the V is the execution step of the project. The right-hand edge of the V is where the commissioning and qualification testing of the installed system is performed. The V-model provides a logical sequence that helps to organize the complex activities of defining a project scope, executing it and qualifying it.

PROJECT PHASE

Validation

The validation documentation and reports should cover the relevant steps of the life cycle. Manufacturers should be able to justify their standards, protocols, acceptance criteria, procedures and records based on their risk assessment. Validation documentation should include change control records (if applicable) and reports on any deviations observed during the validation process. An up to date listing of all relevant systems and their GMP functionality (inventory) should be available.

For critical systems an up to date system description detailing the physical and logical arrangements, data flows and interfaces with other systems or processes, any hardware and software pre-requisites, and security measures should be available. User Requirements Specifications should describe the required functions of the computerized system and be based on documented risk assessment and GMP impact. User requirements should be traceable throughout the life-cycle. The regulated user should take all reasonable steps, to ensure that the system has been developed in accordance with an appropriate quality management system. The supplier should be assessed appropriately. For the validation of bespoke or customized computerized systems there should be a process in place that ensures the formal assessment and reporting of quality and performance measures for all the life-cycle stages of the system.

Evidence of appropriate test methods and test scenarios should be demonstrated. Particularly, system (process) parameter limits, data limits and error handling should be considered. Automated testing tools and test environments should have documented assessments for their adequacy. If data are transferred to another data format or system, validation should include checks that data are not altered in value and/or meaning during this migration process.

Maximize the Benefits of Computer System Validation

Computer validation is more than a compliance requirement. Pharmaceutical computer system validation is a unique opportunity for a business to examine their computer systems to maximize effectiveness and enhance quality. CSV ensures that your validation project clearly documents why your customers should share the high degree of confidence you hold in your company and your systems, while scaling the project to your organizational validation requirements and budget. Drug and medical device manufacturing in the modern world relies increasingly on computerized systems. Being highly regulated industries, ensuring quality and accuracy of data is paramount; and thus, Computer System Validation (CSV) is necessary to assure that critical processes are functioning properly.

Validation: Aspects

CSV is applied to many aspects of the healthcare and other regulated industries and businesses:

- Services
- Equipment
- Computer Systems Cleaning
- Processes

Validation: Objectives

The FDA defines process validation as "establishing documented evidence which provides a high degree of assurance that a specific process will consistently produce a product meeting its predetermined specifications and quality attributes." The objective of validation, therefore, is to produce documented evidence that parts of the facility will work correctly every time, when brought into use. The goal is also to make sure that quality is built in to the system at every step; and not just a factor at the 'output' end of the process chain.

Basic Requirements

Computer system validation requires, first, that you obtain or design a process that can consistently conform to requirements; and then that you run studies demonstrating that this is the case. Both tasks can be performed with the aid of the right statistical tools. Briefly put, the requirements are:

- Development of a validation plan
- Utilization of Standard Operating Procedures (SOPs)
- Documented Training on SOPs
- Development of detailed specifications
- Development of a test plan and/or test scripts

Both the FDA and ISO 13485:2003 [4] require computer system validation.

Computer System Process Validation

Validation and Verification training address some common sense approach to this dilemma; such as having V&V plans and processes that clearly define the completion criteria for a product or process step. In 2001 Software bugs cost the US economy $59.5 billion annually. About a third of the losses ($22.2 billion could have been avoided with a good V&V program. To achieve a good V&V program an organization must address the major problems that creep into the V&V process, and reach a balance between not doing any V&V and testing for 25 years. The presentation will address some common sense approach to this dilemma; such as having V&V plans and processes that clearly define the completion criteria for a product or process step; and to match the V&V process to the product and risk. Instead of cast of thousands for a review maybe only one qualified person can perform this process.

USER REQUIREMENT SPECIFICATIONS (URS)

When utilising a computerised system within a regulated environment it is appropriate to establish system control documentation or a system description, giving a written detailed description of the system, also covering development and maintenance. This system control document may include a record of, or a reference to, the documented 'User Requirement Specifications' (URS), or other life-cycle documents. It should also be the definitive statement of what the system must or must not do. This document is also important for legacy systems and those systems under development.

When properly documented, the URS should be complete, realistic, definitive and testable. Establishment and agreement to the requirements for the software is of paramount importance. Requirements also need to define non-software (*e.g.,* SOPs) and hardware. "User Requirement Specifications", (URS), requirements should satisfy the following criteria:

- Each requirement document should be reviewed, authorised and uniquely catalogued.
- There should be no conflict between requirements.
- Each requirement, particularly those to be met to satisfy G x P expectations, should be specified in a manner such that compliance with the requirements is capable of being verified objectively by an authorized method, *e.g.,* inspection, analysis or test.
- The URS, although independent of the supplier should be understood and agreed by both user and supplier. There should be a clear distinction between mandatory regulatory requirements and optional features.
- The URS should contain functional and non-functional requirements: functionality, effectiveness, maintainability, usability, etc. Requirements should be objectively verifiable.

Evaluation of the URS and the functional specifications should allow identification of the G x P requirements covered by the system. Additionally the URS will provide information as to where there are important interfaces between the system and manual operations. The URS should also form the basis for a risk assessment of the system for G x P compliance requirements, in addition to other risks such as safety. The risk analysis may be based on the FS, which is related to the URS, (*e.g.,* for bespoke systems). The risk assessment and the results including the reasons for the ranking as either: 'critical' or 'not critical' should be documented. The nature of any GxP risks should be clearly stated.

All computerised systems should have been subjected to documented prospective validation or qualification. However, as user's systems evolve through modification, enhancement or integration and in response to additional regulatory requirements, it may be necessary to conduct additional re-qualification and revalidation work on the existing systems. The URS and 'System Description' document should be correspondingly updated as validation life cycle evidence.

FUNCTIONAL SPECIFICATIONS (FS)

From the URS, the supplier (this would include in-house developer) of the software would be able to develop the functional specifications (in the case of bespoke programs) or clearly identify the functional specifications for selection and purchase of off-the-shelf systems. The functional specifications should define a system to meet the URS, *i.e.,* the customer's needs. The functional specifications should provide a precise and detailed description of each of the essential requirements for the computer system and external interfaces. This means descriptions of functions, performances and where applicable, design constraints and attributes. For particular types and levels of systems it may be appropriate to have a combined URS and FS.

The regulated user should be able to provide documentation describing the computer system(s) to include logic flow or block diagrams where practical, also giving an indication of hardware layout, networks and interaction. These basic schematics should align with the functional specification and be traceable to the URS. Within the EU it is logical for this information to be held within the controlled 'System Description' document, required by GMP Annex 11 [5].

TESTING

Assurance of reliability of software is achieved by execution of quality plans and testing during the software development process. The development and testing of hardware and software should be done under a quality assurance system, documented and formally agreed between the various parties. This can ultimately provide evidence in support of G x P quality compliance. Locations and responsibilities for testing (depending on the category of the software and system) are outlined in the GAMP Guide, V.

One of the most critical aspects of development of software is the integration testing phase where individual elements of software code (and hardware, where applicable), are combined and tested during or prior to this stage until the entire system has been integrated. Extra benefits may be achieved by code walkthroughs including evaluation of critical algorithms and/or routines, prior to testing. Errors found at the integration testing phase are much cheaper to correct than errors found at a later stage of testing. Code review (walk-through) is best done as early in the process as possible, preferably before submitting a module to test. Code reviews are best performed before formal unit code testing (*i.e.,* before a unit or module is frozen and enters formal testing).

For some simpler G x P systems, for example certain PLCs and systems based on basic algorithms or logic sets, the functional testing may provide adequate assurance of reliability of the computerised system. For critical and/or more complex systems the verification testing that is conducted at the IQ, OQ & PQ stages provides only a limited level of assurance that the system does what it purports to do, reliably. This level of testing provides only limited assurance of the operation and reliability of hidden functions and code. For complex systems there should also be a high level of assurance that the development of the software has ensured delivery and operation of a quality product that is structurally sound, clearly defined and controlled.

Test scripts should be developed, formally documented and used to demonstrate that the system has been installed, and is operating and performing satisfactorily. These test scripts should be related to the User Requirements Specifications and the Functional specifications for the system. This schedule of testing should be specifically aimed at demonstrating the validation of the system. In software engineering terms satisfactory results obtained from the testing should confirm design validation.

Any processing equipment and activities related to or controlled by the computer system would require additional IQ, OQ and PQ testing regimes. It may be appropriate to combine test phases and test scopes for a group of equipment or activities, and this should be defined in a test plan or strategy. Regulated Users should be able to demonstrate formal acceptance of systems after testing and controlled transfer into the live operational environment.

VALIDATION STRATEGIES AND PRIORITIES

Regulated users need to be able to provide evidence for their computerized systems to demonstrate their range, complexity, functionality, control and validation status. For the validation of computerised systems there should be a system in place that assures the formal assessment and reporting of quality and performance measures for all the life-cycle stages of software and system development, its implementation, qualification and acceptance, operation, modification, requalification, maintenance and retirement. This should enable both the regulated user, and competent authority, to have a high level of confidence in the integrity of both the processes executed within the controlling computer system(s) and in those processes controlled by and/or linked to the computer system(s), within the prescribed operating environment(s).

The regulated user's range of computerised systems needs to be formally listed in an inventory and the scope/extent of validation for each detailed in a consolidated written Validation programme. Validation scope should include G x P compliance criteria, ranked for product/process quality and data integrity risk criticality, should the system fail or malfunction. This process represents one of the most important pre-requisites of Validation Master Planning, in that it is essential to assign priorities and attention to those systems (and features within systems) that represent the highest potential for disaster, should they malfunction or become inoperative. The risk analyses and the results, together with reasoning for critical or non-critical classifications, should be documented. Risks potentially impacting on G x P compliance should be clearly identified. There are a number of techniques to help identify and analyse risks and to select risk reduction and control measures. For further information refer to the GAMP Guide appendix and the GAMP Forum special interest group paper on 'Functional Risk Assessment'. G x P compliance evidence is essential for the following aspects and activities related to computerised systems:

- Data input (capture and integrity), data filing, data-processing, networks, process control and monitoring, electronic records, archiving, retrieval, printing, access, change management, audit trails and decisions associated with any automated G x P related activity; in this context, examples of G x P related activities might include:
- Regulatory submissions,
- R&D,
- Clinical trials,
- Procurement,
- Dispensing/ weighing,
- Manufacturing,
- Assembly,
- Testing,
- Quality control,
- Quality assurance,
- Inventory control,
- Storage and distribution,
- Training,
- Calibration,
- Maintenance,
- Contracts/ technical agreements and associated records and reports.

Historically, these systems have relied on manual systems, some electromechanical controls and paper based documentation. The introduction of computerised systems does not diminish the need for compliance with G x P requirements and guidelines. The current Good Automated Manufacturing Practice (GAMP) Supplier Guide provides essential guidance to suppliers of software to the Industry. The guide also provides a concise explanation of the interrelationship between various stages of software development and the requirements for Installation, Operational and Performance Qualification. The GAMP Guide identifies five different categories of software.

GAMP VALIDATION APPROACH BASED ON DIFFERENT CATEGORIES OF SOFTWARE PRODUCTS

The GAMP Guide may be referred to as appropriate for detailed guidance both in the core project management section, the quality narrative and the specific appendices. Categories summarized from GAMP are given in Table 1:

Table 1: Summary for categories of software

Category	*Software type*	*Validation approach*
1	Operating system	Record version (including service pack). The Operating System will be challenged indirectly by the functional testing of the application. For non-configurable firmware record version. Calibrate instruments as necessary. Verify operation against user requirements.
2	Firmware	For configurable firmware record version and configuration. Calibrate instruments as necessary and verify operation against user requirements. Manage custom (bespoke) firmware as Category 5 software.
3	Standard software package	Record version (and configuration of environment) and verify operation against user requirements. Consider auditing the supplier for critical and complex applications.
4	Configurable software packages	Record version and configuration, and verify operation against user requirements. Normally audit the supplier for critical and complex applications. Manage any custom (bespoke) programming as Category 5.
5	Custom software	Audit supplier and validate complete system.

However, this pre-defined category approach may be difficult to apply to complex integrated computerised systems where different GAMP category 'levels' are effectively combined. Many systems span the category levels. For all critical systems a holistic risk-based approach is necessary. This should consider the risks from the entire pharmaceutical application. Quality assurance controls, qualification work and risk reduction measures can cascade from this to consider each of the elements comprising the computerised system. GAMP guidance is considered to be scaleable for large, medium and small, complex and simple systems. Where software and systems do not appear to fit readily into this category system then it is for users to apply judgement in determining particular quality measures, validation strategies and acceptance criteria. For instance, under particular circumstances the operating system configuration may contribute to the overall risk of the system and the level of validation should reflect this. Inspectors will be interested in the company's approach to identifying G x P risks and the criteria for assessing the fitness for purpose of the system application.

There are a number of additional important aspects that would be required in the documentation and records necessary to support a validation exercise. These aspects relate to on-going evaluation and system maintenance. As a result the documentation and records for validation of a computer system would also require information and records for the following aspects of system control:

- Evaluation records to demonstrate that the system works as described in the URS (verification stage and on-going monitoring).
- Records of operator training (introduction and on-going training).
- Procedure for on-going monitoring, this procedure would interlink the error report system and the deviation reports system with the change control procedure.
- Maintenance of user manuals and SOPs for all systems.

RETROSPECTIVE VALIDATION

Retrospective validation is not equivalent to prospective validation and is not an option for new systems. Firms will be required to justify the continued use of existing computerised systems that have been inadequately documented for validation purposes. Some of this may be based on historical evidence but much will be concerned with re-defining, documenting, re-qualifying, prospectively validating applications and introducing G x P related life-cycle controls. Reference should also be made to GAMP Forum's forthcoming guidance on 'Legacy Systems'. Inspectors may be interested in seeing whether 'system descriptions' are available and that documented evidence exists that the system has been checked/tested against URS and other specifications. Risk and criticality analysis and assessment of supplier may also be relevant. A documented evaluation of system history *i.e.,* error logs, changes made, evaluation of user manuals and SOPs would also be expected to provide some of the documentation relating to the 'controlled system' in place of formal validation evidence.

A significant number of legacy systems may operate satisfactorily and reliably, however, this does not preclude them from a requirement for validation. The approach to be taken is to provide data and information to support the retrospective documentation of the system to provide validation and requalification evidence. G x Ps have required the validation of computerized systems for many years. It should therefore be noted that a lack of prospective validation evidence for computerised systems would increasingly be seen as a serious deviation from G x Ps by a number of regulatory authorities. However retrospective validation might be justified if a non-G x P system is newly classified as a G x P system.

The principles identified above for computer systems validation should be addressed where a retrospective validation approach has been undertaken for a legacy system. For legacy systems, because of their age and unique characteristics, the system development documentation and records appropriate for validation may not be available. As a result the approach taken to establish and document system reliability and on-going assurance based on the "build-in-quality" concept for software development would, of necessity, be different to a current system.

Nevertheless, the validation strategy would be consistent with the principles established for classic retrospective validation where the assurances are established, based on compilation and formal review of the history of use, maintenance, error report and change control system records and risk assessment of the system and its functions. These activities should be based on documented URS's. If historical data do not encompass the current range of operating parameters, or if there have been significant changes between past and current practices, then retrospective data would not of itself support validation of the current system.The validation exercise for on-going evaluation of legacy systems should entail inclusion of the systems under all the documentation, records and procedural requirements associated with a current system. For example, change control, audit trail(s), (where appropriate), data and system security, additional development or modification of software under a QMS, maintenance of data integrity, system back up requirements, operator (user) training and on-going evaluation of the system operations.

What Documentation is Required for Regulatory Validation?

The following documents are what auditors like to see in a Quality System Validation:

- Software Validation Protocol;
- Network Diagram;
- Software Requirements Specification;
- Risk Analysis (the GAMP standard template is recommended);
- Part 11 Compliance Analysis;

- Design Specification (only for systems or areas of the system which contain custom code such as integrations between your Product Lifecycle Management (PLM) and Enterprise Resource Planning (ERP) systems)
- Test Plan;
- Test Specifications/Test Cases; and
- Final Validation Report.

These documents may be combined so long as you capture all of the information.

Validation Plan

There should be a computerized system validation master plan that describes the policy, approach, organization and planning, resources, execution and management of computerized system validation for all of the G x P systems in use on-site.

The computerized system validation master plan (CSVMP) should contain, for example, the scope, risk management approach and a complete inventory list of all G x P systems. The CSVMP should also outline the controls including but not limited to backup and recovery of data, contingency planning, disaster recovery, change control management, configuration management, error handling, maintenance and support, corrective measures and system access control policies, that will be in place to maintain the validated state of the systems.

The CSVMP should refer to protocols and reports as appropriate, for the conduct of validation. Where appropriate, computerized systems should be classified based on risk assessment relating to their G x P impact.

Validation Protocol

Validation should be executed in accordance with the validation protocol and applicable SOPs. A validation protocol should define the validation strategy, including roles and responsibilities and documentation and activities to be performed. The protocol should cover the specification, development, testing, review and release of the computerized system for G x P use. The validation protocol should be tailored to the system type, impact, risks and requirements applicable to the system in which it will be used.

System /Software Requirements Specification

This document details system requirements. However, this is more than just a list of functional requirements it also should capture a good description of the various components that make up the system so that everyone has a clear understanding of what this system involves. The Requirements Specification also needs to include information around physical hardware requirements, physical software requirements, client user requirements, training requirements and detail about any customizations or integration with other systems.

Network Diagram

This required document provides a visual layout of how the system is configured on the network. It serves to demonstrate that you understand how your system is configured for your implementation.

Risk Analysis

This document evaluates application safety and identifies potential hazards, the causes and the effect that each hazard has on the application safety and use. Because this is a business system the risk assessment should focus on the business processes being managed by the system vs. a more traditional FMEA risk assessment for software programs which are part of a device and pose direct patient risk. Not all risks will be solely mitigated by the software, some risks are mitigated procedurally.

21 CFR Part 11 Compliance Analysis

This document evaluates system applicability/requirements for the use of electronic signature as required by the FDA in 21 CFR, Part 11.

Design Specification

Typically a design specification is not required for a purchased configurable business quality system. In the event that major integration or customization is to be performed as part of the project this document may be added as deemed appropriate by the project team and quality reviewer.

Verification Protocol (Test Plan)

This document defines the type of testing to be completed along with the procedures and schedules for those tests.

Test Specifications (Test Cases)

This document contains the system level test cases, based on the functional requirements set forth in the Requirements

Specification

If these are separate or maintained as an attachment to the Verification Protocol it makes it easier to add modules or new phases to the validation package while limiting revision time. Plus they are easier to format and work with testing wise.

Requirements Traceability Matrix

This matrix details all system requirements including Requirements ID, and links them to the Test Case IDs. This is a required document that can be helpful going forward when a change occurs, as it makes it easier to assess and identify where there is impact.

Final Validation Report

The validation report should provide a summary of all documentation associated with the validation of the software and test case results. This report should include both a summary of all the validation activities and define how the system will be managed in production. Information such as what work instructions are used to train users to use the system, what system support is available, how the system will be backed up, and how change control will be managed are extremely important elements captured in this document. In essence it puts a bow on the validation package. A validation summary report should be prepared, summarizing system validation activities. It should outline the validation process and activities and describe and justify any deviations from the process and activities specified in the protocol. The report should include all critical and major test discrepancies that occurred during the verification/ validation testing and describe how these were resolved. The report should be approved after the resolution of any issue identified during validation and the system should then be released and ready for G x P use.

DESIGN QUALIFICATION

A design review should be conducted to verify that the proposed design and configuration of the system is suitable for its intended purpose and will meet all applicable user and functional requirements specifications. This process that may be referred to as design qualification, may include a review of vendor documentation, if applicable, and verification that requirements specifications are traceable to proposed design and configuration specifications.

BUILD AND PROJECT IMPLEMENTATION

Once the system requirements and the system design and configuration are specified and verified, system development or "build and test" activities may begin. The development activities may occur as a dedicated phase following completion of specification of system requirements and design and configuration (such as when adhering to a sequential or "waterfall" development model). Alternatively, development activities may occur iteratively as requirements are specified and verified (such as when prototyping or rapid-development methodologies are employed).

Vendor-Supplied Systems

For vendor-supplied systems, development controls for the vendor-supplied portion of the computerized system should be assessed during the vendor evaluation or supplier qualification. For custom-built systems and configurable systems, as well as for vendor-supplied systems that include custom components (such as custom-coded interfaces or custom report tools) and/or require configuration (such as configuration of security profiles in the software or configuration of the hardware within the network infrastructure), the system should be developed under an appropriate documented quality management system.

Custom-Developed Systems

For custom-developed systems or modules, the quality management system controls should include development of code in accordance with documented programming standards, review of code for adherence to programming standards and design specifications, and development testing that may include unit testing and module/integration testing. System prototyping and rapid, agile development methodologies may be employed during the system build and development testing phase. There should be an adequate level of documentation of these activities.

Preparation for the System Qualification Phases

The system development and build phase should be followed by the system qualification phase. This typically consists of installation, operational and performance testing, but actual qualification required may vary depending on the scope of the validation project as defined in the validation plan and based upon a documented and justified risk assessment.

Prior to the initiation of the system qualification phase, the software program and requirements and specifications documents should be finalized and subsequently managed under formal change control.

Persons who will be conducting the system qualification should be trained to adhere to the following requirements for system qualification:

- Test documentation should be generated to provide evidence of testing;
- Test documentation should comply with good documentation practices;
- Any discrepancies between actual test results and expected results should be documented and adequately resolved based upon risk prior to proceeding to subsequent test phases.

INSTALLATION QUALIFICATION

The first phase of system testing is installation qualification (IQ), also referred to as installation verification testing. IQ should provide documented evidence that the computerized system, including software and associated hardware, is installed and configured in the intended system testing and production environments according to written specifications. The IQ will verify, for example, that the computer hardware on which the software application is installed has the proper firmware and operating system; that all components are present and in the proper condition; and that each component is installed per the manufacturer or developer instructions. IQ should include verification that configurable elements of the system are configured as specified. Where appropriate, this could also be done during OQ.

OPERATIONAL QUALIFICATION

The OQ, or operational/functional verification resting, should provide documented evidence that the software and hardware function as intended throughout anticipated operating ranges.

Functional testing should include, based upon risk:

- An appropriate degree of challenge testing (such as boundary, range, limit, nonsense entry testing) to verify the system appropriately handles erroneous entries or erroneous use;
- Verification that alarms are raised based upon alarm conditions;
- Flags are raised to signal invalid or altered data.

Hardware

The extent of validation should depend on the complexity of the system. Appropriate tests and challenges to the hardware should be performed as part of validation. Hardware is considered to be equipment and the focus should be on location, maintenance and calibration of hardware, as well as on qualification.

The qualification of the hardware should prove:

- That the capacity of the hardware matches its assigned function
- That it operates within the operational limits
- That the hardware configuration settings are appropriate and meet user and functional requirements;
- That it performs acceptably under challenging conditions
- Reproducibility/ consistency.

Some of the hardware qualification may be performed by the computer vendor. However, the ultimate responsibility for the suitability of equipment used remains with the company. Qualification protocols, reports (including data) should be kept by the company for the hardware in its configured state. When qualification information is produced by an outside firm, *e.g.,* computer vendor, the records should be sufficiently complete (including general results and protocols) to allow the company to assess the adequacy of the qualification and verification activities. A mere certification of suitability from the vendor, for example, will be inadequate.

Software

Functional testing of software should provide assurance that computer programs (especially those that control critical activities in manufacturing and processing) will function consistently within pre-established limits for both normal conditions as well as under worst-case conditions (*e.g.,* out-of-limit, out-of-range, alarm conditions). Functional testing, also known as "black box" testing, involves inputting normal and abnormal test cases; then, evaluating outputs against those expected. It can apply to computer software or to a total system (reference: CEFIC GMP).

PERFORMANCE QUALIFICATION AND USER ACCEPTANCE TESTING

PQ, that includes UAT, should be conducted to verify the intended system use and administration outlined in the URS, or equivalent document. The PQ should be conducted in the production environment or in a validation environment that is equivalent to the production environment in terms of overall software and hardware configuration. PQ testing should also include, as applicable, an appropriate degree of stress/ load/ volume testing based upon the anticipated system use and performance requirements in the production environment. In addition, an appropriate degree of end-to-end or regression testing of the system should be conducted to verify the system performs reliably when system components are integrated in the fully-configured system deployed in the production environment.

UAT should be conducted by system users to verify the adequacy of system use SOPs and data review SOP(s) and training programmes. The UAT should include verification of the ability to readily discern invalid and altered data, including the ability to efficiently review electronic data and metadata, such as audit trails. IT system administrators should verify the adequacy of system administration SOP(s) and controls that will be routinely executed during normal operational use and administration of the system, including backup/ restore and archival/ retrieval processes.

Why don't just purchase Validation Documentation?

The FDA requires that verification and validation activities cover how a system is configured in the customer's environment so there is no "one size fits all" validation. Many times software vendors will try to sell prepackaged validation documentation. Because a vendor selling a prepackaged validation does not know your requirements they try and list every functionality that the system has and let you whittle down the list of requirements based on your use of the system. Since they do not know exactly which requirements you are going to keep and which requirements you are going to throw out they can't group the test cases to contain multiple requirements. Again, it looks like a great deal because they can show you all of these test cases that you are going to get with their packaged validation. What they aren't telling you is that sorting out which ones you want and don't want takes a lot of time (possibly weeks) that your team might not have.

Failure of CSV: Common Reasons

Without adequate planning and preparation, computer system validation can encounter several problems, eventually leading to failure of the process. Problems include:

- Inadequate documentation of plans
- Inadequate definition of what constitutes the computer system
- Inadequate definition of expected results
- Inadequate specification of software
- Software that does not meet its specifications
- Unavailable source code for software

If you're looking for detailed recommendations for efficient execution of validation projects, as well as information on user validation [1].

CSV: Common Challenges

Computer system validation can come up against several challenges, including the risk of system failure, restrictive company policies and increasingly stringent regulatory requirements. Another significant issue is when users need to take action to balance the risk *vs.* cost equation after risk categories are defined.

CSV: Planning

It's clear that there is no substitute for proper planning before undertaking computer system validation. Once owners, deliverables and check points are in place, validation can actually be a streamlined and smoothly accomplished. In the validation of moderate and relatively low-risk systems, a risk-based approach is also the ideal way to gain efficiencies. To evaluate a simple method to establish system risk level, a risk based-approach is the most significant means to gain efficiencies in the validation of moderate and low risk systems. The risk level of the system can be used to determine what activities ought to be included in the validation and the rigor and intensity with which those activities are carried out. The FDA guidelines urge regulated companies to base their effort to validate systems on the risks associated with their failure.

How to upgrade or add modules to a Validated System

If you designed your validation documentation well it should be a fairly straight forward change control process to upgrade to new software versions or add new modules/ functionality to your system. If it has been less than one year since the original validation, you should be able to review. the documents by adding requirements for the new functionality into the Software Requirements Specification under the functional requirements section and updating other validation documents accordingly. Then either append the original test case document or add new module test cases as an attachment. Keep in mind you should always retest some of the security elements to make sure there was no impact as well as verify that history files are maintained for new functionality that has a quality impact. If it has been more than one year since the original validation, follow your change control procedure and include an assessment of other changes which may warrant full revalidation. Typically the software manufacturer has a major new software release that you will want to include or you may need/want to upgrade your infrastructure. In this case you need review the previous validation, add new functionality, update the test cases to match current business processes, update work instructions and re-test. Again, this is when those process-based test cases pay off.

CONCLUSIONS

The FDA requires that software systems used for quality purposes in place of paper records be validated for their intended use [Title 21 CFR Part

820(i)]. This means that when using COTS systems, companies must verify that the software is configured correctly to meet their business needs. Even if you are intending to do a relatively "vanilla" implementation you need to have documented evidence verifying that the system was correctly installed and configured correctly for your intended use. Performing software validation right the first time will save medical manufacturers both time and money now and in the future. Reason for computer system validation is as highlighted in Fig. 1.

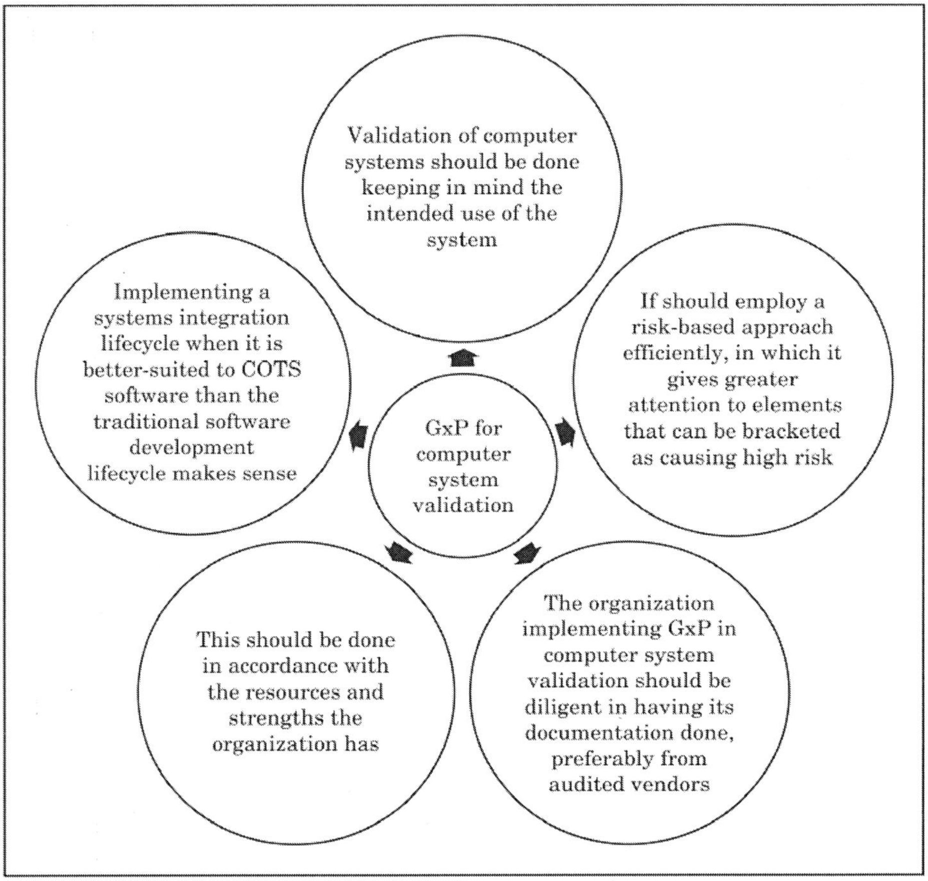

Fig. 1: Reason for computer system validation

Effective, risk-based validation of computerized systems is an important part of maintaining regulatory compliance and product quality in modern laboratories. Inefficient or ineffective CSV processes prevent projects from being delivered on time and within budget and can also result in regulatory action. With regards to the FDA, for example, regulatory action due to failure to perform adequate CSV can be legally and financially devastating to an organization.

Take some time to review regulatory guidance documentation, and not just those that focus on computer system validation (CSV) such as 21 CFR Part 11 and Eudralex 4 Annex 11. Spend time looking at the GCP, GLP, and cGMP predicate rules (21 CFR Parts 58, 211, 820, 600, etc.) for pharmaceutical industry. Specifically look for references to documentation required to support regulated business processes. These form the basis for determining what computerized systems and associated electronic records are subject to regulatory requirements, and their relative patient, quality, and regulatory risk.

Review your internal policies and procedures related to Computer System Validation.

- Are they consistent with requirements from the previously referenced regulatory guidance?
- Have you incorporated risk assessment and management as an integral part of your CSV and system development processes, as outlined in industry best practice?

Having spent some time re-familiarizing yourself with the regulatory basis for CSV requirements, and your internal CSV framework, turn your attention to your existing portfolio of regulated computerized systems.

- Do you have an up-to-date inventory of systems that are subject to validation requirements?
- Do you have a schedule for periodic review of your validated systems in the inventory to ensure incremental changes have not altered the validated status of each system?
- Does your periodic review include potential impacts from changes in regulatory guidance documents?

If you can answer yes to these questions, you can have some confidence in the validated state of your current systems portfolio. If not, this might be a good time to address policy and procedural gaps and move forward with assessing overall compliance of at least your most critical systems.

When reviewing regulatory guidance, don't overlook recent updates to existing or newly issued regulations and related guidance documents. A couple of examples include the non-binding Guidance for Industry and Food and Drug Administration Staff on Mobile Medical Applications issued on September 25, 2013, and the amendment to the Federal Food, Drug, and Cosmetic Act incorporating the Drug Quality and Security Act signed into law on November 27, 2013.

While neither of these actions directly impact existing regulations specifically dealing with computer system validation, they may extend the scope of regulatory oversight for systems used in these areas to deliver safe and reliable products to patients. It will be worth watching specific enforcement activities in the industry segments impacted by such emerging legislation and guidance to see how CSV requirements may be extended. Likewise the increased use of emerging computerized technologies in supporting regulated business processes (mobile devices, cloud computing, big data, etc.) needs to be evaluated for its impact on current internal validation policies and procedures. In looking at your upcoming major computer system projects, incorporating good system and CSV quality practices early on will save time and effort later in implementation and deployment.

REFERENCES

[1] 21 CFR Part 11
[2] EMA Annex 11, Section 4
[3] EMA GMP Annex 11
[4] ISO 134845: 2003
[5] Supplementary guidelines on good manufacturing practice: validation. In: WHO Expert Committee on Specifications for Pharmaceutical Preparations: fortieth report. Geneva: World Health Organization; 2006: Annex 4 (WHO Technical Report Series, No. 937).
[6] WHO guidance on good data and record management practices; 2016: Annex 5 (WHO Technical Report Series, No. 996).

FURTHER READINGS

Supplementary guidelines on good manufacturing practice: validation. Qualification of systems and equipment. *In*: WHO Expert Committee on Specifications for Pharmaceutical Preparations: fortieth report. Geneva: World Health Organization; 2006: Annex 4, Appendix 6 (WHO Technical Report Series, No. 937).

WHO good manufacturing practices for pharmaceutical products: main principles. *In*: WHO Expert Committee on Specifications for Pharmaceutical Preparations: forty-eighth report. Geneva: World Health Organization; 2014: Annex 2 (WHO Technical Report Series, No. 986), also available on CD-ROM and online.

17

Water System Validation

ABSTRACT

Water is widely used as a raw material (excipient / solvent / vehicle) as well as in cleaning applications. The water quality needed can range from general laboratory grade to ultrapure water matching the sensitivity of critical research and analytical techniques. In addition, the water quantity can vary from a few gallons for a single end user to several hundred or thousand gallons per day for an entire facility. Understanding and clearly defining these needs must be the first step in the process for the design and / or selection of any water purification system. In addition, the designer must have in-depth working knowledge and experience in water purification, including an understanding of water contaminants, water purification technologies, and system design. In this informational chapter efforts have been made to include some of the chemical and microbiological concerns unique to water and its preparation and uses. The chapter provides information about water quality attributes and processing techniques that can be used to improve water quality. It also discusses water system validation and gives a description of minimum water quality standards that should be considered when selecting a water source including sampling and system controls. It is equally important for water systems to be operated and maintained in a state of control to provide assurance of operational stability and therefore the capability to provide water that meets established water quality standards. This chapter should be considered as educational, and the user should also refer to existing regulations or guidelines like USP or ICH or WHO issues, as well as operational and engineering guides and / or other regulatory guidance for water. This chapter is not, and should not be considered, an all-inclusive document on pharmaceutical waters.

INTRODUCTION

Basic information and points to be considered for the processing, holding, monitoring, and use of water. It is the user's responsibility to ensure that:

1. The selection of the type and specifications of water is appropriate for its intended use.
2. Water production and quality meet applicable governmental regulations and guidance.
3. The pharmacopeial specifications.
4. Water used in the preparation of reagents for analysis or the performance of required tests meets USP requirements.

Control and monitoring of the chemical and endotoxin purity of waters are important for complying with the requirements of the monographs. More stringent requirements may be needed for some applications to ensure suitability for particular uses. Control of the microbiological quality of water is also important for many of its uses. This chapter contains various chemical, microbiological, processing, and engineering concepts of importance to users of water. Water system validation, process control levels, and specifications are also presented later in this chapter.

SOURCE WATER CONSIDERATIONS

Source (raw) water is the water that enters the facility from natural surface waters like rivers and reservoirs, deep-bed well waters, sea waters, or some combination of these, potentially including multiple locations of each type of source water. Thus, source water can be supplied from these various origins (public or private), from municipalities' on-site water sourcing, or by external delivery such as a truck. It is the responsibility of the users of any source water to ensure that the water used in the production of drug substances, as well as water for indirect drug product contact or for purification system feed water purposes meets, at a minimum, drinking (potable) water standards. It is possible that source water may not be potable and safe to drink, such water may require pretreatment to meet drinking water standards. There are many regulations to establish limits on the types and quantities of certain chemical and microbiological contaminants and ensure that the water will contain safe quantities of chemical and microbial species. Where water supplies are from regulated water utility companies, less stringent monitoring may be possible because the attributes may be tested regularly and ensured by the supplier but if water is withdrawn from a non-regulated supply, it should be sampled and tested appropriately at a suitable frequency that takes into account local environmental and seasonal changes and other quality fluctuations. The chemical and microbial attributes of the starting source water are important to the ability of the water system to remove or reduce these impurities to meet the finished water Specifications. Using the microbial enumeration methods a reasonable maximum bacterial Action Level for source water is 500cfu/ml [1]. This limit should be used as an Action Level indicating the need for improving water purification process to avoid the penetration of any type of microbial flora into the finished drinking water. However it is not a maximum contaminant level (MCL) for drinking water. High microbial and chemical levels in source water may indicate a potable water system upset, a change in the supply or original water source, a broken water main, or inadequate disinfection, and therefore resulting in potentially contaminated water. Considering the potential concern about objectionable microbial and chemical contaminants in the source water, in-house remedial actions is needed which may include performing additional tests on source water (as well as the finished water) or pre-treating the water with additional microbial and chemical purification operations. Control of objectionable chemical contaminants at the source water stage eliminates the need to specifically test for some of them *e.g.,* trihalomethanes and elemental impurities after the water has been further purified, assuming there is no opportunity for recontamination. Source waters can be used for non-product contact purposes such as for non-contact cooling systems. Such water may not normally be required to meet drinking water standards. Under such circumstances, the quality standards for this water when used in a pharmaceutical facility should be subject to quality standards established by the user and defensible to regulatory agencies.

WATERS USED FOR PHARMACEUTICAL MANUFACTURING AND TESTING PURPOSES

There are many different grades of water used for pharmaceutical purposes. These waters can be divided into two general types:

- Bulk waters, which are typically produced on site where they are used;
- Sterile waters, which are produced, packaged, and sterilized to preserve microbial quality throughout their packaged shelf life.

Many times additional substances are added during water system processing but this addition should be justified either to improve water quality or to preserve it from other contamination. It could be understood by following examples.

1. ***The use of softeners is common place:*** A softener is used to remove calcium and magnesium ions so technically two sodium ions are added for each hard ion. The purpose of sodium displacement is to protect downstream equipment from the hard water. The sodium ions are eventually removed sufficiently, and this is proven when the water sample passes the test for Water Conductivity.
2. ***Use of ozone as a sanitant:*** Ozone is added to the storage tank for microbial control. This could be considered an added substance, unless the ozone is destroyed before use, as is normally the case.
3. Other notable examples include the addition of chlorine to kill bacteria in the pretreatment system, use of bisulfite to reduce chlorine to

chloride and protect downstream equipment, and use of a nitrogen blanket for protection from atmospheric contamination.

A brief description of the various types of waters [2] commonly used in pharmaceutical industry is as per Table 1.

Table 1: Various types of waters used in pharmaceutical industry

Type of water	*Considered source water*	*Process used*	*Use in*
Potable water	Raw water from natural source	Filtration	Drinking, Cleaning of equipment
Purified water	Potable water	Deionization, Distillation, Ion exchange, Reverse osmosis, Filtration, Other suitable purification procedures	Non-parenteral manufacturing, Equipment cleaning
Water for injection	Potable water	Distillation,	Parenteral manufacturing, Cleaning of parenteral manufacturing equipment
Water for haemodialysis	Potable water	Purified to reduce chemical and microbiological components	Haemodialysis applications
Pure steam	Potable water	Vaporization	Porous load sterilization processes, Product or cleaning solutions heated by direct steam injection, Humidification of processes
Sterile purified water	Purified water	Sterilization of purified water	Non-parenteral compendial dosage forms, Analytical applications
Sterile water for injection	Water for injection	Sterilization of water for injection	Sterile diluents for parenteral products
Bacteriostatic water for injection	Water for injection	Addition of antimicrobial agent	Diluents for parenteral products (multi-dose units)
Sterile water for irrigation	Water for injection	Sterilization and packaging	Irrigation
Sterile water for inhalation	Water for injection	Packaged and sterilized	Inhalation

VARIOUS CONTAMINANTS IN WATER

Contaminants can be classified into four main groups [2]:

1. Particulates are small particles such as silt and sand that can be visible to the naked eye as well as sub-micron suspended matter (colloids).
2. Inorganics are minerals that dissolve in water to form positive and negative ions, including sodium chloride, hardness ions such as calcium and magnesium, and dissolved carbon dioxide.

3. Organics are chemical contaminants containing carbon that can be naturally occurring (*i.e.,* from decay of vegetation) or man-made (*i.e.,* industrial chemicals, detergents, and pesticides).
4. Microorganisms include algae, bacteria, viruses, and by products of bacteria (endotoxins).

No one technology can remove 100 percent of all four classes of contaminants. Therefore, any water purification system must utilize a combination of technologies to produce pure and ultrapure water.

KEY ELEMENTS IN DESIGNING A HIGH –PURITY WATER SYSTEM

A total water purification system consists of several parts [3]:

Makeup Water Purification System

Using a combination of purification technologies to purify tap feed water, the makeup purification system produces the required water quality and sufficient quantities for the entire facility. The makeup system typically provides the bulk of the purification that is required for the total system, with subsequent steps added to maintain water quality and/or provide higher purity levels.

Storage Reservoir

Purified water from the makeup system typically is stored in a reservoir that helps meet daily needs and cover peak periods of high demand from laboratories. Both the makeup water system's water production rate and the reservoir must be sized to meet the daily and peak usage demands for purified water.

Distribution Loop

An appropriately sized distribution pump ensures water is distributed through the piping network at the correct flow rates and pressures. Distribution equipment often includes additional equipment such as in-line ultraviolet (UV) lamps and filtration to maintain or improve the quality of the water being distributed. Water quality monitoring equipment also may be added to ensure the product water is within specifications.

Point-of-Use Delivery and Polishing

Throughout the piping distribution network, water can be used for feeding instruments, dishwashers, and autoclaves, general glassware rinsing, and buffer and media preparation. Additional point-of-use polishing also can be added to meet ultrapure water quality needs for more sensitive applications.

A Step -by-Step Total Purification System Design

Step 1: Defining User Requirements and Pure Water Specifications

A successful water system design must start with a clear and precise definition of the pure water needs at the facility. Two simple questions need to be answered in detail:

1. What is the purity level required at each point of use?
2. How much water is required at each point of use?

Answering these simple questions is not always an easy task.

The designer, often with help from a water system supplier, must investigate all user requirements before starting the design phase. For example, the requirements may vary from general rinsing to highly sensitive analytical techniques within the same facility. The delivery points also vary from gooseneck faucets and simple valves to instruments and point-of-use ultrapure polishing systems.

Step 1a—Defining Water Purity Level

Too often when end users are asked to define what purity level they use or need, their responses are "DI water," "RO water," or "house DI water." Others may respond, "The water must be really pure." These general responses neither provide the specifics needed to design a water system nor define whether the water quality is adequate for an end user's application. Several organizations provide detailed standards for specific water quality types, including ASTM International, Clinical and Laboratory Standards Institute (CLSI), College of American Pathologists (CAP), International Organization for Standardization (ISO), and United States Pharmacopeia (USP). Most organizations classify water purity levels as Type I, Type II, and Type III, with Type I being the most pure. Although similar, each purity level is slightly different across the different published standards. End users typically follow the standards closely tied to their industry. For example, hospital, medical, and clinical laboratories tend to follow CLSI or CAP standards. University researchers and industrial laboratory technicians follow ASTM. In some cases, end users may specify a variation of the water quality standards to meet a sensitive application requirement. For example, a scientist using gas chromatography-mass spectrometry (GCMS) for trace organic analysis may require total oxidizable carbon (TOC) levels controlled lower than specified by the Type I standard. Therefore, it is important to define the required water quality at each point of use in as much detail as possible. Often end users do not know the required water quality. An experienced designer or water system supplier can help determine the required purity level to match the specific application requirements.

Step 1b—Defining Water Volume Requirements

Once the water quality requirements are defined, the water volume used must be determined. Start by determining all possible usage points from gooseneck faucets at sinks to glassware washers. How much water is used at each use point during a day? when the water is required also must be determined. Is the water used in a normal eight-hour workday or over a full 24-hour day? Is water used on weekdays and/or weekends? Is the usage evenly spread out over the workday, or are there peak demands during a day when high volumes of pure water are needed? For example, a laboratory preparing large volumes of media and/ or buffers might require as much as 80 percent of the water in the first few hours of the day.

It is essential to determine the requirements of instruments that are fed pure water. For example, most glassware washers require a minimum feed pressure and can require several gallons of pure water for rinsing within a few minutes. Fortunately, most manufacturers include this information in instrument specifications with the utility requirements. Estimating maximum simultaneous usage is another factor that needs to be considered when there are multiple points of use. Simply stated, how many points of use are open at one time and for how long? This information ensures the water purification system is sized correctly. An incorrect assessment can be detrimental and result in a shortage of water or an oversized system with higher-than-necessary costs and space. Other important factors to consider include water quality monitoring, ease of use, cost, space requirements, building architecture, and regulatory and validation needs. Therefore, it helps to create a detailed map outlining all pure water requirements, quality, quantity, usage profiles, pressure requirements, and other factors to obtain a successful total pure water system.

Step 2—Pure Water Distribution Design and Equipment

The traditional approach to pure water distribution design has been to lay out a single loop with several hundred or thousand feet of pipe throughout a facility with a single makeup water purification system, storage tank, and distribution pump located in a central location. However, several possible configurations for the design of a total pure water system are available. All these configurations can have an impact on parameters such as flow rate and water quality. These different approaches can help determine and optimize the design that best meets the needs of the facility.

a. ***Approach 1a—Central Location:*** This configuration comprises one large makeup system with storage and distribution equipment located in a central location, with purified water distributed throughout several laboratories or floors and completing a distribution loop that returns back to the storage at the central location.

b. ***Approach 1b—Central Location, Duplex:*** A variation of the first centrally located system is the use of duplex makeup water purification systems providing purified water to the same storage reservoir and distribution equipment. The duplex approach provides some redundancy at the primary makeup level, which reduces the risk of completely shutting down a facility. When one system is down for routine maintenance or service, the second system is still providing purified water to the facility.

c. ***Approach 2—Configuration by Floor or Department:*** This approach divides the total system into parts (floor by floor or department by department) with each smaller system designed to meet specific requirements. Water quality or quantity required from location to location within a facility may be significantly different. A system can be dedicated to areas with similar pure water requirements. For example, a large system with a separate distribution loop can address high volume needs, such as feeding high-volume glassware washers. Other departments or floors can be addressed with smaller systems designed for their needs. This can sometimes be a better approach than trying to build high-consumption requirements into the complete piping distribution network.

d. ***Approach 3—By Floor, Department, and Point of Use:*** This configuration addresses specific needs by using small point-of use systems that include the makeup purification system, storage, and additional polishing as required on a much smaller scale. This approach avoids the need to extend piping to all departments and potentially simplifies the main total water purification system. A small, dedicated system completely independent from the larger central system also allows scientists doing critical research to have full control of their pure water.

Step 3—Water Distribution

Once an approach is selected for facility-wide water distribution, important design considerations should be followed to ensure the distribution piping layout does not compromise water quality. Bacteria control within a distribution piping loop is a key challenge in the design.

a. ***Continuous Recirculation:*** Stagnant water conditions will result in bacteria proliferation and a contaminated system. To avoid water stagnation, it is critical that the loop be designed to circulate the water continuously throughout the entire piping network. Piping should be laid out to re-circulate water to and from every point of use (ideally in one continuous path) and return back to the storage tank.

b. ***Minimize Dead Legs:*** A dead leg is considered any section of the water distribution system where water is not continuously moving. There are published recommendations of good design guidelines. For example, the 6D and 2D rules aim to minimize dead legs. These guidelines recommend that a dead leg branching off a main distribution loop be minimized to six or two times the diameter of the piping run. Thus, if a main piping run is through a ceiling space above point of use locations, it is imperative that the piping run drop down directly to each point-of-use location and then continue back up to the ceiling to continue to the next point-of-use location. Design practices today are moving toward eliminating dead legs as much as possible, including the use of special valves at point-of-use locations. A zero dead leg diaphragm valve (also referred to as a zero-static or T-diaphragm valve) includes a flow through tee built into the valve that allows water from the main piping loop to flow through the main body of the valve. Some manufacturers are making gooseneck faucets with designs that allow continuous recirculation up and through the gooseneck of the faucet.

c. ***Turbulent Flow:*** A distribution loop should be designed to operate with flow rates that ensure turbulent flow. This limits the biofilm formation on pipe walls and minimizes the risk of bacteria proliferation. The Reynolds number, a dimensionless calculation developed by Osborne Reynolds more than 100 years ago, remains the industry standard for determining whether water flow is turbulent. A Reynolds number below 2,300 is considered laminar, 2,300–4,000 is considered a transitional flow range, and greater than 4,000 is turbulent. For pure water piping systems, targeting a flow velocity in the range of approximately 3–5 feet per second (fps) is considered good design practice. A flow velocity of 3 fps is well into the turbulent flow range, and velocity exceeding 5 fps can result in unnecessary pressure losses through the distribution piping.

d. ***Piping Selection:*** If the requirement for total flow through the distribution loop piping is defined as 10 gallons per minute (gpm), 1-inch nominal piping is the correct choice to maintain flow within the targeted velocity range. Construction materials and associated pipe welding methods for assembly are also a key part of the design process. Some common piping materials include PVC, PP, PVDF, and stainless steel. Factors such as overall cleanliness (or the risk of contaminants leaching into the pure water), material cost, installation cost, and cleaning and sanitization compatibility should be considered when selecting a piping system. For most laboratory applications, PP is an excellent choice since it is both very clean and relatively cost-effective.

Installed, PP is significantly lower in cost than PVDF or SST piping systems and is only slightly more expensive to install than a PVC system. Since PP may be thermally welded *via* socket or butt joints, it also eliminates the risk of contamination from solvents or glues commonly used with PVC systems.

e. ***Distribution Pump:*** Selecting the right distribution pump is a frequently overlooked, yet integral part of the design process. At a basic level, this pump must deliver the required flow rate and pressure to all the distribution loop use points. However, several factors need to be considered. Pump selection requires a balance between flow rates, pressure losses, and maintaining the targeted flow velocity of 3–5 fps. The pump distribution flow rate should have been determined in Step 1 of the design process. In addition to flow rate, pressure losses must be considered for all components through which the water will be distributed. Therefore, the total pump pressure needs to be the sum total of the pressure losses through the pipe, fittings, and valves; pressure losses through purification equipment; minimum pressure required throughout the distribution loop; and pressure due to changes in elevation.

f. ***Pressure losses through the pipe, fittings, and valves:*** Most manufacturers can provide guidelines to determine pressure losses through piping systems. The following simplified Hazen-Williams calculation also can be used to determine pressure losses for water flowing through plastic piping under turbulent flow conditions:

$$Hp = 0.000425(L) \times (Q)1.85/(d)4.86$$

Where

Hp = pressure drop in pounds per square inch (psi)

L = pipe length in feet

Q = flow in gpm

d = pipe inside diameter

It is important to note that while pressure loss is proportional to the length of the loop, flow rate and pipe diameter may have a much greater impact on the final pressure loss.

For example, one might consider a change from 1-inch to ¾- inch pipe to be relatively small. At the same flow, this change will result in a pressure increase of more than 300 percent! Pressure loss through fittings and valves can also be determined following manufacturers' guidelines.

g. ***Pressure losses through purification equipment:*** Equipment should be selected to minimize pressure losses as well as meet flow specifications provided by the manufacturer. Pressure losses through the purification equipment should be available from the manufacturer.

h. ***Minimum pressure required in the distribution loop:*** To ensure all points of use have the required pressure and flow, the required minimum pressure should be defined during Step 1 of the design process. The minimum pressure can be controlled using a back-pressure regulating valve installed in-line at the very end of the distribution piping loop. Typically 25–30 psi meets most requirements.

i. ***Change in elevation:*** To ensure minimum pressures are maintained at the highest location of the distribution piping, all elevation changes must be considered. Every 2.31 feet of elevation change results in 1 psi of pressure. The required distribution flow rate, with the sum of the pressure demands, defines the performance requirement for the distribution pump. You can use the manufacturer's pump performance curves to find a pump that meets the required flow rate, with a pressure equaling the sum of all defined pressure demands.

j. ***Distribution Purification Equipment:*** As previously discussed, the makeup system typically provides the bulk of the purification required for the total system with subsequent steps added to maintain water quality or provide higher purity levels. Therefore, distribution equipment selection is based on ensuring the water that re-circulates in the distribution piping reliably meets all point-of-use water quality requirements directly from the piping loop. Purification steps can include UV light for bacteria control (254-nanometer [nm] wavelength), UV light for organic reduction (dual wavelength including 185 nm), mixed-bed ion-exchange for inorganic removal, and membrane filtration options for removal and control of particles, bacteria, and endotoxins. Often a combination of purification technologies is selected to meet point-of-use requirements for each of the four types of contaminants.

k. ***Distribution Monitoring Equipment:*** To verify and document performance, system design should include equipment to monitor distribution loop water quality. Actual requirements should be defined in Step 1, when all user requirements are determined. Common monitoring options include:

- Pressure gauges to monitor pressure at key points (pump pressure, pressure drop across equipment and filters, and pressure at the loop return);
- Conductivity or resistivity monitoring to measure inorganic impurities;
- TOC monitors to measure the total organic content; and
- Sample valves for collection of water samples for bacteria monitoring.

The valve type must be carefully selected to ensure the valve itself does not contribute contamination to the sample.

Step 4—Water Purification Make-up and Storage

The selection and size of the makeup purification system need to be determined together with the selection and size of the storage reservoir to meet water quality requirements and both daily and peak usage demands for purified water in the facility. The makeup purification system produces the total volume of water consumed by a facility each day, starting with tap water and purifying it to a level of water quality that meets laboratory-specific water quality requirements. The selection of purification technologies for the makeup purification system must be linked to the requirements defined in Step 1 of the total design process. Most facilities requiring purified water have a higher volume demand for more general applications (*i.e.,* washing and rinsing glassware) than for critical applications. A practical approach to the total system design is to feed a more general-grade water quality through the primary distribution and polish this water to a Type I level at the points of use where the critical or sensitive work is being performed. A facility with more general applications, requiring Type III quality as the primary water quality throughout the distribution loop, can utilize reverse osmosis as the primary makeup purification technology. A facility with applications requiring Type II or USP purified water quality as the primary water throughout the distribution loop can add an additional purification step of deionization or electro-de-ionization to achieve higher water quality requirements. Electro-de-ionization, as a continuous low-energy process, provides advantages over traditional deionization since there is no need to exchange resin cartridges or to chemically regenerate the resins. The pretreatment system should consider the feed water contaminants found locally in the tap water and be sized to accommodate seasonal variations that may occur. To ensure bacteria control, a UV light (254-nm wavelength) may be added as a final step of the makeup purification system for both the production of Type III and Type II water quality. Water in the storage reservoir serves as a buffer during peak demand periods, allowing the makeup system time to produce the total daily volume needed. For example, a laboratory operating and using pure water (primarily eight to 10 hours per day) can utilize the overnight hours to produce water that fills the storage reservoir. Although at first glance the storage reservoir simply needs to store the water, it is also important that the design of the reservoir not compromise the quality of the water stored. Construction materials and design features, such as a conical bottom, closed design with proper air venting and filtration, and a protected overflow, are important factors that can minimize contamination from materials or from the air.

ADDITIONAL CONSIDERATIONS TO FINALIZE TOTAL SYSTEM DESIGN AND SPECIFICATIONS

The final use or application of the purified water is important to understand when determining the need for additional point-of-use purification polishing systems. Most general, noncritical applications may use the water directly from the distribution system. In contrast, sensitive applications may require water quality targeted for their specific needs. There are several options for final point-of-use polishing systems that combine the necessary purification technologies to meet specific quality requirements of critical applications. Monitoring resistivity and TOC should be included as a final check of the water quality used. Space requirements in the laboratory also must be considered. Installation options should include bench top, under the bench, or wall mounting to optimize space allocation.

Total System Control

Control and coordination of all operating modes, performance parameters, water quality, indicators for routine maintenance, and key alerts and alarms for the total system—from makeup to distribution—also need to be part of the total system design. Easy and user-friendly access must be provided to the controls and displays for simplified, convenient system operation, monitoring, and maintenance. Monitoring water quality at key stages throughout the system is essential for confirming that the system is functioning correctly and final water quality is acceptable. Additional factors in overall system design include the vendor's ability to offer total system design and engineering support, technical and field service support, and qualification and validation support. Increasingly, laboratories are more aware of regulations such as cGMP and GLP. These regulations are aimed at improving the quality and reliability of data produced by a laboratory and ensuring equipment (including water purification equipment) is installed, maintained, calibrated, and performing correctly. In these environments, the ability to validate the water purification equipment is a critical consideration. Technical and field service support capabilities should be evaluated in the process of selecting a total system. The performance of a well-designed total system can be compromised due to improper installation, troubleshooting, repair, or maintenance. As a final step, it is important to prepare detailed documentation that covers user requirements, equipment specification, total system design, control and monitoring, and system performance. This documentation must be reviewed with the principals of the project to ensure a clear link between user requirements and proposed final design.

Meeting the User's Needs

Purified water is an essential resource in all laboratory environments. The complete design process involves a thorough understanding and working knowledge of contaminants in pure water, purification technologies, uses and applications, industry standards, and system design and engineering. Partnering with a supplier that can provide full support through the complete process—from clearly defining user requirements to design, installation, commissioning, and long-term maintenance—can ensure the total water purification system meets all the end user's needs.

VALIDATION AND QUALIFICATION OF WATER PURIFICATION, STORAGE, AND DISTRIBUTION SYSTEMS

Validation Requirement

Establishing the reliability of water purification, storage, and distribution systems requires demonstrating control of the process through an appropriate period of monitoring and observation. The quality of bulk finished water cannot be established by only testing monograph attributes. The unit operations in the pharmaceutical water system need to demonstrate that they are in control through monitoring of the process parameters and water quality. The advent of using conductivity and total organic carbon (TOC) to define chemical purity allows the user to more quantitatively assess the water's chemical purity and its variability as a function of routine treatment system maintenance and regeneration. Treatment processes must also demonstrate control of microbial attributes within the overall system. Some unit operations that are needed for chemical treatment may significantly increase microbial and bacterial endotoxin levels. A typical water system validation program involves an initial increased frequency of monitoring of the treatment system process parameters and sampling and testing of major process points to demonstrate the ability to produce the acceptable water and to characterize the operation of the system. This is followed by a life cycle approach of validation maintenance and monitoring.

Validation Approach

A validation program qualifies and documents the design, installation, operation, and performance of the system. The validation protocol should be based on the boundaries of the water system and the critical water quality and process attributes needed to maintain consistent performance.

Validation elements

Validation is accomplished through the use of a structured, documented process. The phases of this process include Design Qualification (DQ), Installation Qualification (IQ), Operational Qualification (OQ), Performance Qualification (PQ), and Validation Maintenance. Factory Acceptance Testing (FAT), Site Acceptance Testing (SAT), and commissioning testing of the system may supplement qualification tests for IQ or OQ provided that they are properly documented and reviewed; and if it can be shown that the system functionality is not affected by the transport and installation.

User requirements specification and design qualification

The user requirements for the water system should identify the design, operation, maintenance, and quality elements needed to produce the desired water type from the available source water, including its anticipated attribute variability. The essential elements of quality need to be built in at this stage and any GMP risks mitigated to an acceptable level. The review of the specifications, system design, components, functions, and operation should be performed to demonstrate that the system complies with GMPs and verify that the design meets the user requirements. This documented review may be performed as part of the overall design process or as a separate DQ.

Installation qualification

An IQ protocol for a water system confirms that the system has been properly installed and documented. This may include verification of components, piping, installation, and weld quality; documentation of the specifications for all system components present; inspections to verify that the drawings accurately depict the final configuration of the water system and, where necessary, special tests to verify that the installation meets the design requirements.

Operation qualification

The OQ phase consisting of tests and inspections to verify that the equipment, system alerts, and controls are operating reliably and that appropriate Alert and Action Levels are established. SOPs for all aspects of water system operation, maintenance, water use, water sampling, and testing, etc. should be in place and operator training completed. At the completion of the OQ, the water system has demonstrated that the components are operational and the system is producing suitable water.

Performance qualification

The PQ stage considers two aspects of the water system: critical process parameters and critical water attribute parameters. These are evaluated in parallel by monitoring the water quality and demonstrating acceptable quality attributes while demonstrating control of the process parameters. PQ of water system is divided into 3 phases [4].

Phase 1: This PQ stage includes daily sampling and monitoring for approximately 2–4 weeks, to demonstrate that water meeting the appropriate quality attributes is produced and distributed. One of the reasons for this duration is that biofilm, the source of planktonic organisms in water samples, takes time to develop and to determine if the sanitization unit operations and processes are adequate to control microbial proliferation. The chemical control program adequacy is typically apparent in less time than it takes to see microbial control adequacy. However, chemical purification can be compromised by poor microbial control and, to a lesser degree, *vice versa*. During this period, the system should operate continuously without failure or performance deviation. Usually water is not used for "finished pharmaceutical product (FPP) manufacturing during this period. Following activities should be included in the testing approach.

- Undertake chemical and microbiological testing in accordance with a defined plan.
- Sample or continuously monitor the incoming feed-water daily to verify its quality.
- Sample or continuously monitor at each step in the purification process.
- Sample or continuously monitor at each point of use and at other defined sample points.
- Develop appropriate operating ranges.
- Develop and finalize operating, cleaning, sanitizing and maintenance procedures.
- Demonstrate production and delivery of product water of the required quality and quantity.
- Use and refine the standard operating procedures (SOPs) for operation, maintenance, sanitization and troubleshooting.
- Verify provisional alert levels.
- Develop and refine test-failure procedure.

Phase 2: Once a level of control of microbial and chemical attributes has been demonstrated, the next phase of PQ is to continue the frequency of monitoring for approximately 2–4 weeks. Sampling scheme should be the same as that in phase 1. The water may be used for manufacturing at risk, and the associated products may be released only after water quality attributes have been determined to be acceptable and this validation phase has been completed. At the completion of the second phase, the data should be formally reviewed and the system approved for operational use. This phase demonstrate:

- Consistent operation within established ranges;
- Consistent production and delivery of water of the required quantity and quality when the system is operated in accordance with the SOPs.

Phase 3: Phase 3 typically runs for one year after the satisfactory completion of phase 2. Water can be used for FFP manufacturing purposes during this phase which has the following objectives to demonstrate

- Reliable performance over an extended period;
- That seasonal variation is evaluated.

The sample locations, sampling frequencies and tests should be reduced to the normal routine pattern based on established procedures proven during phases 1 and 2.

Continuous Operational Monitoring

When the water system has been placed into operational use, monitoring of the water quality attributes and the system process parameters is performed at a routine frequency to ensure that they remain with a state of control during long-term variability from seasonal variations in source water quality, unit operation maintenance, system sanitization processes, and earlier-established Alert and Action Levels. The water system should continue to be monitored and evaluated on an on-going basis following a life cycle approach using online instruments or samples for laboratory-based testing. The use of online instruments and process automation technology, such as conductivity, TOC, temperature, flow rate, and pressure can facilitate improved operational control of the attributes and parameters and for process release. Manual observation of operating parameters and laboratory-based testing is also appropriate and acceptable for monitoring and trend evaluation.

Monitoring

The frequency of routine monitoring should be based on the criticality of the finished water, capabilities of the process, and ability to maintain product water quality trends. Monitoring may be adjusted from the initial validation monitoring program when there is sufficient data to support a change.

Validation maintenance

WPU systems should be maintained in accordance with a controlled, documented maintenance programme that takes into account the following:

- Defined frequency for system elements;
- The calibration programme;
- SOPs for specific tasks;
- Control of approved spares;
- Issue of a clear maintenance plan and instructions;
- Review and approval of systems for use upon completion of work;
- Record and review of problems and faults during maintenance.

Periodic review

The water system qualification, maintenance history, calibration records, quality and process data, issues with the unit operations and any process variability, change control, and other validation maintenance data should be assessed periodically to determine impact on the state of control. The review may result in adjustments to operating or sanitization processes, calibration or maintenance plans, or monitoring plans. This may also result in additional testing or repeating certain qualification tasks (re-qualification).

DESIGN AND OPERATION OF PURIFIED WATER AND WATER FOR INJECTION SYSTEMS

The design, installation, and operation of systems to produce Purified Water and Water for Injection include similar components, control techniques, and procedures [2,3]. The quality attributes of the two waters differ in their bioburden expectation, the presence of a bacterial endotoxin requirement for Water for Injection, and in their methods of preparation. The similarities in the quality attributes provide considerable common ground in the design of water systems to meet either requirement. The critical difference is the degree of control of the system and the final purification steps needed to ensure removal of bacteria and bacterial endotoxins and reductions in opportunities for biofilm re-development within those purification steps which could become *in situ* sources of bacteria and endotoxin in the finished water. Many aspects of system design and operation relate to control and elimination of biofilm. Unit operations can cause the deterioration of water microbial attributes and the formation of biofilm on unit operation surfaces, even when properly maintained. Production of pharmaceutical water involves sequential unit operations (processing steps) that address specific water quality attributes and protect the operation of subsequent treatment steps. The final unit operation used to produce Water for Injection is limited to distillation or other processes equivalent or superior to distillation in the removal of chemical impurities as well as microorganisms and their components, such as bacterial endotoxins. Distillation coupled with suitable pretreatment technologies has a long history of generally reliable performance (though not completely infallible) and can be validated as a unit operation for the production of Water for Injection. Other combinations of purification technologies may also be suitable in the production of Water for Injection if they can be shown through validation to be as effective and reliable as distillation in the removal of chemicals and microorganisms. The development of new designs and materials of construction for other technologies (such as reverse osmosis, electro-de-ionization, and ultrafiltration) that allow intermittent or continuous operation at hot bactericidal conditions show promise for a valid use in producing Water for Injection.

Unit Operations Considerations

To achieve the quality attributes for pharmaceutical waters, multiple-unit operations are required. The design of the water purification system needs to take into consideration different aspects, including the source water quality, sanitization, pharmaceutical water quality attributes, uses of the water, and maintenance programs. Each unit operation contributes specific purification attributes associated with chemical and microbiological parameters. The following is a brief description of selected unit operations and the design, installation, operation, maintenance, and monitoring parameter considerations associated with them. Not all unit operations are discussed, nor are all potential shortcomings addressed.

Pre-filtration

The purpose of prefiltration or initial, coarse, particulate, or depth filtration is to remove solid contaminants from the incoming source water supply and protect downstream system components from particulates that can inhibit equipment performance and shorten their effective life. This coarse filtration technology primarily uses sieving effects for particle capture and a depth of filtration medium that has a high "dirt load" capacity. Such filtration units are available in a wide range of designs and for various applications. Granular or cartridge prefilters are often used at the beginning of the water purification system prior to unit operations designed to remove the source water disinfectants. Cartridge-type coarse filters may also be used to capture fines released from granular beds such as activated carbon and de-ionization beds. These locations, however, do not preclude the need for periodic microbial evaluation. Design and operational issues that may impact the performance of depth filters include channeling of the filtering media, blockage from silt, microbial growth, and filtering-media loss during improper backwashing. Control methods involve pressure and flow monitoring during use and backwashing, sanitizing, and replacing filtering media.

Activated carbon

Activated carbon beds, depending on the type and placement, are used to adsorb low-molecular-weight organic material, bacterial endotoxins, and oxidizing additives such as chlorine and chloramine compounds, removing them from the water. They are used to achieve certain quality attributes and to protect against reactions with downstream unit operations, stainless steel surfaces, resins, and membranes. The chief operating concerns regarding activated carbon beds include the propensity to support bacterial growth, the potential for hydraulic channeling, the organic adsorption capacity, and insufficient contact time. Operation deficiencies may result in the release of bacteria, endotoxins, organic chemicals, and fine carbon particles. Control measures may involve monitoring water flow rates and differential pressures, sanitizing with hot water or steam, backwashing, testing for adsorption capacity, and frequent replacement of the carbon bed. Monitoring of carbon bed unit operation may also include microbial loading, disinfectant chemical reduction, and TOC if used for TOC reduction.

The use of hot water or steam for carbon bed sanitization is ineffective if there is channeling rather than even permeation through the bed. Channeling can be mitigated through design and proper flow rates during sanitization. Microbial biofilm development on the surface of the granular carbon particles can cause adjacent bed granules to agglomerate. This may result in ineffective removal of trapped debris and fragile biofilm during backwashing, and ineffective sanitization. Alternative technologies to activated carbon beds can be used to avoid their microbial challenges. These include disinfectant-neutralizing chemical additives and intense ultraviolet (UV) light for removal of chlorine, and regenerable organic scavenging deionizing resins for removal of organics.

Additives

Chemical additives are used in water systems

(1) To control microorganisms by use of sanitizing agents, such as chlorine compounds and ozone;
(2) To enhance the removal of suspended solids by use of flocculating agents;
(3) To remove chlorine compounds;
(4) To avoid scaling on reverse osmosis membranes; and
(5) To adjust pH for more effective removal of carbonate and ammonia compounds by reverse osmosis. These additives do not constitute "added substances" as long as they are either removed by subsequent processing steps or are otherwise absent from the finished water. Control of additives to ensure a continuously effective concentration and subsequent monitoring to ensure their removal should be designed into the system and included in the monitoring program.

Organic scavengers

Organic scavenging devices use macro-reticular, weakly basic anion-exchange resins capable of removing negatively charged organic material and endotoxins from the water. Organic scavenger resins can be regenerated with appropriate biocidal caustic brine solutions. Operating concerns are associated with organic scavenging capacity; particulate, chemical, and microbiological fouling of the reactive resin surface; flow rate; regeneration frequency; and shedding of fines from the fragile resins. Control measures include TOC testing of influent and effluent, backwashing, monitoring hydraulic performance, and using downstream filters to remove resin fines.

Softeners

Water softeners may be located either upstream or downstream of disinfectant removal units. They utilize sodium-based cation-exchange resins to remove water-hardness ions, such as calcium and magnesium that could foul or interfere with the performance of downstream processing equipment such as reverse osmosis membranes, deionization devices, and distillation units. Water softeners can also be used to remove other lower affinity cations, such as the ammonium ion, that may be released from chloramine disinfectants commonly used in drinking water. If ammonium removal is one of its purposes, the softener must be located downstream of the disinfectant removal operation. Water softener resin beds are regenerated with concentrated sodium chloride solution (brine). Concerns include microorganism proliferation, channeling, appropriate water flow rates and contact time, ion-exchange capacity, organic and particulate resin fouling, organic leaching from new resins, fracture of the resin beads, resin degradation by excessively chlorinated water, and contamination from the brine solution used for regeneration. Control measures involve recirculation of water during periods of low water use; periodic sanitization of the resin and brine system; use of microbial control devices (*e.g.,* UV light and chlorine); locating the unit upstream of the disinfectant removal step (if used only for softening); appropriate regeneration frequency; effluent chemical monitoring (*e.g.,* hardness ions and possibly ammonium); and downstream filtration to remove resin fines. If a softener is used for ammonium removal from chloramine-containing source water, then the capacity, contact time, resin surface fouling, pH, and regeneration frequency are very important.

De-ionization

De-ionization (DI) and continuous electro-de-ionization (CEDI) are effective methods of improving the chemical quality attributes of water by removing cations and anions. DI systems have charged resins that require periodic regeneration with an acid and base. Typically, cation resins are regenerated with either hydrochloric or sulfuric acid, which replace the captured positive ions with hydrogen ions. Anion resins are regenerated with sodium hydroxide or potassium hydroxide, which replace captured negative ions with hydroxide ions. Because free endotoxin is negatively charged, some removal of endotoxin is achieved by the anion resin. The system can be designed so that the cation and anion resins are in separate or "twin" beds, or they can be blended together to form a "mixed" bed. The CEDI system uses a combination of ion-exchange materials such as resins or grafted material, selectively permeable membranes, and an electric charge, providing continuous flow (of product and waste concentrate) and continuous regeneration. Water enters both the resin section and the waste (concentrate) section. The resin acts as a conductor, enabling the electrical potential to drive the captured cations and anions through the resin and appropriate membranes for concentration and removal in the waste water stream. As the water passes through the resin, it is deionized to become product water. The electrical potential also separates the water in the resin (product) section into hydrogen and hydroxide ions. This permits continuous regeneration of the resin without the need for regenerant additives. However, unlike conventional deionization, CEDI units must start with water that is already partially purified because they generally cannot achieve the conductivity attribute of Purified Water when starting with the heavier ion load of source water. Concerns for all forms of DI units include microbial and endotoxin control; chemical additive impact on resins and membranes; and loss, degradation, and fouling of resin. Issues of concern specific to DI units include regeneration frequency and completeness; channeling caused by biofilm agglomeration of resin particles; organic leaching from new resins; complete resin separation for mixed bed regeneration; and bed fluidization air contamination (mixed beds). Control measures may include continuous recirculation loops, effluent microbial control by UV light, conductivity monitoring, resin testing, microporous filtration of bed fluidization air, microbial monitoring, frequent regeneration to minimize and control microorganism growth, sizing the equipment for suitable water flow and contact time, and use of elevated temperatures. Internal distributor and regeneration piping for DI bed units should be configured to ensure that regeneration chemicals contact all internal bed and piping surfaces and resins. Rechargeable canisters can be the source of contamination and should be carefully monitored. Full knowledge of previous resin use, minimum storage time between regeneration and use, and appropriate sanitizing procedures are critical factors for ensuring proper performance.

Reverse osmosis

Reverse osmosis (RO) units use semi-permeable membranes. The "pores" of RO membranes are inter-segmental spaces among the polymer molecules. They are big enough for permeation of water molecules, but they limit the passage of hydrated chemical ions, organic compounds, and microorganisms. RO membranes can achieve chemical, microbial, and endotoxin quality improvement. Many factors, including pH, temperature, source water hardness, permeate and reject flow rate, and differential pressure across the membrane, affect the selectivity and effectiveness of this permeation. The process streams consist of supply water, product water (permeate), and waste water (reject). Depending on the source water, pretreatment and system configuration variations and chemical additives may be necessary to achieve the desired performance and reliability. For most source waters, a single stage of RO filtration is usually not enough to meet Purified Water conductivity specifications. A second pass of this permeate water through another RO stage usually achieves the necessary permeate purity if other factors such as pH and temperature have been appropriately adjusted and the ammonia from source water that has been previously treated with chloramines is removed. Concerns associated with the design and operation of RO units include membrane materials that are sensitive to sanitizing agents and to particulate, chemical, and microbial membrane fouling;

membrane and seal integrity; and the passage of dissolved gases, such as carbon dioxide and ammonia. Failure of membrane or seal integrity will result in product water contamination. Methods of control involve suitable pretreatment of the influent water stream; appropriate membrane material selection; membrane design and heat tolerance; periodic sanitization; and monitoring of differential pressures, conductivity, microbial levels, and TOC. The development of RO units that can tolerate sanitizing water temperatures and also operate efficiently and continuously at elevated temperatures has added greatly to their microbial control ability and to the avoidance of biofouling. RO units can be used alone or in combination with DI and CEDI units, as well as ultrafiltration, for operational and quality enhancements.

Ultrafiltration

Ultrafiltration is a technology that is often used near the end of a pharmaceutical water purification system for removing endotoxins from a water stream though upstream uses are possible. Ultrafiltration can use semipermeable membranes, but unlike RO, these typically use polysulfone membranes with intersegmental "pores" that have been purposefully enlarged. Membranes with differing molecular weight "cutoffs" can be created to preferentially reject molecules with molecular weights above these ratings. Ceramic ultrafilters are another molecular sieving technology. Ceramic ultrafilters are self-supporting and extremely durable; they can be backwashed, chemically cleaned, and steam sterilized. However, they may require higher operating pressures than do membrane-type ultrafilters. All ultrafiltration devices work primarily by a molecular sieving principle. Ultrafilters with molecular weight cutoff ratings in the range of 10,000–20,000 Da are typically used in water systems for removing endotoxins. This technology may be appropriate as an intermediate or final purification step. As with RO, successful performance is dependent upon pretreatment of the water by upstream unit operations. Issues of concern for ultrafilters include compatibility of membrane material with heat and sanitizing agents, membrane integrity, fouling by particles and microorganisms, and seal integrity. Control measures involve filter membrane composition, sanitization, flow design (dead end *vs*. tangential), cartridge replacement, elevated feed water temperature, and monitoring TOC and differential pressure.

Microbial-retentive filtration

Microbial-retentive membrane filters have a larger effective "pore size" than ultrafilters and are intended to prevent the passage of microorganisms and similarly sized particles without unduly restricting flow. This type of filtration is widely employed within water systems for filtering the bacteria out of both water and compressed gases as well as for vent filters on tanks and stills and other unit operations. In water systems, a filter's microbial retention characteristics exhibit different phenomena than in other aseptic filtration applications. The following factors interact to create the retention phenomena for water system microorganisms: the variability in the range and average pore sizes created by the various membrane fabrication processes; the variability of the surface chemistry and three-dimensional structure related to the different polymers used in these filter matrices; and the size and surface properties of the microorganism intended to be retained by the filters. The typical challenge organism for these filters, *Brevundimonas diminuta*, may not be the best challenge microorganism for demonstrating bacterial retention by 0.2- to 0.22-mm rated filters for use in water systems because this challenge microorganism appears to be more easily retained by these filters than some other water system bacteria. In some situations, the appearance of water system microorganisms on the downstream sides of some 0.2- to 0.22-mm rated filters after a relatively short period of use (days to weeks) seems to support the idea that some penetration phenomenon is at work. It is not known whether this downstream appearance is caused by a "pass-through" phenomenon resulting from tiny cells or less cell "stickiness," or perhaps by a "grow through" phenomenon where cells hypothetically replicate their way through the pores to the downstream side. Whatever the penetration mechanism, 0.2- to 0.22-mm rated membranes may not be the best choice for some water system uses. Nevertheless, microbial retention success in water systems has been reported with the use of filters rated as 0.2 or 0.1 mm. There is general agreement that, for a given manufacturer, their 0.1-mm rated filters are tighter than their 0.2- to 0.22-mm rated filters. However, comparably rated filters from different manufacturers may not have equivalent performance in water filtration applications because of the different filter materials, different fabrication processes, and non-standardized microbial retention challenge processes currently used for defining the 0.1-mm filter rating. It should be noted that filters with a 0.1-mm rating may result in a lower flow rate compared to 0.2- to 0.22-mm filters, so whatever filters are chosen for a water system application, the user must verify that they are suitable for their intended application, use period, and use process, including flow rate. For microbial retentive gas filtrations, the same sieving and adsorptive retention phenomena are at work as in liquid filtration, but the adsorptive phenomenon is enhanced by additional electrostatic interactions between the particles and filter matrix. These electrostatic interactions are so strong, particle retention for a given filter rating is significantly more efficient in gas filtration than in water or product-solution filtrations. These additional adsorptive interactions render filters rated at 0.2–0.22 mm unquestionably suitable for microbial retentive gas filtrations. When microbial retentive filters are used in these applications, the membrane surface is typically hydrophobic (non-wettable by water). A significant area of concern for gas filtration is blockage of tank vents by condensed water vapor, which can cause mechanical damage to the tank. Control measures include electrical or steam tracing and a self-draining orientation of vent filter housings to prevent accumulation of vapor condensate. However, a continuously high filter temperature will take an oxidative toll on polypropylene components of the filter, so sterilization of the unit prior to initial use, and periodically thereafter, as well as regular visual inspections, integrity tests, and filter cartridge changes are recommended control methods. In water applications, microbial retentive filters may be used downstream of unit operations that tend to release microorganisms or upstream of unit operations that are sensitive to microorganisms. Microbial retentive filters may also be used to filter water feeding the distribution system. It should be noted that regulatory authorities allow the use of microbial retentive filters within distribution systems or even at use points if they have been properly validated and are appropriately maintained. A point-of-use filter should only be intended to "polish" the microbial quality of an otherwise well-maintained system and not to serve as the primary microbial control device. The efficacy of system microbial control measures can only be assessed by sampling the water upstream of the filters. As an added measure of protection, in-line UV lamps, appropriately sized for the flow rate, may be used just upstream of microbial retentive filters to inactivate microorganisms prior to their capture by the filter. This tandem approach tends to greatly delay potential microbial penetration phenomena and can substantially extend filter service life.

Ultraviolet light

The use of low-pressure UV lights that emit a 254-nm wavelength for microbial control is discussed in Sanitization, but the application of UV light in chemical purification is also emerging. This 254-nm wavelength is also useful in the destruction of ozone. At wavelengths around 185 nm (as well as at 254 nm), medium-pressure UV lights have demonstrated utility in the destruction of the chlorine-containing disinfectants used in source water as well as for interim stages of water pretreatment. High intensities of 254 nm or in combination with other oxidizing sanitants, such as hydrogen peroxide, have been used to lower TOC levels in recirculating distribution systems. The organics are typically converted to carbon dioxide, which equilibrates to bicarbonate, and incompletely oxidized carboxylic acids, both of which can easily be removed by polishing ion-exchange resins. Areas of concern include inadequate UV intensity and residence time, gradual loss of UV emissivity with bulb age, gradual formation of a UV-absorbing film at the water contact surface, incomplete photodegradation during unforeseen source water hyperchlorination, release of ammonia from chloramine photodegradation, unapparent UV bulb failure, and conductivity degradation in distribution systems using 185-nm UV lights. Control measures include regular inspection or emissivity alarms to detect bulb failures or film occlusions, regular UV bulb sleeve cleaning and wiping, downstream chlorine detectors (when used for dechlorination), downstream polishing deionizers (when used for TOC reduction), and regular (approximately yearly) bulb replacement. UV lamps generate heat during operation, which can cause failure of the lamps or increase the temperature of the water. Precautions should be in place to ensure that water flow is present to control excessive temperature increase.

Distillation

Distillation units provide chemical and microbial purification *via* thermal vaporization, mist elimination, and water vapor condensation. A variety of designs is available, including single effect, multiple effect, and vapor compression. The latter two configurations are normally used in larger systems because of their generating capacity and efficiency. Source water controls must provide for the removal of hardness and silica impurities that may foul or corrode the heat transfer surfaces, as well as the removal of those impurities that could volatize and condense along with the water vapor. In spite of general perceptions, even the best distillation process does not ensure absolute removal of contaminating ions, organics, and endotoxins. Most stills are recognized as being able to accomplish at least a 3–4 log reduction in these impurity concentrations. They are highly effective in sterilizing the feed water. Areas of concern include carry-over of volatile organic impurities such as trihalomethanes and gaseous impurities such as ammonia and carbon dioxide, faulty mist elimination, evaporator flooding, inadequate blow down, stagnant water in condensers and evaporators, pump and compressor seal design, pinhole evaporator and condenser leaks, and conductivity (quality) variations during start-up and operation. Methods of control may involve the following: preliminary steps to remove both dissolved carbon dioxide and other volatile or noncondensable impurities; reliable mist elimination to minimize feed water droplet entrainment; visual or automated highwater- level indication to detect boiler flooding and boil over; use of sanitary pumps and compressors to minimize microbial and lubricant contamination of feed water and condensate; proper drainage during inactive periods to minimize microbial growth and accumulation of associated endotoxin in boiler water; blow down control to limit the impurity concentration effect in the boiler to manageable levels; on-line conductivity sensing with automated diversion to waste to prevent unacceptable water upon still startup or still malfunction from getting into the finished water distribution system; and periodic testing for pinhole leaks to routinely ensure that condensate is not compromised by non-volatized source water contaminants.

Storage tanks

Storage tanks are included in water distribution systems to optimize processing equipment capacity. Storage also allows for routine maintenance within the purification system while maintaining continuous supply to meet manufacturing needs. Design and operation considerations are needed to prevent or minimize the development of biofilm, to minimize corrosion, to aid in the use of chemical sanitization of the tanks, and to safeguard mechanical integrity. Areas of concern include microbial growth or corrosion due to irregular or incomplete sanitization and microbial contamination from unalarmed rupture disk failures caused by condensate-occluded vent filters. Control considerations may include using closed tanks with smooth interiors, the ability to spray the tank headspace using spray balls on re-circulating loop returns, and the use of heated, jacketed/insulated tanks. This minimizes corrosion and biofilm development and aids in thermal or chemical sanitization. Storage tanks require venting to compensate for the dynamics of changing water levels. This can be accomplished with a properly oriented and heat-traced filter housing fitted with a hydrophobic microbial retentive membrane filter affixed to an atmospheric vent. Alternatively, an automatic membrane-filtered compressed gas blanketing system may be used. In both cases, rupture disks equipped with a rupture alarm device should be used as a further safeguard for the mechanical integrity of the tank.

Distribution systems

Distribution system configuration should allow for the continuous flow of water in the piping by means of recirculation. Use of no re-circulating, dead-end, or one-way systems or system segments should be avoided whenever possible. If not possible, these systems should be flushed periodically and monitored more closely. Experience has shown that continuously re-circulated systems are easier to maintain. Pumps should be designed to deliver fully turbulent flow conditions to facilitate thorough heat distribution (for hot-water sanitized systems) as well as thorough chemical sanitant distribution. Turbulent flow also appears to either retard the development of biofilms or reduce the tendency of those biofilms to shed bacteria into the water. If redundant components, such as pumps or filters, are used, they should be configured and used to avoid microbial contamination of the system. Components and distribution lines should be sloped and fitted with drain points so that the system can be completely drained. In distribution systems, dead legs and low-flow conditions should be avoided, and valved tie-in points should have length-to-diameter ratios of six or less. In systems that operate at self-sanitizing temperatures, precautions should be taken to avoid cool points where biofilm development could occur. If drainage of components or distribution lines is intended as a microbial control strategy, they should also be configured to be dried completely using dry compressed gas because drained but still moist surfaces will still support microbial proliferation. Water exiting from the distribution system should not be returned to the system without first passing through all or a portion of the purification system. The distribution design should include the placement of sampling valves in the storage tank and at other locations, such as in the return line of the recirculating water system. Direct connections to processes or auxiliary equipment should be designed to prevent reverse flow into the controlled water system. Hoses and heat exchangers that are attached to points of use to deliver water must not chemically or microbiologically degrade the water quality. The distribution system should permit sanitization for microorganism control. The system may be continuously operated at sanitizing conditions or sanitized periodically.

INSTALLATION, MATERIALS OF CONSTRUCTION, AND COMPONENT SELECTION

Installation techniques are important because they can affect the mechanical, corrosive, and sanitary integrity of the system. Valve installation should promote gravity drainage. Pipe supports should provide appropriate slopes for drainage and should be designed to support the piping adequately under worst-case thermal and flow conditions. The methods of connecting system components—including units of operation, tanks, and distribution piping—require careful attention to preclude potential operational and microbial problems. Stainless steel welds should provide reliable joints that are internally smooth and corrosion-free. Low-carbon stainless steel, compatible wire filler where necessary, inert gas, automatic welding machines, and regular inspection and documentation help to ensure acceptable weld quality. Follow-up cleaning and passivation of metal surfaces after installation are important for removing contamination and corrosion products and to re-establish the passive corrosion-resistant surface. Plastic materials can be fused (welded) in some cases, and also require smooth, uniform internal surfaces. Adhesive glues and solvents should be avoided due to the potential for voids and organic extractables. Mechanical methods of joining, such as flange fittings, require care to avoid the creation of offsets, gaps, penetrations, and voids. Use of plastic materials may contribute to TOC levels. Control measures include good alignment, properly sized gaskets, appropriate spacing, uniform sealing force, and the avoidance of threaded fittings. Materials of construction should be selected to be compatible with control measures such as sanitizing, cleaning, or passivation. Temperature rating is a critical factor in choosing appropriate materials because surfaces may be required to handle elevated operating and sanitization temperatures. If chemicals or additives will be used to clean, passivate, or sanitize the system, materials resistant to these chemicals or additives must be utilized. Materials should be capable of handling turbulent flow and elevated velocities without erosion of the corrosion-resistant film (such as the passive chromium oxide surface of stainless steel) or reduction in wall thickness for plastics. The finish on metallic materials such as stainless steel, whether it is a refined mill finish, polished to a specific grit, or an electropolished treatment, should complement the system design and provide satisfactory corrosion and microbial activity resistance. The finish should also be a material that can be chemically sanitized. Auxiliary equipment and fittings that require seals, gaskets, diaphragms, filter media, and membranes should exclude materials that permit the possibility of extractables, shedding, and microbial activity. Insulating materials exposed to stainless steel surfaces should be free of chlorides to avoid the phenomenon of stress corrosion cracking that can lead to system contamination and the destruction of tanks and critical system components. Specifications are important to ensure proper selection of materials and to serve as a reference for system qualification and maintenance. Information such as the manufacturer's metallurgical reports for stainless steel and reports of composition, ratings, and material-handling capabilities for nonmetallic substances should be reviewed for suitability and retained for reference. Component (auxiliary equipment) selection should be made with assurance that it does not create a source of contamination intrusion. Heat exchangers should be constructed to prevent leakage of heat transfer medium into the pharmaceutical water and, for heat exchanger designs where prevention may fail, there should be a means to detect leakage. Pumps should be of sanitary design with seals that prevent contamination of the water. Valves should have smooth internal surfaces with the seat and closing device exposed to the flushing action of water, such as occurs in diaphragm valves. Valves with pocket areas or closing devices (*e.g.*, ball, plug, gate, globe) that move into and out of the flow area should be avoided [3].

SANITIZATION

Microbial control in water systems is achieved primarily through sanitization practices. Systems can be sanitized using either thermal or (photo-) chemical means [2,4].

Thermal Sanitization

Thermal approaches to system sanitization include periodic or continuously circulating hot water and the use of steam. Temperatures of 65°C–80°C are most commonly used for thermal sanitization. Continuously re-circulating water of at least 65°C at the coldest location in the distribution system has also been used effectively in stainless steel distribution systems when attention is paid to uniformity and distribution of such self-sanitizing temperatures. These techniques are limited to systems that are compatible with the higher temperatures needed to achieve sanitization. Frequent use of thermal sanitization at appropriate temperatures should eliminate the need for other sanitization methods. The use of thermal methods at temperatures above 80°C is contraindicated because it does not add to microbial control of the system or reduction of biofilm. Some methods (*e.g.*, steam sanitizing, hot water circulation at temperatures 100°C) can be less effective or even destructive because of the need to eliminate condensate or manipulate system components, stress materials of construction, deform filters, and its adverse impact on instrumentation. Although thermal methods control biofilm development by either continuously inhibiting its growth or, in intermittent applications, by killing the microorganisms within developing biofilms, they are not effective in removing established biofilms. Killed but intact biofilms can become a nutrient source for rapid biofilm regrowth after the sanitizing conditions are removed or halted. In cases of infrequent thermal sanitizations that allow biofilm development between treatments, a combination of routine thermal treatment and periodic supplementation with chemical sanitization may be more effective. The more frequent the thermal sanitization, the more likely it is that biofilm re-development can be eliminated.

Chemical Sanitization

Chemical methods, where compatible, can be used on a wider variety of construction materials. These methods typically use oxidizing agents such as ozone, hydrogen peroxide, peracetic acid, or combinations thereof. Halogenated compounds can be effective sanitizers but are less aggressive oxidizing agents and may be difficult to flush from the system. Chemical agents may not penetrate the full biofilm matrix or extend into all biofilm locations (such as crevices at gasketed fittings) and may leave biofilms incompletely inactivated. Compounds such as ozone, hydrogen peroxide, and peracetic acid oxidize bacteria and biofilms with reactive peroxides and by forming very reactive free radicals (notably hydroxyl radicals). The short half-life of ozone in particular, and its limitation on achievable concentrations, require that it be added continuously during the sanitization process. Hydrogen peroxide and ozone rapidly degrade to water and/or oxygen, and peracetic acid degrades to oxygen and acetic acid. The ease of degradation of ozone to oxygen using 254-nm UV lights in circulating loops allows it to be used effectively on a continuously sanitizing basis in holding tanks and on an intermittent basis (*e.g.*, daily or weekly) in the distribution loops. The highly reactive nature of ozone requires the use of system materials and components that are even more oxidation resistant than those typically used with the other oxidizing agents. It is important to note that microorganisms in a well-developed biofilm can be extremely difficult to kill, even by using aggressive oxidizing chemicals. The less developed and therefore thinner the biofilm, the more effective the biofilm inactivation. Therefore, optimal microbial control is achieved by using oxidizing chemicals at a frequency that does not permit significant biofilm development between treatments. Validation of chemical sanitization requires demonstration of adequate chemical concentrations throughout the system, exposure to all wetted surfaces including the body of use point valves, and complete removal of the sanitant from the system at the completion of treatment. Methods validation for the detection and quantification of residues of the sanitant or its objectionable degradants is an essential part of the validation program.

UV Sanitization

In-line UV light at a wavelength of 254 nm can also be used to continuously "sanitize" only the water circulating in the system, but these devices must be properly sized for the water flow. Such devices inactivate a high percentage (but not 100%) of microorganisms that flow through the device but cannot be used to directly control existing biofilm upstream or downstream of the device. However, when coupled with conventional thermal or chemical sanitization technologies or located immediately upstream of a microbially retentive filter, UV light is most effective and can prolong the interval between needed system re-sanitizations.

Sanitization Procedures

Sanitization steps require validation to demonstrate the ability to reduce and hold microbial contamination at acceptable levels. Validation of thermal methods should include a heat distribution study to demonstrate that sanitization temperatures are achieved throughout the system, including the body of use point valves; sampling ports; instrument side branches; andfittings, couplings, and adapters, relying on water convection and thermal conduction through system materials for heat transfer to wetted surfaces. The routine frequency of sanitization should be supported by the results of system microbial monitoring. Conclusions derived from trend analysis of the microbiological data should be used as the alert mechanism for the need for extraordinary maintenance. The routine frequency of sanitization should be established in such a way that the system operates in a state of microbiological control and does not regularly exceed Alert and Action Levels.

OPERATION, MAINTENANCE, AND CONTROL

A preventive maintenance program should be established to ensure that the water system remains in a state of control[4]. The program should include

(1) Procedures for operating the system,
(2) Monitoring programs for critical quality attributes and operating conditions including calibration of critical instruments,
(3) Schedule for periodic sanitization,
(4) Preventive maintenance of components, and
(5) Control of changes to the mechanical system and to operating conditions.

Operating Procedures

Operating procedures for the water system and for performing routine maintenance and corrective action should be written, and they should also define the point when action is required. The procedures should be well documented, and should detail the function of each job, assign who is responsible for performing the work, describe how the job is to be done, and identify acceptable operating parameters. The effectiveness of these procedures should be assessed during water system validation.

Process Monitoring Program

A process-monitoring program should establish the critical quality attributes and operating parameters that are documented and monitored. The program may include a combination of in-line sensors and/or automated instruments (*e.g.*, for temperature, TOC conductivity, hardness, and chlorine), automated or manual documentation of operational parameters (such as flow rates or pressure drop across a carbon bed, filter, or RO unit), and laboratory tests (*e.g.*, total microbial counts). The frequency of sampling, the requirement for evaluating test results, and the necessity of initiating corrective action should be included.

Routine Microbial Control

Sanitization may be integral to operation and maintenance, and necessary on a routine basis, depending on system design and the selected units of operation, to maintain the system in a state of microbial control.

SAMPLING

The testing of water samples from a water system is critical to the ongoing control of the system and assessment of the quality of the water being used. If improperly collected, a sample could yield a test result that is unrepresentative of the sample's purpose. This could lead to inaction when remediation is needed or to unnecessary remediation when none is necessary. It could also lead to misinterpretations of product impact. Therefore, properly collecting water samples, understanding their purpose, and establishing appropriate water system sampling plans are essential to water quality control and system control [2,4].

Purposes and Procedures

To assess a particular water quality attribute, a sample of the water usually must be removed from a water system for specific quality attribute testing. This sample may be analyzed by in-line/on-line instruments or it may be completely removed from the system as a "grab sample" in a container for off-line testing. In-line/on-line testing avoids the exogenous contamination potential of grab samples that could lead to artifactually variable data trends and incorrect decisions on system performance, maintenance, and utilized water quality, as well as initiating fruitless causative investigations. However, in-line/on-line testing may not be suitable for the purpose of the resulting data, making the off-line testing of grab samples the only suitable approach. The data from water testing are generally used for one of two purposes: for process control (PC) of the water purification and distribution system or for QC of the water being drawn from the system for some application or use. In many cases, depending on the sampling location and sampling process, the resulting data can be used for both PC and QC purposes.

PC Sampling

Because PC sampling is intended to reflect the quality of the water behind the valve and within the distribution system, coming from the purification system, or between its purification steps, efforts should be made to avoid contaminating the water as it drawn from the system so that its test results accurately reflect the water quality within the system at that location. This may require the use of strategically located sampling ports, in addition to points of use. If microbial testing is needed for PC purposes, the sampling valve should have a properly installed, sanitary design that uses vigorous pre-sampling flushing. This flushing shears off fragile biofilm structures growing on surfaces within the valve and water path before the sample is collected. This avoids biasing the microbial count of perhaps pristine water in the system behind that valve. A fully open valve flush (at >8 ft/s velocity within the valve and connector) for at least 30 s typically provides sufficient shear forces to adequately remove any fragile biofilm structures. Additional control measures for preventing sample contamination could also include stringent pre- and post-sampling outlet sanitation, the use of sterile hoses and gaskets or other connectors to direct the water flow, and other measures. The data from PC sampling indicate how well the system is maintaining the water quality at that sampling location. These data are subsequently used to signal when some extraordinary intervention might be needed, in addition to normal maintenance and system sanitization operations, to restore the system to the expected level of purity. PC sampling can only be used to indicate the quality of the water being delivered to the points of use (for QC purposes) if it has been shown to be representative of that point-of-use quality. This may be possible with chemical attributes which are typically not affected by the fluid path of the water delivery process, but is generally not possible with microbial attributes, which can be greatly affected by localized biofilms along that fluid path. If this fluid path is not utilized for PC sampling, then the resulting data typically cannot be used for QC purposes.

QC Sampling

QC sampling is intended to reflect the quality of water that is being used. These samples should be collected at the true point of use, that is, where the water is delivered for use, not where it leaves the water system. QC sampling must utilize that same delivery path and components utilized for a water transfer during actual water use. This includes the same valves, hoses, heat exchangers, flow totalizers, hard-piped connections, and other components utilized during water use. In addition to the water transfer components, QC sampling must also use the same water transfer process employed during water use, including the same pre-use outlet and delivery path flushing procedure and the same outlet, fitting, and hose sanitization practices employed during actual water use. The water delivery process and components used for QC sampling must be identical to manufacturing practices at every system outlet for the QC sample to mimic the quality of water being used by accumulating the same chemical and microbial contaminant levels it would during actual use from that outlet location. Where permanent connections from the water system to equipment are present, accommodation should be made in the design to collect samples from locations as close to the equipment as possible. *For example*, samples can be collected from special sample ports or other valves near the equipment connection that allow the collected water sample to accurately reflect the water quality that is used. Where the water transfer conduit is designed and/or definitively treated to eliminate all contaminating influences prior to water transfer through that conduit, PC sampling locations within the distribution system can reflect the quality of the water that is actually used for QC purposes at those permanent connections. However, the success of the design and treatments intended to eliminate these contaminating influences must be verified. This is typically done during water system validation. Where routine water use practices involve contamination-prone activities, such as no pre-use flushing or poor hose storage/ sanitization/ replacement practices, these water use practices should be improved to reduce the potential for delivering contaminated water from the water system and for unacceptable QC sample testing results that reflect that same contamination.

Attributes and Sampling Locations

The tests being performed on the samples are relevant to the sampling location and purpose of the sample. In-process monitoring of non-monograph attributes may be indicated for specific unit operations. For instance, before and after a softener, it may be important to determine water hardness to verify softener efficacy. Before and after an activated carbon bed/filter, it may be important to verify chlorine or TOC removal and/or reduction or test for an increase in microbial count. Before a distillation unit, it may be important to quantitate the incoming bacterial endotoxin level to ensure that the still is not being over challenged beyond its typical 3–4 log purification capability. However, once the water is in the distribution system, the compendia attributes of importance typically include at least conductivity, TOC, and microbial count. In Water for Injection systems and other systems or system locations where bacterial endotoxin control is important, endotoxin is also assayed. Other tests may be necessary depending on the intended uses of the water.

Chemical attributes

Dissolved chemical contaminants detected by conductivity or TOC testing tend to be uniformly distributed in the water throughout the water system. However, there are exceptions where localized chemical contamination sources can occur, such as from a coolant-leaking heat exchanger in a sub-loop, or at a point of use, or within a dead leg. These chemical contaminants may only be seen at the associated outlets and not systemically. However, in the absence of localized contamination influences, chemical attributes are candidates for on-line testing at fixed strategic locations within the distribution system, such as near a circulating loop return, and are generally reflective of the same chemical quality at all locations and points of use within the distribution system. Nevertheless, the suitability of the on-line locations of these instruments for QC release purposes must be verified as being representative of the use-point water quality. This is usually done during water system validation.

Microbial attributes

The same uniformity scenario cannot be assumed for microbial attributes. Planktonic organisms in a water sample could have originated from biofilms in the purification or distribution systems releasing more or less uniform levels of planktonic organisms into the circulating water, as detectable in samples from all outlets. However, a local biofilm developing within a water delivery conduit (such as a use-point outlet valve and transfer hose) in an otherwise pristine biofilm-free water system could release planktonic organisms detectable only in water delivered through that conduit. Therefore, QC release samples for assessing the quality of water that is delivered by the system during water use must be collected after the water has traversed the same fluid conduit (including the same preparatory activities such as outlet sanitization and pre-flushing) from the water distribution system to the specific locations where the water is used. On-line microbial water sampling/testing has value in pharmaceutical water systems only for PC purposes unless the water is taken from the point of use in the same manner as routine water usage, in which case the data can also have a QC release purpose. Microbial counts detected from strategic sampling ports continue to have PC and investigational value, but generally cannot be substituted for QC release testing except in certain scenarios, as described in QC Sampling.

Validation Sampling Plans

The initial sampling plan for a pharmaceutical water system is usually developed for a validation program. This strategy is for characterization of the system's ability to purify, distribute, and deliver pharmaceutical water. Typically, the initial validation sampling is for a short duration (*e.g.,* at least 2–4 weeks) at a high sampling frequency to generate a significant body of data that will allow detection of short term or localized chemical or microbial quality deviations from all outlets. These data provide an initial assessment of system performance to guide decisions about using the water for operational purposes. The initial validation sampling plan is re-evaluated when the pharmaceutical water is placed into operation, typically to reduce the amount of data being generated while not compromising the ability to identify anomalous operations/ events, especially during the early life cycle of the water system. In the absence of such quality deviations during the initial sampling period, the sampling frequency can be lessened for a period of time (*e.g.,* at least 2–4 additional weeks) to ensure that somewhat longer-term adverse quality trends are not apparent. During this second period of time, the water may be considered for at risk routine use, pending the acceptable completion of the second validation sampling period. After successful completion, monitoring can eventually be lessened again to what will become the routine sampling plan.

Periodic review of the water system operation and monitoring needs to be performed to assess seasonal source water variability, effectiveness of sanitization, and routine maintenance events. Periodic review should be performed during the complete life cycle of the water system, typically annually, for evidence of longer-term data trends and quality deviations. The routine sampling plan should be re-evaluated periodically based on the available data to determine the appropriate frequency and sample locations. This review offers an opportunity to improve data evaluation and reduce workloads based on what that data indicate relative to process and quality control. The routine sampling plan should have a rationale for the frequency and locations that are selected to justify how the resulting data will be used to characterize the overall operation of the system and the release of the water for use.

Routine Sampling Plans

Source water sampling

As mentioned in Table 1 the source water for pharmaceutical water systems must comply with the standards. When a municipality or other water authority is providing this Drinking Water, they are required to comply with the local Drinking Water Regulations for the water supplied to a drinking or potable water distribution piping grid for that region. The quality of that water by the time it reaches the pharmaceutical user is dependent on a number of factors including distance from the input source, duration of travel within the piping, and condition of the piping in that potable water distribution grid, any of which could have adversely affected some of its initial chemical and/or microbial attributes. Based on a risk assessment, it may be prudent to verify full compliance with regulations using water collected from sample ports prior to the pretreatment system, or other equivalent Drinking Water outlets within the facility. If the water complies, then continued assurance of compliance could be verified using Drinking Water Regulation test results provided by the water authority or by periodic retesting of selected or all the Drinking Water attributes by the user or by both the user and the water authority. If private sourced water is utilized, it is the user's responsibility to demonstrate full Drinking Water regulation compliance, using water samples from such sampling ports on a periodic basis as determined by a risk analysis. These pre-pretreatment sampling ports could, at the user's discretion, be used to periodically monitor other source water attributes that could affect specific pretreatment or purification unit operations. Depending on the user's source water quality consistency and a risk assessment of its potential impact on the purification process, the periodically monitored attributes could include microbial count, absence of coliforms, bacterial endotoxin levels, conductivity, TOC, pH, hardness, chlorine, silica, turbidity or silt density index, and others. These data could be useful in investigations and for operational adjustments to critical unit operation parameters and maintenance procedures, or for feedback to the potable water provider if unusual trends are observed.

Pretreatment and purification system sampling

The location and frequency of sampling from ports within the pretreatment and purification systems may be selected based on a risk analysis of unit operation purpose. The purpose of this sampling is primarily for PC, for example, to ensure maintenance of acceptable unit operation performance, to assess maintenance procedure efficacy, and to investigate the need for remedial action. Quality deviations in the early portions of the purification process can affect unit operation efficiency but usually do not impact the finished water quality or acceptable use.

Purified water distribution system sampling

Purified Water distribution system sampling is intended to provide continuing assurance of ongoing PC and compliance with the user's finished water chemical and microbiological requirements. Generally, the locations for that sampling and the frequency of testing the specific attributes are a matter of process and quality control consistency, as well as risk tolerance in the event of a deviation. Depending on the water system design, the chemical attributes of a water system tend to be relatively constant and more uniformly distributed than the microbiological attributes. Therefore, less frequent sampling at only selected locations could be justified for chemical testing based on familiarity with system design and the existence of historically consistent operational data. However, with some purification system designs, the chemical quality could change dramatically in a short period of time (such as from the exhaustion of deionization beds), so frequent or even continuous in-line/on-line monitoring of the chemical attributes would be advisable to be able to recognize and correct the cause of the problem before non-compliant water is produced and used. For microbial testing, all use points and critical sample ports in a distribution system are typically sampled routinely, including those that are infrequently used by manufacturing. There is no prescribed sampling frequency for Purified Water system outlets, so typical outlet sampling frequencies vary from daily to monthly, with sampling occurring somewhere in the system at least at weekly intervals. A risk analysis is suggested for determining the sampling plan for a Purified Water system. Factors in this analysis could include (but are not limited to) the test result history for the entire water system as well as specific outlets, the criticality of specific outlets to manufacturing, the usefulness of selected sample ports as indicators of ongoing system control, and the scope of impact on products and activities should an unfavorable test result occur. For the scope of impact, the less frequent the sampling, the more products and processes will be impacted by an unfavorable test result.

Water for injection distribution system sampling

The sampling plans for Water for Injection distribution systems (as well as any water system where some level of bacterial endotoxin control is needed) utilize the same general sampling approaches as do Purified Water systems. However, the regulatory expectations for Water for Injection distribution system sampling plans are more prescriptive because microbial control must be much more stringent as it is related to the bacterial endotoxin attribute. In general, water sampling for microbial and bacterial endotoxin testing is expected to occur daily somewhere in the system, with each outlet being sampled periodically, based on a risk assessment, to characterize the quality of the water.

Non-Routine Sampling

Non-routine sampling can also be performed on the water system for episodic events or reasons for which the routine sampling plans are insufficient to capture the needed information. Examples include change control purposes such as evaluating potential changes to sampling, testing, maintenance procedures, or system design; data or event excursion investigation purposes; or simply for long-term informational purposes and establishing baselines for future investigational value. The purpose of the non-routine sampling dictates the sampling procedures to be used, the attributes to be tested, and the location and repeating occurrence (if any) of that testing. It should also be noted that such non-routine sampling may be done from sampling ports that may or may not be routinely tested. Sampling ports can be positioned in a water system purely for investigational, non-routine sampling, and as such, they do not need to be part of a routine sampling plan.

CHEMICAL EVALUATIONS

Chemical Tests for Bulk Waters

The chemical attributes of Purified Water and Water for Injection were specified by a series of chemistry tests for various specific and nonspecific attributes with the intent of detecting chemical species indicative of incomplete or inadequate purification. Although these methods could have been considered barely adequate to control the quality of these waters, they nevertheless stood the test of time. This was partly because the operation of water systems was, and still is, based on on-line conductivity measurements and specifications generally thought to preclude the failure of these archaic chemistry attribute tests. In 1996, USP moved away from these chemical attribute tests, switching to contemporary analytical technologies for the bulk waters Purified Water and Water for Injection. The intent was to upgrade the analytical technologies without tightening the quality requirements. The two contemporary analytical technologies employed were TOC and conductivity. The TOC test replaced the test for Oxidizable Substances that primarily targeted organic contaminants. A multi-staged conductivity test that detects ionic (mostly inorganic) contaminants replaced, with the exception of the test for Heavy Metals, all of the inorganic chemical tests (*i.e.,* Ammonia, Calcium, Carbon Dioxide, Chloride, Sulfate)[2]. Replacing the heavy metals attribute was considered unnecessary because:

(1) The source water specifications [1] for individual heavy metals were tighter than the approximate limit of detection of the Heavy Metals test for USP XXII Water for Injection and Purified Water (approximately 0.1 ppm),

(2) Contemporary water system construction materials do not leach heavy metal contaminants, and

(3) Test results for this attribute have uniformly been negative; there has not been a confirmed occurrence of a singular test failure (failure of only the Heavy Metals test with all other attributes passing) since the current heavy metal drinking water standards have been in place.

Total Solids and pH were the only tests not covered by conductivity testing. The test for Total Solids was considered redundant because the nonselective tests of conductivity and TOC could detect most chemical species other than silica, which could remain undetected in its colloidal form.

Colloidal silica in Purified Water and Water for Injection is easily removed by most water pretreatment steps, and even if present in the water, it constitutes no medical or functional hazard except in extreme and rare situations. In such extreme situations, other attribute extremes are also likely to be detected. It is, however, the user's responsibility to ensure fitness for use. If silica is a significant component in the source water, and the purification unit operations could fail and selectively allow silica to be released into the finished water (in the absence of co-contaminants detectable by conductivity), then either silica-specific testing or a total-solids type testing should be utilized to monitor for and control this rare problem. The pH attribute was eventually recognized to be redundant to the conductivity test (which included pH as an aspect of the test and specification); therefore, pH was discontinued as a separate attribute test. The rationale used by USP to establish its Purified Water and Water for Injection conductivity specifications took into consideration the conductivity contributed by the two least-conductive former attributes of Chloride and Ammonia, thereby precluding their failure had those wet chemistry tests been performed. In essence, the Stage 3 conductivity specifications were established from the sum of the conductivities of the limit concentrations of chloride ions (from pH 5.0 to 6.2) and ammonia ions (from pH 6.3 to 7.0), plus the unavoidable contribution of other conductivity-contributing ions from water (H^+ and OH^-), dissolved atmospheric carbon dioxide (as HCO_3^-), and an electro-balancing quantity of either sodium (Na^+) or chlorine (Cl^-), depending on the pH-induced ionic imbalance. The Stage 2 conductivity specification is the lowest value in this Table, 2.1 mS/cm. The Stage 1 specifications, designed primarily for on-line measurements, were derived by essentially summing the lowest values in the contributing ion columns for each of a series of tables created for each 5° increment between 0° and 100°. As stated above, this rather radical change to utilizing a conductivity attribute as well as the inclusion of a TOC attribute allowed for on-line measurements. This was a major philosophical change and allowed industry to realize substantial savings. The TOC and conductivity tests can also be performed off-line in the laboratories using collected samples, although sample collection tends to introduce opportunities for adventitious contamination that can cause false high readings. The collection of on-line data is not, however, without challenges. The continuous readings tend to create voluminous amounts of data, where previously only a single data point was available. Sampling, continuous in-process data are excellent for understanding how a water system performs during all of its various usage and maintenance events in real time, but this is too much data for QC purposes. Therefore, for example, one can use a justifiable portion of the data (at a designated daily time or at the time of batch manufacturing) or the highest value in a given period as a worst case representation of the overall water quality for that period. Data averaging is generally discouraged because of its ability to obscure short-lived extreme quality events.

Chemical Tests for Sterile Waters

Packaged/sterile waters present a particular dilemma relative to the attributes of conductivity and TOC. The package itself is the major source of chemicals (inorganics and organics) that leach over time into the packaged water and can easily be detected by the conductivity and TOC tests. The irony of organic leaching from plastic packaging is that before the advent of bulk water TOC testing, when the Oxidizable Substances test was the only "organic purity" test for both bulk and packaged/ sterile water monographs in USP, the insensitivity of that test to many of the organic leachables from plastic and elastomeric packaging materials was largely unrecognized, allowing organic levels in packaged/sterile water to be quite high (possibly many times the TOC specification for bulk water). Similarly, glass containers can also leach inorganics, such as sodium, which are easily detected by conductivity but poorly detected by the former wet chemistry attribute tests. Most of these leachables are considered harmless based on current perceptions and standards at the rather significant concentrations present. Nevertheless, they effectively degrade the quality of the high-purity waters placed into these packaging systems. Some packaging materials contain more leachables than others and may not be as suitable for holding water and maintaining its purity. The attributes of conductivity and TOC tend to reveal more about the packaging leachables than they do about the water's original purity. These currently "allowed" leachables could render the sterile packaged versions of originally equivalent bulk water essentially unsuitable for many uses where the bulk waters are perfectly adequate. Therefore, to better control the ionic packaging leachables, is divided into two sections. The first is titled Bulk Water, which applies to Purified Water, Water for Injection, Water for Hemodialysis, and Pure Steam, and includes the three-stage conductivity testing instructions and specifications. The second section is titled Sterile Water, which applies to Sterile Purified Water, Sterile Water for Injection, Sterile Water for Inhalation, and Sterile Water for Irrigation. The Sterile Water section includes conductivity specifications similar to the Stage 2 testing approach because it is intended as a laboratory test, and these sterile waters were made from bulk water that already complied with the three-stage conductivity test. In essence, packaging leachables are the primary target analytes of the conductivity specifications in the Sterile Water section. The effect on potential leachable from different container sizes is the rationale for having two different specifications, one for small packages containing nominal volumes of 10 mL or less and another for larger packages. These conductivity specifications are harmonized with the European Pharmacopoeia conductivity specifications for Sterile Water for Injection. Controlling the organic purity of these sterile packaged waters, particularly those in plastic packaging, is more challenging. Although the TOC test can better detect these impurities and therefore can be better used to monitor and control these impurities than the current Oxidizable Substances test, the latter has a history of use for many decades and has the flexibility to test a variety of packaging types and volumes that are applicable to these sterile packaged waters. Nevertheless, TOC testing of these currently allowed sterile, plastic-packaged waters reveals substantial levels of plastic-derived organic leachables that render the water perhaps orders of magnitude less organically pure than is typically achieved with bulk waters. Therefore, usage of these packaged waters for analytical, manufacturing, and cleaning applications should only be exercised after the purity of the water for the application has been confirmed as suitable.

MICROBIAL EVALUATIONS

This section of the chapter presents a discussion about the types and sources of microorganisms and whether certain microbes are prone to colonize pharmaceutical water systems. This section also addresses microbiological examination of water samples, including a discussion on recovery methods[2].

Microorganism Types

Microorganisms are ubiquitous and their natural habitats are extremely diverse. Based on comparative ribosomal RNA sequencing, the phylogenetic tree of life consists of three domains: Bacteria and Archaea (both prokaryotes), and Eukarya (eukaryotes). Most microorganisms that contaminate pharmaceutical products are prokaryotic bacteria and eukaryotic fungi (yeasts and molds). These microbes are typical isolates from pharmaceutical environments, including the associated personnel, and a few are frank or opportunistic pathogens. Contamination with viruses is a concern in bioprocessing that uses animal cells.

Archaeans

Microbes from the domain Archaea are phylogenetically related to prokaryotes but are distinct from bacteria. Many are extremophiles, with some species capable of growing at very high temperatures (hyperthermophiles) or in other extreme environments beyond the tolerance of any other life form. In general, most extremophiles are anaerobic or microaerophilic chemolithoautotrophs. Because of their unique habitats, metabolism, and nutritional requirements, Archaeans are not known to be frank or opportunistic pathogens, and they are not capable of colonizing a pharmaceutical water system.

Bacteria

Bacteria are of immense importance because of their rapid growth, mutation rates, and ability to exist under diverse and adverse conditions. Some are very small and can pass through 0.2-mm rated filters. Others form spores, which are not part of their reproductive cycle. Bacterial spore formation is a complex developmental process that allows the organisms to produce a dormant and highly resistant cell in times of extreme stress. Bacterial endospores can survive high temperatures, strong UV irradiation, desiccation, chemical damage, and enzymatic destruction, which would normally kill vegetative bacteria. Using a traditional cellular staining technique based on cell wall compositional differences, bacteria are categorized into Gram positive and Gram negative, although many subgroups exist within each category based on genomic similarities and differences. Gram-positive bacteria: Gram-positive bacteria are common in a pharmaceutical manufacturing environment but not in water systems. This is because they are generally not suited to surviving in a liquid environment that has the chemical purity of a pharmaceutical-grade water system. Gram-positive bacteria include the spore-forming bacteria from the genus *Bacillus*, which are common soil and dust contaminants, and the non-sporulating bacteria from the genera *Staphylococcus*, *Streptococcus,* and *Micrococcus*, which normally colonize human skin and mucous membranes. Other types of Gram-positive bacterial contaminants include organisms from the genera *Corynebacterium, Mycobacterium, Arthrobacter, Propionibacterium, Streptomyces,* and *Actinomyces.* This latter group of microbes can be found in various natural habitats including the human skin and soil. Although Gram-positive bacteria can be detected in pharmaceutical water samples, their recovery is often associated with faulty aseptic technique during sampling or testing, or associated with exogenous contamination sources. Although these nonaquatic microorganisms could be present in source water and could, in rare circumstances, make their way into the early stages of a water purification unit operation, Gram-positive bacteria are not known to colonize water systems. In addition, these microbes will likely be removed by one or more of the purification unit operations prior to the ultimate creation of the pharmaceutical-grade water. Gram-negative bacteria: These types of bacteria are found in soil, water, plants, and animals. Gram-negative bacteria are of keen interest to pharmaceutical manufacturers, primarily due to their production of endotoxins, a topic discussed in Endotoxin. Some Gram-negative bacteria prefer aquatic habitats and tend to colonize water systems and other wet environments as biofilms, a topic discussed in Biofilm Formation in Water Systems. *Mycoplasma*: Organisms from the genus *Mycoplasma* are the smallest of the bacteria. Unlike other bacteria, these organisms do not have a cell wall and many exist as intracellular or animal parasites. Mycoplasmas also require specific nutrients for survival, including cholesterol, and they cannot survive in a hypotonic environment such as pure water. Based on these facts, this type of bacteria is not a concern for pharmaceutical-grade water systems.

Fungi

Fungi are mainly aerobic mesophilic microbes. They exist as unicellular (yeast) and multicellular filamentous (mold) organisms. Molds are often found in wet/moist but usually non-aquatic environments, such as soil and decaying vegetation. Examples of common environmental molds include those from the genera *Aspergillus, Penicillium, Fusarium, Cladosporium,* and *Alternaria*. As mold matures it develops spores, which, unlike bacterial spores, are part of their reproductive cycle and are less resistant to adverse conditions. Mold spores are easily spread through air and materials, and could contaminate water samples. Yeasts are often associated with humans and vegetation. Examples of yeasts commonly found in pharmaceutical environments include the genera *Candida, Saccharomyces,* and *Rhodotorula*. Some molds and yeasts are considered human pathogens and a few mold species produce mycotoxins. Neither yeasts nor molds are suited for colonization or survival in pharmaceutical water systems. Their recovery is often associated with faulty aseptic technique during sampling or testing, or associated with exogenous contamination sources. These non-aquatic microorganisms, if present in source water, could make their way into the early stages of a water purification system; however, they will likely be removed by one or more of the purification unit operations.

Viruses

A virus is a small infectious agent unlike eukaryotes and prokaryotes. This is because viruses have no metabolic abilities of their own. Viruses are genetic elements containing either DNA or RNA that replicate within host cells. Human pathogenic viruses, especially those of fecal origin, could be present in source water. However, they are easily neutralized by typical water purification treatments, such as chlorination. Therefore, it is unlikely that viruses will be present or will proliferate (due to the absence of host cells) in pharmaceutical-grade waters.

Thermophiles

Thermophiles are heat-loving organisms and can be either bacteria or molds. Thermophilic and hyperthermophilic aquatic microorganisms require unique environmental and nutritional conditions to survive. These conditions do not exist in the high-purity water of pharmaceutical water systems, whether ambient or hot, to support their growth. Bacteria that are able to inhabit hot pharmaceutical water systems are invariably found in much cooler locations within these hot systems; for example, within infrequently used outlets, ambient subloops off of hot loops, use-point and sub-loop cooling heat exchangers, transfer hoses and connecting pipes, or dead legs. These bacterial contaminants are the same mesophilic (moderate temperature-loving) types found in ambient water systems and are not thermophiles. Based on these facts, thermophilic bacteria are not a concern for hot pharmaceutical-grade water systems.

Biofilm Formation in Water Systems

A biofilm is a three-dimensional structured community of sessile microbial cells embedded in a matrix of extracellular polymeric substances (EPS). Biofilms form when bacteria attach to surfaces in moist environments and produce a slimy, glue-like substance, the EPS matrix, while proliferating at that location. This slimy matrix facilitates biofilm adhesion to surfaces as well as the attachment of additional planktonic cells to form a microbial community. The EPS matrix of biofilms that colonize water systems also facilitates adsorption and concentration of nutrients from the water and retains the metabolites and waste products produced by the embedded biofilm cells, which can serve as nutrients for other biofilm community members. This EPS matrix is also largely responsible for biofilm's resistance to chemical sanitizers, which must penetrate completely through the matrix to contact and kill the biofilm cells within the matrix. Heat sanitization approaches do not generally have these EPS matrix penetration difficulties, so they are usually considered superior to chemicals in killing biofilms where materials of construction allow. The three-dimensional structure of a well-developed biofilm, as well as the biofilm's creation and release of small, motile "pioneer cells" for further colonization, are facilitated through gene expression modulating "quorum sensing" chemicals released in tiny amounts by individual biofilm cells and concentrated to a functional level within this same EPS matrix. So, the EPS matrix of biofilms is primarily responsible for the biofilm's success in colonizing and proliferating in very low nutrient-containing high-purity water systems. The EPS matrix also explains the difficulty in killing and/or removing biofilms from water purification and distribution system surfaces.

Biofilm-forming bacteria in water systems

Common microorganisms recovered from water system samples include Gram-negative bacteria from the genera *Pseudomonas, Ralstonia, Burkholderia, Stenotrophomonas, Comamonas, Methylobacterium,* and many other types of *Pseudomonas*-like organisms known collectively as pseudomonads. These types of microbes, found in soil and source water, tend to colonize all water system distribution and purification system surfaces including activated carbon beds, deionizing resin beds, RO systems, membrane filtration modules, connecting piping, hoses, and valves. If not controlled, they can compromise the functionality of purification steps in the system and spread downstream, possibly forming biofilms on the distribution system surfaces such as tanks, piping, valves, hoses, and other surfaces, from where they can be sheared or otherwise released into the finished water used in processes and products. Some of the biofilm pseudomonads are opportunistic human pathogens and may possess resistance to commonly used pharmaceutical product preservatives, particularly when imbedded in EPS matrix flocs sheared from water system biofilms. Several pseudomonads are also capable of utilizing a wide variety of carbon sources as nutrients, allowing them to colonize austere, adventitious nutrient environments such as water systems. This nutritional diversity also makes them capable of growing to very high numbers in some pharmaceutical products and raw materials, thus leading to product adulteration and potential risk to patient health. Given that these bacteria are commonly found in aqueous environments, endotoxin control for Water for Injection systems (and some Purified Water systems) through biofilm control becomes critical.

Non-biofilm-forming bacteria in water systems

Other types of non-pseudomonad Gram-negative bacteria are generally non-aquatic by nature. They include coliforms from the genera *Escherichia, Salmonella, Shigella, Serratia, Proteus, Enterobacter,* and *Klebsiella*, which are used as indicators of fecal contamination. Although some of these bacteria can be human enteric pathogens, these non-pseudomonads are not suited to colonizing or surviving in pharmaceutical water systems owing to the water's chemical purity. In fact, non-pseudomonad enteric bacteria are extremely unlikely contaminants of pharmaceutical water systems unless local sewage and source water controls are not in place. Such controls are required in order to comply with the source water requirements for making USP-grade waters.

Microorganism Sources

Exogenous contamination

Exogenous microbial contamination of bulk pharmaceutical water comes from numerous possible sources, including source water. At a minimum, source water should meet the microbial quality attributes of Drinking Water, which is the absence of fecal coliforms (*E. coli*). A wide variety of other types of microorganisms, chiefly Gram-negative bacteria, may be present in the incoming water. If appropriate steps are not taken to reduce their numbers or eliminate them, these microorganisms may compromise subsequent water purification steps. Exogenous microbial contamination can also arise from maintenance operations, equipment design, and the process of monitoring, including:

- Unprotected, faulty, or absent vent filters or rupture disks
- Backflow from interconnected equipment
- Non-sanitized distribution system openings for component replacements, inspections, repairs, and expansions
- Inadequate drain air-breaks
- Innate bioburden of activated carbon, ion-exchange resins, regenerant chemicals, and chlorine-neutralizing chemicals

- Inappropriate rinsing water quality after regeneration or sanitization
- Poor sanitization of use points, hard-piped equipment connectors, and other water transfer devices such as hoses
- Deficient techniques for use, sampling, and operation

The exogenous contaminants may not be normal aquatic bacteria but rather microorganisms of soil, air, or even human origin. The detection of non-aquatic microorganisms may be an indication of sampling or testing contamination or a system component failure, which should trigger investigation and remediation. Sufficient care should be given to sampling, testing, system design, and maintenance to minimize microbial contamination from exogenous sources.

Endogenous contamination

Endogenous sources of microbial contamination can arise from unit operations in a water purification system that is not properly maintained and operated. Microorganisms present in source water may adsorb to carbon bed media, ion-exchange resins, filter membranes, and other equipment surfaces, and initiate the formation of biofilms. Downstream colonization can occur when microorganisms are shed from existing biofilm-colonized surfaces and carried to other areas of the water system. Microorganisms may also attach to suspended particles such as carbon bed fines or fractured resin particles. When the microorganisms become planktonic, they serve as a source of contamination to subsequent purification equipment and to distribution systems. Another source of endogenous microbial contamination is the distribution system itself. Microorganisms can colonize pipe surfaces, rough welds, misaligned flanges, valves, and dead legs, where they proliferate and form biofilms. Once formed, biofilms can become a continuous source of microbial contamination, which is very difficult to eradicate. Therefore, biofilm development must be managed by methods such as frequent cleaning and sanitization, as well as process and equipment design.

Endotoxin

Endotoxins are lipopolysaccharides found in and shed from the cell envelope that is external to the cell wall of Gram-negative bacteria. Some grades of pharmaceutical waters, such as those used in parenteral applications (*e.g.*, Water for Injection, Water for Hemodialysis, and the sterilized packaged waters made from Water for Injection) strictly limit the amount of endotoxins that may be present because these compounds are pyrogenic.

Sources

Endotoxins may occur as collections of lipopolysaccharide molecules associated with living microorganisms, fragments of dead microorganisms, the EPS matrix surrounding biofilm bacteria, or free molecular clusters or micelles containing many lipopolysaccharide molecules. The monomeric form of the endotoxin molecule does not exist in high-purity water because of its amphiphilic nature. Endotoxins may be introduced into the system from the source water or may be released from cell surfaces of bacteria that colonize the water system. For example, a spike in endotoxin may occur following sanitization as a result of endotoxin release from killed cells. Endotoxin quantitation in water samples is not a good indicator of the level of biofilm development in a water system because of the multiplicity of endotoxin sources.

Removal and control

To control endotoxin levels in water systems, it is important to control all potential sources of contamination with Gram-negative bacteria as well as free endotoxin in the water. Contamination control includes the use of upstream unit operations to reduce bioburden from incoming water, as well as engineering controls (*e.g.,* heat sanitization, equipment design, UV sanitizers, filters, material surface, and flow velocity) to minimize biofilm development on piping surfaces and to reduce re-inoculation of the system with free-floating bacteria. Endotoxin remediation may be accomplished through the normal exclusion or removal action afforded by various unit operations within the treatment system. Examples of endotoxin removal steps in a water purification train include RO, deionization, ultrafilters, and endotoxin-adsorptive filters.

Test Methods

Microbes in water systems can be detected as exampled in this section or by methods adapted from Microbial Enumeration Tests, Tests for Specified Microorganisms <62>, or the current edition of Standard Methods for the Examination of Water and Wastewater by the American Public Health Association. This section describes classical culture approaches to bioburden testing, with a brief discussion on rapid microbiological methods. Every water system has a unique microbiome. It is the user's responsibility to perform method validation studies to demonstrate the suitability of the chosen test media and incubation conditions for bioburden recovery. In general, users should select the method that recovers the highest planktonic microbial counts in the shortest time, thus allowing for timely investigations and remediation. Such studies are usually performed before or during system validation. In addition, the chosen method should be reassessed periodically, as the microbiome of a new water system gradually establishes a steady state relative to the system's routine maintenance, use, and sanitization procedures. The steady state condition can take months or even years to be achieved, and can be affected by a change in source water quality, changes in finished water purity by using modified or increasingly inefficient purification processes, changes in finished water use patterns and volumes, changes in routine and preventative maintenance or sanitization procedures and frequencies, or any type of system intrusion (*e.g.*, component replacement, removal, or addition).

Microbial enumeration considerations

Most microbial contaminants in water systems are found primarily as biofilms on surfaces, with only a very small percentage of the microbiome suspended in the water, or planktonic, at any given time. Although it would seem logical to directly monitor biofilm development on surfaces, current technology for surface evaluations in an operating water system makes this impractical in a GMP environment. Therefore, an indirect approach must be used: the detection and enumeration of planktonic microorganisms that have been released from biofilms. This planktonic microbiome will impact the processes or products where the water is used. The detection and enumeration of the planktonic microbiome can be accomplished by collecting samples from water system outlets. Planktonic organisms are associated with the presence of biofilms as well as free-floating bacteria introduced into the system (pioneer cells), which may eventually form new biofilms. Therefore, by enumerating the microorganisms in water grab samples, the overall state of control over biofilm development can be assessed. This assessment has historically been accomplished with classical cultural techniques, which are viewed as the traditional method. However, nutritional limitations of the growth media may not satisfy growth requirements of organisms present in the water system that originated from a biofilm. As a result, traditional cultural methods may only detect a fraction of the biofilm bacteria present in the water sample. Other options are available, such as rapid microbiological methods. There is no ideal cultural enumeration method that will detect all microorganisms in a water sample, although some media or incubation temperatures may be better than others. However, from a PC perspective, this limitation is acceptable because it is the relative changes in the trends for water sample microbial counts that indicate the state of PC.

The classical cultural approach

Classical cultural approaches for microbial testing of water include but are not limited to pour plates, spread plates, membrane filtration, and most probable number (MPN) tests. These methods are generally easy to perform, and provide excellent sample processing throughput. Method sensitivity can be increased *via* the use of larger sample sizes. This strategy is used in the membrane filtration method. Cultural approaches are further defined by the type of medium used in combination with the incubation temperature and duration. This combination should be selected according to the monitoring needs of a specific water system and its ability to recover the microorganisms of interest, *i.e.*, those that could have a detrimental effect on the products manufactured or process uses, as well as those that reflect the microbial control status of the system. *Growth media*: The traditional categorization is that there are two basic forms of media available: "high nutrient" and "low nutrient". Those media traditionally categorized as high-nutrient include Plate Count Agar (TGYA), Soybean Casein Digest Agar (SCDA or TSA), and m-HPC Agar (formerly m-SPC Agar). These media are intended for the general isolation and enumeration of heterotrophic or copiotrophic bacteria. Low-nutrient media, such as R2A Agar and NWRI Agar (HPCA), have a larger variety of nutrients than the high-nutrient media. These low-nutrient media were developed for use with potable water due to their ability to recover a more nutritionally diverse population of microorganisms found in these environments. The use of R2A may not be the best choice for high-purity water systems. Even though high-purity water creates an oligotrophic environment, it has been shown empirically that in many high-purity compendial waters, the microbial count disparity between low- and high-nutrient media is dramatically less to nil, compared to potable water. Nevertheless, using the medium that has been demonstrated, through validation studies, to be the most optimal for the microbiome in a particular water system is essential.

Incubation conditions: Duration and temperature of incubation are also critical aspects of microbiological testing. Classical compendial methods specify the use of high-nutrient media, typically incubated at 30°–35° for NLT 48 h. Given the types of microbes found in many water systems, incubation at lower temperatures (*e.g.,* ranges of 20°–25° or 25°– 30°) for longer periods (at least 4 days) could recover higher microbial counts than classical compendial methods. Low-nutrient media typically require longer incubation conditions (at least 5 days) because the lower nutrient concentrations promote slower growth. Even high-nutrient media can sometimes yield higher microbial recovery with longer and cooler incubation conditions. The decision to test a particular system using high- or low-nutrient media, higher or lower incubation temperatures, and shorter or longer incubation times should be based on comparative cultivation studies using the native microbiome of the water system. The decision to use media requiring longer incubation periods to recover higher counts should also be balanced with the timeliness of results. Detection of marginally higher counts at the expense of a significantly longer incubation period may not be the best approach for monitoring water systems. Some cultural conditions using low-nutrient media lead to the development of microbial colonies that are much less differentiated in colonial appearance, an attribute that microbiologists rely on when selecting representative microbial types for further characterization. The nature of some of the slow growers and the extended incubation times needed for their development into visible colonies may also lead to those colonies becoming dysgonic and difficult to subculture. This could limit their further characterization, depending on the microbial identification technology used.

Suggested classical cultural methods

Users should determine through experimentation which methods are best for in-process and QC monitoring, as well as for recovering specific microorganisms that could be found in the water system and might be objectionable for the intended water use. For media growth promotion, use at a minimum *Pseudomonas aeruginosa* ATCC 9027 and *Bacillus subtilis* ATCC 6633. Additional organisms should be used to represent those that are considered objectionable and/or typically isolated from the water system (house isolates).

Microbial identification

In addition to the enumeration of the bioburden in the water, there is a need to identify and/or select certain microbial species that could be detrimental to products or processes. Some bacteria may also be resistant to preservatives and other antimicrobial chemicals used in liquid and semi-solid products, thus leading to potential product spoilage. For example, *Pseudomonas aeruginosa* and *Burkholderia cepacia*, as well as some other pseudomonads, are known opportunistic pathogens. As such, it may be appropriate to consider these species as objectionable microorganisms for the type of water used to manufacture liquid and semi-solid products. There is a higher risk of infection if these organisms are found in products targeted for susceptible patient populations (*e.g.,* the very young, the very old, and the immune-compromised) or products contacting highly susceptible tissues (*e.g.,* inhaled products or some topical products). However, if the product where the water is used carries an absence specification for a particular pathogenic species that is not capable of living in a high-purity water system, then these non-aquatic species should not be candidates for routine water testing. For PC and QC, it is valuable to know the microbial species present in the normal microbiome of a water system, even if they are not specifically objectionable. If a new species is detected, it may be an indication of a subtle process change or an exogenous intrusion. The identity of the microorganism may be a clue as to its origin and can help with implementation of corrective or preventive action. Therefore, it is industry practice to identify the microorganisms in samples that yield results exceeding established Alert and Action Levels. It is also of value to periodically identify the normal microbiome in a water system, even if counts are below established Alert Levels. This information can provide perspective on the species recoveries from Alert and Action Level excursion samples, indicating whether they are new species or just higher levels of the normal microbiome. Water system isolates may be incorporated into a company culture collection for use in tests such as antimicrobial effectiveness tests, microbial method validation/suitability testing, and media growth promotion. The decision to use isolates in these studies should be risk-based because many isolates will not grow on the high nutrient media required in these studies.

Rapid microbiological methods

In recent years, new technologies that enhance microbial detection and the timeliness of test results have been adopted by pharmaceutical QC testing labs. Rapid Microbiological Methods (RMM) are divided into four categories: Growth-Based, Viability-Based, Artifact-Based, and Nucleic Acid-Based. Examples of RMM used for the evaluation of microbial quality of water systems include:

- Microscopic visual epifluorescence membrane counting techniques
- Automated laser scanning membrane counting approaches
- Early colony detection methods based on autofluorescence, adenosine triphosphate (ATP) bioluminescence, or vital staining
- Genetic-based detection/quantitation

ALERT AND ACTION LEVELS AND SPECIFICATIONS

Introduction

Establishment of Alert and Action Levels for any manufacturing process facilitates appropriate and timely control. In the case of a pharmaceutical water system, the key PC parameters can be specific chemical, physical, and microbiological attributes of the water produced. Typically, most chemical attributes can be determined in real time or in the lab within a few min after sample collection. Physical attributes such as the pressure drop across a filter, temperature, and flow rate—which are sometimes considered critical for operation or sanitization of the water system—must be measured in situ during operation. Obtaining timely microbial data is more challenging compared to chemical and physical attributes, often taking several days. This limits the ability to control microbial attributes in a timely manner, and therefore requires a more challenging evaluation of the test results and conservative implementation of PC levels. This section provides guidance on the establishment and use of Alert and Action Levels, as well as Specifications to assess the suitability of the water and the water system for use in production [1,2,4].

Examples of Critical Parameter Measurements

Examples of measurements and parameters that are important to water system processes and products are described below.

- The list, which is not intended to be exhaustive or required, contains some examples of parameters that could be measured to demonstrate that the system is in a state of control.
- Examples of measurements that could be critical to the purification or sanitization process include:

   - Temperature, for thermally sanitized systems
   - % Rejection of an RO system
   - Endotoxin levels of feed water to a distillation system
   - Chlorine presence immediately prior to an RO system
- Examples of measurements that could be critical to the water distribution process include:
   - Return/end-of-loop line pressure, to forewarn of a negative pressure from simultaneous use of too many outlets
   - Beginning and end-of-loop flow rate, to forewarn of an excessively high flow rate at the UV lamps if too many outlets are open
   - Flow rate, to ensure that sufficient water is available for operations
- Examples of measurements that could be critical to final water quality include:
   - Conductivity
   - TOC
   - Endotoxin—for Water for Injection systems
   - Particulate matter
   - Bioburden
   - Ozone or other chemicals—for chemically sanitized systems

Purpose of the Measurements

Although the purpose of each measurement varies, the results can be used to provide system performance feedback, often immediately, serving as ongoing PC and product quality indicators. At the same time, the results provide information necessary for making decisions regarding the immediate processing and usability of the water. However, some attributes may not be monitored continuously or may have a long delay in data availability (*e.g.,* microbial data). Regardless, both real-time data and data with longer cycle times can be used to properly establish Alert and Action Levels, which can serve as an early warning or indication of a potentially approaching quality shift. As PC indicators, Alert and Action Levels are trigger points for the potential need for investigation and/or remedial action, to prevent a system from deviating from normal conditions and producing water unsuitable for its intended use. This "intended use" minimum quality is sometimes referred to as a "Specification" or "Limit", and may include limits for conductivity and TOC listed in water monographs, or other specifications required for these waters that have been defined by the user internally. In all cases, the validity of the data should be verified to ensure that the data are accurate and consistently representative of the water quality in the system, regardless of whether the sample was collected from a sampling port or use point. The resulting data must not be unduly biased, positively or negatively, due to the sampling method, the environment in the vicinity of the sampling location, the test procedure, instrumentation, or other artifacts that could obscure or misrepresent the true quality of the water intended by the purpose of the sampling, *i.e.,* for PC or for QC.

Defining Alert and Action Levels and Specifications

Data generated from routine water system monitoring should be trended to ensure that the system operates in a state of chemical and microbiological control. To assist with the evaluation of system performance, companies should establish inprocess control levels based on historical data or a fraction of the water Specifications (as long as this latter approach yields values with relevance to process performance). When establishing Alert and Action Levels and Specifications, a two- or three-tier approach is typically used. In a three-tier approach, the typical structure is to establish in-process controls using Alert Level, Action Level, and Specifications. Alert and Action Levels are used as proactive approaches to system management prior to exceeding Specifications. The criteria for defining and reacting to adverse trends should be set by the user. These levels should be set at values that allow companies to take action to prevent the system from producing water that is unfit for use. Water Specifications or Limits represent the suitability for use of the water. In a two-tier approach, a combination of the above terminology is used, depending on the parameter to be monitored. For example, if the attribute does have a monograph specification, the two tiers are Alert Level (or Action Level) and Specification. If the attribute does not have a limit/ specification, the two tiers are usually Alert Level and Action Level. A single-tier approach is possible, but this is risky and difficult to manage. With this approach, where the water/ system is either acceptable or not acceptable, the single-tier method does not allow for any adjustment, correction, or investigation prior to stopping production. However, certain sampling locations, such as sampling ports that are not used for manufacturing products or processes, do not represent the finished water quality where a Specification could be applied. In these locations, a two-tier approach (Alert and Action Levels only) could be applied. In some sampling locations, a single PC level might possibly be appropriate, depending on the attribute.

Alert level

An Alert Level for a measurement or parameter should be derived from the normal operating range of the water system. Specifically, Alert Levels are based on the historical operating performance under production conditions, and then are established at levels that are just beyond the majority of the normal historical data. The Alert Level for a parameter is often a single value or a range of values, such as:

- Higher than typical conductivity or TOC
- Higher than typical microbial count

- Higher than typical endotoxin level
- Low temperature during thermal sanitization
- pH range control prior to an RO
- Ozone concentration in a storage tank

Various methods, tools, and statistical approaches are available for establishing Alert Levels, and the user needs to determine the approaches that work for their application. Some numerical examples are two or three standard deviations (or more) in excess of the mean value, or some percentage above the mean value but below a Specification. An event-based example could be the appearance of a new microorganism or a non-zero microbial count where zero is the norm. When an Alert Level is exceeded, this indicates that a process or product may have drifted from its normal operating condition or range. Alert Level excursions represent a warning and do not necessarily require a corrective action. However, Alert Level excursions may warrant notification of personnel involved in water system operation, as well as the quality assurance (QA) personnel. Alert Level excursions may also lead to additional monitoring, with more intense scrutiny of the resulting and neighboring data as well as other process indicators.

Action level

An Action Level is also based on the same historical data, but the levels are established at values (or ranges) that exceed the Alert Levels. The values/ranges are determined using the same types of numerical or event-based tools as the Alert Levels, but at different values. In a three-tier approach, it is good practice to select an Action Level that is more than the Alert Level, but less than the Specification to allow the user to make corrective actions before the water would go out of compliance. Exceeding a quantitative Action Level indicates that the process has allowed the product quality or other critical parameter to drift outside of its normal operating range. An Action Level can also be event-based. In addition to exceeding quantitative Action Levels, some examples of event-based Action Level excursions include, but are not limited to:

- Exceeding an Alert Level repeatedly
- Exceeding an Alert Level in multiple locations simultaneously
- The recovery of specific objectionable microorganisms
- A repeating non-zero microbial count where zero is the norm

If an Action Level is exceeded, this should prompt immediate notification of both QA staff and the personnel involved in water system operations and use, so that corrective actions can be taken to restore the system back to its normal operating range. Such remedial actions should also include investigative efforts to understand what happened and eliminate or reducethe probability of recurrence. Depending on the nature of the Action Level excursion, it may be necessary to evaluate its impact on the water uses during the period between the previous acceptable test result and the next acceptable test result.

Special alert and action level situations

In new or significantly altered water systems, where there is limited or no historical data from which to derive trends, it is common to establish initial Alert and Action Levels based on equipment design capabilities. These initial levels should be within the process and product Specifications where water is used. It is also common for new water systems, especially ambient water systems, to undergo changes, both chemically and microbiologically, over time as various unit operations (such as RO membranes) exhibit the effects of aging. This type of system aging effect is most common during the first year of use. As the system ages, a steady state microbial population (microorganism types and levels) may develop due to the collective effects of system design, source water, maintenance, and operation, including the frequency of re-bedding, backwashing, regeneration, and sanitization. This established or mature microbial population may be higher than the one detected when the water system was new. Therefore, there is cause for the impurity levels to increase over this maturation period and eventually stabilize. Some water systems are so well controlled microbially—such as continuously or intermittently hot Water for Injection distribution systems—that microbial counts and endotoxin levels are essentially nil or below the limit of reasonable delectability. This common scenario often coincides with a very low Specification that is poorly quantifiable due to imprecision (as much as two-fold variability) of the test methods that may be near their limits of detection. In such systems, quantitative data trending has little value, and therefore, quantitative PC levels also have little value. The non-zero values in such systems could be due to sporadic sampling issues and not indicative of a water system PC deviation; however, if these non-zero values occur repeatedly, they could be indicative of process problems. So, an alternative approach for establishing Alert and Action Levels with these data could be the use of the incident rate of non-zero values, with the occasional single non-zero "hit" perhaps being an Alert Level (regardless of its quantitative value), and multiple or sequential "hits" being an Action Level. Depending on the attribute, perhaps single hits may not even warrant being considered an Alert Level, so only a multiple-hit situation would be considered actionable. It is up to the user to decide on their approach for system control, *i.e.,* whether to use one, two, or three levels of controls for a given water system and sampling location, and whether to establish Alert and Action Levels as quantitative or qualitative hit-frequency values.

Specifications

Water Specifications or Limits are set based on direct potential product and/or process impact and they represent the suitability for use of the water. The various bulk water monographs contain tests for Conductivity, TOC, and Bacterial Endotoxins (for Water for Injection). The need for microbial specifications for bulk waters (Purified Water and Water for Injection) depends on the water use(s), some of which may require strict control (*e.g.*, very low bioburden, absence of objectionable organisms, or low ionic strength) while others may require no specification due to the lack of impact. *For example*, microbial specifications are appropriate and typically expected for water that is used in product formulations and final equipment rinses. However, where the water is used for analytical reagent preparation or for cleaning processes that conclude with a final antimicrobial heat drying or solvent rinsing step, the microbial quality of the water is likely less of a concern. The decision to establish microbial Specifications for bulk pharmaceutical waters should be based on a formal risk assessment of its uses and justified by scientific rationale. It is very important to understand the chemical and microbial quality of the water in its final form as it is delivered from a water system to the locations where it is used in manufacturing activities and other points of use. The quality of the water within the water system could be compromised if it picks up chemical or microbial contaminants during its delivery from the system to the points of use. These points of use, where cumulative contamination could be present, are the locations where compliance with all the water Specifications is mandated. As discussed above, compliance with chemical Specifications can be confirmed periodically between uses, immediately prior to use, or even while the water is being utilized in product manufacturing. While the use of RMM may provide for timely microbial data, the use of conventional cultivative microbiological testing usually delays confirmation of microbial compliance until after the water has been used. However, for some applications, this logistical limitation should not eliminate the need for establishing microbial Specifications for this very important raw material. The manufacturing risk imposed by these logistics accentuates the value of validated microbial control for a water system. It also emphasizes the value of unbiased microbial monitoring of samples collected from pertinent locations, with evaluation of the resulting data against well-chosen, preferably trend-derived Alert and Action Levels, which can facilitate remedial PC to preclude Specification excursions. Users should establish their own quantitative microbial Specifications suited to their water uses. But these values should not be greater than 100 cfu/mL for Purified Water or 10 cfu/ 100 mL for Water for Injection unless specifically justified, because these values generally represent the highest microbial levels for pharmaceutical water that are still suitable for manufacturing use. A Specification excursion should prompt an out-of-specification (OOS) investigation. The investigation is performed to determine.

(1) The root cause of the excursion so that CAPA may be taken for remediation purposes, and
(2) Assess the impact on affected processes and finished products where the water was used. Product disposition decisions must be made and are dependent on factors which could include:
    - Role of water in the product or in-process material
    - Chemical or microbial nature of the attribute whose Specification value was exceeded
    - Level of product contamination by the water
    - Presence of objectionable microorganisms
    - Any downstream processing of affected in-process materials that could mitigate the OOS attribute
    - Physical and chemical properties of the finished product where the water was used that could mitigate the OOS attribute
    - Product administration routes and potentially sensitive/susceptible users

CONCLUSIONS

Water is a universal solvent used in the pharmaceutical manufacturing industries for the various purposes as production, processing and cleaning of all equipment hence very keen attention should be given for its purification. There are many types of purified water system used in pharmaceutical facilities. Although most of them share common features, each of system is custom designed for a specific application. Developing a proper design requires a good understanding of system operation and careful attention to details. Simply following common rules of thumb does not necessarily guarantee a reliable system – no matter how much money is spent. On the other hand, with a good under-standing, it is often possible to design, install and validate a functional and reliable Purified Water System with less capital investment and lower operating cost. Water treatment systems must be operated within regulatory guidelines as with pharmaceutical production facilities. Validation of the water system should be performed to prove its reliability and strength of the system for producing water of specified quality with a high degree of assurance and every report should be documented for better work. To validate these systems, there must be documented evidence that the system is operating consistently and according to the desired specifications. Validation is a tool for total quality management and it is necessary for process optimization, safety, efficacy and assurance of quality. Such validation protocols also fulfill regulatory requirements and provide good business sense. Successful accomplishment of validation is ensured by various testing phases. Usually, a three-phase testing approach is recommended over an extended period to prove reliability and robustness of the system for producing water of specified quality with a high degree of assurance.

REFERENCES

[1] Jeffrey Denoncourt; Best practices for water purification system design: 2007; Plumbing system and design, Pg 28-35.
[2] U.S. EPA NPDWR
[3] USP 40, General Information / <1231> Water for Pharmaceutical Purposes, United States Pharmacopeial Convention, Inc., 12601 Twinbrook Parkway, Rockville, MD 20852.
[4] WHO TRS 970 Annex 2 2012 WHO good manufacturing practices: water for pharmaceutical use

18

HVAC System Qualification

ABSTRACT

In pharmaceutical industry HVAC or air handling system acts as a direct impact system in the aseptic practice which has direct impact on product quality and regulatory compliance. The pharmaceutical facilities are closely supervised by regulatory bodies inspectors who have the responsibility to ensure that manufacturing companies conform to cGMP. These inspectors enforce law and required that manufacturers take proactive steps to ensure that their products are safe, pure, and effective. As per GMP regulations, a quality approach of manufacturing, to minimize or eliminate instances of contamination, mix ups, and errors. HVAC services embraces number of issues including air flow, temperature, humidity, pressures, filtration and classification of clean rooms. It also governs the level of control of various parameters regulating acceptance criteria, validation, and documentation for operation and maintenance. The European Community has established a "Guide to Good Manufacturing Practice for Medicinal Products" and in the United Kingdom it is BS 5295. The World Health Organization (WHO) version of GMP is used by pharmaceutical regulators and the pharmaceutical industry in over one hundred countries worldwide, primarily in the developing world. All GMP guideline have one common goal "Hygiene". The level of risk associated with the HVAC system needs to be assessed based on the impact and severity of the probable risk in aseptic practice. After risk assessment, identified control measures and recommended actions are applied to improve cGMP compliance and qualification of the system upgrades. In this chapter we shall discuss for the tests to be performed during qualification of the HVAC system.

INTRODUCTION

Heating, ventilation and air-conditioning (HVAC) is an important component in pharmaceutical premises which ensures environment conditions to manufacture quality products. It not only maintains environment suitable for products but also maintains comfortable conditions for operators. HVAC system design influences architectural layouts with regard to items such as airlock positions, doorways and lobbies. The architectural components affect room pressure differential cascades and cross-contamination control. The prevention of contamination and cross-contamination is an essential design consideration of the HVAC system. Environmental conditions include temperature, relative humidity and differential pressure and parameters are maintained so that these should not adversely affect the quality of pharmaceutical products during their manufacture and storage, or the accurate functioning of equipment. A comprehensive science and risk-based approach should be followed throughout the lifecycle of an HVAC system, including its design, qualification and maintenance. Risk management principles should be applied throughout the life cycle. Risk assessment is however not a substitute for GMP [1, 2].

Many pharmaceutical manufacturers have their own engineering design and qualification standards and requirements may vary from one manufacturer to the next. Design parameters and user requirements should, therefore, be set realistically for each project, with a view to creating a cost-effective design, yet still complying with all regulatory standards and ensuring that product quality and safety are not compromised [3]. The three primary aspects addressed in this manual are the roles that the HVAC system plays in product protection, personnel protection and environmental protection (Fig. 1). Cognisance should be taken of the products to be manufactured when establishing system design parameters. A facility manufacturing multiple different products may have more stringent design parameters with respect to cross-contamination control, compared with a single product facility.

Areas for the manufacture of pharmaceuticals, where pharmaceutical starting materials and products, utensils, primary packing materials and equipment are exposed to the environment, should be defined as “clean areas”, “clean zones”, “controlled areas” or “clean rooms”. The achievement of a particular clean area condition depends on a number of criteria that should be addressed at the design and qualification stages. A suitable balance between the different criteria will be required in order to create an efficient clean area [4]. Some of the basic criteria to be considered which affects room cleanliness should include:

- Building finishes and structure
- Air filtration
- Air change rate or flushing rate
- Room pressure
- Location of air terminals and directional airflow
- Temperature
- Relative humidity

- Material flow
- Personnel flow
- Gowning procedures
- Equipment movement
- Process being carried out (open or closed system)
- Outside air conditions
- Occupancy
- Type of product
- Cleaning standard operating procedures (SOPs).

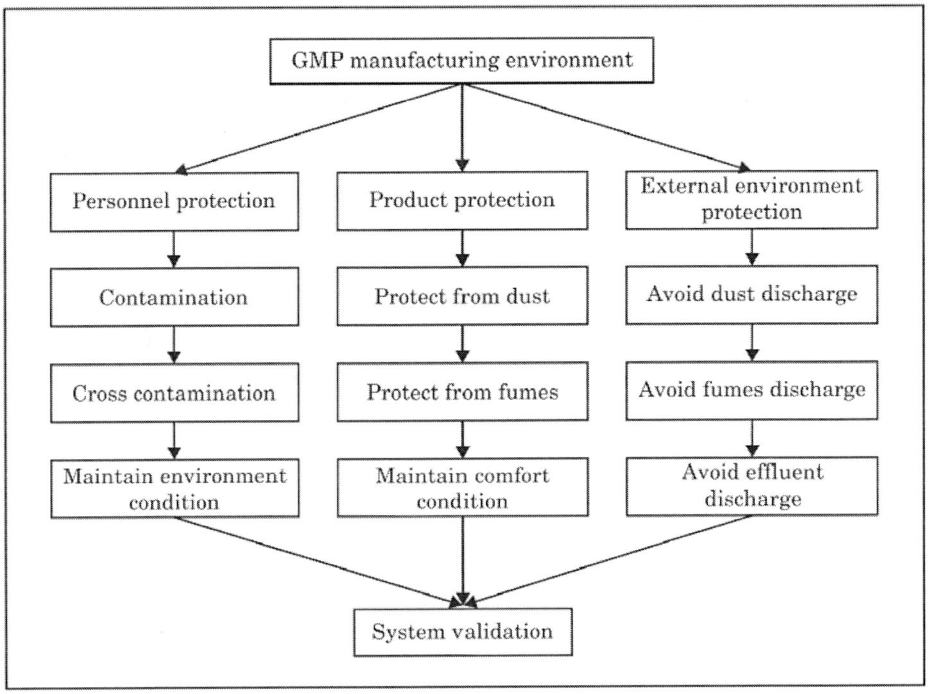

Fig. 1: The guidelines address the various system criteria according to the sequence set out in this diagram

If a clean room classification is specified, the manufacturer should state whether this is achieved under "as-built" (Fig. 2), "at-rest" (Fig. 3) or "operational" (Fig. 4) conditions [4]. Room classification tests in the "as-built" condition should be carried out on the bare room, in the absence of any equipment or personnel. Room classification tests in the "at-rest" condition should be carried out with the equipment operating where relevant, but without any operators. Because of the amounts of dust usually generated in a solid dosage facility, the clean area classifications would be rated for the "at-rest" condition [5]. Room classification tests in the "operational" condition are normally carried out during the normal production process with equipment operating, and the normal number of personnel present in the room.

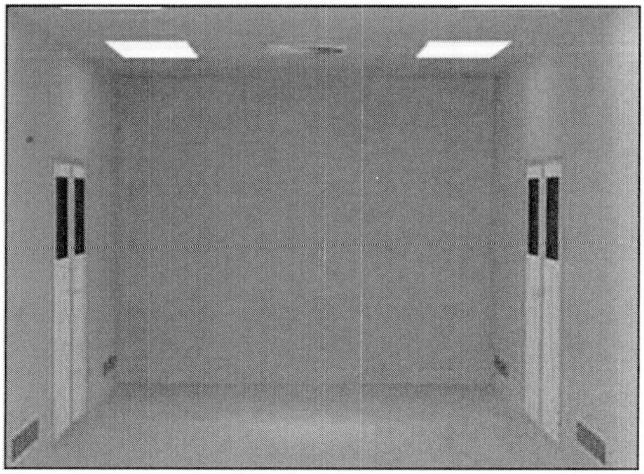

Fig. 2: As built

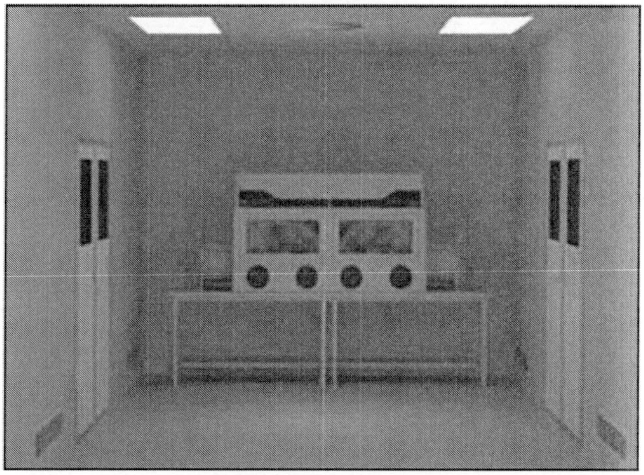

Fig. 3: Rest condition

Generally a room that is tested for an "operational" condition should be able to be cleaned up to the "at-rest" clean area classification after a short clean-up time. The clean-up time should be determined through validation and is generally of the order of 15 minutes [5]. Materials and products should be protected from contamination and cross-contamination during all stages of manufacture. Contaminants may result from inappropriate premises (*e.g.*, poor design, layout or finishing), poor cleaning procedures, contaminants brought in by personnel, poor manufacturing process and a poor HVAC system.

Fig. 4: Operation condition

Airborne contaminants should be controlled through effective ventilation and filtration. External contaminants should be removed by effective filtration of the supply air [6]. Fig. 5 represents an example of a shell-like building layout to enhance containment and protection from external contaminants. Internal contaminants should be controlled by dilution and flushing of contaminants in the room, or by displacement airflow. Airborne particulates and the degree of filtration should be considered critical parameters with reference to the level of product protection required. Personnel should not be a source of contamination. The level of protection and air cleanliness for different areas should be determined according to

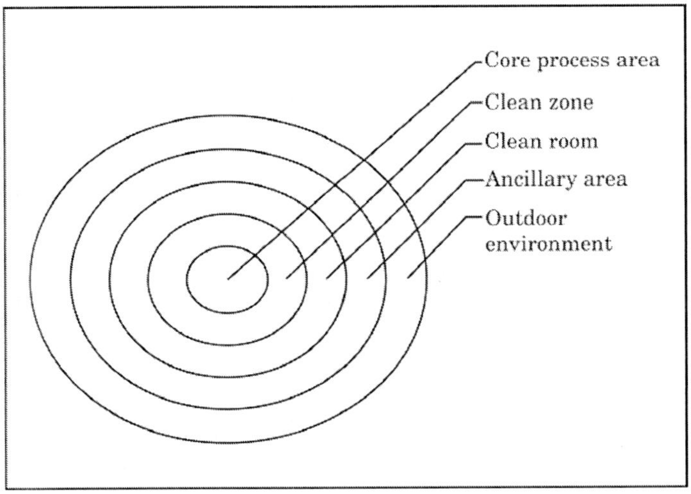

Fig. 5: Shell like containment control concept

the product being manufactured, the process being used and the product's susceptibility to degradation.

DESIGN OF HVAC SYSTEMS AND COMPONENTS

HVAC systems should be designed in such idea to maintain product quality and should be maintained throughout their life cycle. Drawings should be maintained to reflect the current situation, including but not limited to, air supply and extraction, air handling units, room pressure cascades, air flow direction, personnel and material movement and removal [6]. Risk management principles should be applied during the design of an HVAC system. This includes, but is not limited to, appropriate controls of the climatic conditions and the prevention of contamination and cross-contamination [2,6,7]. The HVAC system capacity should be sufficient to ensure that the required performance is maintained during normal use. Materials of construction for components of an HVAC system should not become a source of contamination. Where possible, ducting, piping, fittings, sensors and other components should be clearly marked or labeled for ease of identification, location and direction of flow as appropriate. Air intake and exhaust air terminals should be positioned in a manner in relation to one another that assist in preventing cross-contamination. Air-handling units (AHUs) should be provided with adequate drains to remove condensate that may form in the AHU [8]. Design of AHU/ HVAC system is illustrated in Fig. 6.

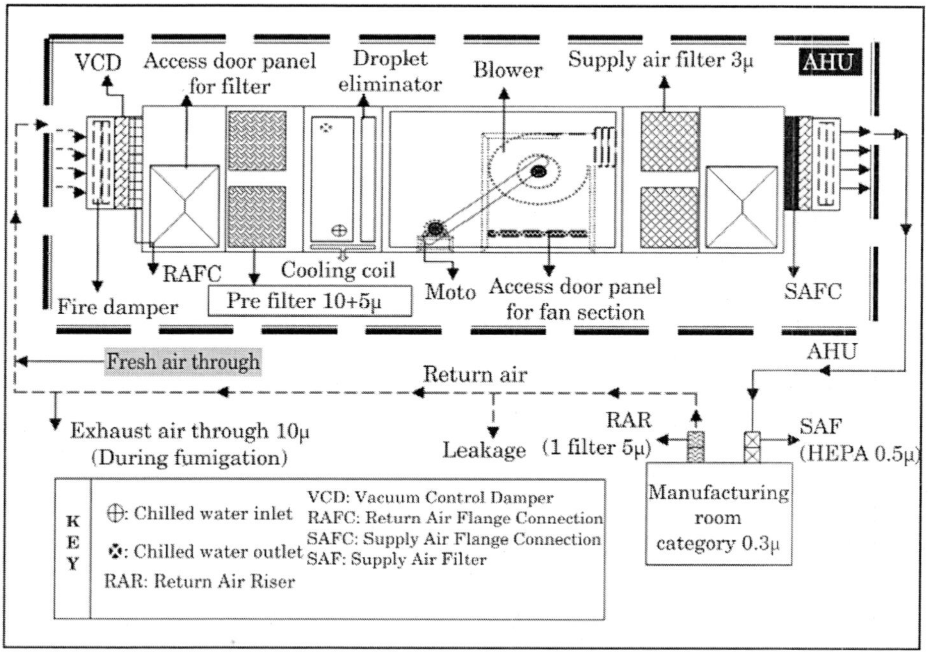

Fig. 6: Flow Diagram of the Air handling unit system

Conditions and limits for parameters such as temperature, relative humidity, air cleanliness and recovery times should be specified and achieved, as needed, for the materials and products handled, as well as process risks[9]. Room recovery rates should demonstrate that the HVAC system is capable of returning an area to a specified level of cleanliness or classification, temperature, relative humidity, room pressure and microbial limits, as appropriate, within the specified time [7]. Possible room pressure changes due to fan failure and partial system shut down with an impact on ease of opening of doors for escape purposes should be considered. The effectiveness of the air distribution and air flow patterns should be appropriate and effective. Air supply and extract grilles should be appropriately located to provide effective room flushing and prevent zones of stagnant air. The performance of HVAC systems should be controlled and monitored to ensure ongoing compliance with defined parameters. Records should be maintained. Limits defined should be justified. Where automated monitoring systems are used, these should be capable of indicating any out-of-specification (OOS) condition by means of an alarm or similar system. Where these systems are identified as G x P systems, they should be appropriately validated [4].

Appropriate alarm systems should be in place to alert personnel in case a critical component of the system fails, *e.g.,* a fan. The effect of fan failure on building and HVAC components should be assessed. Where appropriate provision should be made for a fan interlock failure matrix. Switching off of AHUs at intervals such as overnight or weekends, or reducing supply air volumes during non-production hours, should not compromise product quality. Where this is done, there should be appropriate justification and no risk to materials or products. The procedure and acceptability should be proven through validation and qualification. There should be procedures and records maintained for the start up and shut down sequence of air handling units [10].

FULL FRESH AIR SYSTEMS AND RECIRCULATION SYSTEMS

Full fresh air or recirculation type HVAC systems may be used. Where recirculation systems are used, there should be no risk of contaminants in the return-air system. The re-circulated air should be adequately filtered. HEPA filters may be installed (in the supply air stream or return air stream) to remove contaminants and thus prevent cross- contamination. The HEPA filters in such an application should have an EN 1822 classification of at least H13 or equivalent. HEPA filters may not be required to control cross-contamination where there is evidence that cross-contamination would not be possible due to other robust technical means, or where the air-handling system is serving a single product facility [11]. The amount of fresh air intake required should be determined. As a minimum, the following criteria should be considered:

- Sufficient volume of fresh air to compensate for leakage from the facility and loss through exhaust air systems;
- Operator occupancy;
- Regional or national legislation.

Air that might be contaminated with organic solvents or highly hazardous materials should normally not be re-circulated. The required degree of filtration of the exhaust air should be considered based on risk, exhaust air contaminants and local environmental regulations. Where energy-recovery wheels are used in multiproduct facilities, controls should be in place to ensure that these do not become a source of cross-contamination.

AIR FILTRATION, AIRFLOW DIRECTION AND PRESSURE DIFFERENTIALS

Where different products are manufactured at the same time, such as in different areas or cubicles in a multiproduct manufacturing site, measures should be taken to ensure that dust cannot move from one cubicle to another. Appropriate levels of filtration, airflow direction and a pressure cascade systems can assist in preventing cross-contamination. Filters selected should be appropriate for their intended use and classified according to current international classification.

Airflow directions should be appropriate, taking operator and equipment locations into consideration. The pressure cascade for areas in a facility should be individually assessed according to the products handled and level of protection required. The pressure cascade regime and the direction of airflow should be appropriate to the product and processing method used, and should also provide operator and environmental protection. The pressure cascade should be such that the direction of airflow is from the clean area, resulting in dust containment, *e.g.* from the corridor to the cubicle. The limits for the pressure differential between adjacent areas should be such that there is no risk of overlap in the defined operating ranges. Normally, for cubicles where dust is liberated, the corridor should be maintained at a higher pressure than the cubicles and the cubicles at a higher pressure than atmospheric pressure. Room pressure differential indication should be provided [12].

The pressure indication gauges should have a range and graduation scale which enables the reading to an appropriate accuracy. The normal operating range, alert and action limits should be defined and displayed at the point of indication. Room pressure should be traced back to representative ambient pressure (by summation of the room pressure differentials), in order to determine the room actual absolute pressure. The pressure control and monitoring devices used should be calibrated. Compliance with specifications should be regularly verified and the results recorded. Pressure control devices should be linked to an alarm system which is set according to the levels determined by a risk analysis and justified dead times. Zero setting of gauges should be tamper proof. Zero setting should be checked at regular intervals. Where airlocks are used, the pressure cascade regimes selected should be appropriate. In considering room pressure differentials, transient variations, such as machine extract systems and their impact, should be taken into consideration.

TEMPERATURE AND RELATIVE HUMIDITY

Where appropriate, temperature and relative humidity should be controlled, monitored and recorded to ensure that the conditions are maintained pertinent to the materials and products as required, and provide a comfortable environment for the operators. Limits for minimum and maximum room temperatures and relative humidity should be appropriate. Alert and action limits should be set appropriate to material and product requirements, and to inhibit increased microbial loading. Where steam or humidity is present, controls should be in place to ensure that the HVAC system will remain effective. Precautions should be taken to prevent moisture migration that may increase an uncontrolled load on the HVAC system. Where humidification or dehumidification is required, this should be achieved by appropriate means which does not become a source of contamination. Dehumidification and cooling systems should be well drained. Condensate should not accumulate in air-handling systems and should not become a source of contamination [10].

DUST, VAPOUR AND FUME CONTROL

The location of discharge exhaust points relative to air inlet points should be carefully considered to prevent contamination and cross-contamination. Dust, vapours and fumes could be possible sources of contamination and should be appropriately controlled. Wherever possible, these should be removed at source. The HVAC system should normally not serve as the primary mechanism of dust control. Dust extraction systems should be appropriately designed and installed. Dust should not flow back in the opposite direction, *e.g.,* in the event of component failure or airflow failure. The transfer velocity should be sufficient to ensure that dust is carried away and does not settle in the ducting. The positioning of dust extraction points should be appropriate to prevent dust and powders dropping down from the extract point causing contamination or cross-contamination. Air should not flow through the dust extraction ducting or return air ducting from the room with the higher pressure to the room with the lower pressure. Periodic checks should be performed to ensure that there is no build-up of the dust in the ducting. Dust extraction systems should be interlocked, where appropriate, to the relevant air-handling unit to avoid any risk and impact on pressure cascade imbalances [11,12,13].

PROTECTION OF THE ENVIRONMENT

Where exhaust air from equipment such as fluid bed driers, dust extraction systems and facilities carry dust loads, adequate filtration should be provided to prevent contamination of the ambient air. Waste from wet and dry scrubbers should be disposed of in an appropriate manner. Dust-slurry should be removed by suitable means, *e.g.,* a drainage system or waste removal contractor [4].

COMMISSIONING

Commissioning is a precursor to system qualification and validation, and is normally associated with good engineering practice (GEP).

QUALIFICATION

For general notes on qualification and validation, see WHO Guideline on Validation. HVAC systems, including recirculation and full fresh air systems, should be qualified to ensure continued performance in accordance with specifications and achieving the conditions as specified. The scope and extent of qualification should be determined based on risk management principles. The qualification of the HVAC system should be described in a master plan. The master plan should define the nature and extent of testing, the test procedures and protocols to be followed [3]. Qualification stage for HVAC system is depicted in Fig. 7.

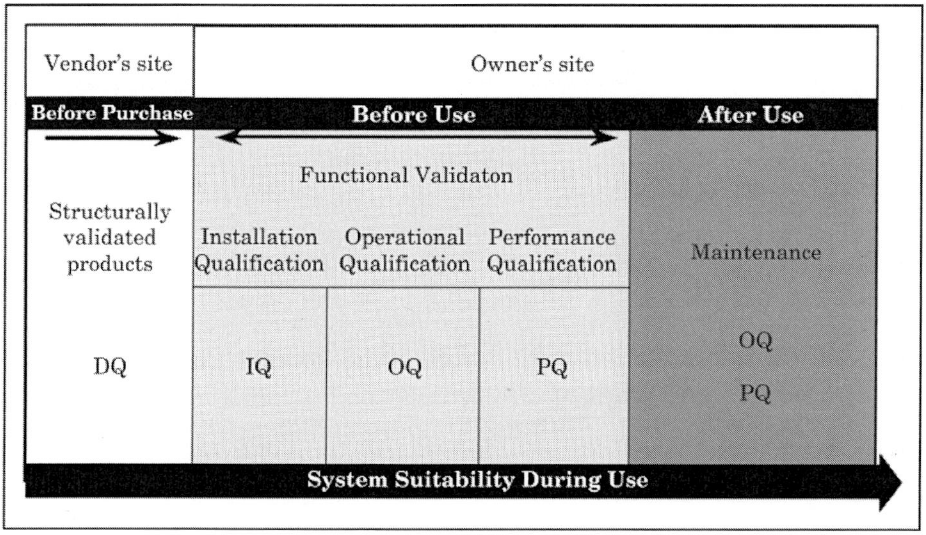

Fig. 7: Qualification stage for HVAC

Where relevant, the procedures followed for the conduct of tests should be in accordance with the appropriate parts as mentioned in ISO 14644 and relevant WHO guidelines. The design condition, operating ranges,alert and action limits should be defined. Alert limits should be based on system capability. Performance parameters to be included in qualification for the HVAC system should be determined by means of a risk assessment. Acceptable tolerances for system parameters, where appropriate, should be specified prior to commencing the physical installation. There should be standard operating procedures describing the action to be taken when alert and action limits are reached. This may include, where relevant:

- Temperature;
- Relative humidity;
- Supply air quantities;
- Return air or exhaust air quantities;
- Room air-change rates;
- Room pressures and pressure differentials;
- Rirflow pattern tests;
- Unidirectional air flow velocities;
- Containment system velocities;
- HEPA filter penetration tests;
- Room particle count tests;
- Duct leakage tests;
- Materials of construction;
- Microbiological counts;
- De-dusting and dust extraction systems.

Where routine or periodic revalidation is done, the frequency should be established based on, *e.g.,* risk, the type of facility, the level of product protection necessary, performance of the system and the extent of routine ongoing monitoring activities. Any change to the HVAC system should be handled according to a change control procedure. The extent of qualification or requalification should be considered based on the scope and impact of the change.

PERFORMANCE QUALIFICATION TESTS

Air Velocity and Air Changes

Velocity at the inlet air grills (supply point) was measured at 5 points (Fig. 8) in a plane parallel to filter face plane and at a distance of about 6 inches (150 mm) from the filter face. The velocity was measured for at least 10 seconds from each point. It is performed by thermal anemometer/

vane type anemometer and average air flow is calculated by following formula:

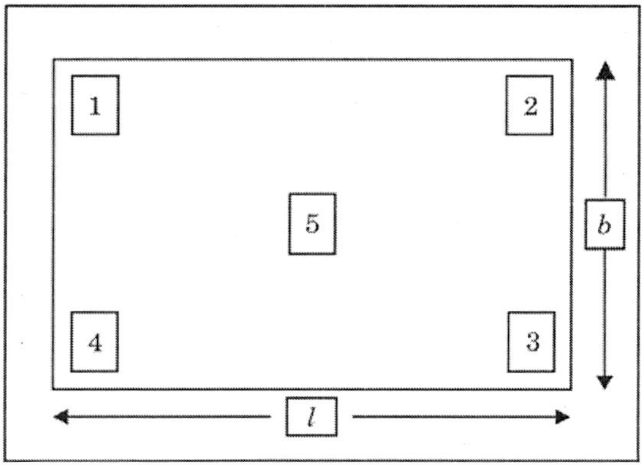

Fig. 8: Air velocity measurement location

$$\text{Mean air flow (a, m/sec)} = \frac{1 + 2 + 3 + 4 + 5}{5}$$

Air volume flow rate in m^3/sec shall be calculated as per the following equation:

Air volume flow rate (y, m^3/sec) = a X area of filter face (l X b)

Air volume flow in 1 hour shall be calculated as per the following equation:

Air volume flow in 1 hour (z, m^3) = y X 60 X 60

ACPH shall be calculated as per the following equation:

ACPH = z/ volume of room

Differential Pressure Test

Measure and record the pressure difference between the room to be tested and any surrounding ancillary environment. This test ensures that the pressure zoning is maintained in the manufacturing area. Pressure zoning for an oral solid manufacturing facility should be as per Fig. 9.

Where CNC = Controlled (For temperature/ relative humidity and pressure) not classified (for particle count and microbial presence) and + sign indicate pressure adjustment.

HEPA Filter Leakage Test

Position the aerosol generator to introduce an aerosol challenge upstream of the HEPA filter to a concentration of 20-100 mg/m^3 (20–100 mg/lit.) of air by opening appropriate number of nozzles. Measure upstream

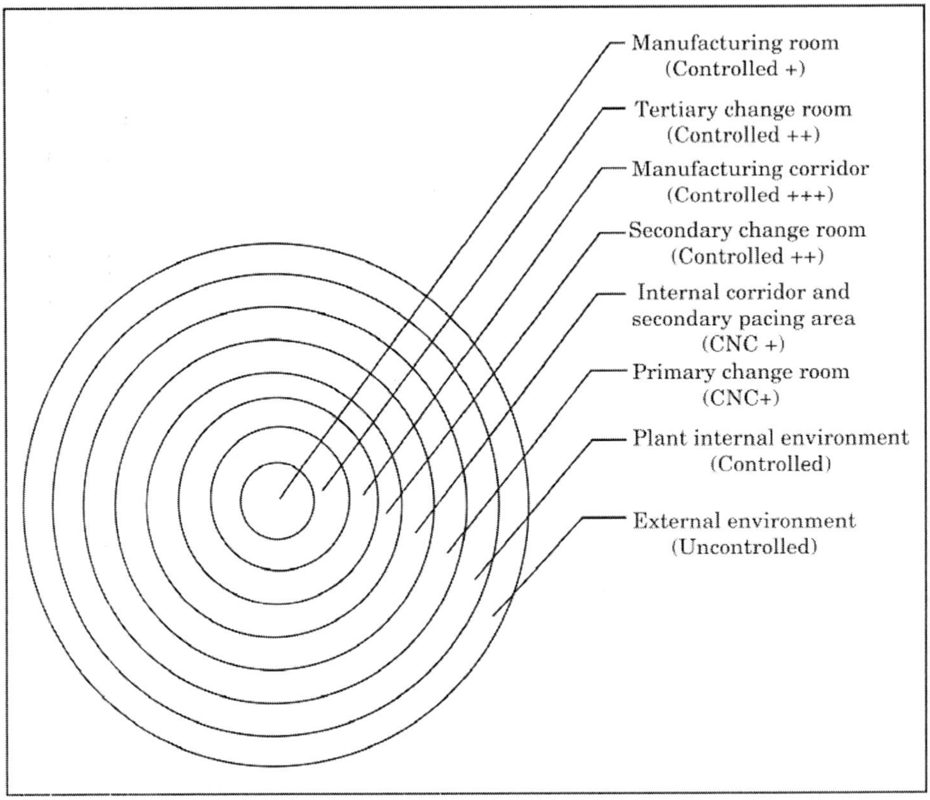

Fig. 9: Pressure zoning in an oral solid manufacturing plant

concentration of aerosol using up-stream port. Adjust the photometer's gain/ span control for a full-scale deflection on 100% range. Scan the downstream side of the HEPA filter. The photometer probe should be about 1 inch from the surface and at a transverse rate not more than 10ft/ minute with a sample flow rate of 1cft/min ± 10%. This test is also called as PAO (Poly alpha olefin) test. Previously it was performed using DOP (Di-octyl phthalate) as aerosol.

Air Flow Visualization (Non-unidirectional flow)

This test is also called as air flow direction test. It is done using water as fogging agent. Water fog is generated using water fogger. Tracer is positioned at the appropriate places like downstream of supply air, return air risers and doors opening. Air direction is visually checked indicating the airflow. Air flow pattern is recorded using photography/ videography.

Non Viable Airborne Particle Count

Number of sampling points shall be selected from the Table 1. Locations shall be selected taking into the consideration for worst points like corners, center, near the equipment, near the risers and near the doors. Particle count is taken at the working height. Particle count shall be calculated in $1m^3$ of the air volume.

Table 1: Sample location number

Area of the room (m^2, less than or equal to)	*Number of sampling locations*
2	1
4	2
6	3
8	4
10	5
24	6
28	7
32	8
36	9
52	10
56	11
64	12
68	13
72	14
76	15
104	16
108	17
116	18
148	19
156	20
192	21
232	22
276	23
352	24
436	25
500	26
1000	27
> 1000	As calculated by equation N

N = (27 X Area of room)/ 1000;

Acceptance criteria for particle count shall be as per Table 2:

Recovery/ Decontamination Rate Test

Take the particle count in the area before aerosol generation under resting conditions. The sampling rate should be 1 CFM. Artificially generate DOP/ PAO aerosol in the classified area and check the count (1000 times more than classified area "at rest"). Record the particle count and time. Stop the aerosol generator. The time at which the aerosol generator is stopped should be the starting time for establishing the recovery rate. Start the particle counting at the specified location at a sampling rate of 1 CFM. Establish the time required for attaining the "at rest" condition. Recovery time should not be more than 15 min.

Table 2: Acceptance criteria

ISO class	***Maximum concentration limit for particles equal to or larger than the considered sizes shown below (particles/m³ of air)***	
	0.5 µm	5.0 µm
5	3520	00
6	35200	293
7	352000	2930
8	3520000	29300

Environmental Conditions - Temperature and Relative Humidity

Digital hygrometers and a Sling hygrometer were used to perform the test for 5 consecutive days for category A1 AHUs and for 3 consecutive days for AHUs of other categories. Readings should be for minimum 16 hours/day at 2 hours interval.

Viable Count Monitoring - Settle Plate and Air Sampling

Settled plates should be of 90 mm diameter and should be exposed for duration of 4 hours. Plates should be exposed at a height above 1 metre from the floor and also at work level for better exposure. For air sampling, 1 m^3 of air from specified locations should be sampled using Soybean Casein Digest Agar. Incubate settle plate at 20 - 25°C for TFC and at 30 - 35°C for TBC.

CONCLUSIONS

In this chapter we discussed about the various air-handling unit validation tests in pharmaceutical industries. It has always been known that facilities and processes involved in pharmaceutical production impact significantly on the quality of the products. AHU or HVAC system plays an important role in product, personnel, environment and machine protection. This can be presented as clean environment, removal of hazard contaminant and provide a suitable temperature and humidity control within acceptable level by providing clean environment. Controls are mandatory in good manufacturing practice (GMP). The purpose is to monitor the manufacturing environment, and hence, its validation is essential. HVAC utility is designed to control the level of viable and non-viable particulate exposure that a drug or medicinal device might receive in addition to regulating temperature and relative humidity conditions. HVAC utility is qualified to demonstrate operating conditions of the area. The areas serviced by the HVAC utility are classified based on viable and non-viable particulate levels during static operating conditions and dynamic operating conditions. Thus HVAC validation is an integral part of quality assurance.

REFERENCES

[1] Agalloco JP, Carleton FJ. Validation of Aseptic Pharmaceutical Process. 2nd ed. New York: Marcel Dekker, Inc., 2–3.

[2] Annex 1. EU Guidelines to Good Manufacturing Practice, Medicinal Products for Human and Veterinary Use. Manufacture of Sterile Medicinal Products, vol. 4. March 2009, 2–9.

[3] Del Valle MA. Keeping clean rooms compliant. Pharm Technol Eur 2006;18(11):1–4.

[4] Dixon AM. Environmental Monitoring for Clean Rooms and Controlled Environments, Drugs and the Pharmaceutical Sciences, vol. 164. USA: *Informa Health Care*; 206–210.

[5] ICH Harmonised Tripartite Guideline on Quality Risk Management (Q9), 2005.

[6] ISO 14644–2015.

[7] Li J, Poulton G. Dynamic zone modeling for HVAC system control. *Int J Model Ident Control* April 2010;9:5–14.

[8] McDowall R. Fundamentals of HVAC Systems, inch edition. USA: American society of heating, refrigerating and air-conditioning Engineer's Inc.; 2006, 2–6.

[9] Nash Robert A, Wachter Alfred H. Qualification of water and air handling systems. Pharmaceutical Process Validation, 3rd ed. vol. 129. Marcel Dekker, 22–24.

[10] Swarbrick J. Encyclopedia of Pharmaceutical Technology, 3rd ed. vol. 1. USA: Informa health care, 127–128.

[11] Tidswell EC, McGarvey B. Quantitative risk modeling in aseptic manufacture. *PDA J Pharm Sci Technol* September 2006; 60:267–269.

[12] WHO guidelines on quality risk management, Annex 2, WHO Technical Report Series, No. 981, 2013.

[13] WHO. Supplementary Training Modules on Good Manufacturing Practice, Heating Ventilation and Air Conditioning (HVAC) Part 1 (a). Introduction and Overview Technical Report Series, no. 937, 2006, 1–26.

FURTHER READINGS

WHO GMP for sterile pharmaceutical products, WHO Technical Report Series, No. 961, Annex 6.

WHO good manufacturing practices for biological products, Annex 3, WHO Technical Report Series, No. 996, 2016.

19

Compressed Air Validation

ABSTRACT

Compressed air is air kept under a pressure that is greater than atmospheric pressure. Compressed Air is a critical component in the production of pharmaceutical industry and effects on the quality of the end product. Compression of ambient air concentrates the normal contaminants already present in the air and can also introduce other contaminants such as Oil mist, water vapor or droplets, solid particles, microbial contaminants. For this reason compressed air needs filtration at every delivery points, if it is coming in direct or indirect contact with products. When properly treated, Compressed air is regarded as a safe, clean utility, as compared to other energy sources. Validation activities can be applied to all aspects of the product in any of its intended environments such as operation, training, manufacturing, maintenance and support services.

INTRODUCTION

Compressed air is a vital energy source and is utilized in multiple operations in pharmaceutical industry. Compressed air is the one of the primary utilities employed in the pharmaceutical industry which is generated by the end-user. Due to this reason end-user and the procedure involved in generating compressed air directly influences its quality. When properly treated, compressed air is considered safe, clean utility, as compared to other energy sources. High quality compressed air is critical for providing products that are not only cost effective to process but also safe. Therefore, it's in best interests for pharmaceutical manufacturers to select the proper compressed air equipment. The ISO 8573 air quality standards and ISO 12500 compressed air filter standards make the basis for air treatment product selection much easier [1].

Air compressors shall essentially meet variety of standards written by various organizations. Among these organizations, the most significant is ASME (American Society of Mechanical Engineers) and ISO. Most standards were written to deal with quality, safety, and efficacy of the individual components of a compressed air system. Analytical standards and procedures are being revised to give the users clear picture of how components will perform the intended activity. One of the key features of ISO requirements is the establishment of facts like capacity of compressed air to be used, its generation cost by a process indicating 'baseline' performance. The purpose of base lining is to establish the current performance levels and costs of a compressed air system, and to correlate the results with the plant's current production levels [2]. As improvements are made to the system, it will be possible to estimate the success by comparing the new measurements with the original baseline. The ASME standard is part of a suite of assessment standards that include compressed air system pumping stems, steam and process heat. ASME requirements are described as follows:

- To understand the international standards for compressed air quality, it is essential to understand the sources of contamination, the individual contaminants found within a compressed air system and the problems that contaminants can cause

ISO 8573 is a multi-part standard, with a total of 9 parts. Part 1 is mainly dealing with classification of type of contaminants and assigning air quality levels, while other parts (2 to 9) define testing methods to accurately measure a full range of contaminants within the end user's facility. The end user-user is responsible for defining the air quality required for their particular application or process. Air treatment manufacturers present technical data in reference to ISO 8573.1. An easy to understand ISO 8573.1 table defines the various air quality classes [3]. The standard also determines that air quality shall be designated by the following nomenclature:

Compressed Air Purity Class A: solid particle class designation,

Compressed Air Purity Class B: humidity and liquid water class designation,

Compressed Air Purity Class C: oil class designation

SOURCES OF CONTAMINATION IN A COMPRESSED AIR SYSTEM

ISO 8573.1 identifies three primary contaminant types as prevalent in a compressed air system. Solid particulates, water and oil (in both aerosol and vapor form) are the most recognized contaminants. Each is categorized and assigned a quality class ranging from class 0, the most stringent, to Class 9, the most relaxed. Contaminants in the form of solid particulates, oil (aerosols and vapor), water (aerosols and vapor), and even unwanted gaseous vapors can be introduced from the plant environment, ingested by the compressors, or created by the air compressor and distribution system. While many compressed air applications require a high degree of purity, all compressed air applications work better if the air is clean and dry [3]. Sources of contaminants in a compressed air system can generally be recognized to the following:

The quality of air being drawn into the compressor

Air compressors draw in large volumes of air from the surrounding atmosphere containing large numbers of airborne contaminants. Contaminants in the surrounding ambient environment are drawn into the air system through the intake of the air compressor. Ingested contaminants appear in the form of water vapor, hydrocarbon vapors, natural particles and airborne particulates. Various types of filters are employed to remove these contaminants from the air at the intake point and other points in the compressed air system.

The type and operation of the air compressor

The air compressor itself can also add contamination as a result of the mechanical compression process. Generated contaminants include compressor lubricant, wear particles and vaporized lubricant.

Compressed air storage devices and distribution systems

The air receiver system and channeling are designed to store and distribute the compressed air to various user points. As a consequence they store large amounts of contamination drawn into the system. Additionally, this piping, tubing and air receivers also cool the moist compressed air forming condensate which causes damage and corrosion. Piping distribution and air storage tanks have contaminant in the form of rust, pipe scale, mineral deposits and bacteria.

Thus the performance of compressed air generation and distribution system can have a dramatic impact on overall plant operational efficiency. Excessive contamination reduces the life of components and systems, adversely affects product quality, can result in excessive maintenance costs, and can even create health and safety problems.

CONTAMINANTS

Contaminants can exist in solid, liquid or gaseous form [3]. They influence each other (*e.g.,* solid particulates agglomerate in the presence of oil or water to form larger particles; oil and water form an emulsion) or condense (*e.g.,* oil vapour or water vapour) inside the pipework of compressed air systems.

Solid

Contaminants in solid form may originate from different sources, *e.g.*, solid particles from source air or atmosphere drawn in by the compressor, or by abrasion or corrosion within the compressed air system or particles generated due to mechanical procedure of equipment. They can range from very large, granular to extremely small submicron-sized particles. Furthermore, solid particles can be either inert particles or viable colony-forming units.

Particle classes 6 and 7

Equipment have been supplied with air filtered by general-purpose filters with a notional particle size rating of 5 µm (class 6) and 40 µm (class 7). These ratings are not absolute particle removal ratings and the air purity delivered by these filters is provided by filters with removal efficiency ratings of at least 95% of the rated particle, *i.e.*, 95% of 5 µm particles for class 6 and 95% of 40 µm particles for class 7, when tested as described in ISO 12500-3. Classes 6 and 7 are used to describe compressed air that is typically too "dirty" to be measured with a particle counter. Instead, mass measurements are used to determine the amount of particulate contamination in the compressed air, according to Part 8 of ISO8573.

Liquid

Liquid contaminants in the compressed air system are mainly water and lubricants or coolant material used in equipment operation. Other liquid contaminants can be present by being drawn into the compressor air intake from the surrounding atmosphere. Concentration of these liquid contaminants is dependent on temperature and pressure of air or environment. Thus liquid droplets can be present due to the condensation of their vapors. Concentration of these liquid contaminants varies from high concentrations of liquid flow to droplets and extremely small submicron-sized aerosols. Liquid contaminants especially water (in droplet form or vapors) can promote corrosion, within the compressor or compressed air distribution system which may generate further contaminants. Liquid contaminants generated from compressor lubricants/ coolants should be compatible with seals and non-ferrous piping, including aluminium and plastic.

Gaseous

Gaseous contaminants in compressed air generally comprised of vapors (either water oil like compressor lubricant or coolants used in equipment). Concentration of gaseous contaminants is dependent on both the temperature and the pressure of the gas. Other gaseous contaminants can be present by being drawn into the compressor air intake from the surrounding atmosphere. Gaseous contaminants can dissolve in liquids that are present or can themselves condense into liquid form by temperature reduction or increasing pressure.

THE PURITY CLASSES

The current version of ISO8573 Part 1 was published in 2010. ISO standards are reviewed periodically to determine whether they are still timely, accurate, and useful to the industries that they serve. There are three categories of contaminants that have been assigned classes in ISO8573.1. The first category is solid particulates. The second category is made up of a combination of liquid water and water vapor. The third category is called oil, and it too consists of the sum of the liquid oil (in aerosol or liquid droplet form) and oil vapor.

The purity classes range from the cleanest, class 0, to the most impure, class 9. Note that not all of the categories have the full range of classes; only the water category does. Also, notice that class 0 does not have any numbers associated with it in any of the categories. In the text of ISO8473.1 class 0 is defined by stating "As specified by the equipment user or supplier and more stringent than class 1". It is very important to understand that class 0 does not imply that there are no contaminants present; it simply means that there are fewer contaminants than in class one [4].

The chart below (Fig. 1) summarizes the three categories of contaminants, and shows the limits of contamination that are required to differentiate one purity class from another.

The International Standard Organization (ISO:8573) sets following quality standards for Compressed air [5]:

Dew Point

The Dew point temperature or Saturation temperature is defined as the temperature at which vapour begins to condense in liquid forms. The quantity of any gas in a mixture can be expressed as a pressure. The major components of compressed air are nitrogen, oxygen, and water vapor, so total atmospheric pressure is composed of the partial pressures of these three gases. While nitrogen and oxygen exist in stable concentrations, the concentration of water vapor is highly variable and must be measured to be determined. Gas of unknown water vapor concentration is passed over a temperature controlled surface. The surface is cooled until condensation forms. The temperature at which condensation forms is called the "Dew Point temperature." Because there is a unique correlation between temperature and saturation vapor pressure, measuring the Dew point temperature of a gas is a direct measurement of the partial pressure of

Class	*Solid particles, Particle size, d (mm)*			*Humidity and liquid water*		*Oil*	
	$0.10 < d \le 0.5$	*$0.5 < d \le 1.0$*	*$1.0 < d \le 5.0$*	*Pressure dew point*		*Total concentration: Aerosol, liquid and vapor*	
	Maximum number of particles per m^3			*°C*	*°F*	*mg/m^3*	*ppm/w/w*
0	As specified			As specified		As specified	
1	100	1	0	≤–70	–94	≤0.01	≤0.008
2	100,000	1,000	10	≤–40	–40	≤0.1	≤0.08
3	-	10,000	500	≤–20	–4	≤1	≤0.8
4	-	-	1,000	≤ + 3	38	≤5	≤04
5	-	-	20,000	≤ + 7	45		
6				≤+10	50		
				Liquid water content Cw g/m^3			
7				$Cw \le 0.5$			
8				$0.5 < Cw \le 5$			
9				$5 < Cw \le 10$			
PER ISO8573–1: 2001 (E)							

Fig. 1: Compressed air contamination

water vapor. Desiccant drying systems absorb water vapor from the air stream and can produce air with a Dew point of –40 °F (–40 °C) and drier if required. Dew point temperatures in compressed air range from ambient down to –112 °F (–80 °C), sometimes lower in special cases.

Oil Content

There are only five classes for oil in the standard, but they describe a wide range of concentrations. Again, class 0 is the most pure, and according to the standard, it describes compressed air that must be more pure than class 1. Classes 1 through 4 cover the range from less than 0.01 mg of oil content per cubic metre of compressed air to less than 5 mg per cubic metre. It is very important to understand that the oil classes can only be determined by adding the contribution from:

(a) Any liquid oil in the compressed air,

(b) The oil aerosols in the compressed air (typically generated by the reciprocal or rotary motion in lubricated compressors), and

(c) Oil vapors that can come from the oil in the compressor crankcase or sump, or from ingestion at the inlet of the compressor.

Liquid oil and oil aerosols are measured using the techniques in ISO8573 Part 2, and the oil vapors are measured using the methods in Part 5. The most scrutinized and often discussed contaminant classified by ISO 8573.1

is oil. Compressed air "free from oil" is a requirement in industry. Most air compressors use oil in the compression stage for sealing, lubrication and cooling. During operation, lubricating oil is carried over into the compressed air system as liquid oil and aerosols. This oil mixes with water vapour in the air and is often very acidic, causing damage to the compressed air storage and distribution system, production equipment and final product. End users are given the choice of selecting from several air compressor technologies, some of which require lubrication in the compression chamber for cooling and sealing purposes, and others that operate less lubricant in the compression chamber. The end user determines which compressor design best meets the desired requirements. The purpose of this discussion is not to tip the scale toward either technology, but to address air treatment requirements in industry. Dependent on the age of the compressor and preventive maintenance programs performed, a lubricated rotary screw air compressor will introduced 2 to 10 ppm/weight of oil into the air system. A well maintained 250 scfm lubricated air compressor, with a conservative 4 ppm carry-over, will add up to 4.8 gallons (18.2 litres) of oil into the air system over an 8000 hour operation. Lubricant free compressor technology presents no risk of lubricant migrating into the process air. Both air compressor technologies are subject to the inherent challenges presented by quality of the intake air. Ingested contamination in the form of water vapor, solid particulate and hydrocarbon vapor must be addressed regardless if the compressor is lubricated or free from lubricant. Depending on the location of the compressor intake, oil vapor levels in industrial areas may contain 20-30 ppm of airborne hydrocarbon aerosols. Hydrocarbon vapors, the primary component of fossil fuel combustion, will condense in a piping system when cooled forming a liquid contaminant.

In addition to dirt and water vapour, atmospheric air also contains oil in the form of unburned hydrocarbons. The unburned hydrocarbons drawn into the compressor intake as well as vaporized oil from the compression stage of a lubricated compressor will carry over into a compressed air system where it can cool and condense, causing the same contamination issues as liquid oil. Typical oil vapour concentrations can vary between 0.05 and 0.5 mg per cubic metre of ambient air. A Compressed Air Oil content test is a measure of the Oil Content of Compressed air systems. The test can accurately determine the amount of Oil flowing in a Compressed Air stream and assess whether the system complies with relevant requirements. Many Compressed air systems are supplied using lubricated compressors. These Compressors often blow small particles of Oil throughout the system, which can cause a range of problems for components when the Oil emulsifies with water in the system. Oil free air is generally required for compressed air system and an oil content of less than 0.01 mg/m^3 is generally specified. Because compressed air may come in direct and indirect contact with pharmaceutical products, an elevated level of filtration is required. A high efficiency coalescing filter capable of removing solids and liquids is recommended. It should be capable of removing solid and liquid aerosols with particle size 0.01 micron and larger. The remaining oil content should be 0.007 ppm, or less. An activated carbon filter, installed in series, is also recommended downstream of the coalescing filter. The adsorption filter will remove trace odors and oil vapor to 0.003 ppm by weight. This filter combination will ensure specified filtration levels achieve ISO 8573.1 Class 1 for oil and vapor removal. Fig. 2 depicts approximate quantity of oil entering the compressed air system per year.

		Gallons of Oil Entering A System Per Year			
Concentration PPM$_M$	***Time (Hours)***	***25 HP (19kW) 100 SCFM***	***50 HP (37kW) 250 SCFM***	***100 HP (75kW) 500 SCFM***	***200 HP (149kW) 1000 SCFM***
2	2000	0.2	0.5	1.2	2.4
	4000	0.5	1.0	2.4	4.8
	8000	1.0	1.9	4.8	9.6
4	2000	0.5	1.2	2.4	4.8
	4000	1.0	2.4	4.8	9.6
	8000	1.9	4.8	9.6	19.2
6	2000	0.7	1.8	3.6	7.2
	4000	1.4	3.6	7.2	14.4
	8000	2.9	7.2	14.4	28.8
8	2000	1.0	2.4	4.8	9.6
	4000	1.9	4.8	9.6	19.2
	8000	3.8	9.6	19.2	38.4
10	2000	1.2	2.9	6.0	12.0
	4000	2.4	5.8	12.0	24.0
	8000	4.8	11.6	24.0	48.0

Fig. 2: Oil used in compressed air system

Particulate Matter

There are eight possible classes for solid particulates, from class 0 to class 7. Class 0 is the most pure, but it is numerically undefined, other than to say that it must be more pure (fewer particles in each size range) than class 1. Classes 0 through 5 are defined by the number of particles in a particular size range, in one cubic metre of compressed air. Measurement methods are described in Part 4 of ISO8573 for classes 0 through 5. In a general industrial area, there are nearly 4,000,000 airborne particles per cubic foot of air. When this ambient air is compressed to 100 psig, the concentration of solid contamination will reach significant proportions. Most air compressor intake filters are rated to capture sold particles 4 to 10 microns in size and larger and are rated at 90-95% efficiency. Approximately 80% of airborne particles are 10 micron or less. Spores, pollen and bacteria are less than 2 micron in size. This may seem like a lot of particulate matter, but keep in mind, a solid particle 40 um in size is barely visible to the naked eye. Even a well maintained and routinely changed intake filter will allow solid particles to enter the air system.

Solid particulate must be removed from process air serving the industry. In pneumatic control circuits, solids particles plug control valve orifices, affect accuracy of gauging and score air cylinders walls, causing leaks. Particles may restrict flow through air jet nozzles used to clean surfaces or adversely affect the consistency of spray coatings applied on products. To achieve the recommended ISO 8573.1 Class 2 classification for solid particulate removal, a micron particulate filter is recommended. The particulate filter will also enhance the service life of high performance coalescing filters by minimizing solid loading. Compressed air is used in a broad range of applications in the industries and used in the mixing of ingredients, cutting, drying of product, transporting/ propelling product through processing systems and packaging of final product. In many of these applications, compressed air is in direct contact or indirect contact with product and the impurities in the compressed air may contaminate the product which can result in change of color and taste, reduced shelf life, in addition to exposure to bacteria and other microorganisms can result in product recalls. Compressed air, which is generated on site by pulling in ambient air and compressing it, contains water vapor, particulate matter (atmospheric air typically contains 140-150 million dirt particles/m^3). More importantly, the filtration systems that are employed are designed to protect process equipment from large slugs of water, oil, rust and pipe scale with a nominal rating of 25 to 40 micron and are not capable of removing submicron contaminates. Compressed Air is generally filtered to remove Particulate Matter to a level less than 0.02 mg/m^3 (size 100% < 0.01 micron).

Moisture

All atmospheric air contains some water vapor which will begin to condense into liquid water in the compressed air or gas system when the air or gas cools past the saturation point, *i.e.,* the point where it can hold no more water vapor. The condensed moisture must be removed by a separator and trap. Moisture in compressed air used in a manufacturing plant causes problems in the operation of pneumatic air systems, solenoid valves and air motors. This moisture causes rust and increased wear of moving parts as it washes away lubrication. Moisture adversely affects the color, adherence, and finish of paint applied by compressed air. Corrosion of air or gas operated instruments from moisture can give false readings, interrupting or shutting down plant processes. The malfunctioning of these controls due to rust, scale, and clogged orifices can result in damage to product or in costly shutdowns. Additionally, the freezing of moisture in control lines in cold weather commonly causes faulty operation of controls. Moisture content should be less than < 0.01% for Compressed Air System. There are ten possible classes for water contamination, from class 0 to class 9. Class 0 is the driest, but it is numerically undefined, other than to say that it must be drier (a lower pressure dew point) than class 1. Classes 0 through 6 are defined by the pressure dew point of the compressed air. Pressure dew point is defined as the temperature at which moisture begins to condense in the pipes and storage tanks of a compressed air system while it is operating, and hence, under pressure. Pressure dew point is a useful method of describing the humidity in compressed air because it tells us that we must keep the ambient temperature that surrounds the compressed air distribution system above the pressure dew point in order to prevent liquid water from condensing inside the piping. Pressure dew point measurements are described in Part 3 of ISO8573.

Classes 7 through 9 are used to describe compressed air that contains liquid water. As mentioned, liquid water appears in the distribution piping and storage when the pressure dew point of the compressed air is higher than the temperature of the ambient air, and it means that the compressed air contains as much water vapor as is possible for it to contain. This condition is usually called "saturated" air. When liquid water is present in the compressed air line, we use the methods described in ISO8573 Part 9 to measure the amount. Water vapor enters the system through the intake of the air compressor. In total volume, condensed water vapor represents the majority of liquid contamination in a compressed air system. On a typical summer day of 80°F (21°C) and 70% relative humidity, approximately 19.5 gallons (73.8 litres) of water enters a 100 scfm (170 nm^3/hr) system in a 24 hour period. This moisture will spoil products, cause pneumatic machinery failure and promote bacterial growth in the compressed air piping. Compressed air systems serving the industry must maintain dry, moisture free conditions mitigating the risk of micro-organism growth. Since compressed air used in operations may come in direct contact with the product, a compressed air dryer producing a sub-zero pressure dew point is required. Dew point, specified as temperature, is the point at which the water vapor held in the compressed air is equal to the compressed air's capacity to hold water vapor. Desiccant dryers using activated alumina will adsorb water vapor from the air most effectively, delivering ISO 8573.1 Quality Class 2 (–40°F/–40°C) pressure dew point), ideal for the industry. At this level of dryness, bacteria will cease to grow. Atmospheric air contains water vapour (water in a gaseous form). The ability of compressed air to hold water vapour is dependent upon its temperature. The higher the temperature, the more water vapour can be held by the air. During compression, the air temperature is increased significantly, which allows it to easily retain the incoming moisture.

After the compression stage, air is normally cooled to a usable temperature. This reduces the air's ability to retain water vapour, resulting in a proportion of the water vapour being condensed into liquid water which is removed by a condensate drain fitted to the compressor after-cooler. The air leaving the after-cooler is now 100% saturated with water vapour and any further cooling of the air will result in more water vapour condensing into liquid water. Condensation occurs at various stages throughout the system as the air is cooled further by the air receiver, piping and the expansion of air in valves, cylinders, tools and machinery. The condensed water and water aerosols cause corrosion to the storage and distribution system, damage production equipment and the end product. It increases both production efficiency and maintenance costs. Water in any form must be removed to enable the system to run correctly and efficiently. Fig. 3 depicts approximate quantity of water entering the compressed air system every day.

Gallons of Water Entering A System Per Day/100 SCFM (170NM^3/HR)									
Temperature of ambient air		***%Relative humidity***							
°F	°C	20%	30%	40%	50%	60%	70%	80%	90%
120°F	49°C	18.6	27.9	37.2	46.5	55.8	65.1	74.4	83.7
110°F	43°C	14.1	21.0	27.9	35.1	42.0	48.9	55.8	63.0
100°F	38°C	10.5	15.6	20.7	26.1	31.2	36.6	41.7	46.8
90°F	32°C	7.8	11.4	15.3	19.2	23.1	26.7	30.6	34.4
80°F	27°C	5.7	8.4	11.1	13.8	16.8	19.5	22.2	24.9
70°F	21°C	3.9	6.0	7.8	9.9	12.0	13.8	15.9	18.0

Fig. 3: Moisture content

Viable Count

Bacteria and viruses will also be drawn into the compressed air system through the compressor intake and warm, moist air provides an ideal environment for the growth of microorganisms. Ambient air can typically contain up to 3,850 micro-organisms per cubic metre. If only a few microorganisms were to enter a clean environment, a sterile process or a production system, enormous damage could because that not only diminishes product quality, but may even render a product entirely unfit for use and subject to a serious recall.

The manufacturer may not realize that the compressed air system could be harboring microorganisms. When the air supply system is operating, it may unleash contaminants which could adversely affect the product, including operational characteristics, by compromising sterile claims, or product aesthetics. The condition or the quality of the supplied air, from a microbiological standpoint, may not be obvious unless microbiological testing is performed. A simple air impaction microbial assay of compressed air lines, however, will alert the manufacturer to the various types of viable microorganisms that might be present. Manufacturers of medical devices, pharmaceutical operations, or those classified as sterile fill, are constantly assessing the environmental impact on the product during the manufacturing process. This assessment usually includes the facility, the equipment, and the personnel involved in the assembly process. Sampling may include, but not limited to, surface sampling, particulate counts, water analysis, and product testing. However, compressed air can easily be overlooked if not initially inserted into the environmental monitoring protocol or identified by an experienced environmental scientist. For Compressed Air System, Viable count should be <100 CFU.

Other Impurities

Atmospheric Dirt

Atmospheric air in an industrial environment typically contains 140 million dirt particles for every cubic metre of air. 80% of these particles are less than 2 microns in size and are too small to be captured by the compressor intake filter, therefore passing directly into the compressed air system.

Rust and Pipe scale

Rust and pipe scale can be found in air receivers and the piping of wet systems purification equipment being installed. Over time, this contamination breaks away to cause damage or blockage in production equipment which can also contaminate final product and processes.

REPORTING THE PURITY CLASSES

According to the standard, the purity classes of compressed air shall be expressed by stating the standard reference number and part, the date of issue, and the three class designations in a specific order: Particulate Water Oil. For example, if the compressed air purity of an audited air system was expressed as ISO8573.1 : 2001 1 2 1, the Particulate Class would be 1, the Water Class would be 2, and the Oil Class would be 1. If the class for a particular category is omitted, then a hyphen is used in its place. Many manufacturers of equipment powered by compressed air are now using this standard to express the purity level of the compressed air supply required in order to keep their tool or process running smoothly and in control. Air tool manufacturers and paint and powder coating suppliers are just two examples of entities that are using ISO8573 to improve their customer's satisfaction with their products [3, 5].

MEETING THE NEWEST CHALLENGE - ISO 12500

The ISO 8573 Air Quality standard is serving the industry well by raising end user awareness of how to measure and define the quality of compressed air. Using this, the end-user can make educated decisions as to the filtration performance required to generate a certain quality level. However, this standard does not address how manufacturers are to test and rate the filters. The playing field is not level and consumers become confused. The ISO 12500 filter standard addresses this issue and establishes how manufacturers test and rate compressed air filters. The standard defines critical performance parameters (namely, inlet oil challenge, inlet compressed air temperature and pressure measurement techniques) that will deliver certifiable filter performance information suitable for comparative purposes. ISO 12500 is a multi-part standard, with ISO 12500-1 encompassing the testing of coalescing filters for oil aerosol removal performance, ISO 12500-2 quantifies vapor removal capacity of adsorption filters, and; ISO 12500-3 outlines requirements to test particulate filters for solid contaminant removal. This Standard covers compressed air systems which are defined as a group of subsystems comprised of integrated sets of components including air compressors, treatment equipment, controls, piping, pneumatic tools, pneumatically powered machinery and process applications utilizing compressed air. The objective is consistent, reliable and efficient delivery of energy to manufacturing equipment and processes. This standard sets the requirements for conducting and reporting the results of a compressed air system assessment that considers the entire system, from energy inputs to the work performed as the result of these inputs. An assessment complying with this standard need not address each individual system component or subsystem within an industrial facility with equal weight. However, it must be sufficiently comprehensive to identify the major energy efficiency opportunities for improving the overall energy performance of the system. This standard is designed to be applied primarily at industrial facilities, but many of the concepts can be used in other facilities such as those in the institutional and commercial sectors. The Standard sets requirements for:

- Organizing and conducting an assessment
- Analyzing the data from an assessment
- Assessment reporting and documentation

Main intention of the standard is to provide industry with set of uniform requirements that must be met during the assessment of particular factory energy system. The U.S. Department of Energy (DOE) is working with the Superior Energy Performance Partnership, the ASME and industry experts in the development of these standards as part of an initiative to improve overall energy efficiency of manufacturing plants in the United States companies, ANSI, U.S. Environmental Protection Agency, and the National Institute of Standards and Technology. Filtration is required to remove the large volume of water aerosols, particulate, rust, Pipe scale and microbiological contamination entering the system. Failure to remove this contamination from the compressed air system can cause numerous problems. Compressed air is a safe and reliable power source that is widely used throughout industry. Approximately 90% of all companies use compressed air in some aspect of their operations. However unlike gas, water and electricity, compressed air is generated on-site, giving the user responsibility for air quality and operational costs. Compressed air is not without its problems, and most systems suffer from some performance and reliability issues. Almost all of these can be directly attributed to contamination. The main sources of contamination in a compressed air system are the ambient air being draw into the compressor, the type of air compressor, the compressed air storage vessels and the distribution pipework. Meeting the Newest Challenge - ISO 12500, ISO 8573, Air Quality Standard is serving the industry well by raising 'end user' awareness of how to measure and define the quality of compressed air. Using this, the end-user can make educated decision as to the filtration performance required to generate a certain quality level. However, this standard does not address how manufacturers are to test and rate the filters. The playing field is not level and consumers become confused. ISO 12500 filter standard addresses this issue and establishes how manufacturers test and rate compressed air filters. The standard defines critical performance parameters (namely, inlet oil challenge, inlet compressed air temperature and pressure measurement techniques) that will deliver certifiable filter performance information suitable for comparative purposes. ISO 12500 is a multi-part standard, with subparts ISO 12500-1, ISO 12500-2, ISO 12500-3 [6].

1. ISO 12500-1: Encompassing the testing of coalescing filters for oil aerosol removal performance.
2. ISO 12500-2: Quantifies vapour removal capacity of adsorption filters.
3. ISO 12500-3: Outlines requirements to test particulate 3000 scfm filters for solid contaminant removal.

CONCLUSIONS

ISO Standards for Air Systems help to harmonize technical specifications of products and services making industry more efficient and breaking down barriers to international trade. Conformity to International Standards helps reassure consumers that products are safe, efficient and good for the environment. These newer standards can have significant impact on plant energy consumption if properly applied.

Monitoring compressed gases is not a frequent event in a facility's environmental monitoring programme. Monitoring is typically performed during the first classification of the clean room. After the initial test, the test should be run monthly for six months, and if these results are satisfactory, the test should be performed quarterly for the rest of the first year. After the first year – and if the results are still satisfactory – the frequency can be lowered to twice per year in an ISO 5 area, corresponding to each clean room verification performed every six months in Europe, but reduced with good justification to once per year in the US. Testing is not frequent, and investing in dedicated equipment with associated costs like validation, maintenance and repair, is difficult to justify financially. However, it is a mandatory regulatory requirement to monitor gases in facilities, with two optional strategies to consider.

REFERENCES

[1] By Dan Ryan, ISO 8573.1 – Contaminants and Purity Classes
[2] Introduction to ISO Air Quality Standards. Parker Hannifin Ltd. Dominick hunter Industrial Division Dukesway.
[3] ISO 12500
[4] ISO Standard 8573:2010 Compressed air 2010
[5] Jay Francis. Air Quality Standards ISO 8573.1 & ISO12500. Compressed air best practices.
[6] Wayne Perry. Standards for Compressed Air System Assessments. Compressed air best practices.

20

Hold Time Study in Pharmaceutical Industry

ABSTRACT

The concept of hold time study was initially developed for the in-process bulk products but with the advent of knowledge and regulatory requirements it became a need of time. Hold time study is performed to make sure that there exists no impact on the pharmaceutical product safety, efficacy and quality during staging period. Manufacturers accepted it to comply with the requirements of the regulatory bodies. Hold time study provides documented evidence that the storage conditions don't have any adverse effects on the product or equipment. Hold time study is now widely accepted for the dispensed raw materials, cleaned equipment, dirty equipment, aqueous solutions, purified water and many more. It gives an assurance that the process and product are efficient enough to maintain quality. In this manuscript an attempt has been made to understand the hold time in a more better and complete way.

INTRODUCTION

As per the regulatory requirements for the industry, it is required that pharmaceutical manufacturers generate a documented evidence to assure that the products under manufacturing process are safe, effective and of the quality required for their intended use.[1] To ensure this, regulatory bodies established various guiding instructions to validate the process, calibrate the instruments and qualify the equipment. Thus the requirement of documented evidences to establish systems is in place to ensure that pharmaceutical products are stored, processed and produced as per the defined procedures and is complying with the established specification. Sometimes, during these processes, it becomes requisite to hold the materials for a period before they are processed for next stage. Thus it becomes necessary to validate the hold time in pharmaceutical industry.[2] During this hold period, raw materials, packaging materials, in-process material, intermediate bulk, finished products, equipment and purified water are required to keep under controlled conditions. As documented evidence, hold time studies assure and rationalise the storage arrangements (environmental conditions, storage containers and time) that it will not deteriorate the product quality with respect to subsequent processing, stability, safety and efficacy on the basis of scientific data.

According to WHO (TRS 992, Annex 4), hold-time studies can be performed either at the development stage or during the later scale-ups.[1] Although WHO did not established minimum or maximum study periods, GMP requirements established the need of validated hold time to ensure that product or equipment can be stored, prior to the next processing step, without impacting the quality of product adversely. This study, establishes time limits for the completion of each phase of production shall be established to assure the quality of the drug product.[3] After WHO the recommendation, these studies became essential part of quality management and assurance during pharmaceutical manufacturing. These hold times should be justified through scientific data, complete analytical data, experimentation and statistical analysis.

Initially hold time studies were developed for the in-process materials or intermediate stages, but with recent developments it has also been explored to give documented proof to establish the quality and efficacy of dispensed materials like API, excipients, colour and flavours. Hold time study for the dispensed raw materials provides assurance that the dispensed raw materials may be used within the hold time period for the manufacturing process. Another fields include clean equipment hold time study, dirty equipment hold time study,[4, 5] storage of purified water, HVAC system.

PURPOSE OF THE STUDY

Approved hold time is considered as the established staging period for which raw materials, in-process bulk or equipment may be kept under specified controlled conditions and will remain within the predetermined specifications when analysed as per the approved testing procedures.[1] These study lay down the basic guide for use by manufacturing planners to plan for future processing. These documents are intended to prescribe to complete a process within the established hold times, and reflect aspects that should be considered during planning of the manufacturing process.

The study manuscripts or documents (matrix, protocol and report) primarily focus on all the required aspects considered in the design of the manufacturing planning. The purpose of these documents is to establish a harmonised procedure and requirements to be performed during the hold time study for in-process materials, dirty equipment, cleaned equipment, purified water and HVAC system in a pharmaceutical manufacturing unit. These documents also make it easy to select the worst case to conduct the hold time studies considered during validation and qualification activity. The selection of worst case products should always be made upon the risk based analysis.[6] These documents should also define the sampling plan and acceptance criteria that should be considered during hold time study.

ASPECTS TO BE CONSIDERED

Hold time studies are intended to establish the maximum time limits to hold the materials or equipment at the controlled conditions to ensure that this staging time does not have an adverse impact on the quality of the product with respect to the stability, safety and efficacy. Thus the design of the study should reflect the aspects to be considered during hold time study at each stage and the test to be performed. Hold times should normally be determined during process design or process qualification stage. Further data can also be collected as part of an investigation of a deviation that occurred during manufacture.[3] A risk based assessment should always be made to analyse the impact of changes in-processes, equipment, storage conditions, starting (raw) material or packaging material.[6]

Manufacturers should develop the process flow chart and summary to review the manufacturing procedure for a product to identify the critical stages of the process on the basis of the time period required for the processing stages, typical pauses in the manufacturing campaign, probable hold time and the potential product quality parameters and attributes on which the storage conditions (storage container, environment conditions and time) will have an impact.

GENERAL CONSIDERATIONS

Considering the statistical analytical requirements, at least study should be performed in the triplicate for hold time study, but there is regulatory obligations regarding the number of study batches. Some regulatory obligations include a well defined study protocol and report. A hold time study protocol should always be prepared, reviewed and approved before execution of the activity and identify the critical stages, quality parameters and quality attributes. It should also include storage condition, sampling plan, sampling frequency, sample quantity, tests to be performed and acceptance criteria. Sampling and testing are performed in accordance to this protocol. Sample quantity and sampling stage can be decided on the basis of type of formulation, strength, and stages involved in its manufacturing. Selection of storage conditions is very important for starting the hold study. These conditions should remain same with the manufacturing area or common hold area conditions maintained in general processes, so these conditions may vary with the type of product.

After completion of the study and tests, a report shall be prepared based on the findings during hold time study and concluding the maximum hold time period which does not have the adverse impact on the product at different process stages. This report shall act as the documented evidence to prove that the staging conditions have no adverse impact on the product quality during the concluded hold time.

Considerations to be made during in-process hold time study

In-process hold time study is established for in-process bulk, intermediate stages and semi finished products. Data to justify the hold time can be collected during development stage on pilot scale batches, during process validation or as a part of a deviation with proper testing.[7] Common considerations to be made during in-process hold time study include storage conditions, containers, duration, quality parameters and attributes, tests to be performed and sample quantity. The tests to be performed are not only limited to the chemical analysis but also extended to the microbiological purity. Thus these tests also establish the extent for microbiological deterioration of the products with time.

Considerations to be made during hold time study of aqueous products

Typically these bulks are intended to be processed immediately after preparations but sometimes due to some process limitations, these could be kept for hold prior to the process.[8] Common considerations to be made during hold time study for such bulk include storage conditions, containers, duration, quality parameters and attributes, bulk uniformity, pH alterations, viscosity changes, loss of water, tests to be performed and sample quantity. Tests to be performed for such bulk should also include microbiological tests along with physical and chemical analysis.

Considerations to be made during hold time study purified water

Purified water is not intended to be stored in pharmaceutical industry as it may lead to the microbial contamination but it can be kept for storage for various manufacturing and cleaning processes. This staging period must be validated and should be established based on the scientific considerations. Common tests to be performed include microbial analysis, conductivity, appearance, total organic content, pH etc.

Considerations to be made during equipment based hold time study

Hold time for the cleaned and dirty equipment is a necessary part of cleaning validation. The ongoing expectation is that equipment cleaning documentation verifies compliance with the validated hold times. A conservative approach uses either the established time for each group of equipment, which makes record keeping difficult, or the shortest established extended hold time for all equipment. There are two aspects of "hold times" generally evaluated for validated cleaning processes in pharmaceutical manufacturing:

Dirty equipment hold time study

Dirty equipment hold time study or DEHT is defined as the time elapsed from the end of manufacturing until the beginning of the cleaning process[4]. DEHT establish the time for which dirty equipment can be kept on hold before cleaning. This study on dirty equipment can be executed after processing for an extended period of time before cleaning. The study has to be executed in triplicate as per the approved protocols.

Microbial sampling has to be performed at regular interval before cleaning to define the DEHT. A thorough cleaning should be carried out immediately after the completion of specified hold time period and chemical and microbial analysis data shall be collected for the same. Main objectives of the dirty equipment hold time study are:

- What is the impact on the surface of the equipment being held for that period of time?
- How is the dirty equipment held so as to not contaminate other items?
- Is there data to support the cleaning of the dirty equipment after it has been held for long periods of time?

Cleaned equipment hold time study

Cleaned equipment hold time or CEHT study is defined as the time elapsed from the end of the cleaning process until the beginning of the use of the cleaned equipment for manufacture of the next product or re-cleaning of the equipment [4]. To assess CEHT, cleaned equipment is left unused for the hold period and analysed for various parameters. The CEHT validation study was conducted independently. After cleaning, the equipment should be analysed for the chemical analysis and thereafter wiped with 70% v/v IPA solution to remove microbial contamination, residual water, dried and covered to prevent any dust or particulate accumulation. The validation study consist several trials for the extended hold time. If the majority of the data showed no significant changes in microbiological burden and all results were below specified alert limit, hold period for re-cleaning is approved.

The results include data from a typical dry-granulation equipment train and a wet granulation equipment train. Main objective of the CEHT include:

- Is this equipment really clean during hold period?
- Do Standard Operating Procedures (SOPs) indicate how long the cleaned equipment can be stored prior to re-cleaning?
- Does adequate data exist to support the storage of the cleaned equipment?

TESTS TO BE PERFORMED DURING HOLD TIME STUDY

Various tests are performed to establish the valid hold time period. These tests include visual inspection, physical, chemical and microbiological tests. These tests are performed for different types of the hold time studies. These are mentioned as below:

Visual Inspection

Before proceeding for the sampling, it is always better to perform the visual inspection of the bulk to be sampled. This inspection should be carried out to detect any change in appearance and other attributes. This shall be carried out for all types of studies.

Physical Analysis

It includes studying the changes in physical properties of the sample during hold period. This shall be applicable for all types of study except CEHT and DEHT.

Chemical Analysis

It includes studying the chemical aspects of the sample during hold period. This shall be applicable for all types of hold time study.

Microbiological Analysis

It includes studying the growth rate of the microbial load during hold period. This shall be applicable to all types of hold time study.

SAMPLING

A sampling plan should be established and followed for taking samples for testing at the different intervals. The amount of sample required should be calculated based on the batch strength, size, study intervals, frequency and the tests to be performed. Results should be compared with the initial baseline data as the control. Samples may be pooled for analysis where appropriate, *e.g.,* when the analysis of a composite sample will not lead to issues that would be detectable in single samples being missed when the samples are pooled. Sampling for different types of tests including physical analysis, chemical analysis and microbial analysis to be performed for hold time studies are collected as per the protocol at the predefined intervals. Sample quantity and frequency need to be predefined in the protocol.

Sampling for cleaned equipment hold time study

Samples are collected at the defined frequency from the defined sampling location, as per the approved protocol, after the cleaning of the equipment once the equipment qualifies the visual inspection test. These samples are to be collected for chemical and microbial analysis in the media as per protocol. Collected swab samples shall be transfered to QC for further analysis.

Sampling for dirty equipment hold time study

Swab samples shall be taken after completion of the process and as per the defined frequency from defined location up to cleaning of the equipment as per the approved protocols. Sample for microbial analysis are collected for the sample frequency before cleaning of the equipment. But chemical and microbial analysis both is required for the sample collected after cleaning.

Bulk sampling for in-process hold time study

A composite sampling is preferred to be done for the in-process hold time study. Composite sample is prepared by performing sampling from different locations or stages and mixing them. Sample is kept in a simulated container under controlled conditions. Sample is kept in the quarantine with proper labelling. A sample is withdrawn from the container at the sampling frequency.

Bulk sampling for aqueous solution

A composite sample is collected from the different locations of the manufacturing vessel. The sample is collected in a stainless steel container with proper closure and label. At the sampling frequency, sample is withdrawn and analysed.

Simulated Bulk sampling for purified water

Purified water is to be used within 24 hours of preparation and is not supposed to be stored. But during manufacturing processes it becomes necessary to store purified water for further processing. So it becomes vital to perform hold time study of purified water. Purified water is stored under simulated conditions in a stainless steel container and analysed at regular intervals.

STAGES FOR THE HOLD TIME

The selection of the stages for the hold time study is very important for starting the hold study. Based on the manufacturing process of the dosage forms hold study stages can be decided. Hold study required stages are summarized in the Tables 1, 2, 3, 4 and 5.

Table 1: Sampling for oral tablets that are coated

Stage	*Considered*	*Test to be conducted*
Granulation	Binder paste	Appearance Viscosity pH Microbial analysis
Drying	Dried granules	Appearance Assay Residual solvent/ loss on drying Particle size distribution Microbial analysis
Lubrication	Lubricated blend	Appearance Assay Particle size distribution Microbial analysis
Compression	Compressed tablet	Appearance Physical properties (dimension) Assay Disintegration Dissolution Friability Uniformity of weight and average weight Hardness Microbial analysis
Coating	Coated tablet	Appearance Physical properties (dimensions) Assay Disintegration Dissolution Uniformity of weight and average weight Microbial analysis
	Coating solution	Appearance Viscosity Microbial analysis

Table 2: Sampling during manufacturing of non sterile liquid products

Dosage form	***Considered***	***Test to be performed***
Solutions	Bulk liquid	Appearance Assay pH Viscosity Microbial analysis
Emulsion	Bulk liquid	Appearance Assay Uniformity of content pH Viscosity Microbial analysis
Suspension	Bulk liquid	Appearance Assay Uniformity of content pH Viscosity Microbial analysis
Dry syrup	Bulk	Appearance Assay Particle size distribution Microbial analysis

WORST CASE SELECTION

Although not suggested by the regulatory guidelines, but a risk based approach could be applied to select the worst case product to study the hold time to reduce the sampling load and tests. This worst case selection helps to easy identification and selection of the product for hold time analysis. Worst case is selected only for the cleaned equipment hold time study and dirty equipment hold time study. This selection is made on the basis of the matrix developed for the cleaning validation study.

Criteria for the selection of equipment for equipment hold time

CEHT and DEHT are required to be performed for all the equipment present in the equipment chain and should be performed for all equipment chains. Worst case selection is required to be made on the basis of a product matrix. This matrix is prepared as per the matrix of cleaning validation.

STORAGE

Hold time sample is stored in a stainless steel container under controlled environmental conditions. Used equipment is stored unused properly in the area dedicated for the cleaning. A Cleaned Equipment shall be stored

Table 3: Sampling during manufacturing of semi-solid external preparation

Dosage form	*Considered*	*Tests to be performed*
Gel	Bulk	Appearance Assay Uniformity of content pH Viscosity Microbial analysis
Cream	Bulk	Appearance Assay Uniformity of content pH Viscosity Microbial analysis
Ointment	Bulk	Appearance Assay Uniformity of content pH Viscosity Microbial analysis
Lotions	Bulk	Appearance Assay Uniformity of content pH Viscosity Microbial analysis
Paste	Bulk	Appearance Assay Uniformity of content pH Viscosity Microbial analysis

properly in the area dedicated for the storage of cleaned equipment. In-process hold time sample are required to be stored in the respective quarantine area under environmental conditions as prescribed[8].

The hold period for each category of material should be established on the basis of the study by keeping the material in either the original or simulated container used in production. The containers in which hold time samples are stored should be the same pack as is used in production unless the pack is exceptionally large, in which case one that is equivalent (constructed of the same material and using the same closure system as the production packaging system) may be used. Reducing the size of container, when this is necessary for testing holding time, should be justified.

Where the headspace of containers used for bulk storage in manufacturing and/or quarantine is important, for example, because of a risk of potential degradation as a result of oxidation, and then the hold time studies should represent worst case conditions. In such cases, the ratio of

Table 4: Sampling during manufacturing of sterile products

Dosage form	*Considered*	*Test to be performed*
Liquid	Bulk Appearance Assay pH Viscosity Microbial analysis	

Table 5: Sampling during the manufacturing of capsules

Dosage form	*Considered*	*Test to be performed*
Hard gelatin capsules	Bulk	Appearance Assay Loss on drying Particle size distribution Microbial analysis
	Filled capsules	Appearance Assay Uniformity of weight Disintegration Dissolution Average weight Microbial analysis
Soft gelatin capsules	Filled capsules	Appearance Assay Uniformity of weight Disintegration Average weight Microbial analysis

headspace to contents in the test containers should be at least as great as the maximum that is possible in routine production (especially taking into account part filled containers). The environmental conditions for sample storage should be the same as those of the quarantine area/ manufacture stage.

PROTOCOL FOR THE HOLD TIME STUDIES

A written protocol, procedure or programme should be followed, which includes, for example, the activities to be performed, test parameters and acceptance criteria appropriate to the material or product under test. The protocol and report should generally include the following: a title; reference number; version; date; objective; scope; responsibility; procedure; description of the material or product; sample quantities; sampling method and criteria; acceptance limits; frequency of sampling; sampling locations; pooling of samples; storage conditions; type of container; methods of analysis; results;

conclusion; recommendation; signatures; and dates. Acceptance criteria are typically more stringent than registered specifications, to provide assurance that the material is well within control. When setting the specifications, any known stability trends will need to be taken into account. Microbiological aspects should also be considered and included. All testing of bulk intermediates and product should be performed using validated stability indicating methods.

Typically study could be performed in duplicate or triplicate, on the basis of justified risk based approach can be used to determine the appropriate number of batches, considering the characteristics of the materials and other relevant aspects to determine hold times. A representative sample of the batch of material or product subjected to the hold time study should be held for the defined hold period. Where appropriate, statistical analysis of the data generated should be performed to identify trends and to justify the limits and hold time set. Normally, intermediate and bulk products should not be stored beyond the established hold time.

CONCLUSIONS

Hold time studies are concluded successful if all the results meet the product specifications. Hold time study shall be carried out with the intended storage container or packing's only. If the dosage form is stored in bulk containers for over 30 days, real-time stability data under specified conditions should be generated to demonstrate comparable stability to the dosage form in the marketed package. Maximum acceptable holding periods should therefore be established to ensure that intermediates and bulk product can be held, pending the next processing step, without producing results outside the acceptance criteria for the quality of the material. The choice of maximum holding period should be supported by relevant data. Studies may extend beyond the chosen maximum hold time but it is not necessary to extend testing to determine the extreme limits at which failure occurs. If any in-process bulk is stored for more time period than the established hold time period it should be re-sampled and shall be commercialised only after release from quality control.

REFERENCES

[1] Agalloco JP, Carleton FJ, (2007) Validation of pharmaceutical processes, 3rd ed. Informa Healthcare: New York; 444-446.
[2] Forsyth RJ (2008) Equipment Hold-Time for Cleaning Validation. Pharm technol.
[3] Huma Ali, Abdul Majid Khatri, Ashish Jain, Ravi Modi, Alpesh Patel, (2011) Standard Practice of sampling, storage and Holding Time for Pharmaceutical Tablet and Injection during manufacturing process. *Drug Invention Today*, 3(7), 157-159.
[4] Mallu UR, Nair AK, Bandaru S, Sankaraiah J (2012) Hold Time Stability Studies in Pharmaceutical Industry: Review. PharmaceutReg Affairs 1:104.

[5] Pawar D P, Shamkuwar P B (2012) Hold Time Study Of Cetirizine Di Hydrochloride Lubricated Granules : *Asian J Pharm Clin Res; Vol 5, Suppl 4, 2012,* 234-236
[6] Quality Risk Management, ICH Q9.
[7] T. Fugate, (2007) "Hold Time Studies: A Lost Parameter for Cleaning Validation," *J. Val. Technol.* 13 (3), 206–209.
[8] WHO Expert Committee on Specifications for Pharmaceutical Preparations Forty-ninth report. TRS 992, Annex 4

21

Common Questions Related to Pharmaceutical Quality Assurance and Their Answers

Q1. What should be the frequency of the product quality review (PQR)?

Ans. The product review is expected annually. Review time frames can be appropriately adjusted based upon manufacturing and campaign duration with adequate justification. The timeframe criteria should be established in a SOP. The trending can include results gathered from the previous period to ensure its robustness. Even if no manufacturing has occurred in the review period, the quality and regulatory review should be conducted and include stability results, returns, complaints, recalls, deviations (including those arising from qualification and validation activities) and regulatory background. The review of the last PQR should also be conducted.

Q2. Should metal detectors be used routinely in manufacturing processes for certain dosage forms *e.g.*, tablet compression and encapsulation processes?

Ans. Metal could originate from raw materials as well as from equipment in manufacturing processes where metal parts could generate fragments due to the conditions of operation or damage to the equipment. It is recommended that metal detection is used for processes prone to this. In order to avoid routine use of metal detectors the company must demonstrate that it has identified and managed the risks such that the use of metal detectors for that particular process is not needed.

Q3. Is it possible to use multiple batch numbers in packaging of medicinal products?

Ans. GMP inspectors have discussed the desirability of more than one batch number appearing on the packaging of medicinal products. It is normal practice for companies to use a bulk batch number that is different from the finished product batch when the bulk is packaged as several sub-batches. There is normally an element in the numbering format common to the bulk batch and finished product batches that clearly ties these together. The difference normally takes the form of a suffix, prefix or both. A matter of concern for the inspectors is when the bulk and finished product batch numbers are completely different and there is no obvious connection between the two. Even though the manufacturer has a system of traceability, the inspectors agree that this is an undesirable practice and should be avoided. The main reasons for this are:

- Patients and healthcare professionals may mistakenly believe that there has been a packaging error;
- Hospitals often remove products from the outer packaging and traceability may therefore be lost;
- Confusion may occur in the case of recall, rendering such action potentially ineffective.

It is accepted that there may be exceptional cases where multiple batch numbers are displayed on a pack, such as in combination product packages. In addition, products that require relabeling following parallel distribution are expected to display the original manufacturer's batch number. Manufacturers are recommended to discuss individual cases with the relevant supervisory authority. In all cases, traceability must be maintained.

Q4. What are the expectations with regard to documentation and verification of the supply chain for active substances?

Ans. The supply chain for each active substance must be established back to the manufacture of the active substance starting materials. This should be documented and must be kept current. The risks associated with this supply chain should be formally documented. Control of each incoming consignment of active substance should include verification that it has been received from the approved supplier and approved manufacturer. The entire supply chain should be verified for a supplied batch periodically to establish a documented trail for the batch back to the manufacturer(s) of the active substance starting materials. The frequency of this verification should be based on risk.

Q5. Is it acceptable to pack (primary and/or secondary packaging) multiple batches of the same product (*e.g.*, tablets, capsules, lozenges) in order to obtain a single batch as a "super batch"?

Ans. Normally, such an approach should be avoided as each batch is made from the same initial quantity of material and should remain as an individual batch of finished medicinal product bearing a unique batch number. Therefore, any other approach should be thoroughly justified by applying the principles of Quality Risk Management (QRM) taking into account at least the following criteria:

- Length of time the equipment has been in use;
- Pharmaceutical form of the drug product that cannot be homogenised (tablet, capsules, etc);
- Expiry date of the drug products;
- Ongoing stability study design and results;
- Reference samples plan for each batch;
- Criticality of the drug product and the risk of shortage that may arise from any quality issue;
- Prior approval of the MAH.

Irrespective of the outcome of the QRM, such an approach can only be accepted if each individual batch of the combined "super batch" undergoes all the in-process control and finished drug product testing as specified in the marketing authorisation dossier. In the event of a recall, the entire "super batch" should be recalled.

Q6. What are the quality defect reporting requirements?

Ans. Suspected product quality defects (*e.g.*, product deterioration, packaging mix-up, among others) should be reported to the competent authority with responsibility for the manufacturing site, and to the competent authority in each market supplied. In case of impact to centrally authorised products, the authority must also be notified. Confirmation of a quality defect does not require completion of the investigation. Reporting should be initiated when available information supports the detection of the issue and when the initial assessment of the potential risks presented to patients/animals indicates that it could result in market action. Notification to competent authorities should typically take place within one working day of confirmation that reporting is required.

In cases where a suspected quality defect involves multiple manufacturing sites, reporting responsibilities should be defined in a technical agreement. It is normal expectation that the MAH and site of final batch certification should take the lead on reporting, unless otherwise justified. Manufacturers are encouraged to notify their national competent authority of confirmed serious GMP issues with the potential to lead to a suspected product defect requiring market action (*e.g.*, media fill failure, serious equipment failure, etc.). Confirmation of a serious GMP issue does not require completion of the investigation; reporting should be initiated when available information confirms the detection of the issue.

Serious GMP issues which may result in an abnormal restriction in supply should be notified to the MAH and relevant competent authorities in accordance with legal obligations. In the event that a medicinal product which is the subject of a marketing authorisation issued by an authority, and which is marketed in another third country (or countries) then the marketing authorisation holder shall forthwith inform the relevant competent authority of any prohibition or restriction imposed by the competent authorities of any country in which the medicinal product is marketed and of any other new information which might influence the evaluation of the benefits and risks of the medicinal product concerned (*e.g.*, recalls or serious GMP issues). This is even if the particular batch subject to the prohibition or restriction is not marketed. In cases where national competent authorities set additional national expectations regarding what quality defects should be reported and the timelines for reporting, these should be complied with.

Q7. For the purposes of product recall, at what stage in the supply chain is a product considered to be 'placed on the market'?

Ans. A batch recall is defined in the Compilation of Community Procedures as "The action of withdrawing a batch from the distribution chain and users. A batch recall may be partial, in that the batch is only withdrawn from selected distributors or users". This definition covers the entire distribution chain from all points following manufacture through to the end user, the patient. Also, it is possible that the MAH or its subsidiaries are actors in the supply chain, acting as the distributor in certain cases. In such cases, the MAH or its subsidiaries should be regarded as also being part of the distribution chain.

A batch of medicinal product is considered to have been 'placed on the market' when one of the following takes place:

- A batch has been Qualified Person (QP) certified and has been made available for sale on the stock management system of the pre-wholesaler/ primary wholesaler, etc.
- A batch has been QP certified and supplied to a facility where the manufacturer has no further control over when the product is transferred to saleable stock. This applies even if within the pre-wholesaler/primary wholesaler network.

In the case of supply chain models where the manufacturer or primary wholesaler supplies direct to the customer (*e.g.,* pharmacy), the batch has been placed on the market from the time of the first customer supply of product from the batch.

National competent authorities should be notified of all recall action proposed after the product has been placed on the market. In situations where the MAH can demonstrate that the batch is reconciled without issuing a recall notice, the national competent authority may agree that public recall communication throughout the distribution network is not necessary.

It is acknowledged that certain short expiry products (*e.g.,* radiopharmaceuticals, advanced therapy medicinal products, etc.) may be shipped under quarantine prior to certification. Retrieval of batches during this quarantine period may be managed within the pharmaceutical quality system.

Q8. How can GMP compliance for active-substance manufacturers be demonstrated?

Ans. Manufacturing-authorisation holders are obliged to use, as starting materials, only active substances that have been manufactured in accordance with the detailed guidelines on GMP for starting materials. Thus the legislation puts the responsibility on the manufacturing-authorisation holders using the active substance and does not foresee mandatory routine inspections of active-substance manufacturers.

To provide guidance on how GMP compliance of active-substance manufacturers should be established, guidance documents have been published on this website, including the 'guidance on the occasions when it is appropriate for competent authorities to conduct inspections at the premises of manufacturers of active substances used as starting materials' as part of the Community procedures. This document states that it is expected that manufacturing-authorisation holders will normally gain assurance that the active substances it uses are manufactured in accordance with GMP through audit of the active-substance suppliers. In addition, a number of questions and answers on audits of active-substance manufacturers on this page provide further guidance.

Q9. Do I need to perform an audit of an active substance supplier if it has been inspected by an inspectorate and a valid GMP certificate is available?

Ans. Manufacturing-authorisation holders sometimes confuse the role of inspectorates with their own obligations but nevertheless, when inspection reports or GMP certificates issued by an agency mutual-recognition-agreement (MRA) partners or other recognised authorities are available, these can provide useful information to manufacturing-authorisation holders. However, these alone cannot fulfil the statutory obligations of the manufacturing authorisation holder or the requirements of the GMP guideline, but the results of inspections may be used together with other supporting information in a risk-based approach by the manufacturer in establishing priorities for its own audit programme of active-substance suppliers.

Q10. Is it acceptable to perform a remote assessment based on, for example, questionnaires, review of documents, International Organization for Standardization 9000 certificate education, results of analytical testing and historical experience with the supplier?

Ans. The EEA inspectorates are not generally in favour of 'paper-based audits' *per se* as they do not provide the same level of assurance as on-site assessments, but do accept that they have a part to play in a risk-based strategy. They may be particularly applicable when recent positive inspection information is available and where satisfactory audits have been concluded in the past. They cannot replace on-site audits of active-substance suppliers but can be a useful interim and temporary measure within the manufacturer's audit programme.

Q11. Is it possible to ask for a voluntary inspection of an active substance manufacturer?

Ans. First, the responsibility for only using active substances that have been manufactured in accordance with GMPs is placed on the holders of a manufacturing authorisation (MA). An inspection of the active substance manufacturer by an authority does not liberate a MA holder from this responsibility. Guidelines have provision for the competent authority of the Member State concerned to carry out inspections of starting material manufacturers at the specific request of the manufacturer. The request for the inspection should be made to the competent authority where the site is located or, in case of sites located in third countries, to a competent authority where the starting material is used in the manufacture of medicinal products. If this is not the case, any authority can be approached.

There is no guarantee that such a request will be fulfilled since competent authorities primarily use risk-based principles to plan starting material inspections. Thus, when a starting material manufacturer applies for a voluntary inspection, this does not constitute an obligation for the competent authority to trigger an inspection.

Q12. The notice to applicants requires the submission of a declaration signed by the qualified person (QP) that the active substance used is manufactured in accordance with GMP. The active substance in my product is widely used, but not normally as a pharmaceutical active substance, and I am having some difficulty in confirming compliance. What should I do to furnish the required declaration?

Ans. Full compliance with GMP for finished products and active substances is a legal obligation for manufacturing-authorisation holders. It is recognised that for a small number of medicinal products, the primary use of the active substance is not in a medicinal product and the producer may therefore not be aiming to meet the specific requirements of pharmaceutical customers that represent an insignificant volume of business. Alternative sources should normally be sought, but in exceptional cases the manufacturing-authorisation holder should assess and document to which extent GMP is complied with and provide a risk-based justification for the acceptance of any derogation. The declaration provided by the QP should set out in detail the basis for declaring that the standards applied provide the same level of assurance as GMP. The European Medicines Agency will collect experience with this approach, which can be used as a basis for discussion on related amendments to guidelines in the future.

Q13. What kind of GMP documentation is needed for an active-substance manufacturer that performs sterilisation of an active substance?

Ans. The GMP basic requirements for active substances used as starting materials only applies to the manufacture of sterile active substances up to the point immediately prior to the active substance being rendered sterile. The sterilisation and aseptic processing of sterile active substances are not covered by this guideline and should be performed in accordance with GMP for medicinal products. This implies that for any active-substance manufacturer that performs sterilisation and subsequent aseptic handling of the active substance, a valid manufacturing authorisation or GMP certificate from an authority or from an authority of countries where MRA or other Community arrangements apply has to be submitted. The active-substance manufacturer also has to submit data on the sterilisation process of the active substance (including validation data) to the marketing-authorisation applicant or holder for inclusion in the dossier submitted for the finished product and approval by the licensing authorities.

Q14. During inspections, why do inspectors sometimes ask to see reports of audits of active substance manufacturers carried out by the medicinal product manufacturer?

Ans. Inspectors may need to see audit reports during inspections as part of the assessment of the manufacturing-authorisation holder's systems for confirming GMP compliance of active substance manufacturers or suppliers. Inspectors will expect to see the full details of these reports upon request, including responses received from the audited site, indication of closure of deficiencies raised or commitments made.

Q15. What expectations do inspectors have for the content of reports of audits of active substance manufacturers carried out by the medicinal product manufacturer?

Ans. As a minimum, the following is expected to be included in the report:

- The full postal address of the site. The auditors must be identified by full name and their employer recorded. If the audit is conducted on behalf of other parties this should be clear in the report. Where an audit report is obtained through a third party, the manufacturing-authorisation holder is responsible for ensuring the validity and impartiality of the audit report.

- The identity of key staff participating in the audit should be recorded along with their roles.
- The full contact details of the person through which the audit was arranged should be recorded including contact details (e-mail address, telephone number).
- The dates of the audit should be recorded, with the full-day equivalents clarified if full days were not spent on site.
- A justification should be recorded for the duration of the audit. If, in exceptional circumstances, the audit had to be restricted to fewer days on site than required by the scope of the audit, the reasons should be explained and the conclusions with respect to the GMP status of the site should be justified.
- Background information on the active substance manufacturer should be recorded; this should include the company ownership, the age of the site, the number of staff employed in total and for the specific products being audited.
- The role of the site in manufacture of the active substances being audited should also be clarified for each of the active substances being audited, *e.g.,* if the site performs the full manufacture or only part of the manufacture.
- The scope of the audit should be clearly stated *e.g.,* what activities were covered.
- The activities which were not covered by the audit should also be clearly recorded.

Auditors should identify the high risk areas for audit specific to the site or products being audited. For example, these could include but not be limited to:

- Process, cleaning or validation;
- Risk of cross-contamination with other active substances or other substances;
- Potential for generation of unknown impurities;
- Risk of mix-up of materials and products through materials handling or packing;
- Change control;
- Deviation recording or management;
- Security sealing of active substance containers and security or temperature control of shipments.

Subsequent audits conducted as part of the ongoing supplier audit program may have a reduced scope focusing on the highest risk areas. In such cases the highest risk areas should be identified and justified. A list should be recorded of all active substances directly included in the audit scope plus other active substances or intermediates (or other products) manufactured at the site. There should be a clear record of the products, the stages of manufacture and the buildings audited. If access was denied to any relevant areas of the site this should be recorded and explained. The list should clarify which of the active substances in the scope of the audit are manufactured in multi-purpose equipment or buildings as either final product or any of the intermediate stages.

Dates of any previous audit conducted by or on behalf of the same manufacturing-authorisation holder should be recorded. If any of the audits did not conclude with a positive GMP compliance status, a brief summary of the reasons for this should be recorded.

Each of the applicable sections should form sections of the report with a summary of what was examined, the key findings and compliance with the requirements of each section. The report should clearly state findings against each activity audited with particular focus on the high risk areas. Any GMP deficiency identified during the audit must be clearly recorded with its criticality defined. An explanation should be given, in the report or in a supporting standard operating procedure, of the categorisation system used to classify deficiencies, *e.g.,* critical, major or minor.

Responses to the audit by the active-substance manufacturer should be reviewed by the auditors. Corrective and preventative actions and timescales for completion should be assessed by the auditors to establish whether these are appropriate to the findings. Further clarification or evidence of completion should be requested, commensurate to the risk.

A summary assessment of the status of corrective and preventive actions should be recorded by the auditors once these have been received and assessed. An overall recommendation should be made in the final report. The summary should include whether the auditor regards the actions as satisfactory. The responsible QP should ensure that he or she, or someone to whom it is delegated, is in agreement with the overall recommendation of the final report. The QP must not release the relevant medicinal products without knowledge of a positive recommendation from the auditors. This recommendation should include the GMP compliance status of the site and whether any reduced controls on materials receipt at the finished product manufacturing site are supported by the auditors. A proposed re-assessment period should be recommended. The final report should be signed and dated by, at least, the lead auditor.

Q16. How should active substance auditors be qualified?

Ans. Auditors should have sufficient scientific, technical and other experience to enable them to perform an adequate and thorough audit of the active substance manufacturer, as related to the planned scope of the audit. Where a proposed auditor lacks an appropriate level of direct experience in the field of active substance manufacture, he or she should undergo a documented training and assessment programme in the areas that are relevant to the audit, taking into account the auditor's anticipated role in the audit and the technologies that are likely to be encountered during the audit. Auditors must also be trained and assessed in their knowledge and understanding of regulatory requirements and in auditing techniques in general. The training and assessment should be fully documented. The qualification and experience of contracted auditors are the same as the requirements for the manufacturing-authorisation holder's own auditors.

Q17. What are the GMP requirements to be applied to the formulation of biological active substances with excipients, when described in the active substance section of a registration dossier?

Ans. For the manufacture of biological active substances, separate requirements the GMP guidelines apply. While quality risk management principles also apply to the formulation of a biological active substance, some aspects of GMP as described below are more appropriate and are expected as a minimum:

- Particular emphasis should be put on the management of the constitutive excipients of the formulated active substance.
- Specifications should be defined for excipients according to GMP and the monographs of the pharmacopoeia should be applied.

- The approval, maintenance and audit of excipient suppliers should be based on quality risk management, in accordance with GMP guidelines on the formalised risk assessment for ascertaining the appropriate good manufacturing practice for excipients of medicinal products for human use.
- An agreement between the medicinal product manufacturer and the excipient manufacturer should be established in accordance with GMP.
- The sampling of excipients used for the formulated active substance should comply with GMP and retention samples of excipients should be kept under the responsibility of the medicinal product manufacturer.
- Excipients used by the manufacturer of the formulated active substance should be included in the Periodic Quality Review (in accordance with GMP).
- Consideration should be given to the inclusion of batches of a finished medicinal product manufactured from formulated active substances, stored for the maximum holding time, in the ongoing stability program of the medicinal product, in accordance with GMP.
- When outsourced, the manufacture of a formulated active substance should be managed in the same way as the outsourcing of the manufacture of an intermediate medicinal product, through full application of the requirements of GMP guideline.

Q18. Are active substances used as starting materials in the production of IMPs subject to GMP?

Ans. Directives include obligations for manufacturing-authorisation holders only to use active substances that have been manufactured in accordance with GMP. Provision is also made for inspections of active-substance manufacturers but only under certain specified circumstances.

GMP guideline does include a short section on new active substances to be used as starting materials for IMPs and these remain as recommendations with no mandatory force. Nevertheless, active substances used in the manufacture of marketed products are already required to comply with GMP irrespective as to whether they may also used in the manufacture of IMPs.

Q19. How should the integrity of sterilising filters be verified?

Ans. Guidelines states, 'the integrity of the sterilised filter should be verified before use and should be confirmed immediately after use by an appropriate method such as a bubble-point, diffusive-flow or pressure-hold test.' The filter-sterilisation process may be physically stressful for the filter. For example, high temperatures during the process may cause the filter to distort, potentially leading to fluid pathways that allow the passage of particles greater than 0.2 μm in size. The performance of a filter can improve with use, as particles begin to block individual pathways and remove larger pathways that smaller particles could successfully navigate. For these reasons, filters should be tested both before use but after sterilisation and again after use. Furthermore, testing should be performed *in situ* in order to verify the integrity of the filter complete with its housing.

Q20. What are the sampling requirements for sterility testing when a finished product batch of a terminally sterilised medicinal product is made up of more than one steriliser load?

Ans. The sampling plan for sterility testing should take account of the definition of a batch as stated in the glossary of the GMP guideline together with the recommendations of guidelines. Each steriliser load is considered to be an independent sub-batch. Consequently, one sterility test should be performed per sub-batch. The number of samples per steriliser load should conform to pharmacopoeia requirements.

Q21. Can there be any exceptions to this rule?

Ans. For large-volume parenterals where the sterilisation cycle has been qualified with an overkill level, an alternative sampling plan in accordance with a specific internal procedure agreed with the supervisory authority can be accepted (unless already specified in the marketing authorisation).

This procedure should state the need to sample from each steriliser load including the coolest location identified during the steriliser qualification. The number of samples per load should be defined based on a risk-based approach and the overall number of samples per batch should conform to pharmacopoeia requirements. An alternative option, which would require a variation to relevant existing marketing authorisations, would be to introduce a system of parametric release, thereby avoiding the need to carry out the sterility test.

Q22. What is the maximum acceptable bioburden level?

Ans. The specification limits for bioburden should be NMT 10 CFU/100 ml, in line with the human and veterinary notes for guidance on manufacture of the finished dosage form.

When a prefilter is installed, unless otherwise justified, a bioburden limit of 10 CFUs/100 ml before first filtration is achievable in principle and is strongly recommended from a GMP point of view. Higher bioburden limits should not be justified by the high capacity of two consecutive bacteria retaining filters.

However, when appropriate justification is submitted (processes involving fermentation or other biological or herbal components, use of purified water for ophthalmic preparations, etc.), a bioburden limit of higher than 10 CFUs/100 ml before prefiltration may be acceptable. In such cases, it should be demonstrated that the first filter has the capability to achieve a bioburden prior to the last filtration of NMT 10 CFUs/100 ml, in line with the notes for guidance on manufacture of the finished dosage form.

Q23. Do I need to follow the requirements of the updated ISO 14644 part 1 standard?

Ans. For qualification or re-qualification of clean room facilities, medicinal product manufacturers may apply the updated ISO standard.

Q24. What is traceability?

Ans. Traceability is the ability to retrieve the history of the manufacturing and distribution operations of a batch of a medicinal product. The data recorded through the traceability system should allow efficient investigation in case an incident occurs and should allow recalls of (potentially) defective products.

In the case of packaged medicinal gases, the packaging components (shells and valves) are reusable. It is therefore necessary to record additional information, in particular in relation to the use and maintenance of these components.

Q25. Which items should be recorded in the case of medicinal gases filled into cylinders to enable traceability?

Ans. Packaging components (shells and valves). The cylinder is the combination of the shell and its valve.

Shell: For safety reasons, shells are individually identified (specific reference). Individual traceability is therefore possible. The date of the last hydrostatic pressure test (or equivalent test) should be recorded.

Valve: Shells may be fitted with simple valves (*e.g.,* pin-index valves) or integrated valves. Integrated valves are individually identified (individual identification reference). Individual traceability is therefore possible. This is not the case for simple valves, which mostly have only a serial number corresponding to a group of valves. The design of integrated valves, which are medical devices, is complex. These valves are also subject to periodic preventive maintenance operations. In terms of risk, more serious incidents have been reported with cylinders having this type of valve. Therefore:

- In the case of simple valves, the type of valve should be recorded, as well as the name of the manufacturer and the serial number, if one is available;
- In the case of integrated valves, traceability should be ensured for each valve. Records should include in particular the type of integrated valve (including the version), the individual identification reference of the valve, the name of the manufacturer, the date of the last (or next) preventive maintenance and details of any preventive maintenance performed on the valve. Each shell-and-valve combination should be traceable.

  Finished product: The manufacturing batch records should include the individual identification references of the cylinders of each batch of finished product.

  Distribution: The distribution records should include the individual identification references of the cylinders delivered to each customer.

Q26. What means should be implemented to ensure traceability?

Ans. In practice, depending on the scale of operation, it may be difficult to ensure effective traceability without a computerised system. Use of bar codes or electronic chips on the cylinders may facilitate this. Any computerised system used to ensure traceability should conform to the requirements of GMP guideline.

Q27. What should be possible through the system of traceability?

Ans. Should a manufacturer of a medicinal gas receive a serious complaint relating to the quality of the medicinal gas itself or the packaging components, the system in place should allow the identification of the affected cylinders and, where necessary, the recall of any affected cylinders from the market.

A defect relating to packaging components may require identification of specific cylinders within a finished product batch or identification of cylinders present in a number of finished product batches in order to establish the extent of any recall required.

For example, an effective traceability system should allow effective recalls of cylinders fitted with defective valves based on:

- Specific type, version or manufacturer's batch for the valves;
- Maintenance and calibration operations for the valves during a specific time period.

Q28. What is the background regarding international incidents of glycerol contamination?

Ans. There is a history of sporadic reports from around the world of supplies of glycerol contaminated with diethylene glycol (DEG) resulting in mortality and serious morbidity in patients receiving contaminated products.

- In late 2006, DEG-contaminated glycerol in cough syrup was the cause of about 50 deaths in Panama.
- DEG-contaminated glycerol in paracetamol syrup was also attributed to at least 80 deaths in a similar incident in Haiti in 1995-1996.
- Other incidents have been reported in Argentina, Bangladesh, India and Nigeria and attributed to the deaths of hundreds of children.
- DEG was also responsible for a poisoning incident resulting in the death of 107 people in the United States in 1937, following ingestion of contaminated sulphanilamide elixir.

These incidents were related to both accidental cross-contamination of glycerol with industrial grade materials and, in some cases, to intentional substitution. Recent cases show the following similarities:

- Pharmaceutical manufacturers of products containing contaminated glycerol did not perform full identity testing or tests to determine DEG on the glycerol raw material;
- Pharmaceutical manufacturers of contaminated products relied on certificates of analysis (COAs) provided by the supplier;
- The origin of glycerine was not apparent from the COA. The COA provided with the glycerol raw material may have been a copy of the original on a distributor letterhead.
- The supply chain for glycerol was not readily known by the medicinal-product manufacturer because the glycerol may have been sold several times between its manufacture and the medicinal-product manufacturer.

Q29. How is the patient protected from similar contamination occurring in products?

Ans. EU GMP requires all manufacturing companies to confirm that all its raw materials are checked on receipt to confirm their identity and quality. Competent authorities expect product manufacturers to routinely ensure that incoming samples of glycerol are tested according to the Pharmacopoeia monograph. Ex. The European Pharmacopoeia monograph for glycerol includes a specific limit test for diethylene glycol (0.1%).

Q30. GMP provides for derogations from the requirement for identity testing of every container where there is a validated supply chain. Can I use this derogation for the glycerol I purchase?

Ans. It is correct that GMP does provide for a relaxation of identity testing of every container, but it also states that this would not normally be possible if brokers or intermediates were involved in the chain of supply. Glycerol is a commercial article that is widely used in the food and other industries. Generally speaking, the supply chain for glycerol tends to be complex and lengthy. The involvement of brokers is common in the supply chain.

Q31. What steps are expected of manufacturers based in the EU when purchasing glycerol or of manufacturers based in third countries supplying glycerol-containing medicines?

Ans. When designing supplier-assurance and incoming-goods-control programmes, companies should consider glycerol a higher-risk material. Companies should be able to exhibit a good knowledge of starting material supply chains and apply this knowledge and principles of quality risk management to their programmes for supply-chain management. Inspectors will look to ensure that the basis for qualification of the supply chain is demonstrably robust for higher-risk materials such as glycerol. It is expected that identity testing and the Pharmacopoeia limit test for DEG will be performed on each container as a matter of routine.

Q32. The European Pharmacopoeia limit test for DEG involves a gas chromatographic method, which may be difficult to perform on a large number of containers.

Ans. This point is acknowledged and currently, alternative tests are under consideration with a view to work up a possible change to the identity tests in the monograph. The European Pharmacopoeia DEG limit test remains the official method for confirmation of compliance with the monograph.

Q33. Are there any considerations applicable to the pharma-aceutical assessment of marketing-authorisation applications?

Ans. In application dossiers for new marketing authorisations (MAs), or in case of relevant variations for existing MAs (for example, replacement of an excipient with glycerol) for medicinal products containing glycerol, confirmation of the tests applied on receipt of batches of glycerol to control the risk from potential DEG contamination in relation to the specific intended use of the product should be provided. A test for DEG content should be conducted in addition to identity testing for glycerol. A suitable control for DEG is included in the European Pharmacopoeia monograph for glycerol. Sufficient information regarding satisfactory control of this risk will be required in the dossier before approval of the MA application or variation.

For existing approved medicinal products, no variation application is required, except for those few specific types of variations referred to in the first paragraph. However, as a minimum, the specific European Pharmacopoeia control for DEG should be conducted along with the identity test at receipt of each batch of glycerol.

The excipient is required to comply with the current European Pharmacopoeia glycerol monograph, and as the specification approved in the dossier will have been that of the European Pharmacopoeia , the risk of DEG contamination will have been appropriately controlled. Compliance with this requirement will be verified during GMP inspections.

Q34. My company manufactures products for external use. Does this guidance apply?

Ans. Where a company manufactures products for external use, and when it has justified that the presence of DEG in these products poses a low risk, the omission of the test for DEG on each container may be accepted by the supervisory authority.

Q35. The registered specifications of our starting materials include conventional or pharmacopoeial methods for the confirmation of identity but we wish to use NIR to perform identity testing on each container of starting materials used in the manufacture of parenteral products. Is the use of this alternative method acceptable?

Ans. GMP guideline states that the identity of a complete batch of starting materials can normally only be ensured if individual samples are taken from all the containers and an identity test performed on each sample. It is permissible to sample only a proportion of the containers where a validated procedure has been established to ensure that no single container of starting material has been incorrectly labelled. However, the annex goes on to say that it is improbable that a procedure could be satisfactorily validated for starting materials for use in parenteral products.

Unless variations are submitted for all affected products, the registered method for confirming identity should be performed. However, there is no restriction on the performance of additional testing and the use of NIR to confirm container-wise confirmation of identity can provide useful information. Under these circumstances, the requirements of the marketing authorisation will be deemed to have been met by carrying out the registered method for confirmation of identity on a statistically representative composite sample when this is supplemented with NIR analysis of every container.

Q36. Appropriate controls for electronic documents such as templates should be implemented. Are there any specific requirements for templates of spreadsheets?

Ans. Templates of spreadsheets help to avoid erroneous calculations from data remaining from previous calculations. They should be suitably checked for accuracy and reliability. They should be stored in a manner which ensures appropriate version control.

Q37. What type of accuracy checks are expected for the use of spreadsheets?

Ans. Data integrity should be ensured by suitably implemented and risk-assessed controls. The calculations and the files should be secured in such a way that formulations are not accidentally overwritten. Accidental input of an inappropriate data type should be prevented or result in an error message (*e.g.*, text in a numeric field or a decimal format into an integer field). So-called 'boundary checks' are encouraged.

Q38. Are there any specific considerations for the validation of spreadsheets?

Ans. Validation is required at least for spreadsheets that contain custom code (*e.g.*, Visual Basic for applications). Formulas or other types of algorithm should be verified for correctness.

Q39. What measures are required to ensure data security of databases?

Ans. Data security includes integrity, reliability and availability of data. During validation of a database-based or inclusive system, consideration should be given to:

- Implementing procedures and mechanisms to ensure data security and keeping the meaning and logical arrangement of data;
- Load-testing, taking into account future growth of the database and tools to monitor the saturation of the database;
- Precautions for necessary migration of data at the end of the life-cycle of the system.

Q40. At which phases of the system life-cycle is risk management recommended?

Ans. Risk management should be applied throughout the whole life-cycle. A first risk assessment should be performed to determine the GMP criticality of the system, *i.e.,* does the system have an impact on patient safety, product quality or data integrity? User-requirement specifications are usually developed with consideration of potential risks and form the basis for the first formal risk assessment. Complex systems should be evaluated in further more detailed risk assessments to determine critical functions. This will help ensure that validation activities cover all critical functions.

Risk management includes the implementation of appropriate controls and their verification.

Q41. Are user requirements needed as part of the retrospective validation of legacy systems?

Ans. The way to check whether a computerised system is fit for its intended purpose is to define user requirements and perform a gap analysis to determine the validation effort for retrospective validation. These user requirements should be verified.

Q42. When do I have to revalidate computerised systems?

Ans. Computerised systems should be reviewed periodically to confirm that they remain in a validated state. Periodic evaluation should include, where applicable, the current range of functionality, deviation records, change records, upgrade history, performance, reliability and security. The time period for revaluation and revalidation should be based on the criticality of the system.

Q43. What are the requirements for storage time of electronic data and documents?

Ans. The requirements for storage of electronically data and documents do not differ from paper documents. It should be ensured that electronic signatures applied to electronic records are valid for the entire storage period for documents.

Q44. What are the relevant validation efforts for small devices?

Ans. Small devices are usually off-the-shelf pieces of equipment that is widely used. In these cases, the development life-cycle is mainly controlled by the vendor. The pharmaceutical customer should therefore reasonably assess the vendor's capability of developing software according to common standards of quality.

A vendor assessment needs to be performed and the application needs to be verified against the requirements for the intended use. From the perspective of the regulated industry, the implementation of such a device is driven by an implementation life-cycle. At minimum the following items need to be addressed:

- Requirement definition for the intended use including process limitations. This should also include a statement indicating whether data are stored or transferred to another system. As per the definition of a small device, data are not stored permanently but temporarily and are not to be modified by a user. Therefore, limited user access handling is acceptable. It needs to be ensured that parameter data influencing the device's behaviour may not be altered without suitable permission;
- Risk assessment, taking into consideration the intended use and the risk to patients for associated with the process supported by the small device;
- Vendor assessment;
- List of available documentation from the vendor, especially those describing the methodology used and the calculation algorithm, if applicable. A vendor certificate or equivalent detailing the testing performed by the vendor may also be included; calibration certificate, if applicable;
- Validation plan according to the risk-assessment results;
- Verification testing proving that the device fulfils the requirements for the intended use. It may be equivalent to a PQ-phase.

Small manufacturing devices are sometimes only equipped with microprocessors and firmware and are not capable of high-level administration functions. Moreover, data is often transient in nature in these devices. Due to the latter there is no risk of inadvertently modifying data. An audit trail is therefore not necessary and user access may be limited to those functions of parameter control.

Q45. What alternative controls are accepted in case a system is not capable to generate print-outs indicating if any of the data has been changed since the original entry?

Ans. As long as this functionality is not supported by the supplier, it may be acceptable to describe in a procedure the fact that a print-out of the related audit trail report must be generated and linked manually to the record supporting batch release.

Q46. How can the QP of a site assure compliance with there requirements of the clinical-trial application in situations where a QP may be required to certify a batch before the application is submitted to, or accepted by, the competent authority?

Ans. The QP of a site that is manufacturing a drug product intermediate should assure that the product is produced and controlled in compliance with the GMP guideline. A product specification file should be developed with contributions from the QPs and other technical personnel of the sites involved with the other manufacturing activities of the IMP. The sponsor of the clinical trial should also be involved in this process. While this may be in a rudimentary form and contain little detail, it should be developed as knowledge of the product evolves and include specifications for critical parameters and controls. The development of the product specification file should be managed under a technical agreement or a number of technical agreements between the various manufacturing sites. These should include the QP responsible for the final certification of the product and the sponsor, if the sponsor has already been appointed. In any event, final release of the product to trial sites should take place only when the sponsor has established that the product has been manufactured in compliance with the terms of the approved clinical-trial application.

Q47. Is it possible to perform packaging or labelling at the investigator site?

Ans. This is normally possible only if a manufacturing authorisation has been granted to the site by the national competent authority.

Q48. Who is responsible for the packaging or labelling activities carried out at the investigator site?

Ans. The sponsor has the ultimate responsibility for all trial activities performed at the investigator site, but should seek the advice of the QP of the IMP manufacturer, if possible, or the clinical-trials pharmacist at the investigator site regarding:

- Adequacy of premises and equipment (storage conditions etc.);
- Adequacy of written standard operating procedures;
- Training of personnel involved, both on GMP requirements and any protocol specific requirements for the IMPs;
- Written instructions to perform activities;
- Forms to document the activities carried out;
- Checks to be done;
- The keeping of retention samples;
- Record-keeping.

Q49. Who is responsible for the transport and storage conditions when an IMP is transported from the manufacturer to the distributor or investigator sites?

Ans. The sponsor should exercise control over the entire chain of distribution of IMPs, from manufacture or importation, through to supply to the investigator sites, so as to guarantee that IMPs are stored, transported, and handled in a suitable manner. When an IMP originates from a third country, the importer is responsible for verifying that the transportation and storage conditions for the product are suitable. For products originating within, the manufacturer is responsible for transportation and storage conditions. The respective responsibilities of the sponsor, manufacturer, importer and, where used, distributor should be defined in a technical agreement.

Q50. What measures should be taken to ensure that the IMPs are kept under suitable conditions during transportation between the manufacturer or distributor and the investigator sites?

Ans. Storage conditions during transportation should be validated or monitored using a suitable temperature-measuring device that is capable of showing fluctuations in temperature *e.g.,* Temperature Logger. The choice of method of transport should be influenced by the nature and sensitivity of the product and should ensure timely delivery of IMPs to the investigator sites. The outer packaging should be labelled showing the final destination, the name of manufacturer or sponsor and the storage conditions required.

Q51. What measures should be taken to ensure that IMPs are kept under suitable conditions during storage at the investigator sites?

Ans. IMPs should be packaged to prevent contamination and unacceptable deterioration during storage. The sponsor should determine acceptable storage temperatures and any other required storage conditions for the IMPs (*e.g.,* protection from light). The sponsor should ensure that all involved parties (*e.g.,* monitors, investigators, pharmacists, storage managers) are aware of these conditions and the actions to be taken in the event that the conditions are not met. Where appropriate, there should be a restricted area for the storage of IMPs. The temperature of the areas and equipment used for the storage should be monitored using suitable means, such as a temperature recorder or, as a minimum, a record of the maximum and minimum temperatures, at a suitable frequency (for example, daily).

Q52. What written procedures should be in place at the investigator site regarding IMPs?

Ans. The sponsor should ensure that written procedures include instructions that the investigator or institution should follow for the handling and storage of IMPs. The procedures should address adequate and safe receipt, handling, storage, where relevant any reconstitution process to be carried out before administration, retrieval of unused product from subjects, and return of unused IMPs to the sponsor (or alternative disposal, if authorised by the sponsor and in compliance with the applicable regulatory requirements). Procedures should also give instructions on the actions to be taken when defined conditions are not met.

Q53. What records must be kept at the investigator site regarding the above mentioned procedures?

Ans. The sponsor should ensure that the documents listed in 'essential documents for the conduct of a clinical trial' of the guideline for good clinical practice are maintained and accessible to those parties authorised to review them.

Q54. Can a site have more than one QP performing certification of batches?

Ans. Legislation requires a manufacturer to have at least one QP at its disposal but a site may have more than one QP who may certify batches on behalf of the manufacturer.

Q55. Can there be more than one QP involved in the certification of a given batch?

Ans. In such cases, the overall responsibility for correct manufacture of the batch lies with the QP performing final certification of the batch before release for sale. It is also possible that, at a single manufacturing site, different QPs could be responsible for certification of different stages of manufacture of the batch. However, as before, the QP performing final certification before release holds overall responsibility for manufacture of the batch in accordance with GMP and the marketing authorisation.

Q56. In the context of handling unexpected deviations, what is included in the scope of registered specifications for medicinal products? What is an 'unexpected' deviation? In the context of handling unexpected deviations, what is included in the scope of registered specifications for medicinal products?

Ans. In order to satisfy the criteria for handling unexpected deviations, all registered specifications for active substances, excipients, packaging materials and medicinal products must be met. Registered specifications for medicinal products include in-process, bulk and finished product specifications which have been included in the MA application.

The criticality of registered in-process specifications may vary depending on the quality attribute tested, the impact to subsequent manufacturing processes and ability to test the quality attribute in the finished product. It may therefore be possible to accept deviation from an in-process specification where risk assessment confirms that there is no impact to manufacturing process or product quality.

Non-compliance with registered specifications (except where excursions from in-process specifications can be accepted based on quality risk management principles) therefore fall outside the scope, and the QP would not be able to certify the affected batches.

Q57. What is an 'unexpected' deviation?

Ans. The process itself should be designed to comply with the registered requirements (fit for purpose). A deviation can be considered as 'unexpected' until the time of discovery. Where the relevant authorities have confirmed the need to avoid supply disruption, repeat deviations thereafter are no longer 'unexpected' but may be considered for QP certification and accepted while corrective and preventive action is in progress. Planned deviations or deviations that are caused by incorrect communication between marketing authorisation holder (MAH) and manufacturers. The marketing authorisation holder should submit an application for a variation to the marketing authorisation, if needed.

Q58. Whether QP is allowed certification of more than one batch affected by the same unexpected deviation?

Ans. If more than one batch has already been manufactured and/ or tested at the time of discovery of the unexpected deviation, then it is acceptable to consider QP certification of all these batches. Following discovery, repeated deviations from the manufacturing process and/or analytical control methods should be considered changes, and variations to the affected marketing authorisations must be submitted. In exceptional circumstances to avoid disruption to supply, it may be possible to continue QP certification while corrective and preventive action is in progress.

Q59. Is it necessary to retain a sufficient number of samples of each batch of a sterile medicinal product in order to carry out a sterility test on two separate occasions?

Ans. For retention purposes, it is not necessary to keep the full number of samples required to repeat the sterility test performed for release purposes, but only a sufficient quantity to allow the carrying out, on two occasions, of a confirmatory test using the minimum quantities described in the monograph.

Q60. In which cases does the exemption for a fully packaged unit as retention sample apply as referred to in section 2.1 of EU GMP Part I, annex 19: "There may be exceptional circumstances where this requirement can be met without retention of duplicate samples *e.g.,* where small amounts of a batch are packaged for different markets or in the production of very expensive medicinal products"?

Ans. Firstly, the supervisory authority should grant such an exemption upon request from the manufacturer. The relevant authority may agree to this when one or more of the following criteria are met:

- A batch size of less than 50 units;
- High value/ low volume medicinal products and the high value price of the medicinal product as determined by each individual competent authority;
- Large size of one packaged unit *e.g.,* some veterinary pre-mixes or hospital packages.

Parallel imported/ distributed medicinal products will not be granted an exemption from keeping a fully packaged unit if the products have been re-packaged. This is because the exemption refers to "duplicate samples", and in these cases no reference sample is required to be kept by the parallel distributor/ importer. On the other hand, where the secondary packaging of the source product is not opened by the parallel importer/distributor only samples of the additional packaging material used needs to be retained.

Q61. In those cases where the supervisory authority agrees that the criteria mentioned in the answer to question 1 are met, what should be retained instead of a fully packaged unit?

Ans. The original batch specific primary packaging material with print/imprint, if any, all the original batch specific secondary packaging materials *e.g.,* labels and leaflets with print/ imprint including Braille, and dosing aids, if any, must be kept. The use of photocopies of the fully packaged unit to replace the retention sample are not acceptable as some details *e.g.,* Braille and holograms may not show correctly.

Q62. Do different requirements for reference and retention samples apply for some medicinal products?

Ans. There may be specific national requirements for compassionate use medicinal products, extemporary produced pharmacy products etc.

Q63. What is a GMP certificate and what is the difference between GMP certificates, certificates of medicinal product (CMPs, also called certificates of pharmaceutical products, CPPs) and certificates of suitability to the monographs of the European Pharmacopoeia (CEPs)?

Ans. A GMP certificate is a certificate issued following a GMP inspection, by the competent authority responsible for carrying out the inspection, to confirm the GMP compliance status of the inspected site.

GMP certificates are site-specific, but can be restricted to particular activities depending on the scope of the inspection (*e.g.,* manufacturing activities related to a specific product). A GMP certificate shall be issued to a manufacturer, if the outcome of the inspection shows that the manufacturer complies with GMP.

CMPs are product-specific certificates issued by the competent authority that granted the marketing authorisation. The European Medicines Agency issues CMPs on behalf of the European Commission for centrally authorised products. CMPs are issued in the context of the World Health Organization certification scheme on the quality of pharmaceutical products moving in international commerce, to confirm the marketing-authorisation status of the products. These certificates also confirm the GMP compliance status of the manufacturing sites. CMPs are mainly used by companies to support applications to export their pharmaceutical products to countries with less-developed regulatory systems.

CEPs are certificates issued by the European Directorate for the Quality of Medicines and Healthcare (EDQM) to confirm that a certain active substance is produced according to the requirements of the relevant monograph of the European

Pharmacopoeia or of the monograph on transmission spongiform encephalopathies. CEPs can be used by companies when submitting an application for marketing authorisation, and replace much of the documentation required for the active substance in the marketing-authorisation dossier. GMP inspections of active-substance manufacturers can be requested by EDQM in the context of the CEP certification scheme.

Q64. How can data risk be assessed?

Ans. Data risk assessment should consider the vulnerability of data to involuntary or deliberate amendment, deletion or recreation. Control measures which prevent unauthorised activity and increase visibility/ detectability can be used as risk mitigating actions. Examples of factors which can increase risk of data integrity failure include complex, inconsistent processes with open-ended and subjective outcomes. Simple tasks which are consistent, well-defined and objective lead to reduced risk. Risk assessment should include a business process focus (*e.g.*, production, QC) and not just consider IT system functionality or complexity. Factors to consider include:

- Process complexity
- Process consistency, degree of automation/ human interface
- Subjectivity of outcome/ result
- Is the process open-ended or well defined

This ensures that manual interfaces with IT systems are considered in the risk assessment process. Computerised system validation in isolation may not result in low data integrity risk, in particular when the user is able to influence the reporting of data from the validated system.

Q65. How can data criticality be assessed?

Ans. The decision which data influences may differ in importance, and the impact of the data to a decision may also vary. Points to consider regarding data criticality include:

- What decision does the data influence? *For example:* when making a batch release decision, data which determines compliance with critical quality attributes is of greater importance than warehouse cleaning records.
- What is the impact of the data to product quality or safety? *For example:* for an oral tablet, active substance assay data is of greater impact to product quality and safety than tablet dimensions' data.

Q66. What does 'Data Lifecycle' refer to?

Ans. 'Data lifecycle' refers to how data are generated, processed, reported, checked, used for decision-making, stored and finally discarded at the end of the retention period. Data relating to a product or process may cross various boundaries within the lifecycle, for example:

- IT systems
- Quality system applications
- Production
- Analytical

- Stock management systems
- Data storage (back-up and archival)
- Organisational
- Internal (*e.g.,* between production, QC and QA)
- External (*e.g.,* between contract givers and acceptors)
- Cloud-based applications and storage

Q67. Why is 'Data lifecycle' management important to ensure effective data integrity measures?

Ans. Data integrity can be affected at any stage in the lifecycle. It is therefore important to understand the lifecycle elements for each type of data or record, and ensure controls which are proportionate to data criticality and risk at all stages.

Q68. What should be considered when reviewing the 'Data lifecycle'?

Ans. The 'Data lifecycle' refers to the:

- Generation and recording of data
- Processing into usable information
- Checking the completeness and accuracy of reported data and processed information
- Data (or results) are used to make a decision
- Retaining and retrieval of data which protects it from loss or unauthorised amendment
- Retiring or disposal of data in a controlled manner at the end of its life

'Data Lifecycle' reviews are applicable to both paper and electronic records, although control measures may be applied differently. In the case of computerised systems, the 'data lifecycle' review should be performed by business process owners (*e.g.,* production, QC) in collaboration with IT personnel who understand the system architecture. The applications of critical thinking skills are important to not only identify gaps in data governance, but to also challenge the effectiveness of the procedural and systematic controls in place.

Segregation of duties between data lifecycle stages provides safeguards against data integrity failure by reducing the opportunity for an individual to alter, misrepresent or falsify data without detection. Data risk should be considered at each stage of the data lifecycle review.

Q69. 'Data lifecycle': What risks should be considered when assessing the generating and recording of data?

Ans. The following aspects should be considered when determining risk and control measures:

- How and where original data are created (*i.e.,* paper or electronic)?
- What metadata is associated with the data, to ensure a complete, accurate and traceable record, taking into account ALCOA principles?
- Does the record permit the reconstruction of the activity?
- Where is the data and metadata located?
- Does the system require that data are saved to permanent memory at the time of recording, or is it held in a temporary buffer?

In the case of some computerised analytical and manufacturing equipment, data may be stored as a temporary local file prior to transfer to a permanent storage location (*e.g.,* server). During the period of 'temporary' storage, there is often limited audit trail provision amending, deleting or recreating data. This is a data integrity risk. Removing the use of temporary memory (or reducing the time period that data are stored in temporary memory) reduces the risk of undetected data manipulation.

Q70. Is it possible to recreate, amend or delete original data and metadata?

Ans. Computerised system controls may be more complex, including setting of user privileges and system configuration to limit or prevent access to amend data. It is important to review all data access opportunities, including IT helpdesk staff, who may make changes at the request of the data user. These changes should be procedurally controlled, visible and approved within the quality system.

Q71. How data are transferred to other locations or systems for processing or storage?

Ans. Data should be protected from possibility of intentional or unintentional loss or amendment during transfer to other systems (*e.g.,* for processing, review or storage). Paper records should be protected from amendment, or substitution. Electronic interfaces should be validated to demonstrate security and no corruption of data, particularly where systems require an interface to present data in a different structure or file format.

Q72. What risks should be considered when assessing the processing data into usable information?

Ans. The following aspects should be considered when determining risk and control measures:

- How are data processed?
  Data processing methods should be approved, identifiable and version controlled. In the case of electronic data processing, methods should be locked where appropriate to prevent unauthorised amendment.
- How are data processing recorded?
  The processing method should be recorded. In situations where raw data have been processed more than once, each iteration (including method and result) should be available to the data checker for verification.
- Does the person processing the data have the ability to influence what data are reported, or how it is presented?

Even 'validated systems' which do not permit the user to make any changes to data may be at risk if the user can choose what data are printed, reported or transferred for processing. This includes performing the activity multiple times as separate events and reporting a desired outcome from one of these repeats.

Data presentation (*e.g.,* changing scale of graphical reports to enhance or reduce presentation of analytical peaks) can also influence decision making, and therefore impact data integrity.

Q73. 'Data lifecycle': What risks should be considered when checking the completeness and accuracy of reported data and processed information?

Ans. The following aspects should be considered when determining risk and control measures:

- Is original data (including the original data format) available for checking? The format of the original data (electronic or paper) should be preserved, and available to the data reviewer in a manner which permits interaction with the data (*e.g.,* search, query). This approach facilitates a risk-based review of the record, and can also reduce administrative burden for instance utilising validated audit trail 'exception reports' instead of an onerous line-by-line review.
- Are there any periods of time when data are not audit trailed? This may present opportunity for data amendment which is not subsequently visible to the data reviewer. Additional control measures should be implemented to reduce risk of undisclosed data manipulation.
- Does the data reviewer have visibility and access to all data generated? This should include any data from failed or aborted activities, discrepant or unusual data which has been excluded from processing or the final decision-making process. Visibility of all data provides protection against selective data reporting or 'testing into compliance'.
- Does the data reviewer have visibility and access to all processing of data? This ensures that the final result obtained from raw data are based on good science, and that any data exclusion or changes to processing method is based on good science. Visibility of all processing information provides protection against undisclosed 'processing into compliance'.

Q74. What risks should be considered when data (or results) are used to make a decision?

Ans. The following aspects should be considered when determining risk and control measures:

- When is the pass / fail decision taken;
- If data acceptability decisions are taken before a record (raw data or processed result) is saved to permanent memory, there may be opportunity for the user to manipulate data to provide a satisfactory result, without this change being visible in audit trail. This would not be visible to the data reviewer. This is a particular consideration where computerised systems alert the user to an out of specification entry before the data entry process is complete (*i.e.,* the user 'saves' the data entry), or saves the record in temporary memory.

Q75. What risks should be considered when retaining and retrieving data to protect it from loss or unauthorised amendment?

Ans. The following aspects should be considered when determining risk and control measures:

- How / where are data stored; Storage of data (paper or electronic) should be at secure locations, with access limited to authorised persons. The storage location must provide adequate protection from damage due to water, fire, etc.

- What are the measures protecting against loss or unauthorised amendment; Data security measures should be at least equivalent to those applied during the earlier Data lifecycle stages. Retrospective data amendment (*e.g.*, via IT helpdesk or data base amendments) should be controlled by the pharmaceutical quality system, with appropriate segregation of duties and approval processes.
- Is data backed up in a manner permitting reconstruction of the activity; Back-up arrangements should be validated to demonstrate the ability to restore data following IT system failure. In situations where metadata (including relevant operating system event logs) are stored in different file locations from raw data, the back-up process should be carefully designed to ensure that all data required to reconstruct a record is included. Similarly, 'true copies' of paper records may be duplicated on paper, microfilm, or electronically, and stored in a separate location.
- What are ownership / retrieval arrangements, particularly considering outsourced activities or data storage; A technical agreement should be in place which addresses the requirements of the GMP guide.

Q76. What risks should be considered when retiring or disposal of data in a controlled manner at the end of its life?

Ans. The following aspects should be considered when determining risk and control measures:

- *The data retention period:* This will be influenced by regulatory requirements and data criticality. When considering data for a single product, there may be different data retention needs for pivotal trial data and manufacturing process / analytical validation data compared to routine commercial batch data.
- *How data disposal are authorised:* Any disposal of data should be approved within the quality system and be performed in accordance with a procedure to ensure compliance with the required data retention period.

Q77. Is it required to implement a specific procedure for data integrity?

Ans. There is no requirement for a specific procedure, however it may be beneficial to provide a summary document which outlines the organisations total approach to data governance. A compliant pharmaceutical quality system generates and assesses a significant amount of data. While all data have an overall influence on GMP compliance, different data will have different levels of impact to product quality. A quality-risk management (ICH Q9) approach to data integrity can be achieved by considering data risk and data criticality at each stage in the Data lifecycle. The effort applied to control measures should be commensurate with this data risk and criticality assessment.

The approach to risk identification, mitigation, review and communication should be iterative, and integrated into the pharmaceutical quality system. This should provide senior management supervision and permit a balance between data integrity and general GMP priorities in line with the principles of ICH Q9 & Q10.

Q78. How should the company design and control their paper documentation system to prevent the unauthorised re-creation of GMP data?

Ans. The template (blank) forms used for manual recordings may be created in an electronic system (Word, Excel, etc.). The corresponding master documents should be approved and controlled electronically or in paper versions. The following expectations should be considered for the template (blank) form:

- Have a unique reference number (including version number) and include reference to corresponding SOP number should be stored in a manner which ensures appropriate version control if signed electronically, should use a secure e-signature
- The distribution of template records (*e.g.*, 'blank' forms) should be controlled. The following expectations should be considered where appropriate, based on data risk and criticality:
- Enable traceability for issuance of the blank form by using a bound logbook with numbered pages or other appropriate system. For loose leaf template forms, the distribution date, a sequential issuing number, the number of the copies distributed, the department name where the blank forms are distributed, etc. should be known
- Distributed copies should be designed to avoid photocoping either by using a secure stamp, or by the use of paper colour code not available in the working areas or another appropriate system.

Q79. What controls should be in place to ensure original electronic data is preserved?

Ans. Computerised systems should be designed in a way that ensures compliance with the principles of data integrity. The system design should make provisions such that original data cannot be deleted and for the retention of audit trails reflecting changes made to original data.

Q80. Why is it important to review electronic data?

Ans. In the case of data generated from an electronic system, electronic data are the original record which must be reviewed and evaluated prior to making batch release decisions and other decisions relating to GMP related activities (*e.g.*, approval of stability results, analytical method validation etc.). In the event that the review is based solely on printouts there is potential for records to be excluded from the review process which may contain un-investigated out of specification data or other data anomalies. The review of the raw electronic data should mitigate risk and enable detection of data deletion, amendment, duplication, reusing and fabrication which are common data integrity failures.

Example of an inspection citing:

- Raw data for HPLC/GC runs which had been invalidated was stored separately to the QC raw data packages and had not been included in the review process.
- In the above situation, the procedure for review of chromatographic data packages did not require a review of the electronic raw data or a review of relevant audit trails associated with the analyses. This lead to the exclusion

of records from the review process and to lack of visibility of changes made during the processing and reporting of the data. The company was unable to provide any explanation for the data which had been invalidated.

Q81. Is a risk-based review of electronic data acceptable?

Ans. Yes. The principles of quality risk management may be applied during the review of electronic data and review by exception is permitted, when scientifically justified.

Exception Reporting is used commonly as a tool to focus the review of electronic data such as (but not limited to) electronic batch records. Exception reporting rapidly highlights to the reviewer one of the most critical elements of batch review, *i.e.,* the exceptions. The level of review of the full electronic batch record can vary based on the exceptions as well as the level of confidence and experience with a particular process. Appropriate testing and validation must be completed for the automated system and the output Batch Exception Report to ensure its functionality meets the business and regulatory requirements as per GMP.

Q82. What are the expectations for the self-inspection program related to data integrity?

Ans. Ongoing compliance with the company's data governance policy/ procedures should be reviewed during self-inspection, to ensure that they remain effective. This may also include elements of the Data lifecycle discussed in Q3-Q9.

Q83. What are my company's responsibilities relating to data integrity for GMP activities contracted out to another company?

Ans. Data integrity requirements should be incorporated into the company's contractor/vendor qualification/ assurance program and associated procedures. In addition to having their own data governance systems, companies outsourcing activities should verify the adequacy of comparable systems at the contract acceptor. The contract acceptor should apply equivalent levels of control to those applied by the contract giver. Formal assessment of the contract acceptors competency and compliance in this regard should be conducted in the first instance prior to the approval of a contractor, and thereafter verified on a periodic basis at an appropriate frequency based on risk.

Q84. How can a recipient (contract giver) build confidence in the validity of documents such as Certificate of Analysis (CoA) provided by a supplier (contract acceptor)?

Ans. The recipient should have knowledge of the systems and procedures implemented at the supplier for the generation of the CoA. Arrangements should be in place to ensure that significant changes to systems are notified and the effectiveness of these arrangements should be subjected to periodic review. Data related to activities which are outsourced are routinely provided as summary data in a report format (*e.g.,* CoA). These summary documents are reviewed on a routine basis by the contract acceptor and therefore the review of data integrity at the contract acceptor site on a regular periodic basis (*e.g.,* during on-site audit) takes on even greater significance, in order to build and maintain confidence in the summary data provided.

Q85. What are the expectations in relation to contract calibration service providers who conduct calibrations on-site and/or off-site? Arc audits of these companies premises required?

Ans. Using the principles of QRM to assess data criticality and risk, the company should include assessment of data governance systems implemented by the service provider when making decisions on service contracts. This may be achieved by on-site audit or desk-based assessment of information submitted by the service provider.

Q86. What is expected of my company in the event that one of my approved contractors (*e.g.,* active substance manufacturer, finished product manufacturer, quality control laboratory etc.) is issued with a warning letter/statement of non-compliance concerning data integrity, from a regulatory authority?

Ans. It is considered that the company should evaluate the risk to its products manufactured/released using the principles of quality risk management. Risk assessments should be made available to Inspectors, on request.

Depending on the outcome of the risk assessment, appropriate action should be taken which may entail delisting the contractor from the approved contractor list. In the event that abnormal disruption in supply may result from a contractor compliance situation, relevant regulatory authorities should be consulted in this regard.

Q87. Where does my company's responsibility begin and end in relation to data integrity aspects of the supply chain for medicinal products?

Ans. All actors in the supply chain play an important part in overall data integrity and assurance of product quality. Data governance systems should be implemented from the manufacture of starting materials right through to the delivery of medicinal products to persons authorised or entitled to supply medicinal products to the public. Relative responsibilities and boundaries should be documented in the contracts between the relevant parties. Final responsibility of ensuring compliance throughout the supply chain rests with batch certifying QP.

Q88. Is it acceptable that storage conditions are not monitored for medicinal products which do not have any predefined storage conditions on the outer packaging?

Ans. No. According to the Guideline on declaration of storage conditions, marketing authorisation holders have to provide stability data for storage conditions at 25°C / 60% relative humidity (RH), or 30°C / 65% RH (long term) and 40°C / 75% RH (accelerated), in order to justify not including a statement in the medicinal product labelling. These stability data are generated according to the temperature and humidity conditions of climate zone I (temperate) and II (Mediterranean/ subtropical) in Europe. No labelling statement means that controls should be in place to maintain conditions relevant to climate zones I and II. Consequently, the temperature should be monitored during storage and transport. Appropriate limits should be set for temperature monitoring to ensure that product stability is not adversely affected.

Subject Index

E

F

G

H

I

K

L

M

N

O